Computer Vision and Image Processing in Intelligent Systems and Multimedia Technologies

Muhammad Sarfraz
Kuwait University, Kuwait

A volume in the Advances in Computational Intelligence and Robotics (ACIR) Book Series

Information Science
REFERENCE
An Imprint of IGI Global

Managing Director:	Lindsay Johnston
Production Editor:	Jennifer Yoder
Development Editor:	Erin O'Dea
Acquisitions Editor:	Kayla Wolfe
Typesetter:	John Crodian
Cover Design:	Jason Mull

Published in the United States of America by
Information Science Reference (an imprint of IGI Global)
701 E. Chocolate Avenue
Hershey PA 17033
Tel: 717-533-8845
Fax: 717-533-8661
E-mail: cust@igi-global.com
Web site: http://www.igi-global.com

Library of Congress Cataloging-in-Publication Data

Computer vision and image processing in intelligent systems and multimedia technologies / Muhammad Sarfraz, editor.
    pages cm.
 Includes bibliographical references and index. ISBN 978-1-4666-6030-4 (hardcover) -- ISBN 978-1-4666-6031-1 (ebook) -- ISBN (invalid) 978-1-4666-6033-5 (print & perpetual access) 1. Intelligent agents (Computer software)--Design. 2. Multimedia systems--Design. 3. Computer vision. 4. Image processing. I. Sarfraz, Muhammad, editor.
  QA76.76.I58C648 2014 006.3'7--dc23
                    2014011688

This book is published in the IGI Global book series Advances in Computational Intelligence and Robotics (ACIR) (ISSN: 2327-0411; eISSN: 2327-042X)

British Cataloguing in Publication Data
A Cataloguing in Publication record for this book is available from the British Library.

For electronic access to this publication, please contact: eresources@igi-global.com.

Advances in Computational Intelligence and Robotics (ACIR) Book Series

ISSN: 2327-0411
EISSN: 2327-042X

MISSION

While intelligence is traditionally a term applied to humans and human cognition, technology has progressed in such a way to allow for the development of intelligent systems able to simulate many human traits. With this new era of simulated and artificial intelligence, much research is needed in order to continue to advance the field and also to evaluate the ethical and societal concerns of the existence of artificial life and machine learning.

The **Advances in Computational Intelligence and Robotics (ACIR) Book Series** encourages scholarly discourse on all topics pertaining to evolutionary computing, artificial life, computational intelligence, machine learning, and robotics. ACIR presents the latest research being conducted on diverse topics in intelligence technologies with the goal of advancing knowledge and applications in this rapidly evolving field.

COVERAGE

- Adaptive & Complex Systems
- Agent Technologies
- Artificial Intelligence
- Cognitive Informatics
- Computational Intelligence
- Natural Language Processing
- Neural Networks
- Pattern Recognition
- Robotics
- Synthetic Emotions

IGI Global is currently accepting manuscripts for publication within this series. To submit a proposal for a volume in this series, please contact our Acquisition Editors at Acquisitions@igi-global.com or visit: http://www.igi-global.com/publish/.

Titles in this Series

For a list of additional titles in this series, please visit: www.igi-global.com

www.igi-global.com

701 E. Chocolate Ave., Hershey, PA 17033
Order online at www.igi-global.com or call 717-533-8845 x100
To place a standing order for titles released in this series, contact: cust@igi-global.com
Mon-Fri 8:00 am - 5:00 pm (est) or fax 24 hours a day 717-533-8661

Table of Contents

Detailed Table of Contents

    Abder-Rahman Ali, Scientific Research Group in Egypt (SRGE), Egypt
    Micael S. Couceiro, University of Coimbra, Portugal & Ingeniarius, Lda., Mealhada,
        Portugal
    Ahmed M. Anter, Scientific Research Group in Egypt (SRGE), Egypt & Mansoura University,
        Egypt
    Aboul Ella Hassanian, Scientific Research Group in Egypt (SRGE), Egypt & Cairo
        University, Egypt

An Evolutionary Particle Swarm Optimization based on the Fractional Order Darwinian method for optimizing a Fast Fuzzy C-Means algorithm is proposed. This chapter aims at enhancing the performance of Fast Fuzzy C-Means, both in terms of the overall solution and speed. To that end, the concept of fractional calculus is used to control the convergence rate of particles, wherein each one of them represents a set of cluster centers. The proposed solution, denoted as FODPSO-FFCM, is applied on liver CT images, and compared with Fast Fuzzy C-Means and PSOFFCM, using Jaccard Index and Dice Coefficient. The computational efficiency is achieved by using the histogram of the image intensities during the clustering process instead of the raw image data. The experimental results based on the Analysis of Variance (ANOVA) technique and multiple pair-wise comparison show that the proposed algorithm is fast, accurate, and less time consuming.

    Ahmed M. Anter, Mansoura University, Egypt & Scientific Research Group in Egypt (SRGE),
        Egypt
    Mohamed Abu ElSoud, Mansoura University, Egypt & Scientific Research Group in Egypt
        (SRGE), Egypt
    Aboul Ella Hassanien, Cairo University, Egypt & Scientific Research Group in Egypt
        (SRGE), Egypt

Internal density of the breast is a parameter that clearly affects the performance of segmentation and classification algorithms to define abnormality regions. Recent studies have shown that their sensitivity is significantly decreased as the density of the breast is increased. In this chapter, enhancement and segmentation process is applied to increase the computation and focus on mammographic parenchyma.

This parenchyma is analyzed to discriminate tissue density according to BIRADS using Local Binary Pattern (LBP), Gray Level Co-Occurrence Matrix (GLCM), Fractal Dimension (FD), and feature fusion technique is applied to maximize and enhance the performance of the classifier rate. The different methods for computing tissue density parameter are reviewed, and the authors also present and exhaustively evaluate algorithms using computer vision techniques. The experimental results based on confusion matrix and kappa coefficient show a higher accuracy is obtained by automatic agreement classification.

Chapter 3

Namita Aggarwal, Jawaharlal Nehru University, India
Bharti Rana, Jawaharlal Nehru University, India
R.K. Agrawal, Jawaharlal Nehru University, India

Early detection of Alzheimer's Disease (AD), a neurological disorder, may help in development of appropriate treatment to slow down the disease's progression. In this chapter, a method is proposed that may assist in diagnosis of AD using T1 weighted MRI brain images. In the proposed method, first-and-second-order-statistical features were extracted from multiple trans-axial brain slices covering hippocampus and amygdala regions, which play a significant role in AD diagnosis. Performance of the proposed approach is compared with the state-of-the-art feature extraction techniques in terms of sensitivity, specificity, and accuracy. The experiment was carried out on two datasets built from publicly available OASIS data, with four well-known classifiers. Experimental results show that the proposed method outperforms all the other existing feature extraction techniques irrespective of the choice of classifier and dataset. In addition, the statistical test demonstrates that the proposed method is significantly better in comparison to the existing methods. The authors believe that this study will assist clinicians/ researchers in classification of AD patients from controls based on T1-weighted MRI.

Chapter 4

Peilin Li, University of South Australia, Australia
Sang-Heon Lee, University of South Australia, Australia
Hung-Yao Hsu, University of South Australia, Australia

In this chapter, the use of two images, the near infrared image and the color image, from a bi-camera machine vision system is investigated to improve the detection of the citrus fruits in the image. The application has covered the design of the bi-camera vision system to align two CCD cameras, the online acquisition of the citrus fruit tree image, and the fusion of two aligned images. In the system, two cameras have been registered with alignment to ensure the fusion of two images. A fusion method has been developed based on the Multiscale Decomposition Analysis (MSD) with a Discrete Wavelet Transform (DWT) application for the two dimensional signal. In the fusion process, two image quality issues have been addressed. One is the detail noise from the background, which is bounded with the envelope spectra and with similar spectra to orange citrus fruit and spatial variance property. The second is the enhancement of the fundamental envelope spectra using two source images. With level of MSD estimated, the noise is reduced by zeroing the high pass coefficients in DWT while the fundamental envelope spectra from the color image are enhanced by an arithmetic pixel level fusion rule. To evaluate the significant improvement of the image quality, some major classification methods are applied to compare the classified results from the fused image with the results from the types of color image. The misclassification error is measured by the empirical type errors using the manual segmentation reference image.

Chapter 5

Shiv Ram Dubey, GLA University Mathura, India
Anand Singh Jalal, GLA University Mathura, India

Diseases in fruit cause devastating problems in economic losses and production in the agricultural industry worldwide. In this chapter, a method to detect and classify fruit diseases automatically is proposed and experimentally validated. The image processing-based proposed approach is composed of the following main steps: in the first step K-Means clustering technique is used for the defect segmentation, in the second step some color and texture features are extracted from the segmented defected part, and finally diseases are classified into one of the classes by using a multi-class Support Vector Machine. The authors have considered diseases of apple as a test case and evaluated the approach for three types of apple diseases, namely apple scab, apple blotch, and apple rot, along with normal apples. The experimental results express that the proposed solution can significantly support accurate detection and automatic classification of fruit diseases. The classification accuracy for the proposed approach is achieved up to 93% using textural information and multi-class support vector machine.

Chapter 6

Esraa El Hariri, Fayoum University, Egypt & Scientific Research Group in Egypt (SRGE),
Egypt
Nashwa El-Bendary, Arab Academy for Science, Technology, and Maritime Transport, Egypt
& Scientific Research Group in Egypt (SRGE), Egypt
Aboul Ella Hassanien, Cairo University, Egypt & Scientific Research Group in Egypt
(SRGE), Egypt
Amr Badr, Cairo University, Egypt

One of the prime factors in ensuring a consistent marketing of crops is product quality, and the process of determining ripeness stages is a very important issue in the industry of (fruits and vegetables) production, since ripeness is the main quality indicator from the customers' perspective. To ensure optimum yield of high quality products, an objective and accurate ripeness assessment of agricultural crops is important. This chapter discusses the problem of determining different ripeness stages of tomato and presents a content-based image classification approach to automate the ripeness assessment process of tomato via examining and classifying the different ripeness stages as a solution for this problem. It introduces a survey about resent research work related to monitoring and classification of maturity stages for fruits/ vegetables and provides the core concepts of color features, SVM, and PCA algorithms. Then it describes the proposed approach for solving the problem of determining different ripeness stages of tomatoes. The proposed approach consists of three phases, namely pre-processing, feature extraction, and classification phase. The classification process depends totally on color features (colored histogram and color moments), since the surface color of a tomato is the most important characteristic to observe ripeness. This approach uses Principal Components Analysis (PCA) and Support Vector Machine (SVM) algorithms for feature extraction and classification, respectively.

It is well known that the careful selection of a set of features, with higher discrimination competence, may increase recognition performance. In general, the magnitude coefficients of some selected orders of ZMs and PZMs have been used as invariant image features. The authors have used a statistical method to estimate the discrimination strength of all the coefficients of ZMs and PZMs. For classification, only the coefficients with estimated higher discrimination strength are selected and are used in the feature vector. The performance of these selected Discriminative ZMs (DZMs) and Discriminative PZMs (DPZMs) features are compared to that of their corresponding conventional approaches on YALE, ORL, and FERET databases against illumination, expression, scale, and pose variations. In this chapter, an extension to these DZMs and DPZMs is presented by exploring the use of phase information along with the magnitude coefficients of these approaches. As the phase coefficients are computed in parallel to the magnitude, no additional time is spent on their computation. Further, DZMs and DPZMs are also combined with PCA and FLD. It is observed from the exhaustive experimentation that with the inclusion of phase features the recognition rate is improved by 2-8%, at reduced dimensions and with less computational complexity, than that of using the successive ZMs and PZMs features.

The Internet is a powerful source of information. However, some of the information that is available on the Internet cannot be shown to every type of public. For instance, pornography is not desirable to be shown to children; pornography is the most harmful content affecting child safety and causing many destructive side effects. A content filter is one of more pieces of software that work together to prevent users from viewing material found on the Internet. In this chapter, the authors present an efficient content-based software system for detecting and filtering pornography images in Web pages. The proposed system runs online in the background of Internet Explorer (IE) for the purpose of restricting access to pornography Web pages. Skin and face detection techniques are the main components of the proposed system. Because the proposed filter works online, the authors propose two fasting techniques that can be used to speed up the filtering system. The results obtained using the proposed system are compared with four commercial filtering programs. The success rate of the proposed filtering system is better than the considered filtering programs.

    Madeena Sultana, University of Calgary, Canada
    Padma Polash Paul, University of Calgary, Canada
    Marina Gavrilova, University of Calgary, Canada

During the Internet era, millions of users are using Web-based Social Networking Sites (SNSs) such as MySpace, Facebook, and Twitter for communication needs. Social networking platforms are now considered a source of big data because of real-time activities of a large number of users. In addition to idiosyncratic personal characteristics, web-based social data may include person-to-person communication, profiles, patterns, and spatio-temporal information. However, analysis of social interaction-based data has not been studied from the perspective of person identification. In this chapter, the authors introduce for the first time the concept of using interaction-based features from online social networking platforms as a novel biometric. They introduce the concept of social behavioral biometric from SNSs to aid the identification process. Analysis of these novel biometric features and their potential use in various security and authentication applications are also presented. Such applications would pave the way for new directions in biometric research.

    Ankit Chaudhary, University of Iowa, USA
    Jagdish Lal Raheja, CEERI/CSIR, India
    Karen Das, Don Bosco University, India
    Shekhar Raheja, TU Kaiserslautern, Germany

In the current age, use of natural communication in human-computer interaction is a known and well-installed thought. Hand gesture recognition and gesture-based applications have gained a significant amount of popularity amongst people all over the world. They have a number of applications ranging from security to entertainment. These applications generally are real time applications and need fast, accurate communication with machines. On the other end, gesture-based communications have few limitations, but bent finger information is not provided in vision-based techniques. In this chapter, a novel method for fingertip detection and for angle calculation of both hands' bent fingers is discussed. Angle calculation has been done before with sensor-based gloves/devices. This study has been conducted in the context of natural computing for calculating angles without using any wired equipment, colors, marker, or any device. The pre-processing and segmentation of the region of interest is performed in a HSV color space and a binary format, respectively. Fingertips are detected using level-set method and angles are calculated using geometrical analysis. This technique requires no training for the system to perform the task.

Chapter 11

Siva Charan Muraharirao, Dhirubhai Ambani Institute of Information and Communication Technology, India

Manik Lal Das, Dhirubhai Ambani Institute of Information and Communication Technology, India

The recent advances in multimedia technology demand protection of digital images from unintentional manipulation for content integrity, copyright, and ownership. Digital watermarking technique has wide acceptance in the industry for anti-piracy, ownership verification, and digital image authentication. There have been a large number of schemes in the literature proposed for digital watermarking using non-cryptographic and cryptographic primitives. Use of Least Significant Bits (LSB) is one of the oldest but classical approaches for digital image authentication. Although LSB approach is efficient, it does not provide adequate security. Cryptographic primitives such as hash function, digital signature, and message authentication codes have been used in several applications including multimedia for data authentication. Digital signature-based image authentication provides strong security, but the approach requires managing public key infrastructure, which is a costly operation. Partial data protection is also an optimal approach for protecting important data while leaving unimportant data unprotected. Considering security weakness of the LSB-based approach and cost overhead of the public key-based approach, the authors present in this chapter a digital image authentication scheme using LSB, keyed hash, and partial encryption. They show that the proposed watermarking scheme is secure and efficient in comparison to other related schemes.

Chapter 12

Noura A. Semary, Menofia University, Egypt & Scientific Research Group in Egypt (SRGE), Egypt

Image colorization is a new image processing topic to recolor gray images to look as like the original color images as possible. Different methods have appeared in the literature to solve this problem, the way that leads to thinking about decolorization, eliminating the colors of color images to just small color keys, aid in the colorization process. Due to this idea, decolorization is considered as a color image encoding mechanism. In this chapter, the authors propose a new decolorization system depends on extracting the color seeds (Representative Pixels [RP]) using morphology operations. Different decolorization methods are studied and compared to the system results using different quality metrics.

Chapter 13

Saif alZahir, The University of North British Columbia, Canada

Large multimedia databases and digital image archival systems are being created in government, academia, military, hospitals, digital libraries, and businesses. Efficient methods to retrieve images from such large databases have become indispensable. In this chapter, the authors present a novel Wavelet Packet (WP)-based method for image identification and retrieval that enables the recovery of the original image from a database even if the image has been subjected to geometric transformations such as size-conserving rotation or flipping operations. The proposed method uses the correlation of wavelet packet coefficients to create an image signature. This signature is comprised of two parts. The first part is a short signature, SS, that represents the location of specific values of the WP coefficient correlations in each frequency band. The second portion is the basis signature of the image, which is a long signature, LS, of 1296 correlation points produced by summing up the correlation values along all frequency bands. Computer simulation results show that the method is extremely fast, has a perfect image retrieval rates (100%), and perfect geometric transformations recognition, if any. In addition, the simulation results show that target images are perfectly identified from an image database of 7500 image signatures within a short period of time (nearly 8 seconds on the average). This method is robust against geometric transformation and requires minimal data transfer and can be used for online image retrieval.

Chapter 14

K. C. Manjunatha, Prakash Steels and Power Private Limited, India
H. S. Mohana, Malnad College of Engineering, India
P. A. Vijaya, Malnad College of Engineering, India

Intelligent process control technology in various manufacturing industries is important. Vision-based non-magnetic object detection on moving conveyor in the steel industry will play a vital role for intelligent processes and raw material handling. This chapter presents an approach for a vision-based system that performs the detection of non-magnetic objects on raw material moving conveyor in a secondary steel-making industry. At single camera level, a vision-based differential algorithm is applied to recognize an object. Image pixels-based differential techniques, optical flow, and motion-based segmentations are used for traffic parameters extraction; the proposed approach extends those futures into industrial applications. The authors implement a smart control system, since they can save the energy and control unnecessary breakdowns in a robust manner. The technique developed for non-magnetic object detection has a single static background. Establishing background and background subtraction from continuous video input frames forms the basis. Detection of non-magnetic materials, which are moving with raw materials, and taking immediate action at the same stage as the material handling system will avoid the breakdowns or power wastage. The authors achieve accuracy up to 95% with the computational time of not more than 1.5 seconds for complete system execution.

Chapter 15

Muhammad Sarfraz, Kuwait University, Kuwait

Corner points or features determine significant geometrical locations of the digital images. They provide important clues for shape representation and analysis. Corner points represent important features of an object that may be useful at subsequent levels of processing. If the corner points are identified properly, a shape can be represented in an efficient and compact way with sufficient accuracy in many shape analysis problem. This chapter reviews some well referred algorithms in the literature together with empirical study. Users can easily pick one that may prove to be superior from all aspects for their applications and requirements.

This chapter proposes a scheme that helps digitizing hand printed and electronic planar objects or vectorizing the generic shapes. An evolutionary optimization technique, namely Genetic Algorithm (GA), is used to solve the problem of curve fitting with cubic and rational cubic spline functions. The underlying scheme is comprised of various phases including data of the image outlines, detection of corner points, using GA for optimal values of shape parameters in the description of spline functions, and fitting curve using spline functions to the detected corner points.

Preface

INTRODUCTION

Computer Vision (CV) and Image Processing (IP) are, although distinct, closely related fields. These are being treated as independent fields of study among the community worldwide. Due to their vital importance, effectiveness, and usefulness, extensive advances and discoveries are taking place everywhere. One can find a huge community worldwide contributing to these fields. In particular, CV and IP play significant roles in the development of Intelligent Systems (IS) and Multimedia Technologies (MT) in real life applications. Such real life applications are continuously needed to improve past and current practices. There is also a severe need to discover new state-of-the-art methodologies and systems for everyday life. There is plenty of literature available in the form of books, journals, conference proceedings, Websites, etc. One can find lot of events being held worldwide, numerous laboratories in function, and plenty of workgroups working in these fields. This book is specifically dedicated to the advances in CV and IP while working towards IS and MT applications.

COMPUTER VISION

Computer Vision (2012; Shapiro & Stockman, 2001; Morris, 2004; Jähne & Haußecker, 2000; Sonka, Hlavac, & Boyle, 2008; Forsyth & Ponce, 2003; Ballard & Brown, 1982; Turek, 2011; Carsten, Ulrich, & Wiedemann, 2007; Davies, 2005; Azad, Gockel, & Dillmann, 2008; Burger & Burge, 2007; Paragios, Chen, & Faugeras, 2005; Fisher, Dawson-Howe, Fitzgibbon, Robertson, & Trucco, 2005; Medioni & Kang, 2004; Hartley & Zisserman, 2003; Trucco & Verri, 1998; Klette, Schluens, & Koschan, 1998; Granlund & Knutsson, 1995; Crowley & Christensen, 1995) is a field that includes methods for acquiring, processing, analyzing, and understanding images and in general, high-dimensional data (Medioni & Kang, 2004; Hartley & Zisserman, 2003; Trucco & Verri, 1998) from the real world in order to produce numerical or symbolic information (Computer Vision, 2012; Shapiro & Stockman, 2001; Morris, 2004). A theme in the development of this field has been to duplicate the abilities of human vision by electronically perceiving and understanding an image (Jähne & Haußecker, 2000). Computer vision is a scientific as well as technological field (Computer Vision, 2012; Shapiro & Stockman, 2001; Morris, 2004; Jähne & Haußecker, 2000; Sonka, Hlavac, & Boyle, 2008). As a scientific field, it is concerned with the theory behind artificial systems that extract information from images. The image data can take many forms, such as video sequences, views from multiple cameras, or multi-dimensional data from a medical scanner. As a technological discipline, computer vision seeks to apply its theories and models to the construction of computer vision systems. Examples of applications of computer vision include detecting events for visual surveillance, navigation of a robot, and automatic inspection in manufacturing applications.

IMAGE PROCESSING

Digital Image Processing (2012; Gonzalez, Woods, & Eddins, 2009; Burger & Burge, 2007; Sarfraz, 2014; Jähne, 2002; Morris, 2004; Sonka, Hlavac, & Boyle, 1999; Stanciu, 2012; Koprowski & Wrobel, 2011; Zheng, 2011; Zhou, Wu, & Zhang, 2010; Young, Gerbrands, & Vliet, 2009; Starck & Murtagh, 2006; Blake & Isard, 2000; Starck, Murtagh, & Bijaoui, 1998; Philipps, 1997; Management Association, 2013; Sarfraz, 2013; Banissi & Sarfraz, 2012; Sargano, Sarfraz, & Haq, 2014) is the use of computer algorithms to perform image processing on digital images. As a subcategory or field of digital signal processing, digital image processing has many advantages over analog image processing. It allows a much wider range of algorithms to be applied to the input data and can avoid problems such as the build-up of noise and signal distortion during processing. Since images are defined over two dimensions (perhaps more), digital image processing may be modeled in the form of multidimensional systems.

Digital image processing allows the use of much more complex algorithms and can offer both more sophisticated performance of simple tasks and the implementation of methods that would be impossible by analog means. In particular, digital image processing is the only practical technology for classification, feature extraction, pattern recognition, projection, and multi-scale signal analysis. Some techniques that are used in digital image processing include pixelation, linear filtering, principal components analysis, independent component analysis, hidden Markov models, anisotropic diffusion, partial differential equations, self-organizing maps, neural networks, and wavelets.

LATEST ADVANCES

The chapters in this comprehensive reference explore the latest developments, methods, and approaches to computer vision and image processing in a wide variety of fields and endeavors, providing researchers, academicians, and readers of backgrounds and methods with an in-depth discussion of the latest advances in IP tools, IS, and MT technologies.

Abder-Rahman Ali et al. begin the book with a discussion of "Evaluating an Evolutionary Particle Swarm Optimization for Fast Fuzzy C-Means Clustering on Liver CT Images." This chapter aims at enhancing the performance of Fast Fuzzy C-Means, both in terms of the overall solution and speed. To that end, the concept of fractional calculus is used to control the convergence rate of particles, wherein each one of them represents a set of cluster centers. The proposed solution, denoted as FODPSO-FFCM, is applied on liver CT images, and compared with Fast Fuzzy C-Means and PSOFFCM, using Jaccard Index and Dice Coefficient. The computational efficiency is achieved by using the histogram of the image intensities during the clustering process instead of the raw image data. The experimental results based on the Analysis of Variance (ANOVA) technique and multiple pair-wise comparison show that the proposed algorithm is fast, accurate, and less time consuming.

This is followed by "Automatic Mammographic Parenchyma Classification According to BIRADS Dictionary" by Ahmed Anter et al. Breast Imaging Reporting and Data System (BIRADS) is becoming a standard for the assessment of mammographic images (American College of Radiology, 1998). Internal density of the breast is a parameter that clearly affects the performance of segmentation and classification algorithms to define abnormality regions. Recent studies have shown that their sensitivity is significantly decreased as the density of the breast is increased. In this chapter, enhancement and segmentation process is applied to increase the computation and focus on mammographic parenchyma. This parenchyma is analyzed to discriminate tissue density according to BIRADS using Local Binary Pattern (LBP), Gray Level Co-Occurrence Matrix (GLCM), Fractal Dimension (FD), and feature fusion technique is applied to maximize and enhance the performance of the classifier rate. The different methods for computing tissue density parameter are reviewed, and the authors also present and exhaustively evaluate algorithms using computer vision techniques. The experimental results based on confusion matrix and kappa coefficient show a higher accuracy is obtained by automatic agreement classification.

Motivated by recent results in diagnosis of Alzheimer's Disease, chapter 3, "Statistical Features-Based Diagnosis of Alzheimer's Disease Using MRI" by Namita Aggarwal et al., addresses the issue of early detection. It may help in development of appropriate treatment to slow down the disease's progression. In this chapter, a method is proposed that may assist in diagnosis of AD using T1 weighted MRI brain images. In the proposed method, first-and-second-order-statistical features were extracted from multiple trans-axial brain slices covering hippocampus and amygdala regions, which play a significant role in AD diagnosis. Performance of the proposed approach is compared with the state-of-the-art feature extraction techniques in terms of sensitivity, specificity, and accuracy. The experiment was carried out on two datasets built from publicly available OASIS data, with four well-known classifiers. Experimental results show that the proposed method outperforms all the other existing feature extraction techniques irrespective of the choice of classifier and dataset. In addition, the statistical test demonstrates that the proposed method is significantly better in comparison to the existing methods. The authors believe that this study will assist clinicians/researchers in classification of AD patients from controls based on T1-weighted MRI.

Machine vision system for citrus fruit harvesting manipulator is one of special applications of pattern recognition by visual perception. Chapter 4, "Use of Bi-Camera and Fusion of Pairwise Real Time Citrus Fruit Images for Classification Application" by PeiLin Li et al. constructs a typical machine vision system by the geometry of image formation, measurement, and interpretation. In this chapter, an application of visual recognition by a bi-camera imaging system is detailed as associated with citrus fruit identification for the citrus fruit harvesting manipulator. The use of bi-camera is enriched by using the measurement and the interpretation method based on the proposal of the use of multisensor from the horticultural industry literature. The application covers the real time citrus fruit image formation by two aligned CCD cameras, the measurement on the citrus fruit tree, and the image data filtering method with fusion approach. The research focuses on the pairwise image filtering method to address the real time citrus fruit image quality issues. One issue is the detail noise from the background of leave or the other, which has similar spectra as citrus fruit. The second issue is the maintenance or enhancement of the fundamental envelopment spectra using two source images. In the filtering method, two issues are addressed by assuming that the real time citrus fruit image is formed by the fundamental envelopment spectra mixed with the local detail noise with spatial variance property. The basis for the bi-camera image-filtering scheme is an approach of Multiscale Decomposition (MSD) by Discrete Wavelet Transform (DWT) using Daubechies wavelets. To a certain level of decomposition and with high-pass filtered coefficients zeroed, the fundamental envelopment spectra from two source images are maintained or enhanced by an arithmetic fusion rule. The pixel level fusion rule index is found by combining the low pass coefficient of the visible image and the low pass coefficient of the near-infrared image convoluted by the complement of local entropy filter from the visible low-pass coefficient. To achieve the function of pairwise images filtering, the prerequisite of the alignment of two cameras is addressed technically from the image formation to the measurement. The citrus fruit tree has been photographed by using a portable bi-camera cold mirror acquisition system. The prototype of the customized fixture has been manufactured to position and align a classical cold mirror with two CCD cameras in relative kinematic position. The algorithmic registration on the pairwise images can be bypassed by both of the alignment of two cameras in spatial coordinate and the triggering synchronization in temporal coordinate during the photographing. After the fused image is transformed reversely into the original resolution image, some clustering or classification methods are applied to segment the fused citrus fruit image. The results have been compared between the fused and the non-fused original color citrus fruit images to evaluate the improvement of the image quality issues. It is found that the citrus identification on the fused artifact image can be improved by comparing the original and the attenuated color image by both the visual perception and the misclassification error estimation. The misclassification error is measured by the empirical weak type error using the weak manual segmentation standard, respectively. The experimental fusion index on low-pass coefficients with high-pass detail coefficients zeroed primarily improves the issue of the similar detail spectra from the non-fruit area and some saturated background noise under the natural illumination condition.

Diseases in fruit cause devastating problem in economic losses and production in agricultural industry worldwide. The next chapter, "Automatic Fruit Disease Classification Using Images" by Shiv Ram Dubey and Anand Singh Jalal, introduces a method to detect and classify fruit diseases automatically. This method to detect and classify fruit diseases automatically is proposed and experimentally validated. The image processing-based proposed approach is composed of the following main steps: in the first step K-Means clustering technique is used for the defect segmentation, in the second step some color and texture features are extracted from the segmented defected part, and finally diseases are classified into one of the classes by using a multi-class Support Vector Machine. The authors have considered diseases of apple as a test case and evaluated the approach for three types of apple diseases, namely apple scab, apple blotch, and apple rot, along with normal apples. The experimental results express that the proposed solution can significantly support accurate detection and automatic classification of fruit diseases. The classification accuracy for the proposed approach is achieved up to 93% using textural information and multi-class support vector machine.

One of the prime factors in ensuring a consistent marketing of crops is product quality, and the process of determining ripeness stages is a very important issue in the industry of (fruits and vegetables) production, since ripeness is the main quality indicator from the customers' perspective. To ensure optimum yield of high quality products, an objective and accurate ripeness assessment of agricultural crops is important. In the next chapter, Esraa El Hariri et al. describe an "Automated Ripeness Assessment System of Tomatoes Using PCA (Principal Components Analysis) and SVM (Support Vector Machine) Techniques." This chapter presents a content-based image classification approach to automate the ripeness assessment process of tomatoes via examining and classifying the different ripeness stages. The proposed system consists of three phases, namely pre-processing, feature extraction, and classification. The classification process depends totally on color features (colored histogram and color moments), since the surface color of tomato is the most important characteristic to observe ripeness. This system uses PCA and SVM algorithms for feature extraction and classification, respectively. The dataset used for experiments was constructed based on real sample images for tomatoes at different stages, which were collected from different farms in Minya city, Upper Egypt. Dataset of total 250 images was used for both training and testing with 10-fold cross-validation. Training dataset is divided into 5 classes representing the different stages of tomato ripeness. Experimental results show that the proposed classification approach has obtained ripeness classification accuracy of 91.20%, using One-Against-One (OAO) multi-class SVM algorithm with linear kernel function and accuracy of 85.60% using One-Against-All (OAA) multi-class SVM algorithm with linear kernel function.

It is well known that the careful selection of a set of features, with higher discrimination competence, may increase the recognition performance. For example, the magnitude coefficients of some selected orders of Zernike Moments (ZMs) and Pseudo-Zernike Moments (PZMs) have been used as invariant image features in the current literature (Nor'aini, Raveendran, & Selvanathan, 2007; Singh, Walia, & Mittal, 2011a, 2011b, 2011c). Neerja Mittal et al., in Chapter 7, "Magnitude and Phase of Discriminative Orthogonal Radial Moments for Face Recognition," proposed a statistical method to estimate the discrimination strength of all the coefficients of ZMs and PZMs. For classification, only the coefficients with estimated higher discrimination strength are selected and are used in the feature vector. The performance of these selected Discriminative ZMs (DZMs) and Discriminative PZMs (DPZMs) features has been compared to that of their corresponding conventional approaches on YALE (Georghiades, 1997), ORL (AT&T Laboratories Cambridge, 2002), and FERET (Phillips, Moon, Rauss, & Rizvi, 2000) databases against illumination, expression, scale, and pose variations. In this chapter, an extension to these DZMs and DPZMs has been presented by exploring the use of phase information along with the magnitude coefficients of these approaches. The phase coefficients are computed in parallel to the magnitude so no additional time is spent on their computation. Further, DZMs and DPZMs are also combined with PCA and Fisher Linear Discriminant (FLD) (Belhumeur, Hespanha, & Kriegman, 1997). It has been observed from the exhaustive experimentation that with the inclusion of phase features the recognition rate is improved by 2-8%, at reduced dimensions and with less computational complexity, than that of using the successive ZMs and PZMs features.

The Internet is a powerful source of information. However, some of the information that is available on the Internet cannot be shown to every type of public. For instance, pornography is not desirable to be shown to children; pornography is the most harmful content affecting child safety and causing many destructive side effects. A content filter is one of more pieces of software that work together to prevent users from viewing material found on the Internet. Chapter 8, "An Efficient System for Blocking Pornography Websites," by Tarek Mahmoud et al., proposes an efficient content-based software system for detecting and filtering pornography images in Web pages. The proposed system runs online in the background of Internet Explorer (IE) for the purpose of restricting access to pornography Web pages. Skin and face detection techniques are the main components of the proposed system. Because the proposed filter works online, the authors propose two fasting techniques that can be used to speed up the filtering system. The results obtained using the proposed system are compared with four commercial filtering programs. The success rate of the proposed filtering system is better than the considered filtering programs.

During the Internet era, millions of users are using Web-based Social Networking Sites (SNSs) such as MySpace, Facebook, and Twitter for communication needs. Social networking platforms are now considered a source of big data because of real-time activities of a large number of users. In addition to idiosyncratic personal characteristics, Web-based social data may include person-to-person communication, profiles, patterns, and spatio-temporal information. However, analysis of social interaction-based data has not been studied from the perspective of person identification. In chapter 9, "Online User Interaction Traits in Web-Based Social Biometrics," Madeena Sultana et al. introduce for the first time the concept of using interaction-based features from online social networking platforms as a novel biometric. They introduce the concept of social behavioral biometric from SNSs to aid the identification process. Analysis of these novel biometric features and their potential use in various security and authentication applications are also presented. Such applications would pave the way for new directions in biometric research.

Chapter 10

In the current age, use of natural communication in human-computer interaction is a known and well-installed thought. Hand gesture recognition and gesture-based applications have gained a significant amount of popularity amongst people all over the world. They have a number of applications ranging from security to entertainment. These applications generally are real time applications and need fast, accurate communication with machines. On the other end, gesture-based communications have few limitations, but bent finger information is not provided in vision-based techniques. The next chapter, "Fingers' Angle Calculation Using Level-Set Method" by Ankit Chaudhary et al., proposes and contributes towards a novel method for fingertip detection and for angle calculation of both hands' bent fingers. Angle calculation has been done before with sensor-based gloves/devices. This study has been conducted in the context of natural computing for calculating angles without using any wired equipment, colors, marker, or any device. The pre-processing and segmentation of the region of interest is performed in a HSV color space and a binary format, respectively. Fingertips are detected using level-set method and angles are calculated using geometrical analysis. This technique requires no training for the system to perform the task.

The recent advances in multimedia technology demand protection of digital images from unintentional manipulation for content integrity, copyright, and ownership. Digital watermarking technique has wide acceptance in the industry for anti-piracy, ownership verification, and digital image authentication. There have been a large number of schemes in the literature proposed for digital watermarking using non-cryptographic and cryptographic primitives. Use of Least Significant Bits (LSB) is one of the oldest but classical approaches for digital image authentication. Although LSB approach is efficient, it does not provide adequate security. Cryptographic primitives such as hash function, digital signature, and message authentication codes have been used in several applications including multimedia for data authentication. Digital signature-based image authentication provides strong security, but the approach requires managing public key infrastructure, which is a costly operation. Partial data protection is also an optimal approach for protecting important data while leaving unimportant data unprotected. Considering security weakness of the LSB-based approach and cost overhead of the public key-based approach, Siva Charan Muraharirao and Manik Lal Das present, in chapter 11, a digital image authentication scheme using LSB, keyed hash, and partial encryption. They show that the proposed watermarking scheme is secure and efficient in comparison to other related schemes.

Next, Noura Semary explores "An Efficient Color Image Encoding Scheme Based on Colorization." Image colorization is a new image processing topic to recolor gray images to look as like the original color images as possible. Different methods have appeared in the literature to solve this problem, the way that leads to thinking about decolorization, eliminating the colors of color images to just small color keys, aid in the colorization process. Due to this idea, decolorization is considered as a color image encoding mechanism. In this chapter, the authors propose that a new decolorization system depends on extracting the color seeds (Representative Pixels [RP]) using morphology operations. Different decolorization methods are studied and compared to the system results using different quality metrics.

Saif al Zahir then presents "A Fast New Rotation Insensitive WP-Based Method for Image Indexing and Retrieval." In this chapter, the author presents a novel Wavelet Packet (WP)-based method for image identification and retrieval that enables the recovery of the original image from a database even if the image has been subjected to geometric transformations such as size-conserving rotation or flip-ping operations. The proposed method uses the correlation of wavelet packet coefficients to create an image signature. This signature is comprised of two parts. The first part is a short signature, SS, that represents the location of specific values of the WP coefficient correlations in each frequency band. The second portion is the basis signature of the image, which is a long signature, LS, of 1296 correlation points produced by summing up the correlation values along all frequency bands. Computer simulation results show that the method is extremely fast, has a perfect image retrieval rates (100%), and perfect geometric transformations recognition, if any. In addition, the simulation results show that target images are perfectly identified from an image database of 7500 image signatures within a short period of time (nearly 8 seconds on the average). This method is robust against geometric transformation and requires minimal data transfer and can be used for online image retrieval.

Intelligent process control technology in various manufacturing industries is important. Vision-based non-magnetic object detection on moving conveyor in the steel industry will play a vital role for intel-ligent processes and raw material handling. In chapter 14, K. C. Manjunatha et al. present an approach for a vision-based system that performs the detection of non-magnetic objects on raw material moving conveyor in a secondary steel-making industry. At single camera level, a vision-based differential al-gorithm is applied to recognize an object. Image pixels-based differential techniques, optical flow, and motion-based segmentations are used for traffic parameters extraction; the proposed approach extends those futures into industrial applications. The authors implement a smart control system, since they can save the energy and control unnecessary breakdowns in a robust manner. The technique developed for non-magnetic object detection has a single static background. Establishing background and background subtraction from continuous video input frames forms the basis. Detection of non-magnetic materials, which are moving with raw materials, and taking immediate action at the same stage as the material handling system will avoid the breakdowns or power wastage. The authors achieve accuracy up to 95% with the computational time of not more than 1.5 seconds for complete system execution.

Next, a review of novel techniques for detecting corner features of planar objects is presented by Muhammad Sarfraz in chapter 15, "Detecting Corner Features of Planar Objects." Corner points or features determine significant geometrical locations of the digital images. They provide important clues for shape representation and analysis. Corner points represent important features of an object that may be useful at subsequent levels of processing. If the corner points are identified properly, a shape can be represented in an efficient and compact way with sufficient accuracy in many shape analysis problem. This chapter reviews some well referred algorithms in the literature together with empirical study. Users can easily pick one that may prove to be superior from all aspects for their applications and requirements.

Finally, in "Outline Capture of Planar Objects by Detecting Corner Features," Misbah Irshad et al. propose a scheme that helps digitizing hand printed and electronic planar objects or vectorizing the generic shapes. An evolutionary optimization technique, namely Genetic Algorithm (GA), is used to solve the problem of curve fitting with cubic and rational cubic spline functions. The underlying scheme is comprised of various phases including data of the image outlines, detection of corner points, using GA for optimal values of shape parameters in the description of spline functions, and fitting curve using spline functions to the detected corner points.

CONCLUSION

In all, the chapters in this book present readers with a full view of some of the most up-to-date discoveries in the fields of computer vision and image processing. The mix of practical applications and theoretical research included in this reference volume effectively illustrate best practices alongside novel techniques, encouraging practitioners and educators to join in creating the next generation of IS and MT technologies and applications.

Muhammad Sarfraz
Kuwait University, Kuwait

REFERENCES

American College of Radiology. (1998). *Illustrated Breast Imaging Reporting and Data System BIRADS* (3rd ed.). American College of Radiology.

AT&T Laboratories Cambridge. (2002). *Olivetti Research Laboratory (ORL) face database*. Retrieved from http://www.cl.cam.ac.uk/research/dtg/attarchive/facedatabase.html

Ballard, D. H., & Brown, C. M. (1982). *Computer Vision*. New York: Prentice Hall.

Banissi, E., & Sarfraz, M. (2012). *Computer Graphics, Imaging and Visualization*. IEEE Computer Society.

Belhumeur, P. N., Hespanha, J. P., & Kriegman, D. J. (1997). Eigenfaces vs. Fisherfaces Recognition using class specific linear projection. *IEEE Transactions on Pattern Analysis and Machine Intelligence, 19*, 711–720. doi:10.1109/34.598228

Blake, A., & Isard, M. (2000). *Active Contours*. Berlin: Springer.

Burger, W., & Burge, M. J. (2007). *Digital Image Processing: An Algorithmic Approach Using Java*. Berlin: Springer.

Burger, W., & Burge, M. J. (2007). *Digital Image Processing: An Algorithmic Approach Using Java*. Berlin: Springer.

Carsten, S., Ulrich, M., & Wiedemann, C. (2007). *Machine Vision Algorithms and Applications*. Hoboken, NJ: Wiley.

Computer Vision. (2012). *Wikipedia*. Retrieved from http://en.wikipedia.org/wiki/Computer_vision

Crowley, J. L., & Christensen, H. I. (Eds.). (1995). *Vision as Process*. Berlin: Springer-Verlag. doi:10.1007/978-3-662-03113-1

Davies, E. R. (2005). Machine Vision: Theory, Algorithms, Practicalities. San Francisco: Morgan Kaufmann. Azad, P., Gockel, T., & Dillmann, R. (2008). Computer Vision – Principles and Practice. Elektor International Media BV.

Digital Image Processing. (2012). *Wikipedia*. Retrieved from http://en.wikipedia.org/wiki/Image_processing#References

Fisher, R., Dawson-Howe, K., Fitzgibbon, A., Robertson, C., & Trucco, E. (2005). *Dictionary of Computer Vision and Image Processing*. Hoboken, NJ: John Wiley. doi:10.1002/0470016302

Forsyth, D. A., & Ponce, J. (2003). *Computer Vision: A Modern Approach*. New York: Prentice Hall.

Georghiades, A. S. (1997). *Yale face database*. Retrieved from http://cvc.yale.edu/projects/yalefaces/yalefaces.html

Gonzalez, R. C., Woods, R. E., & Eddins, S. L. (2009). *Digital Image Processing using MATLAB*. New York: Pearson Education.

Granlund, G. H., & Knutsson, H. (1995). *Signal Processing for Computer Vision*. Dordrecht, The Netherlands: Kluwer Academic Publisher. doi:10.1007/978-1-4757-2377-9

Hartley, R., & Zisserman, A. (2003). *Multiple View Geometry in Computer Vision*. Cambridge, UK: Cambridge University Press.

Jähne, B. (2002). *Digital Image Processing*. New York: Springer. doi:10.1007/978-3-662-04781-1

Jähne, B., & Haußecker, H. (2000). *Computer Vision and Applications: A Guide for Students and Practitioners*. New York: Academic Press.

Klette, R., Schluens, K., & Koschan, A. (1998). *Computer Vision – Three-Dimensional Data from Images*. Berlin: Springer.

Management Association. (2013). *Image Processing: Concepts, Methodologies, Tools, and Applications*. Hershey, PA: IGI Global.

Marcus, D. S., Wang, T. H., Parker, J., Csernansky, J. G., Morris, J. C., & Buckner, R. L. (2007). Open Access Series of Imaging Studies (OASIS), cross-sectional MRI data in young, middle aged, nondemented, and demented older adults. *Journal of Cognitive Neuroscience, 19*(9), 1498–1507. doi:10.1162/jocn.2007.19.9.1498 PMID:17714011

Medioni, G., & Kang, S. B. (2004). *Emerging Topics in Computer Vision*. New York: Prentice Hall.

Morris, T. (2004). *Computer Vision and Image Processing*. New York: Palgrave Macmillan.

Morris, T. (2004). *Computer Vision and Image Processing*. New York: Palgrave Macmillan.

Nor'aini, A. J., Raveendran, P., & Selvanathan, N. (2007). A comparative analysis of Zernike moments and Principal Components Analysis as feature extractors for face recognition. In *Proceedings of 3rd Kuala Lumpur International Conference on Biomedical Engineering*, (Vol. 15, pp. 37-41). Kuala Lumpur, Malaysia: Springer.

Paragios, N., Chen, Y., & Faugeras, O. (2005). *Handbook of Mathematical Models in Computer Vision*. Berlin: Springer.

Philipps, D. (1997). *Image Processing in C: Analyzing and Enhancing Digital Images*. R & D Books.

Phillips, P. J., Moon, H., Rauss, P. J., & Rizvi, S. (2000). *The Facial Recognition Technology (FERET) face database*. Retrieved from http://face.nist.gov/colorferet/request.html

Sarfraz, M. (2013). *Intelligent Computer Vision and Image Processing: Innovation, Application, and Design*. Hershey, PA: IGI Global. doi:10.4018/978-1-4666-3906-5

Sarfraz, M. (2014). *Computer Vision and Image Processing in Intelligent Systems and Multimedia Technologies*. Hershey, PA: IGI Global.

Sargano, A.B., Sarfraz, M., & Haq, N. (2014). An Intelligent System for Paper Currency Recognition with Robust Features. *Journal of Intelligent and Fuzzy Systems*.

Shapiro, L. G., & Stockman, G. C. (2001). *Computer Vision*. New York: Prentice Hall.

Singh, C., Walia, E., & Mittal, N. (2011a). Face Recognition using Zernike and Complex Zernike moment features. *Pattern Recognition and Image Analysis*, *21*(1), 71–81. doi:10.1134/S1054661811010044

Singh, C., Walia, E., & Mittal, N. (2011b). Magnitude and phase coefficients of Zernike and Pseudo Zernike moments for robust face recognition. In *Proceedings of the IASTED international conference on Computer Vision (CV-2011)* (pp. 180-187). Vancouver, Canada: IASTED.

Singh, C., Walia, E., & Mittal, N. (2011c). Rotation Invariant Complex Zernike Moments Features and their Application to Human Face and Character Recognition. *IET Computer Vision*, *5*(5), 255–265. doi:10.1049/iet-cvi.2010.0020

Sonka, M., Hlavac, V., & Boyle, R. (1999). *Image Processing, Analysis, and Machine Vision*. PWS Publishing.

Sonka, M., Hlavac, V., & Boyle, R. (2008). *Image Processing, Analysis, and Machine Vision*. New York: Thomson.

Stanciu, S. G. (2012). *Digital Image Processing. InTech. Koprowski, R., & Wrobel, Z. (2011). Image Processing in Optical Coherence Tomography using Matlab*. University of Silesia.

Starck, J., Murtagh, F. D., & Bijaoui, A. (1998). *Image Processing and Data Analysis: The Multiscale Approach*. Cambridge, UK: Cambridge University Press. doi:10.1017/CBO9780511564352

Starck, J.-L., & Murtagh, F. (2006). *Astronomical Image and Data Analysis*. Berlin: Springer.

Trucco, E., & Verri, A. (1998). *Introductory Techniques for 3-D Computer Vision*. New York: Prentice Hall.

Turek, F. (2011). Machine Vision Fundamentals: How to Make Robots See. *NASA Tech Briefs Magazine*, *35*(6), 60–62.

Zheng, Y. (2011). *Image Fusion and Its Applications*. InTech. doi:10.5772/691

Zhou, H., Wu, J., & Zhang, J. (2010). *Digital Image Processing. BookBoon. Young, I., Gerbrands, J., & Vliet, L.V. (2009). Fundamentals of Image Processing*. Delft University of Technology.

Chapter 1
Evaluating an Evolutionary Particle Swarm Optimization for Fast Fuzzy C–Means Clustering on Liver CT Images

Abder-Rahman Ali
Scientific Research Group in Egypt (SRGE), Egypt

Micael S. Couceiro
University of Coimbra, Portugal & Ingeniarius, Lda., Mealhada, Portugal

Ahmed M. Anter
Scientific Research Group in Egypt (SRGE), Egypt & Mansoura University, Egypt

Aboul Ella Hassanian
Scientific Research Group in Egypt (SRGE), Egypt & Cairo University, Egypt

ABSTRACT

An Evolutionary Particle Swarm Optimization based on the Fractional Order Darwinian method for optimizing a Fast Fuzzy C-Means algorithm is proposed. This chapter aims at enhancing the performance of Fast Fuzzy C-Means, both in terms of the overall solution and speed. To that end, the concept of fractional calculus is used to control the convergence rate of particles, wherein each one of them represents a set of cluster centers. The proposed solution, denoted as FODPSO-FFCM, is applied on liver CT images, and compared with Fast Fuzzy C-Means and PSOFFCM, using Jaccard Index and Dice Coefficient. The computational efficiency is achieved by using the histogram of the image intensities during the clustering process instead of the raw image data. The experimental results based on the Analysis of Variance (ANOVA) technique and multiple pair-wise comparison show that the proposed algorithm is fast, accurate, and less time consuming.

DOI: 10.4018/978-1-4666-6030-4.ch001

1. INTRODUCTION

Image segmentation is the process of subdividing the image to into its constituent parts, and is considered one of the most difficult tasks in image processing. It plays a vital role in any application and its success is based on the effective implementation of the segmentation technique (Annadurai & Shanmugalakshmi, 2006). For many applications, segmentation reduces to finding an object in an image. This involves partitioning the image into two classes, object or background. In the human visual system, segmentation takes place naturally. We are experts on detecting patterns, lines, edges and shapes, and making decisions based upon the visual information. At the same time, we are overwhelmed by the amount of image information that can be captured by today's technology, as it is not feasible to manually process all such images. Instead, we design patterns which looks for certain patterns and objects of interest and put them to our attention (Gunnar, 2010).

Recent advances in a wide range of medical imaging technologies have revolutionized how we view functional and pathological events in the body and define anatomical structures in which these events take place. Medical images in their raw form are represented by arrays of numbers in the computer, with the numbers indicating the values of relevant physical quantities that show contrast between different types of body tissue. Processing and analysis of medical images are useful in transforming raw images into a quantifiable symbolic form for ease of searching and mining, in extracting meaningful quantitative information to aid diagnosis, and in integrating complementary data from multiple imaging modalities. One fundamental problem in medical image analysis is image segmentation, which identifies the boundaries of objects such as organs or tumors in images. Having the segmentation result makes it possible for shape analysis, detecting volume change, and making a precise radiation therapy treatment plan. However, despite the intensive research, segmen-

tation remains a challenging problem due to the diverse image content, cluttered objects, occlusion, image noise, non-uniform image texture, ...etc (Huang & Tsechpenakis, 2009).

Computed Tomography (CT) has rapidly gained acceptance as the preferred technique for routine liver evaluation since it provides image acquisition at the peak enhancement of the liver parenchyma during a single breath hold (Bluemke, & Fishman, 1993) (Zeman et al., 1993) (Bluemke, Urban, & Fishman, 1994).

The liver is a large, meaty organ that sits on the right side of the belly. Weighting about three pounds, the liver is reddish-brown in colour and feels rubbery to the touch (Digestive Disorders Health Center, 2013). It fulfills multiple and finely tuned functions that are critical for the homeostasis of the human body. Although individual pathways for synthesis and breakdown of carbohydrates, lipids, amino acids, proteins, and nucleic acids can be identified in other mammalian cells, only the liver performs all these biochemical transformations simultaneously, and is able to combine them to accomplish its vital biological task. The liver is also the principal site of biotransformation, activation, or inactivation of drugs and synthetic chemicals. Therefore, this organ displays a unique biologic complexity. When it fails, functional replacement presents one of the most difficult challenges in substitutive medicine (Bronzino, 2000).

Due to its unreplaceable attributes, much of the research on medical imaging over the past few years has been centered on studying CT images of the liver. As such, researchers across the globe have been working towards providing a diagnostic support of liver diseases, liver volume measurements, and 3D liver volume rendering, without the need of any manual process and visual inspection, which are a mental work and a huge time consuming process. Image segmentation has been one of the many image processing methods employed on that particular task. Nevertheless, still many challenges remain before one can provide a fully autonomous image segmentation method of liver

CT images. The physical attributes of the liver previously described, combined with the limitations inherent to CT technology, are translated into low-level contrast and blurry edged images, varying from patient to patient and between different CT processes. Additionally, other organs in the vicinities, like spleen and stomach, share similar gray levels, thus making it even harder to clearly identify the liver (Mharib et al., 2012).

In this chapter, we will present a Fast Fuzzy C-Means clustering algorithm, optimized by the Fractional Order Darwinian (FOD) method, and apply the suggested algorithm on liver CT images.

The chapter is organized as follows: Section (2) introduces the classical Fuzzy C-Means clustering, and how it can be extended to Fast Fuzzy C-Means; Section (3) describes Particle Swarm Optimization; Section (4) describes the Fractional Order Darwinian PSO method and fuzzy clustering using this method; Section (5) explains the proposed approach; Section (6) represents the material used in this chapter; Experimental results and discussion are given in Section (7); concluding the chapter in Section (8).

2. FUZZY C-MEANS CLUSTERING

As stated at the beginning of this chapter, image segmentation techniques provide an efficient way to perform image analysis. However, the automatic selection of a robust optimal method remains a challenge in segmentation of medical imaging. Most of the existing image segmentation techniques comprise on threshold, regional, edge detection and clustering methods. Within the class of clustering methods, the Fuzzy C-Means (FCM) clustering algorithm is perhaps the most widely used in image segmentation, due to its overall performance (Oliveira & Pedrycz, 2007).

Clustering is the process of partitioning a data set into different classes, so that the data in each class share same common features according to a defined distance measure. The standard crisp C-Means clustering scheme is very popular in the filed of pattern recognition (Duda, Hart, & Stork, 2001).

However, this scheme uses hard partitioning, in which each data point belongs to exactly one class. The Fuzzy C-Means (FCM) is a generalization of the standard crisp c-means scheme, in which a data point can belong to all classes with different degrees of membership (Bezdek, 1973).

FCM is an unsupervised clustering algorithm that has been successfully applied to a number of problems involving feature analysis, clustering, and classifier design. It divides n vectors into c fuzzy groups, calculates the clustering center to each group, and minimizes the non-similarity index value function. FCM adopts fuzzy partitions to make each given value of data input between 0 and 1 in order to determine the degree of its belonging to a group. With fuzzy partitions, elements of the membership matrix are allowed to have the values between 0 and 1. After normalizing, the combined membership of a dataset would be as follows (Cao et al., 2010):

$$\sum_{i=1}^{c} \mu_{ij} = 1, \forall_j = 1, 2, \ldots, n \tag{1}$$

Let $O = \left\{ o_1, \ldots, o_b, \ldots, o_n \right\}$ be the set of n objects, and $C = \left\{ c_1, \ldots, c_b, \ldots, c_n \right\}$ be the set of c centroids in a p-dimensional feature space. The Fuzzy C-Means partitions O into c clusters by minimizing the following objective function (Maji & Pal, 2008):

$$J = \sum_{j=1}^{n} \sum_{i=1}^{c} \left(\mu_{ij} \right)^m \left\| o_j - c_i \right\|^2 \tag{2}$$

where $1 \leq m \leq \infty$ is the *fuzzifier*, c_i is the ith centroid corresponding to cluster β_i, $\mu_{ij} \in [0, 1]$ is the fuzzy membership of the pattern o_j to cluster β_i, and $\left\| \cdot \right\|$ is the distance norm, such that,

$$\mathbf{c}_i = \frac{1}{n_i} \sum_{j=1}^{n} \left(\mu_{ij}\right)^m \mathbf{o}_j \; where \, n_i = \sum_{j=1}^{n} \left(\mu_{ij}\right)^m \tag{3}$$

and,

$$\mu_{ij} = \frac{1}{\sum_{k=1}^{c} \left(\dfrac{d_{ij}}{d_{kj}}\right)^{\frac{2}{m-1}}}$$

where

$$d_{ij}^{\,2} = \mathbf{o}_j - \mathbf{c}_i^{\,2} \tag{4}$$

FCM starts by randomly choosing c objects as centroids (means) of the c clusters. Memberships are calculated based on the relative distance (Euclidean distance) of the object $\mathbf{o}_j$ to the centroids using Equation (4). After the memberships of all objects have been found, the centroids of the clusters are calculated using Equation (3). The process stops when the centroids from the previous iteration are identical to those generated in the current iteration (Maji & Pal, 2008). Figure 1 summarizes the steps of FCM (Bush, 2013).

In order to obtain a Fast Fuzzy C-Means (FFCM), the histogram of the image intensities is used during the clustering process instead of the raw image data (Semechko, 2013).

3. PARTICLE SWARM OPTIMIZATION

Despite its usefulness, FCM clustering algorithm segmentation is based on a local search mechanism that benefits from a simple climbing technique to find the optimal solution. As such, this sort (Oliveira & Pedrycz, 2007). In addition, the FCM algorithm is also known to present a very slow

Figure 1. FCM flowchart

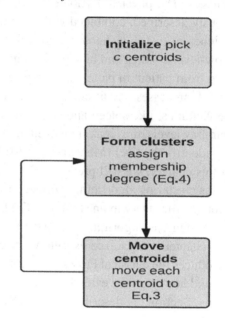

convergence on hard problems, such as grayscale image segmentation with multiple cluster samples.

In spite of these intrinsic limitations, researchers have been proposing several extensions of the FCM over the past few years, in which its combination with well-known Particle Swarm Optimization (PSO) has been one of the most successful ones *e.g.*, (Zhou, 2009), (Izakian & Abraham, 2011).

The PSO algorithm proposed for the first time by (Kennedy & Eberhart, 1995), is a biologically inspired technique derived from the collective behavior of birds flocks.

PSO is an artificial intelligence technique that can be used to find approximate solutions to extremely difficult or impossible numeric maximization and minimization problems (McCaffrey, 2013).

PSO shares many similarities with evolutionary computation techniques such as Genetic Algorithms (GA). The system is initialized with a population of random solutions and searches for optima by updating generations. However, unlike GA, PSO has no evolution operators such as crossover and mutation. In PSO, the potential solutions, called particles, fly through the problem space by following the current optimum particles (Hu, 2013).

In past several years, PSO has been successfully applied in many research and application areas. It is demonstrated that PSO gets better results in a faster, cheaper way compared with other methods. Another reason that PSO is attractive is that there are few parameters to adjust. One version, with slight variations, works well in a wide variety of applications. Particle swarm optimization has been used for approaches that can be used across a wide range of applications, as well as for specific applications focused on a specific requirement (Hu, 2013).

The concept of particle swarms, although initially introduced for simulating human visual behaviors, has become very popular these days as an efficient search and optimization technique. PSO does not require any gradient information of the function to be optimized, uses only primitive mathematical operators, and is conceptually very simple (Kelemen, Abraham, & Chen, 2008).

The stochastic optimization ability of the algorithm is enhanced due to its cooperative simplistic mechanism, wherein each particle presents itself as a possible solution of the problem, e.g., the best cluster centers of a given segmented image. These particles travel through the search space to find an optimal solution, by interacting and sharing information with other particles, namely their individual best solution (local best) and computing the global best (Valle et al., 2008).

In each step t of the PSO the fitness function now represented by Equation (2) is used to evaluate the particles success. To model the swarm, each particle moves in a multidimensional space according to the position $\mathbf{x}_n[t]$, and velocity $\mathbf{v}_n[t]$, which are highly dependent on local best $\breve{x}_n[t]$ and global best $\breve{g}_n[t]$ information:

$$\begin{cases} v_n[t+1] = wv_n[t] + \rho_1 r_1(\breve{g}_n - x_n) + \rho_2 r_2(\breve{x}_n - x_n[t]) \\ \mathbf{x}_n[t+1] = x_n[t] + v_n[t+1] \end{cases}$$

(5)

Coefficients ρ_1 and ρ_2 are assigned weights, which control the inertial influence of "the globally best" and "the locally best", respectively, when the new velocity is determined. Typically, ρ_1 and ρ_2 are constant integer values, which represent "cognitive" and "social" components with $\rho_1 + \rho_2 < 2$ (Couceiro, 2012). However, different results can be obtained by assigning different influences for each component.

The parameter w, commonly known as inertial coefficient, will weigh the influence of the past velocity on determining a new velocity, $0 < w < 1$. It is noteworthy that the w value greatly affects the inertial particles. With a small w, particles ignore their previous activities, thus ignoring the system dynamics and being susceptible to get stuck in local solutions (i.e., exploitation behavior). On the other hand, with a large w, particles will present a more diversified behavior, which allows exploration of new solutions and improves the long-term performance (i.e., exploration behavior). However, if the exploration level is too high, then the algorithm may take too much time to find the global solution. Based on the experimental results from (Eberhart & Shi, 2000), it will be used a fractional coefficient of $w = 0.9$, thus resulting in a balance between exploitation and exploration.

The parameters r_1 and r_2 are random vectors with each component generally a uniform random number between 0 and 1. The intent is to multiply a new random component per velocity dimension, rather than multiplying the same component with each particle's velocity dimension.

It is noteworthy that the velocity dimension, *i.e.*, $\dim v_n[t]$, as well as the position dimension, *i.e.*, $\dim x_n[t]$, corresponds to the total number of desired cluster centers of the image, *i.e.*, $\dim v_n[t] = \dim x_n[t] = c$. In other words, each particle's position will be represented as a c-dimension vector. Moreover, each particle moves in a multidimensional space according to position $x_n[t]$ from the discrete time system (5), wherein

$$x_n[t] \epsilon \, \mathbb{R}^c \wedge [0...0]^T \leq x_n[t] \leq (L-1) \times [1...1]^T.$$

As particles move in that multidimensional space, they share their own solution to their teammates (i.e., other particles inside the same swarm) using the fitness function presented in Equation 2.

4. FRACTIONAL ORDER DARWINIAN PSO

The success of the *PSO* algorithm gave rise to a chain of *PSO*-based alternatives over the last years, so as to overcome its drawbacks, namely, its stagnation. One of the proposed methods was denoted as Darwinian *PSO* (*DPSO*), that comprises on many swarms that individually performs just like an ordinary *PSO* algorithm and some rules govern the whole population of particles, thus mimicking the concepts of natural selection (Tillett et al., 2005). The main idea was to run many simultaneous parallel *PSO* algorithms, each one a different swarm, on the same problem and a simple selection mechanism would be applied. As such, when a search tended to a sub-optimal solution, the search in that area would be simply discarded and another area would be searched instead. In this approach, at each step t, improving swarms would be rewarded (extend particle life or spawn a new descendent) and stagnating swarms would be punished (reduce swarm life or delete particles).

Despite the positive results retrieved by Tillett *et al.* (Tillett et al., 2005), this competitive approach also increases the computational complexity of the optimization method. As many swarms of cooperative test solutions (*i.e.*, particles) run simultaneously in a competitive fashion, the computational requirements increase and, as a consequence, the convergence time also increases for the exact same computer hardware. Therefore, and to further improve the *DPSO* algorithm, an extended version denoted as *Fractional Order Darwinian PSO* was presented in (Couceiro, Rocha, Ferreira, & Machado, 2012), in which fractional calculus is used to control the convergence rate of the algorithm. An important property revealed by fractional calculus is that, while an integer-order derivative just implies a finite series, the fractional-order derivative requires an infinite number of terms. In other words, integer derivatives are 'local' operators while fractional derivatives have, implicitly, a 'memory' of all past events. The characteristics revealed by fractional calculus make this mathematical tool well suited to describe phenomena such as irreversibility and chaos because of its inherent memory property. In this line of thought, the dynamic phenomena of particles' trajectories configure a case where fractional calculus tools fit adequately. In other words, by slightly increasing the memory complexity of the *DPSO* (and *PSO*), one can significantly decrease the computation complexity by increasing the convergence of particles towards the optimal solution.

In estimation problems previously studied in (Couceiro, Luz, Figueiredo, Ferreira, & Dias, 2010), segmentation and classification methods compared in (Ghamisi et al., 2012), the *FODPSO* based on *Grünwald–Letnikov* definition of fractional calculus (Ostalczyk, 2009) has been successfully compared with the *PSO*, the *DPSO* and many other exhaustive and evolutionary methods, depicting a superior performance on every single case. Hence, it was based on such superior performance that a new formulation of the *FODPSO* now proposed, by combining it with the *FCM* algorithm for clustering problems in image segmentation.

4.1 Fuzzy Clustering by FODPSO

This section presents the *FODPSO* as a method to enhance the *FFCM* clustering algorithm. In each step t of the *FODPSO*, the fitness function now represented by Equation 2 is used to evaluate the particles' success. To model the swarm s, each particle n moves in a multidimensional space according to the position $x_n^s[t]$, and velocity $v_n^s[t]$, which are highly dependent on local best $\breve{x}_n^s[t]$ and global best $\breve{g}_n^s[t]$ information (Box 1).

Coefficients ρ_1 and ρ_2 are assigned weights, which control the inertial influence of "the globally best" and "the locally best", respectively, when the new velocity is determined. Typically, ρ_1 and ρ_2 are constant integer values, which represent "cognitive" and "social" components with $\rho_1 + \rho_2 < 2$ (Couceiro, Martins, Rocha, & Ferreira, 2012). However, different results can be obtained by assigning different influences for each component.

The parameter α, commonly known as the fractional coefficient, will weigh the influence of past events on determining a new velocity, $0 < \alpha < 1$. It is noteworthy that the α value greatly affects the inertial particles. With a small α, particles ignore their previous activities, thus ignoring the system dynamics and being susceptible to get stuck in local solutions (*i.e.*, exploitation behavior). On the other hand, with a large α, particles will present a more diversified behavior, which allows exploration of new solutions and improves the long-term performance (*i.e.*, explo-

ration behavior). However, if the exploration level is too high, then the algorithm may take too much time to find the global solution. Based on the experimental results from (Couceiro, Rocha, Ferreira, & Machado, 2012), it will be used a fractional coefficient of $\alpha = 0.6$, thus resulting in a balance between exploitation and exploration.

The parameters r_1 and r_2 are random vectors with each component generally a uniform random number between 0 and 1. The intent is to multiply a new random component per velocity dimension, rather than multiplying the same component with each particle's velocity dimension.

It is noteworthy that the velocity dimension, *i.e.*, $\dim v_n^s[t]$, as well as the position dimension, *i.e.*, $\dim x_n^s[t]$, corresponds to the total number of desired cluster centers of the image, *i.e.*, $\dim v_n^s[t] = \dim x_n^s[t] = C$. In other words, each particle's position will be represented as a C-dimension vector. Moreover, each particle moves in a multidimensional space according to position $x_n^s[t]$ from the discrete time system (5), wherein

$$x_n^s[t] \epsilon \, \mathbb{R}^C \wedge \left[0 \ldots 0\right]^T \leq x_n^s[t] \leq (L-1) \times \left[1 \ldots 1\right]^T.$$

As particles move in that multidimensional space, they share their own solution to their teammates (*i.e.*, other particles inside the same swarm) using the fitness function presented in (2). Following the insights presented for the first time by (Tillett, Rao, Sahin, Rao, & Brockport, 2005) and more recently in (Couceiro, Rocha, Ferreira, & Machado, 2012), a natural selection mechanism based on the Darwinian principle of

Box 1.

$$w_n^s[t+1] = \alpha v_n^s[t] + \frac{1}{2}\alpha(1-\alpha)\, \mathrm{v}_{vn}^s[t-1] + \frac{1}{6}\alpha(1-\alpha)(2-\alpha)\, \mathrm{v}_{vn}^s[t-2] + \frac{1}{24}\alpha(1-\alpha)(2-\alpha)(3-\alpha)\, \mathrm{v}_{vn}^s[t-3]$$

$$v_n^s[t+1] = w_n^s[t] + \rho_1 r_1(\breve{g}_n^s - x_n^s) + \rho_2 r_2(\breve{x}_n^s - x_n^s[t]$$

$$x_n^s[t+1] = x_n^s[t] + v_n^s[t+1]$$

(6)

survival of the fittest is considered. To analyze the general state of each swarm, the fitness of all particles is evaluated and the neighborhood and individual best positions of each of the particles are updated. If a new global solution is found, a new particle is spawned. A particle is deleted if the swarm fails to find a fitter state in a defined number of steps.

Some simple rules are followed to delete a swarm, delete particles, and spawn a new swarm and a new particle: *i*) when the swarm population falls below a minimum bound, the swarm is deleted; and *ii*) the worst performing particle in the swarm is deleted when a maximum threshold number of steps (search counter SC_{max}) without improving the fitness function is reached. After the deletion of the particle, instead of being set to zero, the counter is reset to a value approaching the threshold number, according to:

$$SC^S\left(N_{kill}^s\right) = SC_{max}\left[1 - \frac{1}{N_{kill}^s + 1}\right] \quad (7)$$

where N_{kill}^s is the number of particles deleted from the swarm over a period in which there was no improvement in fitness. To spawn a new swarm, a swarm must not have any particle ever deleted and the maximum number of swarms must not be exceeded. Still, the new swarm is only created with a probability of $p = r / N_{swarms}$, with r being a random uniform number between 0 and 1 and N_{swarms} the number of swarms. This factor avoids the creation of newer swarms when there are large numbers of swarms in existence. The parent swarm is unaffected and half of the parent's particles are selected at random for the child swarm and half of the particles of a random member of the swarm collection are also selected. If the swarm initial population number is not obtained, the rest of the particles are randomly initialized

and added to the new swarm. A particle is spawned whenever a swarm achieves a new global best and the maximum defined population of a swarm has not been reached.

Like the traditional *PSO*, a few parameters, besides the ones from the discrete time system (5), need to be defined to run the algorithm efficiently: *i*) initial swarm population; *ii*) maximum and minimum swarm population; *iii*) initial number of swarms; *iv*) maximum and minimum number of swarms; and *v*) stagnancy threshold.

5. PROPOSED APPROACH

Algorithm 1 describes the proposed approach used in this chapter.

6. ABDOMINAL CT DATA COLLECTION

CT scanning is a diagnostic imaging procedure that uses X-rays in order to present cross-sectional images (slices) of the body. The proposed system will be applied on a complex dataset. The dataset is divided into seven categories, depending on the tumor type: *Benign* (Cyst (CY), *Hemangioma* (HG), *Hepatic Adenoma* (HA), and *Focal Nodular Hyperplasia* (FNH)); or *Malignant* (hepatocellular carcinoma (HCC), *Cholangiocarcinoma* (CC), and *Metastases* (MS)). Each of these categories have more than 15-patients, each patient has more than one hundred slices, and more than one phase of CT scan (arterial, delayed, portal venous, non-contrast). The dataset includes a diagnosis report for each patient. All images are in JPEG format, selected from a DICOM file, and have dimensions of 630×630, with horizontal and vertical resolution of 72 DPI, and bit depth of 24 bits (Anter et al., 2013). All CT images were captured from Radiopaedia[1].

Algorithm 1. FODPSO-FFCM clustering algorithm

Initialize w, ρ_1, ρ_2 // inertial coefficient, global and local weights
Initialize N // initial number of particles within the population
Initialize Δv // maximum number of levels a particle can travel between iterations
Initialize I_T // total number of iterations
Initialize $\begin{bmatrix}0...0\end{bmatrix}^T \leq \mathbf{x}_{\mathbf{n}}^{\mathbf{s}}\begin{bmatrix}0\end{bmatrix} \leq \left(L-1\right) \times \begin{bmatrix}1...1\end{bmatrix}^T$ // randomly initialize the cluster centroids, *i.e.*, position of particles
Initialize $\breve{x}_{\mathbf{n}}^{\mathbf{s}}, \breve{g}_{\mathbf{n}}^{\mathbf{s}}$ based on $x_n^s\begin{bmatrix}0\end{bmatrix}$ // initial local best and global best positions
Initialize $J_n^{\;best}, J_T^{\;best}$ based on $\breve{x}_{\mathbf{n}}^{\mathbf{s}}, \breve{g}_{\mathbf{n}}^{\mathbf{s}}$ // initial local best and global best solution
For each iteration t until I_T // main loop
For each particle n from swarm s
$$\mathbf{w}_{\mathbf{n}}^{\mathbf{s}}\begin{bmatrix}t+1\end{bmatrix} = \alpha\mathbf{v}_{\mathbf{n}}^{\mathbf{s}}\begin{bmatrix}t\end{bmatrix} + \frac{1}{2}\alpha\mathbf{v}_{\mathbf{n}}^{\mathbf{s}}\begin{bmatrix}t-1\end{bmatrix} + \frac{1}{6}\alpha\left(1-\alpha\right)\mathbf{v}_{\mathbf{n}}^{\mathbf{s}}\begin{bmatrix}t-2\end{bmatrix} + \frac{1}{24}\alpha\left(1-\alpha\right)\left(2-\alpha\right)\mathbf{v}_{\mathbf{n}}^{\mathbf{s}}\begin{bmatrix}t-3\end{bmatrix}$$
$$\mathbf{v}_{\mathbf{n}}^{\mathbf{s}}\begin{bmatrix}t+1\end{bmatrix} = \mathbf{w}_{\mathbf{n}}^{\mathbf{s}}\begin{bmatrix}t\end{bmatrix} + \rho_1\mathbf{r}_1\left(\breve{g}_{\mathbf{n}}^{\mathbf{s}} - \mathbf{x}_{\mathbf{n}}^{\mathbf{s}}\right) + \rho_2\mathbf{r}_2\left(\breve{x}_{\mathbf{n}}^{\mathbf{s}} - \mathbf{x}_{\mathbf{n}}^{\mathbf{s}}\begin{bmatrix}t\end{bmatrix}\right)$$
$$\mathbf{x}_{\mathbf{n}}^{\mathbf{s}}\begin{bmatrix}t+1\end{bmatrix} = \mathbf{x}_{\mathbf{n}}^{\mathbf{s}}\begin{bmatrix}t\end{bmatrix} + \mathbf{v}_{\mathbf{n}}^{\mathbf{s}}\begin{bmatrix}t+1\end{bmatrix}, \begin{bmatrix}0...0\end{bmatrix}^T \leq \mathbf{x}_{\mathbf{n}}\begin{bmatrix}t+1\end{bmatrix} \leq \left(L-1\right) \times \begin{bmatrix}1...1\end{bmatrix}^T$$
// compute $J_n\begin{bmatrix}t+1\end{bmatrix}^n$ based on the vector of clusters defined by $x_n\begin{bmatrix}t+1\end{bmatrix}$ $$\mathbf{J}_{\mathbf{n}}\begin{bmatrix}t+1\end{bmatrix} = \sum_{j=1}^{n}\sum_{i=1}^{c}\left(\mathbf{\mu}_{\mathbf{ij}}\right)^m \mathbf{o}_j - \left(\mathbf{x}_{\mathbf{n}}\begin{bmatrix}t+1\end{bmatrix}\right)_i^2$$ $$\left(\mathbf{x}_{\mathbf{n}}\begin{bmatrix}t+1\end{bmatrix}\right)_i = \frac{1}{n_i}\sum_{j=1}^{n}\left(\mathbf{\mu}_{\mathbf{ij}}\right)^m \mathbf{o}_{\mathbf{j}} \text{where} n_i = \sum_{j=1}^{n}\left(\mathbf{\mu}_{\mathbf{ij}}\right)^m$$ $$\mathbf{\mu}_{\mathbf{ij}} = \frac{1}{\sum_{k=1}^{c}\left(\dfrac{d_{ij}}{d_{kj}}\right)^{\frac{2}{m-1}}} \quad \text{where } d_{ij}^{\;2} = \mathbf{o}_{\mathbf{j}} - \left(\mathbf{x}_{\mathbf{n}}\begin{bmatrix}t+1\end{bmatrix}\right)_i^2$$
If $\mathbf{J}_{\mathbf{n}}\begin{bmatrix}t+1\end{bmatrix} < J_n^{\;best}$ // particle n has improved
$$J_n^{\;best} = \mathbf{J}_{\mathbf{n}}\begin{bmatrix}t+1\end{bmatrix}$$

continued on following page

Algorithm 1. Continued

$\breve{x}_{\mathbf{n}}^{\mathbf{s}} = \mathbf{x}_{\mathbf{n}}^{\mathbf{s}}\left[t+1\right]$
For each swarm s
If $\mathbf{J}_{\mathbf{n}}\left[t+1\right] < J_{T}^{\,best}$ // swarm s has improved
$J_{T}^{\,best} = \mathbf{J}_{\mathbf{n}}\left[t+1\right]$
$\breve{g}_{\mathbf{n}}^{\mathbf{s}} = \mathbf{x}_{\mathbf{n}}^{\mathbf{s}}\left[t+1\right]$
$I_{k}^{s} = 0$ // reset stagnancy counter
If $N_{s} < N_{max}$ // the current number of particles within swarm s is inferior to the maximum number of allowed particles
$N_{s} = N_{s} + 1$
Randomly spawns a new particle in swarm s
If $N_{s} < N_{max}^{s}$ and $rand\left(\right)\dfrac{N_{s}}{N_{max}} > rand\left(\right)$ // small probability of creating a new swarm
$N_{s} = N_{s} + 1$
Randomly spawns a new swarm with an initial number of N particles
Else // swarm s has not improved
$I_{k}^{s} = I_{k}^{s} + 1$
If $I_{k}^{s} = I_{kill}^{s}$ // swarm s has improved for too long
If $N_{s} > N_{min}$ // swarm s has currently more than the minimum number of allowed particles to form a swarm
Delete worse particle from swarm s, *i.e.*, lower local solution
Else // swarm s does not currently have the minimum number of allowed particles to form a swarm
Delete whole swarm s, *i.e.*, all particles from swarm s
End

7. EXPERIMENTAL RESULTS AND DISCUSSION

The proposed approach was tested on 30 liver CT images. Figure 2 shows an example of liver CT images, the ground truth for each image, result of FODPSO-FFCM, and the overlap between the result obtained by applying FODPSO-FFCM on the image and its ground truth (shown in grey).

Jaccard index (Jaccard, 1901) (also known as Jaccard similarity coefficient) and Dice Coefficient (Frakes & Baeza-Yates, 1992) were used for evaluation purposes.

Jaccard index is very popular and frequently used as a similarity index for binary data. The area of overlap A_j is calculated between the thresholded binary image B_j and its ground truth image (lesion) G_j as shown in the following equation (Narayana, Sreenivasa Reddy, & Seetharama Prasad, 2012):

$$Jaccard\left(A_i\right) = \frac{\left|B_i \cap G_i\right|}{\left|B_i \cup G_i\right|} \tag{8}$$

If the thresholded object and the corresponding ground truth G_j are exactly identical, then the measure is 1. The measure 0 on the other hand means that they are totally disjoint. Thus, the higher the measure, the higher the similarity is (Albrecht, 2004).

Figure 2. (a) original image; (b) ground truth of (a); (c) result of FODPSO-FFCM for (a); (d) overlap between (b) and (c); (e) original image; (f) ground truth of (e); (g) result of FODPSO-FFCM for (e); (h) overlap between (f) and (g); (i) original image; (j) ground truth of (i); (k) result of FODPSO-FFCM for (i); (l) overlap between (j) and (k)

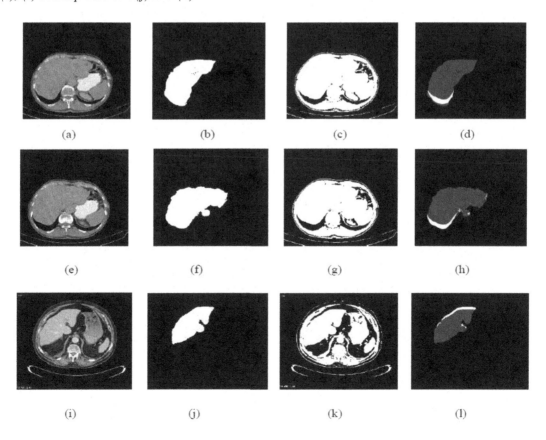

Dice Coefficient is defined as follows (Ashman, 2010):

$$D(A,B) = \frac{2|A \cap B|}{|A| + |B|} \qquad (9)$$

It is one of a number of measures of the extent of spatial overlap between two binary images. It is commonly used in reporting performance of segmentation and gives more weighting to instances where the two images agree. Its values range between 0 (no overlap) and 1 (perfect agreement) (Babalola, 2008).

Table 1 shows a comparison between PSOFFCM, FFCM, and FODPSO-FFCM in terms in terms of Jaccard Index and Dice Coefficient. As can be seen, PSOFFCM and FODPSO-FFCM act pretty much the same, and is better than FFCM.

Figure 3, Figure 4, and Figure 5 show the best similarity indices of PSOFFCM, FFCM, and FODPSO-FFCM, respectively, in terms of Jaccard Index and Dice Coefficient:

Table 1. Comparison between PSOFFCM, FFCM, and FODPSO-FFCM in terms of Jaccard Index and Dice Coefficient

	PSOFFCM		FFCM		FODPSO-FFCM	
Image	Jaccard	Dice	Jaccard	Dice	Jaccard	Dice
1	0.41	0.582	0.401	0.577	0.41	0.582
2	0.37	0.541	0.338	0.505	0.37	0.541
3	0.414	0.586	0.411	0.582	0.414	0.586
4	0.398	0.569	0.393	0.565	0.398	0.569
5	0.411	0.583	0.408	0.58	0.411	0.583
6	0.418	0.59	0.415	0.587	0.418	0.59
7	0.355	0.524	0.322	0.487	0.355	0.524
8	0.299	0.461	0.283	0.441	0.298	0.459
9	0.361	0.531	0.323	0.495	0.36	0.53
10	0.325	0.49	0.304	0.466	0.324	0.489
11	0.396	0.568	0.368	0.538	0.396	0.568
12	0.333	0.5	0.315	0.479	0.333	0.499
13	0.277	0.434	0.264	0.418	0.277	0.434
14	0.274	0.431	0.261	0.413	0.274	0.431
15	0.255	0.406	0.241	0.389	0.255	0.406
16	0.252	0.402	0.24	0.387	0.252	0.402
17	0.51	0.675	0.47	0.64	0.51	0.672
18	0.503	0.669	0.471	0.64	0.503	0.669
19	0.469	0.639	0.451	0.622	0.469	0.639
20	0.499	0.665	0.447	0.618	0.496	0.663
21	0.318	0.482	0.316	0.48	0.317	0.481
22	0.419	0.591	0.418	0.589	0.419	0.59
23	0.407	0.579	0.406	0.577	0.407	0.579
24	0.38	0.551	0.379	0.549	0.38	0.551
25	0.414	0.586	0.413	0.585	0.414	0.586
26	0.402	0.573	0.4	0.571	0.402	0.573
27	0.416	0.588	0.414	0.586	0.415	0.587
28	0.398	0.569	0.397	0.568	0.398	0.569
29	0.362	0.531	0.351	0.52	0.361	0.53
30	0.35	0.519	0.343	0.511	0.35	0.519

Figure 3. PSOFFCM similarity indices in terms of Jaccard Index and Dice Coefficient

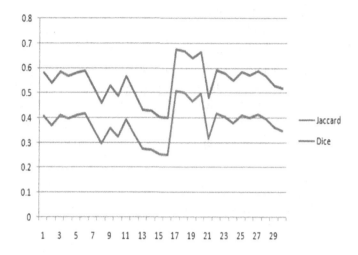

Figure 4. FFCM similarity indices in terms of Jaccard Index and Dice Coefficient

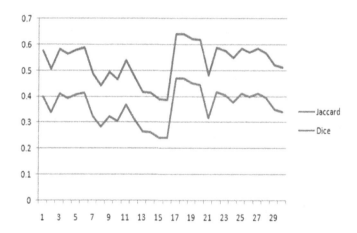

Figure 5. FODPSO-FFCM similarity indices in terms of Jaccard Index and Dice Coefficient

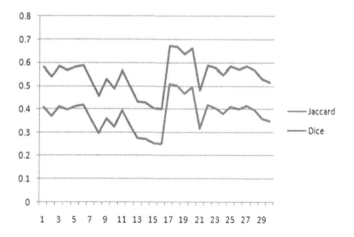

Figure 6 shows the Dice Coefficient values between PSOFFCM, FFCM, and FODPSO-FFCM, where it can be noticed that PSOFFCM and FODPSO-FFCM have pretty much the same values, and are higher and more accurate than FFCM. Figure 7, on the other hand, shows the Jaccard Index values between PSOFFCM, FFCM, and FODPSO-FFCM, where also, PSOFFCM and FODPSO-FFCM can be seen to be better than FFCM.

7.1 ANOVA Analysis

Statistical analysis was performed using one-way ANOVA tests. Analysis of Variance (ANOVA) is a statistical procedure for determining the differences among means of two or more populations. ANOVA tests the null hypothesis of equal means for all populations, where the alternative hypothesis in the population means are not all equal.

Figure 6. Difference between PSOFFCM, FFCM, and FODPSO-FFCM in terms of Dice Coefficient

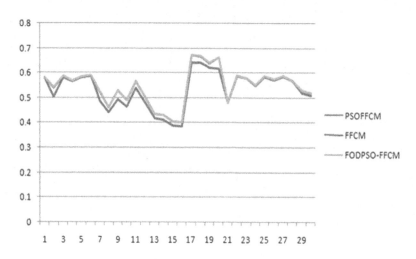

Figure 7. Difference between PSOFFCM, FFCM, and FODPSO-FFCM in terms of Jaccard Index

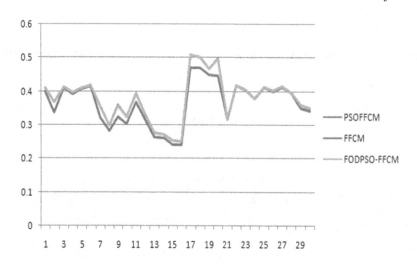

One-way ANOVA is a simple special case of the linear model. The one-way ANOVA form of the model is:

$$y_{ij} = \propto_{.j} + \varepsilon_{.j} \qquad (10)$$

where:

y_{ij} is a matrix of observations in which each column represents a different group

$\alpha_{.j}$ is a matrix whose columns are the group means (the *dot j* notation means that α applies to all rows of column *j*. That is, the value α_{ij} is the same for all *i*).

$\varepsilon_{.j}$ is a matrix of random disturbances

The purpose of ANOVA is to find out whether data from several groups have a common mean. That is, to determine whether the groups are actually different in the measured characteristic (ANOVA, 2013).

In multiple populations, there are two variances taken into account; 1) the variance within each of the samples and, 2) the variance between the samples. We perform Analysis of Invarianc (ANOVA) on each one of the results from FFCM, PSOFFCM, and FODPSO-FFCM.

In Table 2, ANOVA analysis is applied on PSOFFCM, FFCM, and FODPSOFFCM, for two measures, Jaccard Index and Dice Coefficient. As as can be seen from Table 2, PSOFFCM and FODPSO-FFCM have similar results, and give best values in term of Dice Coefficient.

Table 3 shows the results of ANOVA analysis dependency between Jaccard Index and Dice Coefficient for PSOFFCM, FFCM. And FODPSO-FFCM. If the *p-value* is bigger than the specified significance level of *0.05*, this gives us no difference of mean between the groups. The *p-value*

Table 2. ANOVA analysis of PSOFFCM, FFCM, and FODPSO-FFCM for Jaccard Index and Dice Coefficient without any dependency: (SS) Sum of Squares, (df) degree of freedom, (MS) mean squares (SS/df), (s) standard deviation

Method	Similarity Indices	ANOVA Analysis				
		SS	df	MS	Mean	S
PSOFFCM	Jaccard	0.1365	29	0.0047	0.3798	0.0686
	Dice	0.1539	29	0.0053	0.5472	0.0728
FFCM	Jaccard	0.1290	29	0.0044	0.3654	0.0667
	Dice	0.1554	29	0.0054	0.5322	0.0732
FODPSO-FFCM	Jaccard	0.1362	29	0.0047	0.3795	0.0685
	Dice	0.1532	29	0.0053	0.5467	0.0727

Table 3. ANOVA analysis dependency between Jaccard Index and Dice Coefficient for PSOFFCM, FFCM. And FODPSO-FFCM

Method	Similarity Indices	ANOVA Analysis						
		SS	MS	F statistic	P-value	SS err.	MS err.	s
PSOFFCM	Jaccard & Dice	0.42	0.42	83.9017	7.2342e-013	0.2903	0.0050	0.0708
FFCM	Jaccard & Dice	0.417	0.417	85.0567	5.7032e-013	0.2844	0.0049	0.0700
FODPSO-FFCM	Jaccard & Dice	0.4192	0.4192	84.0091	7.0755e-013	0.2894	0.0050	0.0706

here is less than *0.05*. This thus means that Jaccard Index and Dice Coefficient for PSOFFCM, FODPSO-FFCM, and FFCM are significantly different.

7.2 Box and Whisker Plots

Box-and-whisker plots (box plots) were introduced by John Tukey as a means to visualize differences in the distribution of a numeric variable among several groups (Rutledge, 2009).

Box plots show how the data is distributed. They show the median, the quartiles, and the smallest and greatest values in the distribution. They can be very useful in giving a quick picture of a distribution and for comparing two distributions (Hartman, 2006).

The shape of the box and whiskers plot indicates whether the distribution is skewed. If the distribution of the data is symmetrical about the mean, the box and whiskers plot will have a median equidistant from the hinges and whiskers of similar lengths. As the distribution becomes increasingly skewed, the median will become less equidistant from the hinges and the whiskers will have different lengths (McKillup, 2006).

Any values outside the range of the whiskers are called outliers, and should be scrutinised carefully. In some cases, outliers are onviuos mistakes cased by incorrect data entry or recording, faulty equipment, or inappriopriate methodology, in which case, they can justifiably be deleted. When outliers appear to be real, they are of great interest, since they may indicate that something unusual is occuring, especially if they are present in some samples and treatments and not in others (McKillup, 2006).

Figure 8 shows the box plot for PSOFFCM results of the two similarity indices (Jaccard Index, Dice Coefficient), with each represented by a separate box. The central mark is the median. As can be seen from the figure, Dice Coefficient has a vlaue (i.e., 0.55) higher than Jaccard index (i.e., 0.38).

Figure 9, on the other hand, shows the box plot for FFCM results of the two similarity indices (Jaccard Index, Dice Coefficient). The best similarity is Dice Coefficient (i.e., 0.53), which is higher than Jaccard index (i.e., 0.37).

Figure 10 shows the box plot for FODPSO-FFCM results of the two similarity indices (Jaccard Index, Dice Coefficient), with each represented by a separate box. The central mark is the median. As can be seen from the figure, Dice Coefficient has a vlaue (i.e., 0.55) higher than Jaccard index (i.e., 0.38).

From Table 4, ANOVA analysis depicts that the *p-value* is bigger than 0.05. This means that

Figure 8. Box plot of Jaccard Index (1) and Dice Coefficient (2) for PSOFFCM

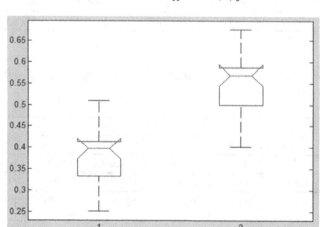

Figure 9. Box plot of Jaccard Index (1) and Dice Coefficient (2) for FFCM

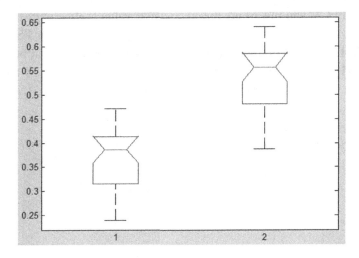

Figure 10. Box plot of Jaccard Index (1) and Dice Coefficient (2) for FODPSO-FFCM

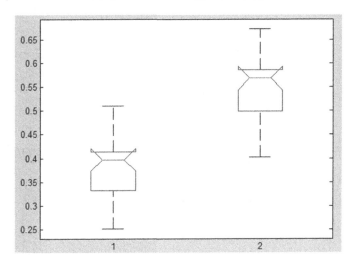

Table 4. Investigation of FDPSO-FCM, FCM-PSO and FCM using Jaccard and Dice similarity measure

Similarity Indices	Methods	ANOVA Analysis						
		SS	MS	F statistic	P-value	SS err.	MS err.	s
Jaccard	FDPSO-FCM, PSO-FCM & FFCM	0.0041	0.0020	0.4401	0.6454	0.4016	0.0046	0.0679
Dice	FDPSO-FCM, PSO-FCM & FFCM	0.0044	0.0022	0.4105	0.6646	0.4625	0.0053	0.0729

Jaccard Index and Dice Coefficient similarity measures for both PSOFFCM and FFCM are not significantly different.

Figure11 shows the box plot of Jaccard Index for PSOFFCM, FFCM, and FODPSO-FFCM. It can be noticed that the best results are of PSOFFCM and FODPSO-FFCM, which has the mean value 0.39. Figure12 shows the box plot of Dice Coefficient for PSOFFCM, FFCM, and FODPSO-FFCM. It can be noticed that the best results are of PSOFFCM and FODPSO-FFCM, having the mean value 0.55.

Figure 11. Box plot difference between (1) PSOFFCM, (2) FFCM, and (3) FODPSO-FFCM in terms of Jaccard Index

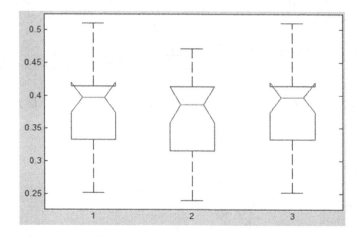

Figure 12. Box plot difference between (1) PSOFFCM, (2) FFCM, and (3) FODPSO-FFCM in terms of Dice Coefficient

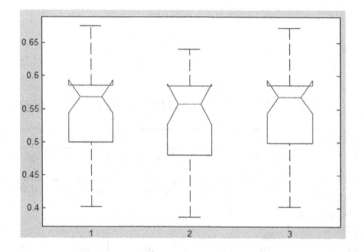

8. CONCLUSION

Optimizing Fast Fuzzy C-Means using the Fractional Order Darwinian method (FODPSO-FFCM), lead to higher values for Jaccard Index and Dice Coefficient when applied on Liver CT images, and thus, indicating higher similarity with the ground truth provided. Based on ANOVA analysis, FODPSO-FFCM showed better results in terms of Dice Coefficient. It also showed better mean values in terms of Jaccard Index and Dice Coefficient based on the box and whisker plots.

REFERENCES

Albrecht, T. et al. (2004). Guidelines for the Use of Contrast Agents in Ultrasound. *Ultraschall in der Medizin (Stuttgart, Germany), 25*(4), 249–256. doi:10.1055/s-2004-813245 PMID:15300497

Annadurai, S., & Shanmugalakshmi, R. (2006). *Fundamentals of Digital Image Processing*. Delhi: Dorling Kindersley.

ANOVA. (2013, December 13). Retrieved from: http://www.mathworks.com/help/stats/anova.html

Anter, A., Azar, A., Hassanien, A., El-Bendary, N., & ElSoud, M. (2013). Automatic Computer Aided Segmentation for Liver and Hepatic Lesions Using Hybrid Segmentations Techniques. In *Proceedings of Federated Conference on Computer Science and Information Systems*, (pp. 193-198). IEEE.

Ashman, J. (2010). *Measuring Named Entity Similarity Through Wikipedia Category Hierarchies*. (MSc thesis). The University of Texas at Arlington, Arlington, TX.

Babalola, K., Patenaude, B., Aljabar, P., Schnabel, J., Kennedy, D., & Crum, W. … Rueckert, D. (2008). Comparison and Evaluation of Segmentation Techniques for Subcortical Structures in Brain MRI. In Medical Image Computing and Computer-Assisted Intervention MICCAI, (LNCS), (Vol. 5241, pp. 409-416). Berlin: Springer.

Bezdek, J. (1973). *Fuzzy Mathematics in Pattern Classification*. (Ph.D. thesis). Applied Mathematic Center, Cornell University, Ithaca, NY.

Bluemke, D., & Fishman, E. (1993). Spiral CT of the liver. *AIR, 160*, 787–792. PMID:8456666

Bluemke, D., Urban, B., & Fishman, E. (1994). Spiral CT of the liver: Current applications. *Seminars in Ultrasound, CT, and MR, 15*, 107–121. doi:10.1016/S0887-2171(05)80093-9 PMID:8198817

Bronzino, J. (2000). *The Biomedical Engineering Handbook 2*. Heidelberg, Germany: Springer.

Bush, B. (2013, December 12). *Fuzzy Clustering Techniques: Fuzzy C-Means and Fuzzy Min-Max Clustering Neural Networks*. Retrieved from http://benjaminjamesbush.com/fuzzyclustering/fuzzyclustering.docx

Cao, B., Wang, G., Chen, S., & Guo, S. (2010). *Fuzzy Information and Engineering 2010* (Vol. 1). Heidelberg, Germany: Springer. doi:10.1007/978-3-642-14880-4

Couceiro, M. S., Luz, J. M., Figueiredo, C. M., Ferreira, N. M., & Dias, G. (2010). Parameter Estimation for a Mathematical Model of the Golf Putting. In V. M. Marques, C. S. Pereira, & A. Madureira (Eds.), *Proceedings of WACI-Workshop Applications of Computational Intelligence* (pp. 1-8). Coimbra, Portugal: ISEC - IPC.

Couceiro, M. S., Martins, F. M., Rocha, R. P., & Ferreira, N. M. (2012). Analysis and Parameter Adjustment of the RDPSO - Towards an Understanding of Robotic Network Dynamic Partitioning based on Darwin's Theory. *International Mathematical Forum, 7*(32), 1587-1601.

Couceiro, M. S., Rocha, R. P., Ferreira, N. M., & Machado, J. T. (2012). *Introducing the Fractional Order Darwinian PSO*. Signal, Image and Video Processing, Fractional Signals and Systems.

Digestive Disorders Health Center. (2013, December 8). Retrieved from http://www.webmd.com/ digestive-disorders/picture-of-the-liver

Duda, R., Hart, P., & Stork, D. (2001). *Pattern Classification* (2nd ed.). Chichester, UK: John Wiley Sons.

Eberhart, R. C., & Shi, Y. (2000). Comparing inertia weights and constriction factors in particle swarm optimization. In *Proceedings of the 2000 Congress on Evolutionary Computation*, (pp. 84-88). IEEE.

Frakes, W. B., & Baeza-Yates, R. (1992). *Information Retrieval, Data Structure and Algorithms*. Prentice Hall.

Ghamisi, P., Couceiro, M. S., Benediktsson, J. A., & Ferreira, N. M. (2012). An Efficient Method for Segmentation of Images Based on Fractional Calculus and Natural Selection. *Expert Systems with Applications, 39*(16), 12407–12417. doi:10.1016/j.eswa.2012.04.078

Gunnar, L. (2010). *Segmentation Methods for Digital Image Analysis: Blood Vessels, Multiscale Filtering, and Level Set Methods*. Linköping studies in science and technology, thesis no. 1434.

Hartman, B. (2006). *Maths AQA*. London: Letts and Lonsdale.

Hu, X. (2013, December 15). *Particle Swarm Optimization*. Retrieved from http://www.swarmintelligence.org/

Huang, X., & Tsechpenakis, G. (2009). *Medical Image Segmentation. Information Discovery on Electronic Health Records*. Boca Raton, FL: Taylor and Francis Group, LLC.

Izakian, H., & Abraham, A. (2011). Fuzzy C-means and Fuzzy Swarm for Fuzzy Clustering Problem. *Expert Systems with Applications, 38*(3), 1835–1838. doi:10.1016/j.eswa.2010.07.112

Jaccard, P. (1901). Etude Comparative de la Distribution Orale Dansune Portion des Alpes et des Jura. *Bulletin de la Société Vaudoise des Sciences Naturelles, 37*, 547–579.

Kelemen, A., Abraham, A., & Chen, Y. (2008). *Computational Intelligence in Bioinformatics*. Heidelberg, Germany: Springer. doi:10.1007/978-3-540-76803-6

Kennedy, J., & Eberhart, R. (1995). A New Optimizer Using Particle Swarm Theory. In *Proceedings of the IEEE Sixth International Symposium on Micro Machine and Human Science* (pp. 39-43). Nagoya, Japan: IEEE.

Maji, P., & Pal, S. (2008). Maximum Class Separability for Rough-Fuzzy CMeans Based Brain MR Image Segmentation. *T. Rough Sets, 9*, 114–134.

McCaffrey, J. (2013, December 15). *Particle Swarm Optimization*. Retrieved from http://msdn.microsoft.com/en-us/magazine/hh335067.aspx

McKillup, S. (2006). *Statistics Explained: An Introductory Guide for Life Scientists*. Cambridge, UK: Cambridge University Press.

Mharib, A., Ramli, A., Mashohor, S., & Mahmood, R. (2012). Survey on Liver CT Image Segmentation Methods. *Artificial Intelligence Review*, *37*(2), 83–95. doi:10.1007/s10462-011-9220-3

Narayana, C., Sreenivasa Reddy, E., & Seetharama Prasad, M. (2012). Automatic Image Segmentation using Ultrafuzziness. *International Journal of Computers and Applications*, *49*(12), 6–13. doi:10.5120/7677-0977

Oliveira, J., & Pedrycz, W. (2007). *Advances in Fuzzy Clustering and its Applications*. John Wiley Sons Ltd. doi:10.1002/9780470061190

Ostalczyk, P. W. (2009). A note on the Grünwald–Letnikov fractional-order backward-difference. *Physica Scripta*, *136*, 1–5.

Rutledge, R. (2009). *Just Enough SAS: A Quickstart Guide to SAS for Engineers*. SAS Institute Inc.

Semechko, A. (2013, December 8). *Fast segmentation of N-dimensional grayscale images*. Retrieved from http://www.mathworks.com/matlabcentral/fileexchange/41967-fastsegmentation-of-n-dimensional-grayscale-images

Tillett, J., Rao, T. M., Sahin, F., Rao, R., & Brockport, S. (2005). Darwinian Particle Swarm Optimization. In B. Prasad (Ed.), *Proceedings of the 2nd Indian International Conference on Artificial Intelligence* (pp. 1474-1487). Pune, India: IEEE.

Valle, Y. D., Venayagamoorthy, G. K., Mohagheghi, S., Hernandez, J. C., & Harley, R. (2008). Particle swarm optimization: Basic concepts, variants and applications in power systems. *IEEE Transactions on Evolutionary Computation*, *2*(2), 171–195. doi:10.1109/TEVC.2007.896686

Zeman, R., Fox, S., & Silverman, P. et al. (1993). Helical (spiral) CT of the abdomen. *AJR*, *160*, 719–725. doi:10.2214/ajr.160.4.8456652 PMID:8456652

Zeman, R., Zeiberg, A., & Davros, W. et al. (1993). Routine helical CT of the abdomen: image quality considerations. *Radiology*, *189*, 395–400. PMID:8210365

Zhou, X.-C. (2009). Image Segmentation Based on Modified Particle Swarm Optimization and Fuzzy C-Means Clustering Algorithm. In *Proceedings of Second International Conference on Intelligent Computation Technology and Automation* (pp. 611-616). IEEE Computer Society.

KEY TERMS AND DEFINITIONS

Analysis of Variance (ANOVA): A statistical procedure for determining the differences among means of two or more populations.

Clustering: The process of partitioning a data set into different classes, so that the data in each class share same common features according to a defined distance measure.

Computed Tomography (CT): An imaging technique that created a series of detailed pictures of areas inside the body.

Dice Coefficient: A measure of the extent of spatial overlap between two binary images.

Fuzzy Set: A set which elements have degrees of membership.

Image Segmentation: The process of subdividing the image into its constituent parts.

Jaccard Index: A similarity index used for binary data.

ENDNOTES

[1] http://radiopaedia.org/search?q=CTscope=all

Chapter 2
Automatic Mammographic Parenchyma Classification According to BIRADS Dictionary

Ahmed M. Anter
Mansoura University, Egypt & Scientific Research Group in Egypt (SRGE), Egypt

Mohamed Abu ElSoud
Mansoura University, Egypt & Scientific Research Group in Egypt (SRGE), Egypt

Aboul Ella Hassanien
Cairo University, Egypt & Scientific Research Group in Egypt (SRGE), Egypt

ABSTRACT

Internal density of the breast is a parameter that clearly affects the performance of segmentation and classification algorithms to define abnormality regions. Recent studies have shown that their sensitivity is significantly decreased as the density of the breast is increased. In this chapter, enhancement and segmentation process is applied to increase the computation and focus on mammographic parenchyma. This parenchyma is analyzed to discriminate tissue density according to BIRADS using Local Binary Pattern (LBP), Gray Level Co-Occurrence Matrix (GLCM), Fractal Dimension (FD), and feature fusion technique is applied to maximize and enhance the performance of the classifier rate. The different methods for computing tissue density parameter are reviewed, and the authors also present and exhaustively evaluate algorithms using computer vision techniques. The experimental results based on confusion matrix and kappa coefficient show a higher accuracy is obtained by automatic agreement classification.

1. INTRODUCTION

Medical image analysis becomes more and more popular in recent years due to the advances of the imaging techniques, including Magnetic Resonance Imaging (MRI), Computer Tomog- raphy (CT), Mammography, Positron emission tomography (PET), X-ray, and Ultrasound or Doppler Ultrasound. It is widely accepted in the medical community that breast tissue density is an important risk factor for the development of breast cancer. Thus, the development of reliable

DOI: 10.4018/978-1-4666-6030-4.ch002

automatic methods for classification of breast tissue is justified and necessary. Every effort has been directed to improving the early detection of breast cancer. Therefore, many computer vision techniques applied to analysis of digital mammograms have been proposed. Most of them require an initial processing step that splits the image into interesting areas, such as the breast region, background and patient markings (El-henawy et.al, 2009). For example, it is well known that information derived from mammographic parenchyma patterns provides one of the most robust indications of risk of developing breast cancer. Moreover, the segmentation method should be robust enough to handle a wide range of mammographic images obtained from different image acquisition systems.

A recent trend in digital mammography is CAD systems, which are computerized tools designed to help radiologists. Most of these systems are used for the automatic detection of abnormalities. However, recent studies have shown that their sensitivity is significantly decreased as the density of the breast is increased. The internal density of the breast is a parameter that clearly affects the performance of segmentation algorithms to define abnormality regions. Surprisingly, most of these segmentation algorithms do not take this information into account leading to many false positive regions, when system identifies abnormality regions.

The computer-aided interpretation systems of mammographic images have two different approaches: 1) a computer-aided detection platform, which processes the mammograms looking for abnormalities 2) a featured computer-aided diagnosis (CAD), which works as a content-based image retrieval (CBIR) (Birdwell et.al, 2001).

CAD systems are being developed to assist radiologists in the evaluation of mammographic images (Freer et.al, 2001). However, recent studies have shown that the sensitivity of these systems is significantly decreased as the density of the breast increases while the specificity of the

systems remains relatively constant (Jain et.al, 1998). From a medical point of view, these studies are disappointing, because it is well-known that there is a strong positive correlation between breast parenchyma density in mammograms and the breast cancer risk (Wolfe, 1976). Therefore, automatic classification of breast tissue will be beneficial for estimating the density of the breast.

As Taylor (Taylor et.al, 1994) suggested, the development of automatic methods for classification of breast tissue are justified by two factors: 1) to permit better use of the time and skills of expert radiologists by allowing the difficult mammograms to be examined by the most experienced readers. 2) to increase the scope for computer-aided detection of abnormalities.

The origin of breast density classification is the work of Wolfe (Wolfe, 1976) and Muhimmah (Muhimmah et.al, 2006), which showed the relationship between mammographic parenchyma patterns and the risk of developing breast cancer, classifying the parenchyma patterns to four categories. Since the discovery of this relationship, automated parenchyma pattern classification has been investigated, as is explained in the next section. However, the American College of Radiology (ACR) Breast Imaging Reporting and Data System (BIRADS) is becoming a standard for the assessment of mammographic images (ACR, 1998). In this standard, breasts are classified into four categories according to their density.

- **BIRADS I:** The breast is almost entirely fatty
- **BIRADS II:** There is some fibro glandular tissue
- **BIRADS III:** The breast is heterogeneously dense
- **BIRADS IV:** The breast is extremely dense.

Automatic tissue classification methods try to imitate radiologist visual judgment. There are a number of different dictionaries for breast tissue classification (Muhimmah et.al, 2006), nowadays, the commonly used is the BIRADS dictionary.

Different approaches based on the use of only histogram information have been proposed for classifying breast tissue (Zhou et.al, 2001). However, it is clear that histogram information alone is not sufficient for classifying mammograms according to the BIRADS categories (Zwiggelaar et.al, 2005). The current systems ignore the texture of the breast tissue, leading to many false-positive regions when the system identifies tumor regions. In this paper, an attempt was made to combine the individual scores from different techniques in order to compensate their individual weakness and to preserve their strength. An automated system was proposed for segmenting the digital mammogram into breast region and background with a new pectoral muscle suppression technique and different approaches were reviewed to automatically classifying the breast according to their internal tissue and a new approach was presented for classifying them according to BIRADS categories. The proposed approach assumes that mammograms belonging to different BIRADS categories are represented by tissue with different texture using Gray level co-occurrence matrix (GLCM), Local Binary Pattern (LBP), Fractal Dimension (FD) and feature fusion between them to increase the performance and classification rate.

The reminder of this paper is ordered as follows. Section 2 discusses the previous work on Mammogram segmentation and tissue classification. Details of the proposed methods and datasets are given in Section 3. The proposed system is presented in Section 4. Section 5 shows the experimental results and analysis. Finally, Conclusion and future work are discussed in Section 6.

2. PREVIOUS WORK

Several researchers have focused their attention on the use of texture features to describe the breast density. Miller and Astley (Miller and Astley,

1992) investigated texture-based discrimination between fatty and dense breast types by applying granulometric techniques and laws texture masks. Byng (Byng et.al, 1996) used measures based on fractal dimensions. Bovis and Singh (Bovis and Singh, 2002) estimated features from the construction of spatial grey level dependency matrices. Recently, Petroudi (Petroudi et.al, 2003) used textons to capture the mammographic appearance within the breast area. Zwiggelaar (Zwiggelaar et.al, 1999), segmented mammograms into density regions based on a set of co-occurrence matrices, and the subsequent density classification used the relative area of the density regions as the feature space. Oliver (Oliver et.al, 2006) use a Fuzzy C-Means algorithm to segment different tissue types (fatty versus dense) in the mammograms. For each tissue region texture features are extracted to characterize the breast tissue to classify the mammograms according to BIRADS categories. Bovis and Singh (Bovis and Singh, 2002) and Petroudi (Petroudi et.al, 2003) extracted the features that treating the global breast as a single region. Edwards (Edwards et.al, 2002) used a minimum error thresholding algorithm to produce an approximation of the dense tissue area.

Table 1 shows the different proposals for breast classification. Moreover, some other characteristics of the works, as the year, features and the type of classifier are shown. Moreover, the classification algorithms are further separated into approaches that extract the features treating the global breast or a single region, and approaches that extract features segmenting the breast according to some parameters.

3. MATERIALS AND METHODS

3.1 Mammography Data Collection

Public and widely known database were used to test the proposed methods. The Mammographic Image Analysis Society Digital Mammogram

Table 1. Shows different proposals for breast feature extraction and classification

Feature Extraction	Author	Year	Classifier	Extraction Global / Local
Co-occurrence	Bovis	2002	KNN	Global
	Blot	2001	KNN	Local
	Zwiggelaar	1999	KNN	Local
Histogram	Zhou	2001	Bayesian	Global
	Martin	2006	KNN	Local
	Edwards	2002	KNN	Global
Fractal Analysis	Byng	1996	KNN	Global
	Caldwell	1990	Bayesian	Global
	Taylor	1994	KNN	Global

database (MIAS) is composed by a set of 322 medio-lateral oblique (MLO) view digitized mammograms corresponding to the left and right breasts of 161 women. The films were extracted from the UK National Breast Screening Program, and digitized to 50 micron pixel. Each pixel was described as an 8-bit word (Suckling et.al, 1994).

The former MIAS only use three classes. As we want to classify the breast in BIRADS categories, two mammographic experts from the Oncology Center – Mansoura University (OCMU) Hospitals have classified all of the MIAS mammograms according to the BIRADS dictionary as fatty tissue 87, glandular tissue 103, heterogeneous tissue 95, and dense tissue 37.

3.2 Image Mammogram Enhancement

Mammographic image preprocessing methods are typically aimed at either improvement of the overall visibility of features or enhancement of a specific sign of malignancy. Image enhancement is one of the most important issues in low-level image processing. Histogram-modeling techniques alter an image in order to ensure that the histogram is of the desired shape. This is useful in stretching the low contrast levels of mammograms with narrow histograms. A typical technique in histogram modeling is histogram equalization, which provides better visualization of a mammogram. It is a probability distribution, based

on information theory, the uniform distribution achieves the maximum entropy, which contains the most information. Therefore, redistribute the grey levels to obtain a histogram as uniform as possible, the mammogram information will be maximized (Duda, Hart and Stork, 2001).

3.3 Breast Segmentation with Pectoral Muscle Suppression

Segmentation is the decomposition of an image into regions. In the context of mammograms, segmentation can be either global or local. Global segmentation of mammograms refers to the separation of a mammogram into two visually distinct regions, namely breast and non-breast regions. Local segmentation refers to further successive division of the breast region into distinct, diagnostically meaningful regions. To achieve the segmentation, we propose a two-phase-based method.

3.3.1 Separate Breast and Non-Breast by Using Connected Component Labeling Algorithm

CCL works by scanning an image pixel by pixel (from top to bottom and left to right) in order to identify connected pixel regions i.e., regions of adjacent pixels which share the same set of intensity values V (Anter et.al, 2013). The CCL operator scans the image by moving along a row until it comes to a point p (where p denotes the pixel to be labeled at any stage in the scanning process) for which V = {1}. When this is true, it examines the four of the neighbors of p which have already been encountered in the scan (i.e., the neighbors (a) to the left of p, (b) above it, and (c and d) the two upper diagonal terms) as seen in Figure 1.

3.3.2 Extract Pectoral Muscle from Breast Parenchyma by Using Region Growing

The region growing (RG) algorithm is one of the simplest region-based segmentation methods. It performs a segmentation of an image with examine the neighboring pixels of a set of points, known as seed points, and determine whether the pixels could be classified to the cluster of seed point or not (Anter et.al, 2013).The advantages of this algorithm is simplest, can correctly separate the regions of same properties, give good shape matching of its results. The algorithm procedure is as follows:

Step 1: Start with a number of clusters and seed points which have been identified from watershed algorithm, cluster called C1, C2,...., Cn. And the positions of initial seed points is set as P1, P2,....., Pn.

Step 2: To compute the difference of pixel value of the initial seed point pi and its neighboring points, if the difference is smaller than the threshold criterion that define, the neighboring point could be classified into Ci, where i = 1, 2,....,n.

Step 3: Recompute the boundary of Ci and set those boundary points as new seed points pi (s). In addition, the mean pixel values of Ci have to be recomputed, respectively.

Step 4: Repeat Step 2 and 3 until all pixels in image have been allocated to a suitable cluster.

3.3.3 Morphological Operator-Based Algorithm

A morphological processing is an obvious choice to refine the segmentation and to smooth the boundary of the breast. Dilation and erosion are the two main morphological processing. Dilation

Figure 1. (a) Binary sub image (b) labeling examples of CCL system

0	1	1	0	1	0	0
0	1	1	0	1	0	1
1	1	1	0	1	0	1
0	0	0	0	1	1	1
0	1	0	0	0	0	0
0	1	1	1	1	1	0
0	1	1	1	0	0	0

(a)

0	1	1	0	2	0	0
0	1	1	0	2	0	2
1	1	1	0	2	0	2
0	0	0	0	2	2	2
0	3	0	0	0	0	0
0	3	3	3	3	3	0
0	3	3	3	0	0	0

(b)

expands objects by a structuring element, filling holes, and connecting disjoint regions. Erosion deletes the small region by a structuring element.

3.4 Features Extraction and Classification

We test and evaluate in this paper different kinds of features extraction Local Binary Pattern (LBP), Fractal Dimension (FD), Grey Level Co-occurrence Matrix (GLCM), and feature fusion between them to maximize and enhance the performance of classifier rate. Classification phase applied using statistical classifier k-nearest neighbors (k-NN).

3.4.1 Local Binary Pattern (LBP)

The LBP operator labels the pixels of an image by thresholding the neighbourhood of each pixel with the centre value and considering the result of this thresholding as a binary number. When all of the image pixels have been labelled with the corresponding LBP codes, the histogram of the labels is computed and used as a texture descriptor (Maenpa, 2003). The LBP code computation for a 3×3 neighborhood is produced by firstly thresholding the neighbour values with the center pixel; such that the pixel greater than or equal to the center pixel will be set to 1, otherwise it will be set to 0. After thresholding the resulted 3×3 window will be multiplied be 3×3 weighted window. Then the central pixel will be replaced by the summation of thresholded multiplied 3×3 window as shown in Equations (1) and (2) respectively. After LBP complete, features will be extracted (Mean, Variance, Standard Division, Skewness, and Kurtosis) to describe breast density.

$$LBP_{p,r} = \sum_{i=0}^{p-1} s(g_i - g_c)x2^i \qquad (1)$$

$$s(x) = \begin{cases} 1, x \geq 0 \\ 0, x < 0 \end{cases} \qquad (2)$$

3.4.2 Fractal Dimension Method

Geometric primitives that are self-similar and irregular in nature are termed as fractals. Fractal Geometry was introduced to the world of research in 1982 by Mandelbrot (Mandelbrot, 1982). The method of self-similarity that used to compute FD is box counting. A self-similar object is exactly or approximately similar to a part of itself. Furthermore, a fractal generally shows irregular shapes that cannot be simply described by Euclidian dimension, but FD has to be introduced to extend the concept of dimension to these objects. Hence features based on fractal dimension were considered. Six features based on fractal dimension used in texture analysis were tried for characterizing breast tissue. Box-counting is useful feature to determine fractal properties, area of ROI, mean, standard derivation, Lacunarity and Haussdorf. These features are extracted to represent ROI.

3.4.3 Grey Level Co-Occurrence Matrices (GLCM)

The GLCMs are essentially two-dimensional histograms of the occurrence of pairs of grey levels for a given displacement vector. Formally, the co-occurrence of grey levels can be specified as a matrix of relative frequencies, in which with two pixels separated by a distance d and angle θ. A set of features derived from co-occurrence matrices was used as texture features (ElSoud and Anter, 2012), as seen in Table 2. Here, we used four different directions: 0°, 45°, 90°, and 135°, and one distance equal to one pixel. Note that these values were empirically determined and are related to the scale of textural features found in mammographic images. A large number of textural features derived from matrices have been proposed. For each co-occurrence matrix, the following statistics were used: angular second moment, energy, entropy, contrast, correlation, dissimilarity, sum average, sum entropy, sum variance, difference variance,

Table 2. List of classical feature functions evaluated on the co-occurrence matrix

Angular Sec. Moment	$f1 = \sum_{i,j=0}^{N-1} P(i,j)^2$	Sum Average	$f7 = \sum_{i=0}^{p-1} s(gi)$
Energy	$f2 = \sqrt{f1}$	Sum Variance	$f8 = \sum_{k=2}^{2N} \sum_{\substack{i,j=0 \\ i+j=k}}^{N-1} (k - f7)^2 P(i,j)$
Entropy	$f3 = \sum_{i,j=0}^{N-1} P(i,j)(-\log P(i,j))$	Sum Entropy	$f9 = -\sum_{k=2}^{2N} \sum_{\substack{i,j=0 \\ i+j=k}}^{N-1} P(i,j)\log(P(i,j))$
Contrast	$f4 = \sum_{i,j=0}^{N-1} P(i,j)(i-j)^2$	Difference Variance	$f10 = \sum_{k=0}^{2N} \sum_{i,j=0}^{N-1} (k - \mu k)^2 P(i,j)$
Homogeneity	$f5 = \sum_{i,j=0}^{N-1} \frac{1}{1+(i-j)^2} P(i,j)$	Difference Entropy	$f11 = \sum_{k=0}^{2N} \sum_{i,j=0}^{N-1} P(i,j) Log(P(i,j))$
Correlation	$f6 = \sum_{i,j=0}^{N-1} \frac{(i-\mu i)(j-\mu j)}{\sqrt{\sigma i^2 \sigma j^2}}$	Dissimilarity	$f12 = \sum_{i,j=0}^{N-1} P(i,j)\,|\,i-j\,|$

difference entropy, and homogeneity features. Each vector consists of 48 values.

3.4.4 K-Nearest Neighbors

The k-NN classifier is a non-parametric statistical method that, like the neural network methods, makes no strong a priori assumptions about the form of the data distribution (Duda, 2001; Gonzalez, 2008). It functions by taking a poll of the K nearest training patterns to the presented pattern, and assigning the presented pattern to the most represented class among them. In effect, this directly estimates the relative densities of patterns from each class in the immediate vicinity of the presented pattern, and selects the most densely represented class. Usually, the Euclidean distance is used as seen in Algorithm (1).

3.5 Classifier Evaluation

3.5.1 Confusion Matrices

A confusion matrix is a visualization tool commonly used in supervised machine learning. It contains information about actual and predicted classifications by a classification system. The confusion matrix is useful for evaluating the performance of a classifier, showing the number per class of well-classified and mislabeled instances. Moreover, it is easy to see if the automatic system is confusing two or more classes (mislabeling one class as another) (Duda, 2001).

3.5.2 Kappa (κ) Coefficient

The kappa (κ) coefficient is another measure which can be extracted from a confusion matrix

Algorithm 1. K-NN algorithm

```
for a fixed K value
        for each point do
                Compute pairwise distances with all others
                for k = 1: 2: K do
                        Take majority class of k nearest neighbours
                end for
        end for
Compare obtained classes with ground truth for each k
Keep k value giving the best good classification rate
```

Table 3. Common interpretation of κ values

K	Agreement
< 0	Poor
[0, 020]	Slight
[0.21, 0.40]	Fair
[0.41, 0.60]	Moderate
[0.61, 0.80]	Substantial
[0.81, 1]	Almost Perfect

introduced by Cohen's (Landis and Koch, 1977), which is a popular statistical measure for estimating agreement in categorical data. It is generally thought to be a more robust measure than simple percent agreement calculation, because κ takes into account the agreement occurring by chance. The motivation for this measure is to extract from the correctly classified percentage the actual percentage expected by chance. Thus, this coefficient is calculated as seen in Table 2.

Where P(D) is the percentage of correctly classified instances (the sum of diagonal terms divided by the sum of total instances) and P(E) is the expected proportion by chance (the sum of the multiplication of the marginal probabilities per class divided by the sum of total instances). A κ coefficient equal to one means a statistically perfect model, whereas a value equal to zero means that every model value was different from the actual value. Table 3 shows a commonly used interpretation of the various κ values.

4. PROPOSED SYSTEM

An automated system is proposed for segmenting the digital mammogram into breast region and background with a new pectoral muscle suppression and classifying the breast tissue according to BIRADS dictionary. The proposed system is comprised from four main phases to segment and classify breast tissue according to BIRADS dictionary as shown in Figure 2.

In the first phase: Image enhancement provides an image with increased focus on the malignant or suspicious area and increased appearance of micro-calcification masses, which are tiny calcifications and appeared in the range from 50 to several hundred microns in diameter, which usually appear in clusters.

In the second phase: After mammogram enhancement, the segmentation process applied to decompose mammogram image into distinct regions to achieve optimal breast parenchyma, this process applied in two steps. In the first step global segmentation of mammograms that refers to the separation of a mammogram into two visually distinct regions, namely breast and non-breast regions using adaptive threshold and CCL algorithm. The result of applying threshold is a collection of different regions. The largest one is the union of the breast and the pectoral muscle. This largest region was extracted using a CCL, is used to label the separate regions in mammogram yielding a new labeled image. The breast region is subsequently identified as the largest non-zero component. In the second step local segmentation that refers to further successive division of the breast region into pectoral muscle and breast parenchyma using RG algorithm.

In the third phase: After enhancement and segmentation techniques are applied, features will be extracted for classification of breast tissue. Four BIRADS category manually selected from MAIS after applying preprocessing methods, enhancement and segmentation, the mammogram will be analyzed to discriminate the tissue density according to BIRADS, different methods are

Figure 2. Architecture of automatic mammogram segmentation and classification

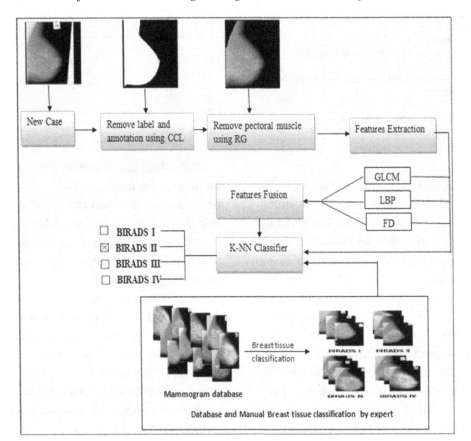

represented by tissue with different texture using Gray level co-occurrence matrix (GLCM), Local Binary Pattern (LBP), Fractal Dimension (FD) and feature fusion between them to increase the performance and classification rate.

In the fourth phase: After features extraction the process of classification applied in two phase learning phase and testing phase using statistical k-NN classifier. It is achieving good accuracy, it expands very quickly and is more and more popular.

5. EXPERIMENTAL RESULTS AND DISCUSSION

Public and widely known database were used to test the proposed methods, the MIAS database. The former only uses three classes. As we want to classify the breast in BIRADS categories, two mammographic experts from Oncology Center - Mansoura University Hospitals (OCMU) have classified all the MIAS mammograms according to the BIRADS dictionary as Fatty tissue (87), Glandular tissue (103), Heterogeneous tissue (95), Dense tissue (37).

5.1 Evaluating Enhancement

Image enhancement provides an image with increased focus on the malignant or suspicious area and increased appearance of micro-calcification masses, which are tiny calcifications and appeared in the range from 50 to several hundred microns in diameter, which usually appear in clusters.

The radiologists in the Oncology Center Mansoura University (OCMU) Hospitals reported that they were able to notice some features of interest in the enhanced images that they were not able to notice in the original images as seen in Figure 3.

5.2 Evaluating Segmentation

The segmentation process applied in two phase. In the first phase global segmentation using adaptive threshold and CCL is applied. The result of applying this adaptive threshold is a collection of different regions, being the biggest the union of the breast and the pectoral muscle. This biggest region can be extracted using a CCL algorithm as seen in Figure 4 (b, c).

In the second phase local segmentation using RG is applied to extract breast from the pectoral muscle. The behavior of the RG algorithm over segmentation of all breasts tissue, two mammo-

gram radiologists from OCMU hospital tested this algorithm over 322 images. The performance and accuracy of segmentation process was evaluated by a visual inspection of the images carried out by experienced radiologists in OCMU hospitals, and we have obtained 99% of good extractions for parenchyma patterns with fatty tissue, glandular tissue, and heterogeneous tissue. However, for breasts with dense tissue, we have obtained 90% of good extraction for pectoral muscle because the tissue is fuzzy. The results obtained by the method show that it is a robust approach. We used this method because it provides useful regions (there is no meaningful loss of information), as seen in Figure 4 (d).

5.3 Features Extraction and Classification

The aim of this phase is to demonstrate the usefulness of computing texture information. Thus, k-NN is used as the classifier to classify breast tissue according to BIRADS, and we compare the results obtained using LBP with those obtained using GLCM and FD. The performance and accuracy of classification evaluated by precision and accuracy extracted from confusion matrix and kappa coefficient. The training phase of clas-

Figure 3. (a) Original mammogram (b) after histogram equalization

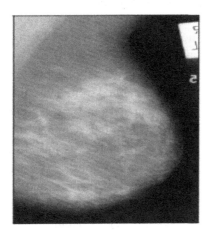
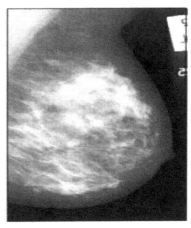

a

b

31

Figure 4. Global and local Segmentation Breast region extraction and pectoral muscle suppression. a) Original Image Mammogram, (b) Label and annotation Remove, (c) Pectoral muscle remove, (d) Global Breast with pectoral muscle suppression.

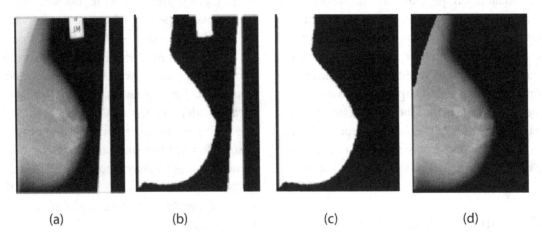

    (a)   (b)   (c)   (d)

sifier applied on 75% of ROI features and testing phase applied on 25% as follow (Fatty tissue (22), Glandular tissue (26), Heterogeneous tissue (24), Dense tissue (10)).

Table 4(a - c) and Figure 5 shows the confusion matrices for all cases, we obtained 80% of correct classification with substantial agreement when using features derived from GLCM, 77% of correct classification with substantial agreement for LBP and 82% of correct classification with substantial agreement for LBP as seen in Table 5.

Finally, a feature fusion approach was adopted to address some of the limitation of the feature extraction techniques utilities. It is a process of combining feature vectors from different sources with the aim of maximizing the useful information content. It improves the reliability or discrimination capability and offers the opportunity to minimize the data retained. The fact of combining multiple features derived from multiple techniques does improve the correct classification rate. Features extracted from GLCM, LBP, and FD is combined to improve the performance of correct classification rate. Table 4(d) and Figure 5 shows the confusion matrices for feature fusion, obtain-

ing 93% as a correct classification with perfect agreement as seen in Table 5 and Figure 6.

5.4 Discussion

This paper has presented different automatic methods to segment and classify mammograms according to the BIRADS categories standard. The radiologists in the OCMU hospitals reported that they were able to notice some features of interest in the enhanced images that they were not able to notice in the original images. This enhancement increased focus on the malignant or suspicious area and increased appearance of micro-calcification masses. About segmentation and muscle subtraction, we have obtained a 99% of good extractions and breasts with dense tissue, we have obtained 90% of good extraction for pectoral muscle. This result is obtained from a visual inspection of the images carried out by experienced radiologists in OCMU hospitals. Comparison with the works which segment breasts into distinct component by Raba (Raba et.al, 2005) have obtained an 86% of good extractions and cases with dense tissue algorithm rejects the muscle detection and provides the region obtained without suppressing

Table 4. Confusion matrices obtained when using (a) GLCM, (b) LBP, and (c) FD for texture extraction and (d) Feature Fusion

Manual / Automatic	BIRADS I	BIRADS II	BIRADS III	BIRADS IV
GLCM				
BIRADS I	19	2	1	0
BIRADS II	2	22	1	1
BIRADS III	0	3	19	2
BIRADS IV	0	1	2	7
LBP				
BIRADS I	18	3	1	0
BIRADS II	2	21	2	1
BIRADS III	1	3	18	2
BIRADS IV	0	1	2	7
FD				
BIRADS I	20	1	1	0
BIRADS II	1	22	2	1
BIRADS III	0	3	20	1
BIRADS IV	0	0	3	7
Feature Fusion				
BIRADS I	21	1	0	0
BIRADS II	2	25	1	0
BIRADS III	0	1	22	1
BIRADS IV	0	0	0	9

Figure 5. BIRADS accuracy extracted for GLCM, LBP, FD and feature fusion

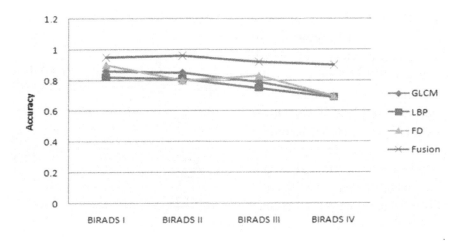

Table 5. Precision and accuracy extracted from confusion matrices for GLCM, LBP, FD and Feature fusion

Parameters		Precision				Overall Accuracy	Kappa Accuracy		
		BIRADS I	BIRADS II	BIRADS III	BIRADS IV		κ	Var.	κ error
Accuracy	GLCM	.86	.85	.79	.70	80	.75	0.0044	0.0588
	LBP	.82	.81	.75	.69	76.75	.70	0.0044	0.0630
	FD	.90	.8	.83	.70	82	.78	0.0045	0.0557
	Fusion	.95	.96	.92	.90	93.25	.89	0.0043	0.0416

Figure 6. Over-all accuracy for GLCM, LBP, FD and feature fusion

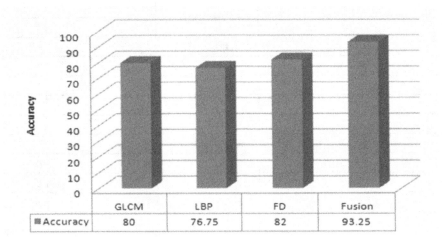

the muscle as a final result. About breast tissue classification, we compare between features extracted from GLCM, LBP, FD, and by ones from combine GLCM, LBP, and FD. We have better performance when using features combination. Comparing with the other previous works which classify the breasts into BIRADS categories, the works of Bovis and Singh (Bovis and Singh, 2002), Petroudi (Petroudi et.al, 2003) and Oliver (Oliver et.al, 2006) have classified breast tissue according to BIRADS categories. Bovis and Singh reached 71% correctly classified mammograms, Petroudi et al. achieved an overall correct classification of 76%, and Oliver achieved an overall correct classification of 86%. A 93.25% of correct classification and perfect agreement were obtained in our experiments, as seen in Table 6.

Table 6. Comparison with existing work, with classification according to BIRADS categories

Authors	Year	Accuracy
Bovis et. al.	2002	71%
Petroudi et al.	2003	76%
Oliver et al.	2006	86%
Proposed system	2013	93.25%

6. CONCLUSION AND FEATURE WORK

We studied the behavior of the RG algorithm over segmentation of all breasts tissue. We have tested these algorithms over 322 images, and we have obtained 99% of good extractions for parenchyma patterns with fatty tissue, glandular tissue, and heterogeneous tissue. For breasts with dense tissue, we have obtained 90% of good extraction for pectoral muscle. The results obtained with the method show that it is a robust approach. We used this method because it provides useful regions (there is no meaningful loss of information).

Once the breast has been segmented from the background and pectoral muscle, texture features are extracted that characterize the breast tissue. The results show that FD and GLCM have better feature extraction from mammogram and k-NN is a good classifier to classify mammogram tissue, and to improve the correct classification rate were using feature fusion techniques utilities, the accuracy of correct BIRADS classification for BIRADS I is around 95%, whilst for the other cases, the percentages are 96% for BIRADS II, 92% for BIRADS III, and 90% for BIRADS IV and for over-all BIRADS accuracy is 93.25%. The kappa κ value is equal to 0.89, this value represent perfect agreement for feature fusion and classifier.

In future work, we plan to assess the performance using a large dataset to evaluate generalization performance of the algorithm that includes a number of parameters in the feature measurement process, which means it might sensitive to size and characteristics of mammogram. More advanced nonlinear classification methods such as fuzzy logic or rough set can be used to improve the classification accuracy.

REFERENCES

Anter, M., Azar, T., Hassanien, E., El-Bendary, N., & ElSoud, A. (2013). Automatic computer aided segmentation for liver and hepatic lesions using hybrid segmentations techniques. In *Proceedings of the 2013 Federated Conference on Computer Science and Information Systems*. IEEE.

Berg, W., Campassi, C., Langenberg, P., & Sexton, M. (2000). Breast Imaging Reporting and Data System: Inter - and Intraobserver Variability. *Feature Analysis and Final Assessment, 174*(6), 1769–1777. PMID:10845521

Birdwell, R., Ikeda, D., Oshaughnessy, K., & Sickles, E. (2001). Mammographic Characteristics of 115 Missed Cancers Later Detected with Screening Mammography and Potential Utility of Computer-aided Detection. *Radiology, 219*, 192–202. doi:10.1148/radiology.219.1.r01ap16192 PMID:11274556

Blot, L., & Zwiggelaar, R. (2001). Background texture extraction for the classification of mammographic parenchymal patterns. *Journal of Medical Image Understanding and Analysis*, 145-148.

Bovis, K., & Singh, S. (2002). Classification of mammographic breast density using a combined classifier paradigm. In *Proc. Medical Image Understanding and Analysis (MIUA) conference*. MIUA.

Byng, W., Boyd, F., Fishell, E., Jong, A., & Yaffe, J. (1996). Automated analysis of mammographic densities. *Physics in Medicine and Biology, 41*(5), 909–923. doi:10.1088/0031-9155/41/5/007 PMID:8735257

Caldwell, B., Stapleton, J., Holdsworth, W., Jong, A., Weiser, J., Cooke, G., & Yaffe, J. (1990). Characterization of mammographic parenchymal pattern by fractal dimension. *Physics in Medicine and Biology*, *35*, 235–247. doi:10.1088/0031-9155/35/2/004 PMID:2315379

Duda, O., Hart, E., & Stork, G. (2001). *Pattern Classification* (2nd ed.). Wiley.

Edwards, C., Kupinski, A., Metz, E., & Nishikawa, M. (2002). Maximum likelihood fitting of FROC curves under an initial detection and candidate analysis model. *Medical Physics*, *29*, 2861–2870. doi:10.1118/1.1524631 PMID:12512721

El-henawy, I., Eisa, M., Elsoud, M., & Anter, M. (2010). Fast mammogram segmentation algorithm for segmentating fibroglandular tissue. *IJICS*, *10*(1), 187–199.

ElSoud, M., & Anter, M. (2012). Automatic mammogram segmentation and computer aided diagnoses for breast tissue density according to BIRADS dictionary. *Int. J. Computer Aided Engineering and Technology*, *4*(2), 165–180. doi:10.1504/IJCAET.2012.045655

Freer, W., & Ulissey, J. (2001). Screening mammography with computer-aided detection, Study 12860 patients in a community breast center. *Radiology*, *220*, 781–786. doi:10.1148/radiol.2203001282 PMID:11526282

Gonzalez, C., & Woods, E. (2008). *Digital Image Processing* (3rd ed.). Prentice-Hall, Inc.

Jain, K., Zhong, Y., & Dubuisson, P. (1998). Deformable template models: a review. *Signal Processing*, *71*(2), 109–129. doi:10.1016/S0165-1684(98)00139-X

Landis, R., & Koch, G. (1977). The measurement of observer agreement for categorical data. *Biometrics*, *33*(1), 159–174. doi:10.2307/2529310 PMID:843571

Maenpa, T. (2003). The local binary pattern approach to texture analysis-extensions and applications. Infotech Oulu and Department of Electrical and Information Engineering, University of Oulu.

Mandelbrot, B. (1983). *The Fractal Geometry of Nature*. John Wiley & Sons, Ltd.

Martin, E., Helvie, A., Zhou, C., Roubidoux, A., Bailey, E., & Paramagul, C. et al. (2006). Mammographic density measured with quantitative computer-aided method: comparison with radiologists estimates and BI-RADS categories. *Radiology*, *240*(3), 656–665. doi:10.1148/radiol.2402041947 PMID:16857974

Miller, P., & Astley, M. (1992). Classification of breast tissue by texture analysis. *Image and Vision Computing*, *10*(5), 277–282. doi:10.1016/0262-8856(92)90042-2

Muhimmah, I., Oliver, A., Denton, E., Pont, J., Perez, E., & Zwiggelaar, R. (2006). *Comparison between Wolfe, Boyd, BI-RADS and Tabar based mammographic risk assessment*. Springer. doi:10.1007/11783237_55

Oliver, A., Mart, J., Mart, R., Bosch, A., & Freixenet, J. (2006). A new approach to the classification of mammographic masses and normal breast tissue. In *Proceedings of International Conference on Pattern Recognition*. Academic Press.

Petroudi, S., Kadir, T., & Brady, M. (2003). Automatic classification of mammographic parenchymal patterns: a statistical approach. In *Proc. International Conference IEEE Engineering in Medicine and Biology Society*, (pp. 798-801). IEEE.

Raba, D., Oliver, A., Mart, J., & Peracaula, M. (2005). Breast segmentation with pectoral muscle suppression on digital mammograms. In *Proceedings of Iberian Conference on Pattern Recognition and Image Analysis*. Academic Press.

Suckling, J., Parker, J., Dance, R., Astley, M., Hutt, I., & Boggis, M. … Savage, J. (1994). The mammographic image analysis society digital mammogram database. In *Proceedings of the 2nd International Workshop on Digital Mammography*. Elsevier.

Taylor, P., Hajnal, S., Dilhuydy, H., & Barreau, B. (1994). Measuring image texture to separate difficult from easy mammograms. *The British Journal of Radiology*, *67*(797), 456–463. doi:10.1259/0007-1285-67-797-456 PMID:8193892

Wolfe, N. (1976). Risk for breast cancer development determined by mammographic parenchymal pattern. *Cancer*, *37*(5), 86–92. doi:10.1002/1097-0142(197605)37:5<2486::AID-CNCR2820370542>3.0.CO;2-8 PMID:1260729

Zhou, C., Chan, P., Petrick, N., Helvie, A., Goodsitt, M., Sahiner, B., & Hadjiiski, M. (2001). Computerized image analysis: estimation of breast density on mammograms. *Medical Physics*, *28*(6), 1056–1069. doi:10.1118/1.1376640 PMID:11439475

Zwiggelaar, R., Muhimmah, I., & Denton, E. (2005). Mammographic density classification based on statistical gray-level histogram modeling. In *Proc. Medical Image Understanding and Analysis*. Academic Press.

Zwiggelaar, R., Parr, C., Schumm, E., Hutt, W., Taylor, J., Astley, M., & Boggis, M. (1999). Model-based detection of spiculated lesions in mammograms. *Medical Image Analysis*, *3*(1), 39–62. doi:10.1016/S1361-8415(99)80016-4 PMID:10709696

KEY TERMS AND DEFINITIONS

BIRADS: American College of Radiology (ACR) Breast Imaging Reporting and Data System (BIRADS) is becoming a standard for the assessment of mammographic images.

CAD System: CAD is computerized tools designed to help radiologists.

Classification: Refers to assigning a physical object or incident into one of a set of predefined categories.

Confusion Matrix: Is a visualization tool commonly used in supervised machine learning. It contains information about actual and predicted classifications by a classification system.

Connected Component Labeling Algorithm (CCL): Is the scanning an image pixel by pixel from top to bottom and left to right in order to identify connected pixel regions which share the same set of intensity.

k-NN Classifier: Is a non-parametric statistical method that, like the neural network methods, makes no strong a priori assumptions about the form of the data distribution.

Mammographic Parenchyma Density: Is considered a risk factor for breast cancer, and it's important in the way in which it affects mammographic screening sensitivity.

Screening Mammography: Is considered one of the most effective ways for the early detection of breast cancer.

Segmentation: The process of subdividing the image into its constituent parts.

Texture: Is one of the important characteristics used in identifying objects or regions of interest in an image.

Chapter 3
Statistical Features–Based Diagnosis of Alzheimer's Disease using MRI

Namita Aggarwal
Jawaharlal Nehru University, India

Bharti Rana
Jawaharlal Nehru University, India

R.K. Agrawal
Jawaharlal Nehru University, India

ABSTRACT

Early detection of Alzheimer's Disease (AD), a neurological disorder, may help in development of appropriate treatment to slow down the disease's progression. In this chapter, a method is proposed that may assist in diagnosis of AD using T1 weighted MRI brain images. In the proposed method, first-and-second-order-statistical features were extracted from multiple trans-axial brain slices covering hippocampus and amygdala regions, which play a significant role in AD diagnosis. Performance of the proposed approach is compared with the state-of-the-art feature extraction techniques in terms of sensitivity, specificity, and accuracy. The experiment was carried out on two datasets built from publicly available OASIS data, with four well-known classifiers. Experimental results show that the proposed method outperforms all the other existing feature extraction techniques irrespective of the choice of classifier and dataset. In addition, the statistical test demonstrates that the proposed method is significantly better in comparison to the existing methods. The authors believe that this study will assist clinicians/researchers in classification of AD patients from controls based on T1-weighted MRI.

DOI: 10.4018/978-1-4666-6030-4.ch003

INTRODUCTION

Availability of various medical imaging modalities namely magnetic resonance imaging (MRI), functional MRI, X-ray, computed tomography, positron emission tomography and single photon emission computed tomography allows in-depth study of anatomy and functionality of human body. In this context, analyses of anatomical brain structures using MRI have become increasingly common for diagnostic purposes and identification of disease progression.

Structural MRI is a non-invasive imaging technique with no side effects of harmful rays. It provides extensive detail about the soft tissue anatomy of the brain. Early detection of subtle structural brain changes could help in development of appropriate treatment and slow down disease progression. However, detection of brain atrophy by visual inspection of MR images is very difficult and time consuming. Moreover, it relies on the expertise of clinicians and lacks the automated technique.

Computer-aided image analysis for studying anatomical brain MR image differences is becoming increasingly important for diagnosis of dementia. Alzheimer's disease (AD) is the most commonly found neurological disorder and common cause of dementia among elderly persons. It causes mental disorder and disturbances in brain functions such as memory, language skills, and perception of reality, time and space.

Many research works have utilized 2D transaxial MRI brain slices to distinguish AD from controls. Bagci & Bai (2007) extracted features using gabor transform, a special variant of short time fourier transform (STFT), which has selective frequency and orientation properties. It extracts both frequency and space information from a non stationary signal with the use of a fixed size window. Unlike Gabor, discrete wavelet transform (DWT) allows analysis of a signal at various levels of resolution which is utilized for feature extraction in the research works (Chaplot,

Patnaik, & Jagannathan, 2006; Dahshan, Hosny, & Salem, 2010). Dahshan, Hosny, & Salem (2010) used principal component analysis to reduced a large number of features obtained using DWT. Maitra & Chatterjee (2006) determined a smaller feature set of size 6 using slantlet transform (ST), a variant of DWT. ST and first-order statistics are used to extract feature set of size 6 by Aggarwal, Rana, & Agrawal (2012a). Aggarwal, Rana, & Agrawal (2012b) utilized first and second order statistics (FSOS) to extract a reduced set of relevant features to distinguish AD from controls. Their experimental results demonstrated the superior performance of FSOS in comparison to the state-of-the-art methods based on 2D slices.

Although analysis of 2D slices is not computationally intensive, it may lose relevant information present in neighboring slices. In order to overcome this problem, research community used 3D brain volumes for classification of AD and controls. Kloppel et al. (2008) proposed approaches based on gray probability maps of 3D volumes of whole brain and volume of interest. However, the size of the feature vector so obtained is large. Hence, it suffers from the curse-of-dimensionality (Bellman, 1961) as available number of samples is small and number of features to represent it is large. The research works (Lao, Shen, Xue, Karacali, Resnick, & Davatzikosx, 2004; Magnin, et al., 2009; Ye, et al., 2008) conducted classification with the help of a labeled atlas. However, this predefined atlas might not be specifically intended to study AD patients. 3D based analysis of MRI brain provides better performance in comparison to 2D based analysis at the cost of computational complexity.

Motivated by the research work (Aggarwal, Rana, & Agrawal, 2012b) and utilizing benefits of both 2D and 3D based approaches, a three-step method is proposed in this chapter. In first step, relevant slices from hippocampus and amygdala, which are good marker to distinguish AD from controls, are considered. In second step, features are extracted using FSOS from each slice. In third step, feature vector is constructed from aggregated values (average) of corresponding features from relevant slices. The performance is evaluated in terms of sensitivity, specificity and classification accuracy. To analyze the robustness of the proposed approach, experiments were conducted with four well-known classifiers on a publicly available OASIS database (Marcus, Wang, Parker, Csernansky, Morris, & Buckner, 2007). The performance of the proposed approach was compared with few research works. Further, a statistical test was conducted to determine significant difference between the classification accuracy of the proposed and existing approaches. We believe that this study will assist clinicians/researchers in classification of AD patients from controls based on T1-weighted MRI.

The rest of the chapter discusses feature extraction methods used in the literature, the proposed method and experimental results.

FEATURE EXTRACTION METHODS

Feature extraction is one of the important components in any pattern recognition system. It is designed to obtain a meaningful representation of observations and reduce the dimension of the feature vector by removing noisy, irrelevant and redundant features. A small set of relevant features may enhance the performance of decision learning system, and take less memory and computation time for training and testing.

Existing feature extraction techniques for AD classification can be grouped into two broad categories: 2D based feature extraction techniques and 3D based feature extraction techniques. These methods are briefly presented in the following paragraphs.

2D Based Feature Extraction Techniques

Gabor Transform

Gabor (Gabor, 1946), a special case of STFT, allows extraction of both frequency and space information of a non stationary signal with the use of a fixed size window. It has selective frequency and orientation properties. In the spatial domain, the 2D gabor filter is a gaussian kernel function modulated by a sinusoidal plane wave. Each gabor filter has a fixed wavelength and orientation, and can be convolved with an image to estimate corresponding magnitude of local frequencies. A 2D gabor filter is given as follows:

$$g(x, y; \lambda, \theta, \psi, \sigma, \gamma) = \exp\left(-\frac{x'^2 + \gamma^2 y'^2}{2\sigma^2}\right) \exp\left(i\left(2\pi\frac{x'}{\lambda} + \psi\right)\right)$$

(1)

where $x' = x\cos(\theta) - y\sin(\theta), y' = -x\sin(\theta) + y\cos(\theta)$, λ represents the wavelength of the sinusoidal factor, θ represents the orientation of the normal to the parallel stripes of a gabor function, ψ is the phase offset, σ is the sigma of the Gaussian envelope and γ is the spatial aspect ratio that specifies the ellipticity of the support of the gabor filter.

The research work (Bagci & Bai, 2007) employed 24 gabor filters (8 orientations, 3 scales) which resulted into 24 gabor filtered images. The upper and lower limit of frequency used were 0.5 cycles/pixel and 0.1 cycles/pixel respectively. A single mean image was obtained using all 24 gabor filtered images and represented in terms of one dimensional feature vector. In this work, it is referred to as 'Gabor'.

Wavelet Transform

Wavelets are mathematical functions that decompose data into different frequency components and allow analysis of each component with a resolution matched to its scale. Both space and frequency contents can be simultaneously analyzed with the use of variable sized windows (Mallat, 1989a; Mallat, 1989b). Wavelet transformation decomposes an image into a series of high-pass and low-pass subbands; at each level, an approximation component and three detailed components *i.e.* horizontal, vertical and diagonal are obtained.

A wavelet can decompose an image with a series of averaging and differencing operations. Wavelets work out average intensity properties as well as several detailed contrast levels distributed throughout the image. The general mother wavelet can be constructed from the scaling function $\varphi(x)$ and wavelet function $\psi(x)$ which is defined as follows:

$$\varphi(x) = \sqrt{2} \sum h(k) \varphi\left(2x - k\right) \qquad (2)$$

$$\psi(x) = \sqrt{2} \sum g(k) \varphi\left(2x - k\right) \qquad (3)$$

where $g(k)=(-1)^k h(N-1-k)$, and N is the number of scaling and wavelet coefficients. The sets of scaling ($h(k)$) and wavelet ($g(k)$) function coefficients vary depending on their corresponding wavelet bases.

With more level of decomposition, compact but coarser approximation of the image is obtained. Thus, wavelets provide a simple hierarchical framework for better interpretation of the image information.

Chaplot, Patnaik, & Jagannathan (2006) used db4 wavelet for feature extraction. In their work, 2-level decomposition is carried out to obtain one approximation, three detailed components at level 2, and three detailed components at level 1. The approximation component is used to construct one dimensional feature vector. In this work, it is referred to as 'Db4'.

Dahshan, Hosny, & Salem (2010) used haar wavelet for feature extraction. They carried out 3-level decomposition of MR brain image and constructed feature vector in terms of approximation coefficients. The size of feature vector is further reduced using principal component analysis. In this work, it is referred to as 'Haar'.

Slantlet Transform

The extent to which wavelet basis in wavelet transform can generate sparse representation of a given signal depends on the two characteristics of basis function namely size of window (support) and number of zero moments. Ideally, short support and more number of zero moments are desirable but difficult to achieve simultaneously. This is due to the fact that the window size also increases with the increase of number of zero moments. Hence, it is pointed out (Selesnick, 1999) that for fixed number of zero moments, classical DWT does not yield optimal discrete time localization. They proposed slantlet transform (ST) with reduced support for a fixed number of zero moments. Moreover, it also maintains inherent properties of DWT namely orthogonal filter bank structure, octave band characteristic (tree like structure) and piecewise linearity.

In general, the *l*-scale filter bank of ST has $2l$ channels. The low-pass filter is denoted by $h_l(n)$ and adjoining by $f_l(n)$. Both $h_l(n)$ and $f_l(n)$ are then down sampled by 2^l. Remaining $2l-2$ channels are obtained by $g_i(n)$ (where $i=1,...,l-1$) and its shifted time reverse filters are down sampled by 2^{i+1}. Filter size of DWT (Daubechies length-4) at scale i is $3 \times 2^i - 2$ in comparison to 2^{i+1} for $g_i(n)$ of ST. It can be noted that the reduction of $2^i - 2$ is achieved at each stage which will grow with increase in level. For coarser scale, this difference approaches to two third of filter size of DWT. Two zero moments are considered to determine filter bank in ST in the research work (Selesnick, 1999).

To achieve this, piecewise linear filters $h_i(n), f_i(n)$ and $g_i(n)$ are required to satisfy the orthogonality and moment conditions. Detailed description is available in the research work (Selesnick, 1999).

Maitra & Chatterjee (2006) used ST on one dimensional intensity histogram of MRI instead of directly applying ST on the 2D image and obtained a total of 256 slantlet coefficients. Then a feature vector of size 6 was constructed by considering only absolute magnitude of dominant values from each detailed scale. In this work, it is referred to as 'Slantlet'.

Aggarwal, Rana and Agrawal (2012a) pointed out that non-dominant values may also be distinguishable marker for classification. In their work, 6 features based on first order statistics of 256 slantlet coefficients were determined. The first order statistics used were mean (m) and five central moments (μ_i) corresponding to i=2,...,6. In this work, it is referred to as 'St_moments'.

First and Second Order Statistics

First and second order statistics (Haralick, Shanmugan, & Dinstein, 1973; Papoulis, 1991) is a well-known approach that can be utilized to extract a minimal set of salient features. Mean (m_1), variance (μ_2), skewness (μ_3), and kurtosis (μ_4) are commonly used first order statistical features (Papoulis, 1991). These are defined as follows:

$$m_1 = E\left[I^1\right] = \sum_{I=0}^{n-1} I^1 P(I) \qquad (4)$$

$$\mu_k = E\left[\left(I - E[I]\right)^k\right] = \sum_{I=0}^{n-1} (I - m_1)^k P(I), \ k = 2, 3, 4 \qquad (5)$$

where random variable I represents the gray levels of image, n is the number of possible gray levels and $P(I)$ denotes first-order histogram defined as:

$$P(I) = \frac{number\ of\ pixels\ with\ gray\ level\ I}{Total\ number\ of\ pixels\ in\ the\ region} \qquad (6)$$

The variance measures the deviation of gray levels from the mean. While variance represents width of the histogram, skewness measures the degree of histogram asymmetry around the mean and kurtosis measures the sharpness of histogram.

Although first-order statistical features capture significant information about gray levels, it do not give any information about the relative positions of the various gray levels within the image. This information can be extracted from the gray-level co-occurrence matrix that measures second-order statistics (Haralick, Shanmugan, & Dinstein, 1973). It determines how often gray values co-occur at two pixels which are separated by a fixed distance and an orientation. A co-occurrence matrix $P_{d,\theta}$ is a two-dimensional array of size $n \times n$, where n is the number of gray levels in the image. The gray-level co-occurrence matrix is defined as

$$P_{d,\theta}(i, j) = n_{ij} \qquad (7)$$

where n_{ij} is the probability of transition from a pixel with intensity i to a pixel with intensity j lying at distance d with a given orientation θ in the image.

Using co-occurrence matrix, features can be defined which quantify coarseness, smoothness and texture related information that have high discriminatory power. Among them (Haralick, Shanmugan, & Dinstein, 1973), angular second moment (ASM), contrast, correlation, homogeneity and entropy are few commonly used measures, which are defined as:

$$ASM = \sum_{i,j} P_{d,\theta}(i, j)^2 \qquad (8)$$

$$Contrast = \sum_{i,j} |i-j|^2 \log P_{d,\theta}(i,j) \qquad (9)$$

$$Correlation = \sum_{i,j} \frac{(i-\mu_1)(j-\mu_2)P_{d,\theta}(i,j)}{\sigma_1 \sigma_2} \qquad (10)$$

$$Homogeneity = \sum_{i,j} \frac{P_{d,\theta}(i,j)}{1+|i-j|^2} \qquad (11)$$

$$Entropy = -\sum_{i,j} P_{d,\theta}(i,j) \log P_{d,\theta}(i,j) \qquad (12)$$

ASM is a feature that measures the smoothness of the image. Less smooth the region is, more uniformly distributed is $P_{d,\theta}(i,j)$ and lower will be the value of ASM. Contrast computes local variations which takes high values for image of high contrast. Correlation is a measure of association between pixels in two different directions. Homogeneity is a measure that takes high values for low-contrast images. Entropy is a measure that captures randomness. For smooth images, it takes low values. Together all these features provide high discriminative power to distinguish two different kind of images.

Aggarwal, Rana and Agrawal (2012b) extracted 14 features from a MRI slice using first and second order statistics (FSOS). While 4 features (mean, variance, skewness, and kurtosis) were derived from first order statistics, 10 were constructed from second order statistics. Second order statistics based features were built from co-occurrence matrix with $d=1$ and $\theta=\{0^0, 45^0, 90^0, 135^0\}$. For each of the five second order measures i.e., angular second moment, contrast, correlation, homogeneity and entropy, mean and range of the resulting values from the four directions were calculated resulting in 10 features.

3D Based Feature Extraction Techniques

In literature, a number of computational methods have been proposed for AD diagnosis using T1-weighted 3D MR brain volumes. Most of the suggested approaches are based on gray matter (GM), which is considered to be the main tissue affected in AD. The different methods compared in this study are briefly described below.

Voxel Value Based

Kloppel et al. (2008) proposed two approaches based on direct voxel values. In their experiment, all T1-weighted MR images were first segmented into GM, white matter (WM) and cerebrospinal fluid (CSF), in native space using the SPM8 (Wellcome-Trust-Centre-for-Neuroimaging, 2009) unified segmentation routine with the default parameters. A template was built with help of all the images via diffeomorphic registration algorithm namely DARTEL (Ashburner, 2007). Further GM maps were normalized to this population template. GM maps were then modulated to ensure that the overall tissue amount remained constant. In the first approach, all the voxels from GM maps were considered as features which resulted into a huge size feature vector. This is referred to as 'Whole' in this work for further reference. The second approach constructed a reduced set of features by considering voxels from a hippocampus based volume of interest. These volumes of interest were defined in terms of rectangular cuboids, centered on x=-17, y=-8, z=-18 and x=16, y=-9, z=-18 in the MNI space and with dimensions 12mm, 16mm and 12mm in the x, y and z directions respectively. This approach is referred to as 'VOI' in this work for further reference. For visualization, a brain slice is shown in transaxial, sagittal and coronal planes in Figure 1. In particular, Figure 1(a) represents a slice of an original 3D MR image, and its corresponding GM probability map, used in 'Whole' method, is shown in Figure 1(b). While Figure 1(c) represents selected VOIs used in 'VOI' method.

Atlas Based

Magnin et al. (2009) proposed an approach, referred to as 'AAL', wherein voxels were grouped into anatomical regions using automatic anatomical labeling atlas (Tzourio-Mazoyer, et al., 2002). A brain slice of this atlas with different region of interest (ROI) is shown in Figure 2 in transaxial, sagittal and coronal planes respectively. In their work, labeled template is denormalized from the MNI space to the space of native individual image using deformation toolbox of SPM8. This parcellated the native image into 116 ROIs, out of which 26 ROIs of cerebellum were excluded. For each ROI, histogram of the frequency of occurrence of intensity in the voxels was created. Further, expectation & maximization (EM) algorithm (Redner &

Walker, 1984) was used to segregate the mixture of three normal distributions corresponding to GM, WM, and CSF. A parameter that represents the relative weight of GM compared to WM and CSF for each ROI was determined and used as a feature vector.

THE PROPOSED METHOD

In literature, MRI based automated classification of AD and controls has been performed using either 2D MR brain slices (Aggarwal, Rana, & Agrawal, 2012a; Aggarwal, Rana, & Agrawal, 2012b; Bagci & Bai, 2007; Chaplot, Patnaik, & Jagannathan, 2006; Dahshan, Hosny, & Salem, 2010) or using 3D MR brain volumes (Kloppel, et al., 2008; Magnin, et al., 2009). Both ways of classification has its own advantages and disadvantages. Classification based on feature extracted from 2D brain slices requires less time and memory, but it may lose brain information present in left out slices that may prove helpful in AD diagnosis.

Figure 1. Brain slice in transaxial, sagittal and coronal plane of (a) original image (b) smooth modulated GM probability map (c) smooth modulated GM probability map with selected VOIs in red color

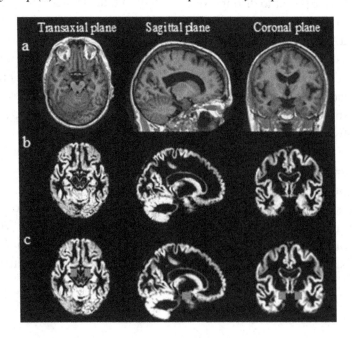

Figure 2. A slice of AAL atlas in (a) transaxial (b) sagittal (c) coronal planes

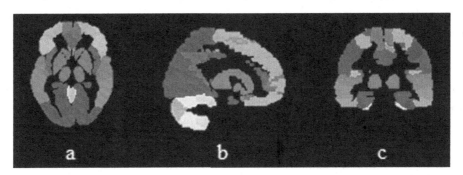

On the other hand, classification based on feature extracted from 3D brain volumes is computationally intensive and requires more memory. In this chapter, an approach is proposed that attempt to cover relevant brain information and at the same time keep both the time and space complexity low. This approach named Ext_FSOS, is an extension of FSOS (Aggarwal, Rana, & Agrawal, 2012b) motivated by good classification performance of FSOS on MR slices in comparison to other existing MR slice based techniques.

Prior to actual feature extraction for classification, brain anatomy was separated from the non-brain anatomy by removing irrelevant tissues external to the brain, such as skull, dura, and eyes using brain extraction tool (BET) (Smith, 2002). This was carried out since the presence of irrelevant and noisy features may degrade the performance of learning system. Figure 3 shows some of the trans-axial slices of original and brain-extracted volume.

Figure 3. (a) Few trans-axial brain slices of original volume and (b) the corresponding brain extracted slices. A distinct oval shaped mark outside the skull boundary in Figure 3(a) is a capsule for marking anatomical side. Note: it is not present in extracted brain.

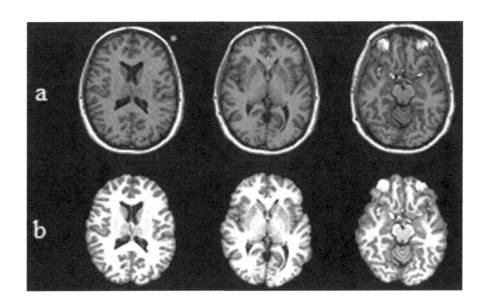

In AD, hippocampus and amygdala located in the medial temporal lobe are preliminary affected regions and may be a good marker to distinguish AD from controls (Bottino, Castro, Gomes, Buchpiguel, Marchetti, & Neto, 2002; Gosche, Mortimer, Smith, Markesbery, & Snowdon, 2002; Van de Pol, et al., 2006). Thus in this work, trans-axial slices from these regions were considered for feature construction. As suggested by (Aggarwal, Rana, & Agrawal, 2012b) only 14 features were extracted from each considered trans-axial slice. Then respective features from each slice were averaged out resulting into a reduced set of relevant features (14 in number). The outline of the proposed Ext_FSOS method is shown in Figure 4.

Similarly, for all existing 2D based feature extraction techniques, features were extracted, as mentioned in their respective research work, from the same trans-axial slices of brain-extracted

volume. Finally a feature vector was constructed by aggregating (averaging) features from selected brain slices. Experiments were also performed by concatenating features from selected slices, but results were not encouraging. It might be attributed to so obtained high dimensional feature vector and availability of small number of samples. Thus in this work, only aggregated features from multiple slices were utilized for implementing all 2D based techniques.

EXPERIMENTAL SETUP AND RESULTS

The performance of the proposed approach was evaluated in terms of sensitivity, specificity and accuracy, where sensitivity=tp/(tp+fn), specificity=tn/(tn+fp) and accuracy=(tp+tn)/

Figure 4. The proposed method

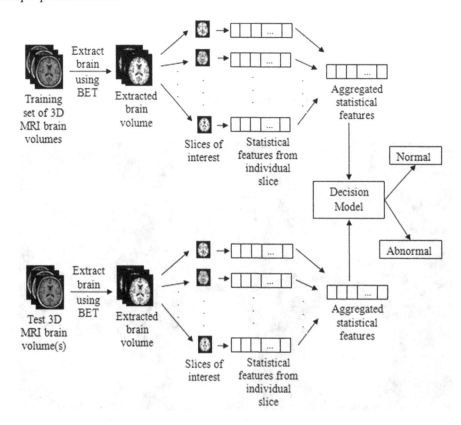

(tp+tn+fp+fn). Here tp, fp, tn and fn denotes true positives, false positives, true negatives and false negatives respectively. In general, sensitivity and specificity measures, how well model identifies positive and negative cases respectively whereas accuracy indicates how well it identifies both categories. We used four widely used classifiers: support vector machine with linear kernel (SVM), *k*-nearest neighbor (KNN), C4.5 and levenberg–marquardt neural classifier (LMNC) in our experiments. The performance of the proposed Ext_FSOS method was compared with the existing 3D and all other extension of 2D based feature extraction techniques.

To evaluate and compare the performance, a publicly available MRI data from Open Access Series of Imaging Studies (OASIS) database (Marcus, Wang, Parker, Csernansky, Morris, & Buckner, 2007) was used. In this database, multiple structural T1-weighted MP-RAGE (Magnetization-Prepared Rapid-Acquisition Gradient Echo) images were acquired on a 1.5-T Vision scanner in a single imaging session for each subject. MRI acquisition details used are as follows: TR=9.7 ms, TE=4.0 ms, Flip angle=100, TI=20ms, TD=200ms, 128 sagittal 1.25 mm slices with pixels resolution of 256×256 (1×1mm) and without gaps. In order to mark anatomical side, a capsule was placed over the left forehead. In this experiment, average registered MRI volumes with corrected bias field were used.

The original dataset comprised of a cross-sectional collection of 416 subjects aged between 18 to 96 years. 181 subjects were excluded whose clinical dementia ratings (CDR) were not provided. CDR of 0 represents no dementia, and CDR of 0.5, 1, and 2 indicate very mild, mild and moderate dementia respectively. Two more subjects which could not be successfully processed were also excluded from our experiment. Two balanced datasets were constructed from the remaining 99 AD subjects and 134 controls. First dataset D_Extremes was constructed based on 30 mild or moderate AD patients, and 30 well matched controls. Second dataset D_Females focused on 48 AD females and 48 age matched control females. This construction was based on the study (Lao, Shen, Xue, Karacali, Resnick, & Davatzikosx, 2004) that brain of a female is different from those of male and could be discriminated via MRI analysis. The demographic and clinical summaries of both the datasets i.e. D_Extremes and D_Females are shown in Table 1. MMSE and SES represent the score of mini-mental state examination and socioeconomic status respectively.

Table 1. Demographic and clinical summaries of AD and controls

| | | D_Extremes | | D_Females | |
		AD	Control	AD	Control
Subjects	no. of subjects (M/F)	30 (10/20)	30 (8/22)	48 (0/48)	48 (0/48)
Age	mean range	78.03 (65-96)	75.33 (61-90)	77.85 (66-96)	77.54 (65-94)
Education Level	mean range	2.53 (1-5)	3.63 (1-5)	2.67 (1-5)	2.90 (1-5)
SES	mean range	2.92 (1-5)	2.37 (1-4)	2.92 (1-5)	2.77 (1-5)
CDR	(0.5/1/2)	(0/28/2)	0	(30/17/1)	0
MMSE	mean range	21.23 (15-29)	29.96 (29-30)	24.15 (15-30)	29 (26-30)

All experiments were carried out using Windows XP environment over Pentium 4 machine, with 8 GB RAM and a processor speed of 3 GHz. We used Image Processing Toolbox from Matlab R2008b, BET (Smith, 2002), SPM8 (Wellcome-Trust-Centre-for-Neuroimaging, 2009), automatic anatomical labeling atlas (Tzourio-Mazoyer, et al., 2002) and Prtools version 4.1 (Duin, Juszcak, Paclik, Pekalska, De Ridder, & Tax, 2004).

Each experiment was executed 10 times on 10-fold cross-validation. In each run, data was partitioned only once corresponding to a 10-fold cross-validation and the same was used throughout the experiment for all methods. The average performance measures along with its standard deviation are reported in Table 2. The best results achieved for each classifier corresponding to different performance measures are shown in italics. Boxplots of classification accuracy of different methods for both datasets with SVM and C4.5 are shown in Figure 5. In box plots, the central mark on each box denotes the median, the edges of the box represent the 25th and 75th percentiles, the whiskers extend to the most extreme data points, and the outliers are plotted individually. Similar trend in boxplots were also observed for other classifiers. Features for each method were extracted as aforementioned.

We observed the following from Table 2 and Figure 5.

- For all classifiers, Ext_FSOS yielded maximum average accuracy and sensitivity in comparison to all other techniques except few cases.
- In most of the cases, Ext_Slantlet technique was leading in terms of specificity. However, the performance is poor in terms of sensitivity using Ext_Slantlet.
- Features obtained with Ext_Db4, Ext_Gabor, Whole and VOI were large and required huge memory. Hence, the learning model could not be built with LMNC classifier.

In addition, a statistical test (two-tailed paired sample t-test at significance level of 0.05) was also performed to validate whether Ext_FSOS is statistically significantly different from other feature extraction techniques. For this, the null hypothesis H_0 is that there is no significant difference between the classification accuracy (μ) of Ext_FSOS and each of the remaining feature extraction techniques. Corresponding alternate hypothesis H_1 is that there is significant difference between the two *i.e.*

$$H_0 : \mu_{Ext\_FSOS} = \mu_X, \quad H_1 : \mu_{Ext\_FSOS} \neq \mu_X$$

where $X \in$
{Ext_Gabor, Ext_Db4, Ext_Haar, Ext_Slantlet, Ext_St_moments, Whole, VOI, AAL}

Table 3 shows t-statistic values of the degree of correspondence between Ext_FSOS and other techniques for both datasets. It is known that at the significance level of 0.05 and degrees of freedom equal to 99 (for 100 runs), the threshold value of t-statistic is 1.984.

Based upon this threshold value, it can be observed from Table 3 that there is a significant difference between Ext_FSOS and other techniques for experimental settings except for a few cases shown in italics.

CONCLUSION AND FUTURE WORK

In this study, a novel method is proposed for efficient AD diagnosis using relevant brain MRI slices instead of conventional approach of using a single slice or whole brain volume. Single slice based methods are fast yet may lose relevant information present in neighboring slices. While whole brain based approaches overcome the drawback of slice based approaches but at the cost of

Table 2. Performance measures (in percentage) for dataset D_Extremes and D_Females

		D_ Extremes			D_ Females		
		Sensitivity	Specificity	Accuracy	Sensitivity	Specificity	Accuracy
		Mean±Std	Mean±Std	Mean±Std	Mean±Std	Mean±Std	Mean±Std
SVM	Ext_Gabor	66.67±5.44	64.67±3.58	65.67±3.7	62.65±3.12	64.8±4.66	63.69±2.41
	Ext_Db4	57±6.75	67.67±3.87	62.33±4.59	56.8±3.28	67.25±3.19	62.03±1.67
	Ext_Haar	57.67±4.98	69.33±4.39	63.5±3.8	53.5±2.57	62.35±3.62	57.92±2.31
	Ext_Slantlet	51.67±3.6	64.67±3.91	58.17±3.28	54.45±1.61	55±2.3	54.83±1.52
	Ext_St_moments	54±2.11	70±3.85	62±2.05	56.3±1.49	72.1±3.11	64.2±1.58
	Ext_FSOS	78.33±4.23	*80±1.57*	79.17±1.96	*75.15±2.01*	*75.2±1.3*	*75.14±1.07*
	Whole	*81.33±1.72*	*80±1.57*	80.67±0.86	64.75±1.75	74.9±3.34	69.82±1.88
	VOI	67.67±2.25	70±2.22	68.83±1.37	68.6±2.84	72.5±2.54	70.61±1.66
	AAL	62±5.71	62.67±5.16	62.33±5.1	53.2±3.43	69.1±5.17	60.92±3.63
KNN	Ext_Gabor	54±3.44	81.67±1.76	67.83±1.58	48.6±3.55	88.4±2.04	68.43±2.15
	Ext_Db4	62.67±3.06	79±3.53	70.83±2.12	44.35±3.97	89.15±2.22	66.69±2.22
	Ext_Haar	62.33±2.74	75.33±3.22	68.83±1.58	52±3.14	80.85±2.58	66.4±1.83
	Ext_Slantlet	36±1.41	87.67±3.16	61.83±2	41.6±1.97	*92.15±3.09*	66.93±2.26
	Ext_St_moments	54.67±6.13	70.67±4.39	62.67±2.51	62.85±2.76	71.6±4.61	67.26±2.12
	Ext_FSOS	*82.67±2.63*	73.67±1.89	*78.17±1.23*	*73.5±3.97*	67.25±3.81	70.11±2.77
	Whole	79±2.74	76.33±3.67	77.67±1.79	55±3.57	71.5±4.28	63.29±2.21
	VOI	63.33±3.14	85.67±2.25	74.5±2.23	63.95±2.74	76.95±1.57	*70.39±1.19*
	AAL	55.67±4.98	64.67±4.22	60.17±3.37	38.45±3.77	70.1±5.02	54.39±2.64
C4.5	Ext_Gabor	70±2.72	69.33±4.1	69.67±2.46	71.15±3.63	67.95±5.23	69.54±3.16
	Ext_Db4	66±7.5	66.67±6.09	66.33±4.7	66.7±3.16	65±5.68	66±2.48
	Ext_Haar	63.33±7.37	66±8.29	64.67±6.13	66.05±6.13	62.35±5.31	64.14±3.16
	Ext_Slantlet	29.33±3.06	*88.33±2.36*	58.83±1.93	59.4±4.02	*81.25±1.09*	70.26±1.87
	Ext_St_moments	51.33±7.57	67.67±6.68	59.5±5.61	65.3±2.39	76.3±2.55	70.67±1.99
	Ext_FSOS	*74±4.1*	76±4.1	*75±2.48*	79.75±1.86	73.7±2.42	*76.81±1.43*
	Whole	60.67±6.63	61.67±8.78	61.17±3.24	65.2±6.98	65±6.67	65.2±3.76
	VOI	66±7.67	64.33±8.17	65.17±5.69	66.9±6.56	64.35±4.64	65.63±4.63
	AAL	52.67±3.44	47.67±9.43	50.17±4.74	62.6±4.48	64.7±7.71	63.53±3.83
LMNC	Ext_Gabor	-	-	-	-	-	-
	Ext_Db4	-	-	-	-	-	-
	Ext_Haar	60±6.09	64.67±5.26	62.33±4.66	57.9±7.96	60.8±6.13	59.29±5.01
	Ext_Slantlet	50.33±7.28	58.67±6.32	54.5±5.16	51.95±3.69	*81.4±2.99*	66.87±2.31
	Ext_St_moments	51.67±5.27	68.33±6.89	60±3.04	64.6±4.23	68.6±5.14	66.58±2.19
	Ext_FSOS	*70.67±4.39*	*69.67±6.37*	*70.17±3.37*	68.6±5.93	67.4±6.78	68.08±3.98
	Whole	-	-	-	-	-	-
	VOI	-	-	-	-	-	-
	AAL	59.33±5.16	65±3.93	62.17±3.69	60.8±6.52	66.15±5.78	63.68±4.45

*Ext stands for extension

Figure 5. Variation in accuracy among different methods for all datasets with (a) SVM and (b) C4.5 classifier using boxplot

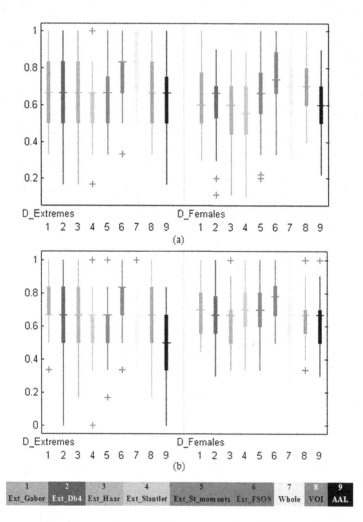

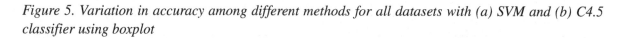

(a)

(b)

Table 3. T-statistic values of the degree of correspondence between Ext_FSOS and other techniques

	D_ Extremes				D_ Females			
	SVM	**KNN**	**C4.5**	**LMNC**	**SVM**	**KNN**	**C4.5**	**LMNC**
Ext_Gabor	6.98	5.34	2.06	-	5.81	*1.02*	3.69	-
Ext_Db4	1.99	4.28	3.05	-	8.38	*1.85*	6.05	-
Ext_Haar	7.22	5.12	3.94	3.88	9.92	2.12	6.69	4.87
Ext_Slantlet	8.63	8.42	7.10	6.15	9.27	*1.72*	3.87	*0.71*
Ext_St_moments	7.58	7.40	5.76	4.43	5.30	*1.42*	3.72	*0.92*
Whole	*-0.84*	*0.21*	5.75	-	3.69	3.41	5.78	-
VOI	6.00	*1.61*	3.65	-	2.74	*-0.13*	5.58	-
AAL	7.31	8.21	10.78	3.18	8.19	7.18	6.98	2.51

high computational complexity. In contrast, the proposed method covers sufficient brain information needed for AD diagnosis and at the same time has low computational complexity. A small set of features were obtained by aggregation of statistical features extracted from multiple slices of brain covering hippocampus and amygdala region. Experiments were performed on two datasets (build from publicly available MRI brain OASIS database) with four well-known classifiers (SVM, KNN, C4.5 and LMNC). Results were compared with five 2D slices based extended methods and three 3D volumes based existing feature extraction techniques. It was observed that the proposed approach provides better classification accuracy in comparison to all existing methods regardless of dataset and classifier. These results were also supported by statistical test.

Although the proposed method outperforms the existing methods, it requires prior knowledge of region of interest. The model can be further enhanced if some component can learn the region of interest from the data itself in absence of prior knowledge. In addition, efficacy of the model may be investigated on different datasets possibly from some different imaging modality, settings or disease.

REFERENCES

Aggarwal, N., Rana, B., & Agrawal, R. K. (2012a). Computer Aided Diagnosis of Alzheimer's Disease from MRI Brain Images. In *Proceedings of International Conference on Image Analysis and Recognition* (pp. 259-267). Aveiro, Portugal: Springer.

Aggarwal, N., Rana, B., & Agrawal, R. K. (2012b). Classification of Alzheimer's from T2 Trans-Axial Brain MR Images: A Comparative Study of Feature Extraction Techniques. *International Journal of Computer Vision and Image Processing*, *2*(3), 50–63. doi:10.4018/ijcvip.2012070103

Ashburner, J. (2007). A fast diffeomorphic image registration algorithm. *NeuroImage*, *38*, 95–113. doi:10.1016/j.neuroimage.2007.07.007 PMID:17761438

Bagci, U., & Bai, L. (2007). A Comparison of Daubechies and Gabor Wavelets for Classification of MR Images. In *Proceedings of International Conference on Signal Processing and Communications* (pp. 676 - 679). Dubai: IEEE.

Bellman, R. (1961). *Adaptive control processes: A guided tour*. Princeton University Press.

Bottino, C. M., Castro, C. C., Gomes, R. L., Buchpiguel, C. A., Marchetti, R. L., & Neto, M. R. (2002). Volumetric MRI measurements can differentiate Alzheimer's disease, mild cognitive impairment, and normal aging. *International Psychogeriatrics*, *14*(1), 59–72. doi:10.1017/S1041610202008281 PMID:12094908

Chaplot, S., Patnaik, L. M., & Jagannathan, N. R. (2006). Classification of magnetic resonance brain images using wavelets as input to support vector machine and neural network. *Biomedical Signal Processing and Control*, *1*(1), 86–92. doi:10.1016/j.bspc.2006.05.002

Dahshan, E.-S. A., Hosny, T., & Salem, A.-B. M. (2010). A hybrid technique for automatic MRI brain images classification. *Digital Signal Processing*, *20*, 433–441. doi:10.1016/j.dsp.2009.07.002

Duin, R., Juszcak, P., Paclik, P., Pekalska, E., De Ridder, D., & Tax, D. (2004, January). *PrTools: The Matlab Toolbox for Pattern Recognition*. Retrieved from http://www.prtools.org

Gabor, D. (1946). Theory of communication. *Journal of the Institution of Electrical Engineers*, *93*(3), 429–457.

Gosche, K. M., Mortimer, J. A., Smith, C. D., Markesbery, W. R., & Snowdon, D. A. (2002). Hippocampal volume as an index of Alzheimer neuropathology: findings from the Nun study. *Neurology*, *58*, 1476–1482. doi:10.1212/WNL.58.10.1476 PMID:12034782

Haralick, R. M., Shanmugan, K., & Dinstein, I. (1973). Textural Features for Image Classification. *IEEE Transactions on Systems: Man, and Cybernetics SMC*, *3*(6), 610–621.

Kloppel, S., Stonnington, C. M., Chu, C., Draganski, B., Scahill, R. I., & Rohrer, J. D. et al. (2008). Automatic classification of MR scans in Alzheimer's disease. *Brain*, *131*(3), 681–689. doi:10.1093/brain/awm319 PMID:18202106

Lao, Z., Shen, D., Xue, Z., Karacali, B., Resnick, S. M., & Davatzikosx, C. (2004). Morphological classification of brains via high-dimensional shape transformations and machine learning methods. *NeuroImage*, *21*(1), 46–57. doi:10.1016/j.neuroimage.2003.09.027 PMID:14741641

Magnin, B., Mesrob, L., Kinkingnéhun, S., Issac, M. P., Colliot, O., & Sarazin, M. et al. (2009). Support vector machine-based classification of Alzheimer's disease from whole-brain anatomical MRI. *Neuroradiology*, *51*(2), 73–83. doi:10.1007/s00234-008-0463-x PMID:18846369

Mallat, S. G. (1989a). A theory for multiresolution signal decomposition: the wavelet representation. *IEEE Transactions on Pattern Analysis and Machine Intelligence*, *11*(7), 674–693. doi:10.1109/34.192463

Mallat, S. G. (1989b). Multiresolution Approximations and Wavelet Orthonormal Bases of L2. *Transactions of the American Mathematical Society*, *315*(1), 69–87.

Marcus, D. S., Wang, T. H., Parker, J., Csernansky, J. G., Morris, J. C., & Buckner, R. L. (2007). Open Access Series of Imaging Studies (OASIS), cross-sectional MRI data in young, middle aged, nondemented, and demented older adults. *Journal of Cognitive Neuroscience*, *19*(9), 1498–14507. doi:10.1162/jocn.2007.19.9.1498 PMID:17714011

Papoulis, A. (1991). *Probability, Random Variables and Stochastic Processes* (3rd ed.). New York: McGraw-Hill.

Redner, R., & Walker, H. (1984). Mixture densities, maximum likelihood and the EM algorithm. *SIAM Review*, *26*, 195–239. doi:10.1137/1026034

Selesnick, I. W. (1999). The Slantlet Transform. *IEEE Transactions on Signal Processing*, *47*(5), 1304–1313. doi:10.1109/78.757218

Smith, S. M. (2002). Fast robust automated brain extraction. *Human Brain Mapping*, *17*(3), 143–155. doi:10.1002/hbm.10062 PMID:12391568

Tzourio-Mazoyer, N., Landeau, B., Papathanassiou, D., Crivello, F., Etard, O., & Delcroix, N. et al. (2002). Automated anatomical labeling of activations in SPM using a macroscopic anatomical parcellation of the MNI MRI single-subject brain. *NeuroImage*, *15*, 273–289. doi:10.1006/nimg.2001.0978 PMID:11771995

Van de Pol, L. A., Hensel, A., Van der Flier, W. M., Visser, P., Pijnenburg, Y. A., & Barkhof, F. et al. (2006). Hippocampal atrophy on MRI in frontotemporal lobar degeneration and Alzheimer's disease. *Journal of Neurology, Neurosurgery, and Psychiatry*, *77*, 439–442. doi:10.1136/jnnp.2005.075341 PMID:16306153

Wellcome-Trust-Centre-for-Neuroimaging. (2009, April). *SPM8 - Statistical Parametric Mapping*. Retrieved from http://www.fil.ion.ucl. ac.uk/spm/software/spm8/

Ye, J., Chen, K., Wu, T., Li, J., Zhao, Z., Patel, R., et al. (2008). Heterogeneous data fusion for Alzheimer's disease study. In *Proceedings of International Conference on Knowledge Discovery and Data Mining* (pp. 1025-1033). New York: ACM.

KEY TERMS AND DEFINITIONS

Alzheimer's Disease (AD): A progressive neurodegenerative disorder that induces impairment in brain functions such as memory, language skills and perception of reality, time and space. Its early symptoms include decline in short-term memory and gradually it affects other cognitive areas such as long-term memory, orientation, language and judgment.

Classification: A process of assigning a class label to a given test sample on the basis of decision rules learnt from available training samples with known class labels.

Clinical Dementia Rating (CDR): Quantifies the severity of dementia by rating it on five-point scale {0, .5, 1, 2, 3} which represents no dementia, very mild dementia, mild dementia, moderate dementia and severe dementia respectively.

Curse of Dimensionality: Refers to the need of exponential number of samples for high dimensional data to achieve better performance.

Feature Extraction: A technique to obtain a compact and meaningful representation of the original data.

Magnetic Resonance Imaging (MRI): A medical imaging modality that utilizes proton (hydrogen nuclei) resonance phenomenon, magnetic fields and radio waves to generate images of internal structure of the human body.

Mini-Mental State Examination (MMSE): A test that quantifies cognitive impairment on 30-point scale with help of series of questions based on arithmetic, memory and orientation where score greater than or equal to 27 indicates a normal cognition.

Voxel: Stands for volumetric picture element that represents a data point in 3D space.

Chapter 4
Use of Bi–Camera and Fusion of Pairwise Real Time Citrus Fruit Image for Classification Application

Peilin Li
University of South Australia, Australia

Sang-Heon Lee
University of South Australia, Australia

Hung-Yao Hsu
University of South Australia, Australia

ABSTRACT

In this chapter, the use of two images, the near infrared image and the color image, from a bi-camera machine vision system is investigated to improve the detection of the citrus fruits in the image. The application has covered the design of the bi-camera vision system to align two CCD cameras, the online acquisition of the citrus fruit tree image, and the fusion of two aligned images. In the system, two cameras have been registered with alignment to ensure the fusion of two images. A fusion method has been developed based on the Multiscale Decomposition Analysis (MSD) with a Discrete Wavelet Transform (DWT) application for the two dimensional signal. In the fusion process, two image quality issues have been addressed. One is the detail noise from the background, which is bounded with the envelope spectra and with similar spectra to orange citrus fruit and spatial variance property. The second is the enhancement of the fundamental envelope spectra using two source images. With level of MSD estimated, the noise is reduced by zeroing the high pass coefficients in DWT while the fundamental envelope spectra from the color image are enhanced by an arithmetic pixel level fusion rule. To evaluate the significant improvement of the image quality, some major classification methods are applied to compare the classified results from the fused image with the results from the types of color image. The misclassification error is measured by the empirical type errors using the manual segmentation reference image.

DOI: 10.4018/978-1-4666-6030-4.ch004

INTRODUCTION

Background

In horticultural industry, the automatic fruit harvesting methods have been researched and investigated since the photometric comparison was proposed (Schertz & Brown, 1968). The vision system for harvesting mechanism is used to detect the fruits by interpreting the information of the location and the depth estimation for the manipulator. However the issues from both the real time measured data and the interpretation methods behind the data are not trivial for the implementation of the vision system on the harvesting mechanism. In visual recognition system, the vision cameras are the main solution to communicate with the environment. The considerable researches have been done in both the vision systems and the interpretation methods in the agricultural harvesting automation applications (A. R. Jimenez, Ceres, & Pons, 2000). The imaging data has covered three main categories: intensity, spectral, and laser range finder. In applications literature, the successful fruit detection rate is averagely around 70% and up to 90% with variation in some cases. The application has covered from the single sensor with physical optical function (A. R. Jimenez et al., 2000; Parrish, Jr, & Goksel, 1977; Slaughter & Harrell, 1987) to the binocular stereoscope based on the photogrammetric principle (Buemi, Massa, & Sandini, 1995; Grasso & Recce, 1996; Plebe & Grasso, 2001; Takahashi, Zhang, & Fukuchi, 2002). Although the depth between the end effecter and the fruit target can be estimated based on the measure of the incremental movement of the sensor and the distortion of the target area (Johan Baeten, 2008). However the prerequisite is the accuracy of the main classification interpretation of the targets in the image. The considerable imaging techniques have been investigated to improve the classification interpretation. In practice, the single sensor scheme for imaging has certain physical limitation

such as the resolution and the spectral waveband. Therefore the image data acquired by the sensor is degraded. On top of that, the spectra is a mixed waveband produced by the potential multifactor under the open natural illumination (Kane & Lee, 2007). By using hyperspectral technique, the certain wide range of spectra can be acquired under the resolution capability. The study of the statistics on the segments of all waveband can provide the features from the waveband for the machine vision system development. However the scanning time in practice depends on both the area to be scanned and the sensor resolution (Okamoto & Lee, 2009). The use of the segments with dominant spectra is fuzzy for the real time applications. Alternatively the multispectral imaging has been proposed to capture and combine more information at the same time with capability of acquiring more wavebands and a smarter image processing technique to improve the detection (Edan, 1995; Kane & Lee, 2006). Instead of dispersing spectra into the discrete numerous wavebands, multispectral technique captures the specific range of wavelength across the electromagnetic spectrum space. The early multispectral scheme was presented using three CCD micro cameras side by side with three different optical waveband filters in terms of 550nm, 650nm, and 950nm wavelength respectively (Rabatel, 1988). Two ratios by using 550nm and 650nm intensity to 950nm intensity were calculated to discriminate the apples from the remaining background. The detection of fruits was about 75% of all existing fruits. This scheme initially gave the implication to possibly detect immature green fruits by combining different waveband spectra. However the failures were detected and the system was not absolutely insensitive to illumination variation. A monochromatic near infrared camera was equipped with multi waveband pass filters to capture citrus fruit tree images(Kane & Lee, 2007). This work was an extension after the measurement done on the green leaves and types of green citrus fruit in seasons (Kane & Lee, 2006). Three waveband filters were attached to the camera respectively to catch waveband spectral area images. The reference index of waveband intensity was used followed by the global optimal discriminant threshold to discriminate the citrus fruits from the background. Averagely 84.5% correct citrus fruit pixels were identified. However the resultant multispectral images were not well synchronized and aligned in dynamic scenes. Another issue was the saturation and the dark area in the image. The reason that the number of leaves caused the diffuse reflectance was theoretically studied as well (Kane & Lee, 2006). It was proposed that the multispectral image should be captured at the same time with capability of acquiring more wavebands and a smarter image processing technique. On top of that, the multispectral scheme has been broadly designed and practiced by research in inspection analysis. Variant sensors have been selected and practiced in special applications (Aleixos, Blasco, Navarron, & Molto, 2002; Lu, 2004). In applications, the multispectral imaging data can be achieved by multisensor shooting the same channel (Aleixos, Blasco et al. 2002) or a single sensor shooting the channel by interchanging certain filters (Lu, 2004). Basically the certain spectral regions and the ratio of the spectral region components in combination are used to contrast the image for the classification interpretation. By comparing with the use of the narrowed waveband image, the potential use of different source images, like NIR image and color image, is not trivial to be justified analytically with fusion method for the improvement of the image quality.

The multisensor fusion technique is a synergistic combination of different sources information. The idea of fusion technique has been broadly researched for various applications such as the medical diagnostic learning, the surveillance, and the inspection application (Blum & Liu, 2006; Wyawahare, Patil, & Abhyankar, 2009). The main information can possibly be enhanced in the fused data by combining the quality of the feature from the sources complementarily. The use of image

fusion technique has two issues to be addressed (Blum & Liu, 2006), namely the registration and the fusion of the data. The registration is the prerequisite of the fusion to align the images precisely (Blum & Liu, 2006). Normally the registration can be done spatially by aligning the multisensor in the same coordinate space using physical optical lens aiming at a prescribed pattern in a template. Most of the registration can be done by the algorithmic method to find the transform matrix based on the control point or the feature in the image (Blum & Liu, 2006). Then the algorithmic registration solves a transform matrix based on the global or the local deformation between the real image and the reference image. For the registration purpose, the frame has been designed in image acquisition for a region of interest in the following study (Bulanon, Burks, & Alchanatis, 2009). The distortion in the image is transformed based on the availability of the information. However the prevalent issue in real time application is the shifting of the objects between the frames due to the time difference by triggering on the sensors in dynamic temporal coordinate (Kane & Lee, 2007). The movement of the objects for example the citrus fruit may be covered and shadowed locally by the neighboring leaves since the ripened developed fruit is heavier than the neighboring leaves. Therefore the local disparity and the uncertainty of the availability of the information cannot be solved by the global transform matrix by the algorithmic method. In dynamic scene, the prerequisite for the use of the multisensor is to register the multisensor closely on both the spatial and the temporal coordinates simultaneously. If the multisensor can capture the same channel closely, the software based registration can be possibly bypassed to improve the efficiency and the accuracy of the following fusion approach. The example to address the registration issue has been detailed with two types of portable multispectral imaging systems, a dual-band spectral imaging system and a three-band spectral imaging system, for contaminant detection in food inspection industry (Kise, Park,

Heitschmidt, Lawrence, & Windham, 2010; Kise, Park, Lawrence, & Windham, 2007). The similar idea has been adopted in this work with more consideration of some flexibility at the terminal of two sensors to acquire the types of citrus fruit image data by applying the combination of some physical optical attenuation filter function in online image acquisition (Li, Lee, & Hsu, 2011). To address the alignment in two coordinates, the hardware alignment and the synchronization technique for triggering in a master and slave architecture are addressed.

On top of the registration, the multisensor fusion technique basically covers the signal level, pixel level, feature level, and the symbol level approaches (Blum & Liu, 2006). The pixel level fuses the images by determine the correlated pixel from each source image. The feature level fusion extracts the feature such as the edge or other feature and combines the feature into the fused image. The feature fusion is selective by application on such as the detail of information. The symbol level fusion processes the information at each source image and then makes decision at high level for abstraction to the fused image. In this application, the pixel level fusion is suited based on the content of the source images from different area of the spectral coordinate. The pixel level fusion is a two dimensional signal level fusion. The fusion methods are generally categorized into the multiscale decomposition based (MSD) and the non-multiscale decomposition based (NMSD). The non-multiscale decomposition based fusion methods approach the fusion on the source images straightforward without addressing the spatial properties (Blum & Liu, 2006). The NMSD methods cover the pixel and the color combination, the nonlinear or the probability estimation, and the advanced neural network architecture. However the citrus fruit image data has certain spatial variance property in frequency domain. The MSD methods are more suited to address the fusion issue in this application. The multiscale decomposition based fusion is performed on each

source image. Then the composite component is transformed reversely to the final fused image. In literature, the commonly used MSD methods are the pyramid transform (PT), the discrete wavelet transform (DWT), and the discrete wavelet frame (DWF). A pyramid structure is an efficient method for representation and computation of the components in decomposition scales. In PT, the low pass filtering and subsampling are the main process followed by the interpolation and the differencing without high pass filtering. On the other hand in DWT, the image is filtered by convolving two coefficient filters such as a low pass and a high pass filter in both rowwise and columnwise successively. The original coefficient is scaled down to decompose the image into four coefficients such as low-low, low-high, high-low, and high-high pass coefficients in current level. The low pass approximation coefficient can be decomposed recursively to the subsequent level. The issue of shift variance property caused by the subsampling in DWT can be addressed by DWF. However this issue will not lead to extra distortion on the fused result if the images are well aligned by the nonparametric registration. Therefore the details with spatial property can be possibly addressed by MSD approach for the following fusion of the source images in spatial resolution. In addition, the discrete Fourier transform (DFT) has been applied in the preliminary study and the result has no enhancement on the fused image. The global effect has a factor of the use of a fixed periodic basis wave set which globally restricts the analysis of high frequency content by DFT. By using the wavelet in MSD, the flexibility is that the detail noise is removed by zeroing the high pass coefficients in each scale level. The fusion in the last level can be achieved by the combination of the fundamental envelope spectra before the reverse transform. However the removal of the detail in high pass coefficients blurs the area of the fruits in the classified result as well. Therefore the enhancement of the fundamental envelope spectra is considered in the fusion rule without losing the main information. The fusion of the coefficients from multisensor has variant arithmetic rules such as maximum, minimum, mean or weighted mean, and majority voting in multi-classifier application on high dimensional coordinate data space (L. O. Jimenez, Morales-Morell, & Creus, 1999; Kittler, Hatef, Duin, & Matas, 1998; Piella, 2003; Yifan Zhang & He, 2009). The fusion rule should maintain the original contrast with possible enhancement by combining another component to improve the final image quality. Normally the features from different area may not have a straightforward correlation. The features to be fused are researched based on the requirement of the particular application and the preliminary study of the fusion rules from the literature.

Motivation of Bi-Camera Fusion Method

Some intractable issues are more complicated from the real time citrus fruit images. The quality issues from the real time citrus fruit image might have multifactor from both the content of the objects and the other factors from the uncontrollable environment. From the preliminary study, the similar spectra appear quite normally on the side or the tip of the leaves when the setup is posed in a wide range of the tree which is covered by the sun light. By using the morphological filter, the size of the structure is difficult to be decided and the citrus fruit area is affected by the structure filter. Normally the details from the background have certain spatial variance property in the image. Therefore two dimensional signal formed in the image can be assumed to be the fundamental envelope spectra bounded with local details in general. The second quality issue is the non-homogeneity of the spectra on the citrus fruit. The main reason is due to the non-Euclidean structure of the citrus fruit posed naturally. The structure is also the reason for the bright value phenomena at the core area of the citrus fruit in the image. The bright value

is close to the saturation of the sensor when the image is captured in front side covered by the sun light. As a result, the part of the citrus fruit has been classified into different cluster by the classification method. The dark area in the image is not considered by the low illumination condition since the data is even difficult to be interpreted after being mapped into a perception color space. To illustrate the image quality issues, the types of color citrus fruit image have been processed by applying the classification methods. The processed types of color image include the attenuated image by physical optical filter function as shown in Figure 1, where (a1) is the normal color image, (a2) is the neutral density filtered color image, and (a3) is the linear polarizer filtered color image; (b1), (b2), and (b3) are the classified results of (a1), (a2), and (a3) respectively. The types of color image are processed with the self-organizing map algorithm. In the results, it is clearly seen that the details noise as mentioned are even difficult to be removed in the attenuated images.

The motivation of the bi-camera scheme is inspired by the issues from the preliminary study and the proposal from the application literature. The information from the color image may not be adequate to discriminate the citrus fruits from the remaining background. The similar reflection area in the background in the image and even in the attenuated image by the uncontrollable factors is one major quality issue. Regardless of the saturated area and the dark illumination which is difficult to be interpreted in a color space, the uncontrollable similar spectral detail noise is intractable to be solved. The use of the bi-camera scheme is an attempt to find the probability of using a more flexible incoming data filtering scheme with fusion solution with source images to improve the image quality for the subsequent interpretation efficiently. Firstly the fusion of source images analysis should be robust against the local spatial detail noise such as the similar spectra blobs as mentioned. The removal of the detail is addressed in a spatial coordinates in frequency domain to

Figure 1. Sample of classification results with SOM algorithm

address the spatial variance property. In addition, the enhancement of the color contrast between the citrus fruit area and the remaining background is also difficult to be addressed. Most literature has been done to find the reference index to contrast between the interest feature and the background in the image. However it is difficult to find the reference index using certain waveband spectra when it is varied with the hyperspectral technique. In this application, the fusion of the source images from different waveband area is focused to enhance the interest feature information by using the fusion technique with NIR (Near InfraRed) image and RGB (Red, Green Blue) color image. After the technical issue of the alignment of two cameras has been addressed (Li et al., 2011), the approached fusion of the aligned images can be verified for the image quality improvement from the classification results.

The contents of this chapter are organized as follows. In next section, the design of the cold mirror and bi-camera acquisition system is summarized. The real time citrus fruit tree image acquisition is practiced using the developed bi-camera imaging assembly under the natural illumination condition. Then the multiscale decomposition based filtering scheme and the fusion of NIR image and RGB color image are developed to address the real time citrus fruit image quality issues. To evaluate the proposed fusion method, some major classification methods are applied to classify the citrus fruit image data. The classified results are evaluated with the empirical type errors. The results of the fusion technique are discussed with classification methods at the end. The final section draws a conclusion for the bi-camera machine vision system and the fusion method.

MATERIAL AND METHODS

The bi-camera machine vision system has covered the image acquisition with alignment, the images fusion process followed by the classification interpretation. The whole experiment includes the indoor alignment with recourse to the software based calibration to quantify the misalignment and the outdoor image acquisition using the bi-camera assembly. The alignment of two images is critical on the use of two cameras. However the quality of the lens collinearity causes the misalignment when the lens physical parameter is adjusted. Hence the alignment of two cameras is important to ensure the subsequent use of two source images with the fusion process.

Assembly of Bi-Camera and Cold Mirror Imaging Vision System

The portable cold mirror and bi-camera fixture has been prototyped for the outdoor citrus fruit tree image acquisition. The nonparametric registration is to align two cameras with the cold mirror in relative kinematic position in both spatial and temporal coordinates. The detail of the bi-camera with cold mirror assembly has been given with the alignment precision quantified by the software based calibration (Li et al., 2011). Two CCD cameras have been aligned on the fixture in 90 degree with each of both with 45 degree to the normal of the cold mirror. The precision of the alignment has been quantified in less than 10 micrometer corresponding to the pairwise pixels distance distributed sparsely on the superposed image. The position of the cold mirror is collimated with two cameras based on the function of the cold mirror. The function of the cold mirror transmits 50% wavelength over 700nm near infrared area and reflect 50% wavelength in the visible area. Since the camera has an IR-cut filter by default on top of the sensor. To suit this application, the IR-cut filter on camera 1 (Figure 2) for acquiring NIR incident light is removed and replaced by other narrow long waveband filter. Two cameras are synchronized by using the embedded optocoupler interface to trigger the second camera closely to the first camera in a master and slave architecture. The triggering on both cameras is less than the minimum shutter

Figure 2. Assembly for citrus fruit image acquisition

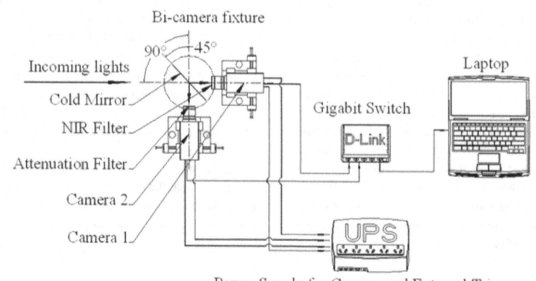

time 10μs regarding the specification from the camera. In real time image acquisition, camera 1 is triggered via software and camera 2 is triggered via hardware by optocoupler. The setup of the image acquisition includes a personal computer, a gigabit Ethernet connector, the UPS power supply for both cameras and two optocoupler interfaces. In online image acquisition, more flexibility is designed at the terminal of two sensors to interchange the filters conveniently by comparing with the multispectral sensor with function embedded and different applications. With standard mounting interface, some attenuation physical optical filters such as the neutral density filter and the linear polarizer filter has been interchanged on camera 2 for capturing the types of color image during the acquisition at the same pose. Therefore the types of the attenuated can be compared with the normal color image (Figure 3).

Citrus Fruit Image Acquisition and Quality Issues from Color Image

Acquisition of citrus fruit tree image has been practiced at the Alverstoke orchard at Waite campus of University of Adelaide and School of Agriculture, Food & Wine under the natural illumination condition without any peripherals. In online image acquisition, the software HALCON is used and programmed to trigger and capture the frames from two cameras closely. The visual

detection of the citrus fruits on the tree is a hierarchical phase (Luo & Kay, 1989; Luo & Lin, 1988). A general paradigm was proposed for the multisensor integration in robotic system based upon four distinct temporal phases in the sensory information acquisition process. The four phases are "far away", "near to", "touching", and "manipulation". Among which the second phase of "near to" is important to detect the citrus fruits on the tree when the manipulator is reaching the object closely. At this close range, the noncontact sensors like proximity sensor or "eye-in-hand" vision system are used and mounted at the end of the gripper of the manipulator. If the information from the phase is confirmed, the robot can proceed to the third phase of "touching". Therefore in the real time image acquisition the "near to" phase is simulated by posing the bi-camera assembly about 1 to 2 meter distance around the citrus fruit tree to capture the image. The most uncertain condition in image acquisition is the weather when the citrus fruit tree image is acquired under the natural outdoor illumination condition. To address the general image quality issues in real time, the acquisition practice has been selected covering from the normal sunny day time, the partial cloudy day time, and the total cloudy day time before the evenfall. Still the low illumination condition is except from the collection of the acquired image. In the preliminary study, the types of image data from have been processed by some major

Figure 3. Combination of image data captured

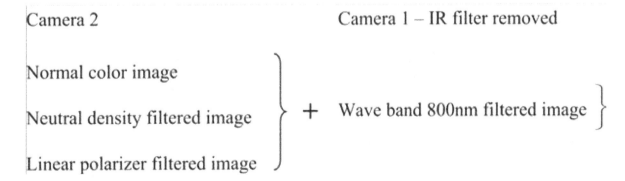

classification methods. The attenuated citrus fruit image data has much improvement by comparing with the normal color image data. However, the stubborn issues such as the similar spectra and the saturated noise from the background such as the leaves are still intractable to be removed in the results (Figure 1). Since the citrus fruits have color contrast with the neighboring feature from the background, it is reasonable to define the details from the background as the local spectra bounded with the fundamental envelope spectra in two dimensional signal formed in the image format. Therefore the main problems for the image quality improvement include both the detail noise with spatial variance property and the enhancement of the envelope spectral wave. The solution of the fusion method with two source images is developed based on the advantages of the multiscale decomposition analysis to address these two problems.

Multiscale Decomposition Analysis and Fusion of Two Images

The difficulty to handle the similar spectral detail in the image is the variance property in spatial coordinate of the frequency domain. The variance in spatial coordinate cannot be addressed by the periodic function such as DFT with the fundamental feature affected globally. The nonperiodic function is considered to handle this kind of issue

by the multiscale decomposition analysis. Hence two aligned images with uncertain background details are considered to be decomposed in segments in spatial coordinate. The measure of the local spatial wave property is by using the wave function which has the wave oscillation to simulate the local wave without effect on the envelope wave in spectral coordinate. In literature, the wavelet transform can be the option to decompose the image into segments with fundamental spectra and high frequency detail separated by different coefficient filters to address this real time citrus fruit image quality issue. In addition, the fundamental spectra from the source images can be researched to enhance the feature for the subsequent interpretation purpose. Hence the idea is formed by including the detail noise removal with certain high pass filters and the combination of the fundamental envelope spectra from the source images by the fusion method. As shown in Figure 4, two original source images are decomposed in levels with certain filters. After the details have been removed, the low pass fundamental envelope spectra are fused for the subsequent interpretation.

Application of Daubechies Wavelet Transform

To acquire the decomposed components of the image in multiscale, the wavelet transform has been selected by using Daubechies wavelet. The

Figure 4. Pairwise images filtering and fusion of fundamental spectra from source images by MSD

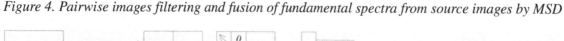
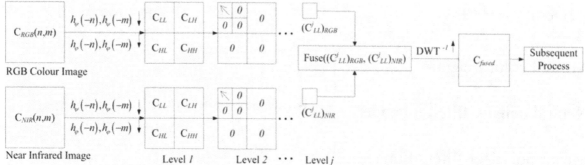

wavelet transform is computed separately for different segments of the time space signal by finite length window or compactly supported function of small wave with oscillatory. The small wave has wave form while dropping the periodicity. The dilation and shift of the mother wavelet function define an orthogonal basis. In DWT, the measure of the signal is computed by inner product with the wavelet orthonormal basis function. The calculated wavelet transform coefficients give rise to the closeness of the signal to the wavelet at current scale. The theory such as the orthogonal or biorthogonal properties has been done mathematically (Daubechies, 1992; Meyer, 1993). On top of the orthogonal basis, the construction of the discrete wavelet transform coefficients is based on the orthogonality condition to satisfy the Fourier transform of the basis coefficients (Fleet, 2007). By comparing with DFT, DWT is a local transform. Two kinds of coefficient vector are arranged in the wavelet transform matrix acting as low pass filter and high pass filter to smooth the data or extract the high frequency detail. The data is then cut into different frequency components by low pass and high pass filters. In each scale level, the image is decomposed and decimated by convolving with two filters on the image in columnwise and then rowwise successively. Therefore four components can be obtained including the low pass and high pass coefficients respectively. The low pass filtered coefficient represents the approximation of the fundamental wave while the high pass filtered coefficient represents the details. The low pass coefficient is decomposed recursively to achieve the depth approximation coefficient in the next scale level. In this application, the Daubechies wavelet of length four is used to decompose both source images in scales with MATLAB (7.11.0.584 (R2010b)) (Gonzalez, Woods, & Eddins, 2004). The detail of the decomposition and the fusion approach on the decomposed coefficients is given in Figure 4. In DWT, $h_\psi(.)$ and $h_\varphi(.)$ are high pass and low pass

coefficient filter for the scaling and the wavelet functions respectively in the wavelet transform matrix. The four term coefficient filter for high pass and low pass filters are solved by the four term nonlinear system using the orthogonality condition (Fleet, 2007).

Definition 1 (Daubechies four-term orthogonal filter): The Daubechies four length filter is defined by the vector $h_\varphi = \left(h_0, h_1, h_2, h_3 \right)$, where h_0, h_1, h_2 and h_3 are given by Equation (1) (Fleet, 2007);

$$h_0 = \frac{1}{4\sqrt{2}}\left(1+\sqrt{3}\right) \qquad h_1 = \frac{1}{4\sqrt{2}}\left(3+\sqrt{3}\right)$$
$$h_2 = \frac{1}{4\sqrt{2}}\left(3-\sqrt{3}\right) \qquad h_3 = \frac{1}{4\sqrt{2}}\left(1-\sqrt{3}\right)$$

$$(1)$$

The high pass filter is defined by $h_\psi = \left(g_0, g_1, g_2, g_3 \right)$ and given by the rule in Equation (2);

$$g_k = \left(-1\right)^k h_{3-k}, \qquad k = 0,1,2,3. \qquad (2)$$

so that the high pass coefficients are formed in Equation (3);

$$g_0 = h_3 \qquad g_1 = -h_2$$
$$g_2 = h_1 \qquad g_3 = -h_0$$

$$(3)$$

Two filters are arranged in the matrix of filter bank (Fleet, 2007). As an example, the low pass and high pass coefficients are calculated by the following Equation (4) to (7) (Gonzalez et al., 2004);

$$C_{LL}\left(j,m,n\right) = h_\varphi(-m) * h_\varphi(-n) * C\left(j-1,m,n\right)$$

$$(4)$$

$$C_{LH}\left(j, m, n\right) = h_{\psi}(-m) * h_{\varphi}(-n) * C\left(j-1, m, n\right) \tag{5}$$

$$C_{HL}\left(j, m, n\right) = h_{\varphi}(-m) * h_{\psi}(-n) * C\left(j-1, m, n\right) \tag{6}$$

$$C_{HH}\left(j, m, n\right) = h_{\psi}(-m) * h_{\psi}(-n) * C\left(j-1, m, n\right) \tag{7}$$

where the previous or original image is denoted as the coefficient by $C\left(j-1, n, m\right)$ with three transform variables involved in the representation of the coefficient image, and j is the scale of current decomposition level starting from one, in here m and n are vertical and horizontal translation in wavelet vectors. In each level, the three coefficients, namely C_{LH}, C_{HL}, and C_{HH}, carry the high pass details in the results and C_{LL} carries the low pass fundamental wave, and '*' is the convolution operator. In MSD, the level of decomposition must be given. In this application, the estimation of the level of MSD is addressed by empirical method based on the entropy filter of high pass coefficients from the coordinates of a color space.

Estimation of Multiscale Decomposition Level

The estimation of the level of multiscale decomposition is based on the empirical heuristic on the information entropy of high pass coefficients in the wavelet transform. In literature, some spectral or spatial metrics have been advocated to estimate the decomposition level (Pradhan, King, Younan, & Holcomb, 2006). However the availability of the reference image of ground truth is still an issue in this application. The spectral quality metrics by using the correlation coefficient has been used to measure the spectral similarity between the original image and the fused image (Lucien, Ranchin, & Mangolini, 1997; Nunez et al., 1999).

The spatial quality metrics have been addressed by the high pass correlation coefficient (Zhou, Civco, & Silander, 1998), quantitative edge analysis (Yun Zhang & Wang, 2004), or the structural and similarity index metrics (Wang, Bovik, Sheikh, & Simoncelli, 2004). These measures are more important for the study on the critical details from the image data in some higher dimensional coordinates space. However to measure the similarity of the edge information between the original and the fused images, the fusion of two images must be applied beforehand. Even the result of the fused image has feature blurred by comparing with the original image in the result.

By recalling the wavelet transform, the low pass approximation coefficient carries the envelope spectra information of the data. The other high pass coefficients carry the detail information in spatial coordinate. It is observed in the citrus fruit image data that the details are found on the side and the tip of the leaves with spatial variance. Therefore the details can be decimated by decomposing the image into segments in the spatial coordinates. In each level, the uncertainty of the details from the high pass coefficients can be measured by the entropy which is a measure of the uncertainty of a random variable respectively. The entropy is the maximum when the probability of all the unit information is equal and decreased and minimised when the probability is less than a uniform. To observe the detail property of the citrus fruit image data in the spatial coordinates, the entropy filter has been calculated and plotted in decomposition levels. Without loss of the generality of the empirical study on the entropy, one example has been randomly selected and given in Figure 5. The entropy filter is calculated on three coordinates from the RGB color space respectively. As shown in the figure, a is the low pass coefficient, h is the horizontal high pass detail coefficient, v is the vertical high pass detail coefficient, and d is the diagonal high pass detail coefficient in DWT transform. It is found that the entropy of the detail coefficients from h, v, and d

Figure 5. Entropy filter of coefficient from components R, G, and B of RGB colour space in levels of decomposition in DWT

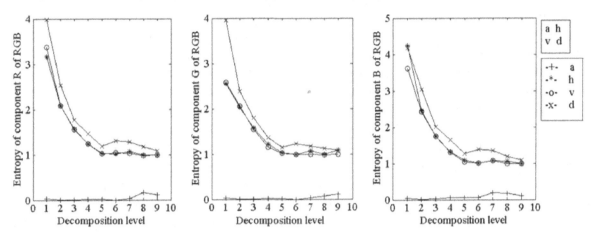

has a tendency of descending in certain level in all three components of R, G, and B from the RGB color space. On the other hand, the entropy filter of the low coefficient *a* is more stable in almost all levels of the decomposition. The descending tendency in entropy filter has variance more or less respectively but without sharp drop generally. However the entropy filter of the component in the decomposition tends to be stable after certain level generally.

By choosing certain threshold for the change of the entropy fore-and-after the levels, the current level can be selected as the decomposition level with a certain level of confidence. After this level there is almost no more variation in the detail information of entropy filter. This empirical method can be seen based on the definition of the entropy about the uncertainty of the information from the coefficients. By zeroing the detail coefficients in the previous level, the variation of the entropy filter of the coefficients in successive decomposition level implies that the main details have been removed in spatial coordinate. Hence the empirical results of the entropy filter from the coefficients have addressed the spatial variance of the background details in spatial coordinate. Therefore the level of the decomposition is proposed to be estimated based on the entropy

filter distortion fore-and-after the levels in DWT. In simulation, the level is estimated when the change of the entropy filter decrease below one and it is assumed that the most of the details has been removed in DWT transform. However the theoretical justification is to be furthered on the heuristic guideline in the uncertainty estimation. Finally the fusion rule by using the low pass coefficients remains experimental in the next section.

Fusion of NIR Image and RGB Color Image

To certain level of the decomposition, the details can be removed in each level. The low pass coefficients which carry the fundamental spectra can be fused in certain level before the reverse transform. In this application, the interest is the area of the citrus fruits in the image. The background details in spatial coordinate are not used. By zeroing the high pass coefficients in each level, the removal of the detail noise blurs the area of the fruits in the classified result as well. Therefore the fundamental spectra need to be enhanced using two low pass coefficients from the source images. The combination of the low pass coefficients from two source images is by heuristic based on the fusion rule from the literature. The variants of the arithmetic fusion rule which have been applied in the preliminary study include such as the maximum, minimum, mean or the weighted mean, and the majority voting (L. O. Jimenez et al., 1999; Kittler et al., 1998). The use of the clustering rules requires the clusters given or found. By assigning the instance with certain metrics in probability, the instance can be selected as the main features to be kept in the composite image. However in the application, the fundamental spectra have not been interpreted by clustering method for classification. The voting of the maximum or the minimum on each instance in pixel cannot be used directly due to the fact that the intensity has not been classified. In addition, the real time intensity of each pixel is more complicated and affected by multifactor like the saturation or the dark illumination. Hence the majority voting rule using the maximum probability with metrics to assign the instance is not applicable. However the mean of two low pass coefficients can be directly applied by arithmetic expectation of two coefficients without the prerequisite of the parameters of the clusters. The result depends on the contrast between features locally in each of two coefficients. It is found that the local entropy filter of the low pass coefficient of the visible component has a high contrast between the fruit and the background in complementary. One example is given by generating the local entropy filter on the coordinates from the RGB color space. The original paired images used are given in Figure 6, where (a) is the color image, and (b) is the aligned company NIR image. The local entropy filter in levels of DWT is given in Figure 7, where the images in first column, second column, and the third column are the entropy filter in MSD levels on the coordinate R, G, and B of RGB color space respectively.

With the details removed in spatial coordinate, the quality of NIR component is more homogeneous than the color image. Use of NIR component is to reduce the non-uniform distribution effect caused by the non-Euclidean structure of the citrus fruit. Considering that the low pass coefficient carries the fundamental envelope spectra, a fusion rule is then introduced using the complementary of the local entropy filter of the low pass coefficient of RGB colour image to the addend of the low pass coefficient of NIR filtered image in the arithmetic combination rule in Equation (11). The construction of the fusion rule follows the operators including the entropy and the convolution operators. The details of the fusion rule with the relative mathematical operators are de-

Figure 6. Original aligned paired citrus images

(a)   (b)

Figure 7. Sample of entropy filter of low pass coefficients from three components, namely R, G and B from colour image of (a) in Figure 6 shown in columns, and in 3 levels of decomposition by DWT in rows

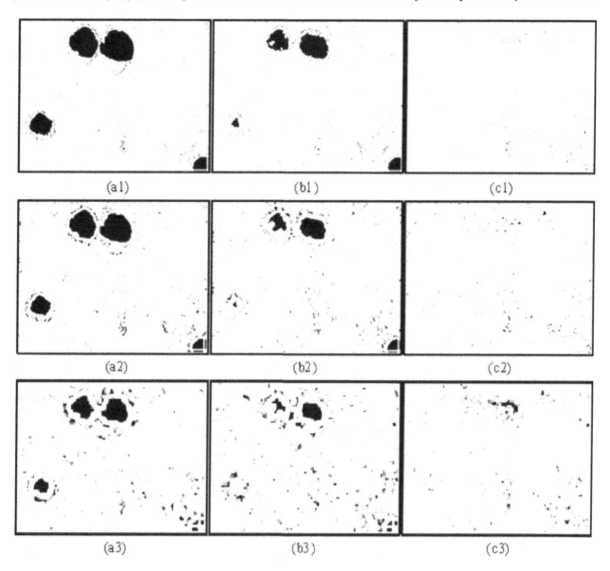

tailed based on the entropy contents as follows. The entropy is a measure of the uncertainty of a random variable. A random event E with a probability of $P(E)$ is said to contain $I(E) = -\log P(E)$ units of information (Gonzalez et al., 2004).

Definition 2: Given a source of random events from the discrete set of possible events $\{x_1, x_2, ..., x_j\}$. The entropy of the source X is defined as the average information of

the events as shown in Equation (8) (Gonzalez et al., 2004);

$$E(X) = \sum_{i=1}^{j} p(x_i) I(x_i) = -\sum_{i=1}^{j} p(x_i) \log p(x_i)$$

(8)

where $I(x_i)$ is units of information and $I(x_i) = \log(1/p(x_i))$.

Definition 3: The entropy filter is defined as the average information of the event source within the neighbourhood of each pixel coordinates in the image (Gonzalez et al., 2004);

$$E_{fitler}\left(X_{i,j}\right) = -\sum_{i-n,j-n}^{i+n,j+n} p(x_{i,j}) \log p\left(x_{i,j}\right) \qquad (9)$$

where $X_{i,j}$ is the source image, $p\left(x_{i,j}\right)$ is defined as the probability of the gray level of the pixel in the histogram of the gray level in image frame, n is the size of the neighbourhood, and (i, j) is the coordinates of the current input pixel. The outside of the coordinates space is padded with zero in operation.

Definition 4: The convolution operator in the digital image processing is the linear spatial filtering. The pixel value from the image and the spatial mask is defined as the function of $f\left(i,j\right)$ and $h\left(i,j\right)$ with respect to the variables of i and j representing the coordinates of the pixel. The operation is by rotating the mask $h\left(i,j\right)$ 180 degree prior to passing it by the image $f\left(i,j\right)$, the convolution operation is by weighted sum of neighbourhood input by the weight mask with zero padded outside the input size as given in Equation (10) (Gonzalez et al., 2004);

$$h\left(i,j\right) * f\left(i,j\right) =$$
$$\frac{1}{MN}\sum_{k_1=0}^{M-1}\sum_{k_2=0}^{N-1} f\left(k_1,k_2\right) h\left(i-k_1,j-k_2\right), \forall k_1, k_2 \qquad (10)$$

where $\left(i,j\right)$ is the coordinate of the pixel in original image and $M \times N$ is the size of the mask from the second image corresponding to the same coordinate. With these definitions, the following arithmetic fusion rule is proposed to combine NIR

filtered image and RGB colour image to enhance the image quality.

Definition 5: The fusion rule is defined by an arithmetic addition by the arithmetic of two parts as given in Equation (11). The first part of the summand is the function of the low pass coefficient of the first source image. The second part is the addend of the function of the low pass coefficient of the second source image convolved with the complementary of the local sliding mask of the local entropy filter from the low pass coefficient of the first source image. The sliding mask is the odd side with 3 by 3 smallest meaningful sizes and the centre of mask is the corresponding coordinates of image pixel in the summand input. The fusion rule is defined as follows;

$$C'(i, j) =$$
$$C_{RGB}(i, j) + \left[J(i, j) - \left(h(i,j)\right)_{(E_{filter})RGB}\right] * C_{NIR}(i, j) \qquad (11)$$

where the first source image is RGB colour image and the second source image is NIR filtered image. C' is the fused coefficient in the subsequent level, C_{RGB} is the function of the low pass coefficient of RGB image, C_{NIR} is the function of the low pass coefficient of the near infrared image, $\left(h(i,j)\right)_{(E_{filter})RGB}$ is the spatial mask function of size 3 by 3 in the sliding window in the resultant image of the entropy filter of C_{RGB} coefficient from Equation (9), $J(i, j)$ is a corresponding mask of all ones with the same dimension as $\left(h(i,j)\right)_{(E_{filter})RGB}$, '*' denotes the convolution operator, (i, j) is the coordinate of the pixel in coefficient image, and the complementary of the entropy filter in the spatial mask is used to convolve with low pass component of NIR image as defined.

Although the current CCD camera 1 for the NIR sensing with band pass filter has no contrast between the citrus fruit and the background in general. However the complementary of the entropy filter converts and highlights the local entropy of the fruit area. If the sensor for the NIR area can detect the contrast, the addend in the convolution of both components can create higher enhancement while maintaining the primary contrast. Therefore the injection of both components of $C_{NIR}(i,j)$ and $\left(h(i,j)\right)_{(E_{filter})RGB}$ contributes to the further enhancement of the final fused image. After the fusion approach, the fused result is transformed reversely to the original resolution. To evaluate the improvement of the fusion approach, some major classification methods are applied on the artifact results. The results from the fused image are compared to the results from the non-fused color image by the accuracy measure using the empirical type errors.

Application of Classification Methods on Citrus Fruit Image Data

The fused artifact image has a precision and quality metrics to evaluate the fusion result in the application. However the ultimate purpose is to detect the citrus fruits area in the image. Therefore some major classification methods have been applied on the same version of MATLAB for the detection accuracy comparison on types of the citrus fruit image data. The methods have covered from the linear projection methods to the multiclass nonlinear methods as follows.

Color Indices

Color indices have been applied in preliminary study including the literature. Two out of those color indices with consistent performance have been given in the study. They are $R - B$ and $2R - G - B$. After the color indices are applied, the global variance discriminant threshold method (Jian-jun, Han-ping, & Su-yu, 2009) has been

used to discriminate the citrus fruits from the remaining background. The mentioned indices can be interpreted as the projection $\mathbf{w}^T\mathbf{x}$ from the coordinates of the RGB colour space in $\mathbf{w}$, where $\mathbf{w}^T = \left(R, G, B\right)$ onto the lower dimensional space of $\mathbf{x}$ where $\mathbf{x}$ is a direction vector. The direction vector is constructed by the coefficients of the colour indices or the normalised indices. However the direction of the projection may not represent the optimal variance direction of two data sets. The spectra of the citrus fruits digitised in image can be fuzzy with some variations generally. To evaluate the consistency of the use of the color indices, the representative major direction in eigenvector by linear discriminant analysis is adopted to verify the consistency of the performance by the projection based method.

Fisher Linear Discriminant Analysis

Fisher linear discriminant analysis (FLDA) is the dimensionality reduction technique from the principal component analysis (PCA). FLDA searches the direction through the data sets with the maximum variance between data cluster sets and the minimum variance within each data cluster sets (Du & Swamy, 2006). The maximization problem is transformed into the Lagrangian optimization to find the major eigenvector corresponding to the eigenvalue of the generalized eigenvalue problem. Without an automatic search method to find these two sets, the image is segmented manually into the foreground of citrus fruits and the remaining background. After the scatter matrix is formed by using these two groups of image data sets, the eigenvector function is used to find the principal eigenvector which is corresponding to the largest eigenvalue uniquely. The classes of data can be projected onto the lower dimensional eigenvector for the following classification application. The classification is done by the nearest neighbor estimation to classify the foreground citrus fruits and the remaining background using the Euclidean metrics for the measurement.

Hyperplane Using SLP and MLP

The hyperplane has been selected based on the assumption that the citrus fruit foreground and the remaining background are two decision regions. The perceptron model based on the McCulloch-Pitts neuron model (McCulloch & Pitts, 1943) has been applied in both single layer perceptron (SLP) and multilayer perceptron (MLP) architectures. The learning algorithm of the perceptron is based on the convergence theorem proved by Rosenblatt (Du & Swamy, 2006) which converges to the unique weight parameters. The weight parameters construct the hyperplane for the dichotomy assignment. The learning algorithm is coded based on the objective function of the optimization defined as the mean squared error (MSE). Considering the probability of introducing the extra local minima from the higher number of layer perceptron (Xiang, Ding, & Lee, 2005). The three-layer perceptron has been coded as a universal approximator. Both SLP and MLP are applied using three learning algorithms from the literature to compare the convergence speed such as the back-propagation (Rumelhart, Hinton, & Williams, 1986), the Levenberg-Marquardt method (More, 1977), and the conjugate-gradient method (Charalambous, 1992). Each local reference foreground of the orange citrus fruits by manual segmentation has been used to train and adjust the connection parameter matrix. The classification is done directly based on the trained weight parameter matrix after the convergence. However the hyperplane only defines the position in the color space. An alternative method by constructing the hyperplane in high dimensional feature coordinate space is also applied.

SVM

The support vector machine (SVM) is the implementation of the structural risk minimization principle to minimize the risk functional in both of empirical and VC-dimension of the functions under the statistical learning theory (Vapnik, 2000). SVM is an alternative to MLP to minimize an upper bound of the generalization error by maximizing the margin of hyperplane in high dimensional feature space to optimal. To overcome the curse of dimensionality, the nonlinear kernel function is adopted to map the input data to higher dimensional space to separate the data. The support vectors on the margin are found via a quadratic optimization method (Haykin, 1999). When the data is a multiclass problem, the one-against-rest or one-against-one methods are used to find the hyperplane SVM (Crammer & Singer, 2001; Weston & Watkins, 1999). Since the training sample is unavailable from the real time citrus fruit image data, the manual segmented reference image sample with citrus fruits foreground is selected against the rest in the study.

Self-Organizing Map

The topology preserved competitive learning method of Kohonen's self-organizing map (SOM) is applied based on the assumption that the citrus fruit image data is a multiclass problem generally. In SOM, the input is connected fully with output associated with the connection weights. The input is presented to the map by instance and the Euclidean metrics is then measured to find the codebook closest to the input. Another feature of SOM is the lateral connection update within the neighboring distance around the winning codebook. The learning is combined with the Hebbian hypothesis and a forgetting term (Haykin, 1999; Kohonen, 2001). Then the update of the connections to the codebook includes the learning rate varied with learning phase and the neighborhood kernel for the lateral connection update damply. In the study, the image frame data has been fully presented into the map once for fast map ordering and followed by the refining phase. In SOM, the input is reconstructed by using the coordinates of a* and b* from CIE Lab color space and the Hue coordinate from HSV color space. Finally the algorithm is forced to terminate when the energy is not changed under certain confidence followed by the classification by the vector quantization.

Evaluation on Classified Citrus Fruit Cluster Image

The evaluation metrics for the fusion result is a difficult proposition. The perceptual evaluation decision by observers is quite subjective response based on both the observer and the background conditions. The objective evaluation metrics could be considered to quantify the fusion quality based on the application such as the mutual information or the quality treatment metrics on the fused result (Stathaki, 2008). The issue regarding the evaluation on the fused image is the availability of the reference with ground truth which is unavailable in special application. The noise to signal measure is another issue on the fused image introduced by the use of different sensors. In addition the information from different sensors may not have direct correlation such as the spectra from the visible and the near infrared area. The internal statistics from the classified clusters conforms to the criteria of the derivation of the methods by objective or metrics function. On top of that, the quality evaluation on the fused result image has no measures on the detection accuracy in the special application. Therefore the segmented results are simply compared using both the visual perception and the proposed empirical weak type error estimation. The weak type error used is defined as Type I error and Type II error. Type I error is defined as the probability of the background pixels being classified as the fruit sets. Type II error is defined as the probability of the fruit sets being excluded as the background pixels. For example given set A as background, set B as fruit foreground, and set R as the classification result, Type I error is estimated by $\Pr\left(A, R\right) / \Pr(A)$, Type II error is estimated by $\left(\Pr(B) - \Pr(B,R)\right) / \Pr(B)$. Note that the set A and B are the empirical refer-

ence image of the background and the fruits foreground with manual scrutinized segmentation. The total error is the weighted sum in terms of the conditional probability of the foreground and the background sets with respect to the whole image data set. Then all the classified results with citrus fruits are compared to the empirical reference image. With manual segmentation error, the primary error can still be quantified in the dominant Type I error to see the difference of pixels from the background on the resultant citrus fruits cluster image.

Results and Discussion

In experiment, two registered citrus fruit images have been processed including the fused and the non-fused citrus fruit image data by the selected methods. The quantified results in Type I, Type II, and total error are given in Table 1 and printed in Figure 8 to Figure 10. The attenuation filter can relax the highly saturation area from the CCD sensor in Type I error. However the heaviest detail noise is still intractable to be removed more from the segmented fruits cluster. The fusion technique used is more robust than the morphological structure filtering in detail noise removal with fundamental envelope spectral contrast enhanced on the citrus fruit area. It can be observed that few intractable images without attenuation have a blurred artifact classification result with citrus fruit area being maintained by comparing with the original image. The NIR area has no average contrast by using the narrow waveband filter on this CCD sensor camera 1. The spectral contrast detection on NIR bandwidth area needs to be researched further. However with recourse to another contribution of the entropy filter from the visible area and the quality of the homogeneity of NIR area in the fusion rule, the overall results by all the classification methods have significant improvement on the classified results. In Table 1, the fused results normally have lower Type I error by comparing with the corresponding color

Table 1. Type I error and Type II error by some major classification methods

Type I Error: background pixels being included; Type II error: foreground pixels being excluded **RGB:** Normal colour image; RGB Fused: normal colour image fused with NIR image **Neut Filt:** Neutral density filtered colour image; Neut Fused: neutral density filtered image fused with NIR image **Pola File:** linear polarizer filtered colour image; Pola Fused: linear polarizer filtered image fused with NIR image							
Methods	**Error type**	**RGB**	**RGB Fused**	**Neut Filt**	**Neut Fused**	**Pola Filt**	**Pola Fused**
SVM	Type I error	10.25%	3.70%	3.71%	2.77%	2.83%	3.60%
	Type II error	1.98%	19.69%	3.89%	28.38%	4.18%	33.39%
	Total error	9.50%	5.16%	3.72%	5.00%	2.94%	6.24%
SOM	Type I error	4.81%	1.83%	2.28%	0.91%	2.09%	1.21%
	Type II error	28.66%	23.85%	23.68%	34.24%	23.24%	39.51%
	Total error	6.98%	3.80%	4.17%	3.75%	4.04%	4.56%
FLDA	Type I error	8.77%	1.54%	2.40%	0.91%	2.06%	1.16%
	Type II error	9.93%	25.31%	15.60%	37.94%	17.58%	44.14%
	Total error	8.89%	3.67%	3.44%	4.06%	3.32%	4.90%
SLP	Type I error	11.47%	3.21%	6.54%	2.15%	5.11%	2.32%
	Type II error	39.18%	53.99%	42.12%	64.86%	47.16%	67.78%
	Total error	13.77%	7.61%	9.31%	7.40%	8.46%	7.97%
MLP	Type I error	12.63%	4.17%	6.99%	2.66%	5.58%	2.88%
	Type II error	33.12%	50.64%	38.75%	61.02%	44.56%	63.97%
	Total error	14.34%	8.19%	9.45%	7.53%	8.69%	8.14%
R - B	Type I error	13.80%	2.62%	4.35%	0.81%	3.21%	2.06%
	Type II error	18.99%	27.80%	19.36%	42.98%	26.42%	48.40%
	Total error	14.37%	4.91%	5.69%	4.31%	5.10%	6.08%
2R - G - B	Type I error	8.69%	1.47%	2.62%	1.27%	2.05%	2.62%
	Type II error	17.39%	28.46%	17.62%	40.34%	22.82%	46.00%
	Total error	9.56%	3.88%	3.96%	4.57%	3.77%	6.45%

Figure 8. Type I error by classification methods on data class

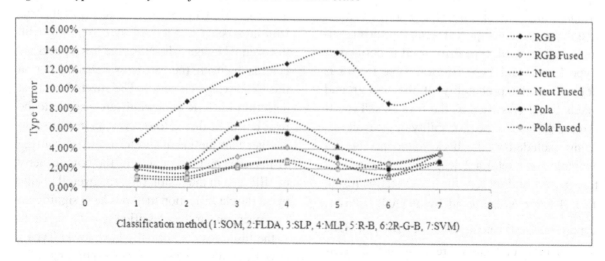

Figure 9. Type II error by classification methods on data class

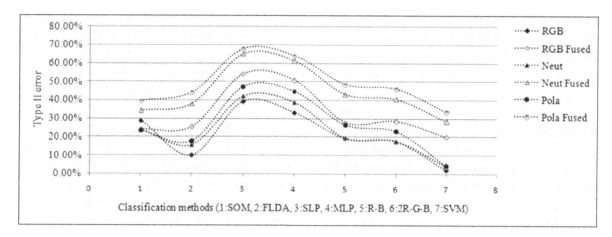

Figure 10. Total error by classification methods on data class

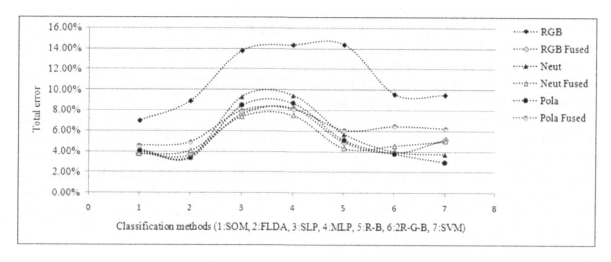

image. The factor for the Type II error is due to the saturated area or the non-homogeneity of the spectral distribution on the citrus fruit area. The part of these areas has been interpreted as different spectra from the citrus fruit spectra in perception colour space. When the classified result is compared with the empirical reference, the removed area is calculated more in Type II error. Hence the Type II error calculated has much difference from each other due to the multifactor for each of different kinds of image as shown in Figure 9. However Type II error does not lower the accuracy of the final detection of the citrus fruit area in the image by comparing with Type I error. The overall weighted error still shows that the fused and the attenuated image have a significant improvement by comparing with the normal color image by all the classification methods.

The methods applied have a tradeoff between the accuracy and the efficiency as referred in both Table 1 and Table 2. SOM shows better classification result with lower Type I error but with long learning time. Color indices can be interpreted as projection direction constructed by the coefficients of the coordinates of the used color space. Therefore color indices have similar mathematical interpretation to FLDA by projecting the image data onto the lower dimensional projection direction. However the direction of the projection is not consistent since the distribution of the spectra is varied and affected by the multifactor. The automatic direction search in data clusters remains in literature of the applications. SLP and MLP give similar even the same result by the hyperplane construction for a dichotomy assignment. The results by both SLP and MLP have much noise in the classified results since the parameters only define the position of the hyperplane. By comparing with MLP, SVM is more general based on the structural minimization principle. Type I error from SVM is close to some other methods. However Type II error is lower significantly while the total error maintains low. The hyperplane in a color space by MLP or in high dimensional feature space by SVM all relies on the credit of the training sample which is unavailable in real time application. From the data processing, the fundamental envelope spectra from the color source images are close to a multiclass issue in general based on all the classification results from this application. However the solutions to the multiclass problem for the fundamental envelope spectra on real time citrus fruit image are to be addressed by the clustering methods in a different research topic. To conclude this work, one example is selected to illustrate the results as given in Figure 11. This example result

is generated by SOM algorithm. The difference of the detail noise removal and the improvement in classified results with SOM can be seen clearly between the last two rows in the figure.

As shown in Figure 11, (a1), (a2), and (a3) are the color image, neutral density filtered image, and linear polarizer filtered image respectively; (b1), (b2), and (b3) are the corresponding company NIR images, while (c1), (c2), and (c3) are the corresponding fused image with the color image and NIR image; (d1), (d2), and (d3) are the classified results of (a1), (a2), and (a3) respectively, and (e1), (e2), and (e3) are the classified results of the fused images (c1), (c2), and (c3) respectively. The improvement of the image quality with the fusion method is illustrated in the last image in the figure.

CONCLUSION

The potential use of multisensor imaging data has been practiced with a bi-camera machine vision system associated with the real time citrus fruit image data classification. The objective is to improve the real time citrus fruit image data quality by developing the fusion method. The fusion method is developed based on the multiscale decomposition analysis with a discrete wavelet transform application using two registered source images, NIR image and RGB color image, from the

Table 2. Processing time for some major classification methods

	R - G	2R - G - B	FLDA	SLP BP	SLP LM	SLP CG	MLP BP	MLP LM	MLP CG	SOM	SVM
LT: The algorithmic learning time (in second) CT: The classification time (in second) BP: Backpropagation method LM: Levenberg-Marquardt method CG: Conjugate-gradient method											
LT	N/A	N/A	3.37	330.55	0.81	0.09	129.78	0.23	0.14	185.73	0.26
CT	0.2802	0.2743	1.27	0.93	0.93	1.35	8.26	7.56	8.84	7.32	108.17

Figure 11. Example of classification results by SOM algorithm on types of fused image and corresponding non-fused color image

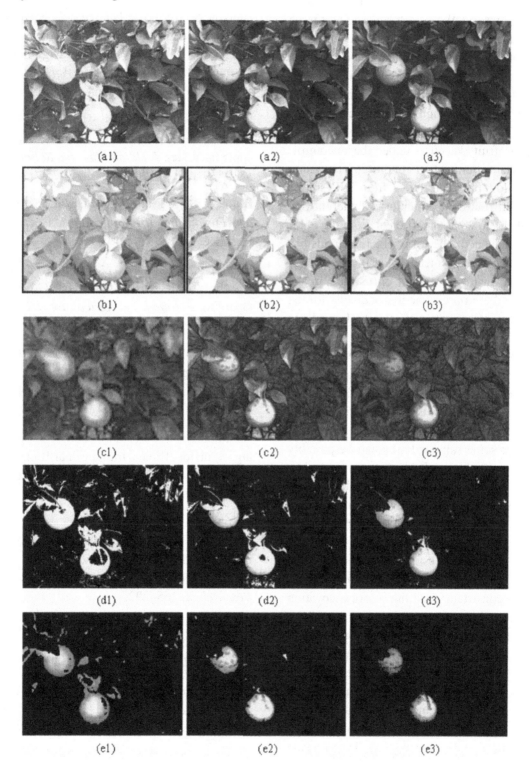

bi-camera vision system. As a result, two aligned source images have been fused by addressing two quality issues in DWT transform. The first issue is the local detail noise removal. The second issue is the combination of the fundamental envelope spectra from two source images. It is found that the fusion of the source images by using the low pass coefficients with the high pass detail coefficients zeroed in DWT transform can possibly improve the citrus fruit detection under the uncontrollable variant illumination condition. The fusion with the low pass coefficient from NIR source image with the complementary of the entropy filter of the low pass coefficient from the color image as addend in the arithmetic fusion rule has the contrast enhancement of the image quality. Therefore the fused artifact citrus fruit image can be used to improve the image quality for the subsequent interpretation efficiently. To evaluate the improvement of the real time citrus fruit image quality, some major classification methods have been applied on the fused artifact image and the non-fused color image respectively. Based on the empirical evaluation of the classification results, the normal detail noise issues such as the similar spectra or some saturated area can be possibly improved with the envelope spectra enhanced by applying the fusion method. The overall classification results from the fused image have a significant improvement in the empirical accuracy measure. However the decision of the decomposition level in DWT transform is estimated empirically and remains experimental. The issue of contrast detection with consistency and the sensor innovation for the near infrared waveband area remain to be researched continually. The measurement is indispensable based on the improvement or the innovation of the sensor applied in the bi-camera vision system. The two dimensional fundamental envelope spectra approximate a multiclass problem based on the evaluation of the classification results by the major classification methods. Therefore the solution to the multiclass problem is addressed in a topic of classification methods.

REFERENCES

Aleixos, N., Blasco, J., Navarron, F., & Molto, E. (2002). Multispectral Inspection of Citrus in Real-time Using Machine Vision and Digital Signal. *Computers and Electronics in Agriculture, 33,* 121–137. doi:10.1016/S0168-1699(02)00002-9

Baeten, Boedrij, Beckers, & Claesen. (2008). Autonomous fruit picking machine: a robotic apple harvester. *Field and Service Robotics, 42,* 531–539. doi:10.1007/978-3-540-75404-6_51

Blum, R. S., & Liu, Z. (2006). *Multi-Sensor Image Fusion and Its Applications.* Boca Raton, FL: CRC Press.

Buemi, F., Massa, M., & Sandini, G. (1995). Agrobot: A Robotic System for Greenhouse Operations. *Robotics in Agriculture & The Food Industry, 4,* 172–184.

Bulanon, D. M., Burks, T. F., & Alchanatis, V. (2009). Image fusion of visible and thermal images for fruit detection. *Biosystems Engineering, 103,* 12–22. doi:10.1016/j.biosystemseng.2009.02.009

Charalambous, C. (1992). Conjugate gradient algorithm for efficient training of artificial neural networks. [). The Institution of Engineering and Technology.]. *Proceedings of the IEEE, 139,* 301–310.

Crammer, K., & Singer, Y. (2001). On the Algorithmic Implementation of Multiclass Kernel-based Vector Machines. *Journal of Machine Learning Research, 2,* 265–292.

Daubechies, I. (1992). *Ten Lectures on Wavelets.* Philadelphia: SIAM. doi:10.1137/1.9781611970104

Du, K.-L., & Swamy, M. N. S. (2006). *Neural Networks in a Softcomputing Framework.* London: Springer-Verlag London Limited.

Edan, Y. (1995). Design of an autonomous agricultural robot. *Applied Intelligence*, *5*, 41–50. doi:10.1007/BF00872782

Fleet, P. J. V. (2007). *Discrete Wavelet Transformations*. John Wiley & Sons, Inc.

Gonzalez, R. C., Woods, R. E., & Eddins, S. L. (2004). *Digital Image Processing Using MATLAB*. Pearson Education, Inc.

Grasso, G. M., & Recce, M. (1996). Scene Analysis for an Orange Picking Robot. In *Proceedings of International Congress for Computer Technology in Agriculture* (pp. 275-280). Wageningen, The Netherlands: VIAS Wageningen, Netherlands.

Haykin, S. (1999). *Neural Network A Comprehensive Foundation* (2nd ed.). Tom Robbins.

Jian-Jun, Y., Han-Ping, M., & Su-Yu, Z. (2009). Segmentation methods of fruit image based on color difference. *Journal of Communication and Computer*, *6*(7), 40–45.

Jimenez, A. R., Ceres, R., & Pons, J. L. (2000). A Survey of Computer Vision Methods for Locating Fruit on Trees. *Transactions of the ASAE. American Society of Agricultural Engineers*, *43*(6), 1911–1920. doi:10.13031/2013.3096

Jimenez, L. O., Morales-Morell, A., & Creus, A. (1999). Classification of Hyperdimensional Data Based on Feature and Decision Fusion Approaches Using Projection Pursuit, Majority Voting, and Neural Networks. *IEEE Transactions on Geoscience and Remote Sensing*, *37*(3), 1360–1366. doi:10.1109/36.763300

Kane, K. E., & Lee, W. S. (2006). Spectral Sensing of Different Citrus Varieties for Precision Agriculture. In *American Society of Agricultural and Biological Engineers. ASABE Paper No. 061065*. St. Joseph, MI: ASABE.

Kane, K. E., & Lee, W. S. (2007). Multispectral Imaging for In-field Green Citrus Identification. In *American Society of Agricultural and Biological Engineers. ASABE Paper No. 073025*. St. Joseph, MI: ASABE.

Kise, M., Park, B., Heitschmidt, G. W., Lawrence, K. C., & Windham, W. R. (2010). Multispectral imaging system with interchangeable filter design. *Computers and Electronics in Agriculture*, *72*, 61–68. doi:10.1016/j.compag.2010.02.005

Kise, M., Park, B., Lawrence, K. C., & Windham, W. R. (2007). Design and calibration of a dual-band imaging system. *Sens., &. Instrumen. Food Qual*, *1*, 113–121. doi:10.1007/s11694-007-9016-y

Kittler, J., Hatef, M., Duin, R. P. W., & Matas, J. (1998). On Combining Classifiers. *IEEE Transactions on Pattern Analysis and Machine Intelligence*, *20*(3), 226–239. doi:10.1109/34.667881

Kohonen, T. (2001). *Self-Organizing Maps* (3rd ed.). Berlin: Springer. doi:10.1007/978-3-642-56927-2

Li, P., Lee, S.-H., & Hsu, H.-Y. (2011). Use of a Cold Mirror System for Citrus Fruit Identification. In *Proceedings of IEEE International Conference on Computer Science and Automation Engineering*, (Vol. 2, pp. 376 - 381). Shanghai, China: IEEE Press.

Lu, R. (2004). Multispectral imaging for predicting firmness and soluble solids content of apple fruit. *Rostharvest Biology and Technology*, *31*, 147–157. doi:10.1016/j.postharvbio.2003.08.006

Lucien, W., Ranchin, T., & Mangolini, M. (1997). Fusion of satellite images of different spatial resolutions: assessing the quality of resulting images. *Photogrammetric Engineering and Remote Sensing*, *63*(6), 691–699.

Luo, R. C., & Kay, M. G. (1989). Multisensor Integration and Fusion in Intelligent Systems. *IEEE Transactions on Systems, Man, and Cybernetics*, *19*(5), 901–931. doi:10.1109/21.44007

Luo, R. C., & Lin, M.-H. (1988). Robot Multi-Sensor Fusion and Integration: Optimum Estimation of Fused Sensor Data. In *Proceedings 1988 IEEE conference on Robotics and Automation*, (Vol. 2, pp. 1076-1081). Philadelphia, PA: IEEE.

McCulloch, W. S., & Pitts, W. (1943). A logical calculus of the ideas immanent in nervous activity. *The Bulletin of Mathematical Biophysics, 5*.

Meyer, Y. (1993). *Wavelets Algorithms & Applications*. Philadelphia: SIAM.

More, J. J. (1977). The Levenberg-Marquardt algorithm: implementation and theory. In *Proceedings of Conference on Numerical Analysis*. University of Dundee.

Nunez, J., Otazu, X., Fors, O., Prades, A., Pala, V., & Arbiol, R. (1999). Multiresolution-based image fusion with additive wavelet decomposition. *IEEE Transactions on Geoscience and Remote Sensing*, *37*(3), 1204–1211. doi:10.1109/36.763274

Okamoto, H., & Lee, W. S. (2009). Green citrus detection using hyperspectral imaging. *Computers and Electronics in Agriculture*, *66*, 201–208. doi:10.1016/j.compag.2009.02.004

Parrish, E. A. Jr, & Goksel, A. K. (1977). Pictorial Pattern Recognition Applied to Fruit Harvesting. *Transactions of the ASAE. American Society of Agricultural Engineers*, *20*(5), 822–827. doi:10.13031/2013.35657

Piella, G. (2003). A general framework for multiresolution image fusion: from pixels to regions. *Information Fusion*, *4*, 259–280. doi:10.1016/S1566-2535(03)00046-0

Plebe, A., & Grasso, G. (2001). Localization of spherical fruits for robotic harvesting. *Machine Vision and Applications*, *13*, 70–79. doi:10.1007/PL00013271

Pradhan, P. S., King, R. L., Younan, N. H., & Holcomb, D. W. (2006). Estimation of the Number of Decomposition Levels for a Wavelet-Based Multiresolution Multisensor Image Fusion. *IEEE Transactions on Geoscience and Remote Sensing*, *44*(12), 3674–3686. doi:10.1109/TGRS.2006.881758

Rabatel, G. (1988). A vision system for Magali, the fruit picking robot. In Agricultural Engineering. Paris: Paper 88293, AGENG88.

Rumelhart, D. E., Hinton, G. E., & Williams, R. J. (1986). Learning representations by back-propagating errors. *Nature*, *323*(9), 533–536. doi:10.1038/323533a0

Schertz, C. E., & Brown, G. K. (1968). Basic considerations in mechanizing citrus harvest. *Transactions of the ASAE. American Society of Agricultural Engineers*, 66–131.

Slaughter, D. C., & Harrell, R. C. (1987). Color vision in robotic fruit harvesting. *American Society of Agricultural Engineers, 30*(4), 1144-1148.

Stathaki, T. (2008). *Image Fusion: Algorithms and Applications*. London: Elsevier Ltd.

Takahashi, T., Zhang, S., & Fukuchi, H. (2002). Measurement of 3-D Locations of Fruit by Binocular Stereo Vision for Apple Harvesting in an Orchard. In *American Society of Agricultural Engineers. ASABE Paper No. 021102*. St. Joseph, MI: ASABE.

Vapnik, V. N. (2000). *The Nature of Statistical Learning Theory* (2nd ed.). New York: Springer-Verlag New York, Inc. doi:10.1007/978-1-4757-3264-1

Wang, Z., Bovik, A. C., Sheikh, H. R., & Simoncelli, E. P. (2004). Image quality assessment: from error visibility to structural similarity. *IEEE Transactions on Image Processing*, *13*(4), 1–14. doi:10.1109/TIP.2003.819861 PMID:15376952

Weston, J., & Watkins, C. (1999). Support Vector Machines for Multi-Class Pattern Recognition. In *Proc European Symp Artif Neural Netw (ESANN)*, (Vol. 99, pp. 61-72). Bruges, Belgium: Univ. Cath. de Louvain - ICTEAM-ELEN - Machine Learning Group.

Wyawahare, M. V., Patil, D. P. M., & Abhyankar, H. K. (2009). Image Registration Techniques: An overview. *Internal Journal of Signal Processing. Image and Processing and Pattern Recognition*, *2*(3), 11–28.

Xiang, C., Ding, S. Q., & Lee, T. H. (2005). Geometrical Interpretation and Architecture Selection of MLP. *IEEE Transactions on Neural Networks*, *16*(1), 84–96. doi:10.1109/TNN.2004.836197 PMID:15732391

Zhang, Y., & He, M. (2009). 3D Wavelet Transform and Its Application in Multispectral and Hyperspectral Image Fusion. In *Proceedings of the 4th IEEE Conference on Industrial Electronics and Applications* (pp. 3643-3647). Xi'an, China: IEEE.

Zhang, Y., & Wang, R. (2004). Multi-resolution and multi-spectral image fusion for urban object extraction. In *Proceeding of 20th ISPRS Congress*, (Vol. 3, pp. 960-966). GeoICT.

Zhou, J., Civco, D. L., & Silander, J. A. (1998). A wavelet transform method to merge Landsat TM and SPOT panchromatic data. *International Journal of Remote Sensing*, *19*(4), 743–757. doi:10.1080/014311698215973

ADDITIONAL READING

Blum, R. S., & Liu, Z. (2006). *Multi-Sensor Image Fusion and Its Applications*. Boca Raton: CRC Press Taylor & Francis Group.

Chen, Y.-R., Chao, K., & Kim, M. S. (2002). Machine Vision Technology for Agricultural Applications. *Computers and Electronics in Agriculture*, *36*, 173–191. doi:10.1016/S0168-1699(02)00100-X

Daubechies, I. (1992). *Ten Lectures on Wavelets*. Philadelphia: SIAM. doi:10.1137/1.9781611970104

Du, K.-L., & Swamy, M. N. S. (2006). *Neural Networks in a Softcomputing Framework*. London: Springer-Verlag London Limited.

Duda, R. O., Hart, P. E., & Stork, D. G. (2000). *Pattern Classification* (2nd ed.). New York: Wiley-Interscience.

Fleet, P. J. V. (2007). *Discrete Wavelet Transformations*. New Jersey: John Wiley & Sons, Inc.

Gonzalez, R. C., Woods, R. E., & Eddins, S. L. (2004). *Digital Image Processing Using MATLAB*. New Jersey: Pearson Education, Inc.

Haykin, S. (1999). *Neural Network A Comprehensive Foundation* (2nd ed.). New Jersey: Tom Robbins.

Jain, A. K. (1989). *Fundamentals of Digital Image Processing*. New Jersey: Prentice-Hall, Inc.

Jain, A. K., & Dubes, R. C. (1988). *Algorithms for Clustering Data*. New Jersey: Prentice-Hall, Inc.

Jain, A. K., Duin, R. P. W., & Mao, J. (2000). Statistical Pattern Recognition: A Review. *IEEE Transactions on Pattern Analysis and Machine Intelligence*, *22*(1), 4–37. doi:10.1109/34.824819

Jain, R., Kasturi, R., & Schunck, B. G. (1995). *Machine Vision*. New York: McGraw-Hill, Inc.

Kohonen, T. (2001). *Self-Organizing Maps* (3rd ed.). Berlin: Springer. doi:10.1007/978-3-642-56927-2

Laliberte, F., Gagon, L., & Sheng, Y. (2003). Registration and Fusion of Retinal Images - An Evaluation Study. *IEEE Transactions on Medical Imaging*, 22(5), 661–673. doi:10.1109/TMI.2003.812263 PMID:12846435

LU, D., & WENG, Q. (2007). A survey of image classification methods and techniques for improving classification performance. *International Journal of Remote Sensing*, 28(5), 823–870. doi:10.1080/01431160600746456

Meyer, Y. (1993). *Wavelets Algorithms & Applications*. Philadelphia: SIAM.

Mitchell, H. B. (2007). *Multi-Sensor Data Fusion - An Introduction*. New York: Springer Berlin Heidelberg.

Nunez, J., Otazu, X., Fors, O., Prades, A., Pala, V., & Arbiol, R. (1999). Multiresolution-based image fusion with additive wavelet decomposition. *IEEE Transactions on Geoscience and Remote Sensing*, 37(3), 1204–1211. doi:10.1109/36.763274

Piella, G. (2003). A general framework for multiresolution image fusion: from pixels to regions. *Information Fusion*, 4, 259–280. doi:10.1016/S1566-2535(03)00046-0

Pradhan, P. S., King, R. L., Younan, N. H., & Holcomb, D. W. (2006). Estimation of the Number of Decomposition Levels for a Wavelet-Based Multiresolution Multisensor Image Fusion. *IEEE Transactions on Geoscience and Remote Sensing*, 44(12), 3674–3686. doi:10.1109/TGRS.2006.881758

Stathaki, T. (2008). *Image Fusion: Algorithms and Applications* (1st ed.). London: Elsevier Ltd.

Wang, Z., Bovik, A. C., Sheikh, H. R., & Simoncelli, E. P. (2004). Image quality assessment: from error visibility to structural similarity. *IEEE Transactions on Image Processing*, 13(4), 1–14. doi:10.1109/TIP.2003.819861 PMID:15376952

Wyawahare, M. V., Patil, D. P. M., & Abhyankar, H. K. (2009). Image Registration Techniques: An overview. *Internal Journal of Signal Processing. Image and Processing and Pattern Recognition*, 2(3), 11–28.

Xydeas, C. S., & Petrovic, V. (2000). Objective image fusion performance measure. *Electronics Letters*, 36(4), 308–309. doi:10.1049/el:20000267

Zhang, Y., & He, M. (2009). *3D Wavelet Transform and Its Application in Multispectral and Hyperspectral Image Fusion*. In *The 4th IEEE Conference on Industrial Electronics and Applications* (pp. 3643-3647). Xi'an, China: IEEE.

Zitova, B., & Flusser, J. (2003). Image registration methods: a survey. *Image and Vision Computing*, 21, 977–1000. doi:10.1016/S0262-8856(03)00137-9

KEY TERMS AND DEFINITIONS

Clustering and Classification: Clustering and classification is an application of pattern recognition by the assignment of the data instance with label. The assignment is realized by the measurement using certain dissimilarity metrics function.

Cold Mirror Function: The function of cold mirror is achieved by using the dielectric coatings to reflect the visible spectra while transmit the long wavelength spectra. In this application the light incidence is separated for each of two CCD cameras for the fusion of two aligned images.

Discrete Wavelet Transform (DWT): Discrete wavelet transform is an implementation for the multiresolution analysis by constructing the filter bank composed of high pass and low pass filters based on the properties of the wavelet function. The image is decomposed successively into series of the downscaled approximations and the details by convoluting high pass and low pass filters followed by the downscale sampling.

Image Registration: Image registration is to transform the data such as the two dimensional signal formed in the image frame from different sensors into the same coordinate space for the use of information from multisensor application. The coordinate space includes the spatial and the temporal coordinate space.

Image Segmentation: Image Segmentation subdivides the image into constituent features with certain dissimilarity properties from each other.

Multiscale Decomposition (MSD): Multiscale decomposition is a multiresolution analysis in Hilbert space. The multiresolution is achieved by the projection of the signal function onto the translations and the dilations of the basis scaling functions. The decomposition of the signal in levels can be achieved by filter bank composed of high pass and low pass filters which are derived from the basis scaling function.

Multisensor Image Fusion: In visual perception application, the multisensor image fusion is the combination of feature information from individual sensor for application purpose such as by using two sensors in this chapter.

Multispectral Image: The multispectral imaging method captures the specific spectral frequency area along the electromagnetic spectrum coordinate. The multispectral image can be achieved by using different sensor with specific physical optical filter functions.

Chapter 5
Automatic Fruit Disease Classification Using Images

Shiv Ram Dubey
GLA University Mathura, India

Anand Singh Jalal
GLA University Mathura, India

ABSTRACT

Diseases in fruit cause devastating problems in economic losses and production in the agricultural industry worldwide. In this chapter, a method to detect and classify fruit diseases automatically is proposed and experimentally validated. The image processing-based proposed approach is composed of the following main steps: in the first step K-Means clustering technique is used for the defect segmentation, in the second step some color and texture features are extracted from the segmented defected part, and finally diseases are classified into one of the classes by using a multi-class Support Vector Machine. The authors have considered diseases of apple as a test case and evaluated the approach for three types of apple diseases, namely apple scab, apple blotch, and apple rot, along with normal apples. The experimental results express that the proposed solution can significantly support accurate detection and automatic classification of fruit diseases. The classification accuracy for the proposed approach is achieved up to 93% using textural information and multi-class support vector machine.

INTRODUCTION

Recognition system is a 'grand challenge' for the computer vision to achieve near human levels of recognition. In the agricultural sciences, images are the important source of data and information. To reproduce and report such data photography was the only method used in recent years. It is difficult to process or quantify the photographic data mathematically. Digital image analysis and image processing technology circumvent these problems based on the advances in computers and microelectronics associated with traditional photography. This tool helps to improve images from microscopic to telescopic visual range and offers a scope for their analysis.

Monitoring of health and detection of diseases is critical in fruits and trees for sustainable agriculture. To the best of our knowledge, no sensor is available commercially for the real time

DOI: 10.4018/978-1-4666-6030-4.ch005

assessment of trees health conditions. Scouting is the most widely used method for monitoring stress in trees, but it is expensive, time-consuming and labor-intensive process. Polymerase chain reaction which is a molecular technique used for the identification of fruit diseases but it requires detailed sampling and processing. The various types of diseases on fruits determine the quality, quantity, and stability of yield. The diseases in fruits not only reduce the yield but also deteriorate the variety and its withdrawal from the cultivation. Early detection of disease and crop health can facilitate the control of fruit diseases through proper management approaches such as vector control through fungicide applications, disease-specific chemical applications and pesticide applications; and improved productivity. The classical approach for detection and identification of fruit diseases is based on the naked eye observation by experts. In some of the developing countries, consultation with experts is a time consuming and costly affair due to the distant locations of their availability. Fruit diseases can cause significant losses in yield and quality appeared in harvesting. For example, soybean rust (a fungal disease in soybeans) has caused a significant economic loss and just by removing 20% of the infection, the farmers may benefit with an approximately 11 million-dollar profit (Roberts et al., 2006). Some fruit diseases also infect other areas of the tree causing diseases of twigs, leaves and branches. An early detection of fruit diseases can aid in decreasing such losses and can stop further spread of diseases.

A lot of work has been done to automate the visual inspection of the fruits by machine vision with respect to size and color. However, detection of defects in the fruits using images is still problematic due to the natural variability of skin color in different types of fruits, high variance of defect types, and presence of stem/calyx. To know what control factors to consider next year to overcome similar losses, it is of great significance to analyze what is being observed. The approach introduced in this chapter can be used for designing automatic

systems for agricultural process using images from distant farm fields. Several applications of image processing technology have been developed for the agricultural operations. These applications involve implementation of the camera based hardware systems or color scanners for inputting the images. We have attempted to extend image processing and analysis technology to a broad spectrum of problems in the field of agriculture. The computer based image processing is undergoing rapid evolution with ever changing computing systems. The dedicated imaging systems available in the market, where user can press a few keys and get the results, are not very versatile and more importantly, they have a high price tag on them. Additionally, it is hard to understand as to how the results are being produced.

Diseases appear as spots on the fruits and if not treated on time, cause severe losses. Excessive uses of pesticide for fruit disease treatment increases the danger of toxic residue level on agricultural products and has been identified as a major contributor to the ground water contamination. Pesticides are also among the highest components in the production cost thus their use must be minimized. Therefore, we have attempted to give an approach which can identify the diseases in the fruits as soon as they produce their symptoms on the growing fruits such that a proper management application can be applied. Some common diseases of apple fruits are apple scab, apple rot, and apple blotch (Hartman, 2010). Apple scabs are gray or brown corky spots. Apple rot infections produce slightly sunken, circular brown or black spots that may be covered by a red halo. Apple blotch is a fungal disease and appears on the surface of the fruit as dark, irregular or lobed edges.

In this chapter, we propose and experimentally evaluate an approach for the detection and classification of fruit diseases using images automatically. The proposed approach is composed of the following steps; in first step the fruit images are segmented using K-Means clustering technique, in second step, some state-of-the-art color and texture features are extracted from the segmented image, and finally, fruit diseases are classified using a Multi-class Support Vector Machine. We show the significance of using clustering technique for the disease segmentation and Multi-class Support Vector Machine as a classifier for the automatic classification of fruit diseases. In order to validate the proposed approach, we have considered three types of the diseases in apple; apple blotch, apple rot and apple scab. The experimental results shows that the proposed approach can significantly achieve accurate detection and automatic classification of fruit diseases.

LITERATURE REVIEW

In this section, we focus on the previous work done by several researchers in the area of image categorization and fruit diseases identification. Fruit disease identification can be seen as an instance of image categorization. Recently, a lot of activity in the area of image categorization has been done. In (Dubey, & Jalal, 2012a; Dubey, & Jalal, 2013; Dubey, 2013; Dubey et al., 2013), a framework for fruits and vegetables recognition and classification is proposed. They have considered images of 15 different types of fruit and vegetable collected from a supermarket. Their approach first segment the image to extract the region of interest and then calculate image features from that segmented region which is further used in training and classification by a multi-class support vector machine. They have also proposed an Improved Sum and Difference Histogram (ISADH) texture feature for this kind of problem. From their results, ISADH outperformed the other image color and texture features. Major works performing defect segmentation of fruits are done using simple threshold approach (Li, Wang, & Gu, 2002; Mehl et al., 2002). A globally adaptive threshold method (modified version of Otsu's approach) to segment fecal contamination defects on apples are presented

by Kim et al. (2005). Classification methods attempt to partition pixels into different classes using different methods. Bayesian classification is the most used method by researchers Kleynen, Leemans, & Destain (2005) and Leemans, Magein, & Destain (1999), where pixels are compared with a pre-calculated model and classified as defected or healthy. Unsupervised classification does not benefit any guidance in the learning process due to lack of target values. This type of approach was used by Leemans, Magein, & Destain (1998) for defect segmentation.

The spectroscopic and imaging techniques are unique disease monitoring approaches that have been used to detect diseases and stress due to various factors, in plants and trees. Current research activities are towards the development of such technologies to create a practical tool for a large-scale real-time disease monitoring under field conditions. Various spectroscopic and imaging techniques have been studied for the detection of symptomatic and asymptomatic plant and fruit diseases. Some the methods are: fluorescence imaging used by Bravo et al. (2004); multispectral or hyperspectral imaging used by Moshou et al. (2006); infrared spectroscopy used by Spinelli, Noferini, & Costa (2006); visible/multiband spectroscopy used by Yang, Cheng, & Chen (2007); Chen et al. (2008), and nuclear magnetic resonance (NMR) spectroscopy used by Choi et al. (2004). Hahn (2009) reviewed multiple methods (sensors and algorithms) for pathogen detection, with special emphasis on postharvest diseases. Several techniques for detecting plant diseases is reviewed by Sankarana et al. (2010) such as, Molecular techniques, Spectroscopic techniques (Fluorescence spectroscopy and Visible and infrared spectroscopy), and Imaging techniques (Fluorescence imaging and Hyperspectral imaging). A ground-based real-time remote sensing system for detecting diseases in arable crops under field conditions is developed by Moshou, (2005), which considers the early stage of disease development. The authors have used hyper-spectral reflection images of infected and healthy plants with an imaging spectrograph under ambient lighting conditions and field circumstances. They have also used multi-spectral fluorescence images simultaneously using UV-blue excitation on the same plants. They have shown that it is possible to detect presence of disease through the comparison of the 550 and 690 nm fluorescence images. Color based features are also used by Singh et al. (2012) and clustering is also performed for human activity recognition (Gupta et al., 2013).

Large scale plantation of oil palm trees requires on-time detection of diseases as the ganoderma basal stem rot disease was present in more than 50% of the oil palm plantations in Peninsular Malaysia. To deal with this problem, airborne hyper-spectral imagery offers a better solution (Shafri & Hamdan, 2009) in order to detect and map the oil palm trees that were affected by the disease on time. Airborne hyper-spectral has provided data on user requirement and has the capability of acquiring data in narrow and contiguous spectral bands which makes it possible to discriminate between healthy and diseased plants better compared to multispectral imagery. Citrus canker is among the most devastating diseases that affect marketability of citrus crops. In (Qin et al., 2009), a hyper-spectral imaging approach is developed for detecting canker lesions on citrus fruit and hyper-spectral imaging system is developed for acquiring reflectance images from citrus samples in the spectral region from 450 to 930 nm. In (Purcell et al., 2009), the authors have investigated the power of NIR spectroscopy as an alternative to rate clones of sugarcane leaf spectra from direct measurement and examined its potential using a calibration model to successfully predict resistance ratings based on a chemometrics approach such as partial least squares. To populate the nature of the NIR sample, they have undertaken a scanning electron microscopy study of the leaf substrate. Marcassa et al. (2006) have applied laser-induced fluorescence spectroscopy to investigate biological processes in orange trees. They have investigated water stress and Citrus Canker, which is a disease produced by the Xanthomonas axonopodis pv. citri bacteria. They have discriminated the Citrus Canker's contaminated leaves from the healthy leaves using a more complex analysis of the fluorescence spectra. However, they were unable to discriminate it from another disease.

Fernando et al. (2010) used an unsupervised method based on a Multivariate Image Analysis strategy which uses Principal Component Analysis (PCA) to generate a reference eigenspace from a matrix obtained by unfolding spatial and color data from defect-free peel samples. In addition, a multiresolution concept is introduced to speed up the process. They tested on 120 samples of mandarins and oranges from four different cultivars: Marisol, Fortune, Clemenules, and Valencia. They reported 91.5% success ratio for individual defect detection, while 94.2% classification ratio for damaged/sound samples. Dubey, & Jalal (2012b) and Dubey, & Jalal (2012c) proposed a method to detect and classify the fruit diseases using image processing techniques. First of all, they detected the defected region by k-means clustering based image segmentation technique then extracted the features from that segmented defected region which is used by a multi-class support vector machine for training and classification purpose.

Gabriel et al. (2013) proposed a pattern recognition method to automatically detect stem and calyx ends and damaged blueberries. First, color and geometrical features were extracted. Second, five algorithms were tested to select the best features. The best classifiers were and Linear Discriminant Analysis. Using Support Vector Machine classifier, they distinguished the blueberries' orientation in 96.8% of the cases. The average performance for mechanically damaged, shriveled, and fungally decayed blueberries were reported as 86%, 93.3%, and 97% respectively. A synthesis segmentation algorithm is developed for the real-time online diseased strawberry images in greenhouse (Ouyang et al., 2013). The impact of uneven illumination is eliminated through the "top-hat" transform, and noise interferences are removed by median filtering. They obtained complete strawberry fruit area of the image after applying the methods of gray morphology, logical operation, OTSU and mean shift segmentation. Then, they normalize the extracted eigenvalues, and used eigenvectors of samples for training the support vector machine and BP neural network. Their Results indicate that support vector machines have higher recognition accuracy than the BP neural network.

AUTOMATIC FRUIT DISEASE CLASSIFICATION

Image categorization, in general, relies on combinations of structural, statistical and spectral approaches. Structural approaches describe the appearance of the object using well-known primitives, for example, patches of important parts of the object. Statistical approaches represent the objects using local and global descriptors such

as mean, variance, and entropy. Finally, spectral approaches use some spectral space representation to describe the objects such as Fourier spectrum (Gonzalez & Woods, 2007).

In this chapter, we introduce a method which exploits statistical color and texture descriptors to identify fruit diseases in a multi-class scenario. The steps of the proposed approach are shown in the Figure 1. Defect segmentation, feature extraction, training and classification are the major tasks to be performed. For the fruit disease identification problem, precise image segmentation is required; otherwise the features of the non-infected region will dominate over the features of the infected region. K-means based defect segmentation is used to detect the region of interest which is the infected part only in the image. The proposed approach operates in two phases, i.e. training and classification. Training is required to learn the system with the characteristics of each type of diseases. First we extract the feature from the segmented portion of the images that are being used for the training and store in a feature database. Then, we train support vector machine with the

Figure 1. Proposed approach for the fruit disease identification

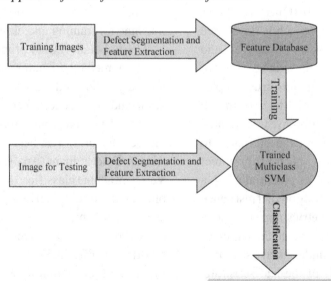

features stored in the feature database. Finally any input image can be classified into one of the classes using feature derived from segmented part of the input image and trained support vector machine.

Defect Segmentation

Image segmentation is a convenient and effective method for detecting foreground objects in images with stationary background. Background subtraction is a commonly used class of techniques for segmenting objects of interest in a scene. This task has been widely studied in the literature. Specular reflections, background clutter, shading and shadows are the major factors that affect the efficiency of the system. Therefore, in order to reduce the scene complexity, it might be interesting to perform image segmentation focusing on the object's description only. K-means clustering technique is used for the defect segmentation. Images are partitioned into four clusters in which one or more cluster contains only infected region of the fruit. K-means clustering algorithm was developed by J. MacQueen (1967) and later by J. A. Hartigan & M. A. Wong (179). The K-means clustering algorithms classify the objects (pixels in our problem) into K number of classes based on a set of features. The classification is carried out by minimizing the sum of squares of distances between the data objects and the corresponding cluster.

K-Means Image Segmentation Algorithm

Step 1: Read input image.
Step 2: Transform image from RGB to L*a*b* color space.
Step 3: Classify colors using K-Means clustering in 'a*b*' space.
Step 4: Label each pixel in the image from the results of K-Means.
Step 5: Generate images that segment the image by color.

Step 6: Select disease containing segment.

In this experiment, squared Euclidean distance is used for the K-means clustering. We use L*a*b* color space because the color information in the L*a*b* color space is stored in only two channels (i.e. a* and b* components), and it causes reduced processing time for the defect segmentation. In this experiment input images are partitioned into four segments. From the empirical observations it is found that using 3 or 4 cluster yields good segmentation results. Figure 2 demonstrates the output of K-Means clustering for an apple fruit infected with apple scab disease. Figure 3 also depicts some more defect segmentation results using the K-mean clustering technique.

Feature Extraction

We have used some state-of-the-art color and texture features to validate the accuracy and efficiency of the proposed approach. The features used for the fruit disease identification problem are Global Color Histogram, Color Coherence Vector, Local Binary Pattern, and Completed Local Binary Pattern.

Global Color Histogram (GCH)

The Global Color Histogram (GCH) is the simplest approach to encode the information present in an image (Gonzalez & Woods, 2007). A GCH is a set of ordered values, for each distinct color, representing the probability of a pixel being of that color. Uniform normalization and quantization are used to avoid scaling bias and to reduce the number of distinct colors (Gonzalez & Woods, 2007).

Color Coherence Vector (CCV)

An approach to compare images based on color coherence vectors are presented by Pass, Zabih, & Miller (1997). They define color coherence as the degree to which image pixels of that color

Figure 2. K-Means clustering for an apple fruit that is infected with apple scab disease (a) The infected fruit image, (b) first cluster, (c) second cluster, (d) third cluster, and (e) fourth cluster, respectively, (f) single gray-scale image colored based on their cluster index

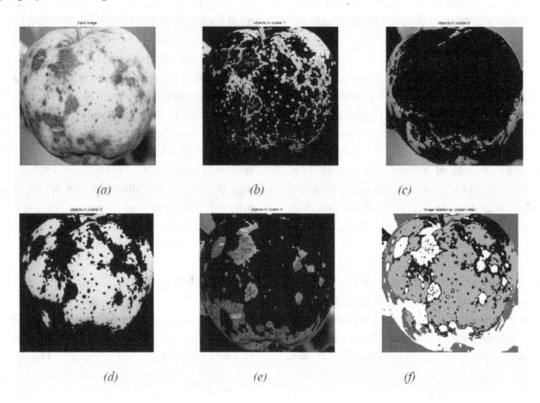

(a)   *(b)*   *(c)*

(d)   *(e)*   *(f)*

are members of a large region with homogeneous color. These regions are referred as coherent regions. Coherent pixels are belongs to some sizable contiguous region, whereas incoherent pixels are not. In order to compute the CCVs, the method blurs and discretizes the image's color-space to eliminate small variations between neighboring pixels. Then, it finds the connected components in the image in order to classify the pixels of a given color bucket is either coherent or incoherent. After classifying the image pixels, CCV computes two color histograms: one for coherent pixels and another for incoherent pixels. The two histograms are stored as a single histogram.

Local Binary Pattern (LBP)

Given a pixel in the input image, LBP is computed by comparing it with its neighbors (Ojala, Pietikainen, & Maenpaa, 2002):

$$LBP_{N,R} = \sum_{n=0}^{n-1} s(v_n - v_c)2^n, s(x) = \begin{cases} 1, x \geq 0 \\ 0, x < 0 \end{cases} \quad (1)$$

where, v_c is the value of the central pixel, v_n is the value of its neighbors, R is the radius of the neighborhood and N is the total number of neighbors. Suppose the coordinate of v_c is (0, 0), then the coordinates of v_n are

Figure 3. Some defect segmentation results (a) Images before segmentation, (b) Images after segmentation

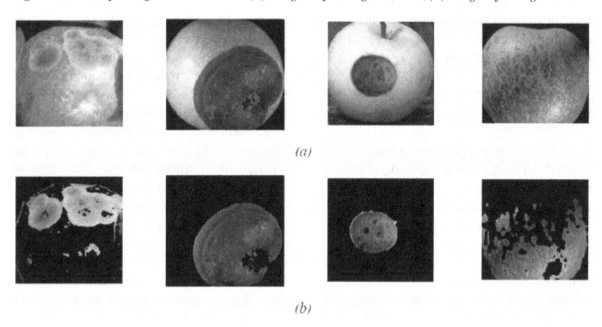

(a)

(b)

$(R\cos(2\pi n / N), R\sin(2\pi n / N))$.

The values of neighbors that are not present in the image grids may be estimated by interpolation. Let the size of image is $I*J$. After the LBP code of each pixel is computed, a histogram is created to represent the texture image:

$$H(k) = \sum_{i=1}^{I}\sum_{j=1}^{J} f(LBP_{N,R}(i,j),k), k \in [0,K],$$

$$f(x,y) = \begin{cases} 1, x = y \\ 0, otherwise \end{cases}$$

$$(2)$$

where, K is the maximal LBP code value. In this experiment the value of 'N' and 'R' are set to '8' and '1' respectively to compute the LBP feature.

Completed Local Binary Pattern (CLBP)

LBP feature considers only signs of local differences (i.e. difference of each pixel with its

neighbors) whereas CLBP feature considers both signs (S) and magnitude (M) of local differences as well as original center gray level (C) value (Guo, Zhang, & Zhang, 2010). CLBP feature is the combination of three features, namely CLBP_S, CLBP_M, and CLBP_C. CLBP_S is the same as the original LBP and used to code the sign information of local differences. CLBP_M is used to code the magnitude information of local differences:

$$CLBP_{N,R} = \sum_{n=0}^{n-1} t(m_n,c)2^n, t(x,c) = \begin{cases} 1, x \geq c \\ 0, x < c \end{cases}$$

$$(3)$$

where, c is a threshold and set to the mean value of the input image in this experiment.

CLBP_C is used to code the information of original center gray level value:

$$CLBP_{N,R} = t(g_c,c_I), t(x,c) = \begin{cases} 1, x \geq c \\ 0, x < c \end{cases} \quad (4)$$

where, threshold c_i is set to the average gray level of the input image. In this experiment the value of 'N' and 'R' are set to '8' and '1' respectively to compute the CLBP feature.

Supervised Learning and Classification

Supervised learning is a machine learning approach that aims to estimate a classification function f from a training data set. The trivial output of the function f is a label (class indicator) of the input object under analysis. The learning task is to predict the function outcome of any valid input object after having seen a sufficient number of training examples. In the literature, there are many different approaches for supervised learning such as Linear Discriminant Analysis (LDA), Support Vector Machines (SVMs), Classification Trees, Neural Networks (NNs), and Ensembles of Classifiers (Bishop, 2006).

Recently, a unified approach is presented by Rocha et al. (2010) that can combine many features and classifiers. The author approaches the multi-class classification problem as a set of binary classification problem in such a way one can assemble together diverse features and classifier approaches custom-tailored to parts of the problem. They define a class binarization as a mapping of a multi-class problem onto two-class problems (divide-and-conquer) and referred binary classifier as a base learner. For N-class problem $N \times (N-1)/2$ binary classifiers will be needed where N is the number of different classes.

According to the author, the ij^{th} binary classifier uses the patterns of class i as positive and the patterns of class j as negative. They calculate the minimum distance of the generated vector (binary outcomes) to the binary pattern (ID) representing each class, in order to find the final outcome. They have categorized the test case into a class for which distance between ID of that class and binary outcomes is minimum. This approach can

be understood by a simple three class problem. Let three classes are x, y, and z. Three binary classifiers consisting of two classes each ($.x \times y$, $x \times z$, and $y \times z$) are used as base learners, and each binary classifier is trained with training images. Each class receives a unique ID as shown in Table 1. To populate the table is straightforward. First, we perform the binary comparison $x \times y$ and tag the class x with the outcome $+1$, the class y with -1 and set the remaining entries in that column to 0. Thereafter, we repeat the procedure comparing $x \times z$, tag the class x with $+1$, the class z with -1, and the remaining entries in that column with 0. In the last, we repeat this procedure for binary classifier $y \times z$, and tag the class y with $+1$, the class z with -1, and set the remaining entries with 0 in that column, where the entry 0 means a "Don't care" value. Finally, each row represents unique ID of that class (e.g., $y = [-1, +1, 0]$). Each binary classifier results a binary response for any input example. Let's say if the outcomes for the binary classifier $x \times y$, $x \times z$, and $y \times z$ are $+1$, -1, and $+1$ respectively, then the input example belongs to that class which have the minimum distance from the vector [$+1$, -1, $+1$]. So the final answer is given by the minimum distance of

$$\min \ \text{dist}\big(\{+1,-1,+1\},\big(\{+1,+1,0\},\{-1,0,+1\},\{0,-1,-1\}\big)\big)$$

In this experiment, we have used Multi-class Support Vector Machine (MSVM) as a set of binary Support Vector Machines (SVMs) for the training and classification.

Table 1. Unique ID of each class

		$x \times y.$	$x \times z$	$y \times z$
x		+1	+1	0
y		-1	0	+1
z		0	-1	-1

RESULTS AND DISCUSSIONS

In this section, first we discuss about the data set of apple fruit diseases and after present a detailed result of the fruit disease identification problem and discuss various issues regarding the performance and efficiency of the system. We consider two color-spaces (i.e. RGB and HSV color-space) and compare the performance of the system under these color spaces.

Data Set Preparation

To demonstrate the performance of the proposed approach, we have used a data set of normal and diseased apple fruits, which comprises four different categories: Apple Blotch (104), Apple rot (107), Apple scab (100), and Normal Apple (80).

The total number of apple fruit images (N) is 391. Figure 4 depicts the classes of the data set. Presence of a lot of variations in the type and color of apple makes the data set more realistic.

Result Discussion

In the quest for finding the best categorization procedure and feature to produce classification, we have analyzed some color and texture based image descriptors derived from RGB and HSV stored images considering Multiclass Support Vector Machine (MSVM) as classifier. If we use M images per class for training then remaining $N-4*M$ are used for testing. The accuracy of the proposed approach is defined as,

Figure 4. Sample images from the data set of type (a) apple scab, (b) apple rot, (c) apple blotch, and (d) normal apple

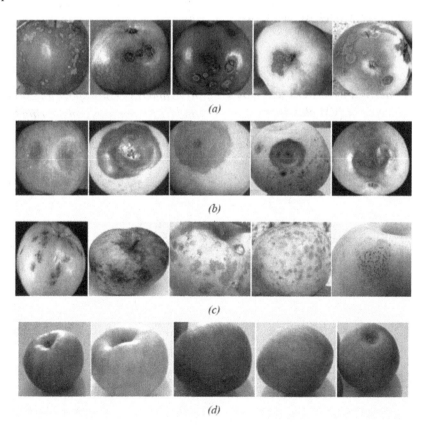

(a)

(b)

(c)

(d)

$$Accuracy(\%) = \frac{Total\ number\ of\ images\ correctly\ classified}{Total\ number\ of\ images\ used\ for\ testing} * 100$$

Figure 5(a) and 5(b) shows the results for different features in the RGB and HSV color spaces respectively. The x-axis represents the number of images per class in the training set and the y-axis represents the accuracy for the test images. This experiment shows that GCH does not perform well and reported accuracy is lowest for it in both the color spaces. One possible explanation is that, GCH feature have only color information, it does not considers neighboring information. GCH uses simply frequency of each color, however CCV uses frequency of each color in coherent and incoherent regions separately and so it performs better than GCH in both color spaces. From the Figure 5, it is clear that LBP and CLBP features yield better result than GCH and CCV features because both LBP and CLBP uses the neighboring information of each pixel in the image. Both LBP and CLBP

are robust to illumination differences and they are more efficient in pattern matching because they use local differences which are computationally more efficient. In HSV color space with 50 training examples per class, the reported classification accuracy is 80.94% for GCH, 86.47% for CCV, 90.97% for LBP, and 93.14% for CLBP feature. The LBP feature uses only the sign information of the local differences, even then, LBP reasonably represent the image local features because sign component preserves the major information of local differences. The CLBP feature exhibits more accurate result than LBP feature because CLBP feature uses both sign and magnitude component of local differences with original center pixel value.

We also observe across the plots that each feature performs better in the HSV color space than the RGB color space as shown in the Figure 6 (a-b). For 45 training examples and CLBP feature, for instance, reported classification error is 88.74% in RGB and 92.65% in HSV. One important aspect when dealing with apple fruit disease classification is the accuracy per class.

Figure 5. Accuracy (%) for the GCH, CCV, LBP, and CLBP features derived from RGB and HSV color images considering MSVM classifier

Figure 6. Comparison of the accuracy achieved in RGB and HSV color space for the GCH, CCV, LBP, and CLBP features considering MSVM classifier

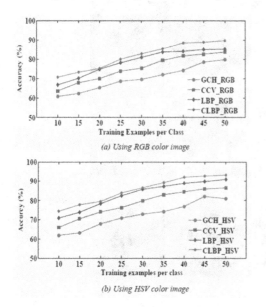

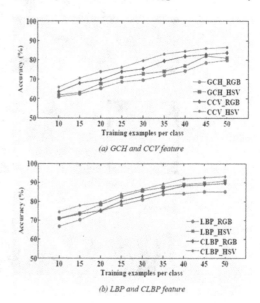

This information points out the classes that need more attention when solving the confusions. Figure 7 and 8 depicts the accuracy for each one of 4 classes using LBP and CLBP features in RGB and HSV color spaces. In the plots of Figure 7 and 8 the lines are crossing so it becomes difficult to know for which class it is better. To cope with the above problem, we also presented area under curve (AUC) for each class in Figure 7 and 8. The value of AUC is more means the accuracy is more for that disease. Clearly, Apple Blotch is one class that needs attention in both color spaces. It yields the lowest accuracy when compared to other classes in both color spaces. Figure 7 and 8 also shows that, the behavior of Apple Rot is nearly same in each scenario. Normal Apples are very easily distinguishable with diseased apples and a very good classification result is achieved

for the Normal Apples in both color spaces as shown in Figure 7 and 8. For CLBP feature and HSV color space, for instance, reported classification accuracy are 89.88%, 90.71%, 96.66%, and 99.33% for the Apple Blotch, Apple Rot, Apple Scab, and Normal Apple respectively, resulting average accuracy 93.14% when training is done with 50 images per class.

CONCLUSION

An image processing based approach is proposed and evaluated in this chapter for fruit disease identification problem. The proposed approach is composed of mainly three steps. In the first step defect segmentation is performed using K-means clustering technique. In the second step features

Figure 7. Accuracy per class for the LBP features in RGB and HSV color spaces using MSVM as a classifier

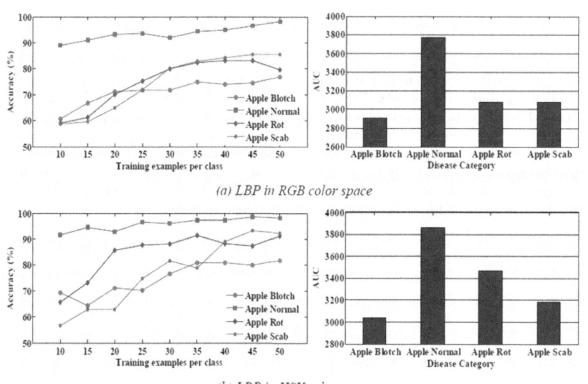

(a) LBP in RGB color space

(b) LBP in HSV color space

Figure 8. Accuracy per class for the CLBP features in RGB and HSV color spaces using MSVM as a classifier

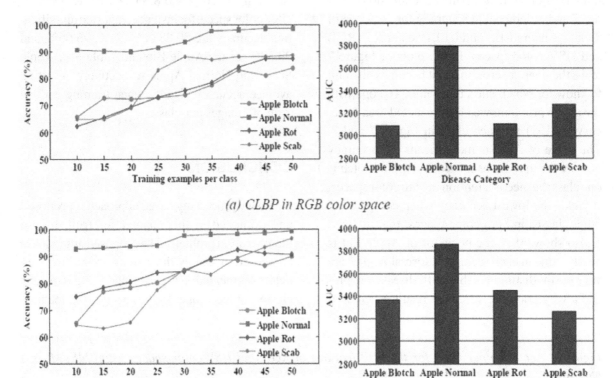

(a) CLBP in RGB color space

(b) CLBP in HSV color space

are extracted. In the third step training and classification are performed on a Multiclass SVM. We have used three types of apple diseases namely: Apple Blotch, Apple Rot, and Apple Scab as a case study and evaluated our program. Our experimental results indicate that the proposed solution can significantly support automatic detection and classification of apple fruit diseases. Based on our experiments, we have found that normal apples are easily distinguishable with the diseased apples and CLBP feature shows more accurate result for the identification of apple fruit diseases and achieved more than 93% classification accuracy. Further work includes consideration of fusion of more than one feature to improve the output of the proposed method.

REFERENCES

Belasque, J. Jr, Gasparoto, M. C. G., & Marcassa, L. G. (2008). Detection of mechanical and disease stresses in citrus plants by fluorescence spectroscopy. *Applied Optics*, *47*(11), 1922–1926. doi:10.1364/AO.47.001922 PMID:18404192

Bishop, C. M. (2006). *Pattern recognition and machine learning* (Vol. 1, p. 740). New York: Springer.

Bravo, C., Moshou, D., Oberti, R., West, J., McCartney, A., Bodria, L., & Ramon, H. (2004). Foliar Disease Detection in the Field using Optical Sensor Fusion. *Agricultural Engineering International: the CIGR Journal of Scientific Research and Development*, *6*, 1–14.

Chen, B., Wang, K., Li, S., Wang, J., Bai, J., Xiao, C., & Lai, J. (2008). Spectrum characteristics of cotton canopy infected with verticillium wilt and inversion of severity level. In Computer and Computing Technologies In Agriculture, (vol. 2, pp. 1169-1180). Springer US.

Choi, Y. H., Tapias, E. C., Kim, H. K., Lefeber, A. W. M., Erkelens, C., & Verhoeven, J. T. J. et al. (2004). Metabolic Discrimination of Catharanthus Roseus Leaves Infected by Phytoplasma using 1H-NMR Spectroscopy and Multivariate Data Analysis. *Plant Physiology*, *135*, 2398–2410. doi:10.1104/pp.104.041012 PMID:15286294

Dubey, S. R. (2012). *Automatic Recognition of Fruits and Vegetables and Detection of Fruit Diseases. (Master's theses)*. India: GLA University Mathura.

Dubey, S. R., Dixit, P., Singh, N., & Gupta, J. P. (2013). Infected fruit part detection using K-means clustering segmentation technique. *International Journal of Artificial Intelligence and Interactive Multimedia*, *2*(2). doi:10.9781/ijimai.2013.229

Dubey, S. R., & Jalal, A. S. (2012a). Robust Approach for Fruit and Vegetable Classification. *Procedia Engineering*, *38*, 3449–3453. doi:10.1016/j.proeng.2012.06.398

Dubey, S. R., & Jalal, A. S. (2012b). Detection and Classification of Apple Fruit Diseases using Complete Local Binary Patterns. In *Proceedings of the 3rd International Conference on Computer and Communication Technology* (pp. 346-351). MNNIT Allahabad.

Dubey, S. R., & Jalal, A. S. (2012c). Adapted Approach for Fruit Disease Identification using Images. *International Journal of Computer Vision and Image Processing*, *2*(3), 51–65. doi:10.4018/ijcvip.2012070104

Dubey, S. R., & Jalal, A. S. (2013). Species and Variety Detection of Fruits and Vegetables from Images. *International Journal of Applied Pattern Recognition*, *1*(1), 108–126. doi:10.1504/IJAPR.2013.052343

Fernando, L.-G., Gabriela, A.-G., Blasco, J., Aleixos, N., & Valiente, J.-M. (2010). Automatic detection of skin defects in citrus fruits using a multivariate image analysis approach. *Computers and Electronics in Agriculture*, *71*(2), 189–197. doi:10.1016/j.compag.2010.02.001

Gabriel, A. L. V., & Aguilera, J. M. (2013). Automatic detection of orientation and diseases in blueberries using image analysis to improve their postharvest storage quality. *Food Control*, *33*(1), 166–173. doi:10.1016/j.foodcont.2013.02.025

Gonzalez, R., & Woods, R. (2007). *Digital Image Processing* (3rd ed.). Prentice-Hall.

Grauman, K., & Darrell, T. (2005, June). Efficient image matching with distributions of local invariant features. In *Proceedings of the IEEE International Conference on Computer Vision and Pattern Recognition*, (Vol. 2, pp. 627-634). IEEE.

Guo, Z., Zhang, L., & Zhang, D. (2010). A Completed Modeling of Local Binary Pattern Operator for Texture Classification. [TIP]. *IEEE Transactions on Image Processing*, *19*(6), 1657–1663. doi:10.1109/TIP.2010.2044957 PMID:20215079

Gupta, J. P., Singh, N., Dixit, P., Semwal, V. B., & Dubey, S. R. (2013). Human Activity Recognition using Gait Pattern. [IJCVIP]. *International Journal of Computer Vision and Image Processing*, *3*(3), 31–53. doi:10.4018/ijcvip.2013070103

Hahn, F. (2009). Actual Pathogen Detection: Sensors and Algorithms—A Review. *Algorithms*, *2*(1), 301–338. doi:10.3390/a2010301

Hartigan, J. A., & Wong, M. A. (1979). Algorithm AS 136: A K-Means Clustering Algorithm. *Journal of the Royal Statistical Society. Series C, Applied Statistics*, *28*, 100–108.

Hartman, J. (2010, April). *Apple Fruit Diseases Appearing at Harvest*. Plant Pathology Fact Sheet, College of Agriculture, University of Kentucky.

Kim, M. S., Lefcourt, A. M., Chen, Y. R., & Tao, Y. (2005). Automated Detection of Fecal Contamination of Apples Based on Multispectral Fluorescence Image Fusion. *Journal of Food Engineering*, *71*, 85–91. doi:10.1016/j.jfoodeng.2004.10.022

Kleynen, O., Leemans, V., & Destain, M. F. (2005). Development of a Multi-Spectral Vision System for the Detection of Defects on Apples. *Journal of Food Engineering*, *69*, 41–49. doi:10.1016/j.jfoodeng.2004.07.008

Leemans, V., Magein, H., & Destain, M. F. (1998). Defect Segmentation on 'Golden Delicious' Apples by using Color Machine Vision. *Computers and Electronics in Agriculture*, *20*, 117–130. doi:10.1016/S0168-1699(98)00012-X

Leemans, V., Magein, H., & Destain, M. F. (1999). Defect Segmentation on 'Jonagold' Apples using Color Vision and a Bayesian Classification Method. *Computers and Electronics in Agriculture*, *23*, 43–53. doi:10.1016/S0168-1699(99)00006-X

Li, Q., Wang, M., & Gu, W. (2002, November). Computer Vision Based System for Apple Surface Defect Detection. *Computers and Electronics in Agriculture*, *36*, 215–223. doi:10.1016/S0168-1699(02)00093-5

Lins, E. C., Junior, J. B., & Marcassa, L. G. (2009). Detection of Citrus Canker in Citrus Plants using Laser Induced Fluorescence Spectroscopy. *Precision Agriculture*, *10*, 319–330. doi:10.1007/s11119-009-9124-2

MacQueen, J. (1967, June). Some methods for classification and analysis of multivariate observations. In *Proceedings of the fifth Berkeley symposium on mathematical statistics and probability*. University of California.

Marcassa, L. G., Gasparoto, M. C. G., Belasque, J., Lins, E. C., Nunes, F. D., & Bagnato, V. S. (2006). Fluorescence Spectroscopy Applied to Orange Trees. *Laser Physics*, *16*(5), 884–888. doi:10.1134/S1054660X06050215

Marszaek, M., & Schmid, C. (2006). Spatial weighting for bag-of-features. In *Proceedings of the IEEE International Conference on Computer Vision and Pattern Recognition*, (Vol. 2, pp. 2118-2125). IEEE.

Mehl, P. M., Chao, K., Kim, M., & Chen, Y. R. (2002). Detection of Defects on Selected Apple Cultivars using Hyperspectral and Multispectral Image Analysis. *Applied Engineering in Agriculture*, *18*, 219–226.

Moshou, D., Bravo, C., Oberti, R., West, J., Bodria, L., McCartney, A., & Ramon, H. (2005). Plant Disease Detection Based on Data Fusion of Hyper-Spectral and Multi-Spectral Fluorescence Imaging using Kohonen Maps. *Real-Time Imaging*, *11*(2), 75–83. doi:10.1016/j.rti.2005.03.003

Moshou, D., Bravo, C., Wahlen, S., West, J., McCartney, A., & De, J. et al. (2006). Simultaneous Identification of Plant Stresses and Diseases in Arable Crops using Proximal Optical Sensing and Self-Organising Maps. *Precision Agriculture*, *7*(3), 149–164. doi:10.1007/s11119-006-9002-0

Ojala, T., Pietikäinen, M., & Mäenpää, T. T. (2002). Multiresolution Gray-Scale and Rotation Invariant Texture Classification with Local Binary Pattern. [TPAMI]. *IEEE Transactions on Pattern Analysis and Machine Intelligence*, *24*(7), 971–987. doi:10.1109/TPAMI.2002.1017623

Ouyang, C., Li, D., Wang, J., Wang, S., & Han, Y. (2013). The Research of the Strawberry Disease Identification Based on Image Processing and Pattern Recognition. *Computer and Computing Technologies in Agriculture VI*, *392*, 69–77. doi:10.1007/978-3-642-36124-1_9

Purcell, D. E., O'Shea, M. G., Johnson, R. A., & Kokot, S. (2009). Near-Infrared Spectroscopy for the Prediction of Disease Rating for Fiji Leaf Gall in Sugarcane Clones. *Applied Spectroscopy*, *63*(4), 450–457. doi:10.1366/000370209787944370 PMID:19366512

Qin, J., Burks, F., Ritenour, M. A., & Bonn, W. G. (2009). Detection of Citrus Canker using Hyper-Spectral Reflectance Imaging with Spectral Information Divergence. *Journal of Food Engineering*, *93*(2), 183–191. doi:10.1016/j.jfoodeng.2009.01.014

Roberts, M. J., Schimmelpfennig, D., Ashley, E., Livingston, M., Ash, M., & Vasavada, U. (2006). *The Value of Plant Disease Early-Warning Systems (No. 18)*. Economic Research Service, United States Department of Agriculture.

Rocha, A., Hauagge, C., Wainer, J., & Siome, D. (2010). Automatic Fruit and Vegetable Classification from Images. *Computers and Electronics in Agriculture*, *70*, 96–104. doi:10.1016/j.compag.2009.09.002

Sankarana, S., Mishraa, A., Ehsania, R., & Davisb, C. (2010). A Review of Advanced Techniques for Detecting Plant Diseases. *Computers and Electronics in Agriculture*, *72*, 1–13. doi:10.1016/j.compag.2010.02.007

Shafri, H. Z. M., & Hamdan, N. (2009). Hyperspectral Imagery for Mapping Disease Infection in Oil Palm Plantation using Vegetation Indices and Red Edge Techniques. *American Journal of Applied Sciences*, *6*(6), 1031–1035. doi:10.3844/ajassp.2009.1031.1035

Singh, N., Dubey, S. R., Dixit, P., & Gupta, J. P. (2012, September). Semantic Image Retrieval by Combining Color, Texture and Shape Features. In *Proceedings of the International Conference on Computing Sciences (ICCS)*, (pp. 116-120). ICCS.

Spinelli, F., Noferini, M., & Costa, G. (2006). Near Infrared Spectroscopy (NIRs), Perspective of Fire Blight Detection in Asymptomatic Plant Material. In *Proceedings of the 10th International Workshop on Fire Blight*, (pp. 87-90). Academic Press.

Yang, C. M., Cheng, C. H., & Chen, R. K. (2007). Changes in Spectral Characteristics of Rice Canopy Infested with Brown Planthopper and Leaffolder. *Crop Science*, *47*, 329–335. doi:10.2135/cropsci2006.05.0335

ADDITIONAL READING

Belasque, L., Gasparoto, M. C. G., & Marcassa, L. G. (2008). Detection of Mechanical and Disease Stresses in Citrus Plants by Fluorescence Spectroscopy. *Applied Optics*, 7(11), 1922–1926. doi:10.1364/AO.47.001922 PMID:18404192

Bennedsen, B. S., & Peterson, D. L. (2004). Identification of apple stem and calyx using unsupervised feature extraction. *Transactions of the ASAE. American Society of Agricultural Engineers*, 47(3), 889–894. doi:10.13031/2013.16086

Berg, A., Berg, T., & Malik, J. (2005). Shape Matching and Object Recognition using Low Distortion Correspondences. In *Proceedings of the IEEE Computer Society Conference on Computer Vision and Pattern Recognition,* San Diego, CA, USA (pp. 26-33).

Bishop, C. M. (2006). *Pattern Recognition and Machine Learning*, 1st Ed., Springer. http://www.springer.com/computer/image+processing/book/978-0-387-31073-2.

Chaerle, L., Lenk, S., Hagenbeek, D., Buschmann, C., & Straeten, D. V. D. (2007). Multicolor Fluorescence Imaging for Early Detection of the Hypersensitive Reaction to Tobacco Mosaic Virus. *Journal of Plant Physiology*, 164(3), 253–262. doi:10.1016/j.jplph.2006.01.011 PMID:16545491

Chen, B., Wang, K., Li, S., Wang, J., Bai, J., Xiao, C., & Lai, J. (2008). Spectrum Characteristics of Cotton Canopy Infected with Verticillium Wilt and Inversion of Severity Level. *Computer and Computing Technologies in Agriculture*, 2, 1169–1180.

Cheng, X., Tao, Y., Chen, Y. R., & Luo, Y. (2003). Nir/mir dual-sensor machine vision system for online apple stem-end/calyx recognition. *Transactions of the ASAE. American Society of Agricultural Engineers*, 46(2), 551–558. doi:10.13031/2013.12944

Choi, Y. H., Tapias, E. C., Kim, H. K., Lefeber, A. W. M., Erkelens, C., & Verhoeven, J. T. J. et al. (2004). Metabolic Discrimination of Catharanthus Roseus Leaves Infected by Phytoplasma using 1H-NMR Spectroscopy and Multivariate Data Analysis. *Plant Physiology*, 135(4), 2398–2410. doi:10.1104/pp.104.041012 PMID:15286294

Du, C. J., & Sun, D. W. (2006). Learning techniques used in computer vision for food quality evaluation: a review. *Journal of Food Engineering*, 72(1), 39–55. doi:10.1016/j.jfoodeng.2004.11.017

Geoola, F., Geoola, F., & Peiper, U. M. (1994). A spectrophotometric method for detecting surface bruises on 'golden delicious' apples. *Journal of Agricultural Engineering Research*, 58(1), 47–51. doi:10.1006/jaer.1994.1034

Gonzalez, J. J., Valle, R. C., Bobro, S., Biasi, W. V., Mitcham, E. J., & McCarthy, M. J. (2001). Detection and monitoring of internal browning development in 'fuji' apples using mri. *Postharvest Biology and Technology*, 22(2), 179–188. doi:10.1016/S0925-5214(00)00183-6

Hahn, F. (2009). Actual Pathogen Detection: Sensors and Algorithms—A Review. *Algorithms*, 2(1), 301–338. doi:10.3390/a2010301

Heidemann, G. (2005). Unsupervised Image Categorization. *Image and Vision Computing*, 23(10), 861–876. doi:10.1016/j.imavis.2005.05.016

Judith, A. A. (1999). Quality measurement of fruits and vegetables. *Postharvest Biology and Technology*, 15(3), 207–225. doi:10.1016/S0925-5214(98)00086-6

Kavdir, I., & Guyer, D. E. (2002). Apple sorting using artificial neural networks and spectral imaging. *Transactions of the ASAE. American Society of Agricultural Engineers*, 45(6), 1995–2005. doi:10.13031/2013.11411

Kavdir, I., & Guyer, D. E. (2004). Comparison of artificial neural networks and statistical classifiers in apple sorting using textural features. *Biosystems Engineering, 89*(3), 331–344. doi:10.1016/j.biosystemseng.2004.08.008

Kim, M. S., Chen, Y. R., & Mehl, P. M. (2001). Hyperspectral reflectance and fluorescence imaging system for food quality and safety. *Transactions of American Society of Agricultural Engineers, 44*(3), 721–729.

Kleynen, O., Leemans, V., & Destain, M.-F. (2003). Selection of the most efficient wavelength bands for 'jonagold' apple sorting. *Postharvest Biology and Technology, 30*(3), 221–232. doi:10.1016/S0925-5214(03)00112-1

Leemans, V., & Destain, M.-F. (2004). A real-time grading method of apples based on features extracted from defects. *Journal of Food Engineering, 61*(1), 83–89. doi:10.1016/S0260-8774(03)00189-4

López, M. M., Bertolini, E., Olmos, A., Caruso, P., Gorris, M. T., & Llop, P. et al. (2003). Innovative Tools for Detection of Plant Pathogenic Viruses and Bacteria. *International Microbiology, 6*(4), 233–243. doi:10.1007/s10123-003-0143-y PMID:13680391

Marcassa, L. G., & Gasparoto, M. C. G., BelasqueJunior, J., Lins, E. C., Nunes, F. D., & Bagnato, V. S. (2006). Fluorescence Spectroscopy Applied to Orange Trees. *Laser Physics, 16*(5), 884–888. doi:10.1134/S1054660X06050215

Moshou, D., Bravo, C., Oberti, R., West, J., Bodria, L., McCartney, A., & Ramon, H. (2005). Plant Disease Detection Based on Data Fusion of Hyper-Spectral and Multi-Spectral Fluorescence Imaging using Kohonen Maps. *Real-Time Imaging, 11*(2), 75–83. doi:10.1016/j.rti.2005.03.003

Moshou, D., Bravo, C., Wahlen, V., West, J., McCartney, A., Baerdemaeker, J. D., & Ramon, H. (2006). Simultaneous Identification of Plant Stresses and Diseases in Arable Crops using Proximal Optical Sensing and Self-Organising Maps. *Precision Agriculture, 7*(3), 149–164. doi:10.1007/s11119-006-9002-0

Penman, D. W. (2001). Determination of stem and calyx location on apples using automatic visual inspection. *Computers and Electronics in Agriculture, 33*(1), 7–18. doi:10.1016/S0168-1699(01)00172-7

Purcell, D. E., O'Shea, M. G., Johnson, R. A., & Kokot, S. (2009). Near-Infrared Spectroscopy for the Prediction of Disease Rating for Fiji Leaf Gall in Sugarcane Clones. *Applied Spectroscopy, 63*(4), 450–457. doi:10.1366/000370209787944370 PMID:19366512

Sankarana, S., Mishraa, A., Ehsania, R., & Davisb, C. (2010). A Review of Advanced Techniques for Detecting Plant Diseases. *Computers and Electronics in Agriculture, 72*(1), 1–13. doi:10.1016/j.compag.2010.02.007

Shafri, H. Z. M., & Hamdan, N. (2009). Hyperspectral Imagery for Mapping Disease Infection in Oil Palm Plantation using Vegetation Indices and Red Edge Techniques. *American Journal of Applied Sciences, 6*(6), 1031–1035. doi:10.3844/ajassp.2009.1031.1035

Sivic, J., Russell, B., Efros, A., Zisserman, A., & Freeman, W. (2005). Discovering Objects and Their Location in Images. In *Proceedings of the Tenth IEEE International Conference on Computer Vision,* Beijing, China (pp. 370-377).

Xing, J., & Baerdemaeker, J. D. (2005). Bruise detection on 'jonagold' apples using hyperspectral imaging. *Postharvest Biology and Technology, 37*(2), 152–162. doi:10.1016/j.postharvbio.2005.02.015

KEY TERMS AND DEFINITIONS

Classification: In machine learning, classification is the problem of identifying to which of a set of categories (sub-populations) a new observation belongs, on the basis of a training set of data containing observations (or instances) whose category membership is known.

Color Histogram: In image processing, a color histogram is a representation of the distribution of colors in an image. For digital images, a color histogram represents the number of pixels that have colors in each of a fixed list of color ranges, that span the image's color space, the set of all possible colors.

Feature Extraction: When the input data to an algorithm is too large to be processed and it is suspected to be notoriously redundant (e.g. the same measurement in both feet and meters) then the input data will be transformed into a reduced representation set of features (also named features vector). Transforming the input data into the set of features is called feature extraction.

Image Segmentation: In computer vision, image segmentation is the process of partitioning a digital image into multiple segments (sets of pixels, also known as super-pixels). The goal of segmentation is to simplify and/or change the representation of an image into something that is more meaningful and easier to analyze.

Image Texture: An image texture is a set of metrics calculated in image processing designed to quantify the perceived texture of an image. Image Texture gives us information about the spatial arrangement of color or intensities in an image or selected region of an image.

K-Means Clustering: K-means clustering is a method of vector quantization, originally from signal processing, that is popular for cluster analysis in data mining.

Machine Learning: It is a branch of artificial intelligence, concerns the construction and study of systems that can learn from data.

Pattern Recognition: In machine learning, pattern recognition is the assignment of a label to a given input value.

Support Vector Machine: In machine learning, support vector machines are supervised learning models with associated learning algorithms that analyze data and recognize patterns, used for classification and regression analysis.

Chapter 6
Automated Ripeness Assessment System of Tomatoes Using PCA and SVM Techniques

Esraa El Hariri
Fayoum University, Egypt & Scientific Research Group in Egypt (SRGE), Egypt

Nashwa El-Bendary
Arab Academy for Science, Technology, and Maritime Transport, Egypt & Scientific Research Group in Egypt (SRGE), Egypt

Aboul Ella Hassanien
Cairo University, Egypt & Scientific Research Group in Egypt (SRGE), Egypt

Amr Badr
Cairo University, Egypt

ABSTRACT

One of the prime factors in ensuring a consistent marketing of crops is product quality, and the process of determining ripeness stages is a very important issue in the industry of (fruits and vegetables) production, since ripeness is the main quality indicator from the customers' perspective. To ensure optimum yield of high quality products, an objective and accurate ripeness assessment of agricultural crops is important. This chapter discusses the problem of determining different ripeness stages of tomato and presents a content-based image classification approach to automate the ripeness assessment process of tomato via examining and classifying the different ripeness stages as a solution for this problem. It introduces a survey about resent research work related to monitoring and classification of maturity stages for fruits/vegetables and provides the core concepts of color features, SVM, and PCA algorithms. Then it describes the proposed approach for solving the problem of determining different ripeness stages of tomatoes. The proposed approach consists of three phases, namely pre-processing, feature extraction, and classification phase. The classification process depends totally on color features (colored histogram and color moments), since the surface color of a tomato is the most important characteristic to observe ripeness. This approach uses Principal Components Analysis (PCA) and Support Vector Machine (SVM) algorithms for feature extraction and classification, respectively.

DOI: 10.4018/978-1-4666-6030-4.ch006

INTRODUCTION

Fruits and vegetables development is characterized by a short period of cell division followed by a longer period of cell elongation by water uptake. The final fruit size mainly depends on initial cell number, rather than cell size(Cowan, Cripps, Richings, & Taylor, 2001). Fruit ripening on the other hand is characterized by the development of color, flavor, texture and aroma. The actual time from anthesis until full maturity can vary tremendously among species/cultivars due to genetic and environmental differences. Even between fruit on the same plant, fruit development and ripening can take more or less time depending on local microclimate conditions and differences in sink/source relations within the plant. In addition, when a fruit is harvested, the time of anthesis of a particular fruit is generally unknown, as is its full history.

Monitoring and controlling produce (fruits and vegetables) ripeness has become a very important issue in the crops industry, since ripeness is perceived by customers as the main quality indicator. Also, the product's appearance is one of the most worrying issues for producers as it has a high influence on product's quality and consumer preferences. However, up to this day, optimal harvest dates and prediction of storage life are still mainly based on subjective interpretation and practical experience.

Hence, automation of this process is a big gain at agriculture and industry fields. For agriculture, it may be used to develop automatic harvest systems and saving crops from damages caused by environmental changes. On the other hand, for industry, it is used to develop automatic sorting system or checking the quality of fruits to increase customer satisfaction level[(Brezmes, Llobet, Vilanova, Saiz, & Correig, 2000),(Elhariri, El-Bendary, Fouad, Plato, Hassanien, & Hussein, 2014)]. So, an objective and accurate ripeness assessment of agricultural crops is important in ensuring optimum yield of high quality products.

Moreover, identifying physiological and harvest maturity of agricultural crops correctly, will ensure timely harvest to avoid cutting of either under- and over-ripe agricultural crops[(Elhariri, El-Bendary, Fouad, Plato, Hassanien, & Hussein, 2014),(May & Amaran, 2011)].

Every fruit shows one or more apparent signs when it reaches physiological maturity or ripeness. Tomatoes, with their continuously prevailing daily nutrition and dietary value, are taking a dominant place among the vegetables all over the world. In Tomatoes, over maturity or over ripening is the stage when the fruit softens and loses part of its characteristic taste and flavor(Camelo, 2004). At this point, it is necessary to differentiate between two types of fruits: climacteric and non-climacteric. Tomato belongs to the group of climacteric agricultural products, which means that it is capable of generating ethylene, the hormone required for ripening even when detached from the mother plant and they reach full red color even when harvested green(Camelo, 2004).On the other hand, bell pepper for example, belongs to the group of non-climacteric agricultural products, which means that ripeness (full red color) is only obtained while fruit is attached to the plant and slight changes in color take place after harvest [(Camelo, 2004), (Coates & Johnson, 1997)].

Tomato maturity has been related to quantifiable parameters that reflect the biochemical changes during ripening. Color is used as a major method in determining maturity of tomato. However, skin color of tomato varies from cultivar to another cultivar even at the same maturity stage [(Molyneux, Lister, & Savage, 2004), (Zhang & McCarthy, 2011)]. During ripening, tomatoes go through a series of highly ordered physiological and biochemical changes, such as chlorophyll degradation and increased activity of cell wall-degrading enzymes, bring on changes in color, firmness, and development of aromas and flavors (Prasanna, Prabha, & Tharanathan, 2007). For tomatoes, ripeness issue is often handled via classifying harvested produce according to discrete color classes going from immature green to mature red, as stated in some recent researches that have classified tomatoes in different maturity stages based on measurements of color [(Hahn, 2002), (Aranda-Sanchez, Baltazar, & Gonzlez-Aguilar, 2009)]. Different tomato products have distinct requirements for maturity to achieve quality standards; hence, tomato maturity is one of the most important factors associated with the quality of processed tomato products.

Recently, utilizing computer vision in food products has become very wide spread, especially for products where measuring color or other spectral features enables estimating the ripeness stage (Rodrguez-Pulido, Gordillo, Gonzlez-Miret, & Heredia, 2013).

This chapter presents a multi-class content-based image classification system to automate the ripeness assessment process of tomato via investigating and classifying the different maturity/ ripeness stages based on the color features. The dataset used for experiments were constructed based on real sample images for tomato at different stages, which were collected from different farms in Minya city, Upper Egypt.

Dataset of total 250 images was used for both training and testing datasets with 10-fold cross-validation. Training dataset is divided into 5 classes representing the different stages of tomato ripeness. The proposed approach consists of three phases; namely pre-processing, feature extraction}, and classification phases. During pre-processing phase, the proposed approach resizes images to 250x250 pixels, in order to reduce their color index, and the background of each image will be removed using background subtraction technique. Also, each image is converted from RGB to HSV color space. For feature extraction phase, Principal Component Analysis (PCA) algorithm is applied in order to generate a feature vector for each image in the dataset. Finally, for classification phase, the proposed approach ap-

plied Support Vector Machine (SVM) algorithm classification of ripeness stages.

The rest of this chapter is organized as follows. Section 2 introduces a survey about resent research work related to monitoring and classification of maturity stages for fruits/vegetables. Section 3 presents the core concepts of color features, SVM and PCA algorithms. Section 4 describes the different phases of the proposed content-based classification system; namely pre-processing, feature extraction, and classification phases. Section 5 discusses the tested image dataset and presented the obtained experimental results. Finally, Section 6 presents conclusions.

BACKGROUND

This section reviews a survey about current approaches which tackling the ripeness assessment and classification problem of tomatoes and other fruits/vegetables.

(Zhang & McCarthy, 2011)offered tomato maturity evaluation approach using magnetic resonance imaging (MRI). The tomatoes used for this approach were collected from the field at different maturity stages. Firstly, MR images were captured, then for each of the MR images, the mean and histogram features of the voxel intensities in the region of interest (RoI) were calculated. Finally, partial least square discriminant analysis (PLS-DA) was applied using both the calculated features and maturity classes variables in order to deduce a maturity classification model and shows that different maturity stages are embedded in MR images signal intensity.

Also, (Baltazar, Aranda, & Gonzalez-Aguilar, 2008)used total of 128 tomatoes samples that were harvested and preliminarily sorted with colorimeter choosing only those with roughly breaker color, which represents the ripeness stage where there is a definite break in color from green to tannish-yellow. So, they firstly applied data fusion to nondestructive image of fresh intact tomatoes by assessing both of colorimeter and nondestructive firmness measurements for the samples at the selected testing days using two sensors placed at different points. Then, the measurements data were normalized. Finally, a three-class Bayesian classifier was applied and the results showed that multi-sensorial data fusion is better than single sensor data and considerably reduces the classification error.

Moreover, (Polder, Heijden, & Young, 2002) proposed an approach based on spectral images analysis to measure the ripeness of tomatoes for automatic sorting. The proposed approach compared hyper-spectral images with standard RGB images for classification of tomatoes ripeness stages. That depends on individual pixels and includes gray reference in each image for obtaining automatic compensation of different light sources. The proposed approach applied the linear discriminant analysis (LDA) as a classification technique depending on pixels values and proved that spectral images are better than standard RGB images for measuring ripeness stages of tomatoes via offering more discriminating power.

In (Ghazali, Samad, Arshad, & Karim, 2009), an approach for automatic grading of oil palm fruits has been presented. The proposed approach based on image processing. Firstly, samples of oil palm fruits were collected at three different ripeness stages(ripe, under ripe, and over ripe), then RGB images were captured using digital camera. The proposed approach removed background pixels, then R,G and B component were analyzed and mean value for each component was computed. After the analysis step a threshold of red components was set. Finally a neural network application was applied for ripeness checking. this approach gave 100% correct classification for ripe stage, but the under ripe and unripe stages have some errors with 20% and 25% respectively.

Also, (May & Amaran, 2011) offered an automated ripeness assessment approach for oil palm fruit in order to assess oil palm ripeness and overcome the problem of subjectivity and inconsistency of manual human grading techniques based on experience to ensure optimum yield of high quality oil.Depending on color intensity palm fruit can be classified into three ripeness stages(under ripe, ripe and overripe).The proposed approach used RGB with fuzzy logic technique to assess the ripeness. Firstly, image is captured and preprocessed, and then RGB features were extracted. Finally fuzzy logic model was applied for the classification purpose. This approach achieved an efficiency of 88.74%.

On the other hand,(Jaffar, Jaafar, Jamil, Low, & Abdullah, 2009) applied a photogrammetric methodology in order to depict a relationship between the color of the palm oil fruits and their ripeness and sort them out physically depending on this relationship. The proposed methodology works as follow, firstly, image were preprocessed for noise removal. Then image segmentation using K-means clustering with the L*a*b* Color Space was applied to images because palm fruit imagesare fused with dirt and branches, this resulting in a difficulty of using the average color digital number values at RGB color space for evaluating ripeness, so the proposed approach applied, after segmentation step color digital numbers calculations were performed. Then, to differentiate ripe FFB from unripe fruits, the calculated color value to R/G and R/B ratios of the digital number of the segmented images was used. This methodology considered the first automation of palm oil grading system.

(Fadilah, Mohamad-Saleh, Halim, Ibrahim, & Ali, 2012)presented an approach for ripeness classification of oil palm fresh fruit bunch. the proposed approach based on image processing, ANN and PCA techniques. Firstly, FFBs were collected at different ripeness stages, then FFBs were classified into four ripeness (unripe, underripe, ripe and overripe). Then for each FFB, four images were captured at different areas of the bunch, after that, images were segmented into two regions fruits area and spikes. Then color features were extracted for fruits part. Finally, an ANN model was applied using two method. the first one used all features as the input parameters of ANN, whereas the other, Firstly it applied PCA for features reduction, then it used the resulting features as the input parameters of ANN. this approach achieved 91.67% accuracy for the first method and 93.33% for the second one.

Furthermore,(Paulraj, Hema, R. Pranesh, & Siti Sofiah, 2009) designed a neural network with image processing approach for color recognition for the problem of identifying the ripe of banana fruit. The proposed approachbased on RGB color components of banana images. It used four sets of bananas used with different type of sizes and ripeness. Each image of the banana is captured in four different positions and the images are captured daily until all bananas turn to be rotten. The images of banana is captured and resized. Later, the image is extracted into the RGB color components and each pixel of the color component is rescaled using a simple heuristic method. As a result, histograms are obtained and used as the feature vector in determining the ripeness of the banana. Then a supervised Neural Network model with utilizing the error back propagation model was applied as a classification technique. It achieved an identification accuracy of 96%.

Also,(Shah Rizam, Farah Yasmin, Ahmad Ihsan, & Shazana, 2009) designed an artificial neural network with image processing approach for measuring and determining the ripeness and quality of watermelon. the proposed approach depends on watermelon colors in YCbCr Color Space. Firstly, the colour in watermelon images is segmented into three regions. Then from each region watermelon was classified into ripe depending on the amount of pixels at each region. Then CbCr colour feature was extracted. Finally, an ANN model was applied for determining ripeness stages. This approach achieved an accuracy of 86.51%.

(Effendi, Ramli, & Ghani, 2010)presented a back propagation neural network approach for the identification of Jatropha curcas fruit maturity. Firstly, Jatropha curcas fruits were collected at three different maturity stages(raw, ripe and overripe) and images were captured using digital camera. Then, the Jatropha fruits were separated from background and segmented to 100 X 100 Pixels. Then features were extracted by classifying Each pixel of a Jatropha curcas fruit image into one of 256 categories, represented by an integer in the range from 0 (black)-255 (white). Finally, Back propagation neural network approach was applied for the identification process of maturity stages. This approach achieved 95% accuracy.

Also, (Syal, Mehta, & Darshni, 2013) proposed a fruit sorting and grading approach based on image processing techniques and fuzzy logics for. The proposed approach depends on three basic features: RGB color components, shape, and size of the fruit object. Jatropha fruit can be classified into three grades(A, B, C) depending on selected features values. In this approach authors Firstly extracted features using image processing techniques, then a fuzzy system is applied to classify the grade of the fruit (A, B or C). it achieves an very promising and accurate results.

Also, (Dadwal & Banga, 2012) proposed an approach based on color image segmentation and fuzzy logic technique to classify the ripeness stages of Apple fruit. Apple fruit can be classified into three stages ripe, under ripe and overripe stages. The proposed approach depends on RGB color components, where Firstly four images are captured from different directions for each fruit. Then a segmentation approach is applied to these images to get region of interest, Then the mean value for each color component (R, G and B) is calculated for the area of interest. Finally the fuzzy logic system is applied to decide the ripeness stages of apple depending on mean values of Red, Green and Blue color components. This system can be applied at many applications.

Furthermore, (balestani, Moghaddam, motlaq, & Dolaty, 2012) designed an approach based on image processing for cherry sorting and grading. it depend on RGB color components of the captured images of cherry. Cherry samples at four different ripeness stages were collected with an interval of 5 days. The proposed sorting system of cherries used color criteria and the TTS(Total Soluble Solids) in fruit to classify it to the right ripeness stage.The reflected light in image was removed in order to minimize the error rate in calculating the average color components.This system achieved 92% accuracy in sorting cherries according to their ripeness.

Also, (Damiri & Slamet, 2012) proposed an approach based on image processing and Artificial Neural Networks for lime maturity and ripeness identification. Lime samples from three levels of maturity and ripeness were collected and used as dataset for this approach. Theproposed approach depends on area, shape factor, RGB color index and texture features of lime to identify its ripeness stages. These features are sent to ANN using back propagation method as inputs for training to perform the classification. Thisapproach achieved 100% accuracy in classifying the maturity and ripeness of lime.

This chapter presents a multi-class content-based image classification system to automate the ripeness assessment process of tomato via investigating and classifying the different maturity/ripeness stages based on the color features. The datasets used for experiments were constructed based on real sample images for tomato at different stages, which were collected from different farms in Minya city, Upper Egypt. Colors features were computed firstly, and thenPrincipal Component Analysis (PCA) algorithm is applied for features extraction in order to generate a feature vector for each image in the dataset. Then, Support Vector Machine (SVM) algorithms were applied for classification of ripeness stages.

PRELIMINARIES

This section presents a brief idea concerning the core concepts of PCA and SVM algorithms that have been utilized for feature extraction and classification, respectively.

Principal Component Analysis (PCA)

Principal component analysis is a statistical common technique, which is widely used in image recognition and compression for a dimensionality reduction, data representation and features extraction tool as it ensures better classification[(Suganthy & Ramamoorthy, 2012),(Xiao, 2010)(El-Bendary, Zawbaa, Hassanien, & Snasel, 2011),(Ada & RajneetKaur, 2012). It basically reduces the dimensionality by avoiding redundant information, and reducing samples features space to features sub-space (smaller space which contains all independent variables which are needed to describe the data) by discarding all un-effective minor components. So, it's necessary to perform various pre-processing steps in order to utilize the PCA method for feature extraction. Steps of PCA algorithm are shown in algorithm (1).

Color Features

A widely used feature in image retrieval and image classification problems is the color, which is as well an important feature for image representation (El-Bendary, Zawbaa, Hassanien, & Snasel, 2011). In this research two color descriptors will be used; namely color moments and color histogram.

Color Moments

The first three color moments, which are mean, standard deviation, and skewness(Shahbahrami, Borodin, & Juurlink, 2008),(Soman, Ghorpade, Sonone, & Chavan, 2012), have been proved to be efficient and effective way for representing

Algorithm 1. Principal component analysis (PCA) algorithm

Step 1: Calculate the sample mean $\overline{\mu}$

$$\overline{\mu} = \frac{\sum_{i=1}^{n} X_i}{n}$$

Step 2: Subtract sample mean from each observation X_i

$$\overline{Z}_i = X_i - \overline{\mu}$$

Step 3: Calculate the covariance matrix C

$$C = \sum_{i=1}^{n} Z_i . Z_i^t$$

Step 4: Calculate the eigenvectors and eigenvalues of the covariance matrix C
Step 5: Rearrange the eigenvectors and eigenvalues and select a subset as basis vectors
Step 6: Project the data

color distribution in any image. Mean, standard deviation, and skewness for a colored image of size N X M pixels are defined by Equations (1), (2), and (3).

$$\overline{x}_i = \frac{\sum_{j=1}^{M.N} x_{ij}}{M.N} \tag{1}$$

$$\partial_i = \sqrt{\left[\frac{1}{M.N} \sum_{j=1}^{M.N} \left(x_{ij} - \overline{x}_1 \right)^2 \right]} \tag{2}$$

$$S_i = \sqrt[3]{\left[\frac{1}{M.N} \sum_{j=1}^{M.N} \left(x_{ij} - \overline{x}_1 \right)^3 \right]} \tag{3}$$

where x_{ij} is the value of image pixel j of color channel i (e.g RGB, HSV and etc..), $\overline{x}_1$. is the mean for each channel i=(H,S and V), ∂_i is the standard deviation and S_i is the skewness for each channel(Shahbahrami, Borodin, & Juurlink, 2008),(Soman, Ghorpade, Sonone, & Chavan, 2012). HSV channels can be computed for RGB channels using Equations (4), (5), and (6), where

R, G and B are color component of RGB color space (Singh & Hemachandra, 2012).

$$H = \cos^{-1} \frac{\frac{1}{2}\left[(R - G) + (R - B) \right]}{\sqrt{(R - G)^2 + (R - B)(G - B)}} \tag{4}$$

$$S = 1 - \frac{3\left[\min(R,\ G,\ B) \right]}{R + G + B} \tag{5}$$

$$V = \left(\frac{R + G + B}{3} \right) \tag{6}$$

where R, G and B are color component of RGB color space.

Color Histogram

Color histogram is a color descriptor that shows representation of the distribution of colors in an image. It represents the number of pixels that have colors in each range of colors (El-Bendary, Zawbaa, Hassanien, & Snasel, 2011). Color histogram can be calculated for many color spaces (e.g. RGB, HSV, etc). It is often used with 3-dimensional spaces like as RGB and HSV color spaces. color histogram is invariant with rotation, translation, and scale (Meskaldji, Boucherkha, & Chikhi, 2009).

Support Vector Machine

One of the most used algorithms at classification problems is the Support Vector Machine. it is a machine learning algorithm which is applied for classification and regression problem of high dimensional datasets with excellent results. [(Wu & Zhou, 2006),(Zawbaa, El-Bendary, Hassanien, & Abraham, SVM-based Soccer Video Summarization System, 2011),(Zawbaa, El-Bendary, Hassanien, & Kim, Machine Learning-Based Soccer Video Summarization System, 2011)].

SVM solves the classification problem via trying to find an optimal separating hyperplane between classes. it depends on the training cases which are placed on the edge of class descriptor this is called support vectors, any other cases are discarded as shown at Figure 1[(A. Tzotsos, 2006),(Zhang, Xie, & Cheng, 2010),(Suralkar, Karode, & Pawad, 2012)].Theoretically, for linearly separable data, there is an infinite number of hyperplanes. thesehyperplanes can classify training data correctly, SVM algorithm seeks to maximize the margin around a hyperplane that separates a positive class from a negative class. [(Wu & Zhou, 2006),(Zawbaa, El-Bendary, Hassanien, & Abraham, SVM-based Soccer Video Summarization System, 2011),(Zawbaa, El-Bendary, Hassanien, & Kim, Machine Learning-Based Soccer Video Summarization System, 2011)]. Given a training dataset are represented by $\{x_i, y_i\}$, i=1,2,3,....., N, where N is the number of training samples, x_i is a features vector and $y_i \in \{-1,+1\}$ is the target label, y=+1 for samples belong to class C_1 and y=-1 for samples belong to class C_2. Classes C_1, C_2 are linearly separable classes. [(Wu & Zhou, 2006),(Zawbaa, El-Bendary, Hassanien, & Abraham, SVM-based Soccer Video Summarization System, 2011),(Zawbaa, El-Bendary, Hassanien, & Kim, Machine Learning-Based Soccer Video Summarization System, 2011)]. Geometrically, the SVM modeling algorithm finds an optimal hyperplane with the maximal margin to separate two classes, which requires to solve the optimization problem, as shown in Equations (7) and (8).

$$\text{maximize}\sum_{i=1}^{n}\alpha_i - \frac{1}{2}\sum_{i,j=1}^{n}\alpha_i\alpha_j y_i y_j.K\left(x_i,x_j\right) \quad (7)$$

$$Subject-to:\sum_{i=1}^{n}\alpha_i y_i, 0 \leq \alpha_i \leq C \quad (8)$$

where, $\pm_i$ is the weight assigned to the training sample x_i. If $\pm_i > 0$, x_i is called a support vector. C is a regulation parameter used to trade-off the training accuracy and the model complexity so that a superior generalization capability can be achieved. K is a kernel function, which is used to measure the similarity between two samples.

Figure 1. SVM procedure

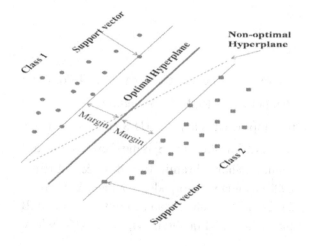

There are many different kernel functions have been applied in the past. Linear, multi-layer perceptron MLP, polynomial and the Gaussian radial basis function (RBF) are the most popular kernel functions[(Boolchandani & Sahula, 2011),(Vanschoenwinkel & Manderick, 2005)].

These kernel functions can be defined by the following Equations(9,10, 11 and 12:

Linear Kernel Function:

$$K\left(X_i, \ X_j\right) = X_i^T X_j \tag{9}$$

RBF Kernel Function:

$$K\left(X_i, \ X_j\right) = e^{\left(-\frac{X_i - X_j^2}{2\lambda^2}\right)} \tag{10}$$

MLP Kernel Function:

$$K\left(X_i, \ X_j\right) = \tanh\left(^2{}_0 X_i^T X_j + {}^2{}_1\right) \tag{11}$$

Polynomial, Order P Kernel Function:

$$K\left(X_i, \ X_j\right) = \left(1 + \ X_i^T X_j\right)^P \tag{12}$$

N-Class Support Vector Machine

SVM is a binary class classification method and our problem is an N-class classification problem. Therefore, in this article, the SVM algorithm is applied to a multi-class problem [(Liu & Zheng, 2005), (Anthony, Gregg, & Tshilidzi, 2007)] and

two different approaches have been applied in order to do that; namely one-against-all (OAA) and one-against-one (OAO) approaches.

The first approach, one-against-all (OAA), worked according to Algorithm (2)

In the second approach, one-against-one (OAO), a SVM classifier was created for each pair of classes (for N-class problem) resulting in $N\left(N - 1\right)/2$ classifiers. The OAO approach worked according to Algorithm (3).

THE PROPOSED APPROACH FOR THE AUTOMATED PROCESS OF RIPENESS ASSESSMENT

The proposed approach for the automated process of ripeness assessment for tomato consists of three phases; namely pre-processing, feature extraction, and classification. Figure 2 describes the general structure of the proposed approach.

The datasets used at this research were prepared from real samples for tomato at different stages, which were collected from different farms at Al-Minya city,which is located approximately 245 km (152 mi) south of Cairo on the western bank of the Nile River. Figure 3 shows some farms.

Tomato fruits can be classified into six different ripeness stages as shown at Figure 4. The ripeness stages are green, breaker, turning, pink, light red and red stages.For green stage, green represents the ripeness stage where fruit surface is completely green, For breaker stage, breaker represents the ripeness stage where there is a definite break in color from green to tannish-yellow, pink or red on not more than 10% of the surface. For turning

Algorithm 2. One-against-all (OAA)

Step 1: Construct N binary SVM.
Step 2: Each SVM separates one class from the rest classes.
Step 3: Train the ith SVM with all training samples of the i^{ti} class with positive labels, and training samples of other classes with negative labels.

Algorithm 3. One-against-one (OAO)

Step 1: Create $N(N-1)/2$ binary SVMs

Step 2: Train $N(N-1)/2$ binary SVMs as follow

$$(1,2), (1,3), \ldots\ldots\ldots, (1,\ k),\ (2,3), (2,4), \ldots\ldots,\ (k1,\ k).$$

Figure 2. Architecture of the proposed ripeness classification approach

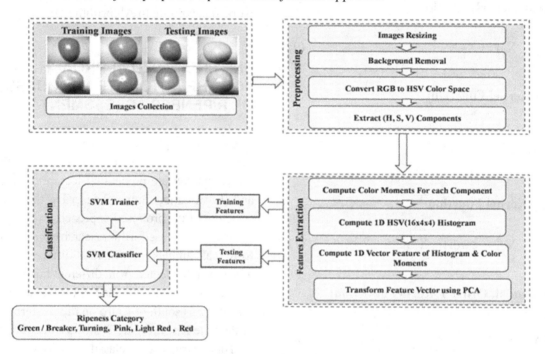

Figure 3. Farms at Al-Minya City

Figure 4. Tomato ripeness stages

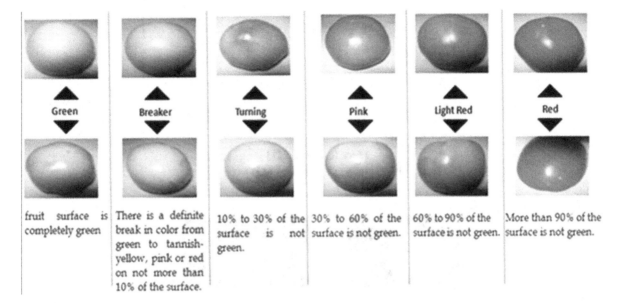

fruit surface is completely green	There is a definite break in color from green to tannish-yellow, pink or red on not more than 10% of the surface.	10% to 30% of the surface is not green.	30% to 60% of the surface is not green.	60% to 90% of the surface is not green.	More than 90% of the surface is not green.

stage, 10% to 30% of the surface is not green. For pink stage, 30% to 60% of the surface is not green. For light red stage, 60% to 90% of the surface is not green. Finally, for red stage, more than 90% of the surface is not green(U.S.D.A., 1991).

Pre-Processing Phase

During pre-processing phase, the proposed approach aimed to preprocess each image for the features extraction phase to get only fruit part. The proposed approach resizes images to 250x250 pixels, in order to reduce their color index, and the background of each image is removed using background subtraction technique. Figure 5 show preprocessing procedure flowchart and Figure 6 shows an example of background removal algorithm. Also, each image is converted from RGB to HSV color space, as it is widely used in the field of color vision and close to the categories of human color perception (Yu, Li, Zhang, & Feng, 2002). Then H,S and V components were extracted individually.

Feature Extraction Phase

As previously stated, since tomato surface color is the most important characteristic to asset the ripeness of tomato, this system uses HSV color

Figure 5. Preprocessing procedure

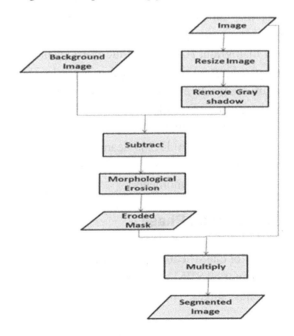

Figure 6. Samples of background removal

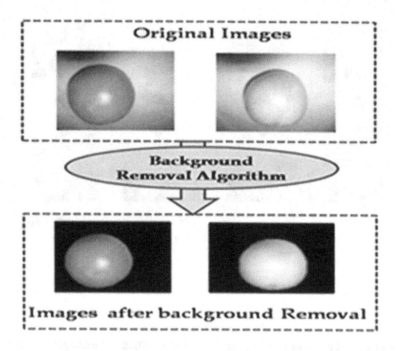

histogram and color moments for ripeness stages classification.

For feature extraction phase, PCA algorithm is applied as features extraction technique in order to generate a feature vector for each image in the dataset.

The proposed approach transforms the input space into sub-spaces for dimensionality reduction. After completing the previous 1D 16x4x4 HSV histogram, 16 levels for hue and 4 levels for each of saturation and value are resulted in 1X256 feature vector. In addition, nine color moments, three for each channel (H, S and V channels) (mean, standard deviation, and skewness), were computed. Then, a 1X265 feature vector was formed as a combination of HSV 1D histogram and the nine color moments.

Classification Phase

Finally, for classification phase, the proposed approach applied SVM algorithm for classification of ripeness stages. The inputs are training dataset feature vectors and their corresponding classes, whereas the outputs are the ripeness stage of each image in the testing dataset. Figure 7 shows a block diagram of classification procedure.

In this phase, the classification approach, previously proposed in (Elhariri, El-Bendary, Fouad, Plato, Hassanien, & Hussein, 2014), has been utilized along with the one-against-one (OAO) approach with 10-fold cross validation for multiclass SVM problems.

EXPERIMENTAL RESULTS

Simulation experiments in this article are done on a PC with Intel Core i7 Q720 @ 1.60 GHZ CPU and 6GB memory. The proposed approach is designed with Matlab running on Windows 7. The datasets used for experiments were constructed based on real sample images for tomato at different ripeness stages, which were collected from different farms in Minya city. The collected datasets contained colored JPEG images of resolution 3664 X 2748

Figure 7. Block diagram for classification procedure

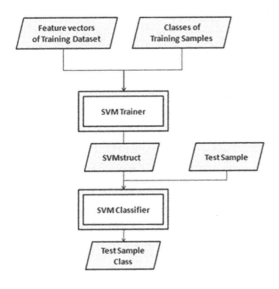

pixels that were captured using Kodak C1013 digital camera of 10.3 megapixels resolution. The dataset is of total 250 images were used for both training and testing datasets with 10-fold cross-validation. Training dataset is divided into 5 classes representing the different stages of tomato ripeness. The classes are Green & Breaker, Turning, Pink, Light Red, and Red stages.

The proposed approach has been implemented considering two scenarios; namely

- **Scenario 1:** One-against-One multi-class SVM system using10-fold cross validation
- **Scenario 2:** One-against-All multi-class SVM system using10-fold cross validation

Scenario 1: One-Against-One Multi-Class SVM System Using10-Fold Cross Validation

The first scenario presents implementing One-against-One multi-class SVM system using10-fold cross-validation and a total of 250 images for both of training and testing datasets. The used features for classification are a combination of color HSV

histogram and color moments and PCA algorithm was applied for features extraction. Moreover, SVM algorithm was employed with different kernel functions that are: Linear kernel, radial basis function (RBF) kernel, and Multi-Layer Perceptron (MLP) kernel and Polynomial kernel for ripeness stage classification. Figure 8 shows classification accuracy obtained via applying each kernel function.

Figures 9 to 16 show 5-class receiver operating characteristic (ROC) curve and area under curve (AUC) for the first two best features resulting from different kernel functions using one-against one multi-class SVM approach with 10-fold cross-validation and total of 250 images (used for both of training and testing). The ROC curve separates each class from other classes.

Figure 9, showing the ROC curve for the best feature using linear kernel function for OAO multi class SVM with cross-validation, the applied approach separated each class from each one of the rest classes by AUCs shown at Table 1.

Figure 10, showing the ROC curve for the second best feature using linear kernel function for OAO multi class SVM with cross-validation, the applied approach separated each class from each one of the rest classes by AUCs shown at Table 2.

Figure 11, showing ROC curve for the best feature using MLP kernel function for OAO

Figure 8. Results for different kernel functions using one-against-one multi-class approach and 10-fold cross-validation

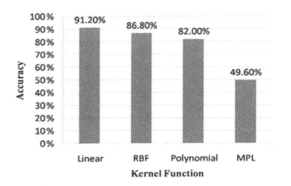

Figure 9. Curve for the best feature using linear kernel function (OAO multi-class SVM with cross-validation), AUC=0.8340

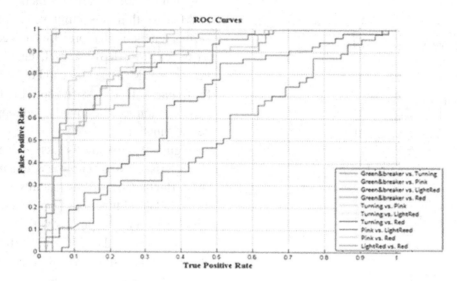

Table 1. AUCs of OAO multiclass-SVM using Linear kernel functions & 10-fold cross validation

	Green & Breaker	Turning	Pink	Light Red	Red
Green & Breaker	-	0.8469	0.9627	0.9612	0.9264
Turning	0.8469	-	0.8969	0.9612	0.9264
Pink	0.9627	0.8969	-	0.5264	0.8592
Light Red	0.9612	0.9612	0.5264	-	0.8298
Red	0.9264	0.9264	0.8592	0.8298	-

Figure 10. Curve for the second best feature using linear kernel function (OAO multi-class SVM with cross-validation), AUC=0.8233

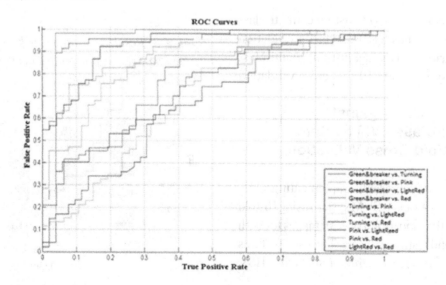

Table 2. AUCs of OAO multiclass-SVM using Linear kernel functions & 10-fold cross validation

	Green & Breaker	Turning	Pink	Light Red	Red
Green & Breaker	-	0.7050	0.8650	0.9424	0.9785
Turning	0.7050	-	0.6759	0.8180	0.9322
Pink	0.8650	0.6759	-	0.6901	0.8639
Light Red	0.9424	0.8180	0.6901	-	0.7615
Red	0.9785	0.9322	0.8639	0.7615	-

Figure 11. Curve for the best feature using MLP kernel function (OAO multi-class SVM with cross-validation), AUC=0.7484

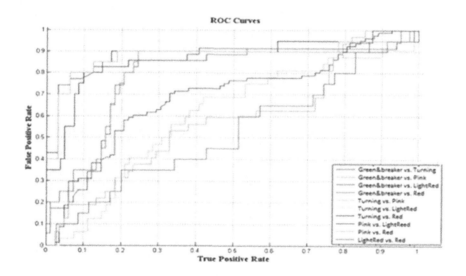

multi-class SVM with cross-validation, the applied approach separated each class from each one of the rest classes by AUCs shown at Table 3.

Figure 12, showing ROC curve for the second best feature using MLP kernel function for OAO multi-class SVM with cross-validation, the applied approach separated each class from each one of the rest classes by AUCs shown at Table 4.

Figure 13, showing ROC curve for the best feature using RBF kernel function for OAO multi-class SVM with cross-validation, the applied approach separated each class from each one of the rest classes by AUCs shown at Table 5.

From Figure 14, showing ROC curve for the second best feature using RBF kernel function for OAO multi-class SVM with cross-validation, the applied approach separated each class from each one of the rest classes by AUCs shown at Table 6.

Figure 15, showing ROC curve for the best feature using Polynomial kernel function for OAO multi-class SVM with cross-validation, the applied approach separated each class from each one of the rest classes by AUCs shown at Table 7.

Figure 16, showing ROC curve for the second best feature using Polynomial kernel function for OAO multi-class SVM with cross-validation, the

Table 3. AUCs of OAO multiclass-SVM using MLP kernel functions & 10-fold cross validation

	Green & Breaker	Turning	Pink	Light Red	Red
Green & Breaker	-	0.6923	0.5774	0.7834	0.7976
Turning	0.6923	-	0.6015	0.8737	0.8741
Pink	0.5774	0.6015	-	0.8799	0.8797
Light Red	0.7834	0.8737	0.8799	-	0.5243
Red	0.7976	0.8741	0.8797	0.5243	-

Figure 12. Curve for the second best feature using MLP kernel function (OAO multi-class SVM with cross-validation), AUC=0.7263

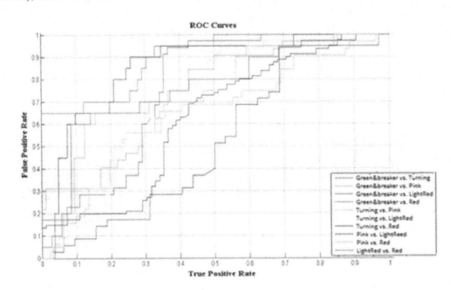

Table 4. AUCs of OAO multiclass-SVM using MLP kernel functions & 10-fold cross validation

	Green & Breaker	Turning	Pink	Light Red	Red
Green & Breaker	-	0.6188	0.7355	0.7549	0.8957
Turning	0.6188	-	0.6431	0.7122	0.8543
Pink	0.7355	0.6431	-	0.5201	0.7469
Light Red	0.7549	0.7122	0.5201	-	0.7543
Red	0.8957	0.8543	0.7469	0.7543	-

Figure 13. ROC curve for the best feature using RBF kernel function (OAO multi-class SVM with cross-validation), AUC=0.8313

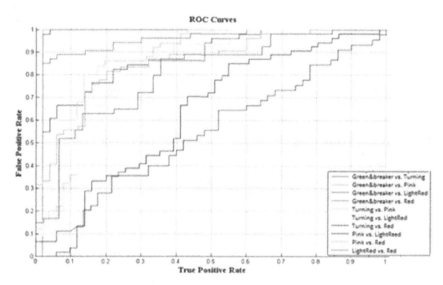

Table 5. AUCs of OAO multiclass-SVM using RBF kernel functions & 10-fold cross validation

	Green & Breaker	Turning	Pink	Light Red	Red
Green & Breaker	-	0.8729	0.9800	0.9796	0.9456
Turning	0.8729	-	0.8678	0.8375	0.6220
Pink	0.9800	0.8678	-	0.5509	0.8552
Light Red	0.9796	0.8375	0.5509	-	0.8012
Red	0.9456	0.6220	0.8552	0.8012	-

applied approach separated each class from each one of the rest classes by AUCs shown at Table 8.

Scenario II: One-Against-All Multi-Class SVM System Using 10-Fold Cross Validation

In the second scenario, the proposed One-against-All multi-class SVM approach was also tested using the previously stated specifications of One-against-One multi-class SVM approach for ripeness stages classification. Figure 17 shows classification accuracy obtained via applying each kernel function.

Figures from 18 to 25 show 5-class receiver operating characteristic (ROC) curve and area under curve (AUC) for the first two best feature for different kernel function using one-against-all multi-class SVM approach with 10-fold cross-validation and total of 250 images (used for both of training and testing).

Figure 18, showing ROC curve for the best feature using linear kernel function for OAA multi class SVM with cross-validation, the applied approach separated each class from each one of the rest classes by AUCs shown at Table 9.

Figure 19, showing ROC curve for the second best feature using linear kernel function for OAA multi class SVM with cross-validation, the applied

Figure 14. ROC curve for the second best feature using RBF kernel function (OAO multi-class SVM with cross-validation), AUC=0.8197

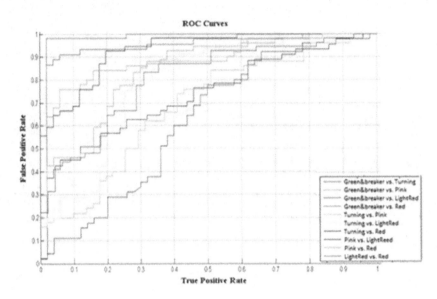

Table 6. AUCs of OAO multiclass-SVM using RBF kernel functions & 10-fold cross validation

	Green & Breaker	Turning	Pink	Light Red	Red
Green & Breaker	-	0.7373	0.8840	0.9467	0.9867
Turning	0.7373	-	0.6808	0.7782	0.9274
Pink	0.8840	0.6808	-	0.6131	0.8422
Light Red	0.9467	0.7782	0.6131	-	0.8008
Red	0.9867	0.9274	0.8422	0.8008	-

Figure 15. ROC curve for the best feature using Polynomial kernel function (OAO multi- class SVM with cross-validation), AUC=0.8223

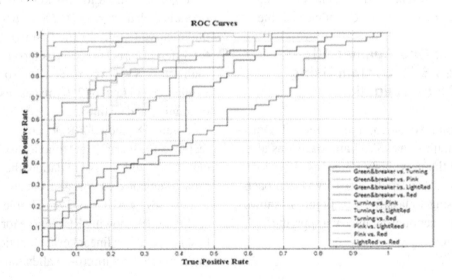

Table 7. AUCs of OAO multiclass-SVM using Polynomial kernel functions & 10-fold cross validation

	Green & Breaker	Turning	Pink	Light Red	Red
Green & Breaker	-	0.8510	0.9804	0.9635	0.9567
Turning	0.8510	-	0.8580	0.8000	0.6338
Pink	0.9804	0.8580	-	0.5724	0.8438
Light Red	0.9635	0.8000	0.5724	-	0.7635
Red	0.9567	0.6338	0.8438	0.7635	-

Figure 16. ROC curve for the second best feature using Polynomial kernel function (OAO multi- class SVM with cross-validation), AUC=0.8205

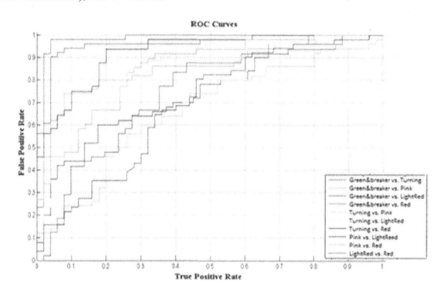

Table 8. AUCs of OAO multiclass-SVM using Polynomial kernel functions & 10-fold cross validation

	Green & Breaker	Turning	Pink	Light Red	Red
Green & Breaker	-	0.7451	0.8502	0.9512	0.9853
Turning	0.7451	-	0.6616	0.8157	0.9225
Pink	0.8502	0.6616	-	0.6845	0.8508
Light Red	0.9512	0.8157	0.6845	-	0.7377
Red	0.9853	0.9225	0.8508	0.7377	-

Figure 17. Results for different kernel functions using one-against-all multi-class approach and 10-fold cross-validation

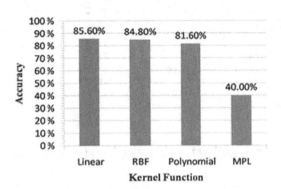

approach separated each class from each one of the rest classes by AUCs shown at Table 10.

Figure 20, showing ROC curve for the best feature using MLP kernel function for OAA multi-class SVM with cross-validation, the applied approach separated each class from each one of the rest classes by AUCs shown at Table 11.

Figure 21, showing ROC curve for the second best feature using MLP kernel function for OAA multi-class SVM with cross-validation, the applied approach separated each class from each one of the rest classes by AUCs shown at Table 12.

Figure 18. ROC curve for the best feature using linear kernel function(OAA multi-class SVM with cross-validation), AUC=0.8233

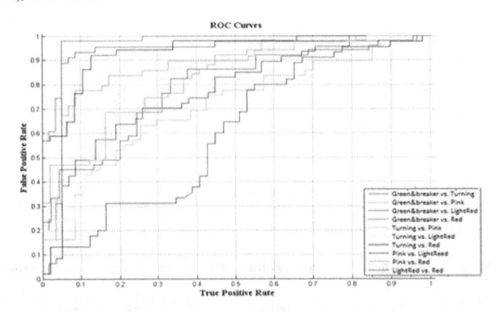

Table 9. AUCs of OAA multiclass-SVM using linear kernel functions & 10-fold cross validation

	Green & Breaker	Turning	Pink	Light Red	Red
Green & Breaker	-	0.7663	0.8776	0.9330	0.9773
Turning	0.7663	-	0.7086	0.8217	0.9378
Pink	0.8776	0.7086	-	0.5998	0.8247
Light Red	0.9330	0.8217	0.5998	-	0.7856
Red	0.9773	0.9378	0.8247	0.7856	-

Figure 19. ROC curve for the second best feature using linear kernel function(OAA multi-class SVM with cross-validation), AUC=0.7882

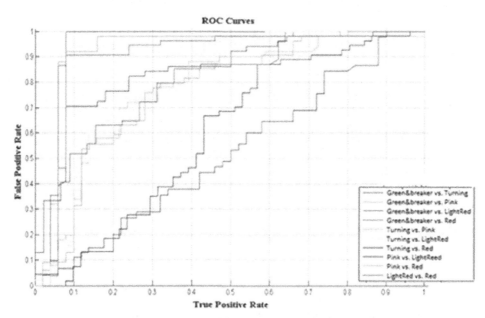

Table 10. AUCs of OAA multiclass-SVM using linear kernel functions & 10-fold cross validation

	Green & Breaker	Turning	Pink	Light Red	Red
Green & Breaker	-	0.8402	0.9264	0.9453	0.9022
Turning	0.8402	-	0.7727	0.8105	0.5951
Pink	0.9264	0.7727	-	0.5176	0.7678
Light Red	0.9453	0.8105	0.5176	-	0.8043
Red	0.9022	0.5951	0.7678	0.8043	-

Figure 22, showing ROC curve for the best feature using RBF kernel function for OAA multi-class SVM with cross-validation, the applied approach separated each class from each one of the rest classes by AUCs shown at Table 13.

Figure 23, showing ROC curve for the second best feature using RBF kernel function for OAA multi-class SVM with cross-validation, the applied approach separated each class from each one of the rest classes by AUCs shown at Table 14.

Figure 24, showing ROC curve for the best feature using Polynomialkernel function for OAA multi-class SVM with cross-validation, the ap-

pliedapproach separated each class from each one of the rest classes by AUCs shown at Table 15.

Figure 25, showing ROC curve for the second best feature using Polynomial kernel function for OAA multi-class SVM with cross-validation, the appliedapproach separated each class from each one of the rest classes by AUCs shown at Table 16.

From the previously depicted experimental results, we found out that the One-against-One multi-class SVM approach is better than the One-against- All multi-class SVM approach, when applied for ripeness stage classification.

Figure 20. ROC curve for the best feature using MLP kernel function (OAA multi-class SVM with cross-validation), AUC=0.7390

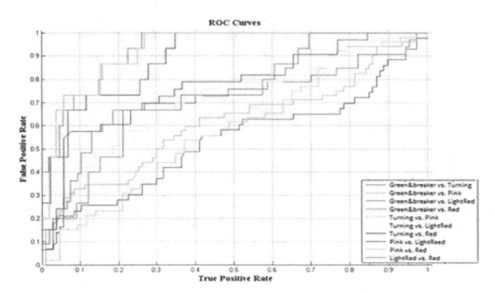

Table 11. AUCs of OAA multiclass-SVM using MLP kernel functions & 10-fold cross validation

	Green & Breaker	Turning	Pink	Light Red	Red
Green & Breaker	-	0.5310	0.6094	0.7133	0.9302
Turning	0.5310	-	0.5814	0.7047	0.8930
Pink	0.6094	0.5814	-	0.7713	0.9282
Light Red	0.7133	0.7047	0.7713	-	0.7273
Red	0.9302	0.8930	0.9282	0.7273	-

Figure 21. ROC curve for the second best feature using MLP kernel function (OAA multi-class SVM with cross-validation), AUC=0.7827

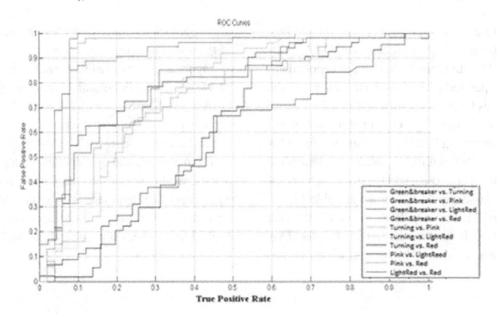

Table 12. AUCs of OAA multiclass-SVM using MLP kernel functions & 10-fold cross validation

	Green & Breaker	Turning	Pink	Light Red	Red
Green & Breaker	-	0.7961	0.9300	0.9498	0.8967
Turning	0.7961	-	0.7575	0.7969	0.5904
Pink	0.9300	0.7575	-	0.5656	0.7437
Light Red	0.9498	0.7969	0.5656	-	0.8004
Red	0.8967	0.5904	0.7437	0.8004	-

Figure 22. ROC curve for the best feature using RBF kernel function(OAA multi-class SVM with cross-validation), AUC=0.8355

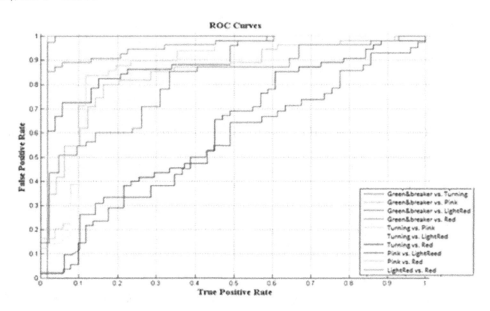

Table 13. AUCs of OAA multiclass-SVM using RBF kernel functions & 10-fold cross validation

	Green & Breaker	Turning	Pink	Light Red	Red
Green & Breaker	-	0.8942	0.9811	0.9807	0.9468
Turning	0.8942	-	0.8796	0.8487	0.6068
Pink	0.9811	0.8796	-	0.5624	0.8505
Light Red	0.9807	0.8487	0.5624	-	0.8043
Red	0.9468	0.6068	0.8505	0.8043	-

Figure 23. ROC curve for the second best feature using RBF kernel function(OAA multi-class SVM with cross-validation), AUC=0.7917

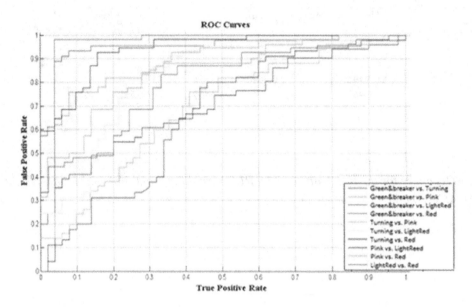

Table 14. AUCs of OAA multiclass-SVM using RBF kernel functions & 10-fold cross validation

	Green & Breaker	Turning	Pink	Light Red	Red
Green & Breaker	-	0.8388	0.9472	0.9609	0.9252
Turning	0.8388	-	0.7982	0.8074	0.5846
Pink	0.9472	0.7982	-	0.5118	0.7641
Light Red	0.9609	0.8074	0.5118	-	0.7790
Red	0.9252	0.5846	0.7641	0.7790	-

Figure 24. ROC curve for the best feature using Polynomial kernel function (OAA multi-class SVM with Cross-validation), AUC=0.8136

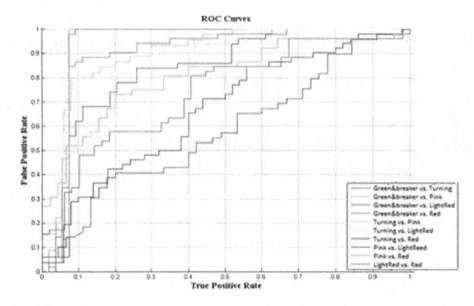

Table 15. AUCs of OAA multiclass-SVM using Polynomial kernel functions & 10-fold cross validation

	Green & Breaker	Turning	Pink	Light Red	Red
Green & Breaker	-	0.8285	0.9403	0.9350	0.8957
Turning	0.8285	-	0.8996	0.8518	0.6627
Pink	0.9403	0.8996	-	0.5785	0.8056
Light Red	0.9350	0.8518	0.5785	-	0.7382
Red	0.8957	0.6627	0.8056	0.7382	-

Figure 26 shows a comparison between accuracies obtained by each of the two approaches.

The accuracy measure is calculated as shown in Equation (9).

$$Accuracy = \frac{number\ of\ correctly\ classified\ images}{total\ number\ of\ testing\ images}$$

FUTURE RESEARCH DIRECTIONS

There are many problem related to this topic. These problems suggest a variety of research directions. One such direction would be to use this system for other crops or apply it to different applications.

another direction is to utilize this system for the whole automation process of harvest. Another direction is to work at the trend of crops diseases and develop automated system for diseases detection and classification.

CONCLUSION

In this chapter, a system for classifying the ripeness stages of tomato has been developed. The proposed system has three main stages; pre-processing, feature extraction and ripeness classification. The proposed classification approach was implemented by applying resizing, background removal,

Figure 25. ROC curve for the second best feature using Polynomial kernel function(OAA multi-class SVM with cross-validation), AUC=0.7937

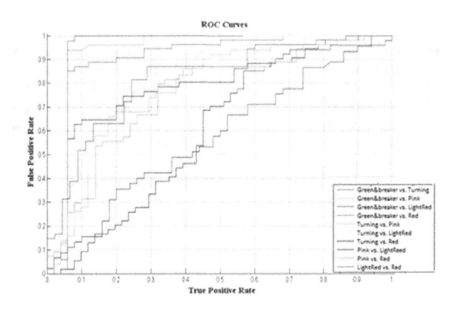

Table 16. AUCs of OAA multiclass-SVM using Polynomial kernel functions & 10-fold cross validation

	Green & Breaker	Turning	Pink	Light Red	Red
Green & Breaker	-	0.7835	0.9338	0.9440	0.9030
Turning	0.7835	-	0.7878	0.8362	0.5984
Pink	0.9338	0.7878	-	0.5758	0.7559
Light Red	0.9440	0.8362	0.5758	-	0.8189
Red	0.9030	0.5984	0.7559	0.8189	-

Figure 26. Comparison between the classification accuracy of OAA and OAO multi-class SVM approaches

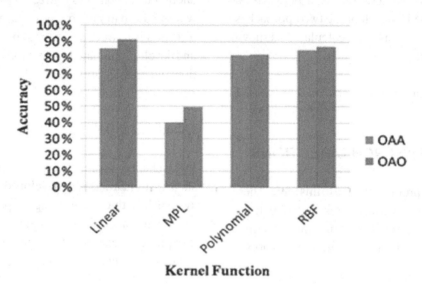

and extracting color components for each image. Then, feature extraction was applied to each preprocessed image, HSV histogram and color moments are obtained as a feature vector, and used as a PCA inputs for transformation.

Finally, SVM model is developed for ripeness stage classification. The proposed approach has been implemented considering two scenarios via applying One-against-One multi-class SVM system using10-fold cross-validation and One-against-All multi-class SVM system using10-fold cross-validation. Based on the obtained the experimental results, the highest ripeness classification accuracies of 91.20% and 85.60% have been achieved by the first scenario and the second scenarios, respectively, using linear kernel function. Thus, it can be concluded that the ripeness classification accuracy obtained by the OAO multi-class SVM approach is better than ripeness classification accuracy obtained by the OAA multi-class SVM approach.

REFERENCES

Ada, & RajneetKaur. (2012). Feature Extraction and Principal Component Analysis for Lung Cancer Detection in CT scan Images. *International Journal of Advanced Research in Computer Science and Software Engineering*, 213-218.

Anthony, G., Gregg, H., & Tshilidzi, M. (2007). Image Classification Using SVMs: One-against-One Vs One-against-All. *in Proc. of the 28th Asian Conference on Remote Sensing*.

Aranda-Sanchez, J., Baltazar, A., & Gonzlez-Aguilar, G. (2009). Implementation of a Bayesian classi. *Biosystems Engineering*, 2(102), 274–284. doi:10.1016/j.biosystemseng.2008.12.005

balestani, A., Moghaddam, P., motlaq, A., & Dolaty, H. (2012). Sorting and Grading of Cherries on the Basis of Ripeness, Size and Defects by Using Image Processing Techniques. *International Journal of Agriculture and Crop Sciences(IJACS)*, 4 (16), 1144-1149.

Baltazar, A., Aranda, J., & Gonzalez-Aguilar, G. (2008). Bayesian classification of ripening stages of tomato fruit using acoustic impact and color-imeter sensor data. *Computers and Electronics in Agriculture*, 60(2), 113–121. doi:10.1016/j.compag.2007.07.005

Boolchandani, D., & Sahula, V. (2011). *Int. Journal of design, analysis, and tools for circuits and systems, 1*, 1-8.

Brezmes, J., Llobet, E., Vilanova, X., Saiz, G., & Correig, X. (2000). Fruit ripeness monitoring using an electronic nose. *Sensors and Actuators B-Chem Journal, 69*, 223–229. doi:10.1016/S0925-4005(00)00494-9

Camelo, A. L. (2004). Manual for the preparation and sale of fruits and vegetables From field to market (version 151 ed.). Rome: in Food ans Agriculture Organization (FAO) of the United Nations (UN), Agricultural Services Bulletin.

Coates, L., & Johnson, G. (1997). Postharvest Diseases of Fruit and Vegetables. In J. Brown, & H. Ogle (Eds.), *Plant pathogens and plant diseases*. Armidale: Rockvale Publications.

Cowan, A., Cripps, R., Richings, E., & Taylor, N. (2001). Fruit size: towards an understanding of the metabolic control of fruit growth using avocado as a model system. *Physiologia Plantarum, 111*, 127–139. doi:10.1034/j.1399-3054.2001.1110201.x

Dadwal, S. M., & Banga, V. (2012). Estimate Ripeness Level of fruits Using RGB Color Space and Fuzzy Logic Technique. [IJEAT]. *International Journal of Engineering and Advanced Technology, 02*(01), 225–229.

Damiri, D., & Slamet, C. (2012). Application of Image Processing and Artificial Neural Networks to Identify Ripeness and Maturity of the Lime(citrus medica). *International Journal of Basic and Applied Science 01*(02), 171–179.

Effendi, Z., Ramli, R., & Ghani, J. (2010). A Back Propagation Neural Networks for Grading Jatropha curcas Fruits Maturity. *American Journal of Applied Sciences*, 390–394. doi:10.3844/ajassp.2010.390.394

El-Bendary, N., Zawbaa, H. M., Hassanien, A. E., & Snasel, V. (2011). PCA-based Home Videos Annotation System. *The International Journal of Reasoning-based Intelligent Systems, 3*(2), 71–79.

El-Bendary, N., Zawbaa, H. M., Hassanien, A. E., & Snasel, V. (2011). PCA-based Home Videos Annotation System. [IJRIS]. *The International Journal of Reasoning-based Intelligent Systems, 3*(2), 71–79.

Elhariri, E., El-Bendary, N., Fouad, M. M., Plato, J., Hassanien, A. E., & Hussein, A. M. (2014). Multi-class SVM Based Classification Approach for Tomato Ripeness. *Innovations in Bio-inspired Computing and Applications* [Springer.]. *Advances in Intelligent Systems and Computing., 237,* 175–186. doi:10.1007/978-3-319-01781-5_17

Fadilah, N., Mohamad-Saleh, J., Halim, Z. A., Ibrahim, H., & Ali, S. S. (2012). Intelligent Color Vision System for Ripeness Classification of Oil Palm Fresh Fruit Bunch. *Sensors (Basel, Switzerland), 12,* 14179–14195. doi:10.3390/s121014179 PMID:23202043

Ghazali, K. H., Samad, R., Arshad, N. W., & Karim, R. A. (2009). Image Processing Analysis of Oil Palm Fruits for Automatic Grading. *International Conference on Instrumentation, Control & Automation* (pp. 75-78). Bandung, Indonesia: ica-itb.

Hahn, F. (2002). Multi-spectral prediction of unripe tomatoes. *Biosystems Engineering, 81*(2), 147–155. doi:10.1006/bioe.2001.0035

Jaffar, A., Jaafar, R., Jamil, N., Low, C. Y., & Abdullah, B. (2009). Photogrammetric Grading of Oil Palm Fresh Fruit Bunches. *International Journal of Mechanical & Mechatronics Engineering, 9*(10), 18–24.

Liu, Y., & Zheng, Y. F. (2005). One-against-all multi-class SVM classification using reliability measures. *in Proc. IEEE International Joint Conference on Neural Networks (IJCNN'05), 2,* pp. 849-854. Montreal, Quebec, Canada.

May, Z., & Amaran, M. H. (2011). Automated Ripeness Assessment of Oil Palm Fruit Using RGB and Fuzzy Logic Technique. *Proceedings of the 13th WSEAS International Conference on Mathematical and Computational Methods in Science and Engineering* (pp. 52-59). World Scientific and Engineering Academy and Society (WSEAS).

Meskaldji, K., Boucherkha, S., & Chikhi, S. (2009). Color quantization and its impact on color histogram based image retrieval accuracy. *Proc. The First International Conference on Networked Digital Technologies(NDT '09),* (pp. 515-517). Ostrava, Czech Republic.

Molyneux, S., Lister, C., & Savage, G. (2004). An investigation of the antioxidant properties and colour of glasshouse grown tomatoes. *International Journal of Food Sciences and Nutrition, 55,* 537–545. doi:10.1080/09637480400015828 PMID:16019297

Paulraj, M., Hema, C. R., & Pranesh, R. K., & Siti Sofiah, M. R. (2009). Color recognition algorithm using a neural network model in determining the ripeness of a Banana. *Proceedings of the International Conference on Man-Machine Systems (ICoMMS 2009)* (pp. 2B71-2B74). Penang, Malaysia: Universiti Malaysia Perlis.

Polder, G., Heijden, G. W., & Young, I. T. (2002). Spectral Image Analysis For Measuring Ripeness Of Tomatoes. *Transactions-American Society of Agricultural Engineers International Journal, 45*(4), 1155–1162.

Prasanna, V., Prabha, T., & Tharanathan, R. (2007). Fruit Ripening Phenomena An Overview. [Taylor & Francis Ltd.]. *Critical Reviews in Food Science and Nutrition,* 1–19. doi:10.1080/10408390600976841 PMID:17364693

Rodrguez-Pulido, F., Gordillo, B., Gonzlez-Miret, M., & Heredia, F. (2013). Analysis of food appearance properties by computer vision applying ellipsoids to colour data. *Computers and Electronics in Agriculture, 99*, 108–115. doi:10.1016/j.compag.2013.08.027

Shah Rizam, M. S., Farah Yasmin, A. R., Ahmad Ihsan, M. Y., & Shazana, K. (2009). Nondestructive Watermelon Ripeness Determination Using Image Processing and Artificial Neural Network (ANN). *International Journal of Intelligent Technology, 4*(2), 130–134.

Shahbahrami, A., Borodin, D., & Juurlink, B. (2008). Comparison between color and texture features for image retrieval. *Proc. 19th Annual Workshop on Circuits, Systems and Signal Processing (ProRisc 2008).* Veldhoven, The Netherlands: STW.

Singh, S., & Hemachandra, K. (2012). Content-Based Image Retrieval using Color Moment and Gabor Based Image Retrieval using Color Moment and Gabor Texture Feature. *IJCSI International Journal of Computer Science Issues, 9* (5).

Soman, S., Ghorpade, M., Sonone, V., & Chavan, S. (2012). Content Based Image Retrieval using Advanced Color and Texture Features. *Proc. International Conference in Computational Intelligence (ICCIA2012).* New York, USA.

Suganthy, M., & Ramamoorthy, P. (2012). Principal Component Analysis Based Feature Extraction, Morphological Edge Detection and Localization for Fast Iris Recognition. *Journal of Computer Science, 8*(9), 1428–1433. doi:10.3844/jcssp.2012.1428.1433

Suralkar, S., Karode, A. H., & Pawad, P. W. (2012). Texture Image Classification Using Support Vector Machine. *International Journal of Computer Applications in Technology, 3*, 71–75.

Syal, S., Mehta, T., & Darshni, P. (2013). Design & Development of Intelligent System for Grading of Jatropha Fruit by Its Feature Value Extraction Using Fuzzy Logics. [IJARCSSE]. *International Journal of Advanced Research in Computer Science and Software Engineering, 3*(7), 1077–1081.

Tzotsos, A. D. A. (2006). A support vector machine approach for object based image analysis. *in Proc. international conference on object based image analysis (OBIA06).* Salzburg, Austria.

U.S.D.A. (1991). Retrieved March 2013, from United States Standards for Grades of Fresh Tomatoes, U.S. Dept. Agric./AMS, Washington, DC: http://www.ams.usda.gov/standards/vegfm.htm

Vanschoenwinkel, B., & Manderick, B. (2005). Appropriate kernel functions for support vector machine learning with sequences of symbolic data. *Deterministic and Statistical Methods in Machine Learning in Computer Science, 3635*, 256–280. doi:10.1007/11559887_16

Wu, Q., & Zhou, D.-X. (2006). Analysis of support vector machine classification. *Journal of Computational Analysis and Applications, 8*, 99119.

Xiao, B. (2010). Principal component analysis for feature extraction of image sequence. *International Conference On Computer and Communication Technologies in Agriculture Engineering (CCTAE). 1*, pp. 250-253. Chengdu, China: IEEE.

Yu, H., Li, M., Zhang, H.-J., & Feng, J. (2002). Color texture moments for content-based image retrieval, " in Proc. International Conference., *3*, pp. 929-932. Rochester, New York, USA.

Zawbaa, H. M., El-Bendary, N., Hassanien, A. E., & Abraham, A. (2011). SVM-based Soccer Video Summarization System. *in Proc. The Third IEEE World Congress on Nature and Biologically Inspired Computing (NaBIC2011)*, (pp. 7-11). Salamanca, Spain.

Zawbaa, H. M., El-Bendary, N., Hassanien, A. E., & Kim, T.-H. (2011). Machine Learning-Based Soccer Video Summarization System. In *Proc. Multimedia, Computer Graphics and Broadcasting FGIT-MulGraB (2). 263, pp* (pp. 19–28). Jeju Island, Korea: Springer. doi:10.1007/978-3-642-27186-1_3

Zhang, L., & McCarthy, M. (2011). Measurement and evaluation of tomato maturity using magnetic resonance imaging. *Postharvest Biology and Technology*, *67*, 37–43. doi:10.1016/j.postharvbio.2011.12.004

Zhang, Y., Xie, X., & Cheng, T. (2010). Application of PSO and SVM in image classification. *in Proc. 3rd IEEE International Conference on Computer Science and Information Technology (ICCSIT)*, *6*, pp. 629-631. Chengdu, China.

KEY TERMS AND DEFINITIONS

Climacteric Fruits: Fruits which can continue ripening after being picked from the mother plant.

Image Classification: The process of analyzing the properties of images features then organizing these images into categories/classes in according to its visual content.

Non-Climacteric Fruits: Fruits which can ripen only when it is attached to the mother plant.

Principal Component Analysis (PCA): PCA is a statistical technique, widely used in recognition, compression for dimensionality reduction, data representation and features extraction.

Ripeness: Ripeness is a process that causes fruits to become more palatable. Simply, a fruit becomes sweeter, less green, and softer as it ripens.

Ripeness Assessment: The process of determining and evaluating ripeness stage of fruits.

Support Vector Machine (SVM): SVM is one of the most used machine learning algorithms for classification and regression problems.

Chapter 7
Magnitude and Phase of Discriminative Orthogonal Radial Moments for Face Recognition

Neerja Mittal
CSIR- Central Scientific Instruments Organisation, India

Ekta Walia
South Asian University, India

Chandan Singh
Punjabi University, India

ABSTRACT

It is well known that the careful selection of a set of features, with higher discrimination competence, may increase recognition performance. In general, the magnitude coefficients of some selected orders of ZMs and PZMs have been used as invariant image features. The authors have used a statistical method to estimate the discrimination strength of all the coefficients of ZMs and PZMs. For classification, only the coefficients with estimated higher discrimination strength are selected and are used in the feature vector. The performance of these selected Discriminative ZMs (DZMs) and Discriminative PZMs (DPZMs) features are compared to that of their corresponding conventional approaches on YALE, ORL, and FERET databases against illumination, expression, scale, and pose variations. In this chapter, an extension to these DZMs and DPZMs is presented by exploring the use of phase information along with the magnitude coefficients of these approaches. As the phase coefficients are computed in parallel to the magnitude, no additional time is spent on their computation. Further, DZMs and DPZMs are also combined with PCA and FLD. It is observed from the exhaustive experimentation that with the inclusion of phase features the recognition rate is improved by 2-8%, at reduced dimensions and with less computational complexity, than that of using the successive ZMs and PZMs features.

DOI: 10.4018/978-1-4666-6030-4.ch007

INTRODUCTION

The main objective of face recognition system is to identify a person in the database of stored face images. These days it is one of the most popular research topics because of having many commercial and law enforcement applications, e.g. criminal identification at public places, human computer interaction, video surveillance, bankcard verification, etc. Although there exist some good reliable methods of human identification such as iris recognition, fingerprint recognition, etc., these methods depend on the cooperation of individuals, whereas a face recognition system can work without the support or knowledge of the targets. Most of the face recognition approaches lack in satisfactory results under the conditions of lighting directions, pose variation, aging, occlusion and real world problems, etc. (Zhao et al., 2003).

In literature, the existing face recognition approaches are broadly classified into two categories, namely, local methods and the global methods (Hjelmas & Low, 2001). In local methods, structural features of facial shape like eyes, nose and mouth are analyzed. These methods are not affected by irrelevant information in the images, but are sensitive to unpredictability of face appearance and noise. Global methods are statistics based methods which use the complete information of faces and are less sensitive to noise. Principal component analysis (PCA) (Burton et al., 2005; Neerja & Walia, 2008; Moon & Phillips, 2001; Turk, 2001), Fisher linear discriminant (FLD) (Belhumeur et al., 2005; Etemad & Chellappa, 1997; Martinez & Kak, 2001), two-dimensional PCA (2DPCA) (Xu et al. 2008), two-directional two-dimensional PCA (2D^{2}PCA) (Daoqiang & Zhi-Hua, 2005) and moment invariants (Singh, 2006; Teh & Chin, 1988; Wee & Paramesran, 2007) fall under the category of global methods. Orthogonal radial moments and their functions have been used as useful image features in a number of applications (Teague, 1980). Among these orthogonal radial moment based methods,

Zernike moments (ZMs) and pseudo-Zernike moments (PZMs) are particularly useful because they are less susceptible to information redundancy and image noise. The magnitude of these orthogonal radial moments is invariant to rotation and under certain geometric transformations they can be made invariant to scale and translation. Some work has already been done to present the usefulness of moment based invariant features for the recognition of face images (Nor'aini et al., 2006; Singh et al., 2011a; Singh et al., 2011b; Singh et al., 2011c). A comparative analysis of different moment invariants is presented in (Faez & Farajzadeh, 2006; Nabatchian et al., 2008). Nor'aini et al. (2006) have observed that the ZMs are able to recognize face images better than PCA because of its characteristics of being invariant to rotation and insensitivity to image noise. PZMs using neural network classifier (Haddandnia et al., 2003) and the ZMs/PZMs using optimal similarity measure (Singh et al., 2011b) gave better results as compared to the Euclidean distance classifier.

The Eigenface based methods like PCA and LDA generate high dimensional feature vectors which make use of large memory space and suffer from high computational time. These methods require eigenvalue decomposition, which is very time consuming for feature vectors with high dimensions. Also in LDA, if number of coefficients in feature vector is more than the number of training images then it creates singularity problem namely small-sample-size problem. To overcome these problems, some preprocessing steps for reducing the size of feature vector, are required by these methods. The PZMs feature vectors of size 100 are provided as input to FLD to obtain an enhanced vector of moment features by maximizing the between-class variance while minimizing the within-class variance (Pang et al., 2006). Kernel Fisher PZMs (KFPZMs) is used to map the moment based features into the high dimensional feature space via kernel function which carry significant information about image (Pang et al., 2005). Prior to applying the FLD approach, the methods of using the moment based features reduce the size of feature vector significantly that provide a stable numerical computation and overcome the small-sample-size problem.

Jing et al. (2004) have proposed an image recognition approach to select the useful DCT frequency bands by using the 2-D separability judgment. Thereafter, it selects the linear discriminative features by an improved Fisherface method followed by the nearest neighbor classifier for classification of images. Detailed analysis proves the theoretical advantages of this approach over other frequency domain transform techniques. Cheng et al. (2010) have designed an incremental discriminant embedding algorithm that preserves local discriminative information for classification. This method learns the discriminative submanifold structures incrementally and extracts the discriminative features in the local discriminant subspace. A discriminative model to recognize the face images in presence of age variation is proposed by Li et al. (2011). In this work, the authors have used scale invariant feature transform (SIFT) and multi-scale local binary patterns (MLBP) as the local descriptors. Also, Multi-feature discriminant analysis (MFDA) is developed to process these two local feature spaces in a unified framework. By random sampling the training set as well as the feature space, multiple LDA-based classifiers are constructed and then combined to generate a robust decision via a fusion rule.

Many practical face recognition applications such as law enhancement, e-passport, and ID card identification, etc. usually enroll a single sample per person (SSPP). Many popular face recognition methods fail to work well in this scenario because there are not enough samples for discriminant learning. In contrast to the conventional appearance-based face recognition methods wherein multiple samples per person are (MSPP) available for discriminative feature extraction during the training phase, Lu et al. (2013) have presented a novel discriminative multimanifold analysis (DMMA) method by learning discriminative

features from image patches. In their approach, each enrolled face image is divided into several non-overlapping patches to form an image set for each sample per person. Then, the SSPP face recognition is framed as a manifold-manifold matching problem and multiple DMMA feature spaces are learned to maximize the manifold margins of different persons and reconstruction-based manifold-manifold distance is used to identify the unlabeled subjects.

Blur-robust face image descriptor based on Local Phase Quantization (LPQ) and its extension to a multiscale framework (MLPQ) has shown promising results against the illumination variation (Chan et al. 2013). To maximize the insensitivity to misalignment, the MLPQ descriptor is computed regionally by adopting a component-based framework. Second, the regional features are combined using kernel fusion. Third, the proposed MLPQ representation is combined with the Multiscale Local Binary Pattern (MLBP) descriptor using kernel fusion to increase insensitivity to illumination. Kernel Discriminant Analysis (KDA) of the combined features extracts discriminative information for face recognition. This approach has been comprehensively evaluated using the combined Yale and Extended Yale database B (degraded by artificially induced linear motion blur) as well as the FERET, FRGC 2.0, and LFW databases. Lu et al. (2012) have carried out a method to learn a discriminative feature subspace by making use of both labeled and unlabeled samples and explore different cost information of all the training samples simultaneously.

BACKGROUND

The success of face recognition system fully depends on the discrimination competence of invariant features obtained from the methods used to represent the facial images. In next step, the classification is performed using these features only. So, the discriminative strength of the selected invariant features should be very high. In practice, all of the extracted image features do not have the same strength of discrimination. If non-discriminative features are selected to perform classification, even the best classifier may also fail to give good recognition performance. In pattern recognition problems, one of the most crucial steps is the selection of highly discriminative features while preserving the reduced size of feature vectors. Statistically, the discriminative features must have the small within-class and large interclass variation. Shen et al. (1999) presented the wavelet moment invariant method that extracts the local and global image features jointly with an approach to select the discriminative features. Kan et al. (2001) have observed in their work that the method proposed by Shen et al. needs large number of training images to have sufficient information to discriminate the objects and secondly, it only uses within-class information to weight the features.

Recently, a lot of work is going on the selection and use of discriminative features for robust classification. Various techniques have been designed, such as LDA for selection of discriminative features (Lei et al. 2012), Sparse Representation Classifier Steered Discriminative Projection (Yang et al. 2013), label consistent K-SVD (LC-KSVD) to learn a discriminative dictionary for sparse coding (Jiang et al. 2013), etc. Lei et al. (2014) have observed that local feature descriptor is an important module for face recognition as Gabor and local binary patterns (LBP) have proven to be one of the effective face descriptors. The authors proposed a method to learn a discriminant face descriptor (DFD) in a data-driven way. The idea is to learn the most discriminant local features that minimize the difference of the features between images of the same person and maximize that between images from different people. Three useful aspects to enhance the discriminative ability of face representation were constructed as the discriminant image filters, the optimal neighborhood sampling strategy and the dominant patterns. Extensive experiments on FERET, CAS-PEAL-R1, LFW,

and HFB face databases validate the effectiveness of the DFD learning on both homogeneous and heterogeneous face recognition problems.

The importance of discrete cosine transform (DCT) together with discrimination power analysis in the area of face recognition has been presented by Dabbaghchian et al. (2010). The authors in this paper have presented a statistical approach to select the discriminative features from a set of premasked DCT coefficients. In their experiments on ORL and Yale face databases, the selected DCT features when combined with PCA and LDA methods produce improved results. However, this approach may not perform well in presence of in-plane image rotation or pose variations as DCT features are not rotation invariant. The usefulness of Gabor phase information as well as its fusion with Gabor magnitude has been investigated for the recognition of face images by Xie et al. (2010). Unlike previous work, this study indicates that Gabor phase might embody more (at least equal) discriminating power than Gabor magnitude, only if it is appropriately exploited. Herein, the authors reveal that methods based on local Gabor patterns work reasonably well under relatively simple testing scenarios but they all degrade abruptly when the testing is challenging with large variations due to unconstrained imaging conditions, e.g., FERET DupI, DupII. This observation might imply that these local pattern methods are sensitive to large extrinsic variations. The challenging problems caused by unconstrained conditions are well addressed by combining local Gabor patterns with the proposed block-based Fisher's linear Discriminant (BFLD) method. Impressive improvements are achieved on FERET DupI, DupII, and FRGC 2.0, which safely validate the effectiveness of BFLD for challenging testing scenarios. Finally, as expected, the fusion of magnitude and phase further enhance the recognition accuracy when they are encoded by local patterns and combined with BFLD. The authors applied score-level fusion and simply combine component classifiers by sum rule. It is evidently not optimal, better statistical fusion schemes may be employed. Additionally, as one statistical learning method, the generalization ability of BFLD method is influenced greatly by the training set and more efforts are required to improve its performance for out-of-sample problem.

We have applied an approach similar to the technique proposed by Dabbaghchian et al. (2010), to measure the discrimination competence of ZMs and PZMs based features. The values depicting the discrimination strength, are estimated for all the coefficients extracted from the ZMs and PZMs approaches. For classification, only the coefficients with higher discrimination values are used in the feature vector. The ZMs and PZMs based approaches comprising of only the highly discriminative features are referred to as discriminative ZMs (DZMs) and discriminative PZMs (DPZMs). The performance of the proposed DZMs and DPZMs approaches is compared to that of their corresponding conventional approaches on Yale, ORL and FERET face databases with illumination, expression, rotation and scale variations. From the extensive experimental analysis, it is observed that the recognition performance of DZMs and DPZMs increases by 2-6% as compared to their non-discriminative counterparts.

Herein, an extension to our previously applied DZMs and DPZMs approaches is presented by including the phase coefficients of these selected discriminative features (along with their magnitude coefficients) which are depicted as DZMs(magPhase) and DPZMs(magPhase). The procedure to remove the effect of rotation from the phase coefficients and to use these values with magnitude features is described by Singh et al., (2011a). Further, DZMs and DPZMs are also combined with PCA and FLD namely discriminative ZMs+PCA (DZMs+PCA), discriminative PZMs+PCA (DPZMs+PCA), discriminative ZMs+FLD (DZMs+FLD) and discriminative PZMs+FLD (DPZMs+FLD). The proposed extension has resulted in significant improvement in recognition performance at reduced dimensions and with less computational complexity.

Zernike Moments (ZMs)

The ZMs features are the projection of the image function $f(x,y)$ on a set of complete orthogonal kernel functions on the unit disk. The Zernike polynomials $V_{nm}(x,y)$ of order n with repetition m, within the unit disc are given by

$$V_{nm}(x,y) = R_{nm}(x,y)e^{jm\theta} \qquad (1)$$

where

$$j = \sqrt{-1},$$

$$\theta = \tan^{-1}\left(\frac{y}{x}\right), \ \theta \in [0, 2\pi], \qquad (2)$$

and

$$R_{nm}(x,y) = \sum_{s=0}^{\frac{n-|m|}{2}} \frac{(-1)^s (x^2+y^2)^{\frac{n-2s}{2}} (n-s)!}{s!\left(\frac{n+|m|}{2}-s\right)!\left(\frac{n-|m|}{2}-s\right)!} \qquad (3)$$

The parameters n and m are integers such that $n \geq 0, |m| \leq n$, and $n - |m| = even$. The ZMs of order n and repetition m of a function $f(x,y)$ are defined by

$$Z_{nm} = \frac{n+1}{\pi} \int_{x^2+y^2\leq 1} \int f(x,y)V_{nm}^*(x,y)dxdy \qquad (4)$$

where $V_{nm}^*(x,y)$ is the complex conjugate of $V_{nm}(x,y)$. To compute the ZMs of a digital image, Zernike basis functions are defined within a unit circle, in which case the pixels located outside the circle are not involved in the calculation. Since there does not exist an analytical solution to Equation (4), the zero[th] order approximation is given by

$$Z_{nm} = \frac{n+1}{\pi} \sum_{\substack{i=0 \\ x_i^2+y_k^2 \le 1}}^{N-1} \sum_{k=0}^{N-1} f(x_i, y_k) V_{nm}^*(x_i, y_k) \Delta x_i \Delta y_k$$

(5)

where

$$x_i = \frac{2i+1-N}{D},$$
$$y_k = \frac{2k+1-N}{D},$$
$$and \quad \Delta x_i = \Delta y_k = \frac{2}{D}$$

(6)

with

$$D = \begin{cases} N, & \text{for inscribed circle} \\ N\sqrt{2}, & \text{for outer circle containing the complete image} \end{cases}$$

(7)

In the present analysis, we have taken $D = N\sqrt{2}$. In this computation, the normalization factor is the number of pixels located in the unit circle (Teh & Chin, 1988; Wee & Paramesran, 2007). The magnitude of ZMs with $m \ge 0$ is only used as feature vector since $Z_{n,-m} = Z_{nm}^*$ and $\left| Z_{n,m} \right| = \left| Z_{n,-m} \right|$. The image can be reconstructed by applying the inverse transformation as:

$$\hat{f}(x_i, y_k) = \sum_{n=0}^{n_{max}} \sum_{m=-n}^{n} Z_{nm} V_{nm}(x_i, y_k)$$

(8)

Pseudo Zernike Moments (PZMs)

The PZMs are similar to the ZMs except for the condition $n - \left| m \right| = even$. This means the definition in Equation (4) is also applicable to PZMs. The kernel functions for PZMs have the same form as defined for ZMs in Equation (1) except for the radial polynomial which are given as:

$$R_{nm}(x, y) = \sum_{s=0}^{n-|m|} \frac{(-1)^s (x^2+y^2)^{n-s}(2n+1-s)!}{s! \left(n + |m| + 1 - s \right)! \left(n - |m| - s \right)!}$$

(9)

and $0 \le \left| m \right| \le n, \ n \ge 0$. For a given maximum order, n_{max}, the total number of PZMs is $(n_{max} + 1)^2$ which is almost double the total number of ZMs for the same n_{max}, i.e

$$\frac{1}{2}(n_{max} + 1)(n_{max} + 2).$$

PCA and FLD

PCA and FLD have become standard techniques in the area of face recognition. For a given p-dimensional vector representation of an image, in a training set of q images, PCA tends to find an q dimensional subspace whose basis vectors correspond to the maximum variance direction in the original image space. The new subspace has a lower dimension compared to the original space $(q \ll p)$. All images of known faces are projected onto the face space to find sets of weights that describe the contribution of each vector. For more details one can refer to the method described by (Turk, 2001). FLD is a class specific method that aims to produce a linear transformation that stresses the between-class differences while minimizing the within-class differences. FLD searches for the projection axes on which the face images of different classes are far from each other and at the same time where the images of the same class are close to each other. The goal is to create a subspace that is linearly separable between-classes (Etemad & Chellappa, 1997). Clearly, FLD aims to find the most discriminative features whereas PCA looks for the features which are good for face representation.

DISCRIMINATIVE FEATURE ANALYSIS AND FEATURE SELECTION

Procedure

The discriminative strength of a feature can be estimated by evaluating the within-class and between-class variance of training images. In case of a particular feature, a large value obtained from the ratio of between-class to within-class variance, demonstrates that the discrimination strength of the said feature is higher than others. In order to estimate the discrimination strength of ZMs and PZMs features, we have used an approach similar to the one proposed by Dabbaghchian et al. (2010). The step by step procedure carried out for the evaluation of discrimination power of the features, is given as follows:

1. Randomly divide the images in the database in training and test sets.
2. Calculate ZMs or PZMs features as described in *Section 2*.
3. Normalize the features in the feature vector.
4. Let n_t be the total number of features in the feature vector before making discriminative analysis. Estimate the value, D_i demonstrating the discrimination strength of ith feature as follows:
   a. Calculate the within-class variance Vw_i for i^{th} feature
   b. Calculate the between-class variance Vb_i for i^{th} feature
   c. Compute $D_i = \dfrac{Vb_i}{Vw_i}$
5. Sort this vector D_i ($1 \leq i \leq n_t$) in descending order and select the top n_f features with highest discrimination values in the final feature vector.
6. Classify the images in test set with some classifier.

Classifier Used

For the classification of test images we have used the Euclidean distance ($L_2 - norm$) classifier. For two vectors $A = \{a_i\}$ and $B = \{b_i\}$, $L_2 - norm$ is computed as:

$$d_2 = \sqrt{\sum_{i=1}^{n_f} (a_i - b_i)^2} \qquad (10)$$

where n_f is the number of features selected for classification.

Analysis

The successive ZMs and PZMs moment features for certain order of moments are normally selected in the feature vector, e.g. on taking the successive features for a maximum order of moments $n_{max} = 12$, a total of 49 elements will be generated in the feature vector. Besides this, the first two features of ZMs ($Z_{0,0}$, $Z_{1,1}$) and first three features of PZMs ($P_{0,0}$, $P_{1,0}$, $P_{1,1}$) are not included in the feature vectors for classification. In this subsection, we have analysed discrimination strength of ZMs and PZMs features at a given maximum order of moments.

The experiments are performed on Yale database (Georghiades, 1997) with illumination and expression variations, ORL database (AT&T, 2002) with expression, scale and small pose variations, grayscale FERET database (Phillips et al., 2000) with yaw rotation (pose) variation. Detailed description of these databases is as follows:

1. **Yale database:** The Yale face database contains 11 images per person for 15 individuals resulting to a total of 165 images. The images in this database reveal major variations of illumination changes, different facial expressions and persons with or with-

out eyeglasses. The original size of images in this database is 243×320 pixels with 256 gray levels. For the experiments, the size of these images is scaled down to 60×80 pixels. Sample images from this database, for one person, are shown in Figure 1(a).

2. **ORL database:** This database contains a total of *400* images of size *112×92* pixels of *40* persons with *10* images per person in different states of variations. All the face images in this database are taken against a dark homogenous background. These images contain pose variation of slight tilt/yaw upto $\pm 20^0$ with some basic facial expressions (smiling/not smiling, open/closed eyes). For the experiments, the size of these images is scaled down to *56×46* pixels. Sample images for one person from this database are shown in Figure 1(b).

3. **FERET database:** We also investigate the performance of these methods on standard and well calibrated FERET grayscale face database with frontal to profile pose variation. We perform the experiments on a subset of this database by randomly selecting *100* persons with seven different poses (yaw) *0°*, *±22.5°*, *±67.5°* and *±90°*. The resolution of the images is *128×128* pixels. The size of these images is scaled down to *64×64* pixels. Sample images from this database for one person are shown in Figure 1(c).

Table 1 presents some sample features used in conventional ZMs and PZMs methods for $n_{max} = 6$. Table 2 presents the top sixteen DZMs and DPZMs according to their discriminative power indicated by the rank value (shown as superscript). The most discriminative feature is ranked one and the least is assigned the value of sixteen. This table presents the complete set of features for moment order $n_{max} = 12$ wherein the selected top sixteen features are highlighted with gray boxes. From these values on three databases with different variations, it has been observed that the middle band of the order and repetition of moments is much more effective than the lower or the higher band. For a set of sample images from Yale database, Table 3 presents the normalized magnitude, average within-class and between-class mean and variance of the ZMs and the PZMs features along with their corresponding estimated value of the discrimination strength (D).

EXPERIMENTS AND RESULTS

In order to evaluate the performance of the proposed DZMs and DPZMs features in comparison to that of the conventional ZMs and PZMs approaches, we have performed various experiments to examine their robustness against different variations present in the face images, taken from the well

Figure 1. Sample images from a) Yale database, b) ORL database and c) FERET database

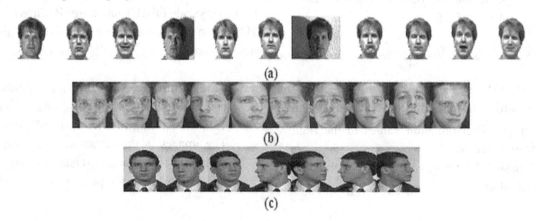

(a)

(b)

(c)

Table 1. Conventional approach to select ZMs and PZMs features

(n)	0	1	2	3	4	5	6	0	1	2	3	4	5	6
2	$Z_{2,0}$		$Z_{2,2}$					$P_{2,0}$	$P_{2,1}$	$P_{2,2}$				
3		$Z_{3,1}$		$Z_{3,3}$				$P_{3,0}$	$P_{3,1}$	$P_{3,2}$	$P_{3,3}$			
4	$Z_{4,0}$		$Z_{4,2}$		$Z_{4,4}$			$P_{4,0}$	$P_{4,1}$	$P_{4,2}$	$P_{4,3}$	$P_{4,4}$		
5		$Z_{5,1}$		$Z_{5,3}$		$Z_{5,5}$		$P_{5,0}$	$P_{5,1}$	$P_{5,2}$	$P_{5,3}$	$P_{5,4}$	$P_{5,5}$	
6	$Z_{6,0}$		$Z_{6,2}$		$Z_{6,4}$		$Z_{6,6}$	$P_{6,0}$	$P_{6,1}$	$P_{6,2}$	$P_{6,3}$	$P_{6,4}$	$P_{6,5}$	$P_{6,6}$

known and suitable Yale, ORL and FERET face databases. The performance of these approaches is compared on the basis of the false recognition rate (*frr*) which measures the percentage of the correct face images rejected by the system. The *frr* can be computed by using the following formula

$$frr = \frac{n_{wc}}{n_{te}} \qquad (11)$$

where n_{wc} is the number of wrongly classified images and n_{te} is the total number of test images. All experiments are performed in Visual C++6.0 under Microsoft Windows environment on a PC with 3.0 GHz CPU and 3 GB RAM.

For performing exhaustive experiments, the images of Yale database are randomly divided into training and test sets. Out of eleven images of each person, six are used in the training set and the remaining five in the test set. The results obtained on this database are the average of more than *120* runs of different possible states of the training and the test sets. Similarly from the ORL database, out of a total of ten images of each person five are used in the training set and the remaining five in the test set. The results on this database are also the average of *120* runs of different possible states of training and test sets. In case of the FE-

RET database, out of a total of seven images (in different pose) of each person, three images are used in the training set and the remaining four are used in the test set. The results on this database are the average of all the possible states of the training and the test sets. The parameters chosen to perform detailed experiments for the analysis of the different approaches considered in this paper are: *effect of order of moments, evaluation of the recognition performance* and *the performance on noisy images.*

Effect of Order of Moments

Conventional ZMs and PZMs approaches normally do not include the values at moment order *0* and *1* in the feature vector because they represent the average of gray values and the variation of gray values from the center of mass. However, orders of moment, selected to extract the invariant features, has a great effect on recognition performance. Haddania et al. (2002) have obtained the better recognition rates by using the higher order features of PZMs. Also, the order of moments has significant effect on the database selected and the kind of variation present in it, e.g. in case of a database with illumination variation, removing the lower order moments improves the results while in a database without illumination variation, the retention of the lower order moments increase the discrimination strength of the features (Dabbaghchian et al., 2010). Therefore, in order to select the most discriminative features, the effect of different order of moments, has been examined on the face images from the three databases in this part of the experiments.

The images in the Yale database contain illumination and expression variations, because of which the low order moment features have less discrimination strength. Hence discarding these

Table 2. List of selected DZMs and DPZMs features after performing discriminative analysis

Method	n_{max}	Yale Database	ORL Database	FERET Database
DZMs	2	$Z_{2,0}$ $Z_{2,2}$	$\overset{9}{Z}_{2,0}$ $Z_{2,2}$	$\overset{3}{Z}_{2,0}$ $Z_{2,2}$
	3	$Z_{3,1}$ $Z_{3,3}$	$Z_{3,1}$ $Z_{3,3}$	$Z_{3,1}$ $\overset{9}{Z}_{3,3}$
	4	$\overset{13}{Z}_{4,0}$ $\overset{14}{Z}_{4,2}$ $Z_{4,4}$	$\overset{16}{Z}_{4,0}$ $\overset{3}{Z}_{4,2}$ $Z_{4,4}$	$\overset{1}{Z}_{4,0}$ $\overset{15}{Z}_{4,2}$ $\overset{10}{Z}_{4,4}$
	5	$\overset{9}{Z}_{5,1}$ $Z_{5,3}$ $Z_{5,5}$	$Z_{5,1}$ $\overset{7}{Z}_{5,3}$ $Z_{5,5}$	$\overset{11}{Z}_{5,1}$ $\overset{2}{Z}_{5,3}$ $Z_{5,5}$
	6	$\overset{7}{Z}_{6,0}$ $\overset{4}{Z}_{6,2}$ $Z_{6,4}$ $Z_{6,6}$	$\overset{11}{Z}_{6,0}$ $Z_{6,2}$ $\overset{13}{Z}_{6,4}$ $\overset{4}{Z}_{6,6}$	$\overset{12}{Z}_{6,0}$ $Z_{6,2}$ $Z_{6,4}$ $Z_{6,6}$
	7	$Z_{7,1}$ $\overset{12}{Z}_{7,3}$ $Z_{7,5}$ $Z_{7,7}$	$Z_{7,1}$ $Z_{7,3}$ $\overset{15}{Z}_{7,5}$ $Z_{7,7}$	$Z_{7,1}$ $Z_{7,3}$ $\overset{7}{Z}_{7,5}$ $\overset{6}{Z}_{7,7}$
	8	$\overset{11}{Z}_{8,0}$ $\overset{6}{Z}_{8,2}$ $Z_{8,4}$ $Z_{8,6}$ $Z_{8,8}$	$Z_{8,0}$ $Z_{8,2}$ $Z_{8,4}$ $\overset{12}{Z}_{8,6}$ $\overset{2}{Z}_{8,8}$	$Z_{8,0}$ $Z_{8,2}$ $Z_{8,4}$ $Z_{8,6}$ $\overset{14}{Z}_{8,8}$
	9	$\overset{3}{Z}_{9,1}$ $Z_{9,3}$ $Z_{9,5}$ $Z_{9,7}$ $Z_{9,9}$	$Z_{9,1}$ $Z_{9,3}$ $Z_{9,5}$ $\overset{5}{Z}_{9,7}$ $Z_{9,9}$	$Z_{9,1}$ $Z_{9,3}$ $Z_{9,5}$ $\overset{16}{Z}_{9,7}$ $\overset{4}{Z}_{9,9}$
	10	$\overset{2}{Z}_{10,0}$ $\overset{8}{Z}_{10,2}$ $Z_{10,4}$ $Z_{10,6}$ $Z_{10,8}$ $Z_{10,10}$	$Z_{10,0}$ $Z_{10,2}$ $Z_{10,4}$ $Z_{10,6}$ $Z_{10,8}$ $\overset{1}{Z}_{10,10}$	$Z_{10,0}$ $Z_{10,2}$ $Z_{10,4}$ $Z_{10,6}$ $Z_{10,8}$ $Z_{10,10}$
	11	$\overset{16}{Z}_{11,1}$ $\overset{10}{Z}_{11,3}$ $\overset{15}{Z}_{11,5}$ $Z_{11,7}$ $Z_{11,9}$ $Z_{11,11}$	$Z_{11,1}$ $Z_{11,3}$ $Z_{11,5}$ $Z_{11,7}$ $\overset{10}{Z}_{11,9}$ $\overset{8}{Z}_{11,11}$	$Z_{11,1}$ $Z_{11,3}$ $Z_{11,5}$ $Z_{11,7}$ $\overset{8}{Z}_{11,9}$ $\overset{5}{Z}_{11,11}$
	12	$\overset{5}{Z}_{12,0}$ $\overset{1}{Z}_{12,2}$ $Z_{12,4}$ ----- $Z_{10,10}$ $Z_{12,12}$	$Z_{12,0}$ $Z_{12,2}$ $\overset{6}{Z}_{12,4}$ ----- $Z_{10,10}$ $\overset{14}{Z}_{12,12}$	$Z_{12,0}$ $Z_{12,2}$ $Z_{12,4}$ ----- $Z_{10,10}$ $\overset{13}{Z}_{12,12}$

continued on following page

Table 2. Continued

Method	n_{max}	Yale Database	ORL Database	FERET Database
DPZMs	2	$P_{2,0}\ P_{2,1}\ P_{2,2}$	$\overset{13}{P}_{2,0}\ P_{2,1}\ P_{2,2}$	$\overset{2}{P}_{20}\ \overset{15}{P}_{21}\ P_{22}$
	3	$\overset{6}{P}_{3,0}\ P_{3,1}\ P_{3,2}\ P_{3,3}$	$\overset{14}{P}_{3,0}\ P_{3,1}\ P_{3,2}\ P_{3,3}$	$P_{30}\ \overset{11}{P}_{31}\ \overset{13}{P}_{32}\ \overset{8}{P}_{33}$
	4	$\overset{1}{P}_{4,0}\ P_{4,1}\ \overset{3}{P}_{4,2}\ \overset{4}{P}_{4,3}\ P_{4,4}$	$P_{4,0}\ P_{4,1}\ P_{4,2}\ P_{4,3}\ \overset{3}{P}_{4,4}$	$\overset{16}{P}_{40}\ P_{41}\ P_{42}\ \overset{9}{P}_{43}\ P_{44}$
	5	$P_{5,0}\ P_{5,1}\ P_{5,2}\ P_{5,3}\ P_{5,4}$ $P_{5,5}$	$P_{5,0}\ P_{5,1}\ P_{5,2}\ P_{5,3}\ \overset{12}{P}_{5,4}\ \overset{6}{P}_{5,5}$	$P_{50}\ P_{51}\ P_{52}\ P_{53}\ P_{54}\ \overset{1}{P}_{55}$
	6	$\overset{7}{P}_{6,0}\ P_{6,1}\ \overset{2}{P}_{6,2}\ P_{6,3}\ P_{6,4}$ $P_{6,5}\ P_{6,6}$	$P_{6,0}\ P_{6,1}\ P_{6,2}\ P_{6,3}\ P_{6,4}\ P_{6,5}$ $\overset{4}{P}_{6,6}$	$P_{60}\ P_{61}\ P_{62}\ P_{63}\ P_{64}\ P_{6,5}$ P_{66}
	7	$P_{7,0}\ P_{7,1}\ \overset{10}{P}_{7,2}\ P_{7,3}\ \_\_\_\_\ P_{7,6}$ $P_{7,7}$	$P_{7,0}\ P_{7,1}\ P_{7,2}\ P_{7,3}\ \_\_\_\ \overset{11}{P}_{7,6}$ $P_{7,7}$	$\overset{7}{P}_{70}\ P_{71}\ P_{72}\ P_{73}\ \_\_\_\_\ P_{76}$ $\overset{5}{P}_{77}$
	8	$\overset{8}{P}_{8,0}\ \overset{13}{P}_{8,1}\ P_{8,2}\ P_{8,3}\ \overset{9}{P}_{8,4}\ \_\_\_$ $\_\_\ P_{8,8}$	$P_{8,0}\ P_{8,1}\ P_{8,2}\ _____\ \overset{15}{P}_{8,6}$ $\overset{2}{P}_{8,7}\ P_{8,8}$	$P_{80}\ P_{81}\ P_{82}\ P_{83}\ \_\_\_\ \overset{14}{P}_{87}$ $\overset{12}{P}_{88}$
	9	$P_{9,0}\ \_\_\_\_\ \overset{14}{P}_{9,3}\ \overset{15}{P}_{9,4}\ \_\_\_\_\ P_{9,7}\ \_\_\_$ $P_{9,9}$	$P_{9,0}\ P_{9,1}\ P_{9,2}\ P_{9,3}\ P_{9,4}\ \_\_\_\_\_$ $\_\_\ \overset{5}{P}_{9,9}$	$P_{9,0}\ P_{9,1}\ P_{9,2}\ P_{9,3}\ P_{9,4}\ \_\_\_$ $\overset{3}{P}_{9,9}$
	10	$\overset{16}{P}_{10,0}\ P_{10,1}\ P_{10,2}\ _____\ P_{10,9}$ $P_{10,10}$	$P_{10,0}\ P_{10,1}\ P_{10,2}\ _____\ \overset{9}{P}_{10,9}$ $\overset{1}{P}_{10,10}$	$P_{10,0}\ P_{10,1}\ P_{10,2}\ _____\ \overset{6}{P}_{10,9}$ $P_{10,10}$
	11	$P_{11,0}\ \overset{12}{P}_{11,1}\ \_\_\ \overset{5}{P}_{11,4}\ _____$ $P_{11,11}$	$P_{11,0}\ \_\_\_\ P_{11,3}\ P_{11,4}\ \_\_\_\_$ $\overset{7}{P}_{11,10}\ \overset{8}{P}_{11,11}$	$P_{11,0}\ \_\_\_\ P_{11,3}\ P_{11,4}\ \_\_\_$ $P_{11,10}\ \overset{4}{P}_{11,11}$
	12	$P_{12,1}\ _____\ P_{12,11}$ $P_{12,12}$	$P_{12,0}\ P_{12,1}\ _____\ \overset{10}{P}_{12,11}$ $\overset{16}{P}_{12,12}$	$P_{12,0}\ P_{12,1}\ _____\ P_{12,11}$ $\overset{10}{P}_{12,12}$

Table 3. Discriminant strength values (mean) of DZMs and DPZMs features on Yale database

	ZMs						PZMs					
Feature	Absolute value for a sample image	Average Within-class mean for a sample class	Average Between-class mean	Vw	Vb	D	Feature	Absolute value for a sample image	Average within-class mean for a sample class	Average Between-class mean	Vw	Vb	D
$Z_{2,0}$	0.778045	0.707893	0.646483	0.022216	0.694555	32.6039	P_{20}	0.553504	0.618981	0.691286	0.025352	0.7872	32.8241
$Z_{2,2}$	0.347527	0.380436	0.406022	0.005804	0.157636	30.966	P_{21}	0.223229	0.368183	0.249294	0.094474	1.91002	22.6725
$Z_{3,1}$	0.242976	0.410013	0.280125	0.136177	2.63964	21.2628	P_{22}	0.347527	0.380436	0.406022	0.005804	0.157636	30.966
$Z_{3,3}$	0.021927	0.04398	0.031074	0.001492	0.02922	19.7976	P_{30} [6]	0.12511	0.170703	0.242422	0.020189	0.979971	49.8667
$Z_{4,0}$ [13]	0.528193	0.64437	0.770845	0.063007	2.14548	35.4586	:						
$Z_{4,2}$ [14]	0.350855	0.426508	0.478791	0.026087	0.780863	34.0985	P_{33}	0.021927	0.04398	0.031074	0.001492	0.02922	19.7976
$Z_{4,4}$	0.280113	0.296553	0.305787	0.001776	0.043093	24.5826	P_{40} [1]	0.106423	0.11032	0.279137	0.018502	1.51374	83.2191
$Z_{5,1}$ [9]	0.204857	0.240836	0.175229	0.012379	0.516315	43.445	P_{41} [3]	0.188388	0.218272	0.166595	0.010003	0.661214	70.1542
$Z_{5,3}$	0.078691	0.104618	0.084426	0.004775	0.097921	21.2573	P_{42} [4]	0.293618	0.22726	0.223204	0.005919	0.371245	65.0251
$Z_{5,5}$	0.007018	0.040643	0.032566	0.016246	0.257147	15.8894	P_{43}	0.080173	0.105985	0.085989	0.004661	0.100537	22.5602

continued on following page

Table 3. Continued

	ZMs							PZMs					
$Z_{6,0}^{7}$	0.209568	0.227825	0.322211	0.025195	1.10927	48.6702	P_{44}	0.280113	0.296553	0.305787	0.001776	0.043093	24.5826
$Z_{6,2}^{4}$	0.280717	0.201289	0.182804	0.01286	0.679587	56.2765	P_{50}	0.149291	0.227399	0.17953	0.01765	0.525466	30.5429
$Z_{6,4}$	0.280563	0.292544	0.310212	0.004145	0.108632	29.6324	:						
$Z_{6,6}$	0.2959	0.304576	0.320762	0.00172	0.050024	31.7743	P_{55}	0.007018	0.040643	0.032566	0.016246	0.257147	15.8894
$Z_{7,1}$	0.130959	0.06974	0.169109	0.022808	0.71591	32.4115	P_{60}^{7}	0.042252	0.058284	0.142947	0.01715	0.833471	49.1914
$Z_{7,3}^{12}$	0.113947	0.182759	0.145395	0.006154	0.225854	40.3416	P_{61}	0.081281	0.083712	0.109076	0.01086	0.396385	36.9437
$Z_{7,5}$	0.031523	0.030927	0.055378	0.027384	0.43857	16.0782	P_{62}^{2}	0.266949	0.291255	0.215918	0.01011	0.813051	82.5275
$Z_{7,7}$	0.001742	0.030794	0.020213	0.005283	0.087104	16.5718	:						
$Z_{8,0}^{11}$	0.157428	0.227875	0.259723	0.031109	1.26499	41.8032	P_{66}	0.2959	0.304576	0.320762	0.00172	0.050024	31.7743
$Z_{8,2}^{6}$	0.256126	0.212072	0.224231	0.007282	0.341043	49.6844	P_{70}	0.012428	0.050302	0.055328	0.007313	0.152865	21.04
$Z_{8,4}$	0.101798	0.090852	0.073572	0.004031	0.100745	26.0563	:						
Z_{86}	0.310194	0.310314	0.335022	0.004102	0.112739	29.8534	P_{73}^{10}	0.061434	0.198884	0.102014	0.004663	0.217467	48.4833

continued on following page

Table 3. Continued

	ZMs							PZMs					
$Z_{8,8}$	0.039639	0.05349	0.045927	0.00089	0.015394	17.7483	..						
$^{3}Z_{9,1}$	0.227357	0.253765	0.192732	0.016025	0.923037	59.2759	P_{77}	0.001742	0.030794	0.020213	0.005283	0.087104	16.5718
$Z_{9,3}$	0.06683	0.112581	0.129234	0.008065	0.183459	23.3919	$^{8}P_{80}$	0.062881	0.075456	0.113963	0.012531	0.606766	48.9042
$Z_{9,5}$	0.059555	0.063303	0.047658	0.003789	0.073992	19.877	$^{13}P_{81}$	0.00998	0.037381	0.098064	0.005356	0.236701	44.9975
$Z_{9,7}$	0.009867	0.03215	0.033538	0.008318	0.137928	16.6655	..						
$Z_{9,9}$	0.001284	0.019256	0.012264	0.002157	0.035468	16.6305	$^{9}P_{84}$	0.038277	0.079737	0.058923	0.001771	0.085987	48.8387
$^{2}Z_{10,0}$	0.019531	0.043274	0.256459	0.031709	1.94277	62.7992	..						
$^{8}Z_{10,2}$	0.277907	0.343048	0.241273	0.0195	0.882459	46.3722	P_{88}	0.039639	0.05349	0.045927	0.00089	0.015394	17.7483
$Z_{10,4}$	0.064051	0.077429	0.068569	0.002547	0.077398	31.5001	P_{90}	0.013456	0.012069	0.06696	0.007723	0.264834	35.3097
$Z_{10,6}$	0.182313	0.214404	0.209321	0.00484	0.10455	22.7137	$^{14}P_{93}$	0.103033	0.141124	0.101144	0.004591	0.200053	44.3732
$Z_{10,8}$	0.043065	0.065461	0.050497	0.002336	0.043802	19.3074	$^{15}P_{94}$	0.017498	0.095438	0.064749	0.003137	0.134833	44.3382
$Z_{10,10}$	0.214216	0.225309	0.233101	0.001111	0.02822	26.6212	P_{99}	0.001284	0.019256	0.012264	0.002157	0.035468	16.6305
$^{16}Z_{11,1}$	0.165234	0.25302	0.201918	0.017501	0.579051	33.5112	$^{16}P_{100}$	0.057391	0.020071	0.120934	0.014051	0.575727	41.5488

continued on following page

Table 3. Continued

	ZMs						P	PZMs					
$^{10}Z_{11,3}$	0.026329	0.13731	0.079753	0.003849	0.162797	42.7848	P_{101}	0.090678	0.078657	0.08376	0.003882	0.181368	47.9092
$^{15}Z_{11,5}$	0.063184	0.075496	0.047824	0.002661	0.081736	34.013	..						
$Z_{11,7}$	0.019349	0.035551	0.050638	0.002025	0.064034	33.0443	P_{1010}	0.214216	0.225309	0.233101	0.001111	0.02822	26.6212
$Z_{11,9}$	0.008674	0.015303	0.017601	0.002837	0.05014	17.9677	P_{110}	0.002503	0.076468	0.081547	0.008145	0.226117	27.9
$Z_{11,11}$	0.000559	0.024572	0.015409	0.004001	0.064853	16.3034	$^{12}P_{111}$	0.041201	0.055062	0.067056	0.00482	0.140005	30.2898
$^{5}Z_{12,0}$	0.076766	0.140948	0.177713	0.030015	1.58608	54.2396	..						
$^{1}Z_{12,2}$	0.272155	0.319594	0.200902	0.013111	0.954723	73.5888	$^{5}P_{114}$	0.133179	0.193154	0.104367	0.004476	0.238741	54.8155
$Z_{12,4}$	0.032693	0.068772	0.059391	0.003062	0.084484	28.5462	..						
$Z_{12,6}$	0.180327	0.22215	0.216491	0.002541	0.077452	31.3676	$^{11}P_{118}$	0.031412	0.057153	0.074314	0.00179	0.081578	48.3787
$Z_{12,8}$	0.083171	0.111972	0.100923	0.001574	0.050019	32.8387	..	0.207514	0.223335	0.228247	0.001534	0.037341	25.6305
$Z_{10,10}$	0.220694	0.236849	0.24266	0.001651	0.040194	25.6356	..						
$Z_{12,12}$	0.074189	0.076495	0.082302	0.000219	0.005757	29.3276	P_{1212}	0.074189	0.076495	0.082302	0.000219	0.005757	29.3276

values from the features vector may significantly improve the performance. However, going beyond the moment order $n_{max} = 20$ reduces the performance gradually because of the fact that the higher order moment features are more prone to numerical stability and image noise. In case of the ORL and FERET databases, removal of the lower order moments from the feature vector degrades the results because of the fact that the said databases do not contain illumination variations. However, going beyond the maximum order of moments $n_{max} > 15$ and $n_{max} > 13$ for the ZMs and the PZMs, respectively, the performance starts reducing. Table 4 and Table 5 present different groups comprising of values for n_{min} and n_{max} used to analyze the effect of order of moments on the determination of discriminative ZMs and PZMs features, respectively for the three databases.

The experimental results are presented in Figure 2 for the ZMs and PZMs approaches. We perform exhaustive experiments by taking differ-

ent number of features and from the results it is observed that better results are obtained when the number of features is around *40*. The results of discriminative features combined with FLD are better as compared to that of the other approaches. On Yale database, taking the lower moment order $n_{min} = 6$ and higher moment order $n_{max} = 17$ performs better for the selection of the discriminative features for the ZMs based approaches while the moment order $n_{min} = 3$ and $n_{max} = 12$ gives the least false recognition rate for the PZMs based approaches. Similarly, for ORL database the order of moments $n_{min} = 1$, $n_{max} = 15$ and $n_{min} = 1$, $n_{max} = 13$ is selected for ZMs and PZMs, respectively. In order to select the discriminative features from FERET database, the orders of moments $n_{min} = 1$, $n_{max} = 13$ and $n_{min} = 1$, $n_{max} = 11$ are taken for the ZMs and the PZMs, respectively. It is pertinent to mention here that the phase coefficients of these selected features are computed in parallel to their magni-

Table 4. List of various groups of moment orders formed for ZMs

Database	Groups (n_{min}, n_{max})										
	1	2	3	4	5	6	7	8	9	10	12
Yale	(3,20)	(4,20)	(5,20)	(6,20)	(7,20)	(8,20)	(9,20)	(6,15)	(6,16)	(6,17)	(6,18)
ORL	(1,16)	(2,16)	(3,16)	(4,16)	(5,16)	(6,16)	(1,12)	(1,13)	(1,14)	(1,15)	-
FERET	(1,15)	(2,15)	(3,15)	(4,15)	(5,15)	(6,15)	(1,13)	(1,14)	(1,16)	-	-

Table 5. List of various groups of moment orders formed for PZMs

Database	Groups (n_{min}, n_{max})									
	1	2	3	4	5	6	7	8	9	10
Yale	(1,15)	(2,15)	(3,15)	(4,15)	(5,15)	(6,15)	(3,10)	(3,11)	(3,12)	(3,13)
ORL	(2,12)	(3,12)	(4,12)	(5,12)	(6,12)	(1,9)	(1,10)	(1,11)	(1,13)	-
FERET	(1,13)	(2,13)	(3,13)	(4,13)	(5,13)	(1,10)	(1,11)	(1,12)	(1,14)	-

Figure 2. Performance (average) of ZMs and PZMs on (a) Yale database, (b) ORL database, and (c) FERET database for different groups of order of moments

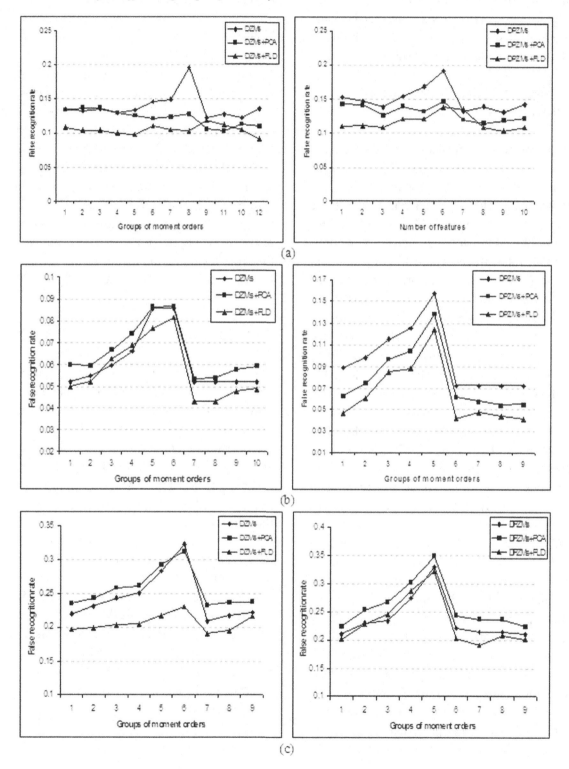

tude coefficients, so no additional time is consumed in their computation. For the performance analysis, the experiments are conducted by using these evaluated groups of the order of moments and are given in detail in next subsection.

Evaluation of the Recognition Performance

This experiment compares the recognition performance of the conventional ZMs and PZMs features with that of the proposed DZMs and DPZMs approaches. The performance of these features combined with PCA and FLD is also analyzed by taking different number of features. Because of the inherent properties of being rotation, scale and translation invariant, we analyzed the performance of these moment based approaches, on three proficient databases with adequate variations. In order to choose the discriminative features, the values of n_{min} and n_{max} are selected from the experiments conducted in previous part of this section. The performance of the proposed discriminative DZMs, DZMs(magPhase), DZMs+PCA, DZMs+FLD, DPZMs, DPZMs(magPhase), DPZMs+PCA and DPZMs+FLD is analyzed for different types of variations present in face images of these databases, in comparison to that of the conventional ZMs, ZMs(magPhase), ZMs+PCA, ZMs+FLD, PZMs, PZMs(magPhase), PZMs+PCA, and PZMs+FLD approaches. Figure 3(a)-(c) present the performance measured in terms of *frr* for the ZMs and PZMs based discriminative and conventional approaches. The experimental results depict significant improvement in performance with the discriminative features because both of the DZMs and the DPZMs based approaches have lower false recognition rates. Further, magPhase features of both of the discriminative and the conventional approaches gives better performance in most of the cases. The recognition results generated by

this set of features are either similar to or better than DZMs+FLD and DPZMs+FLD.

Yale Database

The comparison of highest recognition rate of ZMs and PZMs based approaches on Yale database is presented in Table 6. From this, it can be noticed that the discriminative features performs better than the conventional features with a difference of 2-6% in the recognition rate. The highest recognition rate of the discriminative and conventional ZMs based approaches is *91.3%* and 86.7% which is achieved by DZMs(magPhase) and ZMs+PCA, respectively. In case of PZMs based approaches, the highest recognition rate of *90.8%* and *86.4%* is achieved by DPZMs+PCA and PZMs+PCA, respectively.

ORL Database

There is no illumination variation in images of ORL and FERET face databases therefore the lower order moment features have the higher discrimination strength and because of this the performance of conventional ZMs and PZMs is also good. The comparison of highest recognition rate of ZMs and PZMs based approaches is presented in Table 7. From this, it can be noticed that the discriminative features perform better than the conventional features with a difference of *0.4-2%* in the recognition rate. The highest recognition rate of discriminative and conventional ZMs based approaches is of *96.38%* and *95.9%* which is achieved by DZMs(magPhase) and ZMs+FLD, respectively. In case of PZMs based discriminative and conventional approaches the highest recognition rate of *96.2%* and *94.2%* is achieved by the DPZMs+FLD and PZMs+FLD, respectively.

Figure 3. Performance (average) of ZMs and PZMs on (a) Yale database, (b) ORL database and (c) FERET database

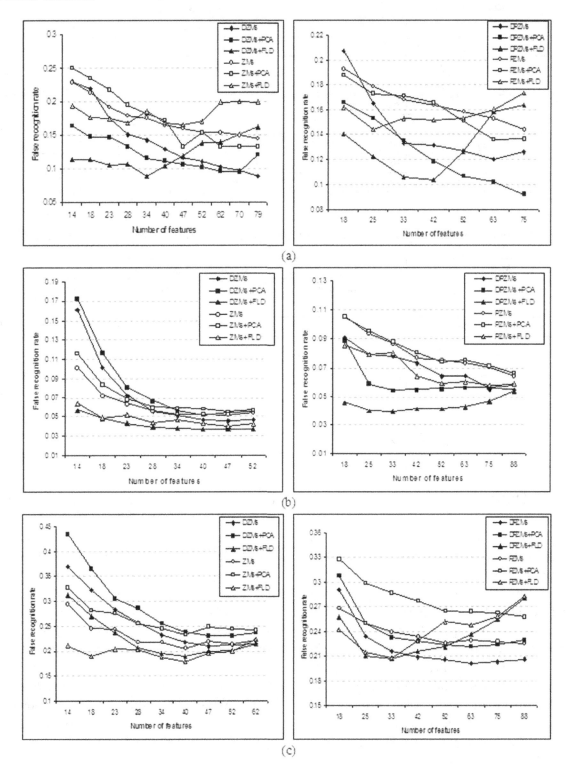

Table 6. Comparison of highest recognition rate of ZMs and PZMs based approaches on Yale database

Method	Recognition Rate (%)		
	Discriminative	Conventional	Difference
ZMs	91.1	85.6	5.5
ZMs(magPhase)	*91.3*	85.6	4.0
ZMs+PCA	90.5	*86.7*	4.0
ZMs+FLD	89.6	83.5	6.1
PZMs	87.96	85.6	2.36
PZMs(magPhase)	90.2	85.9	4.3
PZMs+PCA	*90.8*	*86.4*	4.4
PZMs+FLD	89.6	85.6	4.0

Table 7. Comparison of highest recognition rate of ZMs and PZMs based approaches on ORL database

Method	Recognition Rate (%)		
	Discriminative	Conventional	Difference
ZMs	95.9	94.8	1.1
ZMs(magPhase)	*96.38*	95.72	0.66
ZMs+PCA	94.8	94.48	0.32
ZMs+FLD	96.3	*95.9*	0.4
PZMs	94.5	93.6	0.9
PZMs(magPhase)	95.9	94.11	1.79
PZMs+PCA	94.58	93.35	1.23
PZMs+FLD	96.2	*94.2*	2.0

FERET Database

The evaluation of highly discriminative features is affected by the number of images per person used for training. As in this database, the number of images available per person is very limited and it is not feasible to take more images for training so the methods comprising of selected discriminative features do not generate significant difference in results as compared to that of the conventional approaches. However, the results presented in Figure 3(c) show that on this database, though the performance of DZMs is comparable to the conventional ZMs based approaches, the performance of DPZMs based approaches is better as compared to their conventional PZMs based approaches. The analysis shows that the said results are the outcome of less number of training images, i.e. three training images provide insufficient information for the computation of discrimination strength. In this database, the posed images of *100* persons are considered which in themselves require sufficient number of features in order to generate a large number of basis vectors of the FLD and the same cannot be generated because of only taking some highly discriminative features in the feature vector. As such without this requisite generation of the basis vectors, fewer basis vectors are taken and the same results into decreased performance of the FLD method.

The comparison of highest recognition rate of ZMs and PZMs based approaches is presented in Table 8. From this, it can be noticed that the DZMs(magPhase) has the highest recognition rate. Among conventional approaches, the performance of ZMs+FLD is better. In case of PZMs based approaches, the highest recognition rate of *80.4%* and *79.21%* is achieved by the DPZMs(magPhase) and PZMs+FLD approaches.

Performance on Noisy Images

Most important characteristic of the ZMs and PZMs is the robustness to image noise (Lajevardi & Hussain, 2010). In this part, the effect on recogni-

tion performance in presence of noise is analyzed on the face databases used in experiments. Noise is normally an unwanted variation added to the image intensity. To perform the experiments on noise variation, we manually added the impulsive noise commonly named salt-and-pepper or spike noise to the face images. An image, in presence of impulsive noise, has dark pixels in bright regions and white pixels in dark regions. To generate the noisy image database, the noise density of *0.05* is added in the images of test set and the training is done on the original images, i.e. on images with no noise. Sample noisy images for one person are shown in Figure 4 (a)-(c) for Yale, ORL and FERET databases.

Table 8. Comparison of highest recognition rate of ZMs and PZMs based approaches on FERET database

Method	Recognition Rate (%)		
	Discriminative	**Conventional**	**Difference**
ZMs	79.24	79.1	0.14
ZMs(magPhase)	*81.3*	79.8	1.5
ZMs+PCA	76.95	76.63	0.32
ZMs+FLD	80.99	*81.1*	-0.11
PZMs	80.17	77.5	2.67
PZMs(magPhase)	*80.4*	78.2	2.2
PZMs+PCA	77.8	74.27	3.53
PZMs+FLD	79.29	*79.21*	0.08

Figure 4. Sample noisy images from a) Yale b) ORL c) FERET databases

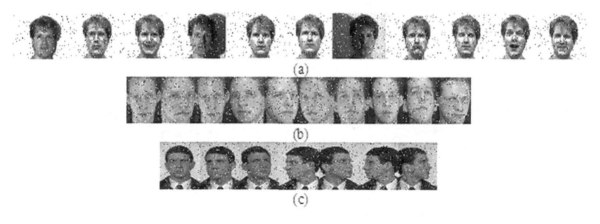

(a)

(b)

(c)

The experimental results with different number of features are presented in Figure 5 (a)-(c) for ZMs and PZMs. From these results it is observed that the DZMs and DPZMs based approaches reveal admirable results as compared to the corresponding conventional ones. As expected, in most of the cases the performance of PZMs based approaches is better than that of the

Figure 5. Performance (average) of ZMs and PZMs for noise variation on (a) Yale database (b) ORL database (c) FERET database

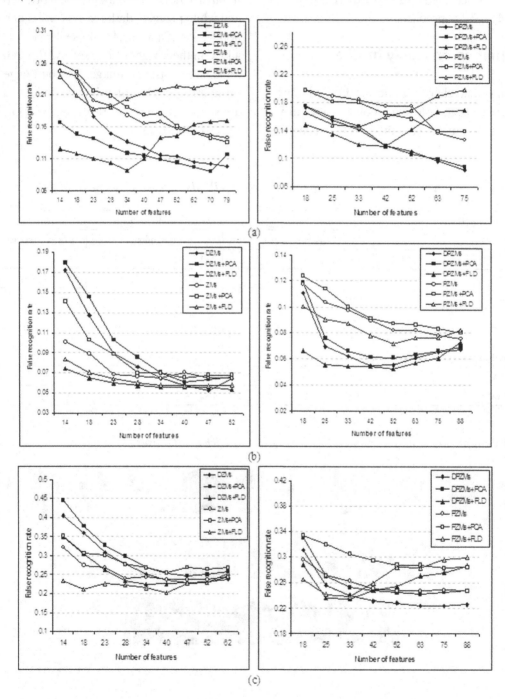

ZMs based approaches. This is because of the PZMs take the lower value of n_{max} than that of the ZMs and it is also well known that the higher order moment features are more prone to image noise. The details of the experiments performed against noise variation and the results observed for the individual face databases are presented in the following subsection.

Yale Database

The highest recognition rates of ZMs and PZMs based approaches are presented in Table 9. From these results, it can be noticed that the PZMs based approaches perform better as compared to the ZMs based approaches against noise variation. The recognition rate of the approaches based on discriminative features is *3-9%* more than that of the conventional approaches. It is obvious that a recognition rate of *90.3%* is achieved by the DZMs while the recognition rate of conventional ZMs is *85.7%*. Similarly, the highest recognition rate of ZMs based approaches is of *91.0%* for DZMs+PCA while the same is *86.4%* for the ZMs+PCA. However, in case of PZMs based approaches, the highest recognition rate of *91.8%* is achieved by the DPZMs(magPhase) whereas the PZMs(magPhase) achieve the recognition rate of *87.45%* only.

ORL Database

The highest recognition rate of ZMs and PZMs based approaches is presented in Table 10. From the experimental results, it can be noticed that for the noise variation on this database the DPZMs based approaches perform better than all of the other approaches. The performance of the DZMs(magPhase) and DPZMs(magPhase) based approaches is better than that of the corresponding conventional approaches with a difference of *0.1-2.4%* in the recognition rate. The highest recognition rates of ZMs based approaches are *95.04%* and *94.92%* in case of DZMs(magPhase) and ZMs(magPhase), respectively. Likewise, the highest recognition rates of *95.26%* and *93.25%* are achieved by the DPZMs(magPhase) and PZMs(magPhase), respectively for the PZMs based approaches. The presented results clearly demonstrate the competence of the phase coefficients of ZMs and PZMs towards the performance improvement.

FERET Database

The results for highest recognition rates on this database for ZMs and PZMs based approaches are presented in Table 11. There is approximately *0.8-4%* improvement in performance with the

Table 9. Highest recognition values of ZMs and PZMs based approaches on Yale database for noise variation

Method	Recognition Rate (%)		
	Discriminative	Conventional	Difference
ZMs	90.3	85.7	4.6
ZMs(magPhase)	89.8	85.9	3.9
ZMs+PCA	91.0	86.4	4.6
ZMs+FLD	90.9	81.2	9.7
PZMs	91.6	87.3	4.3
PZMs(magPhase)	91.8	87.45	4.35
PZMs+PCA	91.1	86.0	5.1
PZMs+FLD	89.2	85.5	3.7

Table 10. Highest recognition values of ZMs and PZMs based approaches on ORL database with noise variation

Method	Recognition Rate (%)		
	Discriminative	Conventional	Difference
ZMs	94.7	93.5	1.2
ZMs(magPhase)	*95.04*	*94.92*	0.12
ZMs+PCA	93.9	93.46	0.44
ZMs+FLD	94.65	94.29	0.36
PZMs	94.89	92.4	2.49
PZMs(magPhase)	95.26	*93.25*	2.01
PZMs+PCA	93.9	91.95	1.95
PZMs+FLD	94.7	92.8	1.9

Table 11. Highest recognition values of ZMs and PZMs based approaches on FERET database with noise variation

Method	Recognition Rate (%)		
	Discriminative	Conventional	Difference
ZMs	77.14	75.9	1.24
ZMs(magPhase)	*78.9*	77.6	1.3
ZMs+PCA	75.3	74.47	0.83
ZMs+FLD	78.16	*78.84*	-0.68
PZMs	77.6	75.2	2.4
PZMs(magPhase)	*78.1*	*76.4*	1.7
PZMs+PCA	75.73	71.66	4.07
PZMs+FLD	77.48	76.14	1.34

use of discriminative features than that of their conventional counterpart. This result demonstrates the advantage of taking the features with higher discrimination competence. The highest recognition rate of conventional and discriminative ZMs based approaches is of *78.84%* and *78.9%* as achieved by ZMs+FLD and DZMs(magPhase), respectively. In case of PZMs based discriminative and conventional approaches the highest recognition rate of *78.1%* and *76.4%* is achieved by DPZMs(magPhase) and PZMs(magPhase), respectively.

Performance Comparison with Other Recent Methods

The performance of the proposed discriminative ZMs and PZMs approaches is better than that of their corresponding conventional approaches. Further, a significant improvement in performance is noticed when these proposed approaches collaborate with standard Eigenface (PCA) and Fisherface (FLD) methods. So far the continuous ongoing research and evolution of Eigenface and Fisherface approaches have been recognized as most popular and standard approaches in the area of face recognition. On ORL and Yale databases, the performance comparison of the proposed approaches and that of some recent well known methods is presented in Table 12. The results show that on these databases, the performance of the proposed approaches is better than that of the recent approaches. The mean results of *120* different states of training/test sets for the proposed DZMs(magPhase) and DZMs+FLD are *96.38%* and *96.3%*, respectively on the ORL database while on Yale database a recognition rate of *91.3%* is achieved by the proposed DZMs(magPhase) approach and the same is better than that of the other approaches listed in the table. Hence, from the analysis performed in this research work, it can be noticed that a better recognition rate (at reduced dimensions) is obtained by the proposed approaches.

FUTURE RESEARCH DIRECTIONS

The future improvement to this work will include allocation of specific weights to highly discrimi-

native features, which we believe may further increase the recognition performance. In addition to this, we will enhance the proposed framework by using some elite classifiers and will employ some advanced technique to use the phase coefficients of ZMs and PZMs. The results may be improved if phase coefficients also contribute towards determination of discriminative strength of individual features.

CONCLUSION

In this research work, the performance of the conventional ZMs and PZMs based approaches is compared to that of the proposed DZMs and DPZMs approaches. The recognition performance of these approaches is analyzed on different types of variations present in face images such as illumination, expression, scale and rotation (pose). The modifications are also made to 1) use the phase coefficients alongwith the magnitude features and 2) combine the feature sets of DZMs and DPZMs with the PCA and the FLD approach, which results in further improvement of recogni-

Table 12. Performance comparison of proposed methods with other latest methods on ORL and Yale databases

Method	Recognition Rate (%)	
	ORL	Yale
PCA (Kwak & Pedrycz, 2005)	93.6	72.22
FLD (Kwak & Pedrycz, 2005)	95.1	87.44
2D-DWLDA (Zhi & Ruan, 2008)	92.5	89.33
2D-PCA with feature fusion (Xu et al., 2008)	94.0	82.7
Discriminative DCT (Dabbaghchian et al., 2010)	96.0	89.0
BLD (Ksantini et al., 2010)	91.9	-
Proposed DZMs	95.9	91.1
Proposed DZMs(magPhase)	*96.38*	*91.3*
Proposed DZMs+FLD	*96.3*	89.6
Proposed DPZMs	94.5	87.96
Proposed DPZMs(magPhase)	95.9	90.2
Proposed DPZMs+FLD	96.2	89.6

tion rate. All these experiments are performed on three proficient face databases, i.e. Yale database with expression and illumination variation, ORL database with scale and small pose variation, FERET database with pose (yaw) variation. From this analysis, the following conclusions are drawn:

1. The selection of only discriminative features in the feature vector, significantly improve the recognition performance at reduced dimensions.
2. DZMs and DPZMs combined with FLD perform better than the conventional approaches analyzed in this work. However, on FERET database, the performance of ZMs+FLD is also good.
3. The phase coefficients of ZMs and PZMs are equally useful and their inclusion alongwith the magnitude coefficient is able to achieve similar or better recognition results than the proposed DZMs and DPZMs combined with FLD approach. In spite of this, as the phase coefficients are computed in parallel to magnitude coefficients, hence it significantly reduces the additional computation time spent on the evaluation of DZMs+FLD and DPZMs+FLD approaches.
4. In order to obtain highly discriminative features sufficient number of images must be available for training.
5. On noisy image test set, in most of the cases the performance of DPZMs based approaches is better than that of the DZMs based approaches.
6. A number of other factors like the type of variation present in the database images, number of discriminative features selected in the classification process and the orders of moments used for computing the discriminative features also affect the results.

Briefly, a careful selection of highly discriminative features may result in significant improvement in the recognition performance as approximately *2-6%* improvement is notified in this analysis.

ACKNOWLEDGMENT

The authors are grateful to All India Council for Technical Education (AICTE), Govt. of India, New Delhi, for supporting the research work vide their file number 8013/RID/BOR/RPS-77/2005-06. We are also grateful to National Institute of Standards and Technology (colorferet@nist.gov) for providing FERET face database.

REFERENCES

AT&T Laboratories Cambridge. (2002). *Olivetti Research Laboratory (ORL) face database*. Retrieved from http://www.cl.cam.ac.uk/research/dtg/attarchive/facedatabase.html

Belhumeur, P. N., Hespanha, J. P., & Kriegman, D. J. (1997). Eigenfaces Vs. Fisherfaces Recognition using class specific linear projection. *IEEE Transactions on Pattern Analysis and Machine Intelligence*, *19*, 711–720. doi:10.1109/34.598228

Burton, A. M., Jenkins, R., Hancock, P. J. B., & White, D. (2005). Robust representations for face recognition: The power of averages. *Cognitive Psychology*, *51*, 256–284. doi:10.1016/j.cogpsych.2005.06.003 PMID:16198327

Cevikalp, H., Yavuz, H. S., Cay, M. A., & Barkana, A. (2009). Two-dimensional subspace classifiers for face recognition. *Neurocomputing*, *72*, 1111–1120. doi:10.1016/j.neucom.2008.02.015

Chan, C. H., Tahir, M. A., Kittler, J., & Pietika, ̈. M. (2013). Multiscale Local Phase Quantization for Robust Component-Based Face Recognition Using Kernel Fusion of Multiple Descriptors. *IEEE Transactions on Pattern Analysis and Machine Intelligence*, *35*(5), 1164–1177. doi:10.1109/TPAMI.2012.199 PMID:23520257

Cheng, M., Fang, B., Tang, Y. Y., Zhang, T., & Wen, J. (2010). Incremental Embedding and Learning in the Local Discriminant Subspace With Application to Face Recognition. *IEEE Transactions on Systems, Man and Cybernetics. Part C, Applications and Reviews*, *40*(5), 580–591. doi:10.1109/TSMCC.2010.2043529

Dabbaghchian, S., Ghaemmaghami, M. P., & Aghagolzadeh, A. (2010). Feature extraction using discrete cosine transform and discrimination power analysis with a face recognition technology. *Pattern Recognition*, *43*, 1431–1440. doi:10.1016/j.patcog.2009.11.001

Daoqiang, Z., & Zhi-Hua, Z. (2005). (2D)^{2}PCA Two directional two dimensional PCA for efficient face representation and recognition. *Neurocomputing*, *69*, 224–231. doi:10.1016/j.neucom.2005.06.004

Etemad, K., & Chellappa, R. (1997). Discriminant analysis for recognition of human face images. *Journal of the Optical Society of America*, *14*, 1724–1733. doi:10.1364/JOSAA.14.001724

Faez, K., & Farajzadeh, N. (2006). A performance comparison of the ZM, PZM and LM in the face recognition system in presence of salt-pepper noise. In *Proceedings of IEEE International Conference on System Man and Cybernetics*, (Vol. 5, pp. 4197-4201). Taipei, Taiwan: IEEE.

Georghiades, A. S. (1997). *Yale face database*. Retrieved from http://cvc.yale.edu/projects/yale-faces/yalefaces.html

Haddandnia, J., Ahmadi, M., & Faez, K. (2003). An efficient feature extraction method with pseudo-Zernike moments in RBF neural network-based human face recognition system. *EURASIP Journal on Applied Signal Processing*, *9*, 890–901. doi:10.1155/S1110865703305128

Haddania, J., Ahmadi, M., & Faez, K. (2002). An efficient method for Recognition of Human Faces Using Higher Orders Pseudo Zernike Moment Invariant. In *Proceedings of 5th International Conference on Automatic Face and Gesture Recognition (FGR'02)* (pp. 330). Washington, DC: FGR.

Hjelmas, E., & Low, B. K. (2001). Face detection A survey. *Computer Vision and Image Understanding*, *83*, 236–274. doi:10.1006/cviu.2001.0921

Jiang, Z., Lin, Z., & Davis, L. S. (2013). Label Consistent K-SVD: Learning a Discriminative Dictionary for Recognition. *IEEE Transactions on Pattern Analysis and Machine Intelligence*, *35*(11), 2651–2654. doi:10.1109/TPAMI.2013.88 PMID:24051726

Jing, X.-Y., & Zhang, D. (2004). A Face and Palmprint Recognition Approach Based on Discriminant DCT Feature Extraction. *IEEE Transactions on Systems, Man, and Cybernetics. Part B, Cybernetics*, *34*(6), 2405–2415. doi:10.1109/TSMCB.2004.837586 PMID:15619939

Kan, C., & Srinath, M. D. (2001). Combined features of cubic B-Spline wavelet moments and Zernike Moments for invariant character recognition. In *Proceedings of International Conference on Information Technology: Coding and Computing (ITCC'01)* (pp. 511-515). Las Vegas, NV: ITCC.

Ksantini, R., Boufama, B., Ziou, D., & Colin, B. (2010). A novel Bayesian logistic discriminant model An application to face recognition. *Pattern Recognition*, *43*, 1421–1430. doi:10.1016/j.patcog.2009.08.021

Kwak, K.-C., & Pedrycz, W. (2005). Face recognition using a fuzzy fisherface classifier. *Pattern Recognition*, *38*, 1717–1732. doi:10.1016/j.patcog.2005.01.018

Lajevardi, S. M., & Hussain, Z. M. (2010). Higher order orthogonal moments for invariant facial expression recognition. *Digital Signal Processing, 20,* 1771–1779. doi:10.1016/j.dsp.2010.03.004

Lei, Z., Liao, S., & Li, S. Z. (2012). *Efficient Feature Selection for Linear Discriminant Analysis and Its Application to Face Recognition.* Paper presented at the 21st International Conference on Pattern Recognition (ICPR 2012). Tsukuba, Japan.

Lei, Z., Pietika, ̈. M., & Li, S. Z. (2014). Learning Discriminant Face Descriptor. *IEEE Transactions on Pattern Analysis and Machine Intelligence, 36*(2), 289–302. doi:10.1109/TPAMI.2013.112 PMID:24356350

Li, Z., Park, U., & Jain, A. K. (2011). A Discriminative Model for Age Invariant Face Recognition. *IEEE Transactions on Information Forensics and Security, 6*(3), 1028–1037. doi:10.1109/TIFS.2011.2156787

Lu, J., Tan, Y.-P., & Wang, G. (2013). Discriminative Multimanifold Analysis for Face Recognition from a Single Training Sample per Person. *IEEE Transactions on Pattern Analysis and Machine Intelligence, 35*(1), 39–51. doi:10.1109/TPAMI.2012.70 PMID:22431525

Lu, J., Zhou, X., Tan, Y.-P., Shang, Y., & Zhou, J. (2012). Cost-Sensitive Semi-Supervised Discriminant Analysis for Face Recognition. *IEEE Transactions on Information Forensics and Security, 7*(3), 944–953. doi:10.1109/TIFS.2012.2188389

Martinez, A. M., & Kak, A. C. (2001). PCA versus LDA. *IEEE Transactions on Pattern Analysis and Machine Intelligence, 23,* 228–233. doi:10.1109/34.908974

Moon, H., & Phillips, P. J. (2001). Computational and performance aspects of PCA-based face recognition algorithms. *Perception, 30,* 303–321. doi:10.1068/p2896 PMID:11374202

Nabatchian, A., Abdel-Raheem, E., & Ahmadi, M. (2008). Human face recognition using different moment invariants: A comparative study. In *Proceedings of IEEE International Congress on Image and Signal Processing* (pp. 661-666). Sanya, China: IEEE.

Neerja & Walia. E. (2008). Face recognition using improved fast PCA algorithm. In *Proceedings of International Congress on Image and Signal Processing,* (vol. 1, pp. 554-558). Sanya, Hainan: Academic Press.

Nor'aini, A. J., Raveendran, P., & Selvanathan, N. (2006). Human face recognition using Zernike moments and nearest neighbor classifier. In *Proceedings of 4th student Conference on Research and Development* (pp. 120-123). Academic Press.

Nor'aini, A. J., Raveendran, P., & Selvanathan, N. (2007). A comparative analysis of Zernike moments and Principal Components Analysis as feature extractors for face recognition. In *Proceedings of 3rd Kuala Lumpur International Conference on Biomedical Engineering,* (Vol. 15, pp. 37-41). Academic Press.

Pang, Y.-H., Teoh, A. B. J., & Ngo, D. C. L. (2005). Enhanced pseudo Zernike moments in face recognition. *IEICE Electronics Express, 2*(3), 70–75. doi:10.1587/elex.2.70

Pang, Y.-H., Teoh, A. B. J., & Ngo, D. C. L. (2006). A discriminant pseudo Zernike moments in face recognition. *Journal of Research and Practice in Information Technology, 38*(2), 197–210.

Phillips, P. J., Moon, H., Rauss, P. J., & Rizvi, S. (2000). *The Facial Recognition Technology (FERET) face database.* Retrieved from http://face.nist.gov/colorferet/request.html

Shen, D., & Ip, H. H. S. (1999). Discriminative wavelet shape descriptors for recognition of 2-D patterns. *Pattern Recognition, 32,* 151–165. doi:10.1016/S0031-3203(98)00137-X

Singh, C. (2006). Improved quality of reconstructed images using floating point arithmetic for moment calculation. *Pattern Recognition, 39,* 2047–2064. doi:10.1016/j.patcog.2006.05.025

Singh, C., Walia, E., & Mittal, N. (2011a). Face Recognition using Zernike and Complex Zernike moment features. *Pattern Recognition and Image Analysis, 21*(1), 71–81. doi:10.1134/S1054661811010044

Singh, C., Walia, E., & Mittal, N. (2011b). Magnitude and phase coefficients of Zernike and Pseudo Zernike moments for robust face recognition. In *Proceedings of the IASTED international conference on Computer Vision (CV- 2011)* (pp. 180-187). Vancouver, Canada: IASTED.

Singh, C., Walia, E., & Mittal, N. (2011c). Rotation Invariant Complex Zernike Moments Features and their Application to Human Face and Character Recognition. *IET Computer Vision, 5*(5), 255–265. doi:10.1049/iet-cvi.2010.0020

Teague, M. R. (1980). Image analysis via the general theory of moments. *Journal of the Optical Society of America, 70,* 920–930. doi:10.1364/JOSA.70.000920

Teh, C. H., & Chin, R. T. (1988). On image analysis by the methods of moments. *IEEE Transactions on Pattern Analysis and Machine Intelligence, 10,* 496–511. doi:10.1109/34.3913

Turk, M. (2001). A random walk through Eigenspace. *IEICE Transactions on Information and Systems. E (Norwalk, Conn.), 84-D*(12), 1586–1595.

Wee, C.-Y., & Paramesran, R. (2007). On the computational aspects of Zernike moments. *Image and Vision Computing, 25,* 967–980. doi:10.1016/j.imavis.2006.07.010

Xie, S., Shan, S., Chen, X., & Chen, J. (2010). Fusing Local Patterns of Gabor Magnitude and Phase for Face Recognition. *IEEE Transactions on Image Processing, 19*(5), 1349–1361. doi:10.1109/TIP.2010.2041397 PMID:20106741

Xu, Y., Zhang, D., Yang, J., & Yang, J.-Y. (2008). An approach for directly extracting features from matrix data and its application in face recognition. *Neurocomputing, 71,* 1857–1865. doi:10.1016/j.neucom.2007.09.021

Yang, J., Chu, D., Zhang, L., Xu, Y., & Yang, J. (2013). Sparse Representation Classifier Steered Discriminative Projection with Applications to Face Recognition. *IEEE Transactions on Neural Networks and Learning Systems, 24*(7), 1023–1035. doi:10.1109/TNNLS.2013.2249088 PMID:24808518

Zhao, W., Chellappa, R., Phillips, P., & Rosenfeld, A. (2003). Face recognition: A literature survey. *ACM Computing Surveys, 35,* 399–458. doi:10.1145/954339.954342

Zhi, R., & Ruan, Q. (2008). Two-dimensional direct and weighted linear discriminant analysis for face recognition. *Neurocomputing, 71,* 3607–3611. doi:10.1016/j.neucom.2008.04.047

APPENDIX

Key Terms and Definitions

Euclidean Distance: It is also known as $L_2 - norm$ or nearest neighbor classifier. The Euclidean distance between two sets of feature vectors is given by

$$d_2(x,y) = \sqrt{\sum_{k=1}^{L} (x_k - y_k)^2}$$

The x and y corresponds to the feature vectors of database and the query images, respectively and L is the size of the feature vectors.

Face Recognition: It is a biometric technique that employs automated methods to verify or recognize the identity of a person based on his/her physiological characteristics.

False Recognition Rate: It measures the percentage of authorized persons falsely rejected by the system. The *frr* can be computed by using the following formula

$$frr = \frac{n_{wc}}{n_{te}}$$

where n_{wc} is the number of wrongly classified images and n_{te} is the total number of test images.

Global Face Recognition Methods: Statistical approaches wherein the features are extracted from whole face image and every element in the feature vector will refer to some holistic characteristic of face images.

Invariant Features: Measurable quantities used to describe the objects are called invariants. These are insensitive to particular deformations, and provide enough discrimination power for distinguishing various objects belonging to different classes.

Local Face Recognition Methods: These structure-based approaches deal with local information, related to some interior parts of the face images that include features of nose patch, distance between the eye-centers, mouth width or height etc.

Recognition Rate: It is a common metric used to evaluate the performance of recognition techniques. Recognition rate can be computed as

$$R = \frac{\text{no. of recognized images}}{\text{total no. of images in test set}}$$

Chapter 8
An Efficient System for Blocking Pornography Websites

Tarek M. Mahmoud
Minia University, Egypt

Tarek Abd-El-Hafeez
Minia University, Egypt

Ahmed Omar
Minia University, Egypt

ABSTRACT

The Internet is a powerful source of information. However, some of the information that is available on the Internet cannot be shown to every type of public. For instance, pornography is not desirable to be shown to children; pornography is the most harmful content affecting child safety and causing many destructive side effects. A content filter is one of more pieces of software that work together to prevent users from viewing material found on the Internet. In this chapter, the authors present an efficient content-based software system for detecting and filtering pornography images in Web pages. The proposed system runs online in the background of Internet Explorer (IE) for the purpose of restricting access to pornography Web pages. Skin and face detection techniques are the main components of the proposed system. Because the proposed filter works online, the authors propose two fasting techniques that can be used to speed up the filtering system. The results obtained using the proposed system are compared with four commercial filtering programs. The success rate of the proposed filtering system is better than the considered filtering programs.

INTRODUCTION

Since the mid-1990s, greater Internet accessibility and advances in file-sharing technology spurred a proliferation in child pornography. The possession of child pornography is extremely troubling when you consider that in each image a child is being forced to engage in a sexual act (Sylvia, 2011). Pornography uses a variety of media, ranging from books, magazines, film and video. However, currently, one of the most prevalent means of distributing pornography is the Internet, by simply typing a few keywords into a search engine (e.g., Google) it is extremely easy to search for pornography on the Internet. The number one search term used on search engine sites is "sex".

DOI: 10.4018/978-1-4666-6030-4.ch008

Users searched for "sex" more than other terms, such as "games, travel, music, jokes, cars, weather, health," and "jobs" combined (Luke, 2010).

According to ConvententEyes report (Luke, 2010) and Internet Pornography Statistics (Ropelato, 2006):

- The largest group of viewers of Internet porn is children between ages 12 and17.
- More than 11 million teenagers view Internet pornography on a regular basis.
- One senior executive spent at least 331 days looking at pornography and chatting online with partially clad or nude women, this cost tax payers anywhere from $13,800 to $58,000.
- One worker perused hundreds of pornographic websites during work hours in a three week time frame in June 2008; that employee received a 10-day suspension.
- 12% (4.2 million websites) of the websites on the Internet are pornographic.
- 25% of daily search engine requests are pornography related.
- 35% of all Internet downloads are pornographic.
- 34% of Internet users received unwanted exposure to sexual material.
- Worldwide Pornography Revenues ballooned to $97.06 billion.
- Every second - 28,258 Internet users are viewing pornography.
- Every 39 minutes: a new pornographic video is being created in the United States.

Different researches and efforts have been carried out recently on how to block the pornography Websites among them content-based filtering is the most effective one (Ahmadi, Fotouhi, & Khaleghi, 2011).

Also, many software packages have been developed (Hammami, Chahir, & Chen, 2006) which mainly employ two kinds of approaches for classifying Web pages: static filtering and dynamic

filtering. Static filtering is based on blocking a specific Web address via searching it in a reference list of black URLs. Although this method has high speed of processing, but its shortcoming is the requirement for instantly update of the URL list. This updating is a very hard task in the rapidly improving Web. Another problem is the high rate of over-blocking the usual pages such as pages with medical, sports, or arts topics, or blocking a Website because of only one immoral page on it. In dynamic filtering, the classification is performed based on the content analysis. First, the content of the pages is analyzed by using learning models and then the page is classified based on the content features. Static and dynamic filters give the parents different degrees of control over the censorship depending on the program.

The outline of the chapter is as follows: Section 2 gives a brief overview of some filtering techniques .Section 3 gives a brief overview of skin detection techniques. Section 4 describes face detection techniques. In Section 5 the Proposed Filtering System is introduced. Experimental results are presented in section 6. Finally, conclusion and future work are presented in section 7.

RELATED WORK

Internet is an infinite information repository that also contains harmful contents like; pornography, violence, and hate messages. It is very important to obstruct these kinds of contents from underage children not to adversely affect their development. To block adult content, many solutions exist, such as filters that are part of image search engines like those of Google or Yahoo! As any user of these services is aware, they often fail to remove pornography images. The reasons are clear in that "current Internet image search technology is based upon words, rather than image content. Generally, there are two main approaches for pornography filtering software classification: classification based on textual content features, and classification based on both visual and textual features. The first group uses textual analysis mainly by searching a list of indicative keywords over the text such as sex, naked, etc. Some representative companies as NetNanny and SurfWatch (Girgis, Mahmoud, & Abd-El-Hafeez, 2010), operate by maintaining lists of URL's and newsgroups and require constant manual updating. In the second methods, textual content-based analysis together with visual features are used to get a more robust classification. Visual features (skin and non-skin pixels) are extracted from the images in the Web pages by utilizing effective skin detection techniques. Numerous techniques are presented in literature for pornography filtering. A web filtering engine combining textual and visual content-based analysis is proposed by Hammami et al. (Hammami, Chahir, & Chen, 2006). In their work, a number of 20 textual and profile features are extracted along with some visual features which are obtained from the skin-area in the images. Hu et al. (Hu, Wu, Chen, Fu, & Maybank, 2007) proposed a framework for recognizing pornographic Web pages. In their work, the Web pages are divided using the C4.5 decision tree algorithm into three categories (continuous text pages, discrete text pages, and image pages) according to content representations. Jones and Rehg (Jones & Rehg, 1999) combine a skin-model-based image detector and a text detector to detect pornographic Web pages and find that this combination improves the detection rate. A statistical approach combines both textual and visual contents is proposed by Chen et al. (Chen, O, Zhu, & W., 2006). Their work consists of three steps: (1) classification based on discrete text (keywords), (2) classification based on continuous text (sentences), and (3) classification through images. Besides using methods like skin color detection, they have also used some other features for image classification based on the Region of Interest (ROI). Bosson et al. (Bosson, Cawley, Chian,, & R., 2002) proposed a method based on visual content features. In the first stage they use a skin filter to localize

skin pixels and generate a skin blob. Then some topological features such as area, the length of the major and minor axis of an ellipse fitted to the blob, are used to classify the page. Girgis et al. (Girgis, Mahmoud, & Abd-El-Hafeez, 2010) presented a system for extracting images from Websites and detecting the skin areas. This system which is called BHO (browser helper object) was an Internet Explorer (IE) accessible object that ran in the background of IE and could extract all images and URL links in the page. Two techniques were introduced for skin detection based on color spaces: YUV and RGB.

SKIN DETECTION TECHNIQUES

Skin detection consists in detecting human skin pixels from an image. The system output is a binary image defined on the same pixel grid as the input image. Skin detection plays an important role in various applications such as face detection, searching and filtering image content on the web. Research has been performed on the detection of human skin pixels in color images by use of various statistical color models. Some researchers have used skin color models such as Gaussian, Gaussian mixture or histograms. Skin detection is the process of finding skin-colored pixels and regions in an image. Numerous techniques for skin color modeling and recognition have been proposed during several past years (Vezhnevets, Sazonov, & Andreeva, 2003). Pixel-based skin detection methods classify each pixel as skin or non-skin individually, independently from its neighbors. In contrast, region-based methods (Kruppa, Bauer, & Schiele, 2002), (Yang & Ahuja, 1998), (Jedynak, Zheng, & Daoudi, 2003) try to take the spatial arrangement of skin pixels into account during the detection stage to enhance the methods performance. The simplest methods in skin detection define or assume skin color to have a certain range or values in some coordinates of a color space. Identifying skin colored pixels involves finding the range of values for which most skin pixels would fall in a given color space (Kakumanu, Makrogiannis, & Bourbakis, 2007). A skin color distribution model based on the RGB, Normalized RGB, and HSV color spaces is constructed using correlation and linear regression (Ahmadi, Fotouhi, & Khaleghi, 2011). RGB is one of the most widely used color spaces for processing and storing of digital image data. HSV is a color model that is more intuitive to humans. To specify a color, one color is chosen and amounts of black and white are added, which gives different shades, tints and tones. In this model, a color is represented by three components: hue, saturation and value. Duan et al. (Duan, Cui, Gao, & Zhang, 2002) convert the pixels' value from RGB to YUV and YIQ respectively. The RGB values are transformed into YIQ values using the formulation:

$$\begin{bmatrix} Y \\ I \\ Q \end{bmatrix} = \begin{bmatrix} 0.2990 & 0.5870 & 0.1140 \\ 0.5957 & -0.2745 & -0.3213 \\ 0.2115 & -0.5226 & 0.3111 \end{bmatrix} \begin{bmatrix} R \\ G \\ B \end{bmatrix}$$

where I is defined as the red-orange axis and Q is roughly orthogonal to I. The less I value means the less blue-green and the more yellow. Converting from RGB to YUV can be accomplished using the formulation:

$$\begin{bmatrix} Y \\ U \\ V \end{bmatrix} = \begin{bmatrix} 0.2990 & 0.587 & 0.1140 \\ -0.147 & -0.289 & 0.436 \\ 0.615 & -0.515 & -0.100 \end{bmatrix} \begin{bmatrix} R \\ G \\ B \end{bmatrix}$$

An excellent survey on pixel-based skin color detection techniques and the different color spaces used for skin modelling can be found in (Vezhnevets, Sazonov, & Andreeva, 2003). Throughout this work, we used a combination between YIQ and YUV color spaces since this combination is more robust than each other (Girgis, Mahmoud, & Abd-El-Hafeez, 2007).

FACE DETECTION TECHNIQUES

Face detection has a wide range of applications on virtual reality, intelligent human machine interface, robotics, videophone system, computer vision communication and automatic access control system. The goal of face detection is to locate all the image regions that contain a face regardless of lighting condition (Jie, Xufeng, Yitan, & Zhonglong, 2008). Numerous techniques for face detection have been proposed during several past years (Amit & Geman, 1999) (Mohan, Papageorgiou, & Poggio, 2001) (Sung & Poggio, 1998) (Viola & Jones, Rapid Object Detection Using a Boosted Cascade of Simple Features, 2001). These techniques can be classified into five categories: knowledge (rules)-based techniques, feature invariant approaches, template matching methods, appearance-based methods, and rapid object detection using a boosted cascade of simple feature (Ge, Yang, Zheng, & F., 2006). Knowledge-based methods encode human knowledge of what constitutes a typical face (usually, the rules capture the relationship between facial features). The aim of feature-based methods is to find structural features that exist even when the pose, viewpoint and lighting conditions vary, and then use these features to locate faces in the arbitrary input image. In template matching methods, several standard patterns of a face are stored in advance to describe the whole face or the separate facial features. The correlations between an input image and the stored patterns are computed for face detection. In contrast to template matching the models (or templates) using appearance-based methods are learned from a set of training images that should capture the representative variability of facial appearance. In general, appearance-based methods mainly depend on techniques from statistical analysis and machine learning to find the relevant characteristics of face and non-face images. The learned characteristics are in the form of distribution models or discriminate functions that are consequently used for face detection. Rapid object detection uses a boosted cascade of simple feature. This method entails a machine learning approach for visual object detection, which is capable of processing images extremely rapidly and achieving high detection rates. First it introduces a new image representation called "integral image" which allows the features used by detector to be computed very quickly. The integral image can be computed from an image using a few operations per pixel. Once computed, any one of these Haar-like features can be computed on any scale or location in constant time. The second is a learning algorithm based on Adaboost, which selects a small number of critical visual features from a large set and yield extremely efficient classifies. The third is a method for combining increasingly more complex classifiers in a "cascade" which allows background regions of the image to be quickly discarded while spends more computation on promising object-like regions (Viola & Jones, Robust Real-Time Face Detection, 2004). An excellent survey on face detection techniques can be found in (Hjelmas, 2001) (Ge, Yang, Zheng, & F., 2006).

The face detection technique used in the proposed filter system is based on Viola and Jones algorithm. This algorithm belongs to rapid object detection using a boosted cascade of simple feature category. The next subsection introduces some details about this algorithm.

Viola and Jones Based Face Detection

The basic principle of the Viola-Jones algorithm is to scan a sub-window capable of detecting faces across a given input image (Viola & Jones, Robust Real-Time Face Detection, 2004). Their face detection procedure classifies images based on the value of simple features. The first step of the Viola-Jones face detection algorithm is to turn the input image into an integral image. This is done by making each pixel equal to the entire sum of all pixels above and to the left of the concerned pixel.

This allows for the calculation of the sum of all pixels inside any given rectangle using only four values. These values are the pixels in the integral image that coincide with the corners of the rectangle in the input image as shown in Figure 1.

The integral image at location x, y contains the sum of the pixels above and to the left of x, y, inclusive:

$$ii(x,y) = \sum_{x' \le x, \; y' \le y} i\left(x', y'\right) \qquad (1)$$

where ii (x, y) is the integral image and i (x, y) is the original image. Using the following pair of recurrences:

$$s\left(x,y\right) = s\left(x, y-1\right) + i\left(x, y\right) \qquad (2)$$

$$ii\left(x,y\right) = ii\left(x-1, y\right) + s\left(x, y\right) \qquad (3)$$

where s(x, y) is the cumulative row sum, s(x, −1) =0, and ii (−1, y) = 0) the integral image can be computed in one pass over the original image.

Figure 1. The value of the integral image at point (x, y) is the sum of all the pixels above and to the left

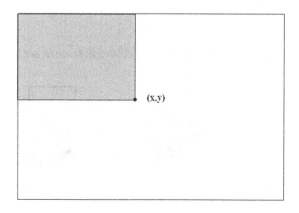

The second step of this technique is a simple and efficient classifier that is built by selecting a small number of important features from a huge library of potential features using AdaBoost.

Viola and Jones detection procedure classifies images based on the value of simple features. The different types of features are shown in Figure 2.

Each feature results in a single value which is calculated by subtracting the sum of the white rectangle(s) from the sum of the black rectangle(s). Viola and Jones have empirically found that a detector with a base resolution of 24×24 pixels gives satisfactory results.

Viola and Jones used a simple and efficient classifier built from computationally efficient features using AdaBoost for feature selection. AdaBoost is a machine learning boosting algorithm capable of constructing a strong classifier through a weighted combination of weak classifiers. (A weak classifier classifies correctly in only a little bit more than half the cases.) To match this terminology to the presented theory each feature is considered to be a potential weak classifier. A weak classifier is mathematically described as:

$$h\left(x, f, p, \theta\right) = \begin{cases} 1 & if\ pf\left(x\right) < p\theta \\ 0 & otherwise \end{cases} \quad (4)$$

where x is a 24×24 pixel sub-window, f is is the applied feature, p the polarity and θ the threshold that decides whether x should be classified as a positive (a face) or a negative (a non-face).

We proposed a hybrid face detection technique (Mahmoud, Abdel-latef, Abd-El-Hafeez, & Omar, 30 June – 3 July, 2011), that combine Viola and Jones face detection technique and skin detection technique to improve to detecting efficiency. The proposed technique can be summarized as follows:

1. Apply Viola & Jones face detection technique.
2. For each detected region f we compute the Skin Percentage SP.
3. If $45 \leq SP \leq 95$ then the detected region represents a face.

THE PROPOSED FILTERING SYSTEM

Girgis et al. (Girgis, Mahmoud, & Abd-El-Hafeez, 2010) presented a filter system for extracting images from Websites and detecting the skin areas, and then prevent Web sites containing pornography images. This system which is called BHO (browser helper object) was an Internet Explorer (IE) accessible object that ran in the background of IE and could extract all images and URL links in the page. The percentage of skin content pixels is used as the criterion for judging if the image contains significant human skin pixels to be classified as pornography or non-pornography. The main drawback of this system is that the images containing faces only are classified as pornography. In order to overcome this drawback we

Figure 2. The Viola–Jones rectangle feature set

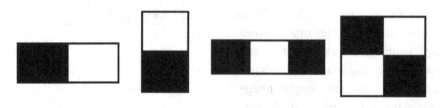

propose a new filter system based on both face and skin detection techniques. We calculate the face skin percentage and then subtract it from the total calculated skin percentage. If skin color pixels are up to the level of between 5% and 10% it indicates a human being is most probably in the image. If the percentage of skin pixels is between 10% and 15%, it is more than likely pornography image. If the percentage of skin pixels is more than 15%, it is a pornography image. The overall algorithm can be described as follows:

1. Start the browser.
2. Set the browser events.
3. Go to the specified URL and execute the extract images phase (described in Section 5.1).
4. Execute the Skin detection phase (described in Section 3).
5. Execute the Face detection phase (described in Section 4.1).
6. Execute the Filter decision phase (described in Section 5.2).
7. Start navigating to different URL.

The proposed system allows the user to choose one of the following filtering techniques:

- Skin detection Filtering.
- Keyword filtering.
- URL filtering.
- Domain Filtering.
- Combination of two or more of the above filtering techniques.

In our filtering system, the blacklist filtering is divided into URL and Domain filtering. If the text Analysis, URL_Analysis, and/or Domain Analysis method returns a non-zero number then:

1. Stop the Web browser (display a window like the case of Internet disconnection), or
2. Redirect the user to the warning page that we are design (see Figure 3).

Once the System classifies the web page as Pornography, it adds this web page to the blacklist automatically, if it is not already there. Figure 4 shows the structure of the filtering system.

Figure 3. The warning page

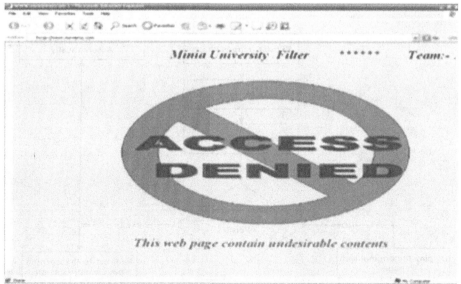

Extracting Images Phase

Girgis et al. (Girgis, Mahmoud, & Abd-El-Hafeez, 2007) introduced three new methods for extracting images from the Web pages. The first method extracts images after loading the Web page. The second method extracts images before loading the Web page physically from the local host. The third method extracts images before loading the Web page from any server. These proposed methods overcome the drawback of the regular expressions method for extracting images suggested by Ilan Assayag (Ilan, 2012). Throughout this work we used the method of extracting images from the

Web pages before loading the Web page from any server. The steps of this method can be described as follows:

1. Read the contents of the Web page.
2. Read the HTML code into an HTML document to enable parsing.
3. Get Image Data from the HTML document.
4. Foreach (HTMLImgClass image in doc. images)
   a. Download the image from the server.

Figure 4. The proposed filtering system structure

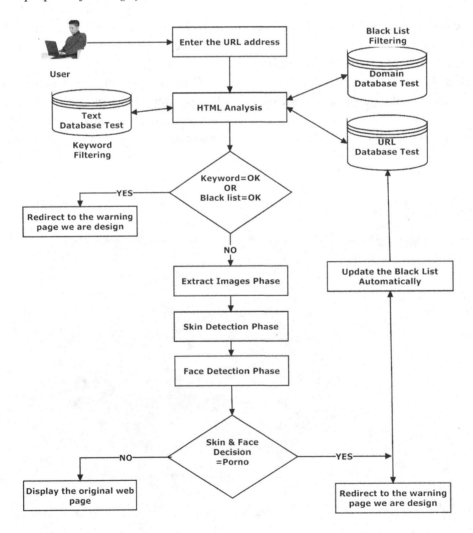

Filter Decision Phase

As described above, the percentage of skin content pixels is used as the criterion for judging if the image contains significant human skin pixels to be classified as pornography or non-pornography. The filter decision phase steps can be described as follows:

- Calculate the Total Skin Percentage (TSP).
- Calculate the Face Skin Percentage (FSP).
- Subtract the Face Skin Percentage (FSP) from the Total Skin Percentage (TSP) and denote this value by NFP.
- If $5\% \leq NFP < 10\%$ then the Web site contains human images.
- Else if $10\% \leq NFP < 15\%$ then the Web site contains likely pornography images.
- Else if $NFP \geq 15\%$ then the Web site contains pornography images.

EXPERIMENTAL RESULTS

This section presents the results of the experiments, which were carried out to evaluate the effectiveness of our system in filtering pornography images. The system is implemented using C# programming language. The experiments are done on an Intel Core 2 Duo 2.93 GHz PC running Microsoft Windows XP Operating System. We conduct three types of experimental methods. The aim of the first experiment was to evaluate the effectiveness of the proposed filtering system. The second experiment was conducted to compare the proposed filtering system with some other existing filtering software. The aim of the last experiment was conducted to improve the CPU time of both skin detection and decision make phases.

Filter Decision Using Face Detection Results

In order to evaluate the proposed filtering system performance, we used different Web pages. Some of these pages include plain-text pages, non-pornographic with the subject of health care, training, scientific news, and sports. As described in Section 5, the percentage of skin content pixels is used as the criterion for judging if the image contains significant human skin pixels to be classified as pornography or non-pornography. Table 1 gives some comparison results between the proposed filtering system and the filtering system proposed by Girgis et al. As can been seen in this Table, the proposed filtering system classifies the

Table 1. Comparison between the proposed filtering system and Girgis et al filtering system

Original Image	The proposed filtering system	Girgis et al Filtering System
	Human Image	Porno Image
	Porno Image	Porno Image
	Human Image	Porno Image
	Porno Image	Porno Image
	Human Image	Porno Image
	Human Image	Porno Image

porno images correctly compared with the other filtering system.

The judgment of both the proposed filtering system and Girgis et al filtering system on the contents of some non-pornographic Web pages is given in Table 2. As can been seen in this Table, the judgment of the proposed filtering system is correct compared to the other system.

Comparison with Other Commercial Filters

Filtering software companies divide their control lists into multiple categories for which they have created unique definitions. Sexually explicit materials, violence, hate speech, gambling, drugs, alcohol, Tobacco, astrology, mysticism, entertainment … etc., are some kinds of these categories (Superkids Educational Software Reviews) (Tom). These filtering programs bring a lot of real-world experience in protecting kids online and the parent has almost complete control over what kind of content is viewable. CYBERsitter, CyberPatrol, NetNanny, and SurfWatch are some of these filtering programs. In order to evaluate the effectiveness of our proposed filtering system, we compare it with these programs. We tested 124 Web pages with different categories (adult/sexually explicit, business, sports, news, and feminist) and some of the comparison results are shown in Tables 3, 4, and 5.

Table 6 summarizes the efficiency percentages of the proposed filtering system compared to these filtering programs in Web sites judgment (blocked or not blocked). The second row shows the total number of errors (false positive and false negative). The last row contains the success percentage of each product and the proposed filtering system. As can been in Table 6:

Table 2. Filter judgment of both the proposed filtering system and Girgis et al filtering system

Web page's URL	The proposed filtering system	Girgis et al filtering system
http://totallylookslike.icanhascheezburger.com/	not blocked	blocked
http://www.facedouble.com/	not blocked	blocked
http://www.nordinho.net/vbull/blogs/tara/index6.html	not blocked	blocked
http://boards.weddingbee.com/topic/look-a-likes	not blocked	blocked
http://www.hairstyle-blog.com/heart-face.html	not blocked	blocked
http://www.lovelyhairstyles.net/short-hairstyles-for-round-faces-2012.html	not blocked	blocked
http://mediumlengthhair-styles.com/	not blocked	blocked
http://www.hairstylesnew2012.tk/uncategorized/best-of-men-hairstyles	not blocked	blocked
http://trendhairstyles.net/tag/men	not blocked	blocked
http://www.hairstylestrend.com/hairstyles-2011/popular-men-hairstyles-2011.html	not blocked	blocked
http://mens-haircuts.net/	not blocked	blocked
http://allentry.blogspot.com/2011/10/different-hair-styles-for-men.html	not blocked	blocked
http://slhairstyles.com/01/2010-shag-hairstyles-the-celebrities-invasion.html	not blocked	blocked
http://www.latesthairstylesdesign.com/category/haircuts-for-round-faces	not blocked	blocked

Table 3. Sex search results

#	URL	CYBERsitter	CyberPatrol	NetNanny	SurfWatch	Proposed Filtering System
	http://www.xtacy.com/	blocked	**not blocked**	**not blocked**	blocked	**Blocked**
	http://www.trailerparktrash.com/	blocked	blocked	**not blocked**	blocked	**Blocked**
	http://www.sexis.com/russia/info.htm	blocked	**not blocked**	**not blocked**	blocked	**Blocked**

Table 4. COPA litigants

URL	CYBERsitter	CyberPatrol	NetNanny	SurfWatch	Proposed Filtering System
http://www.sexualhealth.com/	blocked	blocked	**not blocked**	**not blocked**	**Blocked**
http://www.adlbooks.com/	**blocked**	not blocked	not blocked	not blocked	**Blocked**
http://www.bookweb.org/	not blocked	not blocked	not blocked	not blocked	not blocked
http://www.artnet.com/	not blocked	not blocked	not blocked	not blocked	not blocked
http://www.condomania.com/	blocked	blocked	not blocked	blocked	**Blocked**
http://www.freespeech.org/	not blocked	not blocked	not blocked	blocked	Blocked

Table 5. Feminist sites

URL	CYBERsitter	CyberPatrol	NetNanny	SurfWatch	Proposed Filtering System
http://www.now.org/	**blocked**	not blocked	not blocked	not blocked	not blocked
http://www.feminist.org/	not blocked	not blocked	not blocked	not blocked	not blocked
http://www.guerrillagirls.com/	**blocked**	not blocked	not blocked	not blocked	not blocked
http://www.FeministUtopia.com/	not blocked	not blocked	not blocked	not blocked	not blocked

Table 6. The efficiency comparison of our system and other filtering products

	CYBERsitter	CyberPatrol	NetNanny	SurfWatch	Proposed Filtering System
Total No. of Errors	13.7%	4.8%	9.7%	5.6%	4 %
success %	86.29%	95.16%	90.32%	94.35%	96.77%

- The total number of errors of the proposed filtering system is less than the considered filtering programs.
- The success rate of the proposed filtering system is better than the considered filtering programs.

Improvement the Filtering Decision Time

Because our proposed filter works online, the filtering decision (block or not block) CPU time is an important factor. This section proposes two fasting techniques that can be used to speed up the filtering system. The first technique is used in the skin detection phase of the proposed filtering system. The second technique is used in the filter decision phase.

The Proposed Fast Skin Detection Technique

Most traditional methods used for skin detection represents image pixels in a suitable color space and then test each pixel to label it as skin or non-skin. This approach consumes long time. Tarek (Mahmoud T., 2008) introduced fast skin color detection technique based on skipping a set of pixels instead of testing each image pixel. As can been seen in any pornography image:

- The skin area is often greater than non skin pixels.
- Skin pixels are concentrated at the image center.

So, in our technique we start the pixel testing on the area around the image center. We have conducted many experiments to choose the most appropriate form of the area surrounding the image center. Figure 5 illustrates some of these forms that have been tested. We found that the most appropriate form giving accurate results is as in Figure 5.d.

As can been in Figure 6, the area of selected region is obtained by multiplying its height by half of its width.

The skipping process suggested by Tarek (Mahmoud T., 2008) can be used in our proposed technique. The steps of the proposed method can be described as follows:

Step 1: Extract the images from web pages.
Step 2: Determine the area surrounding the image center (as in Figure 5.d) where Area = height x 1/2 width

Figure 5. Example of tested parts

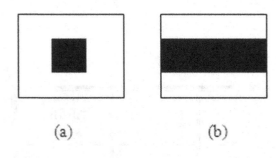 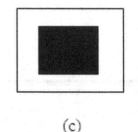 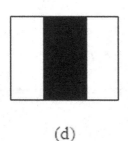

    (a)   (b)   (c)   (d)

Figure 6. Image example centralized human skin

Step 3: Apply the skin color detection on the selected are with skipping a predetermined number of pixels.

Step 4: Record the CPU time of the detection process

Table 7 shows some comparison results of the measured CPU time (in seconds) between the traditional skin detection, the skipping technique proposed by Tarek, and our proposed fast detection technique. We used pornography images with different sizes to evaluate the run time of

the proposed technique. The second and third columns of Table 7 contain the image width and height respectively.

As can be seen in Table 7:

1. Using the proposed skin detection technique speed up the required CPU time compared with the traditional and skipping techniques.
2. The average saving CPU time of the proposed technique compared with the traditional and skipping techniques is approximately 92% and 86% respectively.

Table 7. Measured CPU time in seconds of traditional, skipping, and proposed skin detection techniques

Image No.	Image width	Image height	Traditional technique	Skipping technique	Proposed technique
1	515	380	0.532	0.281	0.062
2	796	550	1.156	0.657	0.094
3	293	400	0.312	0.172	0.016
4	500	758	0.843	0.391	0.047
5	308	450	0.359	0.203	0.032
6	360	524	0.531	0.281	0.031
7	640	480	0.75	0.422	0.063
8	300	225	0.188	0.093	0.016
9	531	542	0.687	0.359	0.047
10	856	684	1.562	0.828	0.109
11	1024	768	2.141	1.203	0.172
12	1427	1019	3.719	2.062	0.281
13	796	550	1.093	0.609	0.078
14	800	600	1.219	0.703	0.109
15	1439	948	3.656	2.093	0.281
16	700	500	0.89	0.516	0.078
17	796	550	1.11	0.625	0.093
18	796	550	1.141	0.641	0.094
19	575	386	0.578	0.344	0.046
20	796	550	1.125	0.625	0.094
21	796	550	1.14	0.641	0.078
22	575	386	0.579	0.313	0.047
23	796	550	1.172	0.641	0.093
24	796	550	1.141	0.625	0.094
Average CPU time			**1.151**	**0.639**	**0.09**

Parallel Process Results

As described above, our proposed filtering technique is based on both face and skin detection techniques. To reduce the CPU time required in the decision phase of the proposed technique, we can execute both face detection and skin detection in parallel. Many experiments were conducted to study the effect of using the parallel processing in our proposed technique. Table 8 gives some CPU time comparison study of these experiments between the traditional filter technique and our proposed filtering technique. Column 1 in Table 8 contains URL of the tested Web site, column 2 contains the number of images existing in the considered Web site, and columns 3 and 4 contain the measured CPU time in seconds.

As can be seen in Table 8:

1. Using the proposed filtering technique speed up the required CPU time compared with the traditional technique.
2. The average saving CPU time of the proposed technique compared with the traditional technique is approximately 92%.

FUTURE RESEARCH DIRECTIONS

There are still many issues to be considered in the future works. Some instances of these issues are: the ability of using machine learning tools as pornography Websites classifiers and comparing them with our proposed technique.

CONCLUSION

In this chapter, we have presented an efficient content based approach to filter pornography Websites. The proposed system runs online in the background of Internet Explorer (IE). Skin and face detection techniques are the main components of the proposed system. We used the percentage of skin content pixels as the criterion for judging if the image contains significant human skin pixels to be classified as pornography or non-pornography. In our implementation, we calculated the face skin percentage and then subtracted it from the total calculated skin percentage to overcome the traditional filtering techniques. According to the experimental results, the success rate of the proposed filtering system was better than four considerable commercial filtering software. Two

Table 8. Traditional and parallel phase decision time comparing

URL	Number of Image	Traditional filtering CPU time in seconds	Proposed filtering CPU time in seconds	Notes
www.softpedia.com	295	70.2	16.3	
http://cima4u.com/	45	100.715	30.64	This Web site contains large size images
http://maktoob.yahoo.com/?p=us	14	9.27	3.63	
http://www.moviemo.com	115	90.65	20.36	This Web site contains small size images

new approaches to improve the consuming CPU time required to judge the Website as pornography or not are introduced.

REFERENCES

Ahmadi, A., Fotouhi, M., & Khaleghi, M. (2011). Intelligent classification of web pages using contextual and visual features. *Applied Soft Computing*, 1638–1647. doi:10.1016/j.asoc.2010.05.003

Amit, Y., & Geman, D. (1999). A computational model for visual selection. *Neural Computation, 11*, 1691–1715. doi:10.1162/089976699300016197 PMID:10490943

Bosson, A., & Cawley, G. C. Y., & R., H. (2002). Blocking pornographic images.Proceedings of the International Conference on the Challenge of Image and Video Retrieval. *Lecture Notes in Computer Science, 2383*, 50–60.

Chen, Z. O, W., Zhu, M., & W., H. (2006). A novel web page filtering system by combining texts and images. In *Proceedings of the 2006 IEEE/WIC/ACM International Conference on Web Intelligence*, (pp. 732-735). Washington, DC: IEEE Computer Society.

Duan, L., Cui, G., Gao, W., & Zhang, H. (2002). Adult image detection method base-on skin color model and support vector machine. In *Proceedings of Asian Conference on computer Vision* (pp. 797-800). Melbourne, Australia: Academic Press.

Ge, X., Yang, J., & Zheng, Z., & F., L. (2006). Multi-view based face chin contour extraction. *Engineering Applications of Artificial Intelligence*, 545–555. doi:10.1016/j.engappai.2005.12.010

Girgis, M. R., Mahmoud, T. M., & Abd-El-Hafeez, T. (2007). An Approach to Image Extraction and Accurate Skin Detection from Web Pages. *International Journal of Computer Science and Engineering, 1* (1307-3699), 88-96.

Girgis, M. R., Mahmoud, T. M., & Abd-El-Hafeez, T. (2010). A New Effective System for Filtering Pornography Images from Web Pages and PDF Files. *International Journal of Web Applications, 2*.

Hammami, M., Chahir, Y., & Chen, L. (2006). WebGuard: a web filtering engine combining textual, structural, and visual content-based analysis. *IEEE Transactions on Knowledge and Data Engineering, 18*, 272–284. doi:10.1109/TKDE.2006.34

Hjelmas, E. (2001). Face Detection: A Survey. *Computer Vision and Image Understanding, 83*, 236–274. doi:10.1006/cviu.2001.0921

Hu, W., Wu, O., Chen, Z., Fu, Z., & Maybank, S. (2007). Recognition of pornographic web pages by classifying texts and Images. *IEEE Transactions on Pattern Analysis and Machine Intelligence, 29*, 1019–1034. doi:10.1109/TPAMI.2007.1133 PMID:17431300

Ilan, A. (2012, January). *Code Project*. Retrieved from http://www.codeproject.com

Jedynak, B., Zheng, H., & Daoudi, M. (2003, June). Statistical models for skin detection. In *Proceedings of IEEE Workshop on Statistical Analysis in Computer Vision. In conjunction with CVPR 2003 Madison*, (pp. 16–22). IEEE.

Jie, Y., Xufeng, L., Yitan, Z., & Zhonglong, Z. (2008). A face detection and recognition system in color image series. *Mathematics and Computers in Simulation*, 531–539. doi:10.1016/j.matcom.2007.11.020

Jones, M., & Rehg, J. (1999). Statistical Color Models with Application to Skin Detection. *International Journal of Computer Vision*, 274–280.

Kakumanu, P., Makrogiannis, S., & Bourbakis, N. (2007). A Survey of Skin-Color Modeling and Detection Methods. *Pattern Recognition, 40*, 1106–1122. doi:10.1016/j.patcog.2006.06.010

Kruppa, H., Bauer, M. A., & Schiele, B. (2002). Skin patch detection in real-world images. In *Proceedings of Annual Symposium for Pattern Recognition of the DAGM 2002,* (LNCS), (vol. 2449, pp. 109–117). Berlin: Springer.

Luke, G. (2010, October). *Covenanteyes.* Retrieved January 2012, from http://www.covenanteyes. com/2010/01/06/updated-pornography-statistics/

Mahmoud, T. (2008). A New Fast Skin Color Detection Technique. *World Academy of Science. Engineering and Technology, 33,* 2070–3740.

Mahmoud, T. M. Abdel- latef, B. A., Abd-El-Hafeez, T., & Omar, A. (2011). An Effective Hybrid Method for Face Detection. In *Proceedings of Fifth International Conference on Intelligent Computing and Information Systems* (ICICIS 2011). Cairo, Egypt: ACM.

Mohan, A., Papageorgiou, C., & Poggio, T. (2001). Example-based object detection in images by components. *IEEE Transactions on Pattern Analysis and Machine Intelligence, 23,* 349–361. doi:10.1109/34.917571

Ropelato, J. (2006). *Internet pornography statistics.* Retrieved from http://internet-filter-review. toptenreviews.com/internet-pornography-statistics.html

Sung, K., & Poggio, T. (1998). Example-based learning for view-based human face detection. *IEEE Transactions on Pattern Analysis and Machine Intelligence, 20,* 39–51. doi:10.1109/34.655648

Superkids Educational Software Reviews. (n.d.). Retrieved january 2012, from http://www. superkids.com/aweb/pages/reviews/kidsafe/1/ sw_sum1.shtml

Sylvia, K. (2011). To block or not to block e European child porno law in question. *Computer Law & Security Report, 27,* 573–584. doi:10.1016/j. clsr.2011.09.005

Tom, I. (n.d.). *Review: CyberPatrol 4 & SurfWatch 3.* Retrieved january 2012, from http://www.atpm. com/4.11/page11.shtml

Vezhnevets, V., Sazonov, V., & Andreeva, A. (2003). A survey on pixel-based skin color detection techniques. In *Proceedings of GraphiCon* (pp. 85–92). GraphiCon.

Viola, P., & Jones, M. J. (2001). Rapid Object Detection Using a Boosted Cascade of Simple Features. In *Proceedings of IEEE Conference Computer Vision and Pattern Recognition, CVPR (1)* (pp. 511-518). IEEE Computer Society.

Yang, M. H., & Ahuja, N. (1998). Detecting human faces in color images. In *Proceedings of International Conference on Image Processing (ICIP),* (vol. 1, pp. 127–130). Chicago: ICIP.

KEY TERMS AND DEFINITIONS

Color Models: Abstract mathematical model describing the way colors can be represented as tuples of numbers.

Content Based Filtering: The classification is performed based on the content analysis.

Face Detection: Determine if the image contains face(s) or not, and if contains return location and size of each detected face.

Internet Pornography: Pornography materials in the internet including video, image, and text.

Pornography Filtering: Prevent access to pornography contents.

Skin Detection: Detect skin pixels in the color image.

URL: Uniform resource locator, also known as web address, is a specific character string that constitutes a reference to a resource.

Chapter 9
Online User Interaction Traits in Web–Based Social Biometrics

Madeena Sultana
University of Calgary, Canada

Padma Polash Paul
University of Calgary, Canada

Marina Gavrilova
University of Calgary, Canada

ABSTRACT

During the Internet era, millions of users are using Web-based Social Networking Sites (SNSs) such as MySpace, Facebook, and Twitter for communication needs. Social networking platforms are now considered a source of big data because of real-time activities of a large number of users. In addition to idiosyncratic personal characteristics, web-based social data may include person-to-person communication, profiles, patterns, and spatio-temporal information. However, analysis of social interaction-based data has not been studied from the perspective of person identification. In this chapter, the authors introduce for the first time the concept of using interaction-based features from online social networking platforms as a novel biometric. They introduce the concept of social behavioral biometric from SNSs to aid the identification process. Analysis of these novel biometric features and their potential use in various security and authentication applications are also presented. Such applications would pave the way for new directions in biometric research.

INTRODUCTION

Biometric identification is defined as "an automated process of recognizing persons from their characteristics" (Jain et al., 2004). Traditionally, two types of biometrics: physiological and behavioural, has been considered (Jain et al., 2004). Physiological biometrics relies on physical attributes of individuals, such as face, palm, fingerprint, iris, ear etc. Behavioural biometrics are based on human activities dictated by person's behaviour, such as handwriting, gait, signature and voice, which also afford discriminability among individuals. Behavioural biometrics are more vola-

DOI: 10.4018/978-1-4666-6030-4.ch009

tile to changes one undergoes through the life time, but have the advantages of being non-intrusive and cost effective over physiological biometrics (Yampolskiy & Govindaraju, 2008). It is gaining an increasing demand for person identification and verification purposes to reduce security threats, especially in the cyber world (Sourin, 2006, Saeed & Nagashima, 2012).

In this chapter, we first classify the existing behavioural biometrics into two main categories: *machine-independent* human behaviour and *machine-dependent* human behaviour. Machine independent behavioural biometrics are well established in the community, with most of the early works falling under this category. For example, person identification from his/her unique signature (Monwar & Gavrilova, 2008, Saeed, 2014), gait or walking style (Bazazian & Gavrilova, 2012), or from a piece of drawing (Al-Zubi et al., 2003) are being studied over last decade. The latter category is emerging compared to the former and more demanding field of research due to increasing number of security threats in virtual domain. Because of the wide range of applications of computing devices and software, users can interact with machine in many ways. We classify machine dependent human behaviours further into the following three sub-categories based on the type of communication with the machine: *interaction- based, style-based, and intelligence-based.*

First subcategory is based on human interaction with input device that does not consider any knowledge or intelligence of the user. Some examples are keystroke dynamics (Bakelman et al., 2013), mouse dynamics (Jorgensen & Yu, 2011), touchscreen interaction (Bo et al., 2013, Frank et al., 2012) etc. Second subcategory takes into account the style or preference of a user during interaction with the computer. Coding style of a programmer (Spafford & Weeber, 1993), browsing style (Olejnik & Castelluccia, 2013) or handshaking style (Guo et al., 2013) would fall into this category. Finally, the third subdivision includes human intelligence, knowledge, and skills

into account during interaction with software such as game playing strategy (Yampolskiy & Govindaraju, 2010), car driving skill (Igarashi et al., 2004), hobby or habits (Jiang et al., 2013) etc.

However, human activities with machine, especially with the computing devices, are not limited to programming, computing, gaming or simply typing. Now, in the era of social networking, our identity as well as everyday activities has been naturally extended into virtual world. According to the statistical report (statisticbrain, 2014), a popular social networking site Twitter has around 5.5 billion of active registered users who produces 58 million tweets per day and 9,100 tweets per second. In addition, 135,000 new users are signing up to Twitter every day. Such statistics demonstrate that activities in online social networking sites are now a part of daily life of millions of humans. Our first hypothesis is that, similarly to a physical world, behavioral patterns and habits are present in the daily activities of virtual world users. Patterns can be found in different online social activities such as: tweets, status updates, 'likes', URLs, photo and video tagging, media sharing, uploads, comments, instant messages, communications, and so on. Our second hypothesis is that a person can be identified based on his activities and information which accumulates through online social networking platforms. Therefore, in this chapter we are introducing the fourth subcategory of machine dependent behavioral biometrics: *web-based social biometrics*. We also investigate the feasibility of using users' web-based social networking activities as novel behavioral biometrics to identify a person in virtual domain. Some identified application domains of the proposed web-based social biometrics are shown in Figure 1. Some of them have been investigated from author authorship attribution (Gray et al., 1997) point of view but rarely been studied from biometric identification perspective.

In this chapter, we introduce *web-based social data as auxiliary behavioral biometric features*. The concept of how these features can be used for

Figure 1. Application domains of web-based social biometrics

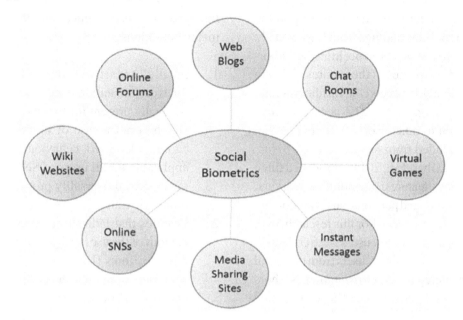

person identification will also be analyzed. Some existing works based on relevant web-based social data are reviewed in the background study. Some state-of-the-art web-based biometric features are analyzed thereafter to understand the significance of the novel biometric. The key challenges and applications are also identified to discover the potential directions for the future research.

BACKGROUND

In this work, we are interested to explore personal characteristics or biometric features from the communicative activities of users on social networking sites. Although human behaviour and communication style through online SNSs are not being investigated from biometric perspective, they have been studied by the researchers of another domain for authorship attribution. In this section, we discuss the approaches to author identification from micro-blogs (e.g. tweets) as well as the differences between the proposed web-based social biometrics and author identification.

In 2010, Shalhoub et al. (Shalhoub et al., 2010) studied the feasibility of applying stylistic features or stylometry for author identification from Twitter. They considered a case where a user's writing profile has to be generated from his books, blogs or other writings. Then this profile would be matched to a writing profile created from tweets. However, the use case authors considered is quite limited in scope since it can only be applied if a user already has some writing samples (book, blogs etc.), which may not be the case. In addition, tweets are usually very unstructured and fragmented because of the length constraint of 140 characters. Therefore, matching two different kind of writing profiles may not produce satisfactory results.

In the same year, Layton et al. (Layton et al., 2010) published the very first work of author identification from microblogs on Twitter. Here, the whole identification process is based on tweets or microblogs collected from Twitter. About 200 tweets from each of the 14000 users were collected initially, and then 50 potential authors were selected for experimentation. Source Code

Authorship Profile (SCAP) and n-gram methods were applied to determine the authorship in the text. Three important findings from Layton et al., 2010 are: a) 140 characters do not limit the authorship identification process if the features are being selected efficiently, b) tweets contain idiosyncratic features of a person, and c) 27% accuracy drops if commination to other users i.e. replies (@) in tweets are excluded from feature set.

Silva et al. (Silva et al., 2011) introduced three type of stylistic features: quantitative markers, marks of emotions, and punctuation for authorship identification from tweets. For this research, over 4 million tweets of 200,000 users were collected. However, only 120 "prolific" users from the initial set were considered for experimentation. Authors showed that good performance (F=0.54) can be obtained by applying all the features to a set of training examples as small as 60 tweets per author.

In another study by MacLeod and Grant (Macleod & Grant, 2012) showed that aggregated tweets produces better results than single tweets as training set. During experimentation, they aggregated messages from 2 to 10 and then extracted a number of features based on grammatical style, lexicons, and punctuations from the aggregated message. For a set of 20 authors, maximum accuracy has been obtained by aggregating 10 messages as one training sample. An additional finding from this work is common phrases such as 'LOL' ('Lough Out Loud') has less contribution than rare ones e.g. 'BBIAB' ('Be Back In A Bit') for the identification purpose.

A comparative analysis of using frequency based features and style based features has been accomplished by Green and Sheppard in (Green & Sheppard, 2013). They found that length constraint of 140 characters of tweets limits the effectiveness of vocabulary based Bag-Of-Words (BOW) method. However, context free style markers such as capitalization, punctuations etc. are much more informative for author identification than traditional BOW method.

All of the above-mentioned works are intended for cyber forensic applications thus have two major limitations:

1. Small closed set of candidates are being used for experimentation since a small suspect list is usually present for forensic applications, which is not a case of biometric identification. Identified behaviours have to be applicable for all users of SNS to maintain the desired universality property of a good biometric trait.

2. Features that indicates communication behaviour of the user such as replies, hashtags, retweets, links (URLs), etc. are ignored to keep the anonymity intact for forensic applications. However, these are very important factors that we want to investigate in our study. According to our second hypothesis, commination factors exhibit strong idiosyncratic behaviour of a person and considering these factors would increase the identification rate. We also want to investigate other factors such as temporal information, connections to other users (friends) to explore a strong behavioural pattern of users in SNSs.

Therefore, author identification from microblogs is a small subset of our investigation towards web-based social biometrics.

STATE-OF-THE-ART BEHAVIORAL BIOMETRICS

One major advantage of behavioural biometric over traditional biometric is it is very difficult to fake. For example, it might be possible to prepare a fake fingerprint but imitating the walking style of a person (i.e. gait) is quite difficult. For this reason, behavioral biometric is becoming a popular alternative to well-established physiological biometrics, such as fingerprints. Many new behavioral biometrics have been proposed within the last few years. A summary of behavioral biometrics until 2011 can be found in (Yampolskiy, 2011). Some state-of-the-art behavioral biometrics proposed since 2012 are listed below:

Continuous Keystroke Dynamics

In 2012, Bours (Bours, 2012) used keystroke dynamics as a behavioral biometric for continuous authentication of a user instead of ordinary static authentication. The concept of continuous authentication is the following. The current user is continuously verified by matching his/her typing pattern to the stored template. Continuous matching does not mean that if the user does any typing mistake the system would be locked out instantly. Only the confidence or trust level of genuine user would decrease and it may increase again if the user's typing matches with the stored template. The system would only be locked out if the trust level decreases below a certain threshold. Thus, typing behavior of the user would serve as a biometric to authenticate the user continuously.

Context-Based Gait Biometric

Bazazian and Gavrilova (Bazazian & Gavrilova, 2012) proposed a novel context based gait biometrics for person identification. In this work, additional information about behavioral patterns of users and the context are fused with gait biometrics to enhance the recognition rate. This work demonstrates that the performance of existing gait recognition systems can be improved up to 100% by fusing distinctive context-based behavioral features of users even at a very low cost.

Touch-Based Biometrics

Frank et al., 2012 (Frank et al., 2012) identified 30 behavioral touch features from raw touchscreen logs of smartphones and named these novel biometric features as *Touchalytics*. This study dem-

onstrates that different users has distinct pattern of navigation and this behavioral pattern exhibits consistency over time. However, *Touchalytic* is not enough for being used as a standalone continuous authentication system for long term; it could be utilized for short-term authentication or as a part of a multimodal biometric authentication system. In 2013, Bo et al. (Bo et al., 2013) showed that considering the fine details of touch pattern improves the uniqueness of the touch-based biometrics. As a result, the user identification rate could reach as high as 99% using solely touch-based micro and large-scale movements on smart phones.

Handshaking Biometrics

Handshaking is a specific set of human actions needed to unlock the screen of the smartphone of a user. Guo et al. (Guo et al., 2013) collected 200 users' handshaking actions with their smart phones. They observed unique, stable, and distinguishable idiosyncratic patterns in shaking behaviors of users. Based on these findings, the authors designed four shaking functions to fetch the unique pattern of user's handshaking actions, which can be used to authenticate a user of a smartphone.

Hobby Driven Biometrics

Jiang et al. (Jiang et al., 2013) proposed a novel behavioral biometric called hobby driven biometric. They presented a comprehensive study on habitual behaviors driven by hobbies. Considering the decorating and tidying style of a room as hobby-driven behavior, they conducted a survey on 225 people of different ages and professions'. They observed unique and steady characteristics based on style, color, position, and habitual operating order of the object for different persons. Their study demonstrates that the novel hobby-driven habitual behavioral biometric-based authentication system is feasible.

Browsing Style

Olejnik and Castelluccia (Olejnik & Castelluccia, 2013) proposed another novel biometric trait based on web browsing habits of users. The authors investigated the potential of this novel biometric based on the browsing data of 4,578 users. Their empirical analysis demonstrates that the idiosyncratic web browsing patterns of users can obtain low False Acceptance Rate and high False Rejection Rate for person authentication. Person authentication, anomaly, and fraud detections etc. could be the potential applications of browsing style-based novel behavioral biometric trait.

From the above summary, it is pertinent that idiosyncratic patterns can be found in every aspect of human actions ranging from walking style in real world to browsing style in cyber world. Therefore, human activities on web-based SNSs should have some patterns for being used as biometric features for person authentication.

Biometric Features from SNS

Behavioral biometric refers to identifying individuals from their very own behavioral characteristics (Yampolskiy & Govindaraju, 2008). The daily activities in SNSs leave a large amount of behavioral footprints (Wang et al. 2011), which are very difficult to fake. However, to identify a set of consistent idiosyncratic activities is the biggest challenge for establishing SNS interactions based social biometrics. Therefore, our first task is to identify a set of consistent features from the wide ranges of social activities and information from web-based SNSs.

We have chosen Twitter for our study for the following reasons:

- Twitter is one of the most popular web-based social networking platform.
- It provides real-time microblogging, which is a great source of social/communication activities of a person.
- Information is publicly available.
- It also provides APIs for data collection.

User profiles are rich source of information about the user and his/her network. In the following section, we would discuss what kind of information could be obtained from a user profile in Twitter and the significance of the information in formation of the proposed web-based social biometrics. A hierarchical view of the identified social biometric features from Twitter is illustrated in Figure 2.

Figure 2. User's social biometric features from Twitter data

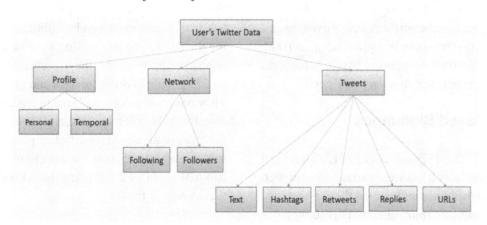

In general following information of a user can be obtained from Twitter:

1. Profile information.
2. Network information.
3. Tweets.

Profile Information

Information is very crucial to profile the behavior of a person. Figure 3 shows a sample of twitter profile of a verified user Bill Gates.

In general, the following information can be obtained from a typical user profile in Twitter (Kumar et al., 2013):

*   **Personal information:** real name, Twitter handle, URL for his personal web page, additional information provided by the user e.g. profession, interests etc.
*   **Temporal information:** location, profile creation date etc.

All the above information can be used as meta data for profiling user's online social networking behavior for further authentication.

Network Information

Twitter also provides information about how and to whom the user is connected. Twitter maintains two types of connection between users (Twitter-glossary): follower and following. A connection can be one way or both ways. For example, if user A wants to get status updates from user B then A can add user B as a following. In this case, user B would see user A as a follower. Again, both way connection may exists between user A and B. In this case, user A would be a follower of B and B would be a follower of A.

Information of the followers and following can be obtained from Twitter. From this information, a social networking graph can be generated to understand the pattern of connection of the user. More inference can be drawn from the analysis

Figure 3. A sample of public user profile in Twitter (twitter.com)

of the network. For example, which community the user belongs to, close friend list and so on.

Tweets

Tweets are real time microblogs posted by the users in Twitter. Though it is limited to 140 characters, still is a rich source of information about the user and his communication behavior. Idiosyncratic pattern of tweets of a user can be explored by analyzing the following features:

- **Text:** The writing style of users, use of special characters, punctuation symbols, emoticons, spelling mistakes, abbreviations can be analyzed to extract discriminant feature set for the user. For this purpose, many well-known text-mining approaches such as bag-of-words, n-grams, style markers analysis, and frequency analysis can be utilized.
- **Hashtags:** Hashtag are used to mark keywords or topics in a Tweet and preceded by # symbol (Twitter-glossary). Just like bag-of-words, bag-of-hashtags can be analyzed to as feature set to identify the user.
- **Retweets:** Retweeting is the act of sharing other user(s) Tweets to all of the followers a user (Twitter-glossary). Analysis of retweets would be useful to build user's behavioral profile in Twitter. Social networking analysis can be applied to analyze the correlation between friends and retweets of the users.
- **Reply:** Replies are Tweets of the users posted in reply to another user's message (Twitter-glossary) in his/her timeline. Analyzing replies would provide us important behavioral information such as – to whom the user replies most, any specific pattern or style followed by the user to reply to a specific person and so on.

- **URLs:** The most frequent URL(s) posted by the user, which URL shorteners are being used etc. can be included based on the frequency analysis of the posted URLs in user's timeline.
- **Other information:** Timestamp, geo-location (if present) etc. of tweets can also be used as either soft biometrics (Jain et al., 2004) or creating behavioral profile for person identification.

A profile can be created based on the above information of the user to represent as a novel biometric trait feature called web-based social biometric. Two main challenges of such data analysis would be:

1. Extraction of features from large apparently random dataset.
2. Selection of a small and consistent behavioral feature set to be used for the identification purpose.

CONCEPT ANALYSIS

In the previous section, we discussed a number of features that could be extracted from tweets to represent personal characteristics of users. Apart from the texts replies, retweets, hashtags, blogs, photo-album organization, discussions, and URLs also represent online social behavior of a person. All the above features can be exploited for person identification in many ways. Background analysis demonstrates that authors can be identified from the personal writing styles of microblogs. In this section, we are analyzing the concept of using interaction or communication-based information as biometric features. The idea of using such features may explore auxiliary biometrics, which may enhance the recognition accuracy of a person. For example, from the frequency analysis of replies of person A the fact may be explored that person A mostly communicate with person B. In addition, further investigation may explore the idiosyncratic way of reply of person A to person B that may play an important role to verify person A.

Online social behaviors of a person can be explored by applying social network analysis on Twitter data. Initially four types of networks can be generated from the Twitter data: *Reply Network, Retweet Network, Hashtags Network, and URL Network*. These four types of networks are explained in the following subsections:

- **Reply Network:** By analyzing the replies of a specific user a weighted network can be generated. Here nodes are the user him/herself and the other users he/she replies. Weights can be the frequency of replies. This network would explore a short list of friends/persons whom the user communicates most. If the network becomes very large for further analysis, some threshold values can be set to prune the network. The thresholds can be frequency based or time based. For example, if a user replies to hundreds of his friends in a day, then we may be interested to find the persons whom the user replies frequently or regularly. Further analysis could be accomplished on the replies to the short listed persons to explore any personal characteristics or communication.

- **Retweet Network**: A weighted retweet network can be generated like the reply network to explore whom the user retweets most. Further behavioral patterns can be found by measuring the similarity of the reply and retweet networks. For example, weight of a person in the user's friend list could be increased if that person exists on both retweet and reply networks. Such analysis may provide further information on the community that the user belongs to,

which eventually could be used as auxiliary biometric features.

- **Hashtag Network:** As we mentioned in the previous section, bag-of-hashtags can be analyzed as a feature set, using method similar to bag-of-words (Singhal, 2001). Unlike in a reply or retweet network, a pre-processing step is required to reduce the number of hashtags on similar topics. The primary goal of the hashtag network is to identify personal interest of the user. Therefore, assigning a general topic of interest as a node would be more meaningful instead of using all hashtags as nodes. For this purpose, all similar or related hashtags could be categorized as one topic of interest and could be weighted based on their frequency. Then, a weighted hashtag network can be generated to explore some behavioral patterns of the user. For example, if some hashtag appear regularly in the tweets of a user over long time, then the user is consistently interested about that issue. Such pattern is an important feature to identify the user in a virtual domain. However, hashtag network should never be used as a static feature; it should be updated after a certain amount of time to cope with the changes of interest of the person over time.

- **URL Network:** URLs are often shared by users in microblogs. Building weighted URL networks may provide personal interest and URL sharing pattern of users. Any correlation between hashtag and URL network may reveal users very own personal choice or interest that would aid person identification in both virtual and real world.

Interested reader can find details on implementation of the above concepts and performance analysis in the journal article on the subject (Sultana et al., 2014).

FUTURE RESEARCH DIRECTIONS

Although behavioral biometric alone is not satisfactorily unique to identify a person with the capacity of real world applications, they can obtain high verification rate and enhance recognition rate of multimodal biometric systems (Ross et al., 2006, Yampolskiy, 2011, Yanushkevich et al. 2007). Such a system takes into consideration more than one single biometric trait, and thus achieves a better recognition rate and ensures tolerance to noise (Gavrilova & Monwar 2013). The proposed online social biometric features can be used to identify person in many ways such as:

- **User Verification of SNS:** Since the social networking sites have access to users' confidential, information some security questions can be auto generated based on that Information to verify a user for that specific SNS. On one hand, it would increase the security to the users' account in SNS. On the other hand, it would lessen the pain of setting security questions and memorizing the corresponding answers for the users.
- **Fraud or Anomaly Detections**: Continuous authentication is another promising application of the proposed web- based social biometric features. For example, instead of static or one time authentication SNSs can authenticate users continuously based on some social biometric features such as posted URLs, lexicons, replies, retweets etc. If the trust level of the current user drops significantly, the system can generate alerts. This application would facilitate anomaly or fraud detection (Abraham & Thomas, 2005) in virtual domain.
- **Multimodal Biometric Systems:** The proposed social biometrics can be integrated to well established physiological biometric traits such as fingerprints (Surmacz et al. 2013, Gavrilova, 2008), iris (Monwar &

Gavrilova, 2013) etc. to enhance the recognition rate of existing biometric systems. In addition, these features can be combined to other behavioral biometrics to improve the uniqueness and aid identification or verification of users in virtual world. For example, tweeting pattern can be integrated with keystroke dynamics (Bakelman et al. 2013) as a multimodal system to enhance the verification rate of users.

- **Forensic Applications:** It is known that author identification often needed for law enforcement and forensic applications of the investigations of cybercrimes. The proposed SNS based biometric features can be utilized for author identification of microblogs.
- **Soft Biometrics:** In addition to the above applications, temporal information collected from SNSs such as time, location etc. can be used as soft biometrics (Jain et al., 1999) to enhance the accuracy and reliability of person authentication systems.

However, security and authentication (Saeed & Mosdorf, 2006) are not the only applications of the proposed social biometric features. Personal choice, interest, community information etc. are of great interest of researchers and industries who work on targeted advertising of product and services. Investigating proposed web-based social biometric features for all the above applications would open new doors for further research.

CONCLUSION

In this chapter, the concept of *social biometrics* based on online social communication of persons has been introduced for the first time. The authors identified web-based social networking sites as a source of mining personal characteristics and behavioral patterns. Proposed novel biometric features are classified as the forth subcategory of the social communication based behavioral biometrics. Although the proposed biometric features may not be strong enough to be utilized in security-critical applications, they can be used for verification or continuous authentication of users in the virtual domains and on-line communities. In addition, performance of existing physiological biometric authentication system can be enhanced by using the proposed personal characteristics as auxiliary biometrics. This process would reduce false acceptance rate even in a critical situation. For example, facial features of twins may be identical but they might have their very own personal interests and way of communication. Therefore, revealing such idiosyncratic characteristics from web-based social interactions and their subsequent use as auxiliary biometrics would aid person identification in both real and virtual domain. Future research includes expanding the concept to include broad range of on-line social environments and introduce new communication-based features.

REFERENCES

Abraham, A., & Thomas, J. (2005). Distributed intrusion detection systems: a computational intelligence approach. In *Applications of information systems to homeland security and defense*. Idea Group Inc. doi:10.4018/978-1-59140-640-2. ch005

Al-Zubi, S., Brömme, A., & Tönnies, K. (2003). Using an active shape structural model for biometric sketch recognition. In *Pattern Recognition* (pp. 187–195). Springer. doi:10.1007/978-3-540-45243-0_25

Bakelman, N., Monaco, J. V., Cha, S. H., & Tappert, C. C. (2013, August). Keystroke biometric studies on password and numeric keypad input. In *Proceedings of Intelligence and Security Informatics Conference (EISIC), 2013 European* (pp. 204-207). Uppsala, Sweden: IEEE.

Bazazian, S., & Gavrilova, M. (2012, May). Context based gait recognition. In SPIE Defense, Security, and Sensing (pp. 84070J-84070J). SPIE Press.

Bo, C., Zhang, L., Li, X. Y., Huang, Q., & Wang, Y. (2013). SilentSense: Silent user identification via touch and movement behavioral biometrics. In *Proceedings of the 19th annual international conference on Mobile computing & networking* (pp. 187-190). New York, NY: ACM.

Bours, P. (2012). Continuous keystroke dynamics: A different perspective towards biometric evaluation. *Information Security Technical Report, 17*(1), 36–43. doi:10.1016/j.istr.2012.02.001

Frank, M., Biedert, R., Ma, E., Martinovic, I., & Song, D. (2013). Touchalytics: On the applicability of touchscreen input as a behavioral biometric for continuous authentication. *Information Forensics and Security. IEEE Transactions on, 8*(1), 136–148.

Gavrilova, M. (Ed.). (2008). *Generalized voronoi diagram: a geometry-based approach to computational intelligence* (Vol. 158). Berlin, Germany: Springer Verlag.

Gavrilova, M. L., & Monwar, M. (2013). *Multimodal biometrics and intelligent image processing for security systems*. IGI Global. doi:10.4018/978-1-4666-3646-0

Gray, A., Sallis, P., & MacDonell, S. (1997). *Software forensics: extending authorship analysis techniques to computer programs* (Information Science Discussion Papers Series No. 97/14). University of Otago. Retrieved from http://hdl.handle.net/10523/872

Green, R. M., & Sheppard, J. W. (2013, May). Comparing Frequency-and Style-Based Features for Twitter Author Identification. In *Proceedings of the Twenty-Sixth International FLAIRS Conference*. AAAI Press.

Guo, Y., Yang, L., Ding, X., Han, J., & Liu, Y. (2013, April). OpenSesame: Unlocking smart phone through handshaking biometrics. In Proceedings IEEE INFOCOM (pp. 365-369). IEEE.

Igarashi, K., Miyajima, C., Itou, K., Takeda, K., Itakura, F., & Abut, H. (2004). Biometric identification using driving behavioral signals. []. IEEE.]. *Proceedings of Multimedia and Expo, 1,* 65–68.

Jain, A. K., Bolle, R. M., & Pankanti, S. (Eds.). (1999). *Biometrics: personal identification in networked society.* Springer. doi:10.1007/b117227

Jain, A. K., Dass, S. C., & Nandakumar, K. (2004). Soft biometric traits for personal recognition systems. In *Biometric Authentication* (pp. 731–738). Berlin, Germany: Springer Berlin Heidelberg. doi:10.1007/978-3-540-25948-0_99

Jain, A. K., Ross, A., & Prabhakar, S. (2004). An introduction to biometric recognition. *Circuits and Systems for Video Technology. IEEE Transactions on, 14*(1), 4–20.

Jiang, W., Xiang, J., Liu, L., Zha, D., & Wang, L. (2013). From mini house game to hobby-driven behavioral biometrics-based password. In *Proceedings of Trust, Security and Privacy in Computing and Communications (TrustCom), 2013 12th IEEE International Conference on* (pp. 712-719). IEEE.

Jorgensen, Z., & Yu, T. (2011, March). On mouse dynamics as a behavioral biometric for authentication. In *Proceedings of the 6th ACM Symposium on Information, Computer and Communications Security* (pp. 476-482). ACM.

Kumar, S., Morstatter, F., & Liu, H. (2013). *Twitter Data Analytics.* Springer.

Layton, R., Watters, P., & Dazeley, R. (2010). Authorship attribution for twitter in 140 characters or less. In *Proceedings of Cybercrime and Trustworthy Computing Workshop (CTC), 2010 Second* (pp. 1-8). IEEE.

Macleod, N., & Grant, T. (2012). *Whose Tweet? Authorship analysis of micro-blogs and other short-form messages.* Aston University Research Archive. Retrieved from http://eprints.aston.ac.uk/19303/1/Authorship_analysis_of_micro_blogs_and_other_short_form_messages.pdf

Monwar, M. M., & Gavrilova, M. (2008). FES: A system for combining face, ear and signature biometrics using rank level fusion. In Proceedings of Information Technology: New Generations, (pp. 922-927). IEEE.

Monwar, M. M., & Gavrilova, M. (2013). Markov chain model for multimodal biometric rank fusion. *Signal. Image and Video Processing, 7*(1), 137–149. doi:10.1007/s11760-011-0226-8

Olejnik, L., & Castelluccia, C. (2013). Towards web-based biometric systems using personal browsing interests. In *Proceedings of Availability, Reliability and Security (ARES), 2013 Eighth International Conference on* (pp. 274-280). IEEE CPS.

Ross, A. A., Nandakumar, K., & Jain, A. K. (2006). *Handbook of multibiometrics* (Vol. 6). Springer.

Saeed, K. (2014). Carathéodory–Toeplitz based mathematical methods and their algorithmic applications in biometric image processing. *Applied Numerical Mathematics, 75,* 2–21. doi:10.1016/j.apnum.2012.05.004

Saeed, K., & Mosdorf, R. (Eds.). (2006). *Biometrics, computer security systems and artificial intelligence applications.* Springer. doi:10.1007/978-0-387-36503-9

Saeed, K., & Nagashima, T. (Eds.). (2012). *Biometrics and Kansei Engineering.* Springer. doi:10.1007/978-1-4614-5608-7

Shalhoub, G., Simon, R., Iyer, R., Tailor, J., & Westcott, S. (2010). Stylometry system–use cases and feasibility study. *Forensic Linguistics, 1,* 8.

Silva, R. S., Laboreiro, G., Sarmento, L., Grant, T., Oliveira, E., & Maia, B. (2011). 'twazn me!!!('automatic authorship analysis of micro-blogging messages. In *Natural Language Processing and Information Systems* (pp. 161–168). Springer. doi:10.1007/978-3-642-22327-3_16

Singhal, A. (2001). Modern information retrieval: A brief overview. *IEEE Data Eng. Bull.*, *24*(4), 35–43.

Sourin, A. (2006). *Computer Graphics: From a Small Formula to Cyberworlds*. Singapore: Prentice-Hall, Inc.

Spafford, E. H., & Weeber, S. A. (1993). Software forensics: Can we track code to its authors? *Computers & Security*, *12*(6), 585–595. doi:10.1016/0167-4048(93)90055-A

Statisticbrain. (n.d.). Retrieved from http://www.statisticbrain.com/twitter-statistics/

Sultana, M., Paul, P. P., & Gavrilova, M. (2014). Social Behavioral Biometrics: An Emerging Trend. *International Journal of Pattern Recognition and Artificial Intelligence*.

Surmacz, K., Saeed, K., & Rapta, P. (2013). An improved algorithm for feature extraction from a fingerprint fuzzy image. *Optica Applicata*, *43*(3), 515–527.

Twitter-glossary. (n.d.). Retrieved from https://support.twitter.com/articles/166337-the-twitter-glossary

Twitter. (n.d.). Retrieved from https://twitter.com/BillGates

Wang, Y., Berwick, R. C., Haykin, S., Pedrycz, W., Kinsner, W., Baciu, G., & Bhavsar, C. (2011). Cognitive Informatics and Cognitive Computing in Year 10 and Beyond. [IJCINI]. *International Journal of Cognitive Informatics and Natural Intelligence*, *5*(4), 1–21. doi:10.4018/jcini.2011100101

Yampolskiy, R. V. (2011). Behavioral, cognitive, and virtual biometrics. In *Computer Analysis of Human Behavior* (pp. 347–385). London, UK: Springer. doi:10.1007/978-0-85729-994-9_13

Yampolskiy, R. V., & Govindaraju, V. (2008). Behavioral biometrics: a survey and classification. *International Journal of Biometrics*, *1*(1), 81–113. doi:10.1504/IJBM.2008.018665

Yampolskiy, R. V., & Govindaraju, V. (2010). Game Playing Tactic as a Behavioral Biometric for Human Identification. In *Behavioral Biometrics for Human Identification: Intelligent Applications*. IGI Global.

Yanushkevich, S., Gavrilova, M., Wang, P., & Srihari, S. (2007). *Image pattern recognition: Synthesis & analysis in biometrics*. Singapore: World Scientific Publishers.

KEY TERMS AND DEFINITIONS

Auxiliary Biometrics: Auxiliary biometrics are some personal features which themselves are not enough to represent standalone biometric traits but can provide additional information about the characteristics of person to aid the person identification process.

Behavioral Biometrics: Behavioral biometrics refer to some behavioral characteristics of human beings which can be used to identify a person.

Biometric Recognition: Recognizing a person by measuring the similarity of some biometric traits of the person stored biometric samples or templates in the system.

Biometric Verification: Verifying the identity of a person that he/she claims to be based on some biometric traits.

Multimodal Biometrics: Use of more than one biometric traits to identify a person.

Social Behavioral Biometrics: Social behavioral biometrics refer to social behaviors or interactions which possess some discriminant characteristics for being used to identify a person.

Unimodal Biometric: Use of a single physiological or behavioral biometric trait to identify a person.

Chapter 10
Fingers' Angle Calculation Using Level–Set Method

Ankit Chaudhary
University of Iowa, USA

Jagdish Lal Raheja
CEERI/CSIR, India

Karen Das
Don Bosco University, India

Shekhar Raheja
TU Kaiserslautern, Germany

ABSTRACT

In the current age, use of natural communication in human-computer interaction is a known and well-installed thought. Hand gesture recognition and gesture-based applications have gained a significant amount of popularity amongst people all over the world. They have a number of applications ranging from security to entertainment. These applications generally are real time applications and need fast, accurate communication with machines. On the other end, gesture-based communications have few limitations, but bent finger information is not provided in vision-based techniques. In this chapter, a novel method for fingertip detection and for angle calculation of both hands' bent fingers is discussed. Angle calculation has been done before with sensor-based gloves/devices. This study has been conducted in the context of natural computing for calculating angles without using any wired equipment, colors, marker, or any device. The pre-processing and segmentation of the region of interest is performed in a HSV color space and a binary format, respectively. Fingertips are detected using level-set method and angles are calculated using geometrical analysis. This technique requires no training for the system to perform the task.

DOI: 10.4018/978-1-4666-6030-4.ch010

1. INTRODUCTION

Robust and natural hand gesture recognition from video or in real time is one of the most important challenges for researchers working in the area of computer vision. Gesture recognition systems are very helpful in general purpose life as they can be used by general people without any training as everybody know how to use hand and what sign would make what mean. So, if computers can understand gestures efficiently, computers would be more useful for all. It can also help in controlling devices, interacting with machine interfaces, monitoring human activities and in many other applications. Generally defined as any meaningful body motion, gestures play a central role in everyday communication and often convey emotional information about the gesticulating person. There are some specific gestures which are pre-defined in a particular community or society as sign language, but many gestures made by hand are just a random shape. Precisely all shapes made by hand gesture are not defined, so one need to track all shapes to efficiently control machines by hand gesture.

During the last few decades researchers have been interested in recognizing automatically human gestures for several applications like sign language recognition, socially assistive robotics, directional indication through pointing, control through gestures, alternative computer interfaces, immersive game technology, virtual controllers, affective computing and remote controlling. For further details on gesture applications see (Chaudhary et al., 2011)(Mitra & Acharya, 2007). Mobile companies are also trying to make handsets which can recognize gestures and operate over small distances (Kroeker, 2010)(Tarrataca, Santos, & Cardoso, 2009). There have been many non-natural methods using devices and color papers/rings. In the past, researchers have employed gloves (Sturman, & Zeltzer, 1994), color strips (Do et al., 2006)(Premaratne, & Nguyen, 2007)(Kohler, 1996)(Bretzner et al., 2001) or full sleeve

shirt (Kim & Fellner, 2004)(Sawah et al., 2007) in image processing based methods to obtain better segmentation results. A preliminary part of this work has been published in (Chaudhary et al., 2012).

It was a well-known fact in advance that natural computing methods will take over other technologies. Pickering (2005) stated "initially touch-based gesture interfaces would be popular, but non-contact gesture recognition technologies would be more attractive finally". Recently human gesture recognition catches the peak attention of the research in both software and hardware environments. Many mobile companies like Samsung, Micromax have implemented hand gesture as a way to control mobile applications, which make it more popular in public domain. It can be used for controlling a robotic hand which can mimic the human hand actions and can secure human life by being used in many commercial and military operations. One such robotic hand is Dexterous from Shadow Robot®.

Many mechanical (Huber & Grupen, 2002) (Lim et al., 2000) and image processing (Nolker & Ritter, 2002) based techniques are available in the literature to interpret single hand gesture. However, in generic scenario humans express their actions with both hands along. it is a new challenge to take into account the gestures depicted by both hands simultaneously. The computational time for both hand gestures would be more compared to that required for a single hand. The approach employed for a single hand can also be used for this purpose with a slight modification in the algorithm for both hands. However, the process may consumes twice time that is required for single hand gesture recognition in serial implementation.

There are certain conditions from (Nolker & Ritter, 2002) . If this algorithm is applied on both hands, it would not always take double time to calculate the finger angles for both hands than time to single hand fingers computation. If the directions of both the hands are the same, the computational time will be similar to the single hand computational time. But in real life, it is not always possible that both hands always pointing towards the same direction. Hence, one has to apply this algorithm twice on the image frame to compute for both hands. That will cause extra expense of time and in real time applications it is very much essential that the computational time should be very small. Therefore, a new approach is required for both hand fingers' angle calculation. Figure 1 shows the block diagram flow of our approach.

2. BACKGROUND WORK

The real time shapes of hand gestures are unknown and could be recognized if the fingers information are correctly known. As the fingertip detection is not possible in bent fingers using color space based techniques, the finger angles need to be computed. The main applications of angle calculation of bent human fingers are in the controlling of machines and robots. Real-time applications need more precise and fast input to machines so that the actuation would be accurate within the given time limit. We couldn't find any previous studies in available literature except (Nolker & Ritter, 2002) that involved calculating the bent fingers' angle without performing any training.

Claudia and Ritter (2002) in her system called 'GREFIT', calculated finger angles with the use of neural network. Chen and Lin (2001) presented a real time parallel segmentation method using mean-C adaptive threshold to detect the region of interest. More applications and segmentation methods for both hands could be found in sign language recognitions and alike systems (Raheja, Chaudhary & Maheswari, 2014)(Alon et al., 2009) (Jeong, Lee & Kim, 2011). In our previous work (Chaudhary & Raheja, 2013), a supervised ANN based method has been presented to calculate one hand fingers' angle calculation when fingers are bending in real time. The real time fingertip and centre of palm detection is shown in Figure 2.

Many researchers (Sawah et al., 2007) (Nolker & Ritter, 2002) (Nguyen, Pham, & Jeon, 2009) (Lee, & Chun, 2009)

(Raheja, Chaudhary, & Singal, 2011) (Gastanldiand et al., 2005) (Kim & Lee, 2008) (Shin, Tsap, & Golgof, 2004)(Zhou, & Ruan, 2006) have used fingertip detection as key to detect shape in their research work according based on their applications. Nguyen, Pham and Jeon (2009) presented fingertip detection of both hands. He implemented Claudia's method for hand segmentation. Lee and Chun (2009) used marker-less method in his augmented reality application to register virtual objects where fingertips were detected on curvature of contour.

Sawah et al. (2007) showed 3D posture estimation using DBN for dynamic hand gesture recognition, but employed a glove to detect fingers and

Figure 1. Algorithmic flow for angle approximation for both hands

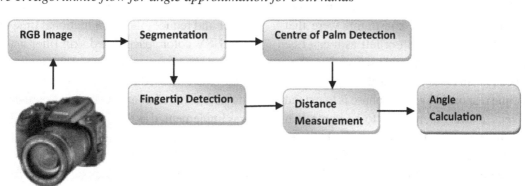

Figure 2. Results of fingertips and centre of palm detection (Chaudhary & Raheja, 2013)

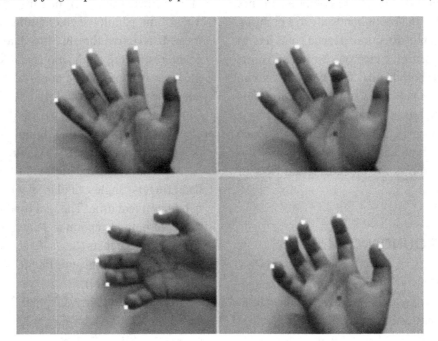

the palm. Raheja, Chaudhary and Singal (2011) have detected fingertips accurately with the help of MS KINECT® but that doesn't fulfill the natural computing requirements addressed in this paper. Gastaldi et al. (2005) used hand perimeter to select points near fingertips and to reduce the computational time. A detailed review on hand pose estimation is presented by Erol et al. (2007).

3. FINGERS' ANGLE CALCULATION

In the first phase of this project (Nolker & Ritter, 2002), milestone was to calculate bent finger angles for one hand. The constraints were that the hand can be either right or left as it can't be say in advance that which hand user will use. The developed system works fine with the requirements of real time response. The next phase is to extend the project, if the system need to be controlled using both hands. To calculate both hands finger angles, there are two ways: firstly repeat the single hand method for both hand but it would take

double time as for single hand method. Hence, to reduce the computational time, it will be better to process both the hands at the same time. The presented method here takes less processing time since both hands are processed simultaneously. The following text describes region of interest segmentation, fingertips detection, centre of palms detection and bended fingers' angle calculation methods respectively.

3.1 Region of Interest Segmentaion

The region of interest (ROI) is needed to extract from original images which makes the work faster and reduces the computational time taken. The HSV color space based skin filter was used to form the binary silhouette of the input image, which will be used to segment hands and masking with original images. The hand segmentation was implemented as described in (Raheja, Das, & Chaudhary, 2011) to obtain the ROI. Essentially, HSV type color spaces are deformations of the RGB color cube and they can be mapped from the

RGB space via a nonlinear transformation. The reason behind the selection of this color space in skin detection is that it allows users to intuitively specify the boundary of the skin color class in terms of the hue and saturation. As 'Value' in HSV provides the brightness information, it is often dropped to reduce illumination dependency of skin color. A more robust learning based skin segmentation method is described in (Chaudhary & Gupta, 2012). The characteristics of skin color with color based segmentation have been discussed in (Raheja et al., 2011).

After the formation of the binary image, BLOBs were collected and the BLOB analysis based on 8 connectivity criteria was applied. As a result of that the two hands were distinguished from each other. They were given different grey values as to ensure that the parameters of one hand are compared against that hand only. Consequently, a mistake, namely consideration of the fingertip of one hand and COP of other hand, is avoided. The hand which seem first in the scene from the left, would be considered as the first hand as there is no concept of right or left hand. The main purpose of BLOB analysis is to extract the two biggest BLOBs to eliminate the false detection of skin pixels and to distinguish the two BLOBs from each other. Figure 3 presents the result of hand segmentation. The brighter BLOB corresponds to the right hand of the main frame and the other BLOB corresponds to the left hand.

3.2 Fingertip Detection

In the available literature, we couldn't find any study related to the detection of fingertips of both hands in parallel. Although for one hand fingertips has been detected in real time (Chaudhary & Raheja, 2013). To process both the hands simultaneously a new approach based on level set method was developed. The circular separability filter (CSF) and concentric circular filter (CCF) which used level set based numeric values for segmentation, has been taken into consideration (Chaudhary et

Figure 3. Result of hands segmentation

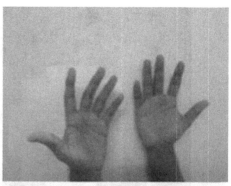

al., 2012). The circular separability filter has the shape of a square with a concentric circle inside as shown in Figure 4. After a number of experiments, the radius of the circle is taken to 5 pixels and the bounding square is considered of 20 pixel length. When the filter response is computed for all the points of the region of interest in the binary image, the filter response for the fingertip regions are found distinctively different from that of other regions because of their boundary characteristics. The candidate fingertip locations are determined by using an appropriate threshold condition.

After getting the fingertips areas from filter, we need to get exact fingertip location. It is calculated in two steps. Firstly, an approximate location for the fingertip is determined and then using orientation of finger, exact location is calculated. In CSF operation the 8-connected points that satisfy the threshold condition for the filter response of the circular separability filter are grouped together. The groups having a number of pixels greater than

Figure 4. Circular separability filter

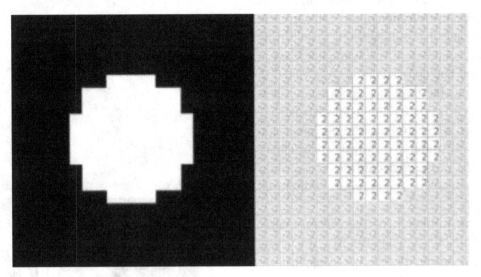

a set threshold, are selected and the centroids of the groups are taken as the approximate fingertip positions. Here the first step completes. Then, the orientation of each finger is determined using a filter with 2-concentric circular regions which is again based on numerical values. The working of CCF filter is described in following text. The concentric circular filter is shown in Figure 5.

The diameters of the inner and outer circular regions of the CC filter are 10 pixels and 20 pixels

respectively. The points inside the inner circle are assigned a value of +2, points in the mid circle are assigned the value of -2, and the points outside the mid circle but inside the bounding square are assigned value of 0, as described in level set method. All these values were set after experimental results. The filter is then applied to the binary silhouette of the hand image which is result of CSF filter. The pixels that lie in the inner circle region are grouped by the 8-connectivity

Figure 5. (a) Concentric circular filter and (b) Concentric circular filter element values

Figure 6. (a) The concentric circular filter being applied on the approximate thumb tip location, (b) Zoomed view of the thumb tip region and (c) Position of the centroid of the largest 8-connected group (region in white) and the angle (θ) with respect to the horizontal

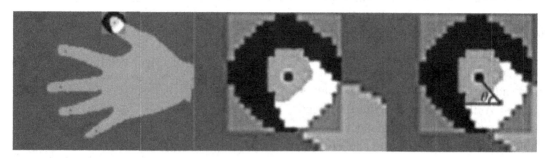

criteria. Then, the largest group is selected and the centroid of the group is calculated.

The orientation of the finger is calculated as the angle (θ) defined by the line joining the centroid of the largest group and the previously calculated approximate fingertip location with the horizontal axis. This process is shown in Figure 6. Then move in this direction several steps with an incremental distance (r) using Equation (1) and (2) till the edge of the finger is reached.

$$R_{new} = R_{old} + r\cos\left(-\theta\right) \qquad (1)$$

$$C_{new} = C_{old} + r\sin\left(-\theta\right) \qquad (2)$$

where *Rold* and *Cold* are the 2D coordinates of the previous trace point, *Rnew* and *Cnew* are the 2D coordinates of the current trace point and *r* is the incremental distance. The values of *Rnew* and *Cnew* after the iterations give the exact coordinates of the fingertips.

3.3 Centre of Palms Detection

The centre of palm (COP) is needed for further processing. The exact location of the COP in the hand is identified by applying a mask of dimension 30x30 to binary silhouette of the image and counting the number of skin pixels lying within the mask. If the count is within a set threshold,

then the centre of the mask will be considered as the candidate for COP. Finally, the mean of all such candidates found in a BLOB are considered as the COP of the hand represented by that BLOB. Since there are two BLOBs, two COPs would be discovered for both the hands. Figure 7 presents the result of fingertip and COP detection. The yellow dots mark the COPs of both the hands while the white points are the detected fingertips.

3.4 Angles Calculation for both Hands' Bent Fingers

The presented geometrical method doesn't need any training or sample data to calculate the angles for both hands. The user can use this application with bare hand just showing hands to camera.

Figure 7. Result of COPs and fingertips detection for both hand

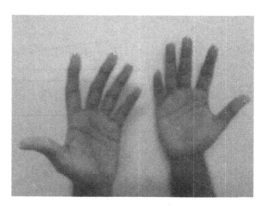

The palm should face the camera for appropriate operation. The distance between each fingertip and COP can be calculated by subtracting their coordinates on the image frames. Initially the user has to show a reference frame to the system in which all fingers are open and the bending angles of all fingers are 180^0. The distance between any fingertip and the COP would be the maximum in this position. As the user starts bending the fingers in either direction, distances among fingertips and COP would decrease. The user can move his hands in front of the camera, it is not necessary to have his hand or arm static. This method will calculate the angles in that case also.

Here the maximum angle calculated would be 90^0 as after this limit the fingertips would not be detected using color space based segmentation. The values calculated from the reference frame are stored for each finger. If the user changes the position of his fingers, the distance between COP and fingertips would be compared with the reference distances. The geometrical analysis as described below, calculate the bending angles. From Figure 8 it is clear thatWhen $d=d_{ref}$, angle $a1=0^0$ andWhen $d=d_{ref}/3$, angle $a1=90^0$.

Hence, we can express angle $a1$ as shown in (3).

$$angle\ a1 = 90^0 - \frac{d - \frac{d_{ref}}{3}}{\frac{2d_{ref}}{3}} * 90^0 \qquad (3)$$

Angle $a2$ of finger bending can be obtained from the Figure 7as

$$angle\ a2 = 180^0 - \left(90^0 - \frac{d - \frac{d_{ref}}{3}}{\frac{2d_{ref}}{3}} * 90^0\right) \qquad (4)$$

$$or\quad angle\ a2 = 90^0 + \frac{d - \frac{d_{ref}}{3}}{\frac{2d_{ref}}{3}} * 90^0 \qquad (5)$$

Here the angle $a2$ stores the value of the finger bending angle for one finger. Figure 9 presents the result of fingers angle detection for both hands simultaneously. The angles are shown on the top of window according to the finger shown sequence. This method work in other conditions like a person

Figure 8. Angle approximation geometry

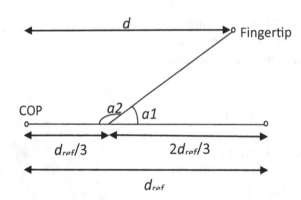

have only eight fingers in both hands, then the system came to know this automatically and will show only eight angles at display.

4. EXPERIMENTAL RESULTS

The experiments were carried out on Intel® i5 processor and 4GB RAM desktop computer. The discussed method is implemented in MATLAB® on Windows® XP. The live video is captured using Logitech® HD webcam with image resolution 240x230. The usage of the system is very similar to what is described in (Chaudhary & Raheja, 2013), only difference is that it will work for both hands simultaneously. If we apply single hand finger's angle calculation method to detect both hands fingers' angle, the computational time come out 294ms. On the other hand, the method proposed in this paper takes only 198ms to perform the same computations.

Both the hands are recognized distinctly, also the system remembers both hands' parameter sepa-

rately. If there is only one hand shown, system will work perform a single hand gesture analysis. This method provides an accuracy of around 90-92% on live input in varying light conditions. Also the systems take care of hand as well as arm movement and form the analysis in the similar way. It can also inform about the displacement of arm. The numbers of fingers are set maximum as ten but if user have less fingers, it system works fine in that case too.

5. CONCLUSION

This paper presents a novel technique for the bent fingers' angle calculation from the hand gesture in real time. The user has to show bare hands to the system and he is free to bend his fingers. The system would describe bend angles in real time in the same sequence as fingers appeared in the scene from left to right. This technique carries tremendous significance since it can be adopted for identifying human gestures, which are often

Figure 9. Finger bending angle approximation of double hand

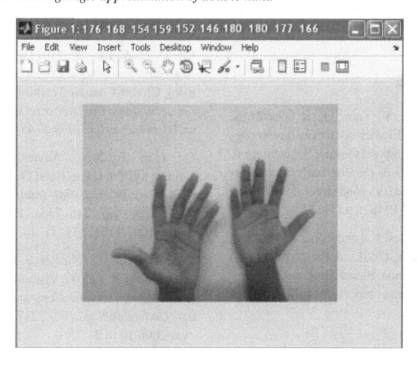

depicted during communication using both hands. The system considered uses no training data and the hands can be used in any direction.

This approach minimizes the processing time of our last algorithm for determining the angles of a single hand. The processing time is reduced by 96ms, which corresponds to a reduction of approximately 33%. This technique can be used in many applications, one which we have tried is in controlling robotic hands which will mimic hand gestures. In the future we would like to enhance this technique by reducing the time computation and making it more robust on background noise. Also more application would be deployed based on this technique, which will be useful for the public daily life operations.

ACKNOWLEDGMENT

This research was carried out at Central Electronics Engineering Research Institute (CEERI) Pilani, a CSIR Laboratory as a part of our project 'Controlling the Robotic Hand using Hand Gesture'. Authors would like to thank Director, CEERI Pilani for providing research facilities and for his support and encouragement.

REFERENCES

Alon, J., Athitsos, V., Yuan, Q., & Sclaroff, S. (2009). A Unified Framework for Gesture Recognition and spatioemporal Gesture Segmentation. *IEEE Transactions on Pattern Analysis and Machine Intelligence*, *31*(9), 1685–1699. doi:10.1109/TPAMI.2008.203 PMID:19574627

Bretzner, L., Laptev, I., Lindeberg, T., Lenman, S., & Sundblad, Y. (2001). A Prototype System for Computer vision Based Human Computer Interaction. Technical report ISRN KTH/NA/P-01/09-SE.

Chaudhary, A., & Gupta, A. (2012). Automated Switching System for Skin Pixel Segmentation in Varied Lightin. In *Proceedings of 19th IEEE International Conference on Mechatronics and Machine Vision in Practice* (pp. 26-31). Auckland, New Zealand: IEEE.

Chaudhary, A., & Raheja, J. L. (2013). Bent fingers' angle calculation using supervised ANN to control electro-mechanical robotic hand. *Computers & Electrical Engineering*, *39*(2), 560–570. doi:10.1016/j.compeleceng.2012.07.012

Chaudhary, A., Raheja, J. L., & Das, K. (2011). A Vision based Real Time System to Control Remote Robotic hand Fingers. In *Proceedings of the IEEE International Conference on Computer Control and Automation* (pp. 118-122). IEEE.

Chaudhary, A., Raheja, J. L., Das, K., & Raheja, S. (2001). A Survey on Hand Gesture Recognition in context of Soft Computing. In *Advanced Computing, CCIS* (pp. 46–55). London: Springer.

Chaudhary, A., Raheja, J. L., Das, K., & Raheja, S. (2012). Both Hands' Fingers' Angle Calculation from Live Video. *International Journal of Computer Vision and Image Processing*, *2*(2), 1–11. doi:10.4018/ijcvip.2012040101

Chen, Y., & Lin, K. (2011). Display Region Segmentation from a Computer Screen Image using Closed-Contour Tracking. In *Proceedings of International Conference on Machine Learning and Cybernetics* (pp. 1739-1745). Academic Press.

Do, J. et al. (2006). Advanced Soft Remote Control System Using Hand Gestures. In *MICAI (Advances in Artificial Intelligence), (LNAI)* (Vol. 4293, pp. 745–755). Berlin: Springer. doi:10.1007/11925231_71

Erol, A., Bebis, G., Nicolescu, M., Boyle, R. D., & Twombly, X. (2007). Vision-based Hand Pose Estimation: A Review. *Computer Vision and Image Understanding*, *108*, 52–73. doi:10.1016/j.cviu.2006.10.012

Gastaldi, G., et al. (2005). A Man-Machine Communication System Based on the Visual Analysis of Dynamic Gestures. In *Proceedings of International Conference on Image Processing* (pp. 397-400). Academic Press.

Huber, M., & Grupen, R. A. (2002). Robust Finger Gaits from Closed-loop controllers. In *Proceedings of IEEE/RSJ International Conference on Intelligent Robots and Systems*, (Vol. 2, pp. 1578-1584). IEEE.

Jeong, E., Lee, J., & Kim, D. (2011). Finger-Gesture Recognition Glove using Velostat. In *Proceedings of 11th International Conference on Control, Automation and Systems* (pp. 206-210). Academic Press.

Kim, H., & Fellner, D. W. (2004). Interaction With Hand Gesture for a Back-Projection Wall. In *Proceedings of Computer Graphics International* (pp. 395–402). Academic Press.

Kim, J. M., & Lee, W. K. (2008). Hand Shape Recognition Using Fingertips. In *Proceedings of fifth International Conference on Fuzzy Systems and Knowledge Discovery* (pp. 44-48). Academic Press.

Kohler, M. (1996). Vision Based Remote Control in Intelligent Home Environments. In 3D Image Analysis and Synthesis, (pp. 147-154). Academic Press. Bretzner, L., Laptev, I., Lindeberg, T., Lenman, S., & Sundblad, Y. (2001). A Prototype System for Computer vision Based Human Computer Interaction. Technical report ISRN KTH/NA/P-01/09-SE.

Kroeker, K. L. (2010). Alternate Interface Technologies Emerge. *Communications of the ACM*, *53*(2), 13–15. doi:10.1145/1646353.1646360

Lee, B., & Chun, J. (2009). Manipulation of Virtual Objects in Marker-Less AR System by Fingertip Tracking and Hand Gesture Recognition. In *Proceedings of 2nd International conference on interaction science: Information Technology, Culture and Human* (pp. 1110-1115). Academic Press.

Lim, M., Oh, S., Son, J., You, B., & Kim, K. (2000). A Human-Like Real-Time Grasp Systhesis Method for Humanoid Robot Hands. *Robotics and Autonomous Systems*, *30*, 261–271. doi:10.1016/S0921-8890(99)00091-3

Mitra, S., & Acharya, T. (2007). Gesture Recognition: A Survey. IEEE Transactions on Systems, Man, and Cybernetics-Part C. *Applications and Review*, *37*(3), 2127–2130.

Nguyen, D. D., Pham, T. C., & Jeon, J. W. (2009). Fingertip Detection with Morphology and Geometric Calculation. In *Proceedings of IEEE/RSJ International Conference on Intelligent Robots and Systems* (pp. 1460-1465). IEEE.

Nolker, C., & Ritter, H. (2002). Visual Recognition of Continuous Hand Postures. *IEEE Transactions on Neural Networks*, *13*(4), 983–994. doi:10.1109/TNN.2002.1021898 PMID:18244493

Pickering, C.A. (2005). The Search for a Safer Driver Interface: A Review of Gesture Recognition Human Machine Interface. *IEE Computing and Control Engineering*, 34-40.

Premaratne, P., & Nguyen, Q. (2007). Consumer electronics control system based on hand gesture moment invariants. *IET Computer Vision*, *1*(1), 35–41. doi:10.1049/iet-cvi:20060198

Raheja, J. L., Chaudhary, A., & Maheshwari, S. (2014). Automatic Gesture Pointing Location Detection. *Optik: International Journal for Light and Electron Optics*, *125*(3), 993–996. doi:10.1016/j.ijleo.2013.07.167

Raheja, J. L., Chaudhary, A., & Singal, K. (2011). Tracking of Fingertips and Centers of Palm Using KINECT. In *Proceedings of 3rd International Conference on Computational Intelligence, Modelling and Simulation* (pp. 248-252). Academic Press.

Raheja, J. L., Das, K., & Chaudhary, A. (2011). Fingertip Detection: A Fast Method with Natural Hand. *International Journal of Embedded Systems and Computer Engineering*, 3(2), 85–89.

Raheja, J. L., Manasa, M. B. L., Chaudhary, A., & Raheja, S. (2011). ABHIVYAKTI: Hand Gesture Recognition using Orientation Histogram in different light conditions. In *Proceedings of 5th Indian International Conference on Artificial Intellige* (pp. 1687-1698). Academic Press.

Sawah, A. E., et al. (2007). A Framework for 3D Hand Tracking and Gesture Recognition Using Elements of Genetic Programming. In *Proceedings of 4th Canadian Conference on Computer and Robot Vision* (pp. 495-502). Montreal, Canada: Academic Press.

Shin, M. C., Tsap, L. V., & Goldgof, D. B. (2004). Gesture Recognition using Bezier Curves for Visualization Navigation from Registered 3-D Data. *Pattern Recognition*, 37(5), 1011–1024. doi:10.1016/j.patcog.2003.11.007

Sturman, D., & Zeltzer, D. (1994). A Survey of Glove-Based Input. *IEEE Transactions on Computer Graphics and Applications*, 14(1), 30–39. doi:10.1109/38.250916

Tarrataca, L., Santos, A. C., & Cardoso, J. M. P. (2009). The current feasibility of gesture recognition for a smartphone using J2ME. In *Proceedings of the ACM Symposium on Applied Computing* (pp.1642-1649). ACM.

Zhou, H., & Ruan, Q. (2006). A Real-time Gesture Recognition Algorithm on Video Surveillance. In *Proceedings of 8th international conference on Signal Processing*. Academic Press.

KEY TERMS AND DEFINITIONS

Bent Finger Detection: In fingertips detection, when fingers are bent, the top part of finger is detected as tip, not the real fingertip. Some mechanisms have been done to detect real fingertips when fingers are closed or bent.

Finger Angle Calculation: In hand gesture recognition, angle fingertips make with the center of palm. It may be very useful in reconstrution the hand posture and understanding the situation.

Gesture Based Systems: The systems operated using gesture, it can be with face or hand or others.

Hand Gesture Recognition: Foregoing the traditional keyboard and mouse setup to interact with a computer, strong gesture recognition could allow users to accomplish frequent or common tasks using hand or face gestures to a camera. Hand gesture provides a naturalness to the user so he feels controlling system like talking to other human.

Human Computer Interface: Human–computer interaction involves the study, planning, design and uses of the interaction between people and computers. It is often regarded as the intersection of computer science, behavioral sciences, design and several other fields of study.

Natural Computing: The computing which is green and offer a natural human like behavior to user. It can be interpreted as working with machines in natural way or machines are working naturally.

Chapter 11
Securing Digital Image with Authentication Code

Siva Charan Muraharirao
Dhirubhai Ambani Institute of Information and Communication Technology, India

Manik Lal Das
Dhirubhai Ambani Institute of Information and Communication Technology, India

ABSTRACT

The recent advances in multimedia technology demand protection of digital images from unintentional manipulation for content integrity, copyright, and ownership. Digital watermarking technique has wide acceptance in the industry for anti-piracy, ownership verification, and digital image authentication. There have been a large number of schemes in the literature proposed for digital watermarking using non-cryptographic and cryptographic primitives. Use of Least Significant Bits (LSB) is one of the oldest but classical approaches for digital image authentication. Although LSB approach is efficient, it does not provide adequate security. Cryptographic primitives such as hash function, digital signature, and message authentication codes have been used in several applications including multimedia for data authentication. Digital signature-based image authentication provides strong security, but the approach requires managing public key infrastructure, which is a costly operation. Partial data protection is also an optimal approach for protecting important data while leaving unimportant data unprotected. Considering security weakness of the LSB-based approach and cost overhead of the public key-based approach, the authors present in this chapter a digital image authentication scheme using LSB, keyed hash, and partial encryption. They show that the proposed watermarking scheme is secure and efficient in comparison to other related schemes.

INTRODUCTION

Recent advances in computing and communication technology allow easy access of digital content through the Internet (Furht, & Kirovski, 2004). The proliferation of Internet technology and ac-cessibility of digital documents across the globe enable increasing copyright fraud, duplication of data and unauthorized distribution of multimedia content. Naturally, controls over copyright, anti-piracy and unauthorized content redistribution are potential challenges in digital economy, which

DOI: 10.4018/978-1-4666-6030-4.ch011

needs significant attention from scientific community. One can use multimedia content from available source, but should take appropriate permission of the content owner and after giving due citation and credits to content owner. Fabrication of multimedia content, in particular manipulation of digital image, is certainly not allowed in any form irrespective of deliberate or (un)intentional attempt. When a dishonest person is getting away by doing such malpractices without being caught then it raises two important concerns - on one hand, the dishonest person knows that s/he can enjoy her/his life in this way without expecting any punishments; and on the other hand, it is because of poor content protection and detection mechanism by the content owner. Finally, it effects on the financial part at the owner side. Therefore, ensuring digital image integrity and image authenticity has become a major concern in multimedia security.

Cryptographic primitives such as encryption and digital signature have been used for data confidentiality and authentication, respectively. However, in multimedia data protection direct use of encryption and digital signature may not be of much help, as the data size is too large and most of the cases data hiding is important than simple encryption. Therefore, these primitives along with other primitives (e.g. hash function, chaotic map, pseudo-noise, etc) must be used for multimedia data protection as per application requirement. In order to protect multimedia data, techniques like digital watermarking, scrambling, authentication, integrity or a combination of these could protect digital content from content tampering. Many techniques (Walton, 1995), (Tang, Hwang, & Yang, 2002), (Hwang, Chang, & Hwang, 1999), (Yeung, & Mintzer, 1997), (Wong, & Memon, 2001), (Chang, Hu, & Lu, 2006), (Ahmed, Siyal, & Abbas, 2010) have been proposed for protecting multimedia data, piracy detection, and copyright and ownership control. Out of several approaches, digital watermarking (Furht, & Kirovski, 2004)

technique has been playing a pivotal role in multimedia data protection.

Digital watermarking (Furht, & Kirovski, 2004) is a technique that inserts a piece of information into a target image, which can be later extracted for a variety of purposes and/or detected in case of malpractices. A watermark can be a binary string, a logo, or some intended features of the multimedia content. Whatever maybe the watermark content, the watermarking technique needs to be designed in such a way that unauthorized entity should not be able to identify any information about the watermarked content and position of it. At the same time, the content owner or authorized entity should be able to identify the watermarked information from the image as and when needed. Digital watermark can use non-cryptographic primitives like LSB (Least Significant Bit) method, chaotic map, or it can use cryptographic primitives such as message authentication codes, digital signature and encryption. The watermarking techniques embed a digital watermark, which asserts the ownership of the digital media such as text, audio, image and video. The embedded watermark is extracted from the watermarked media as and when required and then is used to check its authenticity whether the media is duplicated or fabricated. The main goals of the digital watermarking are the robustness and security of the digital media (Furht, & Kirovski, 2004). A typical work flow of embedding and extraction process of digital watermark in an image is shown in Figure 1.

Watermarking techniques (Furht, & Kirovski, 2004), (Mandhani, 2003), (Hwang, Chang, & Hwang, 1999) can be broadly classified in two categories: visible watermarking and invisible watermarking. Visible watermarking is the classical way of watermark generation, extraction and deletion, where the watermark is inserted into a cover object. Although visible watermarking is useful for identification purpose, it is not secure watermarking for applications such as image authentication, image alteration and copy protec-

Figure 1. Embedding and extraction of watermark

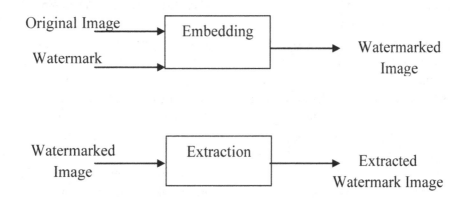

tion. In contrast, invisible watermarking is the modern approach for digital image authentication and piracy detection. LSB technique and parity bit checking have been used in several products as a light-weight image protection mechanism (Walton, 1995). LSB technique makes watermark perceptually invisible and the quality of the image is preserved. The working principle of LSB technique is briefly explained as follows. For embedding process, every pixel in a gray-scale image is represented by a byte, or 8 bits. Each bit from the watermark image is embedded in to the LSB of each pixel. The process is continued until all the pixels in the original image are covered. In extraction process, all LSBs in the stamped image are extracted and reassembled to form the original watermarked image. The process is simple and easy to implement, however, the main drawbacks of this technique are - (i) the watermarked image does not provide security if all the LSBs of the image are changed to 1; (ii) no cryptographic key/ method is used to keep the watermark secure; and (iii) a lossless compression format is needed because of watermarked data lose, possibility, during the transformation of a lossy compression algorithm.

In order to bring robustness and security into multimedia content, cryptographic primitives (Schneier, 1996) such as encryption, digital signature, and message authentication codes can be used for protecting multimedia data from unauthorized data alteration. There are some applications such as currency notes, stamp papers, seals, contracts, which demand cryptographic protection of documents' features. Tang, Hwang, & Yang (2002) proposed a scheme for digital image authentication using the RSA signature scheme (Schneier, 1996). Their scheme uses a 512-bit modulus and each block is protected by 512 bits. Once the signature is generated, the signature is embedded into the LSBs. The image authentication is checked by verifying the signature of the MSBs and the LSBs. Partial encryption (Cheng, & Li, 2000) is another method in which only important part of the data is encrypted and unimportant part remains unencrypted. As the size of the important part is less than that of the original data, there is a significant decrease in encryption and decryption time. Data decomposition and partial encryption are also being used in secure image/video retrieval and real-time data broadcasting scenarios. Fridrich (1999) and Venkatesan, Koon, Jakubowski, & Moulin (2000) proposed a visual hash based watermarking technique for image protection. Recently, Cancellaro, Battisti, Carli, Boato, De-Natale, & Neri (2011) proposed a commutative watermarking and encryption system based on a key dependent transform domain.

Image authentication by digital signature takes more cost in comparison to LSB-based and MAC-based image authentication techniques. Furthermore, digital signature-based approach for digital image protection requires public key infrastructure, whereas, MAC-based approach eliminates such requirement. Digital signature generation and verification on watermark require most computational cost in comparison to MAC-based watermark generation and verification. In order to avoid weaknesses in LSB-based approach, one could consider either digital signature or MAC for achieving strong authentication for digital images. However, we thought that a hybrid approach by considering LSB and MAC as main building blocks for digital image authentication would be an interesting research problem.

In this paper, we present a MAC-based digital image authentication scheme. The proposed scheme uses the concept of the keyed-hash and partial encryption technique. The MAC of the watermark along with the important data of the original image is to be masked in the watermarked image in order to achieve strong security and robustness properties. The proposed scheme provides strong security and takes less computational cost in comparisons with digital signature based watermarking schemes. The proposed scheme can be used for anti-piracy, ownership control and copyright of digital images.

The remaining of the paper is organized as follows. Section 2 reviews watermarking properties and classifies watermarking techniques based on different perceptions. Section 3 presents the proposed scheme. Section 4 analyzes the scheme. We conclude the work in section 5.

WATERMARKING PROPERTIES AND CLASSIFICATIONS

Digital watermarking techniques have played a central role for preserving copyright, ownership, and protecting digital image from piracy and ways to detect unauthorized data alteration as and when necessary. The technique embeds a secret imperceptible signal, a watermark, into the digital image in such a way that it is difficult to detach the watermark from the image. If the watermarked image is altered or watermark is removed from the image then the watermarking techniques should provide an efficient way to detect such alteration of the original image. In order to protect digital image from data piracy and data fabrication, digital watermarking technique typically aims to achieve following properties:

- **Identification:** Watermark can be used as the identity of the original digital image, embedded in the image. On one hand, any alteration of the watermarked image allows identification of the image a pirate copy. On the other hand, extraction of correct watermark from the watermarked image ensures the legitimacy of the image.
- **Authentication:** Watermark can be used to check the authenticity of the image. If extracted watermark from the watermarked image is fragile, then image has been altered. The fragile watermark would also help in supplying the location information as to where the data might have been altered.
- **Robustness:** The watermark should be resilient to standard manipulations of unintentional as well as intentional nature. It allows watermark detector identifying correctly (up to a pre-agreed threshold value) the watermark in the watermarked image even after some unimportant data distortion of the watermarked image.

Based on different perceptions watermarking schemes can be classified into following categories (Mahmoud, Datta, & Flint, 2005).

Inputs and Outputs Perception

- **Private marking system:** In a private marking system, one can locate for possible distortion positions in the watermarked image, and then invert them before applying the watermark detector. Private marking systems usually provide increased robustness (Cox, & Miller, 1997).
- **Semi-private marking system:** In a semi-private marking system, the original watermark checks whether it exists in the cover or not.
- **Public marking system:** In a public marking system, neither the original nor the embedded watermark required.

Workspace Perception

Workspace perception distinguishes watermarking schemes into spatial-domain and frequency-domain depending on whether the watermark is encoded by modifying pixels or by altering some frequency coefficients (obtained by transforming the image into the frequency domain). Spatial domain techniques are cost effective but less robust against tampering in comparison to the watermark based on frequency domain (Langelaar, Setyawan, & Lagendijk, 2000).

Several schemes have been proposed based spatial-domain techniques (van Schyndel, Tirkel, & Osborne, 1994), (Hartung, & Girod, 1996), (Wolfgang, & Delp, 1996), (Fridrich, 1999), (Chang, Tsai & Lin, 2004). For example, the watermarked image $I_w(x, y)$ is created using the watermark $W(x, y)$ and the original image. This can be computed as

$I_w(x, y) = I(x, y) + k*W(x, y)$, where k is a small gain factor.

In order to detect the watermark in a watermarked image $I_w(x, y)$ one calculate the correlation between the watermarked image $I_w(x, y)$ and the watermark $W(x, y)$. It is noted that the watermark detector provides the correlation value high for a pseudorandom pattern generated with the correct key; otherwise, the correlation value would be low.

In contrast, watermarking schemes in frequency-domain hide messages in significant area of the digital image that enables robustness against image tampering. In the frequency-domain, the original image $I(x, y)$ is transformed into coefficients which are perturbed by a small amount in some acceptable way in order to represent the watermark. When the watermarked image $I_w(x, y)$ is compressed, then the required noise is added to the already perturbed coefficients. At the time of watermark detection, it subtracts the received coefficients from the original image ones to obtain the noise perturbation. The watermark is then estimated from the noisy data.

Visibility Perception

Although most of the literature has focused on invisible watermarks, visible watermarks (e.g. company logo, currencies, trademark, and copyright symbol) have also found wider applications. Simply hiding watermark cannot ensure its security and robustness. Instead, a clever approach would be making watermark visible and hiding some important parts of it or masking its digest securely inside the digital image.

Robustness Perception

Robust watermarks have the property that it is infeasible to remove them or make them useless without destroying the object at the same time. In other words, the watermark should be embedded in the most significant portions of the object (Cox, & Miller, 1997) so that image manipulator cannot remove the watermark without removing the watermarked image itself.

Security Perception

Any alteration of the object or embedded watermarks should convey indication at the time of extraction of the watermark and/or at the time of image verification stage. Authentication and integrity could be clubbed together for achieving strong security notion of watermarking techniques. Additionally, hiding important portions of the watermark in the image would be extra measures. With all these measures, the extracted watermark can be verified by the owner of the digital image (Lou, Tso, &Liu, 2007).

SOME EXISTING WATERMARKING SCHEMES BASED ON CRYPTOGRAPHIC PRIMITIVES

Tang, Hwang, & Yang (2002) proposed a signature based watermarking scheme for image authentication using the RSA signature scheme (Schneier, 1996). Their scheme uses a 512-bit modulus and each block is protected by 512 bits. Every pixel in a grey-scale image is represented by 8 bits. Among those 8 bits, the first 5 bits are classified as most significant bits (MSBs) and the last 3 as least significant bits (LSBs). As each signature size is 512 bits, 172 pixels are needed as input to the signature algorithm. Therefore, the number of MSBs and LSBs for 172 pixels is 860 and 516 bits, respectively. Once the signature is generated, the signature is embedded into the LSBs. The image authentication is checked by verifying the signature of the MSBs and the LSBs. The watermark embedding and extraction process are depicted in Figure 2 and 3, respectively.

The steps involved in Tang Hwang, & Yang (2002)scheme are as follows.

1. The 3 bits LSBs of the 172 pixels are formed as w_1. The 5 MSBs of the 172 pixel block are divided into two (86 x 5) sub blocks sb_1 and sb_2. Similarly, the next 172 pixel block is di-

Figure 2. Embedding signature into watermarked image

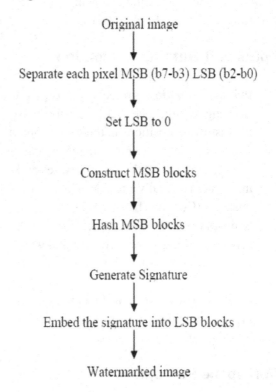

vided into sb_3, sb_4 and w_2. All the subsequent blocks are divided using the same process.

2. The sub blocks b_i are formed as per following arithmetic

$b_1 = sb_1 + sb_2$ and $b_r = sb_{2r-1} + sb_{2r} + sb_{2r+1}$, where $r = 2, 3, 4, \ldots$

The size of b_1 is 172 x 5 bits and that of b_r, $r = 2, 3, 4, \ldots$ is 258 x 5 bits.

3. The signature on b_i is computed as $\sigma_i = \text{Sign}_d(h(b_i))$, $i = 1, 2, \ldots, r$, where d is the signer's private key, e is the corresponding public key, Sign(.) is the RSA signature algorithm, and $h(.)$ is a cryptographically secure hash function. The signature σ_i is embedded into w_i, for $i = 1, 2, \ldots, r$.

Figure 3. Watermarked image verification

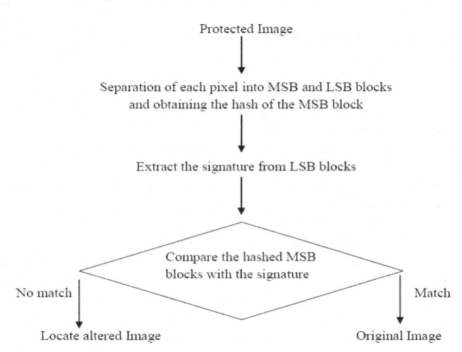

4. The verification of the received image is verified as shown in the Figure 3.

Detection of Tampered image

Detection of the altered location is detected by following logic:

$A = \{sb_i$: a set of the pairs $h(b_i)'$ and $\text{Verify}_e(h(b_i))$ do not match$\}$

$B = \{sb_j$: a set of the pairs $h(b_i)'$ and $\text{Verify}_e(h(b_i))$ match$\}$

$C = \{sb_k$: a set of probable altered sub-blocks$\} = A - B$

The altered location detection is elaborated in Table 1.

Table 1. Detection of tampered location

Case	Sub-block altered	Generalization	A	B	C
1	sb_1	-	sb_1, sb_2	$sb_2, sb_3, sb_4 ..., sb_x$	sb_1
2	sb_1 and sb_2	-	sb_1, sb_2, sb_3, sb_4	$sb_4, sb_5, sb_6 ..., sb_x$	sb_1, sb_2, sb_3
3	sb_2 and sb_3	sb_{2i} and sb_{2i+1}	sb_1, sb_2, sb_3, sb_4	$sb_4, sb_5, sb_6 ..., sb_x$	sb_1, sb_2, sb_3
4	sb_2	sb_{2i}	sb_1, sb_2, sb_3, sb_4	$sb_4, sb_5, sb_6 ..., sb_x$	sb_1, sb_2, sb_3
5	sb_3	sb_{2i+1}	sb_2, sb_3, sb_4	$sb_1, sb_2, sb_4, sb_5, sb_6, ..., sb_x$	sb_3

Our Observation

From Table 1, it is observed that the scheme (Tang, Hwang, & Yang, 2002) can detect alteration of image of block size as small as 86 pixels (Case 1 and Case 5). However, the scheme has a few limitations as follows. From Case 2, the method gives a result which is less accurate than the old technique which accurately detects the tampering in sb_1 and sb_2. The result is same for other two cases, namely 3 and 4. The scheme uses the RSA signature algorithm with modulus of 512 bits, which is not secure and not advisable for use in real-world application (instead, modulus size of 1024 bits or more must be used to provide intended security).

In 1999, Hwang, Chang, & Hwang (1999) proposed a scheme based on the Rabin's scheme (Rabin, 1979). The scheme works as follows. Suppose that the image is represented as m_x x m_y x m_z, where m_x x m_y indicate the size of the image and m_z indicates the size of a pixel in gray-scale, or a pixel in the intensity levels of red, green, and blue color.

Embedding Watermark

The embedding process first calculates the position of the image. The watermark is inserted in to the position of the image sequence. The embedding process works as follows.

1. Choose two large primes numbers p and q, which are kept secret. Compute $n = pq$, and publish n.
2. Secret keys X, Y, Y are calculated as $X = ID^K \bmod n$, $Y = ID^{K2} \bmod n$, $Z = ID^{K4} \bmod n$, where ID denotes the identification of the original image and K is the private key.
3. Position (L_x, L_y, L_z) is calculated as $L_i = i^2 \bmod n$, where $i = X, Y, Z$.
4. Embedding position (x, y, z) is calculated as $j = L_i \bmod n$, where $j = x, y, z$ and $i = X, Y, Z$.

5. One bit of the watermark is embedded in (x, y, z).
6. Now position (L_x, L_y, L_z) is calculated as $L_i = L_i^2 \bmod n$, where $i = X, Y, Z$.
7. Steps (4), (5), (6) are repeated until all the bits of the watermark have been embedded into the original image.

Extraction of Watermark

The extraction process is symmetrical to that of the embedding watermark.

1. Secret keys X, Y, Z are obtained using the same method as in the embedding process.
2. Then position (L_x, L_y, L_z) is calculated.
3. Embedding position (x, y, z) is calculated.
4. Watermark bit from (x, y, z) is retrieved and (L_x, L_y, L_z) is obtained.
5. Steps (3) and (4) are repeated until all the bits of the watermark are extracted.

Detection of Tampered Image

Detection of tampered image is detected by verifying the extracted watermark and checking the same with the original watermark.

Our Observation

We observe that the scheme (Hwang, Chang, & Hwang, 1999) suffers from following weakness. The position (L_x, L_y, L_z) can be chosen repeatedly. Therefore, different bits of the watermark can be embedded into the same position. To avoid this problem, a transient table is used to record all calculated positions. If the calculated position exists already, the watermark bit embedding step is skipped, and else the position is recorded in the transient table. Furthermore, the chosen position (L_x, L_y, L_z) could be an MSB. When (x, y, z) is obtained, if $z = 0$ or $z = 7$, then the watermark bit embedding step is skipped; otherwise, compare z's bit of (x, y) with each bit of the watermark. The process proceeds if they match, else embed the watermark bit in (*x, y, z*) and change another bit (not the one in which the watermark bit was already embedded) such that the difference between the two pixels is minimal. The scheme also suffers from the LSB attack. The attacker destroys the LSBs of the original image without affecting the quality of the image. This does not destroy the watermark since the watermark bit is not always embedded in the LSB.

In (Wong, & Memon, 2001), watermarking schemes using secret key and public key have been proposed. The secret key based watermarking scheme uses cryptographically secure hash function and requires pre-establishment of a secret key between image owner and customer before they start the public key based scheme uses both hash function and public key encryption/decryption algorithm.

THE PROPOSED SCHEME

The proposed scheme uses the message authentication codes (e.g. HMAC (Schneier, 1996)) for protecting digital image against image tampering. The image authentication code is computed as

$$IAC = HMAC_K(OI, ID) \oplus DW$$

where *OI* is the original image, *ID* is the identity of the image, *DW* is the digital watermark, *K* is the secret key and *HMAC*(.) is the keyed hash function. Like other schemes, the proposed scheme has also three phases – watermark insertion, watermark extraction and watermark verification.

Watermark Insertion

We consider a gray-scale image G_i of size *m* x *n*. For each 8 bits pixel of the gray-scale image, the first 5 bits are classified as MSBs (most significant bits) and the last 3 bits as LSBs (least significant bits). The block size of the image is determined in such a way that the LSBs of each block should be big enough to accommodate the output of the image authentication code (*IAC*). The watermark image, *DW*, is formed by taking a binary image of size *u* x *v*, or by taking a smaller binary image *w* and tiling it, i.e., periodically replicating *w* for the desired size. The MSBs of the block are given as input to the *HMAC* along with the image identity *ID*, height *m* of the image, width *n* of the image, and the block number *r*. Then, the output is XORed with the watermark block, and the resultant *IAC* is inserted into the LSB block as shown in Figure 4.

Watermark Extraction

The extraction of watermark, shown in Figure 5, works as follows. The watermarked image is divided into blocks and sub blocks following the same procedure as mentioned in the insertion process. The watermark embedded in the LSB block is now extracted and XORed with the output of

Figure 4. Watermark Insertion

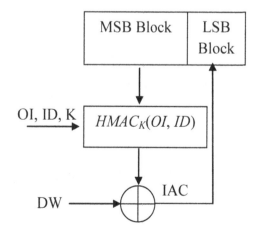

Original Image Block

Figure 5. Watermark extraction

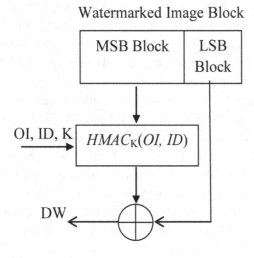

Watermark Verification

The watermark verification, shown in Figure 6, is done as follows:

$$IAC \oplus IAC' = 0$$

where *IAC* is the authentication code of the original image and *IAC'* is the authentication code of the image extracted from the watermark extraction phase.

the *HMAC* of the MSBs block. After the extraction process, all watermarked blocks are collaged together to form the original watermark, DW. It is noted that any noise in the extracted watermark indicates the alteration in the respective block of the watermarked image.

If the outcome is non-zero and above a pre-agreed threshold value, then the image has been altered. In the verification process, the watermark is extracted by XORing the *IAC* of the original image. To attach the *IAC* to the original image, the *IAC* is embedded into the LSBs of the pixels. This works fine because the variation bit value in the LSBs does not change much in the intensity of the pixel. The image is divided into blocks of suitable size, to embed the *IAC* of the MSBs and *DW* into the LSB block. After the watermark extraction process, all watermark blocks are collaged together to form the original watermark.

Figure 6. Watermark verification

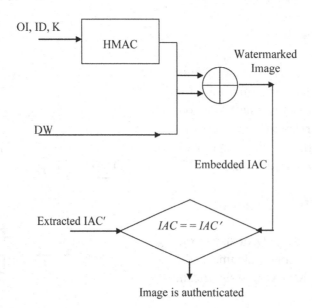

ANALYSIS OF THE PROPOSED SCHEME

The proposed scheme uses a secure keyed function (HMAC) for masking the important portion of the original image and the watermark. The authentication code is embedded in the watermarked image (i.e. in the LSBs) in such a way that the image quality retain in the watermarked image. It is noted that the computation cost of the keyed hash is substantially less than a conventional digital signature computation, and therefore, the proposed scheme is efficient than its contemporary approaches. Additionally, the proposed scheme does not require any public key certificate, so it does not require a trusted party to remain available for certification management. Although computation of keyed hash function requires a secret key, the scheme does not require distribution of the secret key to other party unless any dispute arises for piracy, copyright or ownership issues.

If the watermark is generated and embedded using non-cryptographic technique (e.g. LSB-based, parity-bit), then an attacker can maintain a database of images verified with the same watermark. In that case, there is a possibility that the attacker can choose an arbitrary image and modify it to pass the verification process.

The proposed scheme avoids the above mentioned scenario. Firstly, a unique image identity (ID) is attached at the end of the MSB bit string of each block. Secondly, the block is masked with the watermark using a HMAC. Because of its pre-image resistance property, it is difficult for attacker to find any clue of the watermark. Furthermore, the attacker will not be able to find (in polynomial time) another an object that colludes with the extracted object from the watermarked image, as HMAC seems to be collision resistant. Even the attacker finds a possible candidate; he still cannot get any clue of the watermark without knowing the secret key. Therefore, the proposed scheme provides required security attributes.

The proposed scheme is also robust. The property is achieved with the notion of the partial encryption (in our case, it is partially keyed hashed value). Only important portions (MSBs) of the original image are inputted to HMAC, and LSBs are left unauthenticated. This gives some places to make some manipulation of the image as long as it falls in the LSBs part. In such situation, the extracted object will match to the keyed hashed value (Table 2).

CONCLUSION

We have discussed message authentication code based digital image protection from piracy, copyright violation and ownership dispute. We proposed an efficient watermarking scheme for digital image authentication and integrity using LSBs, partial encryption and message authentication codes. In the proposed scheme, we have considered only important parts of the original image be masked with the watermark, and then the resultant authentication code is embedded into the LSBs of the watermarked image. We have compared the proposed approach with related schemes, and shown that the proposed scheme is secure, robust, and efficient in comparison to other schemes.

Table 2. Comparison of the schemes

Scheme	Cryptographic Primitive / Operation	Comp. cost	Immunization to Attack
Tang Hwang, & Yang (2002)	Modular exponentiation	High	No
Hwang, Chang, & Hwang (1999)	Square root modulo *n*	High	No
Proposed scheme	Keyed hash function	Low	Yes

ACKNOWLEDGMENT

The preliminary version of the work appeared in IJCVIP, 2(2): 36-47 (2012). This is an extended version. The first author of the work carried out this project as a part of his internship at the final year of his B.Tech. program at DA-IICT.

REFERENCES

Ahmed, F., Siyal, M. Y., & Abbas, V. U. (2010). A secure and robust hash-based scheme for image authentication. *Signal Processing*, *90*(5), 1456–1470. doi:10.1016/j.sigpro.2009.05.024

Anderson, R., & Biham, E. (1996). Tiger-A fast new hash function. In *Proc. of Fast Software Encryption*. Cambridge, UK: Academic Press. doi:10.1007/3-540-60865-6_46

Cancellaro, M., Battisti, F., Carli, M., Boato, G., DeNatale, F. G. B., & Neri, A. (2011). A commutative digital image watermarking and encryption method in the tree structured Haar transform domain. *Signal Processing Image Communication*, *26*, 1–12. doi:10.1016/j.image.2010.11.001

Chang, C. C., Hu, Y. S., & Lu, T. C. (2006). A watermarking-based image ownership and tampering authentication scheme. *Pattern Recognition Letters*, *27*(5), 439–446. doi:10.1016/j.patrec.2005.09.006

Chang, C.C., Tsai, P., & Lin, M.H. (2004). An adaptive steganography for index-based images using codeword grouping. *Advances in Multimedia Information Processing*, 731-738.

Cheng, H., & Li, X. (2000). Partial encryption of images and videos. *IEEE Transactions on Signal Processing*, *48*(8), 2439–2451. doi:10.1109/78.852023

Cox, I. J., & Miller, M. L. (1997). A review of watermarking and the importance of perceptual modeling. *SPIE. Human Vision & Electronic Imaging II*, *3016*, 92–99. doi:10.1117/12.274502

Fridrich, J. (1999). Robust bit extraction from images. In *Proc. of International Conference on Multimedia Computing and Systems,* Florence, (pp. 536-540). Academic Press.

Furht, B., & Kirovski, D. (2004). *Multimedia Security Handbook*. CRC Press. doi:10.1201/9781420038262

Hartung, F., & Girod, B. (1996). *Digital watermarking of raw and compressed video* (pp. 205–213). Proc. of Digital Compression Technologies and Systems for Video Communication.

Hwang, M. S., Chang, C. C., & Hwang, K. F. (1999). A watermarking technique based on one-way hash function. *IEEE Transactions on Consumer Electronics*, *45*(2), 286–294. doi:10.1109/30.793411

Langelaar, G. C., Setyawan, I., & Lagendijk, R. L. (2000). Watermarking digital image and video data. *IEEE Signal Processing Magazine*, *17*(5), 20–46. doi:10.1109/79.879337

Lou, D. C., Tso, H. K., & Liu, J. L. (2007). A copyright protection scheme for digital images using visual cryptography technique. *Computer Standards & Interfaces*, *29*, 125–131. doi:10.1016/j.csi.2006.02.003

Mahmoud, K., Datta, S., & Flint, J. (2005). Frequency domain watermarking: An overview. *International Arab Journal of Information Technology, 2*(1), 33–47.

Mandhani, N. K. (2003). *Watermarking using decimal sequences.* (Master thesis). Louisiana State University, Baton Rouge, LA.

Rabin, M. O. (1979). Digital signatures and public-key functions as intractable as factorization. *Technical Report MIT/LCS/TR-212.* Massachusetts Institute of Technology.

Schneier, B. (1996). *Applied cryptography: Protocols, Algorithms, and Source Code in C.* John Wiley & Sons.

Tang, C. W., & Hang, H. M. (2003). A feature-based robust digital image watermarking scheme. *IEEE Transactions on Signal Processing, 51*(4), 950–959. doi:10.1109/TSP.2003.809367

Tang, Y. L., Hwang, M. S., & Yang, C. R. (2002). An image authentication scheme based on digital signatures. *Pakistan Journal of Applied Sciences, 2*(5), 553–557.

van Schyndel, R. G., Tirkel, A. Z., & Osborne, C. F. (1994). A digital watermark. In *Proc. IEEE International Conference of Image Processing,* (vol. 2, pp. 86-90). IEEE.

Venkatesan, R., Koon, S. M., Jakubowski, M. H., & Moulin, P. (2000). Robust image hashing. In *Proc. of the IEEE International Conference on Image Processing,* (vol. 3, pp. 664-666). IEEE.

Walton, S. (1995). Image authentication for a slippery new age. *Dr. Dobb's Journal of Software Tools for Professional Programmers, 20.*

Wolfgang, R. B., & Delp, E. J. (1996). A watermark for digital images. In *Proc. of IEEE International Conference of Image Processing,* (vol. 3, pp. 219-222). IEEE.

Wong, P. W., & Memon, N. (2001). Secret and public key image watermarking schemes for image authentication and ownership verification. *IEEE Transactions on Image Processing, 10*(10), 1593–1601. doi:10.1109/83.951543 PMID:18255501

Yeung, M. M., & Mintzer, F. (1997). An invisible watermarking technique for image verification. In *Proc. of the IEEE International Conference on Image Processing.* IEEE.

KEY TERMS AND DEFINITIONS

Copyright: Copyright is the process of legally granting the exclusive rights to the creator of an original work for its usage and distribution.

Digital Signature: Digital signature is algorithm for demonstrating the authenticity of a digital document.

Digital Watermarking: Digital watermarking is a technique that inserts a piece of information into a target image, which can be later extracted for a variety of purposes and/or detected in case of malpractices.

Image Authentication: Image authentication is a process by which one can confirm whether the image is genuine of not.

Image Protection: Image protection is the way to safeguard the image from malicious or intentional alteration of its content.

Message Authentication Code: Message authentication code is a cryptographic function that takes two inputs, the text and the key, and outputs a digest value of those inputs.

Partial Encryption: Partial encryption is a technique by which the important portions of a target message are encrypted and unimportant portions are left unencrypted.

Chapter 12
An Efficient Color Image Encoding Scheme Based on Colorization

Noura A. Semary
Menofia University, Egypt & Scientific Research Group in Egypt (SRGE), Egypt

ABSTRACT

Image colorization is a new image processing topic to recolor gray images to look as like the original color images as possible. Different methods have appeared in the literature to solve this problem, the way that leads to thinking about decolorization, eliminating the colors of color images to just small color keys, aid in the colorization process. Due to this idea, decolorization is considered as a color image encoding mechanism. In this chapter, the authors propose a new decolorization system depends on extracting the color seeds (Representative Pixels [RP]) using morphology operations. Different decolorization methods are studied and compared to the system results using different quality metrics.

INTRODUCTION

Image colorization is the process of adding colors to black and white images. One of the problems of colorization is how to select the suitable colors, mainly the original colors, to generate a colored image similar to the original color one. Different colorization methods treats this problem in the literature, most of these trials are covered and discussed in our previous publications (Semary, 2011), (Semary, 2012). One of the common colorization methods is A. Levin et al. technique (Levin, Lischinski, & Weiss, 2004) where the user draws some scribbles on a gray image us-

ing a color palette and a brush like tool, then the computer colorizes the image using optimization depending on the fact, the nearby pixels in gray should have the same color.

Levin's method depends on user selection of positions and colors of the scribbles. So it's an important aspect in his method to practice well; where to draw the scribbles and what is the suitable color to be selected for obtaining a color image as the original one. Because of these drawbacks, many researchers like Yao Li et al. (Li, Lizhuang, & Di, 2007) and Liron. Yatziv et al. (Yatziv & Sapiro, 2006) and more appeared in the literature;

DOI: 10.4018/978-1-4666-6030-4.ch012

improve Levin's algorithm quality; speed and the needed number and positions of the scribbles.

Decolorization is a new research field appeared after the fast development in image and video Colorization area. Decolorization means to convert the color image to grayscale by eliminating the colors in the image but keeping some clues refer to the original colors to be used in the Recolorization process; to obtain a recolored image looks like the original one.

From our point of view and literature study, there are two trends for decolorization (Semary, 2011):

Color Embedding: Where the chromatic channels are processed to be hidden or embedded in the gray image. The inverse of the hiding process is performed to extract the color channels back and merge them with the gray (lightness) channel to obtain the color image again, but in lower quality than the original one. This field leads to thinking about encoding color images using decolorization. Ricardo et al. (de Queiroz & Braun, 2006), (de Queiroz, 2010) used wavelet sub-bands to hide chromatic channels. The resulted gray image was a textured one differs a lot from the original gray image but they proposed their method for faxing applications that enables sending the color image by the traditional fax and recolorize them back after receiving. Takahiko Horiuchi et al. (Horiuchi, Nohara, & Tominaga, 2010) used a second-level Haar wavelet transform with a packet assignment technique. The proposed algorithm distributed color information effectively in one-level wavelet subbands for preserving the chroma and spatial resolution. The application permitted color recovery only to a specific user with a key.

Chaumont and Puech (2009) proposed a method to embed the color information of an image in a corresponding grey-level image. This method was made of three major steps which were a fast color quantization, an optimized ordering and an adapted data hiding. The principle was to build an index image which is, in the same time, a semantically intelligible grey-level image. In order to obtain this particular index image, which should be robust to data hiding, a layer running algorithm was proceeded to sort the K colors of the palette.

The algorithm searches for the best scribbles or seeds can be extracted and sent with the gray image to be used in the colorization process. This trend is suitable for user selection colorization techniques, where the decolorization process usually made automatically without user scribbles selection (Vieira, et al., 2003). Next section explains most well-known works in this trend.

RELATED WORKS

One on the simplest methods for color seeds extraction is Brooks' et al. method (Brooks et al., 2007), where the representative pixels (seeds) were selected using sampling (Figure 1).

T. Miyata et al. (Miyata, Komiyama, Sakai, & Inazumi, 2009) proposed a decolorization methodology depends on extracting line segments from the color image to be the scribbles for the colorization process. Their process based on Levin's colorization method, where the colorization process is a basic block in their system framework what leads to a lot of computational time. The authors compared their algorithm results with Cheng's method (Cheng & Vishwanathan, 2007) where the last one algorithm uses active learning feedback to propagate the selection of the seeds and extracts *RP* pixels as seeds instead of lines and scribbles (Figure 2, Figure 3).

Rusu et al. (Rusu & Tsaftaris, 2013) has proposed another iterative method that provides insights as to the relationship between locally vs. globally important scribbles. First, the *RPs* have been selected in random from the image, then the system has to define a scribble contribution measure based on the reconstruction error. Although the main objective of their work is to select the best seeds for colorization process, they assumed the availability of the color image. They didn't

Figure 1. Brooks' system results (Brooks et al., 2007), (left) Color seeds, (right) The colorization result

Figure 2. Cheng's results (Cheng & Vishwanathan, 2007)

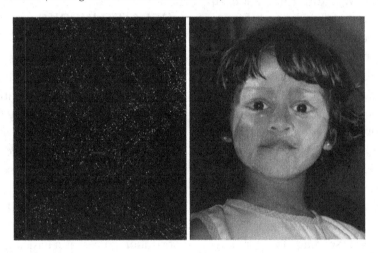

Figure 3. Miyata's result (Miyata et al., 2009)

analysis their system as an encoding system. Their system was tested on Picasso paintings.

Lee et al. (Lee, Park, Oh, & Kang, 2013), (Ryu, Lee, & Lee, 2014) have used the mean shift clustering algorithm (Comaniciu & Meer, 2002) for image compression using inverse colorization (Figure 4). The encoder makes use of the mean shift segmentation algorithm in automatically selecting the *RPs* from the original image from which the colored image is reconstructed by the decoder. Their systems results are better than Cheng's and Miyata's systems but the drawback in is the long time needed to extract the RPs. It's well known that mean shift algorithm is very slow clustering technique besides their system performs mean shift clustering many times and in different scales to get better results.

At the decoder side of all these system, Levin's (Levin et al., 2004) colorization system has been used with the extracted *RPs* to recolorize the encoded image.

In this chapter, we propose a new color encoding system by automatically seeds selection method depends on image morphological operations. Our proposed technique has the following advantages:

- Extracts seeds not scribbles, which results in less number of pixels and thereby a good color compression ratio.
- The extracted seeds are selected well to suit Levin's (Levin et al., 2004), Li's (Li et al., 2007) and Yatziv's (Yatziv & Sapiro, 2006) colorization systems or any colorization system depends on seeds colorization.
- There is no learning or feedbacks what makes it very fast *RPs* extraction algorithm.
- The system parameters affect the quality of both decolorization and colorization but even with high compression ratio/low quality parameters the colorization process obtains very good results.

CHAPTER FUNDAMENTALS

In this section, the basic algorithms used by the proposed system will be presented in some details.

Colorization Using Optimization by A. Levin

Levin's et al. (Levin et al., 2004) colorization algorithm is based on a simple premise: neighboring pixels that have similar intensities should have similar colors.

Figure 4. Lee's colorization system (Ryu et al., 2014)

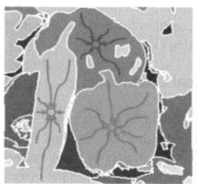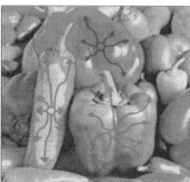

Let n be the number of pixels in the original image and r be an identifier of the pixels in raster-scan order ($1 \leq r \leq n$). u ($u \in R^n$) is assumed to be a one-dimensional vector that contains a color component restored by colorization (denoted as the restoration color component) and is arranged in column in raster-scan order. x ($x \in R^n$) is assumed to be a one-dimensional vector that contains RP values, and x has non-zero values only for RP. $u(r)$ and $x(r)$ are the r-th elements of u and x respectively. $\Omega = \{r|x(r) \neq 0\}$ is a set of positions of RP. Obviously, $|\Omega|$ is the number of RP that have a specific color value, and it corresponds to the amount of information in-colorization based coding. Let $y(r)$ be a luminance component at the r-th pixel. $s \in N(r)$ denotes that the s-th pixel is belonging to the neighbor (defined as 8 surrounding pixels) of the r-th pixel. Levin et al defined a cost function as

$$J\left(u\right) = \sum_{r \notin \Omega}\left(u\left(r\right) - \sum_{s \in N(r)}\omega_{rs}u\left(s\right)\right)^2 + \sum_{r \in \Omega}\left(u\left(r\right) - x\left(r\right)\right)^2$$

(1)

$$w_{rs} \propto e^{-\left(y(r) - y(s)\right)^2/2\sigma_r^2}$$

(2)

where w_{rs} is a weighting function that sums to one. Suppose W is an $n \times n$ matrix that contains w'_{rs}, which is defined as

$$w'_{rs} = \begin{bmatrix} 0 & if & r \in \Omega \\ w_{rs} & otherwise. \end{bmatrix}$$

(3)

When $A = I - W$ (I is the $n \times n$ identity matrix) is an affinity matrix, formula(1) is equal to

$$J\left(u\right) = \left\|x - Au\right\|^2$$

(4)

When $|\Omega| \neq 0$, A is regular matrix and u that fulfills $x = Au$ always exists and minimizes formula

(4). Thus, u is obtained by solving the following equation

$$u = A^{-1}x$$

(5)

They applied their algorithm in the $YCbCr$ color space. Y is the luminance component corresponding to y, and Cb or Cr is the color component corresponding to u.

K-Mean ++ by D. Arther

The K-Means algorithm begins with an arbitrary set of cluster centers. D. Arthur et al. (Arther & Vassilvitskii, 2007) have proposed a specific method of choosing these centers which they have called K-Means++:

1. Choose an initial center c_1 uniformly at random from X.
2. Choose the next center c_i, selecting $c_i = x'$ $\in X$ with probability

$$\frac{D(x')^2}{\sum_{x \in X} D(x)^2}$$

(6)

3. Repeat Step 2 until a total of k centers is chosen.
4. Proceed as with the standard K-Means algorithm.

They called the weighting used in step 2 simply "D^2 weighting", and they finally proved that their algorithm is O (log k).

Morphological Operations

Morphology is a broad set of image processing operations that process bicolor (black and white) images based on shapes. Morphological operations apply a structuring element to an input image, creating an output image of the same size. In a morphological operation, the value of each pixel in the output image is based on a comparison of the corresponding pixel in the input image with its neighbors according to a structure element, which presents the positions of the pixel neighbors. The most basic morphological operations are dilation and erosion. For describing their effect simply, for a binary image presents white objects on black background, dilation adds pixels to the boundaries of the image objects, while erosion removes pixels from objects boundaries. Next subsections present the morphological operations in more details.

Dilation

It means that, the value of the output pixel is the maximum value of all the pixels in the input pixel's neighborhood (structure element). For a binary image A, a structure element B can be presented as binary matrix or as a group of pair wise positions of 1s. The dilation of A by B is defined by:

$$A \oplus B = \bigcup_{b \in B} A_b \qquad (7)$$

For example let B is 3 by 3 structure element where:

$$B = \begin{Bmatrix} (-1,-1) & (-1,0) & (-1,1) \\ (0,-1) & (0,0) & (0,1) \\ (1,-1) & (1,0) & (1,1) \end{Bmatrix} = \begin{vmatrix} 1 & 1 & 1 \\ 1 & 1 & 1 \\ 1 & 1 & 1 \end{vmatrix} \qquad (8)$$

So, A dilated by B means that each object pixel (white=1) will be replaces by its 9 neighbours, so any white object will be enlarged.

Erosion

Erosion is the inverse operation of dilation. It means that, the value of the output pixel is the minimum value of all the pixels in the input pixel's neighborhood. In a binary image, if any of the pixels is set to 0, the output pixel is set to 0.

The erosion of the binary image A by the structuring element B is defined by:$\ominus$

$$A \ominus B = \bigcap_{b \in B} A_{-b} \qquad (9)$$

So, for the same structure element in (8), the effect of eroding A by B is to remove any foreground pixel that is not completely surrounded by other white pixels. Such pixels must lie at the edges of white regions, and so the white regions will shrink.

Opening

In mathematical morphology, opening is the dilation of the erosion of a set A by a structuring element B:

$$A \circ B = (A \ominus B) \oplus B \qquad (10)$$

The effect of the operator is to preserve foreground regions that have a similar shape to this structuring element, or that can completely contain the structuring element, while eliminating all other regions of foreground pixels.

Closing

In mathematical morphology, the closing of a set (binary image) A by a structuring element B is the erosion of the dilation of that set,

$$A \bullet B = (A \oplus B) \ominus B \qquad (11)$$

The effect of the operator is to preserve background regions that have a similar shape to this structuring element, or that can completely contain the structuring element, while eliminating all other regions of background pixels.

Skeletonization

Skeletonization or Medial-axis transform means, to reduce all objects in an image to lines, without changing the essential structure of the image.

In (Lantuéjoul 1977), Lantuéjoul derived the following morphological formula for the skeleton of a continuous binary image *A* (Serra, 1986):

$$S(A)= \bigcup_{\rho>0} \bigcap_{\mu>0} [(A\Theta\,\rho B)\backslash(A\Theta\,\rho B)\circ \mu B] \quad (12)$$

where ρB is an open ball of radius ρ. Another way to think about the skeleton is as the loci of centers of bi-tangent circles that fit entirely within the foreground region being considered. Figure 5 presents an example on object after performing different morphology operations. For more accurate colorization, more seeds may be needed in the center of the object, so the skeleton of the image A_s is obtained. The skeleton is extracted using morphological skeletonization.

ASSESSMENT METHODS

Mean Square Error (*MSE*) and Peak Signal to Noise Ratio (*PSNR*) are the most widely used mage/video quality metrics during last 20 years. *MSE* and *PSNR* are widely used because they are simple and easy to calculate and mathematically easy to deal with for optimization purpose.

MSE and *PSNR* are usually used for evaluating the amount of change between the intensity of two images. So, these measures are suitable for algorithms affect the luminance channel of the image. From the perceptual point of view, chromatic based processing like colorization should resemble the color appearance of the source image, and meanwhile maintain the 'shape' of the target image. Here, 'shape' means the structure information, e.g. the boundaries of target regions. Winkler (Winkler, 2001) has proposed a new quality metric called the Colorfulness Metric (*CM*) to measure the amount of colors in an image. Colorfulness measure was used for assessment in this.

Figure 5. Morphology operations

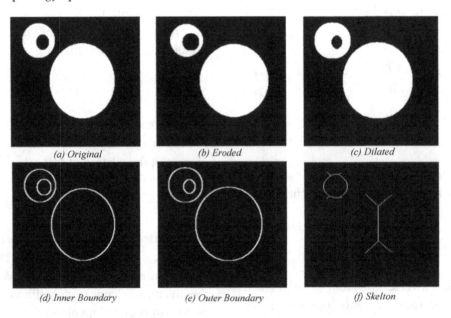

(a) Original (b) Eroded (c) Dilated

(d) Inner Boundary (e) Outer Boundary (f) Skelton

To get a full reference color metric measure (between original and decoded image), the absolute difference between the two images CM is obtained; a low value reflects close colorfulness similarity between the two images, and vice versa. The colorfulness metric presented by (Xiang, Zou, & Li, 2009) is used .

Mean Square Error:

$$MSE = \frac{1}{mn}\sum_{i=0}^{m-1}\sum_{j=0}^{n-1}\left[I(i,j) - K(i,j)\right]^2 \qquad (13)$$

Peak Signal to Noise Ratio:

$$PSNR = 10\log\frac{255^2}{MSE} \qquad (14)$$

Colorfulness Metric:

$$C = \sqrt{\sigma_\alpha^2 + \sigma_\beta^2} + 0.3\sqrt{\mu_\alpha^2 + \mu_\beta^2}$$
$$where$$
$$\alpha = R - G$$
$$\beta = ((R + G\,/\,2)) - B$$

CM Absolute Difference:

$$CM = |C_i\text{-}\, C_j| \qquad (15)$$

where μ and σ are the mean and standard deviations of the pixel cloud along two axes α and β in a simple opponent space .

PROPOSED SYSTEM

In this section the proposed Morphological Decolorization System (MDS) will be presented in details. To extract the suitable seeds, after practicing on seeds colorization systems, we found that most manual seeds or scribbles should be put either near the objects boundaries or in the objects centers or both to obtain better colorization results. From this notice, we thought about extracting the boundaries of each color cluster. This step can be performed by different ways. One of the fast ways to extract objects boundaries is by using the morphological operations. Morphology can be used to extract the inner boundary and the outer boundary of a binary image. Where the inner boundary D_i is the difference between the original binary image A and the eroded image A_e by a structure of size $R \times R$ of ones and the outer boundary D_o is the difference between the original binary image A and the dilated image A_d

$$D_i = A - A_e \qquad (16)$$

$$D_o = A_d - A \qquad (17)$$

The proposed system, presented in Figure 6, states the basic decolorization procedure steps.

First, the image is converted to *YCbCr* color space. The *Cb* and *Cr* channels are used for clustering the image into different color clusters. The clustering is performed using the *K*-Means segmentation technique proposed by D. Arthur et al. (Arther & Vassilvitskii, 2007). The user has to select the number of clusters K given to the clustering technique. Each color cluster is segmented to separated regions which then are converted to binary images to perform the needed morphology operations using $R \times R$ structure element. The inner boundary and the skeleton are detected for each region and the final seeds are extracted from the inner boundaries and/or the skeletons of the regions by sampling with a sampling frequency f.

From the above paragraph, the quality and the compression ratio are related to the system parameters K, R, and f. More additional parameter M is used for eliminating small clusters less than some threshold. The effect of the system variables on the quality and compression ratio is shown in Table 1.

Figure 6. Proposed system flowchart

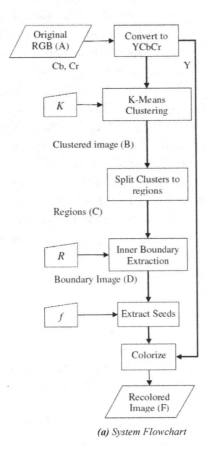

(a) System Flowchart

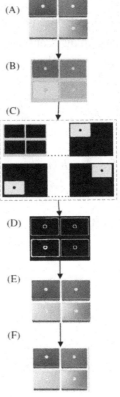

(b) System Visual Steps

In Table 1, Q means the quality which measured by quality assessments; Peak Signal to Noise Ratio (PSNR), Mean Square Error (MSE), Colorfulness Metric, (CM) and CR refers to the compression ratio.

The compression ratio (*CR*) measured in the chapter is calculated by dividing the size of the encoded image by the size of the original image.

Table 1. Relation between system variables and quality and compression ration

Q ~ K	CR ~ 1/K
Q ~ 1/f	CR ~ f
Q ~ R	CR ~ 1/R
Q ~ 1/M	CR ~ M

$$CR = Bytes(encoded)/Bytes(Original) \qquad (18)$$

Each *RP* pixel requires 4 bytes of additional storage: 2 bytes for the *Cb* and *Cr* information, and 2 bytes to encode its location.

EXPERIMENTAL RESULTS AND DISCUSSIONS

The system was implemented in Matlab R2012b on a 2GB RAM, Pentium Dual-Core CPU machine. A lot of images of well-known standard images [1] were used for testing and evaluating the system. Figure 7 presents 12 different size images used in our experiments. *PSNR*, *MSE* and

Figure 7. Test samples

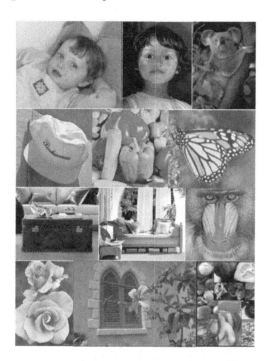

Colorfulness metrics (*CM*) were measured for quality assessment.

Experiment 1: Comparison with Manual Scribbling

Figure 8 shows the most well-known image 'boy' colorized by Levin's manually drawn scribbles and colorization technique. Quality metrics for 'boy' image are *PSNR*= 27.78, *MSE*=33.09 and *CM*=2.3149

Figure 9 presents our system results with inner boundary seeds with quality parameters (*K*=10, *f*=1%, *R*=3) while in Figure 10, skeleton seeds were added to enhance the colorization quality. According to the quality measures presented in Table 2, our system shows better colorization results than manually seeds.

Experiment 2: Comparison with Respect to Chromaticity Compression Ratio

The second type of experimentation tests the system encoding ability. Comparison between our system, Cheng's (Cheng & Vishwanathan, 2007) and Miyata's (Miyata et al., 2009) systems will be discussed in these experiments. In their systems, only the chromaticity values were encoded and attached to the luminance channel as a payload data.

The girl photo (512 × 683) 1,049,088 bytes used in both Cheng's and Miyata's experiments was used in this experiment too. The image was scaled by a scale factor 0.5 as performed in Miyata's system. Cheng's and Miyata's results were presented before in Figures 2, 3 respectively. Different system parameters were used to measure the quality of coloring with respect to compression ratio and presented in Table 3 while Table 4 summaries the quality measures of both Cheng's and Miyata's. N refers to the number of extracted RP. Reader should notice that *CR* usually more

Figure 8. (left) Original, (right) Levin's scribbles and colorization result

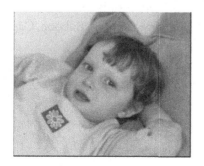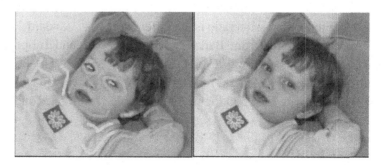

Figure 9. Proposed system results with inner seeds only

 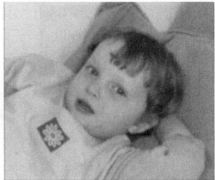

Figure 10. Proposed system results with Inner + Skelton seeds

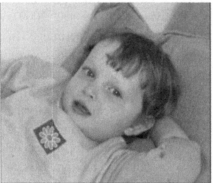 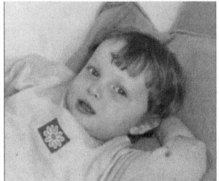

Table 2. Comparison between colorization results using manual scribbles and the proposed system with different seeds selection options

	K	f	R	PSNR	MSE	CM	CR
Manual Seeds				27.78	33.09	2.3149	
Inner Boundary only	10	1%	3	36. 79	10.45	5.44	0.45
Inner + Skelton Seeds	10	1%	3	38.87	5.23	2.32	0.5

than 0.333 (the size of luminance channel), so the chromaticity compression ratio is the difference.

Another example from Berkeley DB[1] ; the Koala photo (321×481) was tested by our system with quality ($k=3, f=1\%, R=3$) and ($k=4, f=50\%, R=3$) . Results are shown in Figure 11 and Table 5. Table 6 presents more results for well-known standard 256×256 images Pepper, Baboon, Caps and Tulips images.

The estimated time for RP seeds extraction for images appear in Table 6 is between 0.1 to 0.5 seconds.

Table 3. Different system parameters

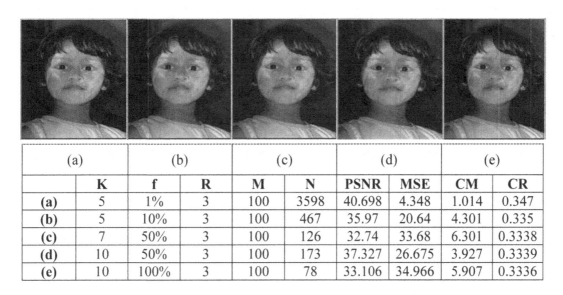

(a)		(b)		(c)		(d)		(e)	
	K	**f**	**R**	**M**	**N**	**PSNR**	**MSE**	**CM**	**CR**
(a)	5	1%	3	100	3598	40.698	4.348	1.014	0.347
(b)	5	10%	3	100	467	35.97	20.64	4.301	0.335
(c)	7	50%	3	100	126	32.74	33.68	6.301	0.3338
(d)	10	50%	3	100	173	37.327	26.675	3.927	0.3339
(e)	10	100%	3	100	78	33.106	34.966	5.907	0.3336

Table 4. Comparison between Cheng's, Miyata's system and the proposed MDS

	N	*PSNR*	*MSE*	*CM*	*Bytes*	*CR*
Miyata's System	456 Line segments	29.448	26.23	3.14	2112	0.335
Cheng's System	2766 Seeds	32.21	17.396	1.20	11064	0.344

Figure 11. Koala (left) Original, (middle) decoded by (3, 1, 3), and (right) decoded by (4, 50, 3)

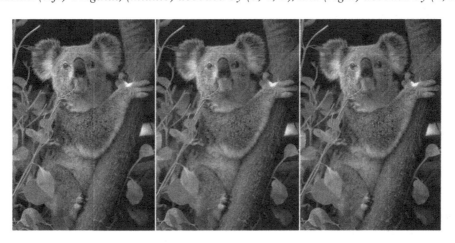

Table 5. Koala results

Q	N	PSNR	MSE	CM	CR	Chroma_CR
(3, 1%, 3)	5053	40.92	5.044	2.79	0.344	0.011
(4, 50%, 3)	1191	38.267	11.86	7.13	0.335	0.003

Table 6. More results

	(256×256) Decoded Images	N	Chroma-Bytes	PSNR	MSE	CM	CR	Chroma_CR
$K=50$ $M=10$ $f=30$ $R=3$		1809	7.07 KB	30.63	27.86	4.61	0.37	0.0368
$K=30$ $M=0$ $f=30$ $R=3$		1654	6.46 KB	28.178	54.33	9.51	0.367	0.0336
$K=10$ $M=10$ $f=10$ $R=3$		1954	7.63 KB	34.135	16.72	3.907	0.373	0.04
$K=20$ $M=5$ $f=20$ $R=3$		2438	9.5 KB	28.276	46.74	9.342	0.383	0.05

Experiment 3: Comparison with JPEG/JPEG2000

In this section, the proposed system is compared to JPEG and JPEG2000. Although the compression ratio obtained from the system is sufficient and less than other decolorization systems, another phase for seeds encoding was added to the system diagram. Huffman encoding method was selected to be used in *MDS* system. It minimizes the size of the extracted seeds and so the compression ratio. Figure 12 shows the diagram of the final encoding procedure.

For performing this comparison, the original color image is converted into *YCbCr* then the chromaticity channels (*Cb* and *Cr*) are encoded using MDS system as previously described. The luminance channel has to be encoded in JPEG/JPEG2000 with encoding quality *Q* for accurate comparison.

At this experiment the 'boy' image was used. First, the image is encoded by JPEG/JPEG2000 with quality $Q = \{4, 8\}$. The same original color image was encoded by the proposed system. MDS parameters used in this experiment are $K=20$, $M=25$, $f= 20\%$ and $R=3$. The number of the extracted seeds are $N=1350$ seeds with compression ratio $CR=0.0057$ after using Huffman coding. *Y* channel was encoded by JPEG/JPEG2000 with $QY=Q$ too. The recolored image then obtained by using the seeds to colorize the decoded *Y* channel. The quality metrics for both images were calculated. Figure 13.a and Figure 13.c present the results of JPEG encoding with quality $Q= \{4, 8\}$ respectively, while Figure 13.b and Figure 13.d present the results of our system using the same JPEG qualities. Table 7 presents the comparison results with JPEG. The same operation has been performed using JPEG2000 instead of standard JPEG. The results are shown in Figure 14 and summarized in Table 8.

More measures have been calculated in this experiment. *MPSNR* is the maximum *PSNR* of *RGB* channels, *APSNR* is the average *PSNR* and *YPSNR* is the *PSNR* calculated on luminance channel. The Mean Structural Similarity Metric (*MSSIM*) also has been calculated for evaluating the change in luminance channel. The max the *MSSIM*, the better is the image.

Although some quality metrics appear better for JPEG and JPEG2000, the proposed system results are subjectively better and the compression ratio is smaller.

Figure 12. Proposed image encoding diagram

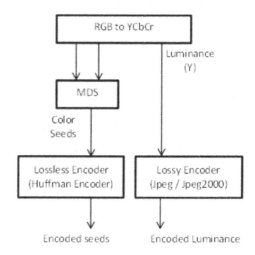

FUTURE WORK DIRECTIONS

The work in this paper could be extended through different directions.

- The number of extracted seeds can be minimized by eliminating the adjacent seeds closer than some threshold.
- There exist many colorization techniques that enhance Levin's system. A colorization algorithm that keep track with image edges may needs fewer number of seeds.
- Instead of sending the seeds as a payload data, seeds could be hided inside the encoded domain (JPEG, JPEG2000) of the luminance channel. Reader can read more about compressed domain in (Mukhopadhyay, 2011).
- Also, the effect of the proposed compression technique on video streams can open new challenges.

Figure 13. Comparison with JPEG. (a)JPEG (Q=8), (b)MDS(Q_Y = 8, K=20, f=20%, M=25), (a)JPEG (Q=4), (b)MDS(Q_Y = 4, K=20, f=20%, M=25), (c)

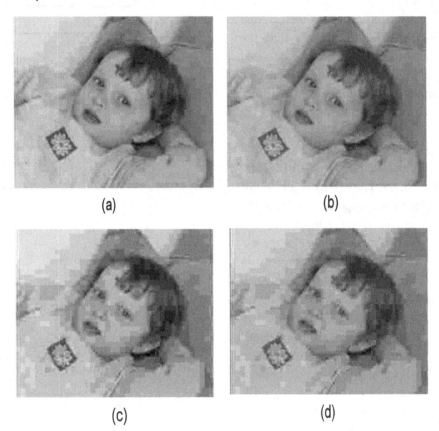

(a)   (b)

(c)   (d)

Table 7. JPEG vs. MDS (Q={4,8})

	MDS-4	JPG-4	MDS-8	JPG-8
MPSNR	32.53	28.73	32.95	31.55
APSNR	28.65	26.88	29.11	29.12
YPSNR	25.3	25.77	26.1	27.5
MSE	45.11	49.81	37.8	30.7
CM	2.83	1.10	3.3	0.03
MSSIM	0.84	0.81	0.89	0.86
CR	0.008	0.008	0.009	0.013

Figure 14. Comparison with JPEG2000. (a)JPEG2000 (Q=8), (b)MDS(Q_Y = 8, K=20, f=20%, M=25), (a)JPEG2000 (Q=4), (b)MDS(Q_Y = 4, K=20, f=20%, M=25), (c)

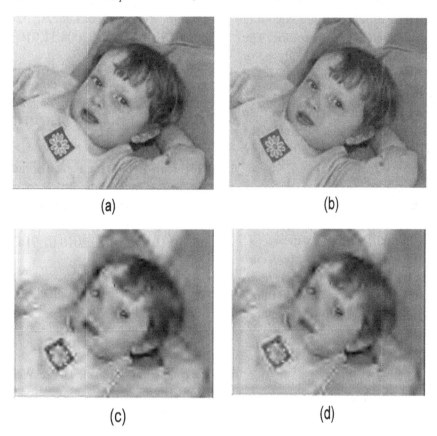

Table 8. JPEG2000 vs. MDS (Q={4,8})

	MDS-4	JPEG2000-4	MDS-8	JPEG2000-8
MPSNR	33.193	29.1279	34.06	34.81
APSNR	29.1539	26.6489	31.21	30.817
YPSNR	26.0537	25.1908	29.87	27.17
MSE	40.6108	49.5698	25.67	14.37
CM	4.8030	0.5777	3.14	1.268
MSSIM	0.8611	0.8394	0.94	0.93
CR	0.0092	0.014474	0.0162	0.04

CONCLUSION

In this chapter we have proposed a new encoding system using morphological decolorization. The proposed system based on automatically color seeds selection from the inner boundaries and the skeleton of the image color clusters. Using morphology, leads to computation time less than methods in the literature besides obtaining the minimum better seeds for efficient recolorization.

REFERENCES

Arther, D., & Vassilvitskii, S. (2007). k-means++: The advantages of careful seeding. *Eighteenth annual ACM-SIAM symposium on Discrete algorithms.* (pp. 1027-1035). Astor Crowne Plaza, New Orleans, Louisiana: Society for Industrial and Applied Mathematics.

Brooks, S., Saunders, I., & Dodgson, N. A. (February 2007). Image compression using sparse colour sampling combined with nonlinear image processin. *The 19th Symposium on Electronic Imaging (SPIE)* (pp. 64920F-64920F). San Jose, California, USA: International Society for Optics and Photonics.

Chaumont, M., & Puech, W. (2009). Protecting the color information by hiding it. *Recent Advances in Signal Processing, 22.*

Cheng, L., & Vishwanathan, S. V. (2007). Learning to compress images and videos. *The 24th international conference on Machine learning* (pp. 161-168). Oregon State University, Oregon, USA: ACM.

Comaniciu, D., & Meer, P. (2002). Mean shift: A robust approach toward feature space analysis. *IEEE Transactions on Pattern Analysis and Machine Intelligence, 24*(5), 603–619. doi:10.1109/34.1000236

de Queiroz, R. L. (2010). Reversible color-to-gray mapping using subband domain texturization. *Pattern Recognition Letters, 31*(4), 269–276. doi:10.1016/j.patrec.2008.11.010

de Queiroz, R. L., & Braun, K. M. (2006). Color to gray and back: color embedding into textured gray images. *IEEE Transactions on Image Processing, 15*(6), 1464–1470. doi:10.1109/TIP.2006.871181 PMID:16764271

Horiuchi, T., Nohara, F., & Tominaga, S. (2010). Accurate reversible color-to-gray mapping algorithm without distortion conditions. *Pattern Recognition Letters, 31*(15), 2405–2414. doi:10.1016/j.patrec.2010.07.014

Lee, S., Park, S.-W., Oh, P., & Kang, M. G. (2013, July). Colorization-Based Compression Using Optimization. *IEEE Transactions on Image Processing, 22*(7), 2627–2636. doi:10.1109/TIP.2013.2253486 PMID:23529096

Levin, A., Lischinski, D., & Weiss, Y. (2004). Colorization using optimization. [TOG]. *ACM Transactions on Graphics, 23*(3), 689–694. doi:10.1145/1015706.1015780

Li, Y., Lizhuang, M., & Di, W. (February, 2007). Fast colorization using edge and gradient constrains. *The 15th International conference in Central Europe on Computer Graphics, Visualization and Computer Vision (WSCG'07)* (pp. 309-315). Plzen - Bory, Czech Republic: Science Press.

Miyata, T., Komiyama, Y., Sakai, Y., & Inazumi, Y. (2009). Novel inverse colorization for image compression. *Picture Coding Symposium (PCS 2009)* (pp. 1-4). Chicago, Illinois, USA: IEEE.

Mukhopadhyay, J. (2011). Image and Video Processing in the Compressed Domain (Har/Cdr ed.). USA: CRC Press.

Rusu, C., & Tsaftaris, S. A. (September 2013). Estimation of Scribble Placement for Painting Colorization. *Image and Signal Processing and Analysis (ISPA)* (pp. 564-569). Trieste, Italy: IEEE.

Ryu, T., Lee, B. G., & Lee, S. (2014). Image Compression System Using Colorization and Meanshift Clustering Methods. *Ubiquitous Information Technologies and Applications*, 165-172.

Semary, N. A. (2011, July). Image Coloring Techniques and Applications. *Ph.D Thesis*, 193. Egypt: Menofia University, Egypt.

Semary, N. A. (2012). *Image coloring Techniques and Applications*. Norderstedt, Germany: GRIN Verlag.

Serra, J. (1986). Introduction to mathematical morphology. *Computer Vision Graphics and Image Processing*, *35*(3), 283–305. doi:10.1016/0734-189X(86)90002-2

Vieira, L. F., Vilela, R. D., & Nascimento, E. R., Jr. F. A., Carceroni, R. L., & Araújo, A. d. (October, 2003). Automatically choosing source color images for coloring grayscale images. *Brazilian Symposium on Computer Graphics and Image Processing (SIBGRAPI)* (pp. 151-158). Sao Carlos, Brazil: IEEE.

Winkler, S. (June 2001). Visual fidelity and perceived quality: Toward comprehensive metrics. *Photonics West 2001-Electronic Imaging* (pp. 114-125). San Jose, California, USA: International Society for Optics and Photonics.

Xiang, Y., Zou, B., & Li, H. (2009). Selective color transfer with multi-source image. *Pattern Recognition Letters*, *30*(7), 682–689. doi:10.1016/j.patrec.2009.01.004

Yatziv, L., & Sapiro, G. (2006). Fast image and video colorization using chrominance blending. *IEEE Transactions on Image Processing*, *15*(5), 1120–1129. doi:10.1109/TIP.2005.864231 PMID:16671293

KEY TERMS AND DEFINITIONS

Colorization: Is the procedure of providing gray images/video with chromatic values.

Decolorization: Is the term refers to converting color images/videos to gray with keeping information about the original colors to be retrieved.

Dilation: Can be described as an expansion made to foreground objects by a specific structure.

Encoding: Refers to minimize the size of a specific data to be saved or processed in smaller space in Hard disk or Memory.

Erosion: Simply is an operation of selecting only the foreground pixels which match a specific structure.

K-Means: It's an iterative supervised clustering technique where each sample data has to be classified to the nearest cluster center out of K clusters.

Morphology: Is a local transformation based on moving foreground pixels according to the structure of their neighbors. The most well-known morphology operations named dilation and erosion.

Representative Pixels: Are the selected color pixels which are considered to be sufficient seeds points for the recolorization stage.

ENDNOTES

1 Berkeley Benchmark: (Online) http://www.eecs.berkeley.edu/Research/Projects/CS/vision/grouping/segbench/

Chapter 13
A Fast New Rotation Insensitive WP–Based Method for Image Indexing and Retrieval

Saif alZahir
The University of North British Columbia, Canada

ABSTRACT

Large multimedia databases and digital image archival systems are being created in government, academia, military, hospitals, digital libraries, and businesses. Efficient methods to retrieve images from such large databases have become indispensable. In this chapter, the authors present a novel Wavelet Packet (WP)-based method for image identification and retrieval that enables the recovery of the original image from a database even if the image has been subjected to geometric transformations such as size-conserving rotation or flipping operations. The proposed method uses the correlation of wavelet packet coefficients to create an image signature. This signature is comprised of two parts. The first part is a short signature, SS, that represents the location of specific values of the WP coefficient correlations in each frequency band. The second portion is the basis signature of the image, which is a long signature, LS, of 1296 correlation points produced by summing up the correlation values along all frequency bands. Computer simulation results show that the method is extremely fast, has a perfect image retrieval rates (100%), and perfect geometric transformations recognition, if any. In addition, the simulation results show that target images are perfectly identified from an image database of 7500 image signatures within a short period of time (nearly 8 seconds on the average). This method is robust against geometric transformation and requires minimal data transfer and can be used for online image retrieval.

INTRODUCTION

The rapid growth of the Internet and the significant expansion of digital multimedia bases in the past years have sharply increased the availability of digital data such as audio, text, images and videos to the public. This huge amount of information offered online and inter-networks require efficient retrieval systems to allow fast access to that incredible amount of content at minimal computational cost. Such requirement represents an interesting challenge especially for image retrieval, which is

DOI: 10.4018/978-1-4666-6030-4.ch013

the focus of this research. This is why so much attention has been drawn towards the development of content-based image retrieval (CBIR) systems as well as other algorithms in the last decade.

This chapter is organized as follows: At first, we present a survey of the previous work done in the area of image retrieval and then we discuss why we chose wavelet packets, WP, over standard wavelets. After the survey, we introduce our image retrieval method. In this section, we explain the way we created the image database and present the simulation results. Finally, we provide the conclusions.

Previous Work

A great deal of work has been done to develop texture, color, shape or content-based indexing procedures for image signature production for image retrieval process (Seng Chua, Tan & Chin Ooi, 1997; AlZahir, 2006; Quellec, Lamard, Cazugue & Cochene, 2010; Schroder & Laurent, 1999; Nicchiotti & Ottaviani, 1999; Kliot & Rivlin, 1998; Wenyin, Wang & Zhang, 2000; Vailaya, Figueiredo, Jain & Zhang, 2001). Because of the many advantages of wavelet representation, some systems use characteristics extracted from wavelet analysis. Venkatachalam (2000) discussed a single stage technique, which addresses the image segmentation / classification problem. This technique is performed at the pixel level using an energy density function based on the wavelet transform, WT. Instantaneous energy distribution, called *Pseudo Power Signature*, is used as the image signature. Its effectiveness and low computational and storage requirements are also discussed.

Romberg, Choi, Baraniuk and Kingsbury (2000) extended on *the hidden Markov tree-modeling* framework of the complex wavelet transforms to take advantage of its near shift-invariance property and improve angular resolution. By focusing on salient signal features, the model can be used to solve the *supervised classification problem* more

efficiently than methods based on traditional WT. However, the required training of the HMT models for each required sample certainly set limits on the technique's practical application.

Scott and Nowak (2000) introduced a hierarchical wavelet-based framework for modeling patterns in digital images. They used the marginal *pdf* of the significant and insignificant wavelet transform coefficients (WTC) to specify the joint distribution of the WTC of a linearly transformed pattern template. With results obtained from real images, the Template Learning from Atomic Representation technique is proven to be efficient in extracting a low dimensional template, representing the defining structure of the pattern while rejecting the noise or the background.

Loupias, Sebe, Bres and Jolion (2000) presented a salient point detector based on Wavelet Transform that extracts points where variations occur in the image. Large WTC at coarse resolution are found and then their largest children coefficients are tracked up to the finest scale. The authors present a retrieval experiment with *Gabor* features and demonstrate that their method performs better than other point detectors.

A method for representing texture information in images using dual tree complex Wavelet Transform (DT-CWT) is presented by Hatipoglu, Mitra, and Kingsbury (2000). The image texture is represented using magnitude quantization of DT-CWT coefficients, to extract the significance of each subband, and separate coding of phase information. In the retrieval process, the similarity of images is defined according to the Euclidean distance between the significant values of their subbands. Using images from real image databases, the authors verified the efficiency of their method in extracting texture features from encoded data.

The abovementioned techniques use WT to extract image signatures based on certain features. In this paper, we present a novel image retrieval method that uses a WP based image signature that requires no prior pre-processing such as feature extraction, indexing, segmentation, and the like.

Wavelets and Wavelet Packets

In this work, we opted to use Wavelet Packets (WP) to generate image signature since they allow better frequency resolution than standard Wavelets (Paquet, Zahir, & Ward, 2002). This is due to the fact that, in the decomposition, not only the output of the low pass filtered image is used for the subsequent level, but also the high pass filters' outputs. This leads to narrower frequency bands at higher frequencies. Besides, the WP allows much higher precision and flexibility in the selection of the band to be used in the extraction of the image signature.

Figure 1 below provides the general filter bank representation of the three levels decomposition for a one-dimensional (1-D) signal using Wavelets (standard). In standard wavelet, subsequent decomposition is applied only to the low pass filters outputs. This yields the frequency decompositions shown in the figure. A down sampling operation is performed after each filtering pass. This process was omitted for the sake of clarity and simplicity of the figures.

Figure 2, on the other hand, gives an example of how the same one-dimensional (1-D) signal is decomposed in frequency bands using wavelet packets (WP). In this type of decomposition, the filters are applied to all outputs of the previous level (i.e., the LP as well as the HP bands) instead of being applied only on the LP band as in the wavelet case, hence resulting in more frequency bands.

As one can see from Figure 2, the wavelet packets approach leads to narrower frequency bands at higher frequencies even if it uses the same basis functions (*i.e.* same filters) as the wavelet analysis. Of course, the same principle can be applied to 2D signals such as images. This is done via considering the rows first then the columns as separate signals. As a result, wavelet packets give more frequency bands to choose from for the purpose of image signature extraction. Besides, if one wants to focus on a particular type of images where the information is contained within a specific frequency range, the wavelet packets will allow the integration of frequency components and spatial characteristics as Wavelets do but also offer much more precision and more flexibility for the selection of the bands to be used in the extraction of the image signature. This has been our main

Figure 1. Wavelets: Octave-band decomposition and resulting frequency bands

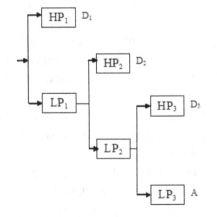
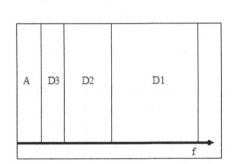

Figure 2. Wavelet Packets: full tree decomposition and resulting frequency bands

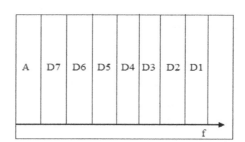

motivation for the choice of wavelet packets to create image signatures as will be described in the following section.

THE ALGORITHM

In this section, we present the image signature extraction process as well as the image signature retrieval process and give a simple example to show the basic calculations required for the proposed algorithm.

Signature Extraction Process

In general, for an image signature to be adopted for image retrieval it must satisfy three basic conditions. The first is that it should accurately represent the image specificities (i.e., must be a unique signature); secondly, it should be represented by much fewer numbers of bits than the original image (i.e., has a minimum transfer of data within the retrieval computer system); thirdly, it should be rotation invariant (i.e., must be robust against common geometric transformations). In our research we chose WP to generate image signatures. While Continuous Wavelet Transform (CWT) is rotation invariant (Strang & Nguyen,

1996) the discrete nature of WP computation yields to variations in coefficients' values introduced by rotating the original image.

A simple but accurate image signature algorithm using WP can be a one-dimensional sequence that contains all WP coefficients of that image. Such simplistic approach is not practical as the number of coefficients may be as large as the number of pixels in the image and has high computational cost due to the WP coefficients calculations. The choice of such image signature contradicts with the second abovementioned criterion for an efficient signature. On the other hand, to meet the third criterion i.e., the robustness, this signature must contain similar number of coefficients for every possible geometric transformation case. Such addition will make the signature huge, impracticable, and worthless. This paper presents a novel method to generate an efficient image signature that satisfies the three-abovementioned criteria. The following are the main steps of the image signature extraction process that we propose:

1. **Image resizing:** An image database may contain images of different sizes, resolutions (binary, greyscale, and color), and characteristics. In this research, the image database we

used contains greyscale images of different sizes (details are found in section 3.0). To obtain WP coefficients for an image, which will be used to produce image signatures, the image must be a square image. Therefore, we had to resize our images in the database to a predetermined square size so as to create the associated image signature database. We chose 128 x 128 pixels for the image size and we used Matlab "imresize" function that uses bilinear interpolation technique to resize the images. We have employed the same Matlab function to resize the test images used for retrieval as well.

2. **Image rotation and WP decomposition:** We have identified six possible image rotation/flipping cases. These cases are: R0: the original (upright position), R1: image rotated by 180°, R2: image rotated by 90°, R3: image flipped about the vertical axis, R4: image rotated by 270° counter clockwise, and R5: image flipped about the horizontal axis. We chose these cases, as they are the most likely cases to occur when creating databases. Other rotations such as 25°, 115°, – 72° or any other angular rotation are unlikely to occur in efficient and reliable image databases, as they do not conserve the image size. The six-abovementioned possible cases (R0-to-R5) are depicted in the Figures 5, 6 and 7. In this step, we generate the two dimensional WP decomposition of the images using three levels Daubechies' 12-tap filter. The choice of Daubechies' filter was motivated by its finite (compact) support and the fact that it is it continuous, yields better frequency resolution than the *Haar* wavelet, and achieves better spatial resolution than other Wavelets (Vetterli & Kovacevic, 1995). The choice of 3 levels decomposition was based on our desire to minimizes the computational cost for analysis and also because further levels decomposition will not add any improvements to the algorithm.

For an image of 128 x 128 pixels size, the 3 levels of Daubechies-12 yields 64 frequency bands (FB) and 1296 coefficients in each frequency band (the number of coefficients is obtained using Matlab).

3. **Image signature generation:** In this step, we create the image signature using the WP coefficient values in step 2. The total image signature, TS, consists of two parts. The first part is the "basis signature" obtained from the image upright position (R0). This is done by calculating the correlation values of every coefficient in each of the 64 FBs with the corresponding coefficients in the other 63 bands. In other words, we first calculate the correlation value of the first WP coefficient of the first FB with the first coefficients of the other 63 FBs. The result of the calculation will produce the first correlation value. Then we calculate the correlation value of the first coefficient of the second FB with the first coefficients of the other 63 FBs to get the second correlation value. Similarly, we get the remaining points of the "basis signature" as shown in Equation 1 $Corr_{(k=1, 1296)}$ below. Once the 1296 points signature is computed, we normalized them between (1 and −1) and then apply a threshold to remove the lowest 15% of the points and replace their values with zeros, hence keeping the original number and location of points in the signature. Such thresholding proved to simplify and speedup our algorithm. We will call the "basis signature" the long signature, LS.

$$Corr_{(k \in 1, 1296)} = \frac{\sum_{j=1}^{64} \sum_{i=1}^{64} (C_{k,j} * C_{k,i})}{64^2} \qquad (1)$$

where k is the number of WP coefficients in each frequency band, C's are the coefficient values in the corresponding frequency bands. The choice for correlation is based on the fact that correlation relationships between variables provide a single number, or index, that measure and describe a relationship between the variables, which is exactly our intent in this case. The reason behind the correlation calculations for each coefficient in each band is to offset a zero value coefficient in a frequency band, which will produce a zero correlation value with all other coefficient, which is not what we want.

4. **Geometric rotation signature:** In this step, we produce the portion of signature that is accountable for recognizing the five rotations – flipping cases in addition to the upright original image position. For this portion of the signature, the correlation values of the WP coefficients are computed within each of the 64 frequency bands as shown Equation (2) below. In other words, for each FB we find one correlation value. This results in 64 correlation values as shown in Equation 2.

$$Corr_{(k \in 1,64)} = \frac{\sum_{m=1}^{1296} \sum_{l=1}^{1296} (C_{k,m} * C_{k,l})}{1296^2} \qquad (2)$$

where k is the number of coefficient in the frequency band, and C is the WP coefficients of each of the 64 FB. The first 64 correlation values represent the upright position case only. Hence this process shall be repeated five more times to cover all cases. This portion of the signature becomes 64 x 6 = 384 points long. At this point we have attempted to shorten this signature in different way to make the retrieval process faster while maintaining its high efficiency. We have decided to replace each of the 64 points representing the R0, R1, R2, R3, R4, and R5 cases by only 4 points. These points are the locations of the maximum, minimum, absolute-maximum, and absolute-minimum of the intra band correlation values in each case making the total number of points equal to 4 X 6 = 24 points. Simulation results showed that these 4-points obtained the same results as the total 384 points. We called this portion of the signature the Short Signature, SS. Figure 3 shows an example of the San Francesco Bridge in its upright position and its 5 rotations/flips.

Figure 3. San Francisco image and its 5- rotation/flipping cases

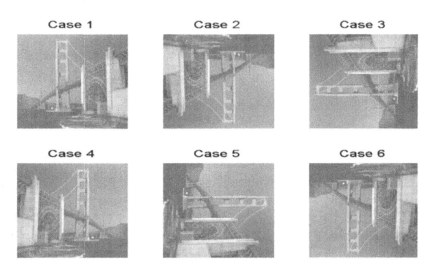

5. Finally we affix the short signatures (for R0-to-R5) at the beginning of the long signature to form the final and total image signature. The total length of image signature, TS = SS + LS = 4 x 6 + 1296= 1320 points.

In Figure 4, a block diagram shows the step-by-step procedure used to extract the total image signature.

Signature Retrieval Process

The image retrieval process is quite simple and straightforward. The following are the main steps in this procedure:

1. Resize the image to be tested, if necessary, to 128 x 128 pixels and extract its short signature as explained above. We allowed a 5% tolerance for the short signature. This is done so as to allow the image under consideration to be shifted or tilted slightly from its original position.
2. In the second step, we compare the first 4-points of the SS of the image with each of SSs in the database. If we find a perfect match then the corresponding image to that signature is identified and hence can be retrieved. If more than one short signature in the database were within the 5% margin of

tolerance we allowed, we compute the LS for the image and then compare it with the long signatures of those identified images only. This means that in nearly 95% of the cases we do not need to resort to the LS. Figure 5 shows a simple schematic of the proposed image retrieval process.

COMPUTER SIMULATIONS AND RESULTS

Experiments were conducted on a reasonable size image database of 267 real images from five different categories. These images differ in size as well as in texture and applications. The composition of this image database is as follows:

1. Twenty miscellaneous natural greyscale images of 256 x 256 pixels from the public domain (web).
2. Eighty greyscale portraits (faces) images of 92 x 112 pixels obtained from the U.K. AT&T Laboratories.
3. Eighty fingerprint greyscale images of 256 x 364 pixels grey obtained from (Paquet, S. Zahir & Ward, 2002).
4. Thirty-five cartographic greyscale images of 512 x 512 pixels modified versions of the maps from (Databases, 2011)

Figure 4. Image signature extraction block diagram

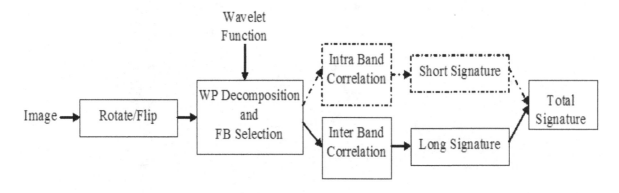

Figure 5. Image retrieval block diagram

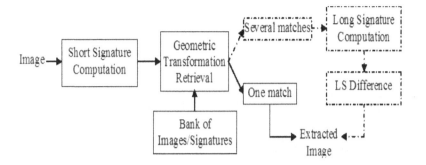

5. Fifty-two scanned text images of 512 x 512 pixels in different languages (English, French and Chinese) and from different media (books, journals, conference proceedings, etc).

These images were first resized to 128 x 128 using Matlab. For each image, we have produced its SS, LS, and TS. This resulted in a total of 267 total signatures. To ensure the high efficiency of our method, we immersed those 267 total signatures into a number of randomly generated fake signatures using Matlab "unifrnd" function. The number of the fake signatures was 7233 so as to make the total number of signatures in the database

7500 signatures, which is reasonably large. The created fake signatures have been generated with similar statistical properties (uniform distribution of same amplitude) as the signature of the particular category of real images in the database. Also, the fake SSs and LSs were generated separately. Figure 6 shows a real image TS in the "centre" and four fake signatures of similar statistics.

Figure 7 shows a sample of the miscellaneous images of the database and their corresponding total signatures and Figure 8 shows another sample of nine (9), face pictures, of the same person but in different orientations. Figure 9 also shows another example of different face images and their signatures.

Figure 6. A real image signature in the center and 4 simulated signatures with similar statistics

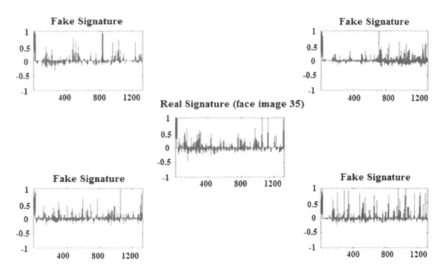

Figure 7. Miscellaneous images and their corresponding signatures

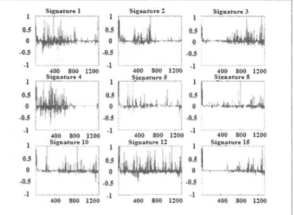

Figure 8. Face images of the same person and their corresponding signatures

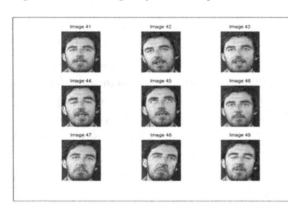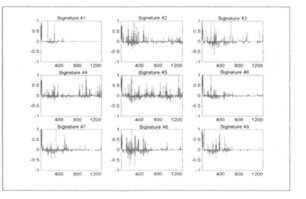

Figure 9. Face images including one image from Figure 6 (centre) and their signatures

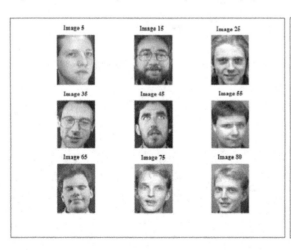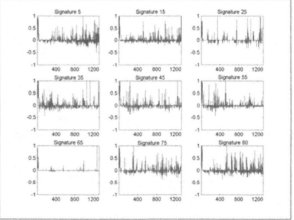

Results

The results of our image retrieval method were exceptional. The retrieval rate was 100% in all five-image categories. For 95% of the cases, the SS was sufficient to identify the image signature perfectly and hence retrieve the image. Only in about 5% of the time we were obliged to refer to the LS to retrieve the image. For large image databases such percentage is extremely favourable and the computational cost is very small. In addition, the average time required for the complete image retrieval process including WP coefficients calculations, SS and LS generation and the search process in the database was nearly eight (8) seconds using Pentium-4 PC computer (1.7 GHz). Approximately, half of this time was consumed in generating the image signature (i.e., nearly 4 second). These results show that our method can support online image retrieval applications. Table 1 shows the successful retrieval rate, the retrieval processing time, and the number of times that the algorithm had to use the LS. The Table shows that for the cartographic images category, the SS was sufficient to retrieve the image in the 210 tests performed. From the 312 tests performed on the text images, only 4 times we needed to use the LS.

This powerful result suggests that four points can represent an image retrieval purposes.

These results led us to examine the possibility of finding four points in an image that uniquely represents it in the spatial domain. Such representation was not possible as there can be many maximum points, many minimum points, many absolute maximum, and many absolute minimum points in the image and to choose one of many can be problematic.

A last question arises. How does our method compare with the straightforward pixel-by-pixel image comparison approach, which has the similar retrieval results (100%)? The time required to retrieve an image using the pixel-by-pixel approach was found to be very long especially if the size of the image and the database are large. Figure 10 shows the time needed to retrieve an image from 30 images of 400 x 400 pixels database. It can be seen from the diagram that for this limited small number of images, this method requires nearly 6.4 second. If the database becomes 7,500 images, (the size of our database), then, the search time for an image will increase to 1575 seconds. This is for the worst-case scenario i.e., we search all 7500 images in the database.

Table 1. Retrieval results

Image Databases Tested	Retrieval Rate		% Of Times when the Main Signature had to be Used	Average Retrieval Time (sec)**
	Image	Orientation		
Miscellaneous	100%	100%	1.6667% (2 out of 120*)	7.84
Faces	100%	100%	5.8333% (28 out of 480*)	8.02
Fingerprints	100%	100%	5.2083% (25 out of 480*	7.81
Maps	100%	100%	0% (0 out of 210*)	7.80
Text	100%	100%	1.2821% (4 out of 312*)	8.64

* This number is the total number of tests done for each database. As we consider 6 rotation/flipping cases, there are 6 different cases for each real image in the bank. For example, there are 20 miscellaneous images that lead to a total of 120 (6*120) tests executed.

**Retrieval time includes the signature extraction (computation) time. The retrieval time ranges between 2 and 6 seconds depending on if the long signature has to be computed.

Figure 10. Time required for searching all images in the database (worst case)

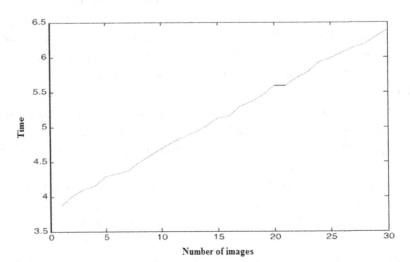

Figure 11. Ship image, its rotated/flipped cases, and the retrieved image

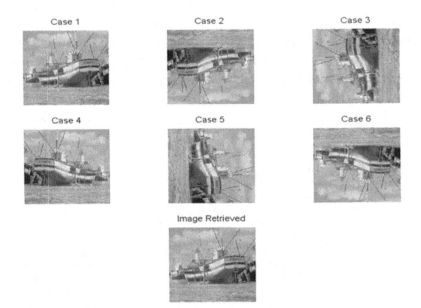

CONCLUSION

We have introduced a novel extremely fast image identification and retrieval method using WP. This method uses WP coefficients correlation along frequency bands for creating signatures of images. This method has perfect (100%) image retrieval and perfect (100%) geometric transformation recognition rates; we have demonstrated that our method is ideal for image identification and retrieval in the context of images databases. Experimentation results show that this method is extremely fast and requires only about eight (8) seconds to complete the process including the signature generation. Such results make our method capable of becoming an online image retrieval system.

REFERENCES

alZahir, S. (2006). A low complexity wavelet-packets based image signature for indexing and retrieval. In *Proceedings of Canadian Conference on Electrical and Computer Engineering* (pp. 2107 - 2111). Ottawa, Canada: IEEE.

Chua, T. S., Tan, K. L., & Chin Ooi, B. (1997). Fast signature based color-spatial image retrieval. In *Proceedings of IEEE International Conference on Multimedia Computing and Systems*, (pp. 362-369). Ottawa, Canada: IEEE.

Databases. (2011). Retrieved November 20, 2011, from http://bias.csr.unibo.it/fvc2000/databases.asp

Daubechies, I. (1992). *Ten lectures on wavelets.* Society for Industrial and Applied Mathematics. doi:10.1137/1.9781611970104

Hatipoglu, S., Mitra, S. K., & Kingsbury, N. (2000). Image texture description using complex wavelet transforms. In *Proceedings of IEEE International Conference on Image Processing*, (pp. 530-533). Vancouver, Canada: IEEE.

Kliot, M., & Rivlin, E. (1998). Invariant-based data model for image databases. In *Proceedings of IEEE International Conference on Image Processing*, (pp. 803-807). Chicago, IL: IEEE.

Liu, J., & Moulin, P. (2000). Analysis of inter-scale and intrascale dependencies between image wavelet coefficients. In *Proceedings of IEEE International Conference on Image Processing*, (pp. 669-672). Vancouver, Canada: IEEE.

Loupias, E., Sebe, N., Bres, S., & Jolion, J. M. (2000). Wavelet-based salient points for image retrieval. In *Proceedings of IEEE International Conference on Image Processing*, (pp. 518-521). Vancouver, Canada: IEEE.

Nicchiotti, G., & Ottaviani, R. (1997). A simple rotation invariant shape signature. In *Proceedings of IEEE International Conference on Image Processing and its Applications*, (pp. 722-726). Dublin, Ireland: IEEE.

Paquet, A., Zahir, S., & Ward, R. (2002). Wavelet-packets-based image retrieval. In *Proc. IEEE International Conference on Acoustics, Speech, and Signal Processing*, (pp. IV-3640 - IV-3643). Orlando, FL: IEEE.

Quellec, G., Lamard, M., Cazugue, G., & Cochene, B. (2010). Adaptive non-separable wavelet transform via lifting and its application to content-based image retrieval. *IEEE Transactions on Image Processing, 19*(1), 25–35. doi:10.1109/TIP.2009.2030479 PMID:19695999

Romberg, J., Choi, H., Baraniuk, R., & Kingsbury, N. (2000). Multi-scale classification using complex wavelets and hidden markov tree models. In *Proceedings of IEEE International Conference on Image Processing*, (pp. 371-374). Vancouver, Canada: IEEE.

Schroder, K., & Laurent, P. (1999). Efficient polygon approximations for shape signatures. In *Proceedings of International Conference on Image Processing*, (pp. 811-814). Kobe, Japan: Academic Press.

Scott, C., & Nowak, R. (2000). Pattern extraction and synthesis using a hierarchical wavelet-based framework. In *Proceedings of IEEE International Conference on Image Processing*, (pp. 383-386). Vancouver, Canada: IEEE.

Strang, G., & Nguyen, T. (1996). *Wavelets and filter banks.* Wellesley-Cambridge Press.

Vailaya, A., Figueiredo, M. A. T., Jain, A. K., & Zhang, H. J. (2001). Image classification for content based indexing. *IEEE Transactions on Image Processing, 10*(1), 117–129. doi:10.1109/83.892448 PMID:18249602

Venkatachalam, V. (2000). Image classification using pseudo power signatures. In *Proceedings of IEEE International Conference on Image Processing*, (pp.796-799). Vancouver, Canada: IEEE.

Vetterli, M., & Kovacevic, J. (1995). *Wavelet and subband coding*. Englewood Cliffs, NJ: Prentice Hall.

Wenyin, L., Wang, T., & Zhang, H. (2000). A hierarchical characterization scheme for image retrieval. In *Proceedings of IEEE International Conference on Image Processing*, (pp. 42-45). Vancouver, Canada: IEEE.

KEY TERMS AND DEFINITIONS

Image Database: A collection of images that are arranged based on certain queries and a classification method(s).

Image Decomposition: The process of analyzing an image based on time, space or frequency.

Image Indexing: The archival process for creating an image database based on some discipline such as texture, color, content.

Image Retrieval: The process of extracting an image from a database. This process must be efficient and fast.

Image Resizing: The process of expansion or reduction of the size of an image so that it suites the processes under consideration.

Image Signature: A signal that faithfully represents the image which can be used to uniquely retrieve an image from a database.

Wavelet Packets (WP): A wavelet transform where the discrete-time signal is passed through more filters than the discrete wavelet transform (DWT), WP, uses both the detail and approximation coefficients to create the full binary tree of an image.

Wavelets: A transform that is concerned with decomposing a signal to its frequency components bands.

Chapter 14

Computer Vision–Based Non–Magnetic Object Detection on Moving Conveyors in Steel Industry through Differential Techniques and Performance Evaluation

K. C. Manjunatha
Prakash Steels and Power Private Limited, India

H. S. Mohana
Malnad College of Engineering, India

P. A. Vijaya
Malnad College of Engineering, India

ABSTRACT

Intelligent process control technology in various manufacturing industries is important. Vision-based non-magnetic object detection on moving conveyor in the steel industry will play a vital role for intelligent processes and raw material handling. This chapter presents an approach for a vision-based system that performs the detection of non-magnetic objects on raw material moving conveyor in a secondary steel-making industry. At single camera level, a vision-based differential algorithm is applied to recognize an object. Image pixels-based differential techniques, optical flow, and motion-based segmentations are used for traffic parameters extraction; the proposed approach extends those futures into industrial applications. The authors implement a smart control system, since they can save the energy and control unnecessary breakdowns in a robust manner. The technique developed for non-magnetic object detection has a single static background. Establishing background and background subtraction from continuous video input frames forms the basis. Detection of non-magnetic materials, which are moving with raw materials, and taking immediate action at the same stage as the material handling system will avoid the breakdowns or power wastage. The authors achieve accuracy up to 95% with the computational time of not more than 1.5 seconds for complete system execution.

DOI: 10.4018/978-1-4666-6030-4.ch014

INTRODUCTION

Computer vision based non-magnetic object recognition and removal has been one of the active research areas in computer vision and industrial smart control. It plays a major role in advanced industrial automation and process control systems. With the aim to recognize non-magnetic moving objects through video monitoring system, it is able to detect and to establish immediate alarm or we can stop the closed loop interlocked system for a moment to remove the non-magnetic material. This can be done in the Programmable Logic Controllers (PLC), by doing suitable preprocessing with Mat Lab platform. Most of the motion pictures analysis presently available, takes considerable computational time, although we have optimized computation technology. Here in this work an attempt is made to introduce a robust, simple and statistical solution to this problem. To reduce the number of frames used for analysis, dynamic selection of images was made. Hence normalized frame to frame difference is obtained and threshold has been fixed to register a subset of images to be used for analysis. The selected subset is compared with reference template which is nothing but the image taken when there is no non-magnetic material on the conveyor. Multiple reference backgrounds have been established to accommodate different illumination conditions. In the second phase of work, reference frame is constantly subtracted from dynamically selected subset. This leads the separation of non-magnetic object pixels, which is corresponding to moving object and the background pixels which are not altered. Counting object pixels and background pixels leads to the flux estimation. To make the design illumination invariant, a section of background is taken as a reference, which will not be affected by the conveyor flow. Comparing illumination of that block of reference with present picture will decide which background must be considered for the purpose of analysis. Discrimination of non-magnetic object pixel and background pixel has shown good repeatability

over many real sequences of images. Threshold is fixed and used to discriminate low, medium, and big size non-magnetic material on the conveyor. There is plot for object pixel count; it is basically number of white pixels versus frame number. Basically object detection is carried out by using this plot and as well as this object pixels count.

Suppose if there is non-magnetic object on the conveyor or in the scene except raw material means, there is drastic change in the white pixel count accordance with the object size. By analyzing this pixels count in various cases, we can detect the non-magnetic object on moving conveyor. Suppose if there is drastic in light illumination and reflectance due to weather change means the background will be changed automatically as per the error. Actually the camera will be fixed inside the shed which preferably closed at the top or we can place the camera at suitable point where there no disturbance. Here we checked up with normal day light and cloudy weather. At the final stage threshold value will be fixed for white pixel count and if the count exceeds the threshold value means, the conveyor will stop by giving an alarm in Supervisory Control and Data Acquisition (SCADA) or Distributed Control Systems (DCS). This paper not only concentrates on the accuracy of non-magnetic object detection but emphasizes on the time and computational complexities of the developed single algorithms as there is a need to detect the object in the real time. Pixel count estimation critically depends on the changes in the intensities of I_{th} image with respect to the reference image at all spatially uniformly spread pixels. One of the assumptions in the present work is that the intensities of the moving objects are preserved during the movement in the view path.

RELATED STUDIES

The review of the literature pertaining to the present topic is presented to the readers. In Spinola, Canero, & Gonzalo (2011) authors worked on image processing based edge inspection and defect detection in the steel rolling mills and they have incorporated twin line camera. Pixel based early fire smoke detection based on improved Gaussian mixture positioning algorithm has been carried out in Wei, Wang, An, and Che (2009). In Barron, Fleet, and Beachemin (1994) authors worked on comparison of different approaches of optical flow estimation. Comparison is done on the basis of accuracy and computational complexities. They have concluded differential technique is best suited for the competition of optical flow and hence the dynamic scene analysis. Entropy based features are used in Hsu, Tyan, Liang, Jeng, and Fan (2005), to check for the existence of vehicles and then tracking is achieved. Though this takes less computational time it suffers serious occlusion problem. Fusion of images and vector maps technique is used in Stilla and Michelses (2002) to discriminate vehicles from objects in the scene. This is suitable for military applications as overall system is complicated and expensive. A comparison of edge element association Edge Element Association (EEA) and marginalized contour approaches for 3D model based vehicle tracking in traffic scenes is implemented in Dehlcamp, Pece, Ottlik, and Nagel (2005). Tracking failures of two approaches, however, usually do not happen at the same time frames which can lead to insights into relative strengths and weakness of the two approaches. Since both the models are to be implemented on every frame computational time frame increases. Recursive optical flow estimation- Adaptive filtering approach is used in (Elad&Fener, 1998). This is modification over Horn and Schunck (Horn &Schunck, 1981) algorithms as it uses only parts of images. Hence sequence of images is used with adaptive filtering technique. The result achieved here is good at cost of linearly growing computational complexities because convergence to be achieved. In Mittrapiyanurk, DeSouza, and Kak (2006) authors

present a new method for tracking rigid objects using a modified version of the Active Appearance Model. It works well with partial and self-occlusion of objects. The layered representation is more flexible than standard image transforms and can capture many important properties of natural image sequences (Wang &Adelson, 1994). The study reveals that increased computational time and complexities are the hurdles in achieving real time analysis at video rate. This fact motivated us to develop the simple technique presented in this paper. Steven S. Beauchemin, Michael A. Bauer (2011) authors described a portable and scalable Vision-Based vehicular instrumentation designed for on-road experimentation and hypothesis verification in the context of designing Advanced Driving Assistance System (i-ADAS) prototypes. ByoungChul, Ko Sooyeong Kwak (2012) authors presented an up-to-date review of five different types of natural disasters and their corresponding warning systems using computer vision and pattern recognition techniques such as wildfire smoke and flame detection, water level detection for flood prevention, coastal zone monitoring, and landslide detection. A communication network for computer vision based system to implement control systems and logistics applications in industrial environment. A robust implementation both with respect to camera packaging and data transmission has been accounted by Taweepol Suesut, Arjin Numsomran, and Vittaya Tipsuwanporn (2010). Changwoo Ha, Ung Hwang, Gwanggil Jeon, Joongwhee Cho, and Jechang Jeong (2012) authors proposed vision-based fire detection algorithm by using optical flow algorithm. H.S. Mohana, M. Aswatha Kumar and G. Shivakumar (2009) authors have implemented vision based traffic vehicles detection and counting through differential analysis. The technique developed for traffic flux estimation is having simple statistical background. Establishing background and background subtraction from continuous video input frames forms the basis. Dynamic selection of images, from the sequence is implemented successfully in order to reduce the computation time.

PROBLEM DEFINITION

Extraction of non-magnetic object on raw material (Iron Ore, Coal, etc.) handling conveyor will be having lots of advantages like energy save and to avoid equipment damages through unnecessary jams in the path of material flow. In the meantime all raw material transfer points should be enabled with dry fog dust suppression system or pressurized water spray nozzles to avoid the dust. Otherwise dust may deposit on the camera face, it leads to an error. In the Figure 1 (a), Figure 1 (b) & Figure 1 (c) shows plastic, rope and wooden pieces blocked the screen and it slow down the rate

of raw material screening process and leads to an energy waste. Figure 1 (d) shows the mechanical chutes, through which the non-magnetic materials will flow and in the next stage, it will cause the jam with equipment (crusher related to Iron Ore/Coal) and its leading to damage equipment.

IMPLEMENTATION

Following general assumptions were made in order to implement the computer vision based system for non-magnetic object detection. Figure 2 shows system implementation flow diagram.

1.   Camera is positioned at a fixed location with predetermined focus. This is to eliminate ego-motion problem.
2.   Video sequences are taken from the oblique view.

Figure 1. Pictures of vibrating screen assembly: (a) Screen blocked with plastic bags & rope, (b) screen blocked with wooden piece, (c) poor screening due to the blockage of plastic bag, and (c) screen transfer chute assembly

Figure 2. System implementation flow diagram

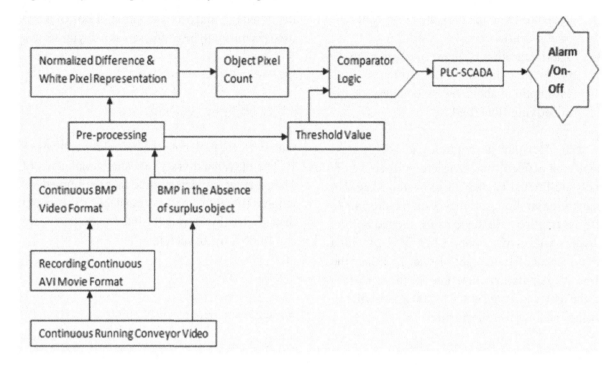

3. Fixed number of frames with fixed camera resolution.
4. Both color and black and white videos are used.
5. Recording in the AVI format and separation of BMP image and Frame.
6. Monocular video is the input for processing.
7. Normalized subtraction and non-magnetic object white pixel separation.
8. Counting non-magnetic object pixel and comparison with the threshold count.
9. Alarming or On/Off with closed loop interlock system as per programmable logic controller (PLC).
10. System configuration:
    a. A simple 5 megapixel video camera in a fixed position.
    b. MATLAB 7.14V Image processing tool box & Simulink Programmable Logic Control (PLC) coder.
    c. ABB PLC Control Builder AC800M 4.0V and Supervisory Control and Data Acquisition (SCADA) Portal 2.0V.
    d. Windows XP Operating System of 2GB RAM.

GENERAL MOTION

In general, an observed motion does not have the simple structure of the spatially constant motion as assumed. Although motions are not constant in space still can make sense. Despite of different processing algorithms, three stages processing is essential to perform computing the motion in spatio-temporal domain.

1. Pre-filtering or smoothening with low-pass or band pass filters in order to extract signal structures of interest and to enhance the signal to noise ratio.

2. The extraction of basic measurements, such as spatio-temporal derivatives or local correlation surfaces.
3. The integration of these measurements to produce 2D flow field, which often involves assumptions about the smoothness of the underlying flow field.

The algorithm description and analysis assumes an affined camera where perspective effects are limited to changes in overall scale. No camera calibration parameters are required since the assumptions are made as mentioned before. Camera used is of resolution 1024×1024 with a video rate of 30 frames per second. To reduce the time of computations, the same has the resolution of the image is scaled down to 200×200 without losing much of the information.

DIFFERENTIAL METHODS

Differential techniques compute motion related information from spatio-temporal derivatives of image intensity. The differential technique developed by Horn and Schunk[6] has been the most widely used algorithm for the optical flow computation Figure 3.

Considering video stream for analysis, that provides continuous image where E(x,y,t)refers

to the gray-level of (x,y) at time t representing the dynamic image as a function of position and time permits it to be expressed as a Taylor series:

$$E(x+u\delta t, y+v\delta t, t+\delta t) = E(x,y,t)$$

$$+E_x \delta x + E_y \delta y + E_t \delta t + O(\partial^2) \qquad (1)$$

where E_x, E_y, E_t denote the partial derivatives of E. The u(x,y) and v(x,y) are the components of optical flow. We can assume that the immediate neighborhood of (x,y) is translated some small distance $(\delta x, \delta y)$ during the interval δt; that is, we can find δx, δy, δt such that

$$\frac{\partial E}{\partial x}\frac{dx}{dt} + \frac{\partial E}{\partial y}\frac{dy}{dt} + \frac{\partial E}{\partial t} = 0$$

which is the expansion of the total derivative

$$\frac{dE}{dt} = 0$$

$$\qquad (2)$$

$$E(x+u\delta t, y+v\delta t, t+\delta t) = E(x,y,t) \qquad (3)$$

The above equation is also known as brightness conservation equation.

If δx, δy, δt are very small, the higher order terms in the equation vanishes. Dividing by δt and taking the limit $\delta t \to 0$, leads to the following

Figure 3. (a) Frame at time t (b) Frame at time t+δt

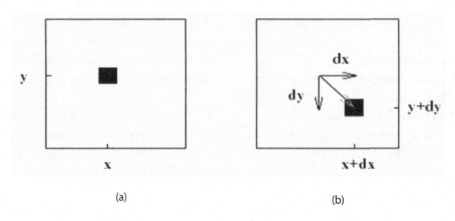

(a)   (b)

expression. Therefore, the brightness constraint equation is given by,

$$E_x u + E_y v + E_t = 0 \qquad (4)$$

Assuming the global smoothness of the brightness changes in the images, one can model the motion field applying the higher order derivatives of the data conservation equation. Iterative solutions of these two or more equations or certain regression methods applied on the relevant set of equations yield the components of the velocity vector field. In the present work we have computed the following differences and are used suitably

$$\frac{dx}{dt}, \frac{dy}{dt}, \frac{\partial E}{\partial t} \qquad (5)$$

Experimentally, it is found that thousands of iterations are needed until convergence. If a second order smoothness criterion is applied, on the other hand the first 10-20 iterations usually leave an error smaller than the required accuracy, and the rest of the iterative process is then very gradual.

ALGORITHM

Here, the images in the sequence are subtracted with established reference background image. Normalized deviation is computed and dynamic selection of images in the sequence is implemented and used in order to compute the non-magnetic object pixels (flux). Line - by- line algorithm is presented below.

1. Selection of reference image in an image sequence: Image with no object in the identified sequence is considered as the reference image shown in the Figure 4 (a).
2. Dynamic selection of images for optical flow computation: Let l be a set of images, ie $l= \{1, 2, 3, 4, 5, ..15, ..30.....\}$. and it is shown in Figure 4 (b)
3. Compute normalized difference,

$$d_{nor} (i,j)= (1/N \times M) \sum_{l\{\}} \; d_l (i,j) - d_{l+1}(i,j) \qquad (5)$$

4. Selection of Images for computation of object flux (non-magnetic object pixels):

If $E_r = \sum \left| d_l (i,j) - d_{l+1}(i,j) \right| \leq \varepsilon_1$, then skip one image $I =I+1$ ... $\qquad (6)$

If $E_r = \sum \left| d_l (i,j) - d_{l+1}(i,j) \right| > \varepsilon_1$ and $< \varepsilon_2$ then skip three images $I =I+3$ ... $\qquad (7)$

If $E_r = \sum \left| d_l (i,j) - d_{l+1}(i,j) \right| > \varepsilon_2$ and $< \varepsilon_3$, then skip five image $I =I+5$ ... $\qquad (8)$

where $\varepsilon_1 < \varepsilon_2 < \varepsilon_3$. This set can be re-ascertained.

Figure 4. (a) Reference image (b) Image i.e.

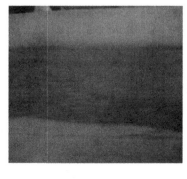 

(a)   (b)

5. Compute the cumulative difference and segment the brighter region using dynamic threshold values. Further link the edges making use of zero crossings in the binary images obtained and shown in figure 5 (a). This is used for computing non-magnetic object white pixels in Figure 5 (b).

6. Compute the normalized average brightness of the segmented region and compute non-magnetic object pixels as a percentage with reference background.

7. Obtained non-magnetic object pixel count as C and it is plotted in Figure 6.

8. Fix the threshold value for pixel count to identify the non-magnetic object.

9. Comparison of actual pixel count with the threshold value.

10. If the actual count is more than the threshold value means either alarm will enable or conveyor will be off along with the closed loop interlock.

11. If the actual count is less than or equal to the threshold value means, the raw material or conveyor circuit will continue.

12. Implemented logic for non-magnetic object recognition.
    a. **r** = Video Stream
    b. **i** = Graph Index for 100 frames
    c. **b2** = Concatenated BMP Image
    d. **neo** = Threshold for Gray Scale Value
    e. **j** = Continuous AVI Video Frames
    f. **a** = Width of the Image Frame
    g. **b** = Height of the Image Frame
    h. **m** = AVI Data file
    i. **c** = Pixel Count
    j. **X (a b)** = Subtracted Image with Gray Scale.
    k. **XX (b,a)** = 255 White Pixel
    l. **XX (b,a)** = 0 Black Pixel
    m. **g** = Graph for Image View
    n. **d (i)** = White Pixel Count
    o. **n** = Threshold value for count
       i. Graph number of frames Vs count. Shown in Figure 5.

```
for i=2:99

grph(i)=0;

end

grph (1)= 0;

grph (100)= 100;
```

ii. Concatenation between the images

```
img = strcat(r, '.bmp');

b2=imread(img);
```

iii. Creating AVI file

```
fileinfo = aviinfo(r);
```

iv. Reading each frames in the AVI file

```
for i=1:1:fileinfo.NumFrames

m=aviread(r,i);

j=m.cdata;
```

v. Initialization of count and obtaining file information

```
c = 0;

for b = 1:fileinfo.Height

for a = 1:fileinfo.Width
```

vi. Normalized subtraction with threshold

```
if b2(b,a) >= j(b,a)
```

```
X (b,a) = b2(b,a) - j(b,a);
else
X (b,a) = j(b,a) - b2(b,a);
end
if X(b,a) >=neo
c = c+1;
XX(b,a) = 255;
else
XX (b,a) = 0;
end
end
end
```

vii. Image view after normalized difference

```
g=3;
while g < 100,
grph(g-1) = grph(g);
g = g+1;
end
```

viii. Object pixel count with threshold

```
d(i)=(c)
grph(99)=d(i);
n = threshold for pixel count;
if d(i) ˃ n
s₁ = s+1;
else
s₁ = s+1;
end ]
```

Figure 5.(a) Binary image (b) White object pixels

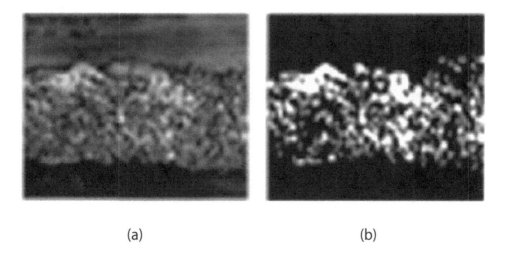

(a)   (b)

13. A non-magnetic plastic bag on moving conveyor is exposed in Figure 7 (a) and equivalent white pixel count shown in Figure 7 (b). In Figure 8 (a) non-magnetic ropes captured from the scene and equivalent white pixel count obtained in Figure 8 (b). Figure 9 (a) and Figure 9 (b) shows an example of non-magnetic wooden piece.

DISCUSSION ON RESULTS

The first set of images is taken in order to establish the reference images under different illumination condition from morning to evening. Four such reference frames have been identified under supervision. In the present work, a platform has been created, so that the complete automation of dynamic and intelligent non-magnetic objects detection system of human intervention. The raw data generation software package developed in

this work is capable of generating the raw data of each pixel in both decimal and hex format. Hence convenient data set can be used for computation. This also provides raw data of each frame in text and data files, it further speeds up computation. The incorporated dynamic selection of images supports the selection of required frames. Four levels of threshold is implemented to mark the difference between two images and assigned with different colors in the output image. From the results obtained it is evident that the implemented algorithm is separating object from the back ground pixels, detection of non-magnetic object on moving conveyor in almost all the cases. Also, it works satisfactorily when there is a change in illumination & reflectance. One of our major investigations has been the identifying confidence measure to establish the validity of the results. This provides means of determining the reliability of the computed non-magnetic object detection.

All techniques produce non-magnetic object classification and count with little deviation al-

Figure 6. White pixel representation with count C

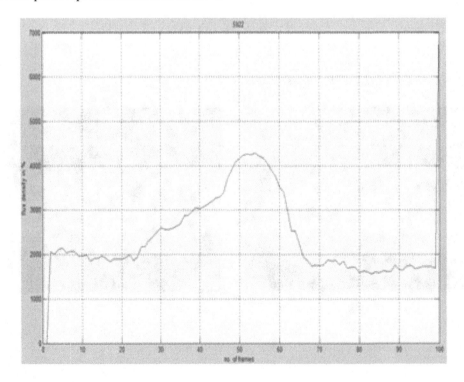

Figure 7. (a) A non-magnetic plastic bag on moving conveyor (b) White pixel representation and resultant count C for plastic bag

(a)

(b)

though the structure of the underlying technique and motion information varies dramatically to the greater extent. Results of non-magnetic object detection system is tabulated in the table 1, it gives the comparison of results estimated for different non-magnetic object cases. Here there are four main category of non-magnetic objects preferred for the computation. Error is the difference between actual and obtained (Error = Actual No. of objects – No. of objects detected), error positive and negative is declared upon the sign of obtained error.

Figure 8. (a) A non-magnetic rope on moving conveyor (b) White pixel representation and resultant count C for rope

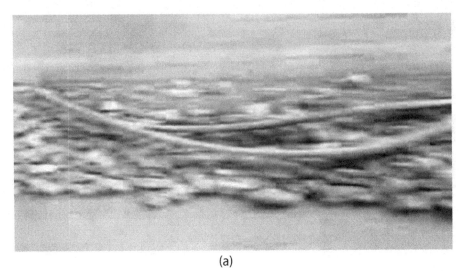

(a)

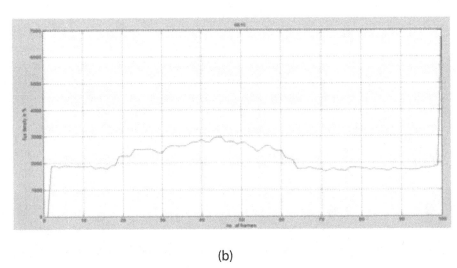

(b)

CONCLUSION

The work carried out has produced very good and consistent results. The small deviations with different video streams taken under different light reflectance and illumination is minimum, this do not really hampers non-magnetic object detection. Further, efforts are going on to relate the above result with quantity of raw material movement on weighment systems. We move towards material weighment through computer vision. If the color of the object and the color of the background are same it may lead to marginally varied object pixel count (approx 5-6%). In weather condition causes subtle variation in estimated non-magnetic object pixel count.

Figure 9. (a) A non-magnetic wooden piece on moving conveyor (b) White pixel representation and resultant count C for wooden piece

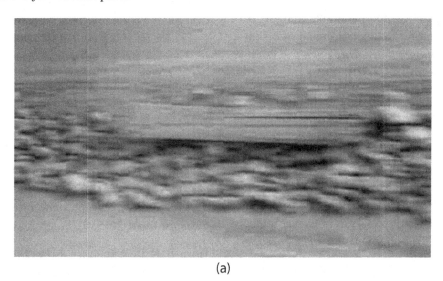

(a)

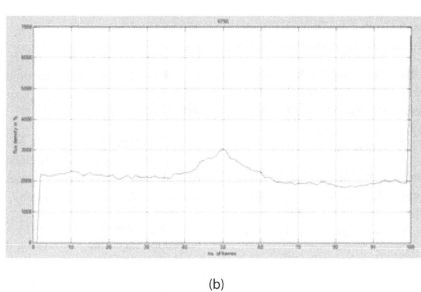

(b)

Table 1. Results of non-magnetic object detection system

Case	Object category	Actual No. of objects	No. of objects detected	Error positive	Error negative	Accuracy (%)
1.	Plastic bags etc.	12	12	0	0	100
2.	Ropes etc.	18	18	0	2	90
3.	Wooden pieces.	9	9	0	0	100
4.	Stone type	24	21	3	0	87.50
Average						**94.35%**

REFERENCES

Anandan, P. (1989). A computational framework and an algorithm for the measurement of visual motion. *International Journal of Computer Vision*, *2*(3), 283–310. doi:10.1007/BF00158167

Barron, J. L., Fleet, D. J., & Beachemin, S. S. (1994). Performance of optical flow techniques. *International Journal of Computer Vision*, *12*(1), 43–77. doi:10.1007/BF01420984

Beauchemin, Bauer, Kowsari, & Cho. (2011). Portable and Scalable Vision Based Vehicular Instrumentation for the Analysis of Driver Intentionality. *IEEE Transactions on Instrumentation and Measurement*.

ByoungChul, & Ko Sooyeong Kwak. (2012). Survey of computer vision–based natural disaster warning systems. *OPTICAL Engineering, 51*(7).

Combs, D., Herman, M., Hong, T., & Nashman, M. (1998). Real time obstacle avoidance using control flow divergence and peripheral flow. *IEEE Transactions on Robotics and Automation*, *14*(1), 49–59. doi:10.1109/70.660840

Dang, G., Changsha, P. R., & Cheng, Z.-Q. (2009). A reverse-projecting pixel-level painting algorithm. In *Proceedings of the IEEE International Conference on Image and Graphics*. Xi'an, China: IEEE.

Dehlcamp, H., Pece, A. E. C., Ottlik, A., & Nagel, H.-H. (2005). Differential analysis of two model based vehicle tracking approaches. In *Proceedings of the 26th DAGM Symposium* (LNCS), (vol. 3175). Tübingen, Germany: Springer.

Elad, M., & Fener, A. (1998). Recursive optical flow estimation. *Journal of Visual Communication and Image Representation*, *9*(2), 119–138. doi:10.1006/jvci.1998.0382

Fermuller, C., Shulman, D., & Akimou, Y. (2001). The statistics of optical flow. *Journal of Computer Vision and Image Understanding, 82*, 1–32. doi:10.1006/ cviu.2000.0900

Gracia, L., Perez-Vidal, C., & Gracia, C. (2011). Computer Vision Applied to Flower, Fruit and Vegetable Processing. *Proceedings of ICPRCV, 7*(78).

Ha, C., & Hwang, U. (2012). Vision-Based Fire Detection Algorithm Using Optical Flow. In *Proceedings of IEEE Sixth International Conference on Complex, Intelligent, and Software Intensive Systems,* (pp. 526-530). Palermo, Italy: IEEE.

Horn, B. K. P., & Schunck, B. G. (1981). Determining optical flow. *Scientific Research in Artificial Intelligence, 17*, 185–203. doi:10.1016/0004-3702(81)90024-2

Hsu, W.-L., Tyan, H.-R., Liang, Y.-M., Jeng, B.-S., & Fan, K.-C. (2005). Real time vehicle tracking on highway. *Journal of Information Science Engineering, 21*, 733–752.

Lin, H., Hong, T. H., Herman, M., & Chellappa, R. (1998). Accuracy Vs efficiency tradeoffs in optical flow algorithms. *Journal of Computer Vision and Image Understanding*, 271–286.

Mittrapiyanurk, P., DeSouza, G. N., & Kak, A. C. (2006). Accurate 3D tracking of rigid objects with occlusion using active appearance models. In *Proceedings of the IEEE Workshop on Motion and Video Computing*. Breckenridge, CO: IEEE.

Mohana, H. S. Aswatha Kumar, & Shivakumar. (2009). Vehicle Detection & Counting by using Real time Traffic Flux Differential Technique & Performance Evaluation. In *Proceedings of IEEE-International Conference on Advanced Computer Control*. IEEE.

Mohana, H. S. AshwathaKumar, A. M., & Shivakumar, G. (n.d.). Statistical approach to real time traffic flux estimation. In *Proceedings of the IEEE International Conference on Signal & Image Processing* (pp. 501-505). Cairo, Egypt: IEEE.

Mohana, H. S., Kumar, A. M., Shivakumar, G., & Ravishankar, K. C. (2006). Vehicle tracking and velocity estimation using cumulative optical flow computation. In *Proceedings of the National Conference on Innovation in Intelligence and Computing Technologies 2006*, (pp. 289-293). Academic Press.

Mohana, H. S., Kumar, M. A., & Shivakumar, G. (2009). Real-time dynamic scene analysis using differential: Technique & performance evaluation with optical flow. In *Proceedings of the IEEE International Conference on Advanced Computer Control*. IEEE.

Razmi, S. M., & Saad, N. (2010). Vision-Based Flame Detection: Motion Detection & Fire Analysis. In *Proceedings of IEEE Student Conference on Research and Development*. IEEE.

Spinola, C. G., Canero, J., & Gonzalo, M.-A. (2011). Real-time image processing for edge inspection and defect detection in stainless steel production lines. In *Proceedings of the IEEE International Conference on Image and Graphics*. Hefei, China: IEEE.

Stilla, U., & Michelses, E. (2002). Estimating vehicle activities using thermal image sequences and maps. In *Proceedings of the Symposium on Geospatial Theory, Processing and Applications*. Academic Press.

Suesut, T., Numsomran, A., & Tipsuwanporn, V. (2010). Vision-based Network System for Industrial Applications. *International Journal of Computer Systems Science and Engineering*, *3*(1), 22–26.

Wang, J. Y. A., & Adelson, E. H. (1994). Representing moving images with layers. *IEEE Transactions on Image Processing*, *3*(5), 625–638. doi:10.1109/83.334981 PMID:18291956

Wei, Z., Wang, X., An, W., & Che, J. (2009, September 20-23). Target-tracking based early fire smoke detection in video. In *Proceedings of the IEEE International Conference on Image and Graphics*, (Vol. 3, pp. 172-176). IEEE.

KEY TERMS AND DEFINITIONS

Conveyor: One that conveys, especially a mechanical apparatus that transports materials, packages, or items being assembled from one place to another.

Dynamic Selection: A non-static selection of image frames. After the selection is created, image frames are added to or removed from it automatically, depending on whether their attribute(s) match the criteria for being included in the selection or not.

Ego-Motion: It is defined as the 3D motion of a camera within an environment. In the field of computer vision, ego motion refers to estimating a camera's motion relative to a rigid scene.

Flux: Flux is the presence of a force field in a specified physical medium, or the flow of energy through a surface.

Pixel Count: A pixel count is the number of pixels in each image.

Programmable Logic Controller (PLC): It is a digital computer used for automation of electromechanical processes.

Supervisory Control and Data Acquisition (SCADA): It is a type of industrial control system (ICS). Industrial control systems are computer-controlled systems that monitor and control industrial processes that exist in the physical world.

Chapter 15
Detecting Corner Features of Planar Objects

Muhammad Sarfraz
Kuwait University, Kuwait

ABSTRACT

Corner points or features determine significant geometrical locations of the digital images. They provide important clues for shape representation and analysis. Corner points represent important features of an object that may be useful at subsequent levels of processing. If the corner points are identified properly, a shape can be represented in an efficient and compact way with sufficient accuracy in many shape analysis problem. This chapter reviews some well referred algorithms in the literature together with empirical study. Users can easily pick one that may prove to be superior from all aspects for their applications and requirements.

INTRODUCTION

Corners in digital images give important clues for shape representation and analysis. Since dominant information regarding shape is usually available at the corners, they provide important features for object recognition, shape representation and image interpretation. Corners are the robust features in the sense that they provide important information regarding objects under translation, rotation and scale change. If the corner points are identified properly, a shape can be represented in an efficient and compact way with sufficient accuracy in many shape analysis problem.

Corner points represent important features of an object that may be useful at subsequent level

of computer vision. Guru at el (Guru at el., 2004) says that information about a shape is concentrated at the corners and corners practically prove to be descriptive primitives in shape representation and image interpretation. Asada and Brady (Asada and Brady, 1986) insist that these points play dominant role in shape perception by humans. Attneave (Attneave, 1954) proposed that information along a visual contour is concentrated in the regions of high magnitude of curvature. Corner points are used in various computer vision, computer graphics, and pattern recognition applications. It can be used as a step in document image analysis, such as chart and diagram processing (Kasturi et el., 1990) and is also important from the view point of understanding human perception of objects (Attneave, 1954). It

DOI: 10.4018/978-1-4666-6030-4.ch015

plays crucial role in decomposing or describing the curve (Abe et el., 19993). It is also used in scale space theory (Deriche & Giraudon, 1990; Mokhtarian & Mackworth, 1992), image representation (Cabrelli & Molter, 1990), stereo vision (Deriche & Faugeras, 1990, Vincent & Laganire, 2001), motion tracking (Dreschler & Nagel, 1982; Wang & Brady, 1995), image matching (Smith et el., 1998; Vincent & Laganiere, 2005), building 2D mosaics (Zoghlami, et el. 1997) and preprocessing phase of outline capturing systems (Sarfraz et el., 2004a; Sarfraz et el., 2004b).

Corner detection schemes can be broadly divided into two categories based on their applications:

- Binary (suitable for binary images) and
- Gray level (suitable for gray level images)

Corner detection approaches for binary images usually involve segmenting the image into regions and extracting boundaries from those regions that contain them. The techniques for gray level images can be categorized into two classes: (a) Template based and (b) gradient based. The template based technique utilizes correlation between a sub image and a template of a given angle. A corner point is selected by finding the maximum of the correlation output. Gradient based techniques require computing curvature of an edge that passes through a neighborhood in a gray level image.

Many corner detection algorithms have been proposed which can be broadly divided into two parts. One is to detect corner points from gray-scale images (Harris & Stephens 1988; Kitchen & Rosenfeld, 1982; Noble, 1988; Smith & Brady, 1995) and other relates to boundary based corner detection (Beus & Tiu, 1987; Chetverikov & Szabo, 1999; Freeman & Davis, 1977; Harris & Stephens 1988; Liu & Srinath, 1990; Pritchard et el., 1993; Rosenfeld & Weszka, 1975; Sarfraz et el., 2006). This chapter mainly deals with techniques adopted for later approach.

BASIC FORMULATION

Visually, corners are the endpoints of straight line segments of polygonal shapes. But, it is difficult and complicated to determine corners in case of non-parametric curves as well as outlines of natural objects especially when the noise is carried. In general, corners represent significant features of an object which human beings would perceive as the meaningful points. Detection of these points is not an easy job since accuracy of detected corners is gauged purely by human judgment and no standard definition/criteria exists. In order to compute the corners, it is important to give them some mathematical representation. In the literature, different authors have described them in different ways. Abe et el (Abe et el., 1993) described corners as local maxima points. They proposed a method for decomposing curves into straight segments and curved arcs, based on the slope at each point. Guru et. al., (Guru et. al., 2004) smoothed the boundary curve and found difference at each curve point called as "cornerity index". The larger values of cornerity index were taken as corners.

Rosenfeld and Johnston (Rosenfeld & Johnston, 1973) took curvature maxima points using k-cosine as corners. Rosenfeld and Weszka (Rosenfeld & Weszka, 1975) proposed a modification of (Rosenfeld & Johnston, 1973) in which averaged k-cosines were used. Freeman and Davis (Freeman & Davis 1977) found corners at maximum curvature change in which a straight line segment moves along the curve. Angular difference between successive segments was used to measure local curvature. Beus and Tiu (Beus & Tiu, 1987) algorithm was similar to (Freeman & Davis 1977) except they proposed arm cutoff parameter τ to limit length of straight line. Davies (Devies, 1988) has described a method for detecting corners using Hough transform. Chetverikov and Szabo (Chetverikov & Szabo, 1999) located corners at significant change in curve slope. In their algorithm, corners are the locations where a triangle of specified size and opening angle can be inscribed in a curve. Pritchard et. al., (Pritchard et. al., 1993) used similar triangles, as in (Chetverikov & Szabo, 1999), to identify the corners in which they compared area of triangle with actual area under the curve.

In general, accuracy of any corner detection algorithm changes with noise, size and resolution of input shape and nature of corner (sharpness). It may perform well for a particular shape and display poor results for others. This does not happen in case of human judgment because they are gifted with adaptive nature and automatically adapt themselves to the changing environment. Study of this human behavior may lead to the developments of adaptive algorithms. Various parameters are generally introduced to compensate for such variations. But, it would be preferable if one can go for an algorithm that covers wide range of shape variations without changing its parameters.

Accuracy of any corner detector can be judged only if the actual corner positions are already known. A panel of 10 human observers was used to judge the actual location of corners for eight test shapes. Corners marked by majority were taken as actual corner positions which were used in measuring accuracy of different corner detec-

tors. Figure 2 shows them as marked with actual corner points on the shapes in Figure 1. Figure 1 shows these test shapes which introduced some noise into the original noise-free pictures. In addition, limited random noise was added to the scanned images to better test the robustness of the algorithms. These shapes (let us call them as im1, im2, …, im3 throughout this Chapter) are available in various references (Chetverikov & Szabo, 1999). These shapes as well as few more shapes will be used to test corner detector algorithms in this Chapter. Six corner detection algorithms have been implemented and tested.

SUMMARY OF COMMONLY REFERRED CORNER DETECTORS

This section is devoted for the summary of four corner detection algorithms used by different authors. The summary is based on the survey (Chetverikov & Szabo, 1999). Each algorithm inputs a chain-coded curve that is converted into a connected sequence of grid points $P_i = (x_i, y_i)$, $i = 1, 2, …, N$. A measure of corner strength ('cornerity') is assigned to each point, then corner points are selected based on this measure. For each

Figure 1. Shapes used in the tests

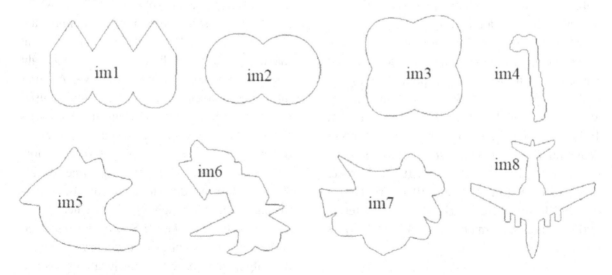

Figure 2. Test shapes marked with actual corner points

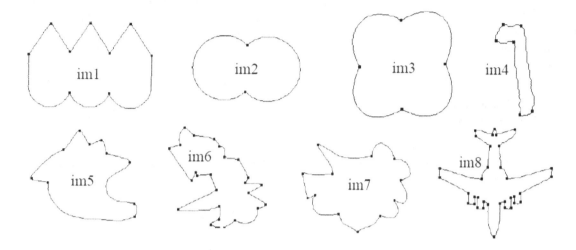

approach, main steps are summarized together with the list of parameters used in the algorithm and their default ('best') values.

When processing a point P_i, the algorithms consider a number of subsequent and previous points in the sequence, as candidates for the arms of a potential corner in P_i. For a positive integer k, the forward and the backward *k-vectors* at point P_i are defined as

$$a_{ik} = \left(x_i - x_{i+k}, \ y_i - y_{i+k}\right) = \left(X_{ik}^+, Y_{ik}^+\right),$$
(1)

$$b_{ik} = \left(x_i - x_{i-k}, \ y_i - y_{i-k}\right) = \left(X_{ik}^-, Y_{ik}^-\right),$$
(2)

where X_{ik}^+, Y_{ik}^+ and X_{ik}^-, Y_{ik}^- are the components of a_{ik} and b_{ik} respectively.

Rosenfeld and Johnston (RJ73) Algorithm

To determine the corner strength, k-cosine of the angle between the k-vectors is used. It is defined as follows:

$$c_{ik} = \frac{\left(a_{ik} \cdot b_{ik}\right)}{\left|a_{ik}\right|\left|b_{ik}\right|}.$$
(3)

where are a_{ik} and b_{ik} explained in Equations (1) and (2) respectively. The selection procedure for the corner points is as follows. Starting from $m = kN$, k is decremented until c_{ik} stops to increase. That is:

$$c_{im} < c_{i,m-1} < ... < c_{in} \not< ci, n-1.$$

Then $k = n$ is selected as the best value for the *i*th point. A corner is indicated in i if $c_{in} > c_{jp}$ for all j such that $\left|i - j\right| \leq n/2$, where p is the best value of k for the *j*th point. The single parameter κ specifies the maximum considered value of k as a fraction of the total number of curve points N. This limits the length of an arm at κN. The default value is taken as $\kappa = 0.05$.

For more details of the algorithm, the reader is referred to (Rosenfeld & Johnston, 1973). Demonstration of the algorithm, for the shapes im1, im2, ..., im8, is made in Figure 19. The choice of the selected parameters, for these figures, can be seen in Table 2. The 'D' in Table 2 is meant for the default values, the deviations from the 'D' are shown otherwise. The proposed algorithm yields reasonable results at the shown values for all the 8 shapes. Points not well located are indicated with arrows.

Rosenfeld and Weszka (RW75) Algorithm

To determine the corner strength, averaged k-cosine of the angle between the k-vectors is used, which is defined as follows:

$$
\overline{c}_{ik} =
\begin{cases}
\dfrac{2}{k+2} \displaystyle\sum_{t=k/2}^{k} c_{it}, & \text{if } k \text{ is even}, \\
\dfrac{2}{k+3} \displaystyle\sum_{t=(k-1)/2}^{k} c_{it}, & \text{if } k \text{ is odd},
\end{cases}
$$

where cit are given by Equation (3). The selection procedure for the corner points is same as in RJ73, but it is performed for $\overline{c}_{ik}$. Similarly, the choice of parameter is also same as in RJ73, with the same default value $\kappa = 0.05$.

For more details of the algorithm, the reader is referred to (Rosenfeld & Weszka, 1975). Demonstration of the algorithm, for the shapes im1, im2, ..., im8, is made in Figure 20. The choice of the selected parameters, for these figures, can be seen in Table 2. The 'D' in Table 2 is meant for the default values, the deviations from the 'D' are shown otherwise. The proposed algorithm yields reasonable results at the shown values for all the 8 shapes. Points not well located are indicated with arrows.

Freeman and Davis (FD77) Algorithm

To determine the corner strength at the ith point, the angle between the x-axis and the backward k-vector defined in Equation (2) is given as:

$$
\theta_{ik} = \theta_{ik} =
\begin{cases}
\tan^{-1}\left(Y_{ik}^{-} / X_{ik}^{-}\right), & \text{if } \left|X_{ik}^{-}\right| \geq \left|Y_{ik}^{-}\right|, \\
\cot^{-1}\left(X_{ik}^{-} / Y_{ik}^{-}\right), & \text{otherwise.}
\end{cases}
$$

The incremental curvature is then defined as

$$
\delta_{ik} = \theta_{i+1,k} - \theta_{i-1,k}. \tag{4}
$$

Finally, the k-strength in i is computed as

$$
S_{ik} = \ln t_1 . \ln t_2 \sum_{j=i}^{i+k} \delta_{jk}, \tag{5}
$$

where

$$
t_1 = \max\left\{t : \delta_{i-v,k} \in (-\Delta, \Delta), \forall\ 1 \leq v \leq t\right\},
$$

and

$$
t_2 = \max\left\{t : \delta_{i+k+v,k} \in (-\Delta, \Delta), \forall\ 1 \leq v \leq t\right\},
$$

account for the effect of the forward and backward arms as the maximum spacings (numbers of steps from i) that still keep the incremental curvature δ_{ik}, within the limit $\pm \Delta$. The Δ is set as follows:

$$
\Delta = \arctan(1 / (k-1)). \tag{6}
$$

The selection procedure for the corner points is as follows. The ith point is selected as a corner if S_{ik} exceeds a given threshold S and individual corners are separated by a spacing of at least k + 1 steps. There is an involvement of two parameters for the procedure. These parameters are the spacing k and the corner strength threshold S. The default values for the parameters are set as k = 5 and S = 1500.

For more details of the algorithm, the reader is referred to (Freeman & Davis, 1977). Demonstration of the algorithm, for the shapes im1, im2, ..., im8, is made in Figure 21. The choice of the selected parameters, for these figures, can be seen in Table 2. The 'D' in Table 2 is meant for the default values, the deviations from the 'D' are shown otherwise. The proposed algorithm yields reasonable results at the shown values for all the 8 shapes.

Beus and Tiu (BT87) Algorithm

The corner strength, for this algorithm, is determined in the same manner as in FD77. However, the following modifications are made. The arm cutoff parameter τ is introduced to specify the upper limit for t_1 and t_2 as a fraction of N. These are explained as follows:

$$t_1 = \max\left\{t : \delta_{i-v,k} \in (-\Delta, \Delta), \forall\ 1 \leq v \leq t,\ \text{and}\ t \leq \tau N\right\},$$

and

$$t_2 = \max\left\{t : \delta_{i+k+v,k} \in (-\Delta, \Delta), \forall\ 1 \leq v \leq t,\ \text{and}\ t \leq \tau N\right\},$$

where δ_{ik} and Δ are given by Equations (4) and (6), respectively. The corner strength is obtained by averaging Equation (5) between two values k_1 and k_2 as follows:

$$S_i = (\sum_{k=k_1}^{k_2} S_{ik}\} / (k_2 - k_1 + 1).$$

The selection procedure follows exactly in the same manner as in FD77. There is an involvement of two parameters for the procedure. These parameters are the averaging limits k_1 and k_2, the arm cutoff parameter τ and the corner strength threshold S. The default values for the parameters

are set as $k_1 = 4$, $k_2 = 7$, $\tau = 0.05$, and $S = 1500$.

For more details of the algorithm, the reader is referred to (Beus & Tiu, 1987). Demonstration of the algorithm, for the shapes im1, im2, ..., im8, is made in Figure 22. The choice of the selected parameters, for these figures, can be seen in Table 2. The 'D' in Table 2 is meant for the default values, the deviations from the 'D' are shown otherwise. The proposed algorithm yields reasonable results at the shown values for all the 8 shapes. Points not well located are indicated with arrows.

CHETVERIKOV AND SZABO (CS99) ALGORITHM

In this algorithm (Chetverikov & Szabo, 1999) a corner point is defined as a point where triangle of specified angle can be inscribed within specified distance from its neighbor points. The number of neighbor points to be checked are also predefined. It is a two pass algorithm. In the first pass, the algorithm scans the sequence of points and selects candidate corner points. The second pass is postprocessing to remove superfluous candidates.

First Pass

In each curve point P, the detector tries to inscribe in the curve a variable triangle $\left(P^-, P, P^+\right)$ constrained by a set of simple rules. For each point P_i, it is checked if triangle of specified size and angle is inscribed or not. Following three conditions are used.

$$d_{\min}^2 \leq \left|P - P_k^+\right|^2 \leq d_{\max}^2, \tag{7}$$

$$d_{\min}^2 \leq \left|P - P_k^-\right|^2 \leq d_{\max}^2, \tag{8}$$

$$\alpha \le \alpha_{max}, \quad (9)$$

where

P is the point under consideration for corner point,
P_k^+ is the kth clockwise neighbor of P,
P_k^- is the kth anti-clockwise neighbor of P.

Taking

$a = \left| P - P_k^+ \right|$, the distance between P and P_k^+

$b = \left| P - P_k^- \right|$, the distance between P and P_k^-

$c = \left| P_k^+ - P_k^- \right|$, the distance between P_k^+ and P_k^-

The angle α can be computed by using cosine law as follows:

$$a^2 + b^2 - c^2 - 2ab\cos\alpha = 0,$$

which yields:

$$\alpha = \cos^{-1}\left(\frac{a^2 + b^2 - c^2}{2ab} \right)$$

All the three conditions described in Equations (7), (8) and (9) are necessary for the first pass. Now each point P may have zero, one or more than one alpha values. Among all alpha values, minimum value is taken as the alpha value of that point P.

Second Pass

Second pass removes some super points. A candidate corner point P from the first pass is discarded if it has a sharper valid neighbor $P_v : \alpha(P) > \alpha(P_v)$. A candidate point P_v is a valid neighbor of P if $\left| P - P_v \right|^2 \le d_{max}^2$. As an alternative definitions, one can use $\left| P - P_v \right|^2 \le d_{min}^2$ or the points adjacent to P in the same manner.

The values d_{min}, d_{max} and α_{max} are the parameters of the algorithm. Small values of d_{min} respond to fine corners. The upper limit d_{max} is necessary to avoid false sharp triangles formed by distant points in highly varying curves. The α_{max} is the angle limit that determines the minimum sharpness accepted as high curvature.

Demonstration

Practical demonstration of the corner detection algorithm CS99 is shown in Figures 3 – 6. Outer boundary of different images are selected to show the results with the default values as well as with different values of d_{min} and α_{max}. The effects of changing the parameters d_{min} and α_{max} are compared in Table 1. Although the algorithm works fine and detects corners correctly in most of the images but, in some cases, it may not find all of the corners at their most appropriate positions such as in the Figures 3 through 6. But the method, in general, takes care of the points which can be considered as corner points for various applications. However, appropriate parameter selection is a manual factor which a user needs to select carefully.

Performance Evaluation

Criteria for performance evaluation of corner detectors were given in (Chetverikov & Szabo, 1999), which is as follows:

- **Selectivity:** It is the most important factor for any corner detector. The rate of correct detections should be high and the wrong ones should be low.

Figure 3. Corner detection with CS99: (a) Corner points at default parameters, (b) Corner points at $d_{min} = 7$ *and* $\alpha_{max} = 160$

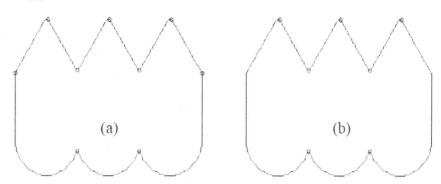

Figure 4. Corner detection with CS99: (a) Corner points at default parameters, (b) Corner points at $d_{min} = 8$ *and* $\alpha_{max} = 160$

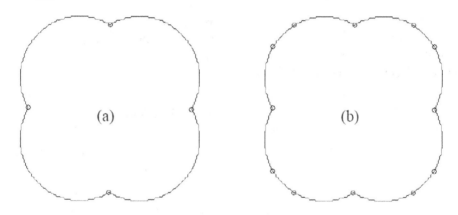

Figure 5. Corner detection with CS99: (a) Corner points at default parameters, (b) Corner points at $d_{min} = 7$ *and* $\alpha_{max} = 140$

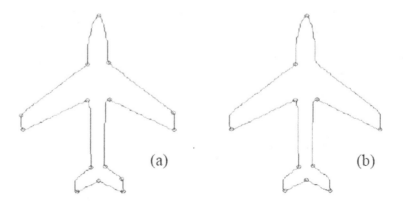

Figure 6. Corner points at default parameters

- **Single response:** Each corner should be detected only once.
- **Precision:** The positions of detected corners should be precise.
- **Robustness to noise:** The algorithm should perform well for noisy shapes as well.
- **Easy setting of parameters:** Parameters should be logical and easy to tune for variety of shapes.
- **Robustness to parameters:** Minor changes in parameter should not cause drastic changes in performance.
- **Speed**

For more details of the algorithm, the reader is referred to (Chetverikov & Szabo, 1999). Demonstration of the algorithm, for the shapes im1, im2, …, im8, is made in Figure 22. The choice of the selected parameters, for these figures, can be seen in Table 2. The 'D' in Table 2 is meant for the default values, the deviations from the 'D' are shown otherwise. The proposed algorithm yields reasonable results at the shown values for all the 8 shapes. Points not well located are indicated with arrows.

It has been observed that, for RJ73 and RW75, somewhat better results can be obtained when the parameters are slightly modified. However, for stable performance, FD77 and BT87 need more frequent modifications of their parameters. In case of BT87, only S needed to be varied. CS99, of course, outperforms RJ73, RW75, FD77 and BT87.

EER ALGORITHM

In EER algorithm (Sarfraz & Swati, 2013), corner detection is based on rectangle R and two ellipses E_1 and E_2 sliding along the given curve. E_1 and E_2 are embedded in R such that $R \supset E_1 \supset E_2$.

Table 1. Effects of changing parameter d_{min} and α_{max} on number of detected corner points

Figure #	d_{min}	α_{max}	No of corner points
3(a)	7	150	9
3(b)	7	160	7
4(a)	7	150	4
4(b)	8	160	12
5(a)	7	150	15
5(b)	7	140	11
6	7	150	2

Table 2. Parameter values for 8 tested shapes

	Parameter Values					
	RJ	**RW**	**FD**	**BT**	**CS**	**EER**
im1	D	D	D	D	D	A=14, B=1.7
im2	k = 0.15	k =0.15	k = 7, S =2500	D	D	D
im3	D	D	S = 6, K= 2500	D	D	D
im4	D	D	k= 5, S= 500	S =500	dmin=8, αmax=140	A=18
im5	k =.06	k=.07	D	S =1000	dmin=8, αmax=140	D
im6	D	D	k= 7, S =1000	S=1300	D	D
im7	D	D	D	D	D	A=16, B=2.42
im8	D	D	D	S =1000	D	A=10

The geometry of the rectangle and two ellipses is shown in Figure 7. To gather information about the locality of neighboring curve points, proposed technique uses rectangle and ellipses shown having common center at p_i (Figure 7).

The mathematical relations of R and two ellipses E_1 and E_2 is described in Equation (1). The geometric structure of Figure 10 has been adopted as follows:

- The length and width of the rectangle R are considered to be the lengths $2A$ and $2B$ respectively.
- The semi minor axis and semi major axis of the ellipse E_1 are considered to be the lengths $3A/4$ and B respectively.
- The semi minor axis and semi major axis of the ellipse E_2 are considered to be the lengths $3A/4$ and $B/2$ respectively.

$$
\left.
\begin{aligned}
R_1 &= 2A \times 2B, \\
E_1 &= \pi \times 3A / 4 \times B, \\
E_2 &= \pi \times 3A / 4 \times B / 2, \\
\theta &= slope\,'S\,'
\end{aligned}
\right\}
\tag{10}
$$

The length of rectangle and semi major axes of ellipses lies in the direction of slope 'S'. Hence the width of rectangle and semi minor axes of ellipses lie at right angle to the slope 'S' of the contour with center at curve point p_i, $1 \leq i \leq n$, where n is the total number of contour points. Slope of curve point at p_i is determined along the line drawn by calculating mean of five points (including p_i) on both sides of p_i.

By taking boundary point p_i as center, the direction of rectangle R is adjusted along major axes of the Ellipses. Similarly, ellipses E_1 and E_2

Figure 7. Geometrical structure of EER Algorithm

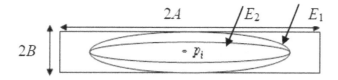

Figure 8. Snapshot of EER algorithm

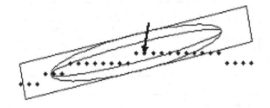

having same center at p_i are configured with same procedure. Thus $R \supset E_1 \supset E_2$.

Combination of rectangle and ellipses slides on given curve and number of adjacent points for rectangle and each ellipse. It is recorded from p_{i-A} to p_{i+A} which lie in the area R, E_1, and E_2. Let nR_i, $nE_{1,i}$ and $nE_{2,i}$ describe the total number of curve points in rectangle R, ellipses E_1, and E_2 respectively, with centers at i^{th} boundary point. For example in Figure 8, $nR_i = 23$, $nE_{1,i} = 18$, and $nE_{2,i} = 15$. Values of nR_i, $nE_{1,i}$ and $nE_{2,i}$, for each boundary point, are finally used while marking the absolute positions of corner points.

The EER algorithm adopts natural corner detection methodology by combining three levels of views. Combination of one rectangle and two ellipses represents three special views of curve points. It traces number of counts nR_i, $nE_{1,i}$ and $nE_{2,i}$, for each boundary point. It calculates sufficient information to mark the absolute corners.

Rectangle R_1 represents global view of boundary points and allowing only those boundary points for which $R_1 - E_1 = 0$. These contour points are represented by set the G in Equations (11).

$$G = \left\{ P = nR_i - nE_{1,i} = 0 \right\}$$
$$\text{Or}$$
$$G = \left\{ P = nR_i - nE_{1,i} \right\} \qquad (11)$$

Set G describes wider view of a shape and does not take false corners (at contour noise/irregularities). This is demonstrated in Figure 9 which shows some snapshots with curves noise/irregularity. Center points p_i's in Figures 9(a) and 9(b) look like corners if the local view of contour is taken, but if we observed the global view (broader part of the curve), these corners are rejected as they do not qualify the Equation (11). In general, $R_1 - E_1 = 0$ pointing with arrows. Curve points in Figures 9(c) and 9(d) are only be considered in group G.

Curve points lying in the set G are corner points in a relative way, they can be considered as candidate corner points. These points describe common region of contour where the actual corner is located as shown in the circled regions in Figure 10. Set G describes connected points that represent

Figure 9. Some snapshots of the EER Algorithm for irregular boundary. (a), (b) are not qualified by G, and (c) is rejected due threshold 'η'.

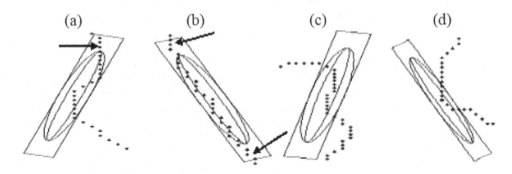

Figure 10. Some shapes marked (bold) with contour points in set G. Corners are marked in grey.

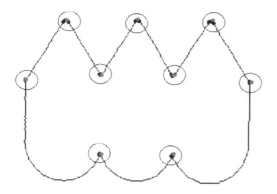

Figure 11. Algorithm for EER corner detector

For each contour point P_i
      Count nR_i, $nE_{1,i}$, $nE_{2,i}$
End For
$G = \{P_i : nR_i = nE_{1,i}\}$
Make groups of connected points in G
For each group G_k
      $Corner = \min_{nE_{2,j}} \{G_{k,j} : nE_{2,j} < \eta\}$

Demonstration

a group and there is a possibility that more than one group may exist in set G. For each group, there is only single point which represents actual corner. The curve points in $E_{2,i}$ of values $nE_{2,i}$ less than threshold 'η' are calculated for every group and smallest value $nE_{2,i}$ is selected as a corner. If in a group the number of points in $E_{2,i}$ are lower than 'η' then it means that corner point does not exist in that group.

The EER corner detection algorithm is given in Figure 11. In this algorithm, default value of A is 14. $A/8$ and $3A/4$ is assigned to B and η, respectively. All other parameters are relative to A (Figure 7). Value of parameter A depends upon the size of boundary, noise, and resolution of image. Assigned values to semi major axis, semi minor axis, length, and width of ellipses and rectangle are suitable to a certain range of size and resolution, which covers all demonstrated shapes in this Chapter. These sizes were found after extensive testing on many images of similar size and resolution. The relationship between relative size of ellipses and rectangle is set (again with extensive testing) for convenience of using these parameters. The user needs to tune only one parameter i.e. A instead of three. However, accuracy can improve by assigning independent sizes, but this would be at the cost of complex tuning of parameters.

Criteria for performance evaluation, in this algorithm, is same as given by (Chetverikov & Szabo, 1999). Test results of this algorithm are compared with five corner detectors presented in (Chetverikov & Szabo, 1999). These are based on scanned images presented in (Davies, 1988) and with the inclusion of some noise into the original noise free pictures. It also uses the same noisy test shapes, which were downloaded from the website (Liu & Srinath, 1990). Very minor variations in demonstrated test shapes from (Chetverikov & Szabo, 1999) are possible, however efforts have been made to keep them close to (Chetverikov & Szabo, 1999).

Comparative results are demonstrated for eight different shapes (im1 to im8, see Figure 1). Results of all the six algorithms are presented together for each shape to have an effective comparison (see Figures 12 to 19). Parameters assigned in each test are summarized in Table 2. In that table, parameter value 'D' stands for default value. For BT87, corner strength parameter S was modified for im4, im5, im6 and im8. For FD77, spacing parameter k and corner strength parameter S were modified for im2, im3, im4 and im6. For RW75 & RJ73, parameter k was modified for im2. For details of these parameters, the reader is referred to (Beus & Tiu, 1987; Chetverikov & Szabo, 1999; Davies, 1988; Sarfraz, et el., 2006).

Figure 12. Detected corner points for im1 as per parameters given in Table 2. (a) EER. (b) CS99. (c) BT87. (d) FD77. (e) RW75. (f) RJ73.

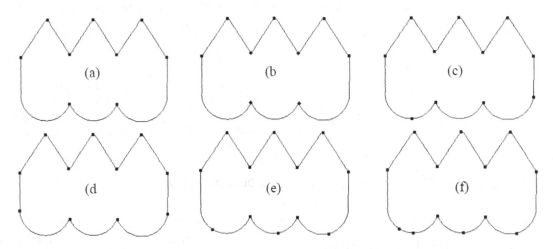

Figure 13. Detected corner points for im2 as per parameters given in Table 2. (a) EER. (b) CS99. (c) BT87. (d) FD77. (e) RW75. (f) RJ73.

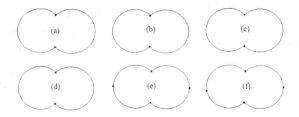

Figure 14. Detected corner points for im3 as per parameters given in Table 2. (a) EER. (b) CS99. (c) BT87. (d) FD77. (e) RW75. (f) RJ73.

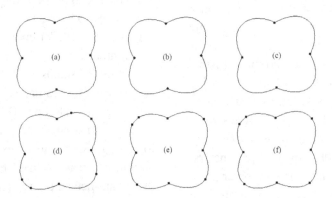

Figure 15. Detected corner points for im4 as per parameters given in Table 2. (a) EER. (b) CS99. (c) BT87. (d) FD77. (e) RW75. (f) RJ73.

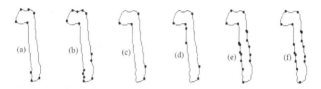

Figure 16. Detected corner points for im5 as per parameters given in Table 2. (a) EER. (b) CS99. (c) BT87. (d) FD77. (e) RW75. (f) RJ73.

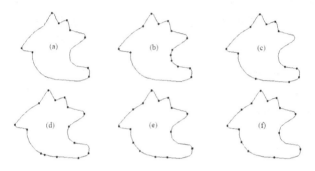

Figure 17. Detected corner points for im6 as per parameters given in Table 2. (a) EER. (b) CS99. (c) BT87. (d) FD77. (e) RW75. (f) RJ73.

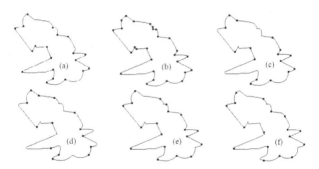

Figure 18. Detected corner points for im7 as per parameters given in Table 2. (a) EER. (b) CS99. (c) BT87. (d) FD77. (e) RW75. (f) RJ73.

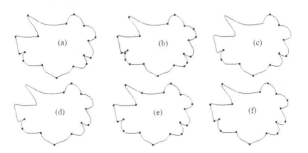

It can be observed in all above demonstrated results of EER that the rate of selecting wrong corners is almost 1%. This is also reflected in Tables 3 and 4.

CONCLUDING REMARKS

Corners are not simply the local maxima, high curvature or dominant points. Points of abrupt change from where the shape can be segmented and which human beings perceive as meaningful points are the true corners. Five corner detection approaches namely BT87, RJ73, RW75, FD77, and CS99, have been discussed, experimented, and analyzed. An extended review of EER has been made. EER algorithm has been found most accurate and efficient as it does not involve curvature analysis and determination of trigonometric functions like cosine angle. A comparative study, based on proposed parameters, shows that EER algorithm has various advantages over previous techniques. Some of the advantages are that it is: (1) most consistent with human judgment of corners; (2) ratio of false detection is extremely low; (3) computationally efficient; (4) invariant to transformation changes; (5) highly insensitive to noise/irregularities along the curve; (6) robust to minor changes in size and resolution; and (7) very suitable for natural shapes/objects. Independent tuning of the parameters can further fine tune the results if needed in some extreme case.

ACKNOWLEDGMENT

This work was supported by Kuwait University, Research Grant No. [QS 01/13].

Table 3. Number of correctly and incorrectly detected corner points

	Correct						Incorrect					
	RJ	RW	FD	BT	CS	EER	RJ	RW	FD	BT	CS	EER
im1	9	9	9	8	9	9	3	3	2	2	0	0
im2	2	2	2	2	2	2	2	2	0	0	0	0
im3	4	4	3	4	4	4	5	5	5	0	0	0
im4	5	5	4	4	6	6	11	12	3	1	4	0
im5	7	8	9	10	9	9	3	3	6	3	0	0
im6	13	17	12	16	24	24	4	2	2	0	4	1
im7	12	12	8	7	12	11	5	6	3	3	9	0
im8	16	15	14	22	25	35	2	2	0	1	1	0

Table 4. Correct and incorrect detected corners by each algorithm

	RJ	RW	FD	BT	CS	EER
% Correct	67	71	60	72	90	98
% Incorrect	35	35	21	10	17	1

REFERENCES

Abe, K., Morii, R., Nishida, K., & Kadonaga, T. (1993). Comparison of Methods for Detecting Corner Points From Digital Curves—A Preliminary Report. In *Proceedings of International Conference on Document Analysis and Recognition.* Tsukuba Science City, Japan: IEEE.

Asada, H., & Brady, M. (1986). The curvature primal sketch. *IEEE Transactions on Pattern Analysis and Machine Intelligence, 8,* 2–4. doi:10.1109/TPAMI.1986.4767747 PMID:21869318

Attneave, F. (1954). Some Informational Aspects of Visual Perception. *Psychological Review, 61,* 183–193. doi:10.1037/h0054663 PMID:13167245

Beus, H. L., & Tiu, S. S. H. (1987). An Improved Corner Detection Algorithm based on Chain Coded Plane Curves. *Pattern Recognition, 20,* 291–296. doi:10.1016/0031-3203(87)90004-5

Cabrelli, C. A., & Molter, U. M. (1990). Automatic representation of binary images. *IEEE Transactions on Pattern Analysis and Machine Intelligence, 12,* 1190–1196. doi:10.1109/34.62608

Chetverikov, D., & Szabo, Z. (1999). A Simple and Efficient Algorithm for Detection of High Curvature Points in Planner Curves. In *Proceedings of 23rd Workshop of Australian Pattern Recognition Group,* (pp. 175-184). Academic Press.

Davies, E. R. (1988). Application of generalized Hough transform to corner detection. *IEE Proceedings, 135E*(1), 49-54.

Deriche, R., & Faugeras, O. D. (1990). 2D curve matching using high curvature points: Application to stereo vision. In *Proceedings of 10th International Conference on Pattern Recognition.* Atlantic City, NJ: IEEE.

Deriche, R., & Giraudon, G. (1990). Accurate corner detection: An analytical study. In *Proceedings of 3rd International Conference on Computer Vision.* Osaka, Japan: IEEE.

Dreschler, L., & Nagel, H. H. (1982). On the selection of critical points and local curvature extrema of region boundaries for interframe matching. In *Proceedings of International Conference on Pattern Recognition.* Munich, Germany: Springer.

Freeman, H., & Davis, L. S. (1977). A Corner Finding Algorithm for ChainCoded Curves. *IEEE Transactions on Computers, 26,* 297–303. doi:10.1109/TC.1977.1674825

Guru, D. S., Dinesh, R., & Nagabhushan, P. (2004). Boundary based corner detection and localization using new 'cornerity' index: a robust approach. In *Proc. 1st Canadian Conference on Computer and Robot Vision.* London, Canada: IEEE.

Harris, C., & Stephens, M. (1988). A combined corner and edge detector. In *Proceedings of the Fourth Alvey Vision Conference.* Manchester, UK: Alvety Vision Club.

Kadonaga, T., & Abe, K. (1996). Comparison of Methods for Detecting Corner Points from Digital Curves, Graphics Recognition Methods and Applications. *Lecture Notes in Computer Science, 1072,* 23–34. doi:10.1007/3-540-61226-2_3

Kasturi, R., Siva, S., & O'Gorman, L. (1990). Techniques for line drawing interpretation: an overview. In *Proc. IAPR Workshop on Machine Vision Applications.* IAPR.

Kitchen, L., & Rosenfeld, A. (1982). Gray-level corner detection. *Pattern Recognition Letters, 1,* 95–102. doi:10.1016/0167-8655(82)90020-4

Liu, H. C., & Srinath, L. S. (1990). Corner Detection from Chain-Code. *Pattern Recognition, 23,* 51–68. doi:10.1016/0031-3203(90)90048-P

Mokhtarian, F., & Mackworth, A. K. (1992). A Theory of Multiscale, Curvature-Based Shape Representation for Planar Curves. *IEEE Transactions on Pattern Analysis and Machine Intelligence, 14,* 789–805. doi:10.1109/34.149591

Noble, J. A. (1988). Finding corners. *Image and Vision Computing*, 6, 121–128. doi:10.1016/0262-8856(88)90007-8

Pritchard, A. J., Sangwine, S. J., & Horne, R. E. N. (1993). Corner and curve detection along a boundary using line segment triangles. *Electronics Division Colloquium on Hough Transforms*, 106, 1–4.

Rattarangsi, A., & Chin, R. T. (1992). Scale-Based Detection of Corners of Planar Curves. *Transactions on Pattern Analysis and Machine Intelligence*, 14, 430–449. doi:10.1109/34.126805

Ray, B. K., & Pandyan, R. (2003). ACORD – an adaptive corner detector for planar curves. *Pattern Recognition*, 36, 703–708. doi:10.1016/S0031-3203(02)00084-5

Rosenfeld, A., & Johnston, E. (1973). Angle Detection on Digital Curves. *IEEE Transactions on Computers*, 22, 875–878. doi:10.1109/TC.1973.5009188

Rosenfeld, & Weszka. (n.d.). An Improved Method of Angle Detection on Digital Curves. *IEEE Transactions on Computers, 24*, 940-941.

Rutkowski, W. S., & Rosenfeld, A. (1978). *A comparison of corner-detection techniques for chain-coded curves (TR-623)*. Computer Science Center, University of Maryland.

Sarfraz, M., Asim, M. R., & Masood, A. (2004a). Capturing Outlines using Cubic Bézier Curves. In *Proc. of IEEE 1st International Conference on Information & Communication Technologies: from Theory to Applications*. IEEE.

Sarfraz, M., Asim, M. R., & Masood, A. (2004b). A Web Based System for Capturing Outlines of 2D Objects. In *Proceedings of The International Conference on Information and Computer Science*, (pp. 575 – 586). King Fahd University of Petroleum and Minerals.

Sarfraz, M., Asim, M. R., & Masood, A. (2006). A New Approach to Corner Detection. In *Computer Vision and Graphics*. Springer. doi:10.1007/1-4020-4179-9_75

Sarfraz, M., & Swati, Z. N. K. (2013). Mining Corner Points on the Generic Shapes. *Open Journal of Applied Sciences*, 3(1B), 10–15. doi:10.4236/ojapps.2013.31B003

Smith, P., Sinclair, D., Cipolla, R., & Wood, K. (1998). Effective Corner Matching. In *Proceedings of the 9th British Machine Vision Conference*, (vol. 2, pp. 545-556). BMVA Press.

Smith, S., & Brady, J. (1995). SUSAN — a new approach to low level image processing. *International Journal of Computer Vision*, 23, 45–78. doi:10.1023/A:1007963824710

Teh, C. H., & Chin, R. (1990). On the detection of dominant points on digital curves. *IEEE Transactions on Pattern Analysis and Machine Intelligence*, 11(8), 859–873. doi:10.1109/34.31447

Vincent, E., & Laganiere, R. (2005). Detecting and matching feature points. *Journal of Visual Communication and Image Representation*, 16(1), 38–54. doi:10.1016/j.jvcir.2004.05.001

Vincent, E., & Laganire, R. (2001). Matching feature points in stereo pairs: a comparative study of some matching strategies. *Machine Graphics and Vision*, 10, 237–259.

Wang, H., & Brady, M. (1995). Real-time corner detection algorithm for motion estimation. *Image and Vision Computing*, 13(9), 695–703. doi:10.1016/0262-8856(95)98864-P

Zoghlami, I., Faugeras, O., & Deriche, R. (1997). Using geometric corners to build a 2D mosaic from a set of images. In *Proceedings of the Conference on Computer Vision and Pattern Recognition*. IEEE Computer Society.

KEY TERMS AND DEFINITIONS

Algorithm: An algorithm is a step-by-step procedure for calculations.

Bitmap Image: An image represented as a two dimensional array of brightness values for pixels.

Computer Vision: Computer vision is a field that includes methods for acquiring, processing, analyzing, and understanding images and, in general, high-dimensional data from the real world in order to produce numerical or symbolic information, e.g., in the forms of decisions.

Corner Detector: Corner detection is an approach used within computer vision systems to extract certain kinds of features and infer the contents of an image.

Corner Point: A corner point is the point that lies in the solution region where two boundary lines intersect.

Digital Image: A digital image is a numeric representation (normally binary) of a two-dimensional image. Depending on whether the image resolution is fixed, it may be of vector or raster type. By itself, the term "digital image" usually refers to raster images or bitmapped images.

Feature Detection: In computer vision and image processing the concept of feature detection refers to methods that aim at computing abstractions of image information and making local decisions at every image point whether there is an image feature of a given type at that point or not.

Image Processing: Image processing is any form of signal processing for which the input is an image, such as a photograph or video frame; the output of image processing may be either an image or a set of characteristics or parameters related to the image.

Plane Curve: A plane curve is a curve in a Euclidean plane.

Raster Image: A raster image, or bitmap, is a dot matrix data structure representing a generally rectangular grid of pixels, or points of color, viewable via a monitor, paper, or other display medium. Raster images are stored in image files with varying formats.

Vector Graphics: Vector graphics is the use of geometrical primitives such as points, lines, curves, and shapes or polygons—all of which are based on mathematical expressions—to represent images in computer graphics.

Chapter 16
Outline Capture of Planar Objects by Detecting Corner Features

Misbah Irshad
University of the Punjab, Pakistan

Muhammad Sarfraz
Kuwait University, Kuwait

Malik Zawwar Hussain
University of the Punjab, Pakistan

ABSTRACT

This chapter proposes a scheme that helps digitizing hand printed and electronic planar objects or vectorizing the generic shapes. An evolutionary optimization technique, namely Genetic Algorithm (GA), is used to solve the problem of curve fitting with cubic and rational cubic spline functions. The underlying scheme is comprised of various phases including data of the image outlines, detection of corner points, using GA for optimal values of shape parameters in the description of spline functions, and fitting curve using spline functions to the detected corner points.

INTRODUCTION

Fitting curves to the data extracted from generic planar shapes is the problem which is immensely worked on during last two decades. It still grabs the attention of researchers due to its applications in diverse fields and its demands in the industry. The process of vectorizing outlines of the images consists of several mathematical and computational phases and stages. This process aims to fit an optimal curve to the data extracted from the boundary of the image (Hou, Z. J. and Wei, G.W. (2002), Kirkpatrick, S., Gelatt, C. D. Jr., Vecchi, M. P. (1983), Sarfraz, M. (2004), Sarfraz, M. and Khan, M. A. (2004), Sarfraz, M., Hussain, M. Z. & Chaudary, F. S. (2005)). Although many contributions in the literature (Harada, T., Yoshimoto, F., and Aoyama, Y. (2000),Horng, J. H. (2003), Lavoue, G., Dupont, F. and Baskurt, A. (2005), Moriyama, M., Yoshimoto, F. and Harada,

DOI: 10.4018/978-1-4666-6030-4.ch016

T. (1998), Sarfraz, M. (2006), Sarfraz, M. and Rasheed, A. (2007), Sarfraz, M. (2010), Yang, H., Wang, W. and Sun, J. (2004),Yang, X.N. and Wang, G.Z. (2001), Yang, Z. Deng, J. and Chen, F. (2005)) can be found in this area, there is still room for making more advancements and finding interactive approaches.

Least square fitting is common in optimization problems in which splines and higher order polynomials are used to approximate the data. One can see a cubic spline technique Sarfraz, M. and Khan, M. A. (2004) with least square fitting. Squared distance minimization has been used on B-spline curves in Yang, X. (2004). It uses iterative process to achieve an optimal curve.

Instead of parametric form, implicit form of the polynomial is also used for this purpose. Implicit B-spline curves Lavoue, G., Dupont, F. and Baskurt, A. (2005) are used to solve curve reconstruction problem by approximating the point clouds. It uses the heuristic of trust region algorithm. In (Jüttler, B. and Felis, A. (2002), Morse, B. S., Yoo, T. S., Chen, D. T., Rheingans, P., and Subramanian, K. R. (2001), Yang, X.N. and Wang, G.Z. (2001)), schemes were proposed for fitting implicitly defined algebraic spline curves and surfaces. This was achieved over the scattered data by simultaneously approximating points and associated normal vectors.

In this paper, a soft computing technique namely Genetic Algorithm (GA) Goldberg, D. E. (1989) is proposed to find the optimal spline curves to the data extracted from the boundaries of the generic images. This evolutionary technique incorporates the corner points from the outline of the input image. The detection of corner points is quite significant as it helps minimizing the time to achieve desired curve to the outline of the image. Curve fitting in this scheme is done by using cubic and rational cubic spline functions which contain shape parameters in their description. Basic target is to find those values of the parameters which assure minimum error between detected boundary of the image and the fitted spline curve.

The paper is organized in a way that the first and second steps (outline estimation and corner detection) of the proposed scheme are described, a generalized cubic spline curve scheme is given, Genetic Algorithm is explained, the proposed scheme is discussed and demonstrated with examples. Finally, the paper is concluded.

COUNTOUR EXTRACTION AND SEGMENTATION

First step in proposed scheme of vectorization of planar objects is to extract data from the boundary of the bitmap image or a generic shape. In this procedure, a bitmap image of the generic shape is used as an input. In order to get the image, software like Paint and Adobe Photoshop can be used or some other appropriate way can be adopted. After saving the bitmap image to the system, the chain code method [Avrahami, G. Pratt, V. (1991), Hou, Z. J. and Wei, G.W. (2002)] is used to extract boundary of the image. Chain codes represent the direction of the image and help to attain the geometric data from outline of the image.

In the next step, the data extracted from the outline needs to be subdivided into smaller segments for curve fitting. For this purpose corner points or significant points are detected. Detection of these points is not an easy task as exactness of detected corners can only be judged by human eye and no other standard criterion exist. Then accuracy of any corner detection scheme can only be examined if the original corner positions are known. Generally corner detection can be defined as an approach which extracts the dominating features of an image and consequently helps deducing contents of the image. Plenty of corner detection schemes can be found in the literature [Beus, H.L., and Tiu, S.S.H. (1987), Chetrikov, D. and Zsabo, S. (1999), Freeman, H., and Davis, L.S. (1977),Jüttler, B. and Felis, A. (2002)]. In this paper, the scheme presented in Chetrikov, D. and Zsabo, S. (1999) is used to divide the boundary into smaller segments. Each segment of the boundary consists of two consecutive corner points and the data points in between them. These corner points would be used for curve fitting.

GENERALIZED SPLINE FUNCTIONS

Finding corner leads to subdivision of the data obtained by the boundary of the bitmap image into pieces. Each piece consists of two successive corner points and the data points in between them. Thus if there are m corner points $F_1, ..., F_m$ then there will be m pieces $P_1, ..., P_m$. Each piece is treated separately and spline is fitted to it.

First piece consists of all the contour points in between F_1 and F_2 inclusive. Second piece contains all contour points in between F_2 and F_3 inclusive. Consequently, the mth piece includes all contour points between F_m and F_1 inclusive. In general, the ith piece contains all the data points between F_i and F_{i+1} inclusive.

Cubic Spline Function

As a curve fitting technique, the algorithm proposed in Section 5 makes use of a generalized cubic spline method. This spline embodies a number of desirable features needed for an optimum solution. The curve-fitting method employed here seeks the cubic spline for the determination of good shape parameters in its description.

Cubic spline function, Sarfraz, M., Hussain, M. Z. & Chaudary, F. S. (2005), is used for fitting curves at corner points. Let F_i, F_{i+1}, $i \in Z$ be the two corner points of ith piece. Also let D_i and D_{i+1} be the corresponding tangents at corner points. Then the cubic function, where v_i and w_i are shape parameters, is defined by:

$$P\big|_{[t_i, t_{i+1}]}(t) = F_i(1-t)^3 + 3V_i(1-t)^2 t + 3W_i(1-t)t^2 + F_{i+1}t^3, \tag{1}$$

where

$$V_i = F_i + \frac{v_i h_i D_i}{3}, \tag{2}$$

$$W_i = F_{i+1} - \frac{w_i h_i D_{i+1}}{3}, \tag{3}$$

$$h_i = t_{i+1} - t_i > 0.$$

Equation (1) can be rewritten as:

$$P\big|_{(t_i, t_{i+1})}(t) = R_{0,i}(t)F_i + R_{1,i}(t)V_i + R_{2,i}(t)W + R_{3,i}(t)F_{i+1}, \tag{4}$$

where

$$\left. \begin{aligned} R_{0,i}(t) &= (1-t)^3, \\ R_{1,i}(t) &= 3t(1-t)^2, \\ R_{2,i}(t) &= 3t^2(1-t), \\ R_{3,i}(t) &= t^3. \end{aligned} \right\} \tag{5}$$

The functions $R_{j,i}$, $j = 0,1,2,3$ are Bernstein Bézier like basis functions, such that

$$\sum_{j=0}^{3} R_{j,i}(t) = 1. \tag{6}$$

The cubic function (1) has the following properties:

Figure 1. Demonstration of cubic function (1) for different values of parameters

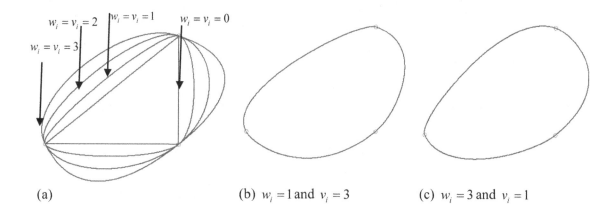

(a)   (b) $w_i = 1$ and $v_i = 3$ (c) $w_i = 3$ and $v_i = 1$

$$P\left(t_i\right) = F_i,\ P\left(t_{i+1}\right) = F_{i+1},$$

$$P^{(1)}\left(t_i\right) = v_i D_i,\ \text{and}\ P^{(1)}\left(t_{i+1}\right) = v_i D_{i+1},\ i \in Z.$$

$$P(t) = P_i(t) =$$
$$\frac{F_i(1-\theta)^3 + v_i V_i (1-\theta)^2\theta + w_i W_i (1-\theta)\theta^2 + F_{i+1}\theta^3}{(1-\theta)^3 + v_i(1-\theta)^2\theta + w_i(1-\theta)\theta^2 + \theta^3}$$

$$(7)$$

Figure 1 represents curve fitting to the given data by using cubic function (1) for assigning the different values to the parameters v_i and w_i. The effect of different values of the shape parameters on the shape of the curve are also shown in Figure 1. In Figure 1(a) cubic curve (1) is fitted to the data with the values of parameters as: $v_i = w_i = 0$, $v_i = w_i = 1$, $v_i = w_i = 2$ and $v_i = w_i = 3$. Figure 1(b) and Figure 1(c) show cubic curves with parameters $v_i = 3$, $w_i = 1$ and $v_i = 1$, $w_i = 3$ respectively.

Rational Cubic Spline Function

A piecewise rational cubic parametric function $P \in C^1[t_i, t_{i+1}]$, with shape parameters $v_i, w_i \geq 0$, $i = 1,...,n$, is used for curve fitting to the corner points detected from the boundary of the bitmap image, the rational cubic function is defined for $t \in [t_i, t_{i+1}]$, $i = 1,...,n$, as follows:

where F_i and F_{i+1} are two corner points (given control points) of the ith segment of the boundary with $h_i = t_{i+1} - t_i$,

$$V_i = F_i + \frac{h_i D_i}{v_i}\ \text{and}\ W_i = F_{i+1} - \frac{h_i D_{i+1}}{w_i}$$

$$(8)$$

where D_i, $i = 1,...,n+1$ are the first derivative values at the knots t_i, $i = 1,...,n+1$.

Effect of the shape parameters v_i, w_i, $i = 1,...,n$, on the curve is shown in Figure 2 and Figure 3. Moreover, for $v_i, w_i = 3$, $i = 1,...,n$, (7) reduces to cubic Hermite interpolation. If $v_i, w_i \to \infty$, then the rational cubic function (7) converges to linear interpolant $L_i(t) = (1-\theta)F_i + \theta F_{i+1}$ as shown in Figure 2. Furthermore it can be observed that the function (7) may have two sub cases as:

Figure 2. Demonstration of rational cubic function (7) for case 1

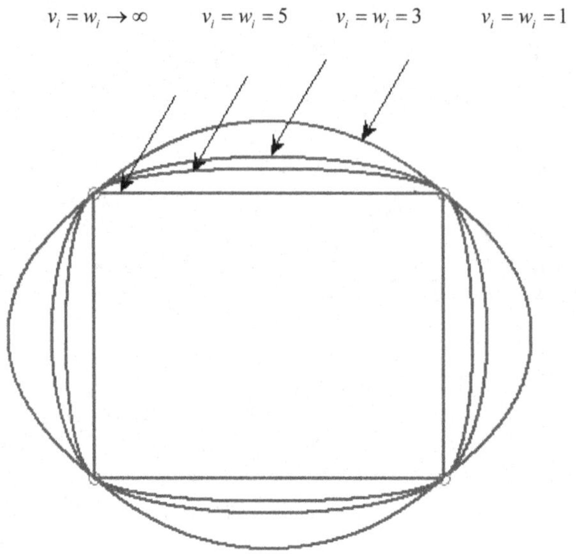

$v_i = w_i \to \infty$ $v_i = w_i = 5$ $v_i = w_i = 3$ $v_i = w_i = 1$

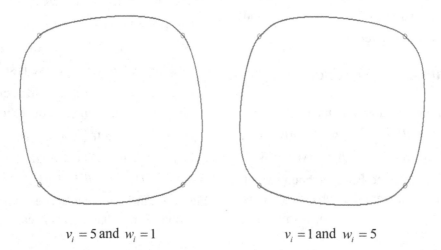

Case 1: $v_i = w_i$, $i = 1, ..., n$

Case 2: $v_i \neq w_i$, $i = 1, ..., n$

In this paper both the cases are discussed for the curve fitting.

For $v_i = w_i$, $i = 1, ..., n$ equation (7) can be written in the form

$$P_i(t_i; v_i) =$$
$$R_0(\theta; v_i)F_i + R_1(\theta; v_i)V_i + R_2(\theta; v_i)W_i + R_3(\theta; v_i)F_{i+1}$$

$$(9)$$

where V_i and W_i are given in equation (8) and $R_j(\theta; v_i)$, $j = 0, 1, 2, 3$ are rational Bernstein-Bezier weight functions such that $\sum_{j=0}^{3} R_j(\theta; v_i) = 1$.

Figure 3. Demonstration of rational cubic function (7) for case 2

$v_i = 5$ and $w_i = 1$ $v_i = 1$ and $w_i = 5$

Similarly for $v_i, w_i \neq 0$ equation (7) will become

$$P_i(t_i; v_i, w_i) =$$
$$R_0(\theta; v_i, w_i)F_i + R_1(\theta; v_i, w_i)V_i + \qquad (10)$$
$$R_2(\theta; v_i, w_i)W_i + R_3(\theta; v_i, w_i)F_{i+1}$$

where $R_j(\theta; v_i, w_i)$, $j = 0, 1, 2, 3$ are rational Bernstein-Bezier weight functions such that $\sum_{j=0}^{3} R_j(\theta; v_i, w_i) = 1$, V_i and W_i are given in equation (8).

Parameterization

Number of parameterization techniques can be found in literature for instance uniform parameterization, linear or chord length parameterization, parabolic parameterization and cubic parameterization. In this paper, chord length parameterization is used to estimate the parametric value t associated with each point. It is as follows:

$$t_i = \begin{cases} 0 & if\ i = 1 \\ \dfrac{|p_1 p_2| + |p_2 p_3| + ... + |p_i p_{i+1}|}{|p_1 p_2| + |p_2 p_3| + ... + |p_{n-1} p_n|} & if\ 2 \leq i \leq n-1 \\ 1 & if\ i = n \end{cases}$$

It can be observed that t_i is in normalized form and varies from 0 to 1. Consequently, in our case, h_i is always equal to 1.

Estimation of Tangent Vectors

A distance based choice of tangent vectors D_i's at F_i's is used which is defined as:

For open curves:

$$\left.\begin{aligned} D_0 &= 2(F_1 - F_0) - (F_2 - F_0)/2, \\ D_n &= 2(F_n - F_{n-1}) - (F_n - F_{n-2})/2, \\ D_i &= a_i(F_i - F_{i-1}) - (1 - a_i)(F_{i+1} - F_i), \\ & i = 1, 2, ..., n-1. \end{aligned}\right\} \qquad (11)$$

For close curves:

$$\left.\begin{aligned} F_{-1} &= F_{n-1}, F_{n+1} = F_1, \\ D_i &= a_i(F_i - F_{i-1}) - (1 - a_i)(F_{i+1} - F_i), \\ & i = 0, 1, ..., n. \end{aligned}\right\} \qquad (12)$$

where

$$a_i = \frac{|F_{i+1} - F_i|}{|F_{i+1} - F_i| + |F_i - F_{i-1}|}, \qquad (13)$$
$$i = 0, 1, ..., n.$$

GENETIC ALGORITHM

Genetic Algorithms (GAs) are the evolution based search techniques. In GAs, every solution, in a given well-defined search space, is represented by a bit string. This bit string is called a chromosome. Selection, crossover and mutation are the three operators used in a genetic algorithm Goldberg, D. E. (1989). A GA creates a population of chromosomes iteratively and is attempted to improve on the quality of chromosomes.

A GA allows a population composed of many individuals to evolve under specified selection rules to a state that maximizes the "fitness" (i.e., minimizes the cost function). A set of input variable, in the form of a chromosome solution, is represented in a well-defined search space. A cost function, which may be a game, or an experiment or a mathematical function, is used to generate an optimal output from the chromosome.

The GA begins by defining a chromosome or an array of variable values to be optimized. The variable values are represented in binary form, so the binary GA works with bits. However, the cost function normally needs continuous variable to use in its description. Therefore, the chromosome is decoded whenever the cost function is evaluated.

How, a chromosome is encoded in binary for, is shown in Figure 4.

The GA starts with a group of chromosomes known as the population. Next the variables are passed to the cost function for evaluation. Natural Selection process leads to Survival of the fittest i.e. discarding the chromosomes with the highest cost. Natural selection occurs in each generation or iteration of the algorithm. It is somewhat arbitrary to discard the undesired chromosomes or to keep the desired ones. If only very few chromosomes are allowed to survive for the next generation, it limits the available genes in the offspring. Similarly, if too many chromosomes are allowed to stay for next generation, the bad performers get a chance to contribute to the next generation in a bad way. Therefore, to have a natural selection process, it is recommended to keep 50% of the chromosomes.

Thresholding is another approach to the process of natural selection. All the chromosomes having a cost value less than some threshold are assumed to be survived in this approach. In order that parents produce offspring, the threshold allows some of the chromosomes to continue. Otherwise, to find some chromosomes that pass the test, there would be the case that the whole new population would be generated. In the whole process, in the beginning, a small number of chromosomes may survive. However, in the generations afterwards, most of the chromosomes will survive provided the threshold is not changed.

In process of matchmaking, two chromosomes are selected from the mating pool of survived chromosomes to produce two new offspring. There are several schemes for parent selection like roulette wheel, tournament selection, random pairing etc. The next step after selecting parents is mating to create one or more offspring.

The crossover operator is a commonly used form of mating. It deals with two parents to produce two offspring. The first and the last bits of the parent's chromosomes are used to randomly select a crossover point. The left of the crossover point to the first offspring is passed the binary code of the first parent. In the same way, the left of the crossover point to the second offspring is passed the binary code of the second parent. Moreover, the binary code to the right of the crossover point of first parent goes to second offspring and second parent passes its right side's code to first offspring. As a result of crossover operator the offspring contain parts of both the parents. Crossover operator is demonstrated in Figure 5.

Another way of creating new chromosomes is mutation in which new traits can be introduced to chromosomes that are not present in the original population. A single point mutation changes a 1 to a 0, and vice versa is shown in Figure 6.

The process of GA described is iterated and would be repeated until the achievement of best solution for the problem. Flowchart of GA is shown in Figure 7.

Figure 4. Example of binary encoding

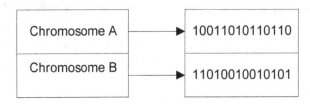

Figure 5. Example of crossover operator

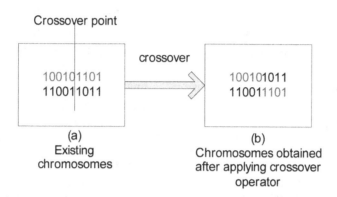

Figure 6. Example of mutation operator

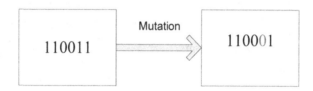

Figure 7. Flow diagram of genetic algorithm

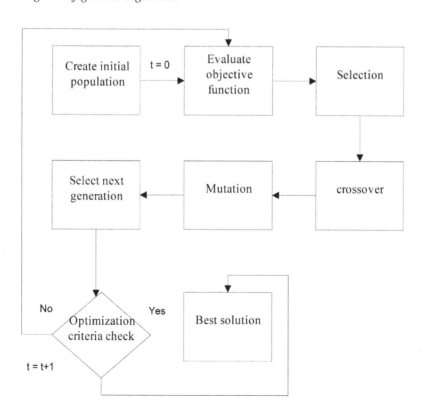

PROPOSED APPROACH

In this Section the proposed scheme to the curve fitting problem is described. It includes the phases of problem matching with Genetic Algorithm using cubic and rational cubic spline functions.

Problem Mapping

In this section Genetic Algorithm formulation of the problem discussed in this paper is described in detail, process described in this section would be applied one by one on both the spline functions described above.

Suppose, for $i = 0, 1, ..., n-1$, the data segments $P_{i,j} = \left(x_{i,j}, y_{i,j} \right)$, $j = 1, 2, ..., m_i$ are given as ordered sets of the universal set of data points. Then the squared sums S_i's of distance between $P_{i,j}$'s and their corresponding parametric points $P\left(t_j \right)$'s on the curve are determined as

$$ S_i = \sum_{j=1}^{m_i} \left[P_i(u_{i,j}) - P_{i,j} \right]^2, \quad i = 0, 1, 2, ..., n-1 $$

where u's are parameterized in reference to chord length parameterization. For the best fitting of the curve to given data, such values of parameter v_i and w_i, are required so that the sums S_i's are minimal. Genetic Algorithm is used to optimize this value for the fitted curve. We start with initial population of values of v_i and w_i chosen randomly. Successive application of search operations to this population leads to optimal values of v_i and w_i.

Initialization

Once we have the bitmap image shown in Figure 8(a), Figure 9(a) and Figure 10(a), the method described earlier is used to extract the boundary of the image. The boundary of the image is then used to detect the corner points in the next phase. It uses the corner detection method pointed out earlier. Figure (8b and 8c, Figure (9b and 9c and Figure (10b and 10c, show boundary of the bitmap images and detected corner points respectively. Table 1 gives number of contour points and initial corner points of the images.

Curve Fitting

Detection of the corner points leads towards the subdivision of the boundary of the image into segments. One interpolating spline functions stated above is then used to approximate each segment of the boundary. Each spline function has the parameters v and w in its description. The initial solution of the parameters v and w is randomly selected. After an initial approximation for the segment is obtained, The GA is run to get the optimal solution of v and w. Genetic Algorithm helps to obtain better approximations to achieve optimal solution.

Breaking Segment

For some segments, the best fit obtained through iterative improvement may not be satisfactory. In that case, we subdivide the segment into smaller segments at points where the distance between the boundary and parametric curve exceeds some predefined threshold; such points are termed as *intermediate points*. A new parametric curve is fitted for each new segment as shown in Figure 8((e) and (f)), Figure 9((e) and (f)) and Figure 10((e) and (f)). In Table 2, number of intermediate points is presented which is obtained while fitting the optimized cubic and rational cubic spline for different iterations of GA, whereas Table 3 gives maximum number of iterations and time elapsed while running GA for both the spline functions for both cases.

Figure 8. Image of plane with detected corner points and fitted cubic curve

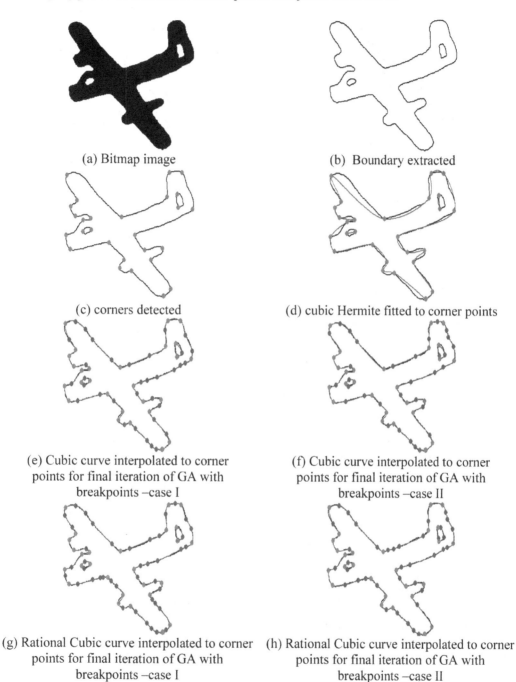

(a) Bitmap image

(b) Boundary extracted

(c) corners detected

(d) cubic Hermite fitted to corner points

(e) Cubic curve interpolated to corner points for final iteration of GA with breakpoints –case I

(f) Cubic curve interpolated to corner points for final iteration of GA with breakpoints –case II

(g) Rational Cubic curve interpolated to corner points for final iteration of GA with breakpoints –case I

(h) Rational Cubic curve interpolated to corner points for final iteration of GA with breakpoints –case II

Figure 9. Image of fork with detected corner points and fitted cubic curve

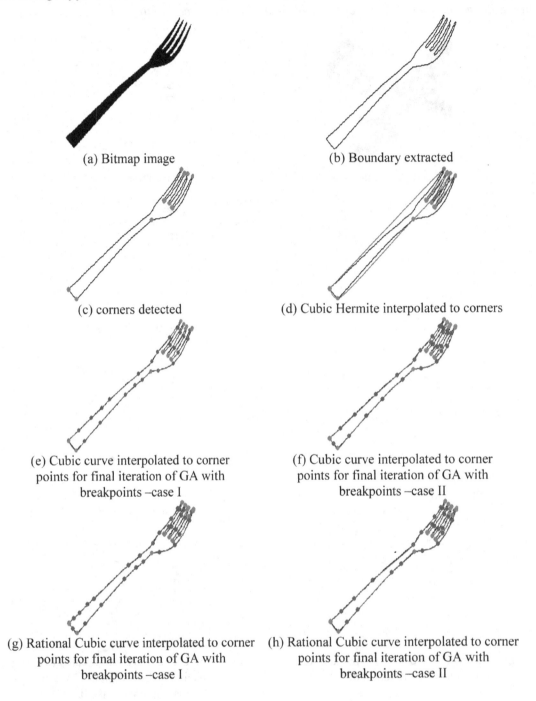

(a) Bitmap image

(b) Boundary extracted

(c) corners detected

(d) Cubic Hermite interpolated to corners

(e) Cubic curve interpolated to corner
points for final iteration of GA with
breakpoints –case I

(f) Cubic curve interpolated to corner
points for final iteration of GA with
breakpoints –case II

(g) Rational Cubic curve interpolated to corner
points for final iteration of GA with
breakpoints –case I

(h) Rational Cubic curve interpolated to corner
points for final iteration of GA with
breakpoints –case II

Figure 10. Image of fish with detected corner points and fitted cubic curve

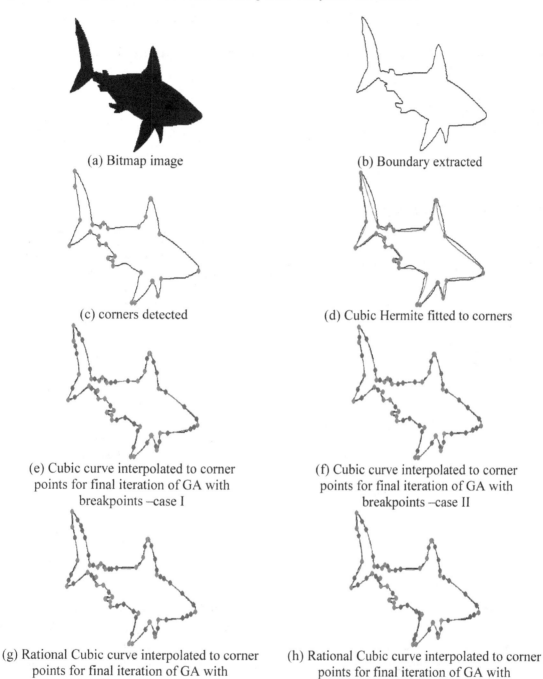

(a) Bitmap image

(b) Boundary extracted

(c) corners detected

(d) Cubic Hermite fitted to corners

(e) Cubic curve interpolated to corner points for final iteration of GA with breakpoints –case I

(f) Cubic curve interpolated to corner points for final iteration of GA with breakpoints –case II

(g) Rational Cubic curve interpolated to corner points for final iteration of GA with breakpoints –case I

(h) Rational Cubic curve interpolated to corner points for final iteration of GA with breakpoints –case II

Table 1. Details of digital contours and corner points

Image	Name	# of contours	# of contour points	# of initial corner points
	Fork.bmp	1	673	15
	Plane.bmp	3	915+36+54	28
	Fish.bmp	1	975	32

Table 2. Number of intermediate points using GA

Image Name	# of contours	# of boundary Points	# of initial corner points	# of intermediate points for different splines with threshold value 3 using GA in final fitted curve			
				Cubic spline		Rational cubic spline	
				Case1	Case2	Case1	Case2
Fork	1	673	15	31	28	28	24
Plane	3	915+36+54	28	34	32	42	38
Fish	1	976	31	32	28	38	35

Table 3. Number of iterations and time ellapsed to achieve final fitted curve using GA

Image Name	Number of iterations to achieve final fitted curve and time elapsed for GA							
	Cubic spline				Rational cubic spline			
	Case I		Case II		Case I		Case II	
	Iteration	Time(sec)	Iteration	Time(sec)	Iteration	Time(sec)	Iteration	Time(sec)
Fork	6	1.45	6	1.50	5	9.34	5	9.45
Plane	5	1.60	4	1.33	5	13.60	5	14.11
Fish	5	1.62	4	1.59	5	14.94	5	15.24

DEMONSTRATION

Curve fitting scheme, proposed above, has been implemented on different images. Flowchart for proposed algorithm is given in Figure 18. In Figure 8 ((a) represents original image, (b) shows outline of the image, (c) demonstrates corner points (d), (e) and (f) give fitted outline for final iterations for threshold 3 using cubic spline, case I and II respectively and (g) and (h) portray final iterations

for threshold 3 using rational cubic spline, case I and II respectively along with Genetic Algorithms, together with corner points and intermediate points). Figures 9 and 10 can also be described in similar fashion.

Figures 11-15 show behaviors of fitness function for the image of fish on running GA again and again. It can be observed in Figure 11 that minimum value of cost function is achieved after iteration 20, whereas Figure 12 and Figure 13 in-

Figure 11. Graph of fitness function

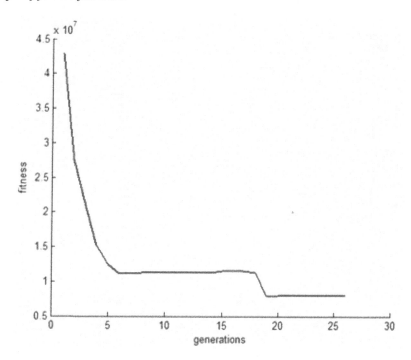

Figure 12. Behavior of fitness function

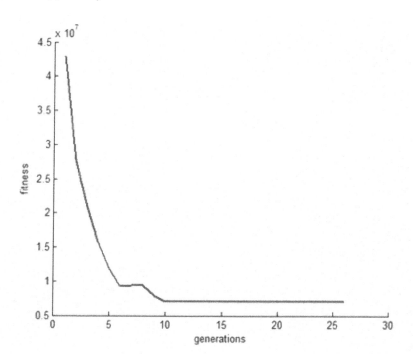

Figure 13. Fitness function for different iterations

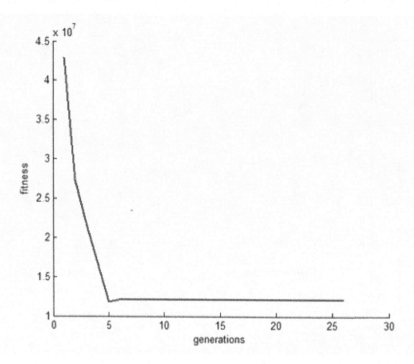

Figure 14. Mix behavior of fitness function

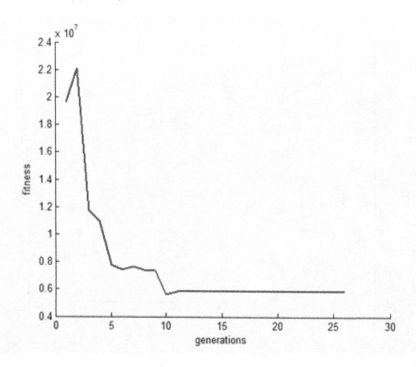

Figure 15. Increasing and decreasing fitness function

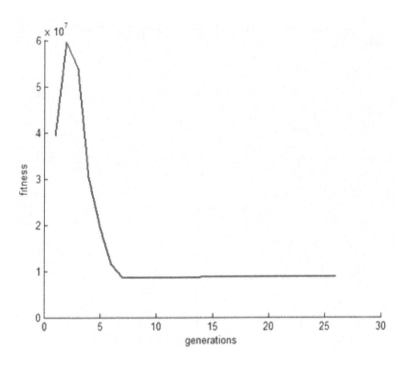

dicate that minimum fitness function is obtained at iteration 10 and iteration 5 respectively. While Figure 14 and Figure 15 depict a bit different behavior as in these cases initially fitness function increases and then it starts decreasing.

In Figure 16, stopping criteria followed to run GA is given and in Figure 17 best (^), worst (o) and mean (*) values of objective functions are shown in each iteration for the image of fish.

Figure 16. Stopping crieteria met by GA in %

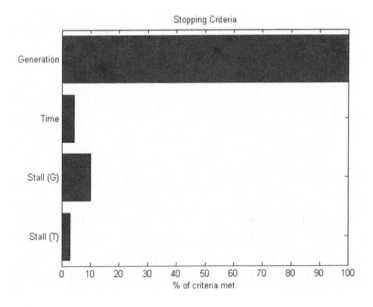

Figure 17. Best, worst and mean scores in different iterations

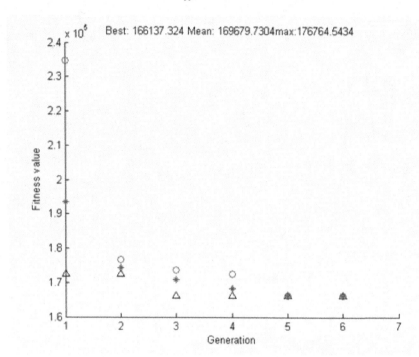

Figure 18. Outline of proposed algorithm

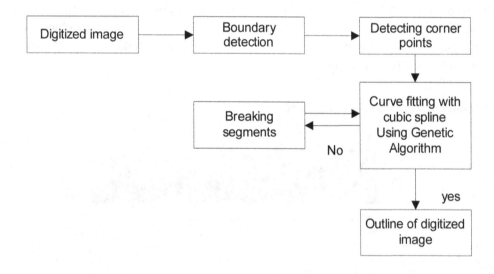

CONCLUSION

In this paper a scheme is presented which vectorizes the generic shapes. Cubic spline and rational cubic spline functions are used for curve fitting and a soft computing technique genetic algorithm is used to find optimal values of the parameters in the description of the spline functions. The method proposed starts with initial random population of parameters and find those values of the parameters which can assure best optimal curve to the data extracted by bitmap images. The scheme presented is automatic and no human intercession is required. It also ensures computational efficiency as far as curve fitting is concerned.

Finally, from Table 2 and Table 3 it may be concluded that, cubic spline functions give relatively better results numerically and graphically than rational cubic spline functions.

REFERENCES

Avrahami, G., & Pratt, V. (1991). Sub-pixel edge detection in character digitization. In *Proceedings of International Conference on Raster Imaging and Digital Typography II*. Cambridge University Press.

Beus, H. L., & Tiu, S. S. H. (1987). An improved corner detection algorithm based on chain coded plane curves. *Pattern Recognition*, *20*, 291–296. doi:10.1016/0031-3203(87)90004-5

Chetrikov, D., & Zsabo, S. (1999). A simple and efficient algorithm for detection of high curvature points in planar curves. *Electronic Publishing*, *6*(3), 195–198.

Freeman, H., & Davis, L. S. (1977). A Corner finding algorithm for chain-coded curves. *IEEE Transactions on Computers*, *26*, 297–303. doi:10.1109/TC.1977.1674825

Goldberg, D. E. (1989). Genetic algorithms in search. In *Optimization and Machine Learning*. Addison-Wesley.

Harada, T., Yoshimoto, F., & Aoyama, Y. (2000). Data fitting using a genetic algorithm with real number genes. In *Proceedings of the IASTED International Conference on Computer Graphics and Imaging*, (pp. 131-138). IASTED.

Horng, J. H. (2003). An adaptive smooting approach for fitting digital planar curves with line segments and circular arcs. *Pattern Recognition*, *24*(1-3), 565–577. doi:10.1016/S0167-8655(02)00277-5

Hou, Z. J., & Wei, G. W. (2002). A new approach to edge detection. *Pattern Recognition*, *35*(7), 1559–1570. doi:10.1016/S0031-3203(01)00147-9

Hu, W.-C. (2005). Multiprimitive segmentation based on meaningful breakpoints for fitting digital planar curves with line segments and conic arcs. *Image and Vision Computing*, *23*(9), 783–789. doi:10.1016/j.imavis.2005.05.004

Jüttler, B., & Felis, A. (2002). Least square fitting of algebraic spline surfaces. *Advances in Computational Mathematics*, *17*, 135–152. doi:10.1023/A:1015200504295

Jyoti, M., Ratna, D., & Sainarayanan, G. (2011). Harris operator corner detection using sliding window method. *International Journal of Computers and Applications*, *22*(1), 28–37. doi:10.5120/2546-3489

Kano, H., Nakata, H., & Martin, C. F. (2005). Optimal curve fitting and smoothing using normalized uniform B-splines: A tool for studying complex systems. *Applied Mathematics and Computation*, *169*(1), 96–128. doi:10.1016/j.amc.2004.10.034

Kirkpatrick, S., Gelatt, C. D. Jr, & Vecchi, M. P. (1983). Optimization by simulated annealing. *Science*, *220*(4598), 671–680. doi:10.1126/science.220.4598.671 PMID:17813860

Lavoue, G., Dupont, F., & Baskurt, A. (2005). A new subdivision based approach for piecewise smooth approximation of 3D polygonal curves. *Pattern Recognition*, *38*(8), 1139–1151. doi:10.1016/j.patcog.2005.02.002

Moriyama, M., Yoshimoto, F., & Harada, T. (1998). A method of plane data fitting with a genetic algorithm. In *Proceeding of the IASTED International Conference on Computer Graphics and Imaging*. IASTED.

Morse, B. S., Yoo, T. S., Chen, D. T., Rheingans, P., & Subramanian, K. R. (2001). Interpolating implicit surfaces from scattered surface data using compactly supported radial basis functions. In *Proceedings of Conference on Shape Modeling and Applications*, (pp. 89-98). IEEE.

Sarfraz, M. (2004). Some algorithms for curve design and automatic outline capturing of images. *International Journal of Image and Graphics*, 4(2), 301–324. doi:10.1142/S0219467804001427

Sarfraz, M. (2006). Computer-Aided reverse engineering using simulated evolution on NURBS. *International Journal of Virtual and Physical Prototyping*, 1(4), 243–257. doi:10.1080/17452750601130492

Sarfraz, M. (2010). Vectorizing outlines of generic shapes by cubic spline using simulated annealing. *International Journal of Computer Mathematics*, 87(8), 1736–1751. doi:10.1080/00207160802452519

Sarfraz, M., Hussain, M. Z., & Chaudary, F. S. (2005). Shape preserving cubic spline for data visualization. *Computer Graphics and CAD/CAM*, 1(6), 185-193.

Sarfraz, M., & Khan, M. A. (2004). An automatic algorithm for approximating boundary of bitmap characters. *Future Generation Computer Systems*, 20(8), 1327–1336. doi:10.1016/j.future.2004.05.024

Sarfraz, M., & Rasheed, A. (2007). A randomized knot insertion algorithm for outline capture of planar images using cubic spline. In *Proceedings of The 22th ACM Symposium on Applied Computing* (ACM SAC-07), (pp. 71 – 75). ACM.

Sarfraz, M., & Raza, A. (2002). Visualization of Data using Genetic Algorithm. In *Soft Computing and Industry: Recent Applications*. Springer. doi:10.1007/978-1-4471-0123-9_45

Yang, H., Wang, W., & Sun, J. (2004). Control point adjustment for B-spline curve approximation. *Computer Aided Design*, 36(7), 639–652. doi:10.1016/S0010-4485(03)00140-4

Yang, X. (2004). Curve fitting and fairing using conic splines. *Computer Aided Design*, 36(5), 461–472. doi:10.1016/S0010-4485(03)00119-2

Yang, X. N., & Wang, G. Z. (2001). Planar point set fairing and fitting by arc splines. *Computer Aided Design*, 33(1), 35–43. doi:10.1016/S0010-4485(00)00059-2

Yang, Z., Deng, J., & Chen, F. (2005). Fitting unorganized point clouds with active implicit B-spline curves. *The Visual Computer*, 21(1), 831–839. doi:10.1007/s00371-005-0340-0

KEY TERMS AND DEFINITIONS

Bitmap Image: An image represented as a two dimensional array of brightness values for pixels.

Evolution: A process of growth in which something passes by different stages.

Optimization Problem: In optimization problem one seeks values of the variables that lead to an optimal value of the function that is to be optimized.

Parameter: A constant in the equation of a curve that can be varied to yield a family of similar curves.

Simulation: The act of imitating.

Related References

To continue our tradition of advancing information science and technology research, we have compiled a list of recommended IGI Global readings. These references will provide additional information and guidance to further enrich your knowledge and assist you with your own research and future publications.

Adam, C., Gaudou, B., Login, D., & Lorini, E. (2011). Logical Modeling of Emotions for Ambient Intelligence. In N. Chong, & F. Mastrogiovanni (Eds.), *Handbook of Research on Ambient Intelligence and Smart Environments: Trends and Perspectives* (pp. 108–127). Hershey, PA: Information Science Reference. doi:10.4018/978-1-61692-857-5.ch007

Adeyeye, M. (2013). Provisioning Converged Applications and Services via the Cloud. In D. Kanellopoulos (Ed.), *Intelligent Multimedia Technologies for Networking Applications: Techniques and Tools* (pp. 248–269). Hershey, PA: Information Science Reference.

Albertos, P., Sala, A., & Ramírez, M. (2011). Perspectives of Multivariable Fuzzy Control. In J. Jozefczyk, & D. Orski (Eds.), *Knowledge-Based Intelligent System Advancements: Systemic and Cybernetic Approaches* (pp. 283–314). Hershey, PA: Information Science Reference.

Alexandre de França, J., Stemmer, M. R., França, M. B., & Palácios, R. H. (2012). Camera Calibration with 1D Objects. In V. Mago, & N. Bhatia (Eds.), *Cross-Disciplinary Applications of Artificial Intelligence and Pattern Recognition: Advancing Technologies* (pp. 65–85). Hershey, PA: Information Science Reference.

Alharbi, H. M., Kwan, P., Jayawardena, A., & Sajeev, A. S. (2013). Fuzzy Image Segmentation for Mass Detection in Digital Mammography: Recent Advances and Techniques. In I. Management Association (Ed.), Image Processing: Concepts, Methodologies, Tools, and Applications (pp. 769–792). Hershey, PA: Information Science Reference. doi: doi:10.4018/978-1-4666-3994-2.ch040

Almomani, R., & Dong, M. (2013). Building a Multiple Object Tracking System with Occlusion Handling in Surveillance Videos. In I. Management Association (Ed.), Image Processing: Concepts, Methodologies, Tools, and Applications (pp. 1051-1063). Hershey, PA: Information Science Reference. doi: doi:10.4018/978-1-4666-3994-2.ch053

Almustafa, M. M., & Alkhaldi, D. (2014). Business Intelligence and Agile Methodology for Risk Management in Knowledge-Based Organizations. In I. Management Association (Ed.), Software Design and Development: Concepts, Methodologies, Tools, and Applications (pp. 1710-1735). Hershey, PA: Information Science Reference. doi: doi:10.4018/978-1-4666-4301-7

Alonso, E., & Mondragón, E. (2011). Computational Models of Learning and Beyond: Symmetries of Associative Learning. In E. Alonso, & E. Mondragón (Eds.), *Computational Neuroscience for Advancing Artificial Intelligence: Models, Methods and Applications* (pp. 316–332). Hershey, PA: Medical Information Science Reference.

Alsmadi, I. (2014). How Much Automation can be done in Testing? In I. Management Association (Ed.), Software Design and Development: Concepts, Methodologies, Tools, and Applications (pp. 1828-1849). Hershey, PA: Information Science Reference. doi: doi:10.4018/978-1-4666-4301-7.ch087

Amirante, A., Castaldi, T., Miniero, L., & Romano, S. P. (2013). Protocol Interactions among User Agents, Application Servers, and Media Servers: Standardization Efforts and Open Issues. In D. Kanellopoulos (Ed.), *Intelligent Multimedia Technologies for Networking Applications: Techniques and Tools* (pp. 48–63). Hershey, PA: Information Science Reference.

Ane, B. K., & Roller, D. (2013). Adaptive Intelligent Systems for Recognition of Cancerous Cervical Cells Based on 2D Cervical Cytological Digital Images. In I. Management Association (Ed.), Image Processing: Concepts, Methodologies, Tools, and Applications (pp. 793-831). Hershey, PA: Information Science Reference. doi: doi:10.4018/978-1-4666-3994-2.ch041

Angelopoulos, N., Hadjiprocopis, A., & Walkinshaw, M. D. (2011). Learning Binding Affinity from Augmented High Throughput Screening Data. In H. Lodhi, & Y. Yamanishi (Eds.), *Chemoinformatics and Advanced Machine Learning Perspectives: Complex Computational Methods and Collaborative Techniques* (pp. 212–234). Hershey, PA: Medical Information Science Reference.

Antúnez, E., Haxhimusa, Y., Marfil, R., Kropatsch, W. G., & Bandera, A. (2013). Artificial Visual Attention Using Combinatorial Pyramids. In I. Management Association (Ed.), Image Processing: Concepts, Methodologies, Tools, and Applications (pp. 455-472). Hershey, PA: Information Science Reference. doi: doi:10.4018/978-1-4666-3994-2.ch023

Aranda, S. E., Sentí, E. E., Díaz, E. D., Díaz, A. P., Soto, M. D., Soto, A. T., & Ortiz Zezzatti, C. A. (2012). An Evolutionary Algorithm for Graph Drawing with a Multiobjective Approach. In C. Ortiz Zezzatti, C. Chira, A. Hernandez, & M. Basurto (Eds.), *Logistics Management and Optimization through Hybrid Artificial Intelligence Systems* (pp. 113–140). Hershey, PA: Information Science Reference. doi:10.4018/978-1-4666-0297-7.ch005

Arjunan, S., Kumar, D. K., Weghorn, H., & Naik, G. (2012). Facial Muscle Activity Patterns for Recognition of Utterances in Native and Foreign Language: Testing for its Reliability and Flexibility. In V. Mago, & N. Bhatia (Eds.), *Cross-Disciplinary Applications of Artificial Intelligence and Pattern Recognition: Advancing Technologies* (pp. 212–231). Hershey, PA: Information Science Reference.

Arsénio, A. M. (2013). Developmental Language Learning from Human/Humanoid Robot Social Interactions: An Embodied and Situated Approach. In L. Gogate, & G. Hollich (Eds.), *Theoretical and Computational Models of Word Learning: Trends in Psychology and Artificial Intelligence* (pp. 197–223). Hershey, PA: Information Science Reference. doi:10.4018/978-1-4666-2973-8.ch009

Arsenio, A. M. (2013). Intelligent Approaches for Adaptation and Distribution of Personalized Multimedia Content. In D. Kanellopoulos (Ed.), *Intelligent Multimedia Technologies for Networking Applications: Techniques and Tools* (pp. 197–224). Hershey, PA: Information Science Reference.

Asghari-Oskoei, M., & Hu, H. (2011). Using Myoelectric Signals to Manipulate Assisting Robots and Rehabilitation Devices. In E. Alonso, & E. Mondragón (Eds.), *Computational Neuroscience for Advancing Artificial Intelligence: Models, Methods and Applications* (pp. 166–185). Hershey, PA: Medical Information Science Reference.

Azar, A. T. (2013). Statistical Analysis for Radiologists' Interpretations Variability in Mammograms. In I. Management Association (Ed.), Image Processing: Concepts, Methodologies, Tools, and Applications (pp. 753-768). Hershey, PA: Information Science Reference. doi: doi:10.4018/978-1-4666-3994-2.ch039

Babu, T. R., Danivas, C. S., & Subrahmanya, S. (2012). Adaptive Face Recognition of Partially Visible Faces. In V. Mago, & N. Bhatia (Eds.), *Cross-Disciplinary Applications of Artificial Intelligence and Pattern Recognition: Advancing Technologies* (pp. 194–211). Hershey, PA: Information Science Reference.

Bakshi, K., Chandra, S., Konar, A., & Tibarewala, D. (2012). Hand Tremor Prediction and Classification Using Electromyogram Signals to Control Neuro-Motor Instability. In V. Mago, & N. Bhatia (Eds.), *Cross-Disciplinary Applications of Artificial Intelligence and Pattern Recognition: Advancing Technologies* (pp. 651–673). Hershey, PA: Information Science Reference.

Balasundaram, P. (2012). Effective Open-Source Performance Analysis Tools. In J. Leng, & W. Sharrock (Eds.), *Handbook of Research on Computational Science and Engineering: Theory and Practice* (pp. 98–118). Hershey, PA: Engineering Science Reference.

Barrass, I., & Leng, J. (2012). Improving Computational Models and Practices: Scenario Testing and Forecasting the Spread of Infectious Disease. In J. Leng, & W. Sharrock (Eds.), *Handbook of Research on Computational Science and Engineering: Theory and Practice* (pp. 432–455). Hershey, PA: Engineering Science Reference.

Benitez, D. (2012). High-Performance Customizable Computing. In J. Leng, & W. Sharrock (Eds.), *Handbook of Research on Computational Science and Engineering: Theory and Practice* (pp. 48–77). Hershey, PA: Engineering Science Reference.

Beynier, A., & Mouaddib, A. (2012). Applications of DEC-MDPs in Multi-Robot Systems. In L. Sucar, E. Morales, & J. Hoey (Eds.), *Decision Theory Models for Applications in Artificial Intelligence: Concepts and Solutions* (pp. 361–384). Hershey, PA: Information Science Reference.

Bhattacharyya, S. (2012). Neural Networks: Evolution, Topologies, Learning Algorithms and Applications. In V. Mago, & N. Bhatia (Eds.), *Cross-Disciplinary Applications of Artificial Intelligence and Pattern Recognition: Advancing Technologies* (pp. 450–498). Hershey, PA: Information Science Reference.

Biancolini, M. E. (2012). Mesh Morphing and Smoothing by Means of Radial Basis Functions (RBF): A Practical Example Using Fluent and RBF Morph. In J. Leng, & W. Sharrock (Eds.), *Handbook of Research on Computational Science and Engineering: Theory and Practice* (pp. 347–380). Hershey, PA: Engineering Science Reference.

Bichot, C. (2013). Unsupervised and Supervised Image Segmentation Using Graph Partitioning. In I. Management Association (Ed.), *Image Processing: Concepts, Methodologies, Tools, and Applications* (pp. 322-344). Hershey, PA: Information Science Reference. doi: doi:10.4018/978-1-4666-3994-2.ch018

Bisset, D. (2011). Designing Useful Robots: Is Neural Computation the Answer? In E. Alonso, & E. Mondragón (Eds.), *Computational Neuroscience for Advancing Artificial Intelligence: Models, Methods and Applications* (pp. 250–269). Hershey, PA: Medical Information Science Reference.

Blasco, J., Aleixos, N., Cubero, S., Albert, F., Lorente, D., & Gómez-Sanchis, J. (2013). In-Line Sorting of Processed Fruit Using Computer Vision: Application to the Inspection of Satsuma Segments and Pomegranate Arils. In I. Management Association (Ed.), *Image Processing: Concepts, Methodologies, Tools, and Applications* (pp. 874-895). Hershey, PA: Information Science Reference. doi: doi:10.4018/978-1-4666-3994-2.ch044

Bortfeld, H., Shaw, K., & Depowski, N. (2013). The Miracle Year: From Basic Structure to Social Communication. In L. Gogate, & G. Hollich (Eds.), *Theoretical and Computational Models of Word Learning: Trends in Psychology and Artificial Intelligence* (pp. 153–171). Hershey, PA: Information Science Reference. doi:10.4018/978-1-4666-2973-8.ch007

Boudreaux, A., & Primeaux, B. (2014). Modular Game Engine Design. In I. Management Association (Ed.), *Software Design and Development: Concepts, Methodologies, Tools, and Applications* (pp. 1179-1199). Hershey, PA: Information Science Reference. doi: doi:10.4018/978-1-4666-4301-7.ch058

Bouillet, E., Feblowitz, M., Liu, Z., Ranganathan, A., & Riabov, A. (2012). Semantic Matching, Propagation and Transformation for Composition in Component-Based Systems. In Y. Wang (Ed.), *Software and Intelligent Sciences: New Transdisciplinary Findings* (pp. 122–141). Hershey, PA: Information Science Reference. doi:10.4018/978-1-4666-0261-8.ch008

Brito, P. H., Bittencourt, I. I., Machado, A. P., Costa, E., Holanda, O., Ferreira, R., & Ribeiro, T. (2014). A Systematic Approach for Designing Educational Recommender Systems. In I. Management Association (Ed.), Software Design and Development: Concepts, Methodologies, Tools, and Applications (pp. 1264-1288). Hershey, PA: Information Science Reference. doi: doi:10.4018/978-1-4666-4301-7.ch062

Bunke, H., & Riesen, K. (2013). Graph Embedding Using Dissimilarities with Applications in Classification. In I. Management Association (Ed.), Image Processing: Concepts, Methodologies, Tools, and Applications (pp. 363-380). Hershey, PA: Information Science Reference. doi: doi:10.4018/978-1-4666-3994-2.ch020

Casali, A., Gerling, V., Deco, C., & Bender, C. (2012). A Recommender System for Learning Objects Personalized Retrieval. In O. Santos, & J. Boticario (Eds.), *Educational Recommender Systems and Technologies: Practices and Challenges* (pp. 182–210). Hershey, PA: Information Science Reference.

Cederborg, T., & Oudeyer, P. (2013). Learning Words by Imitating. In L. Gogate, & G. Hollich (Eds.), *Theoretical and Computational Models of Word Learning: Trends in Psychology and Artificial Intelligence* (pp. 296–326). Hershey, PA: Information Science Reference. doi:10.4018/978-1-4666-2973-8.ch013

Chen, P., Ding, W., & Ding, C. (2012). A Lexical Knowledge Representation Model for Natural Language Understanding. In Y. Wang (Ed.), *Software and Intelligent Sciences: New Transdisciplinary Findings* (pp. 193–210). Hershey, PA: Information Science Reference. doi:10.4018/978-1-4666-0261-8.ch012

Chen, S., & Liu, C. (2012). Eye Detection Using Color, Haar Features, and Efficient Support Vector Machine. In V. Mago, & N. Bhatia (Eds.), *Cross-Disciplinary Applications of Artificial Intelligence and Pattern Recognition: Advancing Technologies* (pp. 286–309). Hershey, PA: Information Science Reference.

Chen, S., Tai, C., Wang, T., & Wang, S. G. (2011). Social Simulation with Both Human Agents and Software Agents: An Investigation into the Impact of Cognitive Capacity on Their Learning Behavior. In S. Chen, Y. Kambayashi, & H. Sato (Eds.), *Multi-Agent Applications with Evolutionary Computation and Biologically Inspired Technologies: Intelligent Techniques for Ubiquity and Optimization* (pp. 95–117). Hershey, PA: Medical Information Science Reference.

Chen, S., & Wang, S. G. (2011). Neuroeconomics: A Viewpoint from Agent-Based Computational Economics. In S. Chen, Y. Kambayashi, & H. Sato (Eds.), *Multi-Agent Applications with Evolutionary Computation and Biologically Inspired Technologies: Intelligent Techniques for Ubiquity and Optimization* (pp. 35–49). Hershey, PA: Medical Information Science Reference.

Chen, S., Zeng, R., Yu, T., & Wang, S. G. (2011). Bounded Rationality and Market Micro-Behaviors: Case Studies Based on Agent-Based Double Auction Markets. In S. Chen, Y. Kambayashi, & H. Sato (Eds.), *Multi-Agent Applications with Evolutionary Computation and Biologically Inspired Technologies: Intelligent Techniques for Ubiquity and Optimization* (pp. 78–94). Hershey, PA: Medical Information Science Reference. doi:10.4018/978-1-61350-456-7.ch518

Chesi, G., & Hung, Y. S. (2012). Certain and Uncertain Triangulation in Multiple Camera Vision Systems via LMIs. In V. Mago, & N. Bhatia (Eds.), *Cross-Disciplinary Applications of Artificial Intelligence and Pattern Recognition: Advancing Technologies* (pp. 53–64). Hershey, PA: Information Science Reference.

Chiprianov, V., Kermarrec, Y., & Rouvrais, S. (2014). Integrating DSLs into a Software Engineering Process: Application to Collaborative Construction of Telecom Services. In I. Management Association (Ed.), *Software Design and Development: Concepts, Methodologies, Tools, and Applications* (pp. 570-595). Hershey, PA: Information Science Reference. doi: doi:10.4018/978-1-4666-4301-7.ch028

Chira, C., & Gog, A. (2012). Recombination Operators in Permutation-Based Evolutionary Algorithms for the Travelling Salesman Problem. In C. Ortiz Zezzatti, C. Chira, A. Hernandez, & M. Basurto (Eds.), *Logistics Management and Optimization through Hybrid Artificial Intelligence Systems* (pp. 268–285). Hershey, PA: Information Science Reference. doi:10.4018/978-1-4666-0297-7.ch010

Chiu, M. M., & Chen, G. (2014). Statistical Discourse Analysis: Testing Educational Hypotheses with Large Datasets of Electronic Discourse. In H. Lim, & F. Sudweeks (Eds.), *Innovative Methods and Technologies for Electronic Discourse Analysis* (pp. 285–303). Hershey, PA: Information Science Reference.

Cho, S., Teoh, T., & Nguwi, Y. (2011). Facial Expression Analysis by Machine Learning. In Y. Zhang (Ed.), *Advances in Face Image Analysis: Techniques and Technologies* (pp. 239–258). Hershey, PA: Medical Information Science Reference.

Chohra, A., Kanaoui, N., Amarger, V., & Madani, K. (2011). Hybrid Intelligent Diagnosis Approach Based On Neural Pattern Recognition and Fuzzy Decision-Making. In J. Jozefczyk, & D. Orski (Eds.), *Knowledge-Based Intelligent System Advancements: Systemic and Cybernetic Approaches* (pp. 372–394). Hershey, PA: Information Science Reference. doi:10.4018/978-1-60960-818-7.ch307

Cirillo, M., Pecora, F., & Saffiotti, A. (2011). Proactive Assistance in Ecologies of Physically Embedded Intelligent Systems: A Constraint-Based Approach. In N. Chong, & F. Mastrogiovanni (Eds.), *Handbook of Research on Ambient Intelligence and Smart Environments: Trends and Perspectives* (pp. 534–557). Hershey, PA: Information Science Reference. doi:10.4018/978-1-61692-857-5.ch025

Corona, E., & Sucar, L. E. (2012). Task Coordination for Service Robots Based on Multiple Markov Decision Processes. In L. Sucar, E. Morales, & J. Hoey (Eds.), *Decision Theory Models for Applications in Artificial Intelligence: Concepts and Solutions* (pp. 343–360). Hershey, PA: Information Science Reference.

Costen, F., & Balasko, A. (2012). Opportunities and Challenges in Porting a Parallel Code from a Tightly-Coupled System to the Distributed EU Grid, Enabling Grids for E-sciencE. In J. Leng, & W. Sharrock (Eds.), *Handbook of Research on Computational Science and Engineering: Theory and Practice* (pp. 197–217). Hershey, PA: Engineering Science Reference.

Cowell, R. A., Bussey, T. J., & Saksida, L. M. (2011). Using Computational Modelling to Understand Cognition in the Ventral Visual-Perirhinal Pathway. In E. Alonso, & E. Mondragón (Eds.), *Computational Neuroscience for Advancing Artificial Intelligence: Models, Methods and Applications* (pp. 15–45). Hershey, PA: Medical Information Science Reference.

Cruz-Chávez, M. A., Rodríguez-León, A., Rivera-López, R., Juárez-Pérez, F., Peralta-Abarca, C., & Martínez-Oropeza, A. (2012). Grid Platform Applied to the Vehicle Routing Problem with Time Windows for the Distribution of Products. In C. Ortiz Zezzatti, C. Chira, A. Hernandez, & M. Basurto (Eds.), *Logistics Management and Optimization through Hybrid Artificial Intelligence Systems* (pp. 52–81). Hershey, PA: Information Science Reference. doi:10.4018/978-1-4666-0297-7.ch003

Csapo, A., Resko, B., Lind, M., Baranyi, P., & Tikk, D. (2012). A Generic Framework for Feature Representations in Image Categorization Tasks. In Y. Wang (Ed.), *Software and Intelligent Sciences: New Transdisciplinary Findings* (pp. 491–512). Hershey, PA: Information Science Reference. doi:10.4018/978-1-4666-0261-8.ch029

Cucchiarini, C., & Strik, H. (2014). Second Language Learners' Spoken Discourse: Practice and Corrective Feedback through Automatic Speech Recognition. In H. Lim, & F. Sudweeks (Eds.), *Innovative Methods and Technologies for Electronic Discourse Analysis* (pp. 169–189). Hershey, PA: Information Science Reference.

Cuevas, E., Zaldivar, D., & Perez-Cisneros, M. (2012). Corner Detection Using Fuzzy Principles. In V. Mago, & N. Bhatia (Eds.), *Cross-Disciplinary Applications of Artificial Intelligence and Pattern Recognition: Advancing Technologies* (pp. 270–285). Hershey, PA: Information Science Reference.

Da Silva, M. P., & Courboulay, V. (2013). Implementation and Evaluation of a Computational Model of Attention for Computer Vision. In I. Management Association (Ed.), Image Processing: Concepts, Methodologies, Tools, and Applications (pp. 422-454). Hershey, PA: Information Science Reference. doi: doi:10.4018/978-1-4666-3994-2.ch022

Daradoumis, T., & Lafuente, M. M. (2014). Studying the Suitability of Discourse Analysis Methods for Emotion Detection and Interpretation in Computer-Mediated Educational Discourse. In H. Lim, & F. Sudweeks (Eds.), *Innovative Methods and Technologies for Electronic Discourse Analysis* (pp. 119–143). Hershey, PA: Information Science Reference.

Daskalaki, A., Giokas, K., & Koutsouris, D. (2013). Surgeon Assistive Augmented Reality Model with the use of Endoscopic Camera for Line of Vision Calculation. In I. Management Association (Ed.), Image Processing: Concepts, Methodologies, Tools, and Applications (pp. 658-674). Hershey, PA: Information Science Reference. doi: doi:10.4018/978-1-4666-3994-2.ch034

Davis, B., & Mason, P. (2014). Positioning Goes to Work: Computer-Aided Identification of Stance Shifts and Semantic Themes in Electronic Discourse Analysis. In H. Lim, & F. Sudweeks (Eds.), *Innovative Methods and Technologies for Electronic Discourse Analysis* (pp. 394–413). Hershey, PA: Information Science Reference.

Davy-Jow, S. L., Decker, S. J., & Schofield, D. (2013). Virtual Forensic Anthropology: Applications of Advanced Computer Graphics Technology to the Identification of Human Remains. In I. Management Association (Ed.), Image Processing: Concepts, Methodologies, Tools, and Applications (pp. 832-849). Hershey, PA: Information Science Reference. doi: doi:10.4018/978-1-4666-3994-2.ch042

Defourny, B., Ernst, D., & Wehenkel, L. (2012). Multistage Stochastic Programming: A Scenario Tree Based Approach to Planning under Uncertainty. In L. Sucar, E. Morales, & J. Hoey (Eds.), *Decision Theory Models for Applications in Artificial Intelligence: Concepts and Solutions* (pp. 97–143). Hershey, PA: Information Science Reference.

de Mingo, L. F., Gómez, N., Arroyo, F., & Castellanos, J. (2012). Hierarchical Function Approximation with a Neural Network Model. In Y. Wang (Ed.), *Software and Intelligent Sciences: New Transdisciplinary Findings* (pp. 466–479). Hershey, PA: Information Science Reference. doi:10.4018/978-1-4666-0261-8.ch027

Deplano, M., & Ruffo, G. (2013). GWAP as a Tool to Analyze, Design, and Test Geo-Social Systems. In D. Kanellopoulos (Ed.), *Intelligent Multimedia Technologies for Networking Applications: Techniques and Tools* (pp. 380–407). Hershey, PA: Information Science Reference.

Devyatkov, V., & Alfimtsev, A. (2013). Human-Computer Interaction in Games Using Computer Vision Techniques. In I. Management Association (Ed.), Image Processing: Concepts, Methodologies, Tools, and Applications (pp. 1210-1231). Hershey, PA: Information Science Reference. doi: doi:10.4018/978-1-4666-3994-2.ch061

Díez, F. J., & van Gerven, M. A. (2012). Dynamic LIMIDS. In L. Sucar, E. Morales, & J. Hoey (Eds.), *Decision Theory Models for Applications in Artificial Intelligence: Concepts and Solutions* (pp. 164–189). Hershey, PA: Information Science Reference.

Dobrescu, R., & Popescu, D. (2013). Image Processing Applications Based on Texture and Fractal Analysis. In I. Management Association (Ed.), Image Processing: Concepts, Methodologies, Tools, and Applications (pp. 235-259). Hershey, PA: Information Science Reference. doi: doi:10.4018/978-1-4666-3994-2.ch014

Dobrescu, R., & Popescu, D. (2013). Real-Time Primary Image Processing. In I. Management Association (Ed.), Image Processing: Concepts, Methodologies, Tools, and Applications (pp. 33-53). Hershey, PA: Information Science Reference. doi: doi:10.4018/978-1-4666-3994-2.ch003

Dodson, C. T. (2012). Some Illustrations of Information Geometry in Biology and Physics. In J. Leng, & W. Sharrock (Eds.), *Handbook of Research on Computational Science and Engineering: Theory and Practice* (pp. 287–315). Hershey, PA: Engineering Science Reference.

Dornaika, F., Dornaika, F., Raducanu, B., & Raducanu, B. (2011). Subtle Facial Expression Recognition in Still Images and Videos. In Y. Zhang (Ed.), *Advances in Face Image Analysis: Techniques and Technologies* (pp. 259–278). Hershey, PA: Medical Information Science Reference.

Douglas, I. (2012). Medical Critiquing Systems. In R. Magdalena-Benedito, E. Soria-Olivas, J. Martínez, J. Gómez-Sanchis, & A. Serrano-López (Eds.), *Medical Applications of Intelligent Data Analysis: Research Advancements* (pp. 209–222). Hershey, PA: Information Science Reference. doi:10.4018/978-1-4666-1803-9.ch014

Drigas, A., Kouremenos, D., & Vrettaros, J. (2011). Learning Applications for Disabled People. In P. Ordóñez de Pablos, J. Zhao, & R. Tennyson (Eds.), *Technology Enhanced Learning for People with Disabilities: Approaches and Applications* (pp. 44–57). Hershey, PA: Information Science Reference.

Droege, D. (2013). Image Analysis. In I. Management Association (Ed.), Image Processing: Concepts, Methodologies, Tools, and Applications (pp. 1-14). Hershey, PA: Information Science Reference. doi: doi:10.4018/978-1-4666-3994-2.ch001

Dromzée, C., Laborie, S., & Roose, P. (2013). A Semantic Generic Profile for Multimedia Document Adaptation. In D. Kanellopoulos (Ed.), *Intelligent Multimedia Technologies for Networking Applications: Techniques and Tools* (pp. 225–246). Hershey, PA: Information Science Reference.

Duan, Y. (2012). A Dualism Based Semantics Formalization Mechanism for Model Driven Engineering. In Y. Wang (Ed.), *Software and Intelligent Sciences: New Transdisciplinary Findings* (pp. 211–230). Hershey, PA: Information Science Reference. doi:10.4018/978-1-4666-0261-8.ch013

Dubey, S. R., & Jalal, A. S. (2013). Adapted Approach for Fruit Disease Identification using Images. In I. Management Association (Ed.), Image Processing: Concepts, Methodologies, Tools, and Applications (pp. 1395-1409). Hershey, PA: Information Science Reference. doi: doi:10.4018/978-1-4666-3994-2.ch069

El Sayed, M. S., Nasr, M., & Sultan, T. I. (2013). Enhancing e-Learning Environment with Embedded Recommender Systems. In F. Albadri (Ed.), *Information Systems Applications in the Arab Education Sector* (pp. 234–253). Hershey, PA: Information Science Reference.

Elias, R. (2013). Projective Geometry for 3D Modeling of Objects. In I. Management Association (Ed.), Image Processing: Concepts, Methodologies, Tools, and Applications (pp. 125-144). Hershey, PA: Information Science Reference. doi: doi:10.4018/978-1-4666-3994-2.ch008

El-said, S. A., Hussein, K. F., & Fouad, M. M. (2013). Image Compression Technique for Low Bit Rate Transmission. In I. Management Association (Ed.), Image Processing: Concepts, Methodologies, Tools, and Applications (pp. 1306-1322). Hershey, PA: Information Science Reference. doi: doi:10.4018/978-1-4666-3994-2.ch064

Erfurth, C., & Schau, V. (2011). Software Agents for Human Interaction in Social Networks. In G. Kreuzberger, A. Lunzer, & R. Kaschek (Eds.), *Interdisciplinary Advances in Adaptive and Intelligent Assistant Systems: Concepts, Techniques, Applications, and Use* (pp. 177–198). Hershey, PA: Information Science Reference.

Fang, N., Luo, X., & Xu, W. (2012). Measuring Textual Context Based on Cognitive Principles. In Y. Wang (Ed.), *Software and Intelligent Sciences: New Transdisciplinary Findings* (pp. 169–192). Hershey, PA: Information Science Reference. doi:10.4018/978-1-4666-0261-8.ch011

Fleury, M., Ali, I., Qadri, N., & Ghanbari, M. (2013). Intra-Refresh Techniques for Mobile Video Streaming. In D. Kanellopoulos (Ed.), *Intelligent Multimedia Technologies for Networking Applications: Techniques and Tools* (pp. 102–125). Hershey, PA: Information Science Reference.

Fleury, M., & Al-Jobouri, L. (2013). Techniques and Tools for Adaptive Video Streaming. In D. Kanellopoulos (Ed.), *Intelligent Multimedia Technologies for Networking Applications: Techniques and Tools* (pp. 65–101). Hershey, PA: Information Science Reference.

Fries, T. P. (2014). Reengineering Structured Legacy System Documentation to UML Object-Oriented Artifacts. In I. Management Association (Ed.), Software Design and Development: Concepts, Methodologies, Tools, and Applications (pp. 749-771). Hershey, PA: Information Science Reference. doi: doi:10.4018/978-1-4666-4301-7.ch036

Furtado, V., Melo, A., Coelho, A. L., Menezes, R., & Belchior, M. (2011). Simulating Crime Against Properties Using Swarm Intelligence and Social Networks. In I. Management Association (Ed.), Gaming and Simulations: Concepts, Methodologies, Tools and Applications (pp. 1142-1159). Hershey, PA: Information Science Reference. doi: doi:10.4018/978-1-60960-195-9.ch416

Gallegos, J. C., Aguilera, F. S., Aguilar, J. A., & Villalón, C. J. (2012). Logistics for the Garbage Collection through the use of Ant Colony Algorithms. In C. Ortiz Zezzatti, C. Chira, A. Hernandez, & M. Basurto (Eds.), *Logistics Management and Optimization through Hybrid Artificial Intelligence Systems* (pp. 33–51). Hershey, PA: Information Science Reference. doi:10.4018/978-1-4666-0297-7.ch002

García, G. B., Rojo, M. G., Morales, R. G., Suárez, O. D., & González, J. G. (2011). Grid Architecture and Components in Diagnostic Pathology. In E. Kldiashvili (Ed.), *Grid Technologies for E-Health: Applications for Telemedicine Services and Delivery* (pp. 105–116). Hershey, PA: Medical Information Science Reference.

Gavrilov, A. V. (2012). Hybrid Intelligent Systems in Ubiquitous Computing. In I. Management Association (Ed.), Computer Engineering: Concepts, Methodologies, Tools and Applications (pp. 100-119). Hershey, PA: Engineering Science Reference. doi: doi:10.4018/978-1-61350-456-7.ch107

Gavrilova, M. L. (2012). Adaptive Computation Paradigm in Knowledge Representation: Traditional and Emerging Applications. In Y. Wang (Ed.), *Software and Intelligent Sciences: New Transdisciplinary Findings* (pp. 142–156). Hershey, PA: Information Science Reference. doi:10.4018/978-1-4666-0261-8.ch009

Génova, G., Llorens, J., & Morato, J. (2014). Software Engineering Research: The Need to Strengthen and Broaden the Classical Scientific Method. In I. Management Association (Ed.), Software Design and Development: Concepts, Methodologies, Tools, and Applications (pp. 1639-1658). Hershey, PA: Information Science Reference. doi: doi:10.4018/978-1-4666-4301-7.ch079

Geramifard, O., Xu, J., & Zhou, J. (2013). A Temporal Probabilistic Approach for Continuous Tool Condition Monitoring. In S. Kadry (Ed.), *Diagnostics and Prognostics of Engineering Systems: Methods and Techniques* (pp. 205–228). Hershey, PA: Engineering Science Reference.

Gesquière, G., & Manin, A. (2013). 3D Visualization of Urban Data Based on CityGML with WebGL. In I. Management Association (Ed.), Image Processing: Concepts, Methodologies, Tools, and Applications (pp. 1410-1425). Hershey, PA: Information Science Reference. doi: doi:10.4018/978-1-4666-3994-2.ch070

Girotto, I., & Farber, R. M. (2012). Multi-Threaded Architectures: Evolution, Costs, Opportunities. In J. Leng, & W. Sharrock (Eds.), *Handbook of Research on Computational Science and Engineering: Theory and Practice* (pp. 22–47). Hershey, PA: Engineering Science Reference.

Gogate, L., & Hollich, G. (2013). Timing Matters: Dynamic Interactions Create Sensitive Periods for Word Learning. In L. Gogate, & G. Hollich (Eds.), *Theoretical and Computational Models of Word Learning: Trends in Psychology and Artificial Intelligence* (pp. 28–48). Hershey, PA: Information Science Reference. doi:10.4018/978-1-4666-2973-8.ch002

Goka, M., & Ohkura, K. (2011). Autonomous Specialization in a Multi-Robot System using Evolving Neural Networks. In S. Chen, Y. Kambayashi, & H. Sato (Eds.), *Multi-Agent Applications with Evolutionary Computation and Biologically Inspired Technologies: Intelligent Techniques for Ubiquity and Optimization* (pp. 156–173). Hershey, PA: Medical Information Science Reference.

Gopalakrishnan, V. (2012). Computer Aided Knowledge Discovery in Biomedicine. In I. Management Association (Ed.), Machine Learning: Concepts, Methodologies, Tools and Applications (pp. 1389-1403). Hershey, PA: Information Science Reference. doi: doi:10.4018/978-1-60960-818-7.ch512

Gottschalk, P. (2011). Stages of Information Systems in E-Government for Knowledge Management: The Case of Police Investigations. In V. Weerakkody (Ed.), *Applied Technology Integration in Governmental Organizations: New E-Government Research* (pp. 270–280). Hershey, PA: Information Science Reference.

Grois, D., & Hadar, O. (2013). Advances in Region-of-Interest Video and Image Processing. In I. Management Association (Ed.), Image Processing: Concepts, Methodologies, Tools, and Applications (pp. 1257-1305). Hershey, PA: Information Science Reference. doi: doi:10.4018/978-1-4666-3994-2.ch063

Grois, D., & Hadar, O. (2013). Recent Advances in Computational Complexity Techniques for Video Coding Applications. In D. Kanellopoulos (Ed.), *Intelligent Multimedia Technologies for Networking Applications: Techniques and Tools* (pp. 156–195). Hershey, PA: Information Science Reference.

Guan, P. P., & Yan, H. (2013). A Hierarchical Multilevel Image Thresholding Method Based on the Maximum Fuzzy Entropy Principle. In I. Management Association (Ed.), Image Processing: Concepts, Methodologies, Tools, and Applications (pp. 274-302). Hershey, PA: Information Science Reference. doi: doi:10.4018/978-1-4666-3994-2.ch016

Guéhéneuc, Y. (2012). A Theory of Program Comprehension: Joining Vision Science and Program Comprehension. In Y. Wang (Ed.), *Software and Intelligent Sciences: New Transdisciplinary Findings* (pp. 352–371). Hershey, PA: Information Science Reference. doi:10.4018/978-1-4666-0261-8.ch020

Günel, B., & Hacihabiboglu, H. (2011). Sound Source Localization: Conventional Methods and Intensity Vector Direction Exploitation. In W. Wang (Ed.), *Machine Audition: Principles, Algorithms and Systems* (pp. 126–161). Hershey, PA: Information Science Reference.

Guo, Y., & Li, R. (2011). A Multi-Agent Machine Learning Framework for Intelligent Energy Demand Management. In G. Trajkovski (Ed.), *Developments in Intelligent Agent Technologies and Multi-Agent Systems: Concepts and Applications* (pp. 198–212). Hershey, PA: Information Science Reference. doi:10.4018/978-1-60960-818-7.ch214

Grzes, M., & Kudenko, D. (2011). Reward Shaping and Mixed Resolution Function Approximation. In G. Trajkovski (Ed.), *Developments in Intelligent Agent Technologies and Multi-Agent Systems: Concepts and Applications* (pp. 95–115). Hershey, PA: Information Science Reference.

Hafner, M., & Koeppl, H. (2012). Stochastic Simulations in Systems Biology. In J. Leng, & W. Sharrock (Eds.), *Handbook of Research on Computational Science and Engineering: Theory and Practice* (pp. 267–286). Hershey, PA: Engineering Science Reference.

Haftor, D. M. (2011). Moral Considerations for the Development of Information and Communication Technology. In D. Haftor, & A. Mirijamdotter (Eds.), *Information and Communication Technologies, Society and Human Beings: Theory and Framework (Festschrift in honor of Gunilla Bradley)* (pp. 477–492). Hershey, PA: Information Science Reference.

Hammal, Z. (2013). From Face to Facial Expression. In I. Management Association (Ed.), Image Processing: Concepts, Methodologies, Tools, and Applications (pp. 1508-1531). Hershey, PA: Information Science Reference. doi: doi:10.4018/978-1-4666-3994-2.ch074

Han, Y., Wang, B., Koike, H., & Idesawa, M. (2012). Object Recognition with a Limited Database Using Shape Space Theory. In V. Mago, & N. Bhatia (Eds.), *Cross-Disciplinary Applications of Artificial Intelligence and Pattern Recognition: Advancing Technologies* (pp. 128–147). Hershey, PA: Information Science Reference.

Haq, S., & Jackson, P. J. (2011). Multimodal Emotion Recognition. In W. Wang (Ed.), *Machine Audition: Principles, Algorithms and Systems* (pp. 398–423). Hershey, PA: Information Science Reference.

Harandi, M., Taheri, J., & Lovell, B. C. (2013). Machine Learning Applications in Computer Vision. In I. Management Association (Ed.), Image Processing: Concepts, Methodologies, Tools, and Applications (pp. 896-926). Hershey, PA: Information Science Reference. doi: doi:10.4018/978-1-4666-3994-2.ch045

Harbers, M., van den Bosch, K., & Meyer, J. C. (2011). Agents with a Theory of Mind in Virtual Training. In M. Beer, M. Fasli, & D. Richards (Eds.), *Multi-Agent Systems for Education and Interactive Entertainment: Design, Use and Experience* (pp. 172–187). Hershey, PA: Information Science Reference.

Hayashi, H., & Minazuki, A. (2013). Study on Image Quality Assessment with Scale Space Approach Using Index of Visual Evoked Potentials. In I. Management Association (Ed.), Image Processing: Concepts, Methodologies, Tools, and Applications (pp. 927-938). Hershey, PA: Information Science Reference. doi: doi:10.4018/978-1-4666-3994-2.ch046

Hemanth, D. J., & Anitha, J. (2013). Computational Intelligence Techniques for Pattern Recognition in Biomedical Image Processing Applications. In I. Management Association (Ed.), Image Processing: Concepts, Methodologies, Tools, and Applications (pp. 710-724). Hershey, PA: Information Science Reference. doi: doi:10.4018/978-1-4666-3994-2.ch037

Henderson, A. M., & Sabbagh, M. A. (2013). Learning Words from Experience: An Integrated Framework. In L. Gogate, & G. Hollich (Eds.), *Theoretical and Computational Models of Word Learning: Trends in Psychology and Artificial Intelligence* (pp. 109–131). Hershey, PA: Information Science Reference. doi:10.4018/978-1-4666-2973-8.ch005

Hine, M. J., Farion, K. J., Michalowski, W., & Wilk, S. (2011). Decision Making by Emergency Room Physicians and Residents: Implications for the Design of Clinical Decision Support Systems. In J. Tan (Ed.), *New Technologies for Advancing Healthcare and Clinical Practices* (pp. 131–148). Hershey, PA: Medical Information Science Reference. doi:10.4018/978-1-60960-780-7.ch008

Hiremath, P. S., & Humnabad, I. Y. (2013). Color Image Segmentation of Endoscopic and Microscopic Images for Abnormality Detection in Esophagus. In I. Management Association (Ed.), Image Processing: Concepts, Methodologies, Tools, and Applications (pp. 725-752). Hershey, PA: Information Science Reference. doi: doi:10.4018/978-1-4666-3994-2.ch038

Hoey, J., Poupart, P., Boutilier, C., & Mihailidis, A. (2012). POMDP Models for Assistive Technology. In L. Sucar, E. Morales, & J. Hoey (Eds.), *Decision Theory Models for Applications in Artificial Intelligence: Concepts and Solutions* (pp. 294–314). Hershey, PA: Information Science Reference.

Hoffman, M., & de Freitas, N. (2012). Inference Strategies for Solving Semi-Markov Decision Processes. In L. Sucar, E. Morales, & J. Hoey (Eds.), *Decision Theory Models for Applications in Artificial Intelligence: Concepts and Solutions* (pp. 82–96). Hershey, PA: Information Science Reference.

Hofkirchner, W. (2011). Information and Communication Technologies for the Good Society. In D. Haftor, & A. Mirijamdotter (Eds.), *Information and Communication Technologies, Society and Human Beings: Theory and Framework (Festschrift in honor of Gunilla Bradley)* (pp. 434–444). Hershey, PA: Information Science Reference. doi:10.4018/978-1-60960-472-1.ch710

Holecek, P., Talašová, J., & Müller, I. (2012). Fuzzy Methods of Multiple-Criteria Evaluation and Their Software Implementation. In V. Mago, & N. Bhatia (Eds.), *Cross-Disciplinary Applications of Artificial Intelligence and Pattern Recognition: Advancing Technologies* (pp. 388–411). Hershey, PA: Information Science Reference.

Honey, R. C., & Grand, C. S. (2011). Application of Connectionist Models to Animal Learning: Interactions between Perceptual Organization and Associative Processes. In E. Alonso, & E. Mondragón (Eds.), *Computational Neuroscience for Advancing Artificial Intelligence: Models, Methods and Applications* (pp. 1–14). Hershey, PA: Medical Information Science Reference.

Houston-Price, C., & Law, B. (2013). How Experiences with Words Supply All the Tools in the Toddler's Word-Learning Toolbox. In L. Gogate, & G. Hollich (Eds.), *Theoretical and Computational Models of Word Learning: Trends in Psychology and Artificial Intelligence* (pp. 81–108). Hershey, PA: Information Science Reference. doi:10.4018/978-1-4666-2973-8.ch004

Hu, Y., Gopalakrishnan, V., & Rajan, D. (2013). Modeling Visual Saliency in Images and Videos. In I. Management Association (Ed.), Image Processing: Concepts, Methodologies, Tools, and Applications (pp. 79-100). Hershey, PA: Information Science Reference. doi: doi:10.4018/978-1-4666-3994-2.ch005

Huang, Y. (2013). Hypergraph Based Visual Segmentation and Retrieval. In I. Management Association (Ed.), Image Processing: Concepts, Methodologies, Tools, and Applications (pp. 345-362). Hershey, PA: Information Science Reference. doi: doi:10.4018/978-1-4666-3994-2.ch019

Hummel, H. (2014). Topology Aggregating Routing Architecture (TARA): A Concept for Scalable and Efficient Routing. In M. Boucadair, & D. Binet (Eds.), *Solutions for Sustaining Scalability in Internet Growth* (pp. 98–125). Hershey, PA: Information Science Reference.

Husbands, P., Philippides, A., & Seth, A. K. (2011). Artificial Neural Systems for Robots. In E. Alonso, & E. Mondragón (Eds.), *Computational Neuroscience for Advancing Artificial Intelligence: Models, Methods and Applications* (pp. 214–248). Hershey, PA: Medical Information Science Reference.

Iannizzotto, G., & La Rosa, F. (2013). A Modular Framework for Vision-Based Human Computer Interaction. In I. Management Association (Ed.), Image Processing: Concepts, Methodologies, Tools, and Applications (pp. 1188-1209). Hershey, PA: Information Science Reference. doi: doi:10.4018/978-1-4666-3994-2.ch060

Jakóbczak, D. (2013). Object Recognition via Contour Points Reconstruction Using Hurwitz - Radon Matrices. In I. Management Association (Ed.), Image Processing: Concepts, Methodologies, Tools, and Applications (pp. 998-1018). Hershey, PA: Information Science Reference. doi: doi:10.4018/978-1-4666-3994-2.ch050

James, A. P. (2013). Machine Intelligence Using Hierarchical Memory Networks. In S. Bhattacharyya, & P. Dutta (Eds.), *Handbook of Research on Computational Intelligence for Engineering, Science, and Business* (pp. 62–74). Hershey, PA: Information Science Reference.

Jan, T., & Wang, W. (2011). Cocktail Party Problem: Source Separation Issues and Computational Methods. In W. Wang (Ed.), *Machine Audition: Principles, Algorithms and Systems* (pp. 61–79). Hershey, PA: Information Science Reference.

Jennings, D. J., Alonso, E., Mondragón, E., & Bonardi, C. (2011). Temporal Uncertainty During Overshadowing: A Temporal Difference Account. In E. Alonso, & E. Mondragón (Eds.), *Computational Neuroscience for Advancing Artificial Intelligence: Models, Methods and Applications* (pp. 46–55). Hershey, PA: Medical Information Science Reference.

Jones, C. (2012). Positive and Negative Innovations in Software Engineering. In Y. Wang (Ed.), *Software and Intelligent Sciences: New Transdisciplinary Findings* (pp. 252–263). Hershey, PA: Information Science Reference. doi:10.4018/978-1-4666-0261-8.ch015

Jorge, R. R., Salgado, G. R., & Sánchez, V. G. (2012). An Enhanced Petri Net Model to Verify and Validate a Neural-Symbolic Hybrid System. In Y. Wang (Ed.), *Software and Intelligent Sciences: New Transdisciplinary Findings* (pp. 434–450). Hershey, PA: Information Science Reference. doi:10.4018/978-1-4666-0261-8.ch025

Jost, G., & Koniges, A. E. (2012). Hardware Trends and Implications for Programming Models. In J. Leng, & W. Sharrock (Eds.), *Handbook of Research on Computational Science and Engineering: Theory and Practice* (pp. 1–21). Hershey, PA: Engineering Science Reference.

Kacprzyk, J., & Zadrozny, S. (2012). Protoforms of Linguistic Database Summaries as a Human Consistent Tool for Using Natural Language in Data Mining. In Y. Wang (Ed.), *Software and Intelligent Sciences: New Transdisciplinary Findings* (pp. 157–168). Hershey, PA: Information Science Reference. doi:10.4018/978-1-4666-0261-8.ch010

Kambayashi, Y., Tsujimura, Y., Yamachi, H., & Takimoto, M. (2011). A Multi-Robot System Using Mobile Agents with Ant Colony Clustering. In S. Chen, Y. Kambayashi, & H. Sato (Eds.), *Multi-Agent Applications with Evolutionary Computation and Biologically Inspired Technologies: Intelligent Techniques for Ubiquity and Optimization* (pp. 174–192). Hershey, PA: Medical Information Science Reference.

Kanaga, E. G., Valarmathi, M., & Darius, P. S. (2012). A Novel 3D Approach for Patient Schedule Using Multi-Agent Coordination. In V. Mago, & N. Bhatia (Eds.), *Cross-Disciplinary Applications of Artificial Intelligence and Pattern Recognition: Advancing Technologies* (pp. 544–563). Hershey, PA: Information Science Reference.

Karpinsky, N., & Zhang, S. (2013). 3D Shape Compression Using Holoimage. In I. Management Association (Ed.), Image Processing: Concepts, Methodologies, Tools, and Applications (pp. 939-956). Hershey, PA: Information Science Reference. doi: doi:10.4018/978-1-4666-3994-2.ch047

Kashima, H., Saigo, H., Hattori, M., & Tsuda, K. (2011). Graph Kernels for Chemoinformatics. In H. Lodhi, & Y. Yamanishi (Eds.), *Chemoinformatics and Advanced Machine Learning Perspectives: Complex Computational Methods and Collaborative Techniques* (pp. 1–15). Hershey, PA: Medical Information Science Reference.

Kelly, D., Hook, D., & Sanders, R. (2012). A Framework for Testing Code in Computational Applications. In J. Leng, & W. Sharrock (Eds.), *Handbook of Research on Computational Science and Engineering: Theory and Practice* (pp. 150–176). Hershey, PA: Engineering Science Reference.

Kenny, P. G., & Parsons, T. D. (2011). Embodied Conversational Virtual Patients. In D. Perez-Marin, & I. Pascual-Nieto (Eds.), *Conversational Agents and Natural Language Interaction: Techniques and Effective Practices* (pp. 254–281). Hershey, PA: Information Science Reference. doi:10.4018/978-1-60960-617-6.ch011

Khan, O. Z., Poupart, P., & Black, J. P. (2012). Automatically Generated Explanations for Markov Decision Processes. In L. Sucar, E. Morales, & J. Hoey (Eds.), *Decision Theory Models for Applications in Artificial Intelligence: Concepts and Solutions* (pp. 144–163). Hershey, PA: Information Science Reference.

Khosla, M., Sarin, R. K., Uddin, M., Singh, S., & Khosla, A. (2012). Realizing Interval Type-2 Fuzzy Systems with Type-1 Fuzzy Systems. In V. Mago, & N. Bhatia (Eds.), *Cross-Disciplinary Applications of Artificial Intelligence and Pattern Recognition: Advancing Technologies* (pp. 412–427). Hershey, PA: Information Science Reference.

Kinsner, W. (2012). Challenges in the Design of Adoptive, Intelligent and Cognitive Systems. In Y. Wang (Ed.), *Software and Intelligent Sciences: New Transdisciplinary Findings* (pp. 47–67). Hershey, PA: Information Science Reference. doi:10.4018/978-1-4666-0261-8.ch004

Klavdianos, P. B., Brasil, L. M., & Melo, J. S. (2013). Face Recognition with Active Appearance Model (AAM). In I. Management Association (Ed.), Image Processing: Concepts, Methodologies, Tools, and Applications (pp. 1124-1144). Hershey, PA: Information Science Reference. doi: doi:10.4018/978-1-4666-3994-2.ch057

Kldiashvili, E. (2011). The Application of Virtual Organization Technology for eHealth. In E. Kldiashvili (Ed.), *Grid Technologies for E-Health: Applications for Telemedicine Services and Delivery* (pp. 1–17). Hershey, PA: Medical Information Science Reference.

Kleese van Dam, K., James, M., & Walker, A. M. (2012). Integrating Data Management and Collaborative Sharing with Computational Science Research Processes. In J. Leng, & W. Sharrock (Eds.), *Handbook of Research on Computational Science and Engineering: Theory and Practice* (pp. 506–538). Hershey, PA: Engineering Science Reference.

Kolomvatsos, K., & Hadjiefthymiades, S. (2012). On the Use of Fuzzy Logic in Electronic Marketplaces. In V. Mago, & N. Bhatia (Eds.), *Cross-Disciplinary Applications of Artificial Intelligence and Pattern Recognition: Advancing Technologies* (pp. 609–632). Hershey, PA: Information Science Reference.

Kouskouridas, R., & Gasteratos, A. (2012). From Object Recognition to Object Localization. In V. Mago, & N. Bhatia (Eds.), *Cross-Disciplinary Applications of Artificial Intelligence and Pattern Recognition: Advancing Technologies* (pp. 1–17). Hershey, PA: Information Science Reference.

Kovács, J., Bokor, L., Kanizsai, Z., & Imre, S. (2013). Review of Advanced Mobility Solutions for Multimedia Networking in IPv6. In D. Kanellopoulos (Ed.), *Intelligent Multimedia Technologies for Networking Applications: Techniques and Tools* (pp. 25–47). Hershey, PA: Information Science Reference.

Krieg-Brückner, B., Shi, H., Gersdorf, B., Döhle, M., & Röfer, T. (2011). Context-Sensitive Spatial Interaction and Ambient Control. In N. Chong, & F. Mastrogiovanni (Eds.), *Handbook of Research on Ambient Intelligence and Smart Environments: Trends and Perspectives* (pp. 513–533). Hershey, PA: Information Science Reference. doi:10.4018/978-1-61692-857-5.ch024

Lacuesta, R., Fernández-Sanz, L., & Romay, M. D. (2014). Requirements Specification as Basis for Mobile Software Quality Assurance. In I. Management Association (Ed.), Software Design and Development: Concepts, Methodologies, Tools, and Applications (pp. 719-732). Hershey, PA: Information Science Reference. doi: doi:10.4018/978-1-4666-4301-7.ch034

LeGrand, R., Roden, T., & Cytron, R. K. (2012). Nonmanipulable Collective Decision-Making for Games. In A. Kumar, J. Etheredge, & A. Boudreaux (Eds.), *Algorithmic and Architectural Gaming Design: Implementation and Development* (pp. 67–81). Hershey, PA: Information Science Reference. doi:10.4018/978-1-4666-1634-9.ch004

Leng, J., Rhyne, T., & Sharrock, W. (2012). Visualization: Future Technology and Practices for Computational Science and Engineering. In J. Leng, & W. Sharrock (Eds.), *Handbook of Research on Computational Science and Engineering: Theory and Practice* (pp. 381–413). Hershey, PA: Engineering Science Reference.

Lenskiy, A. A., & Lee, J. (2012). Detecting Eyes and Lips Using Neural Networks and SURF Features. In V. Mago, & N. Bhatia (Eds.), *Cross-Disciplinary Applications of Artificial Intelligence and Pattern Recognition: Advancing Technologies* (pp. 338–354). Hershey, PA: Information Science Reference.

Leni, P., Fougerolle, Y. D., & Truchetet, F. (2013). The Kolmogorov Spline Network for Image Processing. In I. Management Association (Ed.), Image Processing: Concepts, Methodologies, Tools, and Applications (pp. 54-78). Hershey, PA: Information Science Reference. doi:10.4018/978-1-4666-3994-2.ch004

Li, F. F., Kendrick, P., & Cox, T. J. (2011). Machine Audition of Acoustics: Acoustic Channel Modeling and Room Acoustic Parameter Estimation. In W. Wang (Ed.), *Machine Audition: Principles, Algorithms and Systems* (pp. 424–446). Hershey, PA: Information Science Reference.

Li, Z., Liu, F., & Boyer, J. (2011). Amusing Minds for Joyful Learning through E-Gaming. In I. Management Association (Ed.), Gaming and Simulations: Concepts, Methodologies, Tools and Applications (pp. 1280-1297). Hershey, PA: Information Science Reference. doi:doi:10.4018/978-1-60960-195-9.ch503

Lodhi, H. (2011). Learning Methodologies for Detection and Classification of Mutagens. In H. Lodhi, & Y. Yamanishi (Eds.), *Chemoinformatics and Advanced Machine Learning Perspectives: Complex Computational Methods and Collaborative Techniques* (pp. 274–288). Hershey, PA: Medical Information Science Reference.

Logenthiran, T., & Srinivasan, D. (2011). Management of Distributed Energy Resources Using Intelligent Multi-Agent System. In S. Chen, Y. Kambayashi, & H. Sato (Eds.), *Multi-Agent Applications with Evolutionary Computation and Biologically Inspired Technologies: Intelligent Techniques for Ubiquity and Optimization* (pp. 208–231). Hershey, PA: Medical Information Science Reference.

Lucas da Silva, D., Souza, R. R., & Almeida, M. B. (2012). Ontologies and Controlled Vocabulary: Comparison of Building Methodologies. In I. Management Association (Ed.), Computer Engineering: Concepts, Methodologies, Tools and Applications (pp. 46-60). Hershey, PA: Engineering Science Reference. doi:doi:10.4018/978-1-61350-456-7.ch104

Ludvig, E. A., Bellemare, M. G., & Pearson, K. G. (2011). A Primer on Reinforcement Learning in the Brain: Psychological, Computational, and Neural Perspectives. In E. Alonso, & E. Mondragón (Eds.), *Computational Neuroscience for Advancing Artificial Intelligence: Models, Methods and Applications* (pp. 111–144). Hershey, PA: Medical Information Science Reference.

Luna, F., Romo, J. C., Mora-González, M., Martínez-Cano, E., & Rivas, V. L. (2012). Handwritten Signature Verification Using Multi Objective Optimization with Genetic Algorithms in a Forensic Architecture. In C. Ortiz Zezzatti, C. Chira, A. Hernandez, & M. Basurto (Eds.), *Logistics Management and Optimization through Hybrid Artificial Intelligence Systems* (pp. 141–180). Hershey, PA: Information Science Reference. doi:10.4018/978-1-4666-0297-7.ch006

Ma, B., Li, C., Wang, Y., & Bai, X. (2013). Salient Region Detection for Biometric Watermarking. In I. Management Association (Ed.), Image Processing: Concepts, Methodologies, Tools, and Applications (pp. 201-219). Hershey, PA: Information Science Reference. doi: doi:10.4018/978-1-4666-3994-2.ch012

Madureira, A. M. (2012). Hybrid Meta-Heuristics Based System for Dynamic Scheduling. In I. Management Association (Ed.), Machine Learning: Concepts, Methodologies, Tools and Applications (pp. 428-435). Hershey, PA: Information Science Reference. doi: doi:10.4018/978-1-60960-818-7.ch305

Mahalakshmi, G. S., & Geetha, T. V. (2012). Requirements Elicitation by Defect Elimination: An Indian Logic Perspective. In Y. Wang (Ed.), *Software and Intelligent Sciences: New Transdisciplinary Findings* (pp. 372–391). Hershey, PA: Information Science Reference. doi:10.4018/978-1-4666-0261-8.ch021

Maharana, S. K., & Prabhakar, P. G., & Bhati, A. (2013). A Study of Cloud Computing for Retinal Image Processing through MATLAB. In I. Management Association (Ed.), Image Processing: Concepts, Methodologies, Tools, and Applications (pp. 101-111). Hershey, PA: Information Science Reference. doi: doi:10.4018/978-1-4666-3994-2.ch006

Mahmood, M. T., & Choi, T. (2013). Image Focus Measure Based on Energy of High Frequency Components in S-Transform. In I. Management Association (Ed.), Image Processing: Concepts, Methodologies, Tools, and Applications (pp. 162-180). Hershey, PA: Information Science Reference. doi: doi:10.4018/978-1-4666-3994-2.ch010

Malhotra, R., Kaur, A., & Singh, Y. (2012). Comparative Analysis of Random Forests with Statistical and Machine Learning Methods in Predicting Fault-Prone Classes. In V. Mago, & N. Bhatia (Eds.), *Cross-Disciplinary Applications of Artificial Intelligence and Pattern Recognition: Advancing Technologies* (pp. 428–449). Hershey, PA: Information Science Reference.

Mariappanadar, S. (2012). Motivational Gratification: An Integrated Work Motivation Model with Information System Design Perspective. In Y. Wang (Ed.), *Software and Intelligent Sciences: New Transdisciplinary Findings* (pp. 403–418). Hershey, PA: Information Science Reference. doi:10.4018/978-1-4666-0261-8.ch023

Marichal, G. N., & González, E. J. (2012). Intelligent MAS in System Engineering and Robotics. In I. Management Association (Ed.), Machine Learning: Concepts, Methodologies, Tools and Applications (pp. 175-182). Hershey, PA: Information Science Reference. doi: doi:10.4018/978-1-60960-818-7.ch204

Mastrogiovanni, F., Scalmato, A., Sgorbissa, A., & Zaccaria, R. (2012). On the Representation and Recognition of Temporal Patterns of Activities in Smart Environments. In S. Hazarika (Ed.), *Qualitative Spatio-Temporal Representation and Reasoning: Trends and Future Directions* (pp. 363–385). Hershey, PA: Information Science Reference. doi:10.4018/978-1-61692-868-1.ch012

Masutani, Y., Nemoto, M., Nomura, Y., & Hayashi, N. (2013). Clinical Machine Learning in Action: CAD System Design, Development, Tuning, and Long-Term Experience. In I. Management Association (Ed.), Image Processing: Concepts, Methodologies, Tools, and Applications (pp. 621-638). Hershey, PA: Information Science Reference. doi:10.4018/978-1-4666-3994-2.ch032

Mauk, M. G. (2013). Image Processing for Solar Cell Analysis, Diagnostics and Quality Assurance Inspection. In I. Management Association (Ed.), Image Processing: Concepts, Methodologies, Tools, and Applications (pp. 1426-1462). Hershey, PA: Information Science Reference. doi: doi:10.4018/978-1-4666-3994-2.ch071

McCarthy, P. M., & McNamara, D. S. (2012). The User-Language Paraphrase Corpus. In C. Boonthum-Denecke, P. McCarthy, & T. Lamkin (Eds.), *Cross-Disciplinary Advances in Applied Natural Language Processing: Issues and Approaches* (pp. 73–89). Hershey, PA: Information Science Reference.

McLaren, I. (2011). APECS: An Adaptively Parameterised Model of Associative Learning and Memory. In E. Alonso, & E. Mondragón (Eds.), *Computational Neuroscience for Advancing Artificial Intelligence: Models, Methods and Applications* (pp. 145–164). Hershey, PA: Medical Information Science Reference.

McMurray, B., Zhao, L., Kucker, S. C., & Samuelson, L. K. (2013). Pushing the Envelope of Associative Learning: Internal Representations and Dynamic Competition Transform Association into Development. In L. Gogate, & G. Hollich (Eds.), *Theoretical and Computational Models of Word Learning: Trends in Psychology and Artificial Intelligence* (pp. 49–80). Hershey, PA: Information Science Reference. doi:10.4018/978-1-4666-2973-8.ch003

McNeal, M., & Newyear, D. (2013). Chatbots: Automating Reference in Public Libraries. In E. Iglesias (Ed.), *Robots in Academic Libraries: Advancements in Library Automation* (pp. 101–114). Hershey, PA: Information Science Reference. doi:10.4018/978-1-4666-3938-6.ch006

Merad, S., de Lemos, R., & Anderson, T. (2014). A Game Theoretic Solution for the Optimal Selection of Services. In I. Management Association (Ed.), Software Design and Development: Concepts, Methodologies, Tools, and Applications (pp. 1481-1497). Hershey, PA: Information Science Reference. doi: doi:10.4018/978-1-4666-4301-7.ch072

Mir, U., Merghem-Boulahia, L., & Gaïti, D. (2012). On Using Multiagent Systems for Spectrum Sharing in Cognitive Radios Networks. In P. Cong-Vinh (Ed.), *Formal and Practical Aspects of Autonomic Computing and Networking: Specification, Development, and Verification* (pp. 377–415). Hershey, PA: Information Science Reference.

Mishra, B., & Shukla, K. K. (2014). Data Mining Techniques for Software Quality Prediction. In I. Management Association (Ed.), Software Design and Development: Concepts, Methodologies, Tools, and Applications (pp. 401-428). Hershey, PA: Information Science Reference. doi: doi:10.4018/978-1-4666-4301-7.ch021

Misra, S. (2012). Measurement of Cognitive Functional Sizes of Software. In Y. Wang (Ed.), *Software and Intelligent Sciences: New Transdisciplinary Findings* (pp. 392–402). Hershey, PA: Information Science Reference. doi:10.4018/978-1-4666-0261-8.ch022

Mohammadian, M. (2011). Application of Fuzzy Cognitive Maps in IT Management and Risk Analysis. In P. Ordóñez de Pablos, M. Lytras, W. Karwowski, & R. Lee (Eds.), *Electronic Globalized Business and Sustainable Development Through IT Management: Strategies and Perspectives* (pp. 90–99). Hershey, PA: Business Science Reference.

Mohan, S., & Murali, S. (2013). Image Based 3D Modeling and Rendering from Single View Perspective Images. In I. Management Association (Ed.), Image Processing: Concepts, Methodologies, Tools, and Applications (pp. 604-620). Hershey, PA: Information Science Reference. doi: doi:10.4018/978-1-4666-3994-2.ch031

Mondal, K. (2013). A Novel Fuzzy Rule Guided Intelligent Technique for Gray Image Extraction and Segmentation. In I. Management Association (Ed.), Image Processing: Concepts, Methodologies, Tools, and Applications (pp. 303-321). Hershey, PA: Information Science Reference. doi: doi:10.4018/978-1-4666-3994-2.ch017

Morales, E. F., & Zaragoza, J. H. (2012). An Introduction to Reinforcement Learning. In L. Sucar, E. Morales, & J. Hoey (Eds.), *Decision Theory Models for Applications in Artificial Intelligence: Concepts and Solutions* (pp. 63–80). Hershey, PA: Information Science Reference.

Morales, E. F., & Zaragoza, J. H. (2012). Relational Representations and Traces for Efficient Reinforcement Learning. In L. Sucar, E. Morales, & J. Hoey (Eds.), *Decision Theory Models for Applications in Artificial Intelligence: Concepts and Solutions* (pp. 190–217). Hershey, PA: Information Science Reference.

Morell-Gimenez, V., Orts-Escolano, S., García-Rodríguez, J., Cazorla, M., & Viejo, D. (2013). A Review of Registration Methods on Mobile Robots. In I. Management Association (Ed.), Image Processing: Concepts, Methodologies, Tools, and Applications (pp. 562-574). Hershey, PA: Information Science Reference. doi: doi:10.4018/978-1-4666-3994-2.ch029

Moro, M. M., Weber, T., & Freitas, C. M. (2012). Women in Brazilian CS Research Community: The State-of-the-Art. In I. Management Association (Ed.), Computer Engineering: Concepts, Methodologies, Tools and Applications (pp. 1824-1839). Hershey, PA: Engineering Science Reference. doi: doi:10.4018/978-1-61350-456-7.ch801

Moudani, W., & Mora-Camino, F. (2013). Dynamic Assignment of Crew Reserve in Airlines. In P. Yin (Ed.), *Trends in Developing Metaheuristics, Algorithms, and Optimization Approaches* (pp. 264–288). Hershey, PA: Information Science Reference.

Mukherjee, P., Sen, S., & Airiau, S. (2011). Norm Emergence with Biased Agents. In G. Trajkovski (Ed.), *Developments in Intelligent Agent Technologies and Multi-Agent Systems: Concepts and Applications* (pp. 168–179). Hershey, PA: Information Science Reference.

Mukherji, P., & Rege, P. (2012). Devnagari Script Recognition: Techniques and Challenges. In V. Mago, & N. Bhatia (Eds.), *Cross-Disciplinary Applications of Artificial Intelligence and Pattern Recognition: Advancing Technologies* (pp. 249–269). Hershey, PA: Information Science Reference.

Mulak, K. E., & Best, C. T. (2013). Development of Word Recognition across Speakers and Accents. In L. Gogate, & G. Hollich (Eds.), *Theoretical and Computational Models of Word Learning: Trends in Psychology and Artificial Intelligence* (pp. 242–269). Hershey, PA: Information Science Reference. doi:10.4018/978-1-4666-2973-8.ch011

Muldner, K., & Conati, C. (2012). A Decision-Theoretic Tutor for Analogical Problem Solving. In L. Sucar, E. Morales, & J. Hoey (Eds.), *Decision Theory Models for Applications in Artificial Intelligence: Concepts and Solutions* (pp. 219–247). Hershey, PA: Information Science Reference.

Munipov, V. (2011). Psychological and Social Problems of Automation and Computerization. In D. Haftor, & A. Mirijamdotter (Eds.), *Information and Communication Technologies, Society and Human Beings: Theory and Framework (Festschrift in honor of Gunilla Bradley)* (pp. 136–146). Hershey, PA: Information Science Reference.

Naik, G., Kumar, D. K., & Arjunan, S. (2012). ICA as Pattern Recognition Technique for Gesture Identification: A Study Using Bio-Signal. In V. Mago, & N. Bhatia (Eds.), *Cross-Disciplinary Applications of Artificial Intelligence and Pattern Recognition: Advancing Technologies* (pp. 367–387). Hershey, PA: Information Science Reference.

Nehmzow, U. (2011). Modelling and Analysis of Agent Behaviour. In E. Alonso, & E. Mondragón (Eds.), *Computational Neuroscience for Advancing Artificial Intelligence: Models, Methods and Applications* (pp. 186–212). Hershey, PA: Medical Information Science Reference.

Nemoianu, I., & Pesquet-Popescu, B. (2013). Network Coding for Multimedia Communications. In D. Kanellopoulos (Ed.), *Intelligent Multimedia Technologies for Networking Applications: Techniques and Tools* (pp. 1–24). Hershey, PA: Information Science Reference.

Nguyen, H. T., Franke, K., & Petrovic, S. (2013). Feature Extraction Methods for Intrusion Detection Systems. In I. Management Association (Ed.), Image Processing: Concepts, Methodologies, Tools, and Applications (pp. 1064-1092). Hershey, PA: Information Science Reference. doi: doi:10.4018/978-1-4666-3994-2.ch054

Nijholt, A., Heylen, D., & Rienks, R. (2011). Creating Social Technologies to Assist and Understand Social Interactions. In I. Management Association (Ed.), Virtual Communities: Concepts, Methodologies, Tools and Applications (pp. 450-462). Hershey, PA: Information Science Reference. doi: doi:10.4018/978-1-60960-100-3.ch205

Nissen, H. (2011). Services Rendered By Computers and Their Explications. In D. Haftor, & A. Mirijamdotter (Eds.), *Information and Communication Technologies, Society and Human Beings: Theory and Framework (Festschrift in honor of Gunilla Bradley)* (pp. 283–292). Hershey, PA: Information Science Reference.

Noguez, J., Muñoz, K., Neri, L., Robledo-Rella, V., & Aguilar, G. (2012). Dynamic Decision Networks Applications in Active Learning Simulators. In L. Sucar, E. Morales, & J. Hoey (Eds.), *Decision Theory Models for Applications in Artificial Intelligence: Concepts and Solutions* (pp. 248–270). Hershey, PA: Information Science Reference.

Nóvoa, F. J., Curra, A., López, M. G., & Mato, V. (2011). Angiographic Images Segmentation Techniques. In I. Management Association (Ed.), Clinical Technologies: Concepts, Methodologies, Tools and Applications (pp. 368-376). Hershey, PA: Medical Information Science Reference. doi: doi:10.4018/978-1-60960-561-2.ch209

Orito, Y., Kambayashi, Y., Tsujimura, Y., & Yamamoto, H. (2011). An Agent-based Model for Portfolio Optimization Using Search Space Splitting. In S. Chen, Y. Kambayashi, & H. Sato (Eds.), *Multi-Agent Applications with Evolutionary Computation and Biologically Inspired Technologies: Intelligent Techniques for Ubiquity and Optimization* (pp. 19–34). Hershey, PA: Medical Information Science Reference.

Ortiz Zezzatti, C. A., Bustillos, S., Reyes, Y., Tagliarducci-Tcherassi, A., & Jaramillo, R. (2012). Crowdfunding to improve Environmental Projects' Logistics. In C. Ortiz Zezzatti, C. Chira, A. Hernandez, & M. Basurto (Eds.), *Logistics Management and Optimization through Hybrid Artificial Intelligence Systems* (pp. 287–309). Hershey, PA: Information Science Reference. doi:10.4018/978-1-4666-0297-7.ch011

Ortiz Zezzatti, C. A., Castillo, N., Martínez, W., & Velázquez, S. (2012). Logistics Applied to Improve Bottling Water Distribution. In C. Ortiz Zezzatti, C. Chira, A. Hernandez, & M. Basurto (Eds.), *Logistics Management and Optimization through Hybrid Artificial Intelligence Systems* (pp. 1–32). Hershey, PA: Information Science Reference. doi:10.4018/978-1-4666-0297-7.ch001

Ortiz Zezzatti, C. A., Martínez, J., Castillo, N., González, S., & Hernández, P. (2012). Improve Card Collection from Memory Alpha using Sociolinguistics and Japanese Puzzles. In C. Ortiz Zezzatti, C. Chira, A. Hernandez, & M. Basurto (Eds.), *Logistics Management and Optimization through Hybrid Artificial Intelligence Systems* (pp. 310–326). Hershey, PA: Information Science Reference. doi:10.4018/978-1-4666-0297-7.ch012

Ortiz Zezzatti, C. A., Young, D., Chira, C., Azpeitia, D., & Calvillo, A. (2012). Mass Media Strategies: Hybrid Approach using a Bioinspired Algorithm and Social Data Mining. In C. Ortiz Zezzatti, C. Chira, A. Hernandez, & M. Basurto (Eds.), *Logistics Management and Optimization through Hybrid Artificial Intelligence Systems* (pp. 327–354). Hershey, PA: Information Science Reference. doi:10.4018/978-1-4666-0297-7.ch013

Osowski, S., Kruk, M., Koktysz, R., & Kurek, J. (2013). Image Processing for Localization and Parameterization of the Glandular Ducts of Colon in Inflammatory Bowel Diseases. In I. Management Association (Ed.), Image Processing: Concepts, Methodologies, Tools, and Applications (pp. 688-708), Hershey, PA: Information Science Reference. doi: doi:10.4018/978-1-4666-3994-2.ch036

Papageorgiou, E. I. (2012). Fuzzy Cognitive Map Reasoning Mechanism for Handling Uncertainty and Missing Data: Application in Medical Diagnosis. In V. Mago, & N. Bhatia (Eds.), *Cross-Disciplinary Applications of Artificial Intelligence and Pattern Recognition: Advancing Technologies* (pp. 583–608). Hershey, PA: Information Science Reference.

Papakostas, G., Karakasis, E., & Koulouriotis, D. (2012). Orthogonal Image Moment Invariants: Highly Discriminative Features for Pattern Recognition Applications. In V. Mago, & N. Bhatia (Eds.), *Cross-Disciplinary Applications of Artificial Intelligence and Pattern Recognition: Advancing Technologies* (pp. 34–52). Hershey, PA: Information Science Reference.

Park, S. H. (2012). Classification with Axis-Aligned Rectangular Boundaries. In V. Mago, & N. Bhatia (Eds.), *Cross-Disciplinary Applications of Artificial Intelligence and Pattern Recognition: Advancing Technologies* (pp. 355–366). Hershey, PA: Information Science Reference.

Pedrycz, W. (2012). Hierarchies of Architectures of Collaborative Computational Intelligence. In Y. Wang (Ed.), *Software and Intelligent Sciences: New Transdisciplinary Findings* (pp. 32–46). Hershey, PA: Information Science Reference. doi:10.4018/978-1-4666-0261-8.ch003

Peña de Carrillo, C. I., Choquet, C., Després, C., Iksal, S., Jacoboni, P., Lekira, A., et al. (2014). Engineering and Re-engineering of Technology Enhanced Learning Scenarios Using Context Awareness Processes. In I. Management Association (Ed.), Software Design and Development: Concepts, Methodologies, Tools, and Applications (pp. 1289-1313). Hershey, PA: Information Science Reference. doi: doi:10.4018/978-1-4666-4301-7.ch063

Pérez-Suárez, D., Higgins, P. A., Bloomfield, D. S., McAteer, R. J., Krista, L. D., Byrne, J. P., & Gallagher, P. T. (2013). Automated Solar Feature Detection for Space Weather Applications. In I. Management Association (Ed.), Image Processing: Concepts, Methodologies, Tools, and Applications (pp. 979-997). Hershey, PA: Information Science Reference. doi: doi:10.4018/978-1-4666-3994-2.ch049

Poggi, A., & Tomaiuolo, M. (2012). Rule Engines and Agent-Based Systems. In I. Management Association (Ed.), Machine Learning: Concepts, Methodologies, Tools and Applications (pp. 211-218). Hershey, PA: Information Science Reference. doi: doi:10.4018/978-1-60960-818-7.ch206

Polovina, S., & Andrews, S. (2011). A Transaction-Oriented Architecture for Structuring Unstructured Information in Enterprise Applications. In V. Sugumaran (Ed.), *Intelligent, Adaptive and Reasoning Technologies: New Developments and Applications* (pp. 285–299). Hershey, PA: Information Science Reference. doi:10.4018/978-1-60960-595-7.ch016

Poupart, P. (2012). An Introduction to Fully and Partially Observable Markov Decision Processes. In L. Sucar, E. Morales, & J. Hoey (Eds.), *Decision Theory Models for Applications in Artificial Intelligence: Concepts and Solutions* (pp. 33–62). Hershey, PA: Information Science Reference.

Prabhakar, C. (2012). Analysis of Face Space for Recognition using Interval-Valued Subspace Technique. In V. Mago, & N. Bhatia (Eds.), *Cross-Disciplinary Applications of Artificial Intelligence and Pattern Recognition: Advancing Technologies* (pp. 108–127). Hershey, PA: Information Science Reference.

Prabhakar, C., Kumar, P. P., & Hiremath, P. (2013). 3D Reconstruction of Underwater Natural Scenes and Objects Using Stereo Vision. In I. Management Association (Ed.), Image Processing: Concepts, Methodologies, Tools, and Applications (pp. 957-978). Hershey, PA: Information Science Reference. doi: doi:10.4018/978-1-4666-3994-2.ch048

Quinaz, F., Fazendeiro, P., Castelo-Branco, M., & Araújo, P. (2013). Soft Methods for Automatic Drug Infusion in Medical Care Environment. In M. Cruz-Cunha, I. Miranda, & P. Gonçalves (Eds.), *Handbook of Research on ICTs and Management Systems for Improving Efficiency in Healthcare and Social Care* (pp. 830–854). Hershey, PA: Medical Information Science Reference. doi:10.4018/978-1-4666-3990-4.ch043

R., R. A., C., E. O., H., H. F., R., L. C., & F., J. A. (2012). Looking for Reverse Transformations between NP-Complete Problems. In C. Ortiz Zezzatti, C. Chira, A. Hernandez, & M. Basurto (Eds.) *Logistics Management and Optimization through Hybrid Artificial Intelligence Systems* (pp. 181-206). Hershey, PA: Information Science Reference. doi:10.4018/978-1-4666-0297-7.ch007

Rajasingham, L. (2011). The E-Learning Phenomenon: A New University Paradigm? In I. Management Association (Ed.), Virtual Communities: Concepts, Methodologies, Tools and Applications (pp. 161-181). Hershey, PA: Information Science Reference. doi: doi:10.4018/978-1-60960-100-3.ch112

Ramos da Silva, R., & Romero, R. A. (2013). Computer Vision for Learning to Interact Socially with Humans. In I. Management Association (Ed.), Image Processing: Concepts, Methodologies, Tools, and Applications (pp. 1162-1187). Hershey, PA: Information Science Reference. doi: doi:10.4018/978-1-4666-3994-2.ch059

Ratto, M. (2012). CSE as Epistemic Technologies: Computer Modeling and Disciplinary Difference in the Humanities. In J. Leng, & W. Sharrock (Eds.), *Handbook of Research on Computational Science and Engineering: Theory and Practice* (pp. 567–586). Hershey, PA: Engineering Science Reference.

Rebedea, T., Trausan-Matu, S., & Chiru, C. (2014). Inter-Animation between Utterances in Collaborative Chat Conversations. In H. Lim, & F. Sudweeks (Eds.), *Innovative Methods and Technologies for Electronic Discourse Analysis* (pp. 63–93). Hershey, PA: Information Science Reference.

Rene, E. R., Kim, S. J., Lee, D. H., Je, W. B., López, M. E., & Park, H. S. (2012). Artificial Neural Network Modelling of Sequencing Batch Reactor Performance. In J. Leng, & W. Sharrock (Eds.), *Handbook of Research on Computational Science and Engineering: Theory and Practice* (pp. 456–479). Hershey, PA: Engineering Science Reference.

Resconi, G., & Kovalerchuk, B. (2011). Agents in Quantum and Neural Uncertainty. In S. Chen, Y. Kambayashi, & H. Sato (Eds.), *Multi-Agent Applications with Evolutionary Computation and Biologically Inspired Technologies: Intelligent Techniques for Ubiquity and Optimization* (pp. 50–77). Hershey, PA: Medical Information Science Reference.

Reyes, A., & Elizalde, F. (2012). An Intelligent Assistant for Power Plant Operation and Training Based on Decision-Theoretic Planning. In L. Sucar, E. Morales, & J. Hoey (Eds.), *Decision Theory Models for Applications in Artificial Intelligence: Concepts and Solutions* (pp. 271–293). Hershey, PA: Information Science Reference.

Reyes, L. C., Santillán, C. G., Quiroz, M., Alvim, A., Melin, P., Vanoye, J. R., & Najera, V. L. (2012). Heuristic Algorithms: An Application to the Truck Loading Problem. In C. Ortiz Zezzatti, C. Chira, A. Hernandez, & M. Basurto (Eds.), *Logistics Management and Optimization through Hybrid Artificial Intelligence Systems* (pp. 238–267). Hershey, PA: Information Science Reference. doi:10.4018/978-1-4666-0297-7.ch009

Reynolds, R. G., O'Shea, J., Che, X., Gawasmeh, Y., Meadows, G., & Fotouhi, F. (2011). The AGILE Design of Reality Game AI. In S. Chen, Y. Kambayashi, & H. Sato (Eds.), *Multi-Agent Applications with Evolutionary Computation and Biologically Inspired Technologies: Intelligent Techniques for Ubiquity and Optimization* (pp. 193–207). Hershey, PA: Medical Information Science Reference.

Riaz, Z., Gedikli, S., Beetz, M., & Radig, B. (2013). 3D Face Modeling for Multi-Feature Extraction for Intelligent Systems. In I. Management Association (Ed.), Image Processing: Concepts, Methodologies, Tools, and Applications (pp. 1145-1161). Hershey, PA: Information Science Reference. doi: doi:10.4018/978-1-4666-3994-2.ch058

Robbin, A. (2011). Multitasking: Some Consequences of the Convergence of Technologies in the Workplace. In D. Haftor, & A. Mirijamdotter (Eds.), *Information and Communication Technologies, Society and Human Beings: Theory and Framework (Festschrift in honor of Gunilla Bradley)* (pp. 76–95). Hershey, PA: Information Science Reference.

Rodríguez-Sánchez, A. J., & Tsotsos, J. K. (2013). The Roles of Endstopped and Curvature Tuned Computations in a Hierarchical Representation of 2D Shape. In I. Management Association (Ed.), Image Processing: Concepts, Methodologies, Tools, and Applications (pp. 1338-1360). Hershey, PA: Information Science Reference. doi: doi:10.4018/978-1-4666-3994-2.ch066

Rosenbaum, R. (2013). Large Imagery on Small Screens: Novel Technology for Device Adaptation in Mobile Services. In I. Management Association (Ed.), Image Processing: Concepts, Methodologies, Tools, and Applications (pp. 1361-1378). Hershey, PA: Information Science Reference. doi: doi:10.4018/978-1-4666-3994-2.ch067

Rosipal, R. (2011). Nonlinear Partial Least Squares An Overview. In H. Lodhi, & Y. Yamanishi (Eds.), *Chemoinformatics and Advanced Machine Learning Perspectives: Complex Computational Methods and Collaborative Techniques* (pp. 169–189). Hershey, PA: Medical Information Science Reference.

Ruotsalainen, L., & Kuusniemi, H. (2013). Visual Positioning in a Smartphone. In I. Management Association (Ed.), Image Processing: Concepts, Methodologies, Tools, and Applications (pp. 575-603). Hershey, PA: Information Science Reference. doi: doi:10.4018/978-1-4666-3994-2.ch030

Ryman-Tubb, N. F. (2011). Neural-Symbolic Processing in Business Applications: Credit Card Fraud Detection. In E. Alonso, & E. Mondragón (Eds.), *Computational Neuroscience for Advancing Artificial Intelligence: Models, Methods and Applications* (pp. 270–314). Hershey, PA: Medical Information Science Reference.

Sadrnia, A., Nezamabadi-Pour, H., Nikbakht, M., & Ismail, N. (2013). A Gravitational Search Algorithm Approach for Optimizing Closed-Loop Logistics Network. In P. Vasant (Ed.), *Meta-Heuristics Optimization Algorithms in Engineering, Business, Economics, and Finance* (pp. 616–638). Hershey, PA: Information Science Reference.

Saigo, H., & Tsuda, K. (2011). Graph Mining in Chemoinformatics. In H. Lodhi, & Y. Yamanishi (Eds.), *Chemoinformatics and Advanced Machine Learning Perspectives: Complex Computational Methods and Collaborative Techniques* (pp. 95–128). Hershey, PA: Medical Information Science Reference.

Sakellarios, A. A., Bourantas, C. V., Athanasiou, L. S., Fotiadis, D. I., & Michalis, L. K. (2013). IVUS Image Processing Methodologies. In I. Management Association (Ed.), Image Processing: Concepts, Methodologies, Tools, and Applications (pp. 639-657). Hershey, PA: Information Science Reference. doi: doi:10.4018/978-1-4666-3994-2.ch033

Samuelson, L. K., Spencer, J. P., & Jenkins, G. W. (2013). A Dynamic Neural Field Model of Word Learning. In L. Gogate, & G. Hollich (Eds.), *Theoretical and Computational Models of Word Learning: Trends in Psychology and Artificial Intelligence* (pp. 1–27). Hershey, PA: Information Science Reference. doi:10.4018/978-1-4666-2973-8.ch001

Sannakki, S. S., Rajpurohit, V. S., Nargund, V. B., Kumar, A. R., & Yallur, P. S. (2013). Computational Intelligence for Pathological Issues in Precision Agriculture. In I. Management Association (Ed.), Image Processing: Concepts, Methodologies, Tools, and Applications (pp. 850-873). Hershey, PA: Information Science Reference. doi: doi:10.4018/978-1-4666-3994-2.ch043

Santillán, C. G., Reyes, L. C., Rodríguez, M. L., Barbosa, J. J., López, O. C., Zarate, G. R., & Hernández, P. (2012). Variants of VRP to Optimize Logistics Management Problems. In C. Ortiz Zezzatti, C. Chira, A. Hernandez, & M. Basurto (Eds.), *Logistics Management and Optimization through Hybrid Artificial Intelligence Systems* (pp. 207–237). Hershey, PA: Information Science Reference. doi:10.4018/978-1-4666-0297-7.ch008

Sato, H., Kubo, M., & Namatame, A. (2011). Evolution of Agents in a Simple Artificial Market. In S. Chen, Y. Kambayashi, & H. Sato (Eds.), *Multi-Agent Applications with Evolutionary Computation and Biologically Inspired Technologies: Intelligent Techniques for Ubiquity and Optimization* (pp. 118–133). Hershey, PA: Medical Information Science Reference.

Sarma, K. K., & Mitra, A. (2012). Estimation of MIMO Wireless Channels Using Artificial Neural Networks. In V. Mago, & N. Bhatia (Eds.), *Cross-Disciplinary Applications of Artificial Intelligence and Pattern Recognition: Advancing Technologies* (pp. 509–543). Hershey, PA: Information Science Reference.

Sasi, S. (2013). Security Applications Using Computer Vision. In I. Management Association (Ed.), Image Processing: Concepts, Methodologies, Tools, and Applications (pp. 1093-1110). Hershey, PA: Information Science Reference. doi: doi:10.4018/978-1-4666-3994-2.ch055

Sato, Y., Ji, Z., & van Dijk, S. (2013). I Think I Have Heard That One Before: Recurrence-Based Word Learning with a Robot. In L. Gogate, & G. Hollich (Eds.), *Theoretical and Computational Models of Word Learning: Trends in Psychology and Artificial Intelligence* (pp. 327–349). Hershey, PA: Information Science Reference. doi:10.4018/978-1-4666-2973-8.ch014

Schmajuk, N. A., & Kutlu, M. G. (2011). An Associative Approach to Additivity and Maximality Effects on Blocking. In E. Alonso, & E. Mondragón (Eds.), *Computational Neuroscience for Advancing Artificial Intelligence: Models, Methods and Applications* (pp. 57–80). Hershey, PA: Medical Information Science Reference.

Segal, J., & Morris, C. (2012). Developing Software for a Scientific Community: Some Challenges and Solutions. In J. Leng, & W. Sharrock (Eds.), *Handbook of Research on Computational Science and Engineering: Theory and Practice* (pp. 177–196). Hershey, PA: Engineering Science Reference.

Sensakovic, W. F., & Armato, S. G. (2013). Techniques for the Automated Segmentation of Lung in Thoracic Computed Tomography Scans. In I. Management Association (Ed.), Image Processing: Concepts, Methodologies, Tools, and Applications (pp. 675-687). Hershey, PA: Information Science Reference. doi: doi:10.4018/978-1-4666-3994-2.ch035

Shabayek, A. E., Morel, O., & Fofi, D. (2013). Visual Behavior Based Bio-Inspired Polarization Techniques in Computer Vision and Robotics. In I. Management Association (Ed.), Image Processing: Concepts, Methodologies, Tools, and Applications (pp. 1463-1491). Hershey, PA: Information Science Reference. doi: doi:10.4018/978-1-4666-3994-2.ch072

Sharma, D., Walia, E., & Sinha, H. (2012). Feature Set Reduction in Rotation Invariant CBIR Using Dual-Tree Complex Wavelet Transform. In V. Mago, & N. Bhatia (Eds.), *Cross-Disciplinary Applications of Artificial Intelligence and Pattern Recognition: Advancing Technologies* (pp. 232–248). Hershey, PA: Information Science Reference.

Sharma, N., Singh, K., & Goyal, D. (2014). Software Engineering, Process Improvement, and Experience Management: Is the Nexus Productive? Clues from the Indian Giants. In I. Management Association (Ed.), Software Design and Development: Concepts, Methodologies, Tools, and Applications (pp. 1401-1414). Hershey, PA: Information Science Reference. doi: doi:10.4018/978-1-4666-4301-7.ch068

Singh, S., Khosla, A., & Saini, J. S. (2014). Nature-Inspired Toolbox to Design and Optimize Systems. In I. Management Association (Ed.), Software Design and Development: Concepts, Methodologies, Tools, and Applications (pp. 644-662). Hershey, PA: Information Science Reference. doi: doi:10.4018/978-1-4666-4301-7.ch031

Snášel, V., Platoš, J., Krömer, P., & Abraham, A. (2012). Designing Light Weight Intrusion Detection Systems: Non-negative Matrix Factorization Approach. In I. Management Association (Ed.), Machine Learning: Concepts, Methodologies, Tools and Applications (pp. 304-317). Hershey, PA: Information Science Reference. doi: doi:10.4018/978-1-60960-818-7.ch213

Song, P., & Wu, X. (2013). Multi-View Stereo Reconstruction Technique. In I. Management Association (Ed.), Image Processing: Concepts, Methodologies, Tools, and Applications (pp. 145-161). Hershey, PA: Information Science Reference. doi: doi:10.4018/978-1-4666-3994-2.ch009

Stoklasa, J. (2012). A Fuzzy Approach to Disaster Modeling: Decision Making Support and Disaster Management Tool for Emergency Medical Rescue Services. In V. Mago, & N. Bhatia (Eds.), *Cross-Disciplinary Applications of Artificial Intelligence and Pattern Recognition: Advancing Technologies* (pp. 564–582). Hershey, PA: Information Science Reference.

Sucar, L. E. (2012). Introduction to Bayesian Networks and Influence Diagrams. In L. Sucar, E. Morales, & J. Hoey (Eds.), *Decision Theory Models for Applications in Artificial Intelligence: Concepts and Solutions* (pp. 9–32). Hershey, PA: Information Science Reference.

Sucar, L. E., Morales, E., & Hoey, J. (2012). Introduction. In L. Sucar, E. Morales, & J. Hoey (Eds.), *Decision Theory Models for Applications in Artificial Intelligence: Concepts and Solutions* (pp. 1–8). Hershey, PA: Information Science Reference.

Takahashi, H., & Terano, T. (2011). Agent-Based Modeling Bridges Theory of Behavioral Finance and Financial Markets. In S. Chen, Y. Kambayashi, & H. Sato (Eds.), *Multi-Agent Applications with Evolutionary Computation and Biologically Inspired Technologies: Intelligent Techniques for Ubiquity and Optimization* (pp. 134–155). Hershey, PA: Medical Information Science Reference.

Takaki, O., Seino, T., Izumi, N., & Hasida, K. (2014). User-Centered Business Process Modeling and Pattern-Based Development for Large Systems. In I. Management Association (Ed.), Software Design and Development: Concepts, Methodologies, Tools, and Applications (pp. 1014-1035). Hershey, PA: Information Science Reference. doi: doi:10.4018/978-1-4666-4301-7.ch049

Taksa, I., Zelikovitz, S., & Spink, A. (2011). Non-Topical Classification of Query Logs Using Background Knowledge. In C. Wei, & Y. Li (Eds.), *Machine Learning Techniques for Adaptive Multimedia Retrieval: Technologies Applications and Perspectives* (pp. 194–212). Hershey, PA: Information Science Reference. doi:10.4018/978-1-60960-818-7.ch314

Tamisier, T., & Feltz, F. (2013). Intelligent Agent for Modeling and Processing Decisional Workflows in Logistics. In S. Nasir (Ed.), *Modern Entrepreneurship and E-Business Innovations* (pp. 198–206). Hershey, PA: Business Science Reference.

Tennyson, R. D. (2011). Computer Interventions for Children with Disabilities: Review of Research and Practice. In P. Ordóñez de Pablos, J. Zhao, & R. Tennyson (Eds.), *Technology Enhanced Learning for People with Disabilities: Approaches and Applications* (pp. 10–33). Hershey, PA: Information Science Reference.

Thackray, S. D., Bourantas, C. V., Loh, P. H., Tsakanikas, V. D., & Fotiadis, D. I. (2013). Optical Coherence Tomography Image Interpretation and Image Processing Methodologies. In I. Management Association (Ed.), Image Processing: Concepts, Methodologies, Tools, and Applications (pp. 513-528). Hershey, PA: Information Science Reference. doi: doi:10.4018/978-1-4666-3994-2.ch026

Thomaz, C. E., do Amaral, V., Giraldi, G. A., Kitani, E. C., Sato, J. R., & Gillies, D. (2012). A Multi-Linear Statistical Method for Discriminant Analysis of 2D Frontal Face Images. In V. Mago, & N. Bhatia (Eds.), *Cross-Disciplinary Applications of Artificial Intelligence and Pattern Recognition: Advancing Technologies* (pp. 18–33). Hershey, PA: Information Science Reference.

Tiwari, R., Shukla, A., & Kala, R. (2013). Graph Based Path Planning. In Intelligent Planning for Mobile Robotics: Algorithmic Approaches (pp. 26-53). Hershey, PA: Information Science Reference. doi: doi:10.4018/978-1-4666-2074-2.ch002

Tomasiello, S. (2012). DQ Based Methods: Theory and Application to Engineering and Physical Sciences. In J. Leng, & W. Sharrock (Eds.), *Handbook of Research on Computational Science and Engineering: Theory and Practice* (pp. 316–346). Hershey, PA: Engineering Science Reference.

Topaloglu, R. O., Manjari, S. R., & Nayak, S. K. (2012). High-Performance Computing for Theoretical Study of Nanoscale and Molecular Interconnects. In J. Leng, & W. Sharrock (Eds.), *Handbook of Research on Computational Science and Engineering: Theory and Practice* (pp. 78–97). Hershey, PA: Engineering Science Reference.

Torii, I., Okada, Y., Onogi, M., & Ishii, N. (2013). Inexpensive, Simple and Quick Photorealistic 3DCG Modeling. In I. Management Association (Ed.), Image Processing: Concepts, Methodologies, Tools, and Applications (pp. 550-561). Hershey, PA: Information Science Reference. doi: doi:10.4018/978-1-4666-3994-2.ch028

Torres, M. D., Soto, A. T., Ortiz Zezzatti, C. A., Sentí, E. E., Díaz, E. D., Landín, C. J., & Amador, C. E. (2012). Hybrid Algorithm Applied to the Identification of Risk Factors on the Health of Newly Born in Mexico. In C. Ortiz Zezzatti, C. Chira, A. Hernandez, & M. Basurto (Eds.), *Logistics Management and Optimization through Hybrid Artificial Intelligence Systems* (pp. 83–112). Hershey, PA: Information Science Reference. doi:10.4018/978-1-4666-0297-7.ch004

Trajkovski, G., Stojanov, G., Collins, S., Eidelman, V., Harman, C., & Vincenti, G. (2011). Cognitive Robotics and Multiagency in a Fuzzy Modeling Framework. In G. Trajkovski (Ed.), *Developments in Intelligent Agent Technologies and Multi-Agent Systems: Concepts and Applications* (pp. 132–152). Hershey, PA: Information Science Reference.

Tsai, J. J., Zhang, J., Huang, J. J., & Yang, S. J. (2012). Supporting CSCW and CSCL with Intelligent Social Grouping Services. In Y. Wang (Ed.), *Software and Intelligent Sciences: New Transdisciplinary Findings* (pp. 420–433). Hershey, PA: Information Science Reference. doi:10.4018/978-1-4666-0261-8.ch024

Twomey, K. E., Horst, J. S., & Morse, A. F. (2013). An Embodied Model of Young Children's Categorization and Word Learning. In L. Gogate, & G. Hollich (Eds.), *Theoretical and Computational Models of Word Learning: Trends in Psychology and Artificial Intelligence* (pp. 172–196). Hershey, PA: Information Science Reference. doi:10.4018/978-1-4666-2973-8.ch008

Ueno, M. (2011). Intelligent LMS with an Agent that Learns from Log Data in a Virtual Community. In B. Daniel (Ed.), *Handbook of Research on Methods and Techniques for Studying Virtual Communities: Paradigms and Phenomena 2 (Vols.)* (pp. 303–317). Hershey, PA: Information Science Reference.

Vallverdú, J., & Casacuberta, D. (2011). Modelling Hardwired Synthetic Emotions: TPR 2.0. In I. Management Association (Ed.), Gaming and Simulations: Concepts, Methodologies, Tools and Applications (pp. 807-818). Hershey, PA: Information Science Reference. doi: doi:10.4018/978-1-60960-195-9.ch314

van Dam, H. J. (2012). Parallel Quantum Chemistry at the Crossroads. In J. Leng, & W. Sharrock (Eds.), *Handbook of Research on Computational Science and Engineering: Theory and Practice* (pp. 239-266). Hershey, PA: Engineering Science Reference.

Vargas-Vera, M., Nagy, M., Zyskowski, D., Haniewicz, K., & Abramowicz, W. (2011). Challenges on Semantic Web Services. In I. Management Association (Ed.), Virtual Communities: Concepts, Methodologies, Tools and Applications (pp. 2134-2157). Hershey, PA: Information Science Reference. doi:doi:10.4018/978-1-60960-100-3.ch702

Veale, R. (2013). A Neurorobotics Approach to Investigating Word Learning Behaviors. In L. Gogate, & G. Hollich (Eds.), *Theoretical and Computational Models of Word Learning: Trends in Psychology and Artificial Intelligence* (pp. 270-295). Hershey, PA: Information Science Reference. doi:10.4018/978-1-4666-2973-8.ch012

Vento, M., & Foggia, P. (2013). Graph Matching Techniques for Computer Vision. In I. Management Association (Ed.), Image Processing: Concepts, Methodologies, Tools, and Applications (pp. 381-421). Hershey, PA: Information Science Reference. doi: doi:10.4018/978-1-4666-3994-2.ch021

Verma, A., & Liu, C. (2012). Efficient Iris Identification with Improved Segmentation Techniques. In V. Mago, & N. Bhatia (Eds.), *Cross-Disciplinary Applications of Artificial Intelligence and Pattern Recognition: Advancing Technologies* (pp. 148-164). Hershey, PA: Information Science Reference.

Vogel, E. H., & Ponce, F. P. (2011). Empirical Issues and Theoretical Mechanisms of Pavlovian Conditioning. In E. Alonso, & E. Mondragón (Eds.), *Computational Neuroscience for Advancing Artificial Intelligence: Models, Methods and Applications* (pp. 81-110). Hershey, PA: Medical Information Science Reference.

Vogt, M., & Bajorath, J. (2011). Virtual Screening Methods Based on Bayesian Statistics. In H. Lodhi, & Y. Yamanishi (Eds.), *Chemoinformatics and Advanced Machine Learning Perspectives: Complex Computational Methods and Collaborative Techniques* (pp. 190-211). Hershey, PA: Medical Information Science Reference.

Walczak, S., Brimhall, B. B., & Lefkowitz, J. B. (2011). Diagnostic Cost Reduction Using Artificial Neural Networks. In I. Management Association (Ed.), Clinical Technologies: Concepts, Methodologies, Tools and Applications (pp. 1812-1830). Hershey, PA: Medical Information Science Reference. doi: doi:10.4018/978-1-60960-561-2.ch614

Walia, E., & Suneja, A. (2013). Fast and High Capacity Digital Image Watermarking Technique Based on Phase of Zernike Moments. In I. Management Association (Ed.), Image Processing: Concepts, Methodologies, Tools, and Applications (pp. 221-234). Hershey, PA: Information Science Reference. doi: doi:10.4018/978-1-4666-3994-2.ch013

Walk, A. M., & Conway, C. M. (2013). Two Distinct Sequence Learning Mechanisms for Syntax Acquisition and Word Learning. In L. Gogate, & G. Hollich (Eds.), *Theoretical and Computational Models of Word Learning: Trends in Psychology and Artificial Intelligence* (pp. 350-369). Hershey, PA: Information Science Reference. doi:10.4018/978-1-4666-2973-8.ch015

Wang, Y. (2012). Convergence of Software Science and Computational Intelligence: A New Transdisciplinary Research Field. In Y. Wang (Ed.), *Software and Intelligent Sciences: New Transdisciplinary Findings* (pp. 1-13). Hershey, PA: Information Science Reference. doi:10.4018/978-1-4666-0261-8.ch001

Wang, Y. (2013). Inference Algebra (IA): A Denotational Mathematics for Cognitive Computing and Machine Reasoning (I). In Y. Wang (Ed.), *Cognitive Informatics for Revealing Human Cognition: Knowledge Manipulations in Natural Intelligence* (pp. 159-177). Hershey, PA: Information Science Reference.

Wang, Y. (2012). On Abstract Intelligence: Toward a Unifying Theory of Natural, Artificial, Machinable, and Computational Intelligence. In Y. Wang (Ed.), *Software and Intelligent Sciences: New Transdisciplinary Findings* (pp. 14-31). Hershey, PA: Information Science Reference. doi:10.4018/978-1-4666-0261-8.ch002

Wang, Y. (2012). On Cognitive Computing. In Y. Wang (Ed.), *Software and Intelligent Sciences: New Transdisciplinary Findings* (pp. 83–97). Hershey, PA: Information Science Reference. doi:10.4018/978-1-4666-0261-8.ch006

Wang, Y. (2012). On the Cognitive Complexity of Software and its Quantification and Formal Measurement. In Y. Wang (Ed.), *Software and Intelligent Sciences: New Transdisciplinary Findings* (pp. 264–286). Hershey, PA: Information Science Reference. doi:10.4018/978-1-4666-0261-8.ch016

Wang, Y. (2012). On Visual Semantic Algebra (VSA): A Denotational Mathematical Structure for Modeling and Manipulating Visual Objects and Patterns. In Y. Wang (Ed.), *Software and Intelligent Sciences: New Transdisciplinary Findings* (pp. 68–81). Hershey, PA: Information Science Reference. doi:10.4018/978-1-4666-0261-8.ch005

Wang, Y. (2012). The Formal Design Model of a Telephone Switching System (TSS). In Y. Wang (Ed.), *Software and Intelligent Sciences: New Transdisciplinary Findings* (pp. 302–326). Hershey, PA: Information Science Reference. doi:10.4018/978-1-4666-0261-8.ch018

Wang, Y., Anand, V., & Cao, X. (2014). Waveband Switching: A Scalable and Cost Efficient Solution for the Internet Backbone. In M. Boucadair, & D. Binet (Eds.), *Solutions for Sustaining Scalability in Internet Growth* (pp. 195–217). Hershey, PA: Information Science Reference.

Wang, Y., Ngolah, C. F., Ahmadi, H., Sheu, P., & Ying, S. (2012). The Formal Design Model of a Lift Dispatching System (LDS). In Y. Wang (Ed.), *Software and Intelligent Sciences: New Transdisciplinary Findings* (pp. 327–351). Hershey, PA: Information Science Reference. doi:10.4018/978-1-4666-0261-8.ch019

Wang, Y., & Patel, S. (2012). Exploring the Cognitive Foundations of Software Engineering. In Y. Wang (Ed.), *Software and Intelligent Sciences: New Transdisciplinary Findings* (pp. 232–251). Hershey, PA: Information Science Reference. doi:10.4018/978-1-4666-0261-8.ch014

Wang, Y., Zadeh, L. A., & Yao, Y. (2012). On the System Algebra Foundations for Granular Computing. In Y. Wang (Ed.), *Software and Intelligent Sciences: New Transdisciplinary Findings* (pp. 98–121). Hershey, PA: Information Science Reference. doi:10.4018/978-1-4666-0261-8.ch007

Watts, C. (2014). Connection, Fragmentation, and Intentionality: Social Software and the Changing Nature of Expertise. In I. Management Association (Ed.), Software Design and Development: Concepts, Methodologies, Tools, and Applications (pp. 883-901). Hershey, PA: Information Science Reference. doi: doi:10.4018/978-1-4666-4301-7.ch042

Williams, J. D. (2012). A Case Study of Applying Decision Theory in the Real World: POMDPs and Spoken Dialog Systems. In L. Sucar, E. Morales, & J. Hoey (Eds.), *Decision Theory Models for Applications in Artificial Intelligence: Concepts and Solutions* (pp. 315–342). Hershey, PA: Information Science Reference.

Wong, C. Y., Seet, G., Sim, S. K., & Pang, W. C. (2014). A Hierarchically Structured Collective of Coordinating Mobile Robots Supervised by a Single Human. In I. Management Association (Ed.), Software Design and Development: Concepts, Methodologies, Tools, and Applications (pp. 1142-1164). Hershey, PA: Information Science Reference. doi: doi:10.4018/978-1-4666-4301-7.ch056

Worth, D., Greenough, C., & Chin, S. (2012). Pragmatic Software Engineering for Computational Science. In J. Leng, & W. Sharrock (Eds.), *Handbook of Research on Computational Science and Engineering: Theory and Practice* (pp. 119–149). Hershey, PA: Engineering Science Reference.

Wrede, B., Schillingmann, L., & Rohlfing, K. J. (2013). Making Use of Multi-Modal Synchrony: A

Model of Acoustic Packaging to Tie Words to Actions L. Gogate, & G. Hollich (Eds.), *Theoretical and Computational Models of Word Learning: Trends in Psychology and Artificial Intelligence* (pp. 224–240). Hershey, PA: Information Science Reference.

Yahya, A., Ghani, F., Ahmad, R. B., Rahman, M., Syuhada, A., Sidek, O., & Salleh, M. F. (2012). Development of an Efficient and Secure Mobile Communication System with New Future Directions. In J. Leng, & W. Sharrock (Eds.), *Handbook of Research on Computational Science and Engineering: Theory and Practice* (pp. 219–238). Hershey, PA: Engineering Science Reference.

Yap, M. H., & Ugail, H. (2013). Facial Image Processing in Computer Vision. In I. Management Association (Ed.), Image Processing: Concepts, Methodologies, Tools, and Applications (pp. 1111-1123). Hershey, PA: Information Science Reference. doi: doi:10.4018/978-1-4666-3994-2.ch056

Ye, S., Park, R., & Lee, D. (2012). Object Segmentation Based on a Nonparametric Snake with Motion Prediction in Video. In V. Mago, & N. Bhatia (Eds.), *Cross-Disciplinary Applications of Artificial Intelligence and Pattern Recognition: Advancing Technologies* (pp. 86–107). Hershey, PA: Information Science Reference.

Yu, C., & Smith, L. B. (2013). A Sensory-Motor Solution to Early Word-Referent Learning. In L. Gogate, & G. Hollich (Eds.), *Theoretical and Computational Models of Word Learning: Trends in Psychology and Artificial Intelligence* (pp. 133–152). Hershey, PA: Information Science Reference. doi:10.4018/978-1-4666-2973-8.ch006

Zakrzewska, D. (2011). Validation of Clustering Techniques for Student Grouping in Intelligent E-learning Systems. In J. Jozefczyk, & D. Orski (Eds.), *Knowledge-Based Intelligent System Advancements: Systemic and Cybernetic Approaches* (pp. 232–251). Hershey, PA: Information Science Reference.

Zarandi, M. H., & Avazbeigi, M. (2012). A New Optimization Approach to Clustering Fuzzy Data for Type-2 Fuzzy System Modeling. In V. Mago, & N. Bhatia (Eds.), *Cross-Disciplinary Applications of Artificial Intelligence and Pattern Recognition: Advancing Technologies* (pp. 499–508). Hershey, PA: Information Science Reference.

Zarandi, M. H., Avazbeigi, M., & Alizadeh, M. (2012). A Neuro-Fuzzy Expert System Trained by Particle Swarm Optimization for Stock Price Prediction. In V. Mago, & N. Bhatia (Eds.), *Cross-Disciplinary Applications of Artificial Intelligence and Pattern Recognition: Advancing Technologies* (pp. 633–650). Hershey, PA: Information Science Reference.

Zemcik, P., Spanel, M., Krsek, P., & Richter, M. (2013). Methods of 3D Object Shape Acquisition. In I. Management Association (Ed.), Image Processing: Concepts, Methodologies, Tools, and Applications (pp. 473-497). Hershey, PA: Information Science Reference. doi: doi:10.4018/978-1-4666-3994-2.ch024

Zeng, C., Jia, W., He, X., & Xu, M. (2013). Recent Advances on Graph-Based Image Segmentation Techniques. In I. Management Association (Ed.), Image Processing: Concepts, Methodologies, Tools, and Applications (pp. 1323-1337). Hershey, PA: Information Science Reference. doi: doi:10.4018/978-1-4666-3994-2.ch065

Zhang, B., Schwartz, F. W., & Tong, D. (2012). Application of Artificial Neural Computation in Topex Waveform Data: A Case Study on Water Ratio Regression. In Y. Wang (Ed.), *Software and Intelligent Sciences: New Transdisciplinary Findings* (pp. 480–490). Hershey, PA: Information Science Reference. doi:10.4018/978-1-4666-0261-8.ch028

Zhang, D. (2012). Machine Learning and Value-Based Software Engineering. In Y. Wang (Ed.), *Software and Intelligent Sciences: New Transdisciplinary Findings* (pp. 287–301). Hershey, PA: Information Science Reference. doi:10.4018/978-1-4666-0261-8.ch017

Zhang, S. (2011). Application of Machine Leaning in Drug Discovery and Development. In H. Lodhi, & Y. Yamanishi (Eds.), *Chemoinformatics and Advanced Machine Learning Perspectives: Complex Computational Methods and Collaborative Techniques* (pp. 235–256). Hershey, PA: Medical Information Science Reference. doi:10.4018/978-1-60960-818-7.ch517

Zhao, J., & Wang, G. (2012). System Uncertainty Based Data-Driven Knowledge Acquisition. In Y. Wang (Ed.), *Software and Intelligent Sciences: New Transdisciplinary Findings* (pp. 451–465). Hershey, PA: Information Science Reference. doi:10.4018/978-1-4666-0261-8.ch026

Zhou, M., & Xu, Y. (2012). Challenges to Use Recommender Systems to Enhance Meta-Cognitive Functioning in Online Learners. In O. Santos, & J. Boticario (Eds.), *Educational Recommender Systems and Technologies: Practices and Challenges* (pp. 282–301). Hershey, PA: Information Science Reference. doi:10.4018/978-1-4666-2455-9.ch099

Zhou, X., & Fujita, H. (2013). Automatic Organ Localization on X-Ray CT Images by Using Ensemble-Learning Techniques. In I. Management Association (Ed.), Image Processing: Concepts, Methodologies, Tools, and Applications (pp. 1379-1394). Hershey, PA: Information Science Reference. doi: doi:10.4018/978-1-4666-3994-2.ch068

Compilation of References

Abe, K., Morii, R., Nishida, K., & Kadonaga, T. (1993). Comparison of Methods for Detecting Corner Points From Digital Curves—A Preliminary Report. In *Proceedings of International Conference on Document Analysis and Recognition*. Tsukuba Science City, Japan: IEEE.

Abraham, A., & Thomas, J. (2005). Distributed intrusion detection systems: a computational intelligence approach. In *Applications of information systems to homeland security and defense*. Idea Group Inc. doi:10.4018/978-1-59140-640-2.ch005

Ada, & RajneetKaur. (2012). Feature Extraction and Principal Component Analysis for Lung Cancer Detection in CT scan Images. *International Journal of Advanced Research in Computer Science and Software Engineering*, 213-218.

Aggarwal, N., Rana, B., & Agrawal, R. K. (2012a). Computer Aided Diagnosis of Alzheimer's Disease from MRI Brain Images. In *Proceedings of International Conference on Image Analysis and Recognition* (pp. 259-267). Aveiro, Portugal: Springer.

Aggarwal, N., Rana, B., & Agrawal, R. K. (2012b). Classification of Alzheimer's from T2 Trans-Axial BrainMR Images: A Comparative Study of Feature Extraction Techniques. *International Journal of Computer Vision and Image Processing*, 2(3), 50–63. doi:10.4018/ijcvip.2012070103

Ahmadi, A., Fotouhi, M., & Khaleghi, M. (2011). Intelligent classification of web pages using contextual and visual features. *Applied Soft Computing*, 1638–1647. doi:10.1016/j.asoc.2010.05.003

Ahmed, F., Siyal, M. Y., & Abbas, V. U. (2010). A secure and robust hash-based scheme for image authentication. *Signal Processing*, 90(5), 1456–1470. doi:10.1016/j.sigpro.2009.05.024

Albrecht, T. et al. (2004). Guidelines for the Use of Contrast Agents in Ultrasound. *Ultraschall in der Medizin (Stuttgart, Germany)*, 25(4), 249–256. doi:10.1055/s-2004-813245 PMID:15300497

Aleixos, N., Blasco, J., Navarron, F., & Molto, E. (2002). Multispectral Inspection of Citrus in Real-time Using Machine Vision and Digital Signal. *Computers and Electronics in Agriculture*, 33, 121–137. doi:10.1016/S0168-1699(02)00002-9

Alon, J., Athitsos, V., Yuan, Q., & Sclaroff, S. (2009). A Unified Framework for Gesture Recognition and spatioemporal Gesture Segmentation. *IEEE Transactions on Pattern Analysis and Machine Intelligence*, 31(9), 1685–1699. doi:10.1109/TPAMI.2008.203 PMID:19574627

alZahir, S. (2006). A low complexity wavelet-packets based image signature for indexing and retrieval. In *Proceedings of Canadian Conference on Electrical and Computer Engineering* (pp. 2107 - 2111). Ottawa, Canada: IEEE.

Al-Zubi, S., Brömme, A., & Tönnies, K. (2003). Using an active shape structural model for biometric sketch recognition. In *Pattern Recognition* (pp. 187–195). Springer. doi:10.1007/978-3-540-45243-0_25

American College of Radiology. (1998). *Illustrated Breast Imaging Reporting and Data System BIRADS* (3rd ed.). American College of Radiology.

Amit, Y., & Geman, D. (1999). A computational model for visual selection. *Neural Computation*, *11*, 1691–1715. doi:10.1162/089976699300016197 PMID:10490943

Anandan, P. (1989). A computational framework and an algorithm for the measurement of visual motion. *International Journal of Computer Vision*, *2*(3), 283–310. doi:10.1007/BF00158167

Anderson, R., & Biham, E. (1996). Tiger-A fast new hash function. In *Proc. of Fast Software Encryption*. Cambridge, UK: Academic Press. doi:10.1007/3-540-60865-6_46

Annadurai, S., & Shanmugalakshmi, R. (2006). *Fundamentals of Digital Image Processing*. Delhi: Dorling Kindersley.

ANOVA. (2013, December 13). Retrieved from: http://www.mathworks.com/help/stats/anova.html

Anter, A., Azar, A., Hassanien, A., El-Bendary, N., & ElSoud, M. (2013). Automatic Computer Aided Segmentation for Liver and Hepatic Lesions Using Hybrid Segmentations Techniques. In *Proceedings of Federated Conference on Computer Science and Information Systems*, (pp. 193-198). IEEE.

Anthony, G., Gregg, H., & Tshilidzi, M. (2007). Image Classification Using SVMs: One-against-One Vs One-against-All. *in Proc. of the 28th Asian Conference on Remote Sensing*.

Aranda-Sanchez, J., Baltazar, A., & Gonzlez-Aguilar, G. (2009). Implementation of a Bayesian classi. *Biosystems Engineering*, *2*(102), 274–284. doi:10.1016/j.biosystemseng.2008.12.005

Arther, D., & Vassilvitskii, S. (2007). k-means++: The advantages of careful seeding. *Eighteenth annual ACM-SIAM symposium on Discrete algorithms*. (pp. 1027-1035). Astor Crowne Plaza, New Orleans, Louisiana: Society for Industrial and Applied Mathematics.

Asada, H., & Brady, M. (1986). The curvature primal sketch. *IEEE Transactions on Pattern Analysis and Machine Intelligence*, *8*, 2–4. doi:10.1109/TPAMI.1986.4767747 PMID:21869318

Ashburner, J. (2007). A fast diffeomorphic image registration algorithm. *NeuroImage*, *38*, 95–113. doi:10.1016/j.neuroimage.2007.07.007 PMID:17761438

Ashman, J. (2010). *Measuring Named Entity Similarity Through Wikipedia Category Hierarchies*. (MSc thesis). The University of Texas at Arlington, Arlington, TX.

AT&T Laboratories Cambridge. (2002). *Olivetti Research Laboratory (ORL) face database*. Retrieved from http://www.cl.cam.ac.uk/research/dtg/attarchive/facedatabase.html

Attneave, F. (1954). Some Informational Aspects of Visual Perception. *Psychological Review*, *61*, 183–193. doi:10.1037/h0054663 PMID:13167245

Avrahami, G., & Pratt, V. (1991). Sub-pixel edge detection in character digitization. In *Proceedings of International Conference on Raster Imaging and Digital Typography II*. Cambridge University Press.

Babalola, K., Patenaude, B., Aljabar, P., Schnabel, J., Kennedy, D., & Crum, W. … Rueckert, D. (2008). Comparison and Evaluation of Segmentation Techniques for Subcortical Structures in Brain MRI. In Medical Image Computing and Computer-Assisted Intervention MIC-CAI, (LNCS), (Vol. 5241, pp. 409-416). Berlin: Springer.

Baeten, Boedrij, Beckers, & Claesen. (2008). Autonomous fruit picking machine: a robotic apple harvester. *Field and Service Robotics*, *42*, 531–539. doi:10.1007/978-3-540-75404-6_51

Bagci, U., & Bai, L. (2007). A Comparison of Daubechies and Gabor Wavelets for Classification of MR Images. In *Proceedings of International Conference on Signal Processing and Communications* (pp. 676-679). Dubai: IEEE.

Bakelman, N., Monaco, J. V., Cha, S. H., & Tappert, C. C. (2013, August). Keystroke biometric studies on password and numeric keypad input. In *Proceedings of Intelligence and Security Informatics Conference (EISIC), 2013 European* (pp. 204-207). Uppsala, Sweden: IEEE.

balestani, A., Moghaddam, P., motlaq, A., & Dolaty, H. (2012). Sorting and Grading of Cherries on the Basis of Ripeness, Size and Defects by Using Image Processing Techniques. *International Journal of Agriculture and Crop Sciences(IJACS)*, *4* (16), 1144-1149.

Ballard, D. H., & Brown, C. M. (1982). *Computer Vision*. New York: Prentice Hall.

Baltazar, A., Aranda, J., & Gonzalez-Aguilar, G. (2008). Bayesian classification of ripening stages of tomato fruit using acoustic impact and colorimeter sensor data. *Computers and Electronics in Agriculture*, *60*(2), 113–121. doi:10.1016/j.compag.2007.07.005

Banissi, E., & Sarfraz, M. (2012). *Computer Graphics, Imaging and Visualization*. IEEE Computer Society.

Barron, J. L., Fleet, D. J., & Beachemin, S. S. (1994). Performance of optical flow techniques. *International Journal of Computer Vision*, *12*(1), 43–77. doi:10.1007/BF01420984

Bazazian, S., & Gavrilova, M. (2012, May). Context based gait recognition. In SPIE Defense, Security, and Sensing (pp. 84070J-84070J). SPIE Press.

Beauchemin, Bauer, Kowsari, & Cho. (2011). Portable and Scalable Vision Based Vehicular Instrumentation for the Analysis of Driver Intentionality. *IEEE Transactions on Instrumentation and Measurement*.

Belasque, J. Jr, Gasparoto, M. C. G., & Marcassa, L. G. (2008). Detection of mechanical and disease stresses in citrus plants by fluorescence spectroscopy. *Applied Optics*, *47*(11), 1922–1926. doi:10.1364/AO.47.001922 PMID:18404192

Belhumeur, P. N., Hespanha, J. P., & Kriegman, D. J. (1997). Eigenfaces Vs. Fisherfaces Recognition using class specific linear projection. *IEEE Transactions on Pattern Analysis and Machine Intelligence*, *19*, 711–720. doi:10.1109/34.598228

Bellman, R. (1961). *Adaptive control processes: A guided tour*. Princeton University Press.

Berg, W., Campassi, C., Langenberg, P., & Sexton, M. (2000). Breast Imaging Reporting and Data System: Inter - and Intraobserver Variability. *Feature Analysis and Final Assessment*, *174*(6), 1769–1777. PMID:10845521

Beus, H. L., & Tiu, S. S. H. (1987). An Improved Corner Detection Algorithm based on Chain Coded Plane Curves. *Pattern Recognition*, *20*, 291–296. doi:10.1016/0031-3203(87)90004-5

Bezdek, J. (1973). *Fuzzy Mathematics in Pattern Classification*. (Ph.D. thesis). Applied Mathematic Center, Cornell University, Ithaca, NY.

Birdwell, R., Ikeda, D., Oshaughnessy, K., & Sickles, E. (2001). Mammographic Characteristics of 115 Missed Cancers Later Detected with Screening Mammography and Potential Utility of Computer-aided Detection. *Radiology*, *219*, 192–202. doi:10.1148/radiology.219.1.r01ap16192 PMID:11274556

Bishop, C. M. (2006). *Pattern recognition and machine learning* (Vol. 1, p. 740). New York: Springer.

Blake, A., & Isard, M. (2000). *Active Contours*. Berlin: Springer.

Blot, L., & Zwiggelaar, R. (2001). Background texture extraction for the classification of mammographic parenchymal patterns. *Journal of Medical Image Understanding and Analysis*, 145-148.

Bluemke, D., & Fishman, E. (1993). Spiral CT of the liver. *AIR*, *160*, 787–792. PMID:8456666

Bluemke, D., Urban, B., & Fishman, E. (1994). Spiral CT of the liver: Current applications. *Seminars in Ultrasound, CT, and MR*, *15*, 107–121. doi:10.1016/S0887-2171(05)80093-9 PMID:8198817

Blum, R. S., & Liu, Z. (2006). *Multi-Sensor Image Fusion and Its Applications*. Boca Raton, FL: CRC Press.

Bo, C., Zhang, L., Li, X. Y., Huang, Q., & Wang, Y. (2013). SilentSense: Silent user identification via touch and movement behavioral biometrics. In *Proceedings of the 19th annual international conference on Mobile computing & networking* (pp. 187-190). New York, NY: ACM.

Boolchandani, D., & Sahula, V. (2011). *Int. Journal of design, analysis, and tools for circuits and systems*, *1*, 1-8.

Bosson, A., & Cawley, G. C. Y., & R., H. (2002). Blocking pornographic images. Proceedings of the International Conference on the Challenge of Image and Video Retrieval. *Lecture Notes in Computer Science*, *2383*, 50–60.

Bottino, C. M., Castro, C. C., Gomes, R. L., Buchpiguel, C. A., Marchetti, R. L., & Neto, M. R. (2002). Volumetric MRI measurements can differentiate Alzheimer's disease, mild cognitive impairment, and normal aging. *International Psychogeriatrics*, *14*(1), 59–72. doi:10.1017/S1041610202008281 PMID:12094908

Bours, P. (2012). Continuous keystroke dynamics: A different perspective towards biometric evaluation. *Information Security Technical Report*, *17*(1), 36–43. doi:10.1016/j.istr.2012.02.001

Bovis, K., & Singh, S. (2002). Classification of mammographic breast density using a combined classifier paradigm. In *Proc. Medical Image Understanding and Analysis (MIUA) conference*. MIUA.

Bravo, C., Moshou, D., Oberti, R., West, J., McCartney, A., Bodria, L., & Ramon, H. (2004). Foliar Disease Detection in the Field using Optical Sensor Fusion. *Agricultural Engineering International: the CIGR Journal of Scientific Research and Development*, *6*, 1–14.

Bretzner, L., Laptev, I., Lindeberg, T., Lenman, S., & Sundblad, Y. (2001). A Prototype System for Computer vision Based Human Computer Interaction. Technical report ISRN KTH/NA/P-01/09-SE.

Brezmes, J., Llobet, E., Vilanova, X., Saiz, G., & Correig, X. (2000). Fruit ripeness monitoring using an electronic nose. *Sensors and Actuators B-Chem Journal*, *69*, 223–229. doi:10.1016/S0925-4005(00)00494-9

Bronzino, J. (2000). *The Biomedical Engineering Handbook 2*. Heidelberg, Germany: Springer.

Brooks, S., Saunders, I., & Dodgson, N. A. (February 2007). Image compression using sparse colour sampling combined with nonlinear image processin. *The 19th Symposium on Electronic Imaging (SPIE)* (pp. 64920F-64920F). San Jose, California, USA: International Society for Optics and Photonics.

Buemi, F., Massa, M., & Sandini, G. (1995). Agrobot: A Robotic System for Greenhouse Operations. *Robotics in Agriculture & The Food Industry*, *4*, 172–184.

Bulanon, D. M., Burks, T. F., & Alchanatis, V. (2009). Image fusion of visible and thermal images for fruit detection. *Biosystems Engineering*, *103*, 12–22. doi:10.1016/j.biosystemseng.2009.02.009

Burger, W., & Burge, M. J. (2007). *Digital Image Processing: An Algorithmic Approach Using Java*. Berlin: Springer.

Burton, A. M., Jenkins, R., Hancock, P. J. B., & White, D. (2005). Robust representations for face recognition: The power of averages. *Cognitive Psychology*, *51*, 256–284. doi:10.1016/j.cogpsych.2005.06.003 PMID:16198327

Bush, B. (2013, December 12). *Fuzzy Clustering Techniques: Fuzzy C-Means and Fuzzy Min-Max Clustering Neural Networks*. Retrieved from http://benjaminjamesbush.com/fuzzyclustering/fuzzyclustering.docx

Byng, W., Boyd, F., Fishell, E., Jong, A., & Yaffe, J. (1996). Automated analysis of mammographic densities. *Physics in Medicine and Biology*, *41*(5), 909–923. doi:10.1088/0031-9155/41/5/007 PMID:8735257

ByoungChul, & Ko Sooyeong Kwak. (2012). Survey of computer vision–based natural disaster warning systems. *OPTICAL Engineering*, *51*(7).

Cabrelli, C. A., & Molter, U. M. (1990). Automatic representation of binary images. *IEEE Transactions on Pattern Analysis and Machine Intelligence*, *12*, 1190–1196. doi:10.1109/34.62608

Caldwell, B., Stapleton, J., Holdsworth, W., Jong, A., Weiser, J., Cooke, G., & Yaffe, J. (1990). Characterization of mammographic parenchymal pattern by fractal dimension. *Physics in Medicine and Biology*, *35*, 235–247. doi:10.1088/0031-9155/35/2/004 PMID:2315379

Camelo, A. L. (2004). Manual for the preparation and sale of fruits and vegetables From field to market (version 151 ed.). Rome: in Food ans Agriculture Organization (FAO) of the United Nations (UN), Agricultural Services Bulletin.

Cancellaro, M., Battisti, F., Carli, M., Boato, G., DeNatale, F. G. B., & Neri, A. (2011). A commutative digital image watermarking and encryption method in the tree structured Haar transform domain. *Signal Processing Image Communication*, *26*, 1–12. doi:10.1016/j.image.2010.11.001

Cao, B., Wang, G., Chen, S., & Guo, S. (2010). *Fuzzy Information and Engineering 2010* (Vol. 1). Heidelberg, Germany: Springer. doi:10.1007/978-3-642-14880-4

Carsten, S., Ulrich, M., & Wiedemann, C. (2007). *Machine Vision Algorithms and Applications*. Hoboken, NJ: Wiley.

Cevikalp, H., Yavuz, H. S., Cay, M. A., & Barkana, A. (2009). Two-dimensional subspace classifiers for face recognition. *Neurocomputing*, *72*, 1111–1120. doi:10.1016/j.neucom.2008.02.015

Chan, C. H., Tahir, M. A., Kittler, J., & Pietika, ¨. M. (2013). Multiscale Local Phase Quantization for Robust Component-Based Face Recognition Using Kernel Fusion of Multiple Descriptors. *IEEE Transactions on Pattern Analysis and Machine Intelligence, 35*(5), 1164–1177. doi:10.1109/TPAMI.2012.199 PMID:23520257

Chang, C.C., Tsai, P., & Lin, M.H. (2004). An adaptive steganography for index-based images using codeword grouping. *Advances in Multimedia Information Processing, 731*-738.

Chang, C. C., Hu, Y. S., & Lu, T. C. (2006). A watermarking-based image ownership and tampering authentication scheme. *Pattern Recognition Letters, 27*(5), 439–446. doi:10.1016/j.patrec.2005.09.006

Chaplot, S., Patnaik, L. M., & Jagannathan, N. R. (2006). Classification of magnetic resonance brain images using wavelets as input to support vector machine and neural network. *Biomedical Signal Processing and Control, 1*(1), 86–92. doi:10.1016/j.bspc.2006.05.002

Charalambous, C. (1992). Conjugate gradient algorithm for efficient training of artificial neural networks.[]. The Institution of Engineering and Technology.]. *Proceedings of the IEEE, 139*, 301–310.

Chaudhary, A., & Gupta, A. (2012). Automated Switching System for Skin Pixel Segmentation in Varied Lightin. In *Proceedings of 19th IEEE International Conference on Mechatronics and Machine Vision in Practice* (pp. 26-31). Auckland, New Zealand: IEEE.

Chaudhary, A., Raheja, J. L., & Das, K. (2011). A Vision based Real Time System to Control Remote Robotic hand Fingers. In *Proceedings of the IEEE International Conference on Computer Control and Automation* (pp. 118-122). IEEE.

Chaudhary, A., & Raheja, J. L. (2013). Bent fingers' angle calculation using supervised ANN to control electro-mechanical robotic hand. *Computers & Electrical Engineering, 39*(2), 560–570. doi:10.1016/j.compeleceng.2012.07.012

Chaudhary, A., Raheja, J. L., Das, K., & Raheja, S. (2001). A Survey on Hand Gesture Recognition in context of Soft Computing. In *Advanced Computing, CCIS* (pp. 46–55). London: Springer.

Chaudhary, A., Raheja, J. L., Das, K., & Raheja, S. (2012). Both Hands' Fingers' Angle Calculation from Live Video. *International Journal of Computer Vision and Image Processing, 2*(2), 1–11. doi:10.4018/ijcvip.2012040101

Chaumont, M., & Puech, W. (2009). Protecting the color information by hiding it. *Recent Advances in Signal Processing, 22.*

Chen, B., Wang, K., Li, S., Wang, J., Bai, J., Xiao, C., & Lai, J. (2008). Spectrum characteristics of cotton canopy infected with verticillium wilt and inversion of severity level. In Computer and Computing Technologies In Agriculture, (vol. 2, pp. 1169-1180). Springer US.

Chen, Y., & Lin, K. (2011). Display Region Segmentation from a Computer Screen Image using Closed-Contour Tracking. In *Proceedings of International Conference on Machine Learning and Cybernetics* (pp. 1739-1745). Academic Press.

Chen, Z. O, W., Zhu, M., & W., H. (2006). A novel web page filtering system by combining texts and images. In *Proceedings of the 2006 IEEE/WIC/ACM International Conference on Web Intelligence,* (pp. 732-735). Washington, DC: IEEE Computer Society.

Cheng, L., & Vishwanathan, S. V. (2007). Learning to compress images and videos. *The 24th international conference on Machine learning* (pp. 161-168). Oregon State University, Oregon, USA: ACM.

Cheng, H., & Li, X. (2000). Partial encryption of images and videos. *IEEE Transactions on Signal Processing, 48*(8), 2439–2451. doi:10.1109/78.852023

Cheng, M., Fang, B., Tang, Y. Y., Zhang, T., & Wen, J. (2010). Incremental Embedding and Learning in the Local Discriminant Subspace With Application to Face Recognition. *IEEE Transactions on Systems, Man and Cybernetics. Part C, Applications and Reviews, 40*(5), 580–591. doi:10.1109/TSMCC.2010.2043529

Chetrikov, D., & Zsabo, S. (1999). A simple and efficient algorithm for detection of high curvature points in planar curves. *Electronic Publishing, 6*(3), 195–198.

Chetverikov, D., & Szabo, Z. (1999). A Simple and Efficient Algorithm for Detection of High Curvature Points in Planner Curves. In *Proceedings of 23rd Workshop of Australian Pattern Recognition Group*, (pp. 175-184). Academic Press.

Choi, Y. H., Tapias, E. C., Kim, H. K., Lefeber, A. W. M., Erkelens, C., & Verhoeven, J. T. J. et al. (2004). Metabolic Discrimination of Catharanthus Roseus Leaves Infected by Phytoplasma using 1H-NMR Spectroscopy and Multivariate Data Analysis. *Plant Physiology, 135*, 2398–2410. doi:10.1104/pp.104.041012 PMID:15286294

Chua, T. S., Tan, K. L., & Chin Ooi, B. (1997). Fast signature based color-spatial image retrieval. In *Proceedings of IEEE International Conference on Multimedia Computing and Systems*, (pp. 362-369). Ottawa, Canada: IEEE.

Coates, L., & Johnson, G. (1997). Postharvest Diseases of Fruit and Vegetables. In J. Brown, & H. Ogle (Eds.), *Plant pathogens and plant diseases*. Armidale: Rockvale Publications.

Comaniciu, D., & Meer, P. (2002). Mean shift: A robust approach toward feature space analysis. *IEEE Transactions on Pattern Analysis and Machine Intelligence, 24*(5), 603–619. doi:10.1109/34.1000236

Combs, D., Herman, M., Hong, T., & Nashman, M. (1998). Real time obstacle avoidance using control flow divergence and peripheral flow. *IEEE Transactions on Robotics and Automation, 14*(1), 49–59. doi:10.1109/70.660840

Computer Vision. (2012). *Wikipedia*. Retrieved from http://en.wikipedia.org/wiki/Computer_vision

Couceiro, M. S., Luz, J. M., Figueiredo, C. M., Ferreira, N. M., & Dias, G. (2010). Parameter Estimation for a Mathematical Model of the Golf Putting. In V. M. Marques, C. S. Pereira, & A. Madureira (Eds.), *Proceedings of WACI-Workshop Applications of Computational Intelligence* (pp. 1-8). Coimbra, Portugal: ISEC - IPC.

Couceiro, M. S., Martins, F. M., Rocha, R. P., & Ferreira, N. M. (2012). Analysis and Parameter Adjustment of the RDPSO - Towards an Understanding of Robotic Network Dynamic Partitioning based on Darwin's Theory. *International Mathematical Forum, 7*(32), 1587-1601.

Couceiro, M. S., Rocha, R. P., Ferreira, N. M., & Machado, J. T. (2012). *Introducing the Fractional Order Darwinian PSO*. Signal, Image and Video Processing, Fractional Signals and Systems.

Cowan, A., Cripps, R., Richings, E., & Taylor, N. (2001). Fruit size: towards an understanding of the metabolic control of fruit growth using avocado as a model system. *Physiologia Plantarum, 111*, 127–139. doi:10.1034/j.1399-3054.2001.1110201.x

Cox, I. J., & Miller, M. L. (1997). A review of watermarking and the importance of perceptual modeling. *SPIE. Human Vision & Electronic Imaging II, 3016*, 92–99. doi:10.1117/12.274502

Crammer, K., & Singer, Y. (2001). On the Algorithmic Implementation of Multiclass Kernel-based Vector Machines. *Journal of Machine Learning Research, 2*, 265–292.

Crowley, J. L., & Christensen, H. I. (Eds.). (1995). *Vision as Process*. Berlin: Springer-Verlag. doi:10.1007/978-3-662-03113-1

Dabbaghchian, S., Ghaemmaghami, M. P., & Aghagolzadeh, A. (2010). Feature extraction using discrete cosine transform and discrimination power analysis with a face recognition technology. *Pattern Recognition, 43*, 1431–1440. doi:10.1016/j.patcog.2009.11.001

Dadwal, S. M., & Banga, V. (2012). Estimate Ripeness Level of fruits Using RGB Color Space and Fuzzy Logic Technique. [IJEAT]. *International Journal of Engineering and Advanced Technology, 02*(01), 225–229.

Dahshan, E.-S. A., Hosny, T., & Salem, A.-B. M. (2010). A hybrid technique for automatic MRI brain images classification. *Digital Signal Processing, 20*, 433–441. doi:10.1016/j.dsp.2009.07.002

Damiri, D., & Slamet, C. (2012). Application of Image Processing and Artificial Neural Networks to Identify Ripeness and Maturity of the Lime(citrus medica). *INTERNATIONAL JOURNAL OF BASIC AND APPLIED SCIENCE, 01*(02), 171–179.

Dang, G., Changsha, P. R., & Cheng, Z.-Q. (2009). A reverse-projecting pixel-level painting algorithm. In *Proceedings of the IEEE International Conference on Image and Graphics*. Xi'an, China: IEEE.

Daoqiang, Z., & Zhi-Hua, Z. (2005). (2D)^{2}PCA Two directional two dimensional PCA for efficient face representation and recognition. *Neurocomputing, 69*, 224–231. doi:10.1016/j.neucom.2005.06.004

Databases. (2011). Retrieved November 20, 2011, from http://bias.csr.unibo.it/fvc2000/databases.asp

Daubechies, I. (1992). *Ten Lectures on Wavelets*. Philadelphia: SIAM. doi:10.1137/1.9781611970104

Davies, E. R. (1988). Application of generalized Hough transform to corner detection. *IEE Proceedings, 135E*(1), 49-54.

Davies, E. R. (2005). Machine Vision: Theory, Algorithms, Practicalities. San Francisco: Morgan Kaufmann. Azad, P., Gockel, T., & Dillmann, R. (2008). Computer Vision – Principles and Practice. Elektor International Media BV.

de Queiroz, R. L. (2010). Reversible color-to-gray mapping using subband domain texturization. *Pattern Recognition Letters, 31*(4), 269–276. doi:10.1016/j.patrec.2008.11.010

de Queiroz, R. L., & Braun, K. M. (2006). Color to gray and back: color embedding into textured gray images. *IEEE Transactions on Image Processing, 15*(6), 1464–1470. doi:10.1109/TIP.2006.871181 PMID:16764271

Dehlcamp, H., Pece, A. E. C., Ottlik, A., & Nagel, H.-H. (2005). Differential analysis of two model based vehicle tracking approaches. In *Proceedings of the 26th DAGM Symposium* (LNCS), (vol. 3175). Tübingen, Germany: Springer.

Deriche, R., & Faugeras, O. D. (1990). 2D curve matching using high curvature points: Application to stereo vision. In *Proceedings of 10th International Conference on Pattern Recognition*. Atlantic City, NJ: IEEE.

Deriche, R., & Giraudon, G. (1990). Accurate corner detection: An analytical study. In *Proceedings of 3rd International Conference on Computer Vision*. Osaka, Japan: IEEE.

Digestive Disorders Health Center. (2013, December 8). Retrieved from http://www.webmd.com/digestive-disorders/picture-of-the-liver

Digital Image Processing. (2012). *Wikipedia*. Retrieved from http://en.wikipedia.org/wiki/Image_processing#References

Do, J. et al. (2006). Advanced Soft Remote Control System Using Hand Gestures. In *MICAI (Advances in Artificial Intelligence), (LNAI)* (Vol. 4293, pp. 745–755). Berlin: Springer. doi:10.1007/11925231_71

Dreschler, L., & Nagel, H. H. (1982). On the selection of critical points and local curvature extrema of region boundaries for interframe matching. In *Proceedings of International Conference on Pattern Recognition*. Munich, Germany: Springer.

Duan, L., Cui, G., Gao, W., & Zhang, H. (2002). Adult image detection method base-on skin color model and support vector machine. In *Proceedings of Asian Conference on computer Vision* (pp. 797-800). Melbourne, Australia: Academic Press.

Dubey, S. R., & Jalal, A. S. (2012b). Detection and Classification of Apple Fruit Diseases using Complete Local Binary Patterns. In *Proceedings of the 3rd International Conference on Computer and Communication Technology* (pp. 346-351). MNNIT Allahabad.

Dubey, S. R. (2012). *Automatic Recognition of Fruits and Vegetables and Detection of Fruit Diseases. (Master's theses)*. India: GLA University Mathura.

Dubey, S. R., Dixit, P., Singh, N., & Gupta, J. P. (2013). Infected fruit part detection using K-means clustering segmentation technique. *International Journal of Artificial Intelligence and Interactive Multimedia, 2*(2). doi:10.9781/ijimai.2013.229

Dubey, S. R., & Jalal, A. S. (2012a). Robust Approach for Fruit and Vegetable Classification. *Procedia Engineering, 38*, 3449–3453. doi:10.1016/j.proeng.2012.06.398

Dubey, S. R., & Jalal, A. S. (2012c). Adapted Approach for Fruit Disease Identification using Images. *International Journal of Computer Vision and Image Processing*, 2(3), 51–65. doi:10.4018/ijcvip.2012070104

Dubey, S. R., & Jalal, A. S. (2013). Species and Variety Detection of Fruits and Vegetables from Images. *International Journal of Applied Pattern Recognition*, 1(1), 108–126. doi:10.1504/IJAPR.2013.052343

Duda, R., Hart, P., & Stork, D. (2001). *Pattern Classification* (2nd ed.). Chichester, UK: John Wiley Sons.

Duin, R., Juszcak, P., Paclik, P., Pekalska, E., De Ridder, D., & Tax, D. (2004, January). *PrTools: The Matlab Toolbox for Pattern Recognition*. Retrieved from http://www.prtools.org

Du, K.-L., & Swamy, M. N. S. (2006). *Neural Networks in a Softcomputing Framework*. London: Springer-Verlag London Limited.

Eberhart, R. C., & Shi, Y. (2000). Comparing inertia weights and constriction factors in particle swarm optimization. In *Proceedings of the 2000 Congress on Evolutionary Computation*, (pp. 84-88). IEEE.

Edan, Y. (1995). Design of an autonomous agricultural robot. *Applied Intelligence*, 5, 41–50. doi:10.1007/BF00872782

Edwards, C., Kupinski, A., Metz, E., & Nishikawa, M. (2002). Maximum likelihood fitting of FROC curves under an initial detection and candidate analysis model. *Medical Physics*, 29, 2861–2870. doi:10.1118/1.1524631 PMID:12512721

Effendi, Z., Ramli, R., & Ghani, J. (2010). A Back Propagation Neural Networks for Grading Jatropha curcas Fruits Maturity. *American Journal of Applied Sciences*, 390–394. doi:10.3844/ajassp.2010.390.394

Elad, M., & Fener, A. (1998). Recursive optical flow estimation. *Journal of Visual Communication and Image Representation*, 9(2), 119–138. doi:10.1006/jvci.1998.0382

El-Bendary, N., Zawbaa, H. M., Hassanien, A. E., & Snasel, V. (2011). PCA-based Home Videos Annotation System. *The International Journal of Reasoning-based Intelligent Systems*, 3(2), 71–79.

Elhariri, E., El-Bendary, N., Fouad, M. M., Plato, J., Hassanien, A. E., & Hussein, A. M. (2014). Multiclass SVM Based Classification Approach for Tomato Ripeness. *Innovations in Bio-inspired Computing and Applications*[Springer.]. *Advances in Intelligent Systems and Computing.*, 237, 175–186. doi:10.1007/978-3-319-01781-5_17

El-henawy, I., Eisa, M., Elsoud, M., & Anter, M. (2010). Fast mammogram segmentation algorithm for segmentating fibroglandular tissue. *IJICS*, 10(1), 187–199.

ElSoud, M., & Anter, M. (2012). Automatic mammogram segmentation and computer aided diagnoses for breast tissue density according to BIRADS dictionary. *Int. J. Computer Aided Engineering and Technology*, 4(2), 165–180. doi:10.1504/IJCAET.2012.045655

Erol, A., Bebis, G., Nicolescu, M., Boyle, R. D., & Twombly, X. (2007). Vision-based Hand Pose Estimation: A Review. *Computer Vision and Image Understanding*, 108, 52–73. doi:10.1016/j.cviu.2006.10.012

Etemad, K., & Chellappa, R. (1997). Discriminant analysis for recognition of human face images. *Journal of the Optical Society of America*, 14, 1724–1733. doi:10.1364/JOSAA.14.001724

Fadilah, N., Mohamad-Saleh, J., Halim, Z. A., Ibrahim, H., & Ali, S. S. (2012). Intelligent Color Vision System for Ripeness Classification of Oil Palm Fresh Fruit Bunch. *Sensors (Basel, Switzerland)*, 12, 14179–14195. doi:10.3390/s121014179 PMID:23202043

Faez, K., & Farajzadeh, N. (2006). A performance comparison of the ZM, PZM and LM in the face recognition system in presence of salt-pepper noise. In *Proceedings of IEEE International Conference on System Man and Cybernetics*, (Vol. 5, pp. 4197-4201). Taipei, Taiwan: IEEE.

Fermuller, C., Shulman, D., & Akimou, Y. (2001). The statistics of optical flow. *Journal of Computer Vision and Image Understanding*, 82, 1–32. doi:10.1006/cviu.2000.0900

Fernando, L.-G., Gabriela, A.-G., Blasco, J., Aleixos, N., & Valiente, J.-M. (2010). Automatic detection of skin defects in citrus fruits using a multivariate image analysis approach. *Computers and Electronics in Agriculture*, 71(2), 189–197. doi:10.1016/j.compag.2010.02.001

Fisher, R., Dawson-Howe, K., Fitzgibbon, A., Robertson, C., & Trucco, E. (2005). *Dictionary of Computer Vision and Image Processing*. Hoboken, NJ: John Wiley. doi:10.1002/0470016302

Fleet, P. J. V. (2007). *Discrete Wavelet Transformations*. John Wiley & Sons, Inc.

Forsyth, D. A., & Ponce, J. (2003). *Computer Vision: A Modern Approach*. New York: Prentice Hall.

Frakes, W. B., & Baeza-Yates, R. (1992). *Information Retrieval, Data Structure and Algorithms*. Prentice Hall.

Frank, M., Biedert, R., Ma, E., Martinovic, I., & Song, D. (2013). Touchalytics: On the applicability of touchscreen input as a behavioral biometric for continuous authentication. *Information Forensics and Security. IEEE Transactions on*, 8(1), 136–148.

Freeman, H., & Davis, L. S. (1977). A Corner Finding Algorithm for Chain Coded Curves. *IEEE Transactions on Computers*, 26, 297–303. doi:10.1109/TC.1977.1674825

Freer, W., & Ulissey, J. (2001). Screening mammography with computer-aided detection, Study 12860 patients in a community breast center. *Radiology*, 220, 781–786. doi:10.1148/radiol.2203001282 PMID:11526282

Fridrich, J. (1999). Robust bit extraction from images. In *Proc. of International Conference on Multimedia Computing and Systems*, Florence, (pp. 536-540). Academic Press.

Furht, B., & Kirovski, D. (2004). *Multimedia Security Handbook*. CRC Press. doi:10.1201/9781420038262

Gabor, D. (1946). Theory of communication. *Journal of the Institution of Electrical Engineers*, 93(3), 429–457.

Gabriel, A. L. V., & Aguilera, J. M. (2013). Automatic detection of orientation and diseases in blueberries using image analysis to improve their postharvest storage quality. *Food Control*, 33(1), 166–173. doi:10.1016/j.foodcont.2013.02.025

Gastaldi, G., et al. (2005). A Man-Machine Communication System Based on the Visual Analysis of Dynamic Gestures. In *Proceedings of International Conference on Image Processing* (pp. 397-400). Academic Press.

Gavrilova, M. (Ed.). (2008). *Generalized voronoi diagram: a geometry-based approach to computational intelligence* (Vol. 158). Berlin, Germany: Springer Verlag.

Gavrilova, M. L., & Monwar, M. (2013). *Multimodal biometrics and intelligent image processing for security systems*. IGI Global. doi:10.4018/978-1-4666-3646-0

Georghiades, A. S. (1997). *Yale face database*. Retrieved from http://cvc.yale.edu/projects/yalefaces/yalefaces.html

Ge, X., Yang, J., & Zheng, Z., & F., L. (2006). Multi-view based face chin contour extraction. *Engineering Applications of Artificial Intelligence*, 545–555. doi:10.1016/j.engappai.2005.12.010

Ghamisi, P., Couceiro, M. S., Benediktsson, J. A., & Ferreira, N. M. (2012). An Efficient Method for Segmentation of Images Based on Fractional Calculus and Natural Selection. *Expert Systems with Applications*, 39(16), 12407–12417. doi:10.1016/j.eswa.2012.04.078

Ghazali, K. H., Samad, R., Arshad, N. W., & Karim, R. A. (2009). Image Processing Analysis of Oil Palm Fruits for Automatic Grading. *International Conference on Instrumentation, Control & Automation* (pp. 75-78). Bandung, Indonesia: ica-itb.

Girgis, M. R., Mahmoud, T. M., & Abd-El-Hafeez, T. (2007). An Approach to Image Extraction and Accurate Skin Detection from Web Pages. *International Journal of Computer Science and Engineering*, 1(1307-3699), 88-96.

Girgis, M. R., Mahmoud, T. M., & Abd-El-Hafeez, T. (2010). A New Effective System for Filtering Pornography Images from Web Pages and PDF Files. *International Journal of Web Applications*, 2.

Goldberg, D. E. (1989). Genetic algorithms in search. In *Optimization and Machine Learning*. Addison-Wesley.

Gonzalez, C., & Woods, E. (2008). *Digital Image Processing* (3rd ed.). Prentice-Hall, Inc.

Gonzalez, R. C., Woods, R. E., & Eddins, S. L. (2009). *Digital Image Processing using MATLAB*. New York: Pearson Education.

Gosche, K. M., Mortimer, J. A., Smith, C. D., Markesbery, W. R., & Snowdon, D. A. (2002). Hippocampal volume as an index of Alzheimer neuropathology: findings from the Nun study. *Neurology*, 58, 1476–1482. doi:10.1212/WNL.58.10.1476 PMID:12034782

Gracia, L., Perez-Vidal, C., & Gracia, C. (2011). Computer Vision Applied to Flower, Fruit and Vegetable Processing. *Proceedings of ICPRCV*, 7(78).

Granlund, G. H., & Knutsson, H. (1995). *Signal Processing for Computer Vision*. Dordrecht, The Netherlands: Kluwer Academic Publisher. doi:10.1007/978-1-4757-2377-9

Grasso, G. M., & Recce, M. (1996). Scene Analysis for an Orange Picking Robot. In *Proceedings of International Congress for Computer Technology in Agriculture* (pp. 275-280). Wageningen, The Netherlands: VIAS Wageningen, Netherlands.

Grauman, K., & Darrell, T. (2005, June). Efficient image matching with distributions of local invariant features. In *Proceedings of the IEEE International Conference on Computer Vision and Pattern Recognition*, (Vol. 2, pp. 627-634). IEEE.

Gray, A., Sallis, P., & MacDonell, S. (1997). *Software forensics: extending authorship analysis techniques to computer programs* (Information Science Discussion Papers Series No. 97/14). University of Otago. Retrieved from http://hdl.handle.net/10523/872

Green, R. M., & Sheppard, J. W. (2013, May). Comparing Frequency-and Style-Based Features for Twitter Author Identification. In *Proceedings of the Twenty-Sixth International FLAIRS Conference*. AAAI Press.

Gunnar, L. (2010). *Segmentation Methods for Digital Image Analysis: Blood Vessels, Multi-scale Filtering, and Level Set Methods*. Linköping studies in science and technology, thesis no. 1434.

Guo, Y., Yang, L., Ding, X., Han, J., & Liu, Y. (2013, April). OpenSesame: Unlocking smart phone through handshaking biometrics. In Proceedings IEEE INFOCOM (pp. 365-369). IEEE.

Guo, Z., Zhang, L., & Zhang, D. (2010). A Completed Modeling of Local Binary Pattern Operator for Texture Classification.[TIP]. *IEEE Transactions on Image Processing*, 19(6), 1657–1663. doi:10.1109/TIP.2010.2044957 PMID:20215079

Gupta, J. P., Singh, N., Dixit, P., Semwal, V. B., & Dubey, S. R. (2013). Human Activity Recognition using Gait Pattern.[IJCVIP]. *International Journal of Computer Vision and Image Processing*, 3(3), 31–53. doi:10.4018/ijcvip.2013070103

Guru, D. S., Dinesh, R., & Nagabhushan, P. (2004). Boundary based corner detection and localization using new 'cornerity' index: a robust approach. In *Proc. 1st Canadian Conference on Computer and Robot Vision*. London, Canada: IEEE.

Ha, C., & Hwang, U. (2012). Vision-Based Fire Detection Algorithm Using Optical Flow. In *Proceedings of IEEE Sixth International Conference on Complex, Intelligent, and Software Intensive Systems*, (pp. 526-530). Palermo, Italy: IEEE.

Haddandnia, J., Ahmadi, M., & Faez, K. (2003). An efficient feature extraction method with pseudo-Zernike moments in RBF neural network-based human face recognition system. *EURASIP Journal on Applied Signal Processing*, 9, 890–901. doi:10.1155/S1110865703305128

Haddania, J., Ahmadi, M., & Faez, K. (2002). An efficient method for Recognition of Human Faces Using Higher Orders Pseudo Zernike Moment Invariant. In *Proceedings of 5th International Conference on Automatic Face and Gesture Recognition (FGR'02)* (pp. 330). Washington, DC: FGR.

Hahn, F. (2002). Multi-spectral prediction of unripe tomatoes. *Biosystems Engineering*, 81(2), 147–155. doi:10.1006/bioe.2001.0035

Hahn, F. (2009). Actual Pathogen Detection: Sensors and Algorithms—A Review. *Algorithms*, 2(1), 301–338. doi:10.3390/a2010301

Hammami, M., Chahir, Y., & Chen, L. (2006). WebGuard: a web filtering engine combining textual, structural, and visual content-based analysis. *IEEE Transactions on Knowledge and Data Engineering*, 18, 272–284. doi:10.1109/TKDE.2006.34

Harada, T., Yoshimoto, F., & Aoyama, Y. (2000). Data fitting using a genetic algorithm with real number genes. In *Proceedings of the IASTED International Conference on Computer Graphics and Imaging*, (pp. 131-138). IASTED.

Haralick, R. M., Shanmugan, K., & Dinstein, I. (1973). Textural Features for Image Classification. *IEEE Transactions on Systems: Man, and Cybernetics SMC*, *3*(6), 610–621.

Harris, C., & Stephens, M. (1988). A combined corner and edge detector. In *Proceedings of the Fourth Alvey Vision Conference*. Manchester, UK: Alvety Vision Club.

Hartigan, J. A., & Wong, M. A. (1979). Algorithm AS 136: A K-Means Clustering Algorithm. *Journal of the Royal Statistical Society. Series C, Applied Statistics*, *28*, 100–108.

Hartley, R., & Zisserman, A. (2003). *Multiple View Geometry in Computer Vision*. Cambridge, UK: Cambridge University Press.

Hartman, J. (2010, April). *Apple Fruit Diseases Appearing at Harvest*. Plant Pathology Fact Sheet, College of Agriculture, University of Kentucky.

Hartman, B. (2006). *Maths AQA*. London: Letts and Lonsdale.

Hartung, F., & Girod, B. (1996). *Digital watermarking of raw and compressed video* (pp. 205–213). Proc. of Digital Compression Technologies and Systems for Video Communication.

Hatipoglu, S., Mitra, S. K., & Kingsbury, N. (2000). Image texture description using complex wavelet transforms. In *Proceedings of IEEE International Conference on Image Processing*, (pp. 530-533). Vancouver, Canada: IEEE.

Haykin, S. (1999). *Neural Network A Comprehensive Foundation* (2nd ed.). Tom Robbins.

Hjelmas, E., & Low, B. K. (2001). Face detection A survey. *Computer Vision and Image Understanding*, *83*, 236–274. doi:10.1006/cviu.2001.0921

Horiuchi, T., Nohara, F., & Tominaga, S. (2010). Accurate reversible color-to-gray mapping algorithm without distortion conditions. *Pattern Recognition Letters*, *31*(15), 2405–2414. doi:10.1016/j.patrec.2010.07.014

Horn, B. K. P., & Schunck, B. G. (1981). Determining optical flow. *Scientific Research in Artificial Intelligence*, *17*, 185–203. doi:10.1016/0004-3702(81)90024-2

Horng, J. H. (2003). An adaptive smooting approach for fitting digital planar curves with line segments and circular arcs. *Pattern Recognition*, *24*(1-3), 565–577. doi:10.1016/S0167-8655(02)00277-5

Hou, Z. J., & Wei, G. W. (2002). A new approach to edge detection. *Pattern Recognition*, *35*(7), 1559–1570. doi:10.1016/S0031-3203(01)00147-9

Hsu, W.-L., Tyan, H.-R., Liang, Y.-M., Jeng, B.-S., & Fan, K.-C. (2005). Real time vehicle tracking on highway. *Journal of Information Science Engineering*, *21*, 733–752.

Hu, X. (2013, December 15). *Particle Swarm Optimization*. Retrieved from http://www.swarmintelligence.org/

Huang, X., & Tsechpenakis, G. (2009). *Medical Image Segmentation. Information Discovery on Electronic Health Records*. Boca Raton, FL: Taylor and Francis Group, LLC.

Huber, M., & Grupen, R. A. (2002). Robust Finger Gaits from Closed-loop controllers. In *Proceedings of IEEE/RSJ International Conference on Intelligent Robots and Systems*, (Vol. 2, pp. 1578-1584). IEEE.

Hu, W.-C. (2005). Multiprimitive segmentation based on meaningful breakpoints for fitting digital planar curves with line segments and conic arcs. *Image and Vision Computing*, *23*(9), 783–789. doi:10.1016/j.imavis.2005.05.004

Hu, W., Wu, O., Chen, Z., Fu, Z., & Maybank, S. (2007). Recognition of pornographic web pages by classifying texts and Images. *IEEE Transactions on Pattern Analysis and Machine Intelligence*, *29*, 1019–1034. doi:10.1109/TPAMI.2007.1133 PMID:17431300

Hwang, M. S., Chang, C. C., & Hwang, K. F. (1999). A watermarking technique based on one-way hash function. *IEEE Transactions on Consumer Electronics*, *45*(2), 286–294. doi:10.1109/30.793411

Igarashi, K., Miyajima, C., Itou, K., Takeda, K., Itakura, F., & Abut, H. (2004). Biometric identification using driving behavioral signals.[]. IEEE.]. *Proceedings of Multimedia and Expo*, *1*, 65–68.

Ilan, A. (2012, January). *Code Project*. Retrieved from http://www.codeproject.com

Izakian, H., & Abraham, A. (2011). Fuzzy C-means and Fuzzy Swarm for Fuzzy Clustering Problem. *Expert Systems with Applications*, *38*(3), 1835–1838. doi:10.1016/j.eswa.2010.07.112

Jaccard, P. (1901). Etude Comparative de la Distribution Orale Dansune Portion des Alpes et des Jura. *Bulletin de la Société Vaudoise des Sciences Naturelles*, *37*, 547–579.

Jaffar, A., Jaafar, R., Jamil, N., Low, C. Y., & Abdullah, B. (2009). Photogrammetric Grading of Oil Palm Fresh Fruit Bunches. *International Journal of Mechanical & Mechatronics Engineering*, *9*(10), 18–24.

Jähne, B., & Haußecker, H. (2000). *Computer Vision and Applications: A Guide for Students and Practitioners*. New York: Academic Press.

Jain, A. K., Bolle, R. M., & Pankanti, S. (Eds.). (1999). *Biometrics: personal identification in networked society*. Springer. doi:10.1007/b117227

Jain, A. K., Dass, S. C., & Nandakumar, K. (2004). Soft biometric traits for personal recognition systems. In *Biometric Authentication* (pp. 731–738). Berlin, Germany: Springer Berlin Heidelberg. doi:10.1007/978-3-540-25948-0_99

Jain, A. K., Ross, A., & Prabhakar, S. (2004). An introduction to biometric recognition. *Circuits and Systems for Video Technology*. *IEEE Transactions on*, *14*(1), 4–20.

Jain, K., Zhong, Y., & Dubuisson, P. (1998). Deformable template models: a review. *Signal Processing*, *71*(2), 109–129. doi:10.1016/S0165-1684(98)00139-X

Jedynak, B., Zheng, H., & Daoudi, M. (2003, June). Statistical models for skin detection. In *Proceedings of IEEE Workshop on Statistical Analysis in Computer Vision. In conjunction with CVPR 2003 Madison*, (pp. 16–22). IEEE.

Jeong, E., Lee, J., & Kim, D. (2011). Finger-Gesture Recognition Glove using Velostat. In *Proceedings of 11th International Conference on Control, Automation and Systems* (pp. 206-210). Academic Press.

Jiang, W., Xiang, J., Liu, L., Zha, D., & Wang, L. (2013). From mini house game to hobby-driven behavioral biometrics-based password. In *Proceedings of Trust, Security and Privacy in Computing and Communications (TrustCom), 2013 12th IEEE International Conference on* (pp. 712-719). IEEE.

Jiang, Z., Lin, Z., & Davis, L. S. (2013). Label Consistent K-SVD: Learning a Discriminative Dictionary for Recognition. *IEEE Transactions on Pattern Analysis and Machine Intelligence*, *35*(11), 2651–2654. doi:10.1109/TPAMI.2013.88 PMID:24051726

Jian-Jun, Y., Han-Ping, M., & Su-Yu, Z. (2009). Segmentation methods of fruit image based on color difference. *Journal of Communication and Computer*, *6*(7), 40–45.

Jie, Y., Xufeng, L., Yitan, Z., & Zhonglong, Z. (2008). A face detection and recognition system in color image series. *Mathematics and Computers in Simulation*, 531–539. doi:10.1016/j.matcom.2007.11.020

Jimenez, A. R., Ceres, R., & Pons, J. L. (2000). A Survey of Computer Vision Methods for Locating Fruit on Trees. *Transactions of the ASAE. American Society of Agricultural Engineers*, *43*(6), 1911–1920. doi:10.13031/2013.3096

Jimenez, L. O., Morales-Morell, A., & Creus, A. (1999). Classification of Hyperdimensional Data Based on Feature and Decision Fusion Approaches Using Projection Pursuit, Majority Voting, and Neural Networks. *IEEE Transactions on Geoscience and Remote Sensing*, *37*(3), 1360–1366. doi:10.1109/36.763300

Jing, X.-Y., & Zhang, D. (2004). A Face and Palmprint Recognition Approach Based on Discriminant DCT Feature Extraction. *IEEE Transactions on Systems, Man, and Cybernetics. Part B, Cybernetics*, *34*(6), 2405–2415. doi:10.1109/TSMCB.2004.837586 PMID:15619939

Jones, M., & Rehg, J. (1999). Statistical Color Models with Application to Skin Detection. *International Journal of Computer Vision*, 274–280.

Jorgensen, Z., & Yu, T. (2011, March). On mouse dynamics as a behavioral biometric for authentication. In *Proceedings of the 6th ACM Symposium on Information, Computer and Communications Security* (pp. 476-482). ACM.

Jüttler, B., & Felis, A. (2002). Least square fitting of algebraic spline surfaces. *Advances in Computational Mathematics*, *17*, 135–152. doi:10.1023/A:1015200504295

Jyoti, M., Ratna, D., & Sainarayanan, G. (2011). Harris operator corner detection using sliding window method. *International Journal of Computers and Applications*, *22*(1), 28–37. doi:10.5120/2546-3489

Kadonaga, T., & Abe, K. (1996). Comparison of Methods for Detecting Corner Points from Digital Curves, Graphics Recognition Methods and Applications. *Lecture Notes in Computer Science*, *1072*, 23–34. doi:10.1007/3-540-61226-2_3

Kakumanu, P., Makrogiannis, S., & Bourbakis, N. (2007). A Survey of Skin-Color Modeling and Detection Methods. *Pattern Recognition*, *40*, 1106–1122. doi:10.1016/j.patcog.2006.06.010

Kan, C., & Srinath, M. D. (2001). Combined features of cubic B-Spline wavelet moments and Zernike Moments for invariant character recognition. In *Proceedings of International Conference on Information Technology: Coding and Computing (ITCC'01)* (pp. 511-515). Las Vegas, NV: ITCC.

Kane, K. E., & Lee, W. S. (2006). Spectral Sensing of Different Citrus Varieties for Precision Agriculture. In *American Society of Agricultural and Biological Engineers. ASABE Paper No. 061065*. St. Joseph, MI: ASABE.

Kane, K. E., & Lee, W. S. (2007). Multispectral Imaging for In-field Green Citrus Identification. In *American Society of Agricultural and Biological Engineers. ASABE Paper No. 073025*. St. Joseph, MI: ASABE.

Kano, H., Nakata, H., & Martin, C. F. (2005). Optimal curve fitting and smoothing using normalized uniform B-splines: A tool for studying complex systems. *Applied Mathematics and Computation*, *169*(1), 96–128. doi:10.1016/j.amc.2004.10.034

Kasturi, R., Siva, S., & O'Gorman, L. (1990). Techniques for line drawing interpretation: an overview. In *Proc. IAPR Workshop on Machine Vision Applications*. IAPR.

Kelemen, A., Abraham, A., & Chen, Y. (2008). *Computational Intelligence in Bioinformatics*. Heidelberg, Germany: Springer. doi:10.1007/978-3-540-76803-6

Kennedy, J., & Eberhart, R. (1995). A New Optimizer Using Particle Swarm Theory. In *Proceedings of the IEEE Sixth International Symposium on Micro Machine and Human Science* (pp. 39-43). Nagoya, Japan: IEEE.

Kim, J. M., & Lee, W. K. (2008). Hand Shape Recognition Using Fingertips. In *Proceedings of fifth International Conference on Fuzzy Systems and Knowledge Discovery* (pp. 44-48). Academic Press.

Kim, H., & Fellner, D. W. (2004). Interaction With Hand Gesture for a Back-Projection Wall. In *Proceedings of Computer Graphics International* (pp. 395–402). Academic Press.

Kim, M. S., Lefcourt, A. M., Chen, Y. R., & Tao, Y. (2005). Automated Detection of Fecal Contamination of Apples Based on Multispectral Fluorescence Image Fusion. *Journal of Food Engineering*, *71*, 85–91. doi:10.1016/j.jfoodeng.2004.10.022

Kirkpatrick, S., Gelatt, C. D. Jr, & Vecchi, M. P. (1983). Optimization by simulated annealing. *Science*, *220*(4598), 671–680. doi:10.1126/science.220.4598.671 PMID:17813860

Kise, M., Park, B., Heitschmidt, G. W., Lawrence, K. C., & Windham, W. R. (2010). Multispectral imaging system with interchangeable filter design. *Computers and Electronics in Agriculture*, *72*, 61–68. doi:10.1016/j.compag.2010.02.005

Kise, M., Park, B., Lawrence, K. C., & Windham, W. R. (2007). Design and calibration of a dual-band imaging system. *Sens., &. Instrumen. Food Qual*, *1*, 113–121. doi:10.1007/s11694-007-9016-y

Kitchen, L., & Rosenfeld, A. (1982). Gray-level corner detection. *Pattern Recognition Letters*, *1*, 95–102. doi:10.1016/0167-8655(82)90020-4

Kittler, J., Hatef, M., Duin, R. P. W., & Matas, J. (1998). On Combining Classifiers. *IEEE Transactions on Pattern Analysis and Machine Intelligence*, *20*(3), 226–239. doi:10.1109/34.667881

Klette, R., Schluens, K., & Koschan, A. (1998). *Computer Vision – Three-Dimensional Data from Images*. Berlin: Springer.

Kleynen, O., Leemans, V., & Destain, M. F. (2005). Development of a Multi-Spectral Vision System for the Detection of Defects on Apples. *Journal of Food Engineering*, *69*, 41–49. doi:10.1016/j.jfoodeng.2004.07.008

Kliot, M., & Rivlin, E. (1998). Invariant-based data model for image databases. In *Proceedings of IEEE International Conference on Image Processing*, (pp. 803-807). Chicago, IL: IEEE.

Kloppel, S., Stonnington, C. M., Chu, C., Draganski, B., Scahill, R. I., & Rohrer, J. D. et al. (2008). Automatic classification of MR scans in Alzheimer's disease. *Brain*, *131*(3), 681–689. doi:10.1093/brain/awm319 PMID:18202106

Kohler, M. (1996). Vision Based Remote Control in Intelligent Home Environments. In 3D Image Analysis and Synthesis, (pp. 147-154). Academic Press.

Kohonen, T. (2001). *Self-Organizing Maps* (3rd ed.). Berlin: Springer. doi:10.1007/978-3-642-56927-2

Kroeker, K. L. (2010). Alternate Interface Technologies Emerge. *Communications of the ACM*, *53*(2), 13–15. doi:10.1145/1646353.1646360

Kruppa, H., Bauer, M. A., & Schiele, B. (2002). Skin patch detection in real-world images. In *Proceedings of Annual Symposium for Pattern Recognition of the DAGM 2002*, (LNCS), (vol. 2449, pp. 109–117). Berlin: Springer.

Ksantini, R., Boufama, B., Ziou, D., & Colin, B. (2010). A novel Bayesian logistic discriminant model An application to face recognition. *Pattern Recognition*, *43*, 1421–1430. doi:10.1016/j.patcog.2009.08.021

Kumar, S., Morstatter, F., & Liu, H. (2013). *Twitter Data Analytics*. Springer.

Kwak, K.-C., & Pedrycz, W. (2005). Face recognition using a fuzzy fisherface classifier. *Pattern Recognition*, *38*, 1717–1732. doi:10.1016/j.patcog.2005.01.018

Lajevardi, S. M., & Hussain, Z. M. (2010). Higher order orthogonal moments for invariant facial expression recognition. *Digital Signal Processing*, *20*, 1771–1779. doi:10.1016/j.dsp.2010.03.004

Landis, R., & Koch, G. (1977). The measurement of observer agreement for categorical data. *Biometrics*, *33*(1), 159–174. doi:10.2307/2529310 PMID:843571

Langelaar, G. C., Setyawan, I., & Lagendijk, R. L. (2000). Watermarking digital image and video data. *IEEE Signal Processing Magazine*, *17*(5), 20–46. doi:10.1109/79.879337

Lao, Z., Shen, D., Xue, Z., Karacali, B., Resnick, S. M., & Davatzikosx, C. (2004). Morphological classification of brains via high-dimensional shape transformations and machine learning methods. *NeuroImage*, *21*(1), 46–57. doi:10.1016/j.neuroimage.2003.09.027 PMID:14741641

Lavoue, G., Dupont, F., & Baskurt, A. (2005). A new subdivision based approach for piecewise smooth approximation of 3D polygonal curves. *Pattern Recognition*, *38*(8), 1139–1151. doi:10.1016/j.patcog.2005.02.002

Layton, R., Watters, P., & Dazeley, R. (2010). Authorship attribution for twitter in 140 characters or less. In *Proceedings of Cybercrime and Trustworthy Computing Workshop (CTC), 2010 Second* (pp. 1-8). IEEE.

Lee, B., & Chun, J. (2009). Manipulation of Virtual Objects in Marker-Less AR System by Fingertip Tracking and Hand Gesture Recognition. In *Proceedings of 2nd International conference on interaction science: Information Technology, Culture and Human* (pp. 1110-1115). Academic Press.

Leemans, V., Magein, H., & Destain, M. F. (1998). Defect Segmentation on 'Golden Delicious' Apples by using Color Machine Vision. *Computers and Electronics in Agriculture*, *20*, 117–130. doi:10.1016/S0168-1699(98)00012-X

Lee, S., Park, S.-W., Oh, P., & Kang, M. G. (2013, July). Colorization-Based Compression Using Optimization. *IEEE Transactions on Image Processing*, *22*(7), 2627–2636. doi:10.1109/TIP.2013.2253486 PMID:23529096

Lei, Z., Liao, S., & Li, S. Z. (2012). *Efficient Feature Selection for Linear Discriminant Analysis and Its Application to Face Recognition*. Paper presented at the 21st International Conference on Pattern Recognition (ICPR 2012). Tsukuba, Japan.

Lei, Z., Pietika, ˝. M., & Li, S. Z. (2014). Learning Discriminant Face Descriptor. *IEEE Transactions on Pattern Analysis and Machine Intelligence*, *36*(2), 289–302. doi:10.1109/TPAMI.2013.112 PMID:24356350

Levin, A., Lischinski, D., & Weiss, Y. (2004). Colorization using optimization.[TOG]. *ACM Transactions on Graphics*, *23*(3), 689–694. doi:10.1145/1015706.1015780

Li, P., Lee, S.-H., & Hsu, H.-Y. (2011). Use of a Cold Mirror System for Citrus Fruit Identification. In *Proceedings of IEEE International Conference on Computer Science and Automation Engineering*, (Vol. 2, pp. 376 - 381). Shanghai, China: IEEE Press.

Li, Y., Lizhuang, M., & Di, W. (February, 2007). Fast colorization using edge and gradient constrains. *The 15th International conference in Central Europe on Computer Graphics, Visualization and Computer Vision (WSCG'07)* (pp. 309-315). Plzen - Bory, Czech Republic: Science Press.

Lim, M., Oh, S., Son, J., You, B., & Kim, K. (2000). A Human-Like Real-Time Grasp Systhesis Method for Humanoid Robot Hands. *Robotics and Autonomous Systems*, *30*, 261–271. doi:10.1016/S0921-8890(99)00091-3

Lin, H., Hong, T. H., Herman, M., & Chellappa, R. (1998). Accuracy Vs efficiency tradeoffs in optical flow algorithms. *Journal of Computer Vision and Image Understanding*, 271–286.

Lins, E. C., Junior, J. B., & Marcassa, L. G. (2009). Detection of Citrus Canker in Citrus Plants using Laser Induced Fluorescence Spectroscopy. *Precision Agriculture*, *10*, 319–330. doi:10.1007/s11119-009-9124-2

Li, Q., Wang, M., & Gu, W. (2002, November). Computer Vision Based System for Apple Surface Defect Detection. *Computers and Electronics in Agriculture*, *36*, 215–223. doi:10.1016/S0168-1699(02)00093-5

Liu, J., & Moulin, P. (2000). Analysis of interscale and intrascale dependencies between image wavelet coefficients. In *Proceedings of IEEE International Conference on Image Processing*, (pp. 669-672). Vancouver, Canada: IEEE.

Liu, Y., & Zheng, Y. F. (2005). One-against-all multi-class SVM classification using reliability measures. *in Proc. IEEE International Joint Conference on Neural Networks (IJCNN'05)*, *2*, pp. 849-854. Montreal, Quebec, Canada.

Liu, H. C., & Srinath, L. S. (1990). Corner Detection from Chain-Code. *Pattern Recognition*, *23*, 51–68. doi:10.1016/0031-3203(90)90048-P

Li, Z., Park, U., & Jain, A. K. (2011). A Discriminative Model for Age Invariant Face Recognition. *IEEE Transactions on Information Forensics and Security*, *6*(3), 1028–1037. doi:10.1109/TIFS.2011.2156787

Lou, D. C., Tso, H. K., & Liu, J. L. (2007). A copyright protection scheme for digital images using visual cryptography technique. *Computer Standards & Interfaces*, *29*, 125–131. doi:10.1016/j.csi.2006.02.003

Loupias, E., Sebe, N., Bres, S., & Jolion, J. M. (2000). Wavelet-based salient points for image retrieval. In *Proceedings of IEEE International Conference on Image Processing*, (pp. 518-521). Vancouver, Canada: IEEE.

Lucien, W., Ranchin, T., & Mangolini, M. (1997). Fusion of satellite images of different spatial resolutions: assessing the quality of resulting images. *Photogrammetric Engineering and Remote Sensing*, *63*(6), 691–699.

Lu, J., Tan, Y.-P., & Wang, G. (2013). Discriminative Multimanifold Analysis for Face Recognition from a Single Training Sample per Person. *IEEE Transactions on Pattern Analysis and Machine Intelligence*, *35*(1), 39–51. doi:10.1109/TPAMI.2012.70 PMID:22431525

Lu, J., Zhou, X., Tan, Y.-P., Shang, Y., & Zhou, J. (2012). Cost-Sensitive Semi-Supervised Discriminant Analysis for Face Recognition. *IEEE Transactions on Information Forensics and Security*, *7*(3), 944–953. doi:10.1109/TIFS.2012.2188389

Luke, G. (2010, October). *Covenanteyes*. Retrieved January 2012, from http://www.covenanteyes.com/2010/01/06/updated-pornography-statistics/

Luo, R. C., & Lin, M.-H. (1988). Robot Multi-Sensor Fusion and Integration: Optimum Estimation of Fused Sensor Data. In *Proceedings 1988 IEEE conference on Robotics and Automation*, (Vol. 2, pp. 1076-1081). Philadelphia, PA: IEEE.

Luo, R. C., & Kay, M. G. (1989). Multisensor Integration and Fusion in Intelligent Systems. *IEEE Transactions on Systems, Man, and Cybernetics*, *19*(5), 901–931. doi:10.1109/21.44007

Lu, R. (2004). Multispectral imaging for predicting firmness and soluble solids content of apple fruit. *Rostharvest Biology and Technology*, *31*, 147–157. doi:10.1016/j.postharvbio.2003.08.006

Macleod, N., & Grant, T. (2012). *Whose Tweet? Authorship analysis of micro-blogs and other short-form messages.* Aston University Research Archive. Retrieved from http://eprints.aston.ac.uk/19303/1/Authorship_analysis_of_micro_blogs_and_other_short_form_messages.pdf

MacQueen, J. (1967, June). Some methods for classification and analysis of multivariate observations. In *Proceedings of the fifth Berkeley symposium on mathematical statistics and probability.* University of California.

Maenpa, T. (2003). The local binary pattern approach to texture analysis-extensions and applications. Infotech Oulu and Department of Electrical and Information Engineering, University of Oulu.

Magnin, B., Mesrob, L., Kinkingnéhun, S., Issac, M. P., Colliot, O., & Sarazin, M. et al. (2009). Support vector machine-based classification of Alzheimer's disease from whole-brain anatomical MRI. *Neuroradiology, 51*(2), 73–83. doi:10.1007/s00234-008-0463-x PMID:18846369

Mahmoud, T. M. Abdel- latef, B. A., Abd-El-Hafeez, T., & Omar, A. (2011). An Effective Hybrid Method for Face Detection. In *Proceedings of Fifth International Conference on Intelligent Computing and Information Systems* (ICICIS 2011). Cairo, Egypt: ACM.

Mahmoud, K., Datta, S., & Flint, J. (2005). Frequency domain watermarking: An overview. *International Arab Journal of Information Technology, 2*(1), 33–47.

Mahmoud, T. (2008). A New Fast Skin Color Detection Technique. *World Academy of Science. Engineering and Technology, 33*, 2070–3740.

Maji, P., & Pal, S. (2008). Maximum Class Separability for Rough-Fuzzy CMeans Based Brain MR Image Segmentation. *T. Rough Sets, 9*, 114–134.

Mallat, S. G. (1989a). A theory for multiresolution signal decomposition: the wavelet representation. *IEEE Transactions on Pattern Analysis and Machine Intelligence, 11*(7), 674–693. doi:10.1109/34.192463

Mallat, S. G. (1989b). Multiresolution Approximations and Wavelet Orthonormal Bases of L2. *Transactions of the American Mathematical Society, 315*(1), 69–87.

Management Association. (2013). *Image Processing: Concepts, Methodologies, Tools, and Applications.* Hershey, PA: IGI Global.

Mandelbrot, B. (1983). *The Fractal Geometry of Nature.* John Wiley & Sons, Ltd.

Mandhani, N. K. (2003). *Watermarking using decimal sequences.* (Master thesis). Louisiana State University, Baton Rouge, LA.

Marcassa, L. G., Gasparoto, M. C. G., Belasque, J., Lins, E. C., Nunes, F. D., & Bagnato, V. S. (2006). Fluorescence Spectroscopy Applied to Orange Trees. *Laser Physics, 16*(5), 884–888. doi:10.1134/S1054660X06050215

Marcus, D. S., Wang, T. H., Parker, J., Csernansky, J. G., Morris, J. C., & Buckner, R. L. (2007). Open Access Series of Imaging Studies (OASIS), cross-sectional MRI data in young, middle aged, nondemented, and demented older adults. *Journal of Cognitive Neuroscience, 19*(9), 1498–14507. doi:10.1162/jocn.2007.19.9.1498 PMID:17714011

Marszaek, M., & Schmid, C. (2006). Spatial weighting for bag-of-features. In *Proceedings of the IEEE International Conference on Computer Vision and Pattern Recognition,* (Vol. 2, pp. 2118-2125). IEEE.

Martin, E., Helvie, A., Zhou, C., Roubidoux, A., Bailey, E., & Paramagul, C. et al. (2006). Mammographic density measured with quantitative computer-aided method: comparison with radiologists estimates and BI-RADS categories. *Radiology, 240*(3), 656–665. doi:10.1148/radiol.2402041947 PMID:16857974

Martinez, A. M., & Kak, A. C. (2001). PCA versus LDA. *IEEE Transactions on Pattern Analysis and Machine Intelligence, 23*, 228–233. doi:10.1109/34.908974

May, Z., & Amaran, M. H. (2011). Automated Ripeness Assessment of Oil Palm Fruit Using RGB and Fuzzy Logic Technique. *Proceedings of the 13th WSEAS International Conference on Mathematical and Computational Methods in Science and Engineering* (pp. 52-59). World Scientific and Engineering Academy and Society (WSEAS).

McCaffrey, J. (2013, December 15). *Particle Swarm Optimization.* Retrieved from http://msdn.microsoft.com/en-us/magazine/hh335067.aspx

McCulloch, W. S., & Pitts, W. (1943). A logical calculus of the ideas immanent in nervous activity. *The Bulletin of Mathematical Biophysics, 5*.

McKillup, S. (2006). *Statistics Explained: An Introductory Guide for Life Scientists*. Cambridge, UK: Cambridge University Press.

Medioni, G., & Kang, S. B. (2004). *Emerging Topics in Computer Vision*. New York: Prentice Hall.

Mehl, P. M., Chao, K., Kim, M., & Chen, Y. R. (2002). Detection of Defects on Selected Apple Cultivars using Hyperspectral and Multispectral Image Analysis. *Applied Engineering in Agriculture*, *18*, 219–226.

Meskaldji, K., Boucherkha, S., & Chikhi, S. (2009). Color quantization and its impact on color histogram based image retrieval accuracy. *Proc.The First International Conference on Networked Digital Technologies(NDT '09)*, (pp. 515-517). Ostrava, Czech Republic.

Meyer, Y. (1993). *Wavelets Algorithms & Applications*. Philadelphia: SIAM.

Mharib, A., Ramli, A., Mashohor, S., & Mahmood, R. (2012). Survey on Liver CT Image Segmentation Methods. *Artificial Intelligence Review*, *37*(2), 83–95. doi:10.1007/s10462-011-9220-3

Miller, P., & Astley, M. (1992). Classification of breast tissue by texture analysis. *Image and Vision Computing*, *10*(5), 277–282. doi:10.1016/0262-8856(92)90042-2

Mitra, S., & Acharya, T. (2007). Gesture Recognition: A Survey. IEEE Transactions on Systems, Man, and Cybernetics-Part C. *Applications and Review*, *37*(3), 2127–2130.

Mittrapiyanurk, P., DeSouza, G. N., & Kak, A. C. (2006). Accurate 3D tracking of rigid objects with occlusion using active appearance models. In *Proceedings of the IEEE Workshop on Motion and Video Computing*. Breckenridge, CO: IEEE.

Miyata, T., Komiyama, Y., Sakai, Y., & Inazumi, Y. (2009). Novel inverse colorization for image compression. *Picture Coding Symposium (PCS 2009)* (pp. 1-4). Chicago, Illinois, USA: IEEE.

Mohana, H. S. AshwathaKumar, A. M., & Shivakumar, G. (n.d.). Statistical approach to real time traffic flux estimation. In *Proceedings of the IEEE International Conference on Signal & Image Processing* (pp. 501-505). Cairo, Egypt: IEEE.

Mohana, H. S. Aswatha Kumar, & Shivakumar. (2009). Vehicle Detection & Counting by using Real time Traffic Flux Differential Technique & Performance Evaluation. In *Proceedings of IEEE-International Conference on Advanced Computer Control*. IEEE.

Mohana, H. S., Kumar, A. M., Shivakumar, G., & Ravishankar, K. C. (2006). Vehicle tracking and velocity estimation using cumulative optical flow computation. In *Proceedings of the National Conference on Innovation in Intelligence and Computing Technologies 2006*, (pp. 289-293). Academic Press.

Mohana, H. S., Kumar, M. A., & Shivakumar, G. (2009). Real-time dynamic scene analysis using differential: Technique & performance evaluation with optical flow. In *Proceedings of the IEEE International Conference on Advanced Computer Control*. IEEE.

Mohan, A., Papageorgiou, C., & Poggio, T. (2001). Example-based object detection in images by components. *IEEE Transactions on Pattern Analysis and Machine Intelligence*, *23*, 349–361. doi:10.1109/34.917571

Mokhtarian, F., & Mackworth, A. K. (1992). A Theory of Multiscale, Curvature-Based Shape Representation for Planar Curves. *IEEE Transactions on Pattern Analysis and Machine Intelligence*, *14*, 789–805. doi:10.1109/34.149591

Molyneux, S., Lister, C., & Savage, G. (2004). An investigation of the antioxidant properties and colour of glasshouse grown tomatoes. *International Journal of Food Sciences and Nutrition*, *55*, 537–545. doi:10.1080/09637480400015828 PMID:16019297

Monwar, M. M., & Gavrilova, M. (2008). FES: A system for combining face, ear and signature biometrics using rank level fusion. In Proceedings of Information Technology: New Generations, (pp. 922-927). IEEE.

Monwar, M. M., & Gavrilova, M. (2013). Markov chain model for multimodal biometric rank fusion. *Signal. Image and Video Processing*, *7*(1), 137–149. doi:10.1007/s11760-011-0226-8

Moon, H., & Phillips, P. J. (2001). Computational and performance aspects of PCA-based face recognition algorithms. *Perception*, *30*, 303–321. doi:10.1068/p2896 PMID:11374202

More, J. J. (1977). The Levenberg-Marquardt algorithm: implementation and theory. In *Proceedings of Conference on Numerical Analysis*. University of Dundee.

Moriyama, M., Yoshimoto, F., & Harada, T. (1998). A method of plane data fitting with a genetic algorithm. In *Proceeding of the IASTED International Conference on Computer Graphics and Imaging*. IASTED.

Morris, T. (2004). *Computer Vision and Image Processing*. New York: Palgrave Macmillan.

Morse, B. S., Yoo, T. S., Chen, D. T., Rheingans, P., & Subramanian, K. R. (2001). Interpolating implicit surfaces from scattered surface data using compactly supported radial basis functions. In *Proceedings of Conference on Shape Modeling and Applications*, (pp. 89-98). IEEE.

Moshou, D., Bravo, C., Oberti, R., West, J., Bodria, L., McCartney, A., & Ramon, H. (2005). Plant Disease Detection Based on Data Fusion of Hyper-Spectral and Multi-Spectral Fluorescence Imaging using Kohonen Maps. *Real-Time Imaging*, *11*(2), 75–83. doi:10.1016/j.rti.2005.03.003

Moshou, D., Bravo, C., Wahlen, S., West, J., McCartney, A., & De, J. et al. (2006). Simultaneous Identification of Plant Stresses and Diseases in Arable Crops using Proximal Optical Sensing and Self-Organising Maps. *Precision Agriculture*, *7*(3), 149–164. doi:10.1007/s11119-006-9002-0

Muhimmah, I., Oliver, A., Denton, E., Pont, J., Perez, E., & Zwiggelaar, R. (2006). *Comparison between Wolfe, Boyd, BI-RADS and Tabar based mammographic risk assessment*. Springer. doi:10.1007/11783237_55

Mukhopadhyay, J. (2011). Image and Video Processing in the Compressed Domain (Har/Cdr ed.). USA: CRC Press.

Nabatchian, A., Abdel-Raheem, E., & Ahmadi, M. (2008). Human face recognition using different moment invariants: A comparative study. In *Proceedings of IEEE International Congress on Image and Signal Processing* (pp. 661-666). Sanya, China: IEEE.

Narayana, C., Sreenivasa Reddy, E., & Seetharama Prasad, M. (2012). Automatic Image Segmentation using Ultrafuzziness. *International Journal of Computers and Applications*, *49*(12), 6–13. doi:10.5120/7677-0977

Neerja & Walia. E. (2008). Face recognition using improved fast PCA algorithm. In *Proceedings of International Congress on Image and Signal Processing*, (vol. 1, pp. 554-558). Sanya, Hainan: Academic Press.

Nguyen, D. D., Pham, T. C., & Jeon, J. W. (2009). Fingertip Detection with Morphology and Geometric Calculation. In *Proceedings of IEEE/RSJ International Conference on Intelligent Robots and Systems* (pp. 1460-1465). IEEE.

Nicchiotti, G., & Ottaviani, R. (1997). A simple rotation invariant shape signature. In *Proceedings of IEEE International Conference on Image Processing and its Applications*, (pp.722-726). Dublin, Ireland: IEEE.

Noble, J. A. (1988). Finding corners. *Image and Vision Computing*, *6*, 121–128. doi:10.1016/0262-8856(88)90007-8

Nolker, C., & Ritter, H. (2002). Visual Recognition of Continuous Hand Postures. *IEEE Transactions on Neural Networks*, *13*(4), 983–994. doi:10.1109/TNN.2002.1021898 PMID:18244493

Nor'aini, A. J., Raveendran, P., & Selvanathan, N. (2006). Human face recognition using Zernike moments and nearest neighbor classifier. In *Proceedings of 4th student Conference on Research and Development* (pp. 120-123). Academic Press.

Nor'aini, A. J., Raveendran, P., & Selvanathan, N. (2007). A comparative analysis of Zernike moments and Principal Components Analysis as feature extractors for face recognition. In *Proceedings of 3rd Kuala Lumpur International Conference on Biomedical Engineering*, (Vol. 15, pp. 37-41). Academic Press.

Nor'aini, A. J., Raveendran, P., & Selvanathan, N. (2007). A comparative analysis of Zernike moments and Principal Components Analysis as feature extractors for face recognition. In *Proceedings of 3rd Kuala Lumpur International Conference on Biomedical Engineering*, (Vol. 15, pp. 37-41). Kuala Lumpur, Malaysia: Springer.

Nunez, J., Otazu, X., Fors, O., Prades, A., Pala, V., & Arbiol, R. (1999). Multiresolution-based image fusion with additive wavelet decomposition. *IEEE Transactions on Geoscience and Remote Sensing*, *37*(3), 1204–1211. doi:10.1109/36.763274

Ojala, T., Pietikäinen, M., & Mäenpää, T. T. (2002). Multiresolution Gray-Scale and Rotation Invariant Texture Classification with Local Binary Pattern. [TPAMI]. *IEEE Transactions on Pattern Analysis and Machine Intelligence*, 24(7), 971–987. doi:10.1109/TPAMI.2002.1017623

Okamoto, H., & Lee, W. S. (2009). Green citrus detection using hyperspectral imaging. *Computers and Electronics in Agriculture*, 66, 201–208. doi:10.1016/j.compag.2009.02.004

Olejnik, L., & Castelluccia, C. (2013). Towards web-based biometric systems using personal browsing interests. In *Proceedings of Availability, Reliability and Security (ARES), 2013 Eighth International Conference on* (pp. 274-280). IEEE CPS.

Oliveira, J., & Pedrycz, W. (2007). *Advances in Fuzzy Clustering and its Applications*. John Wiley Sons Ltd. doi:10.1002/9780470061190

Oliver, A., Mart, J., Mart, R., Bosch, A., & Freixenet, J. (2006). A new approach to the classification of mammographic masses and normal breast tissue. In *Proceedings of International Conference on Pattern Recognition*. Academic Press.

Ostalczyk, P. W. (2009). A note on the Grünwald–Letnikov fractional-order backward-difference. *Physica Scripta*, 136, 1–5.

Ouyang, C., Li, D., Wang, J., Wang, S., & Han, Y. (2013). The Research of the Strawberry Disease Identification Based on Image Processing and Pattern Recognition. *Computer and Computing Technologies in Agriculture VI*, 392, 69–77. doi:10.1007/978-3-642-36124-1_9

Pang, Y.-H., Teoh, A. B. J., & Ngo, D. C. L. (2005). Enhanced pseudo Zernike moments in face recognition. *IEICE Electronics Express*, 2(3), 70–75. doi:10.1587/elex.2.70

Pang, Y.-H., Teoh, A. B. J., & Ngo, D. C. L. (2006). A discriminant pseudo Zernike moments in face recognition. *Journal of Research and Practice in Information Technology*, 38(2), 197–210.

Papoulis, A. (1991). *Probability, Random Variables and Stochastic Processes* (3rd ed.). New York: McGraw-Hill.

Paquet, A., Zahir, S., & Ward, R. (2002). Wavelet-packets-based image retrieval. In *Proc. IEEE International Conference on Acoustics, Speech, and Signal Processing*, (pp. IV-3640 - IV-3643). Orlando, FL: IEEE.

Paragios, N., Chen, Y., & Faugeras, O. (2005). *Handbook of Mathematical Models in Computer Vision*. Berlin: Springer.

Parrish, E. A. Jr, & Goksel, A. K. (1977). Pictorial Pattern Recognition Applied to Fruit Harvesting. *Transactions of the ASAE. American Society of Agricultural Engineers*, 20(5), 822–827. doi:10.13031/2013.35657

Paulraj, M., Hema, C. R., & Pranesh, R. K., & Siti Sofiah, M. R. (2009). Color recognition algorithm using a neural network model in determining the ripeness of a Banana. *Proceedings of the International Conference on Man-Machine Systems (ICoMMS 2009)* (pp. 2B71-2B74). Penang, Malaysia: Universiti Malaysia Perlis.

Petroudi, S., Kadir, T., & Brady, M. (2003). Automatic classification of mammographic parenchymal patterns: a statistical approach. In *Proc. International Conference IEEE Engineering in Medicine and Biology Society*, (pp. 798-801). IEEE.

Philipps, D. (1997). *Image Processing in C: Analyzing and Enhancing Digital Images*. R & D Books.

Phillips, P. J., Moon, H., Rauss, P. J., & Rizvi, S. (2000). *The Facial Recognition Technology (FERET) face database*. Retrieved from http://face.nist.gov/colorferet/request.html

Pickering, C.A. (2005). The Search for a Safer Driver Interface: A Review of Gesture Recognition Human Machine Interface. *IEE Computing and Control Engineering*, 34-40.

Piella, G. (2003). A general framework for multiresolution image fusion: from pixels to regions. *Information Fusion*, 4, 259–280. doi:10.1016/S1566-2535(03)00046-0

Plebe, A., & Grasso, G. (2001). Localization of spherical fruits for robotic harvesting. *Machine Vision and Applications*, 13, 70–79. doi:10.1007/PL00013271

Polder, G., Heijden, G. W., & Young, I. T. (2002). Spectral Image Analysis For Measuring Ripeness Of Tomatoes. *TRANSACTIONS-AMERICAN SOCIETY OF AGRICULTURAL ENGINEERS International Journal*, 45(4), 1155–1162.

Pradhan, P. S., King, R. L., Younan, N. H., & Holcomb, D. W. (2006). Estimation of the Number of Decomposition Levels for a Wavelet-Based Multiresolution Multisensor Image Fusion. *IEEE Transactions on Geoscience and Remote Sensing, 44*(12), 3674–3686. doi:10.1109/TGRS.2006.881758

Prasanna, V., Prabha, T., & Tharanathan, R. (2007). Fruit Ripening Phenomena An Overview.[Taylor & Francis Ltd.]. *Critical Reviews in Food Science and Nutrition,* 1–19. doi:10.1080/10408390600976841 PMID:17364693

Premaratne, P., & Nguyen, Q. (2007). Consumer electronics control system based on hand gesture moment invariants. *IET Computer Vision, 1*(1), 35–41. doi:10.1049/iet-cvi:20060198

Pritchard, A. J., Sangwine, S. J., & Horne, R. E. N. (1993). Corner and curve detection along a boundary using line segment triangles. *Electronics Division Colloquium on Hough Transforms, 106,* 1–4.

Purcell, D. E., O'Shea, M. G., Johnson, R. A., & Kokot, S. (2009). Near-Infrared Spectroscopy for the Prediction of Disease Rating for Fiji Leaf Gall in Sugarcane Clones. *Applied Spectroscopy, 63*(4), 450–457. doi:10.1366/000370209787944370 PMID:19366512

Qin, J., Burks, F., Ritenour, M. A., & Bonn, W. G. (2009). Detection of Citrus Canker using Hyper-Spectral Reflectance Imaging with Spectral Information Divergence. *Journal of Food Engineering, 93*(2), 183–191. doi:10.1016/j.jfoodeng.2009.01.014

Quellec, G., Lamard, M., Cazugue, G., & Cochene, B. (2010). Adaptive non-separable wavelet transform via lifting and its application to content-based image retrieval. *IEEE Transactions on Image Processing, 19*(1), 25–35. doi:10.1109/TIP.2009.2030479 PMID:19695999

Raba, D., Oliver, A., Mart, J., & Peracaula, M. (2005). Breast segmentation with pectoral muscle suppression on digital mammograms. In *Proceedings of Iberian Conference on Pattern Recognition and Image Analysis.* Academic Press.

Rabatel, G. (1988). A vision system for Magali, the fruit picking robot. In Agricultural Engineering. Paris: Paper 88293, AGENG88.

Rabin, M. O. (1979). Digital signatures and public-key functions as intractable as factorization. *Technical Report MIT/LCS/TR-212.* Massachusetts Institute of Technology.

Raheja, J. L., Chaudhary, A., & Singal, K. (2011). Tracking of Fingertips and Centers of Palm Using KINECT. In *Proceedings of 3rd International Conference on Computational Intelligence, Modelling and Simulation* (pp. 248-252). Academic Press.

Raheja, J. L., Manasa, M. B. L., Chaudhary, A., & Raheja, S. (2011). ABHIVYAKTI: Hand Gesture Recognition using Orientation Histogram in different light conditions. In *Proceedings of 5th Indian International Conference on Artificial Intellige* (pp. 1687-1698). Academic Press.

Raheja, J. L., Chaudhary, A., & Maheshwari, S. (2014). Automatic Gesture Pointing Location Detection. *Optik: International Journal for Light and Electron Optics, 125*(3), 993–996. doi:10.1016/j.ijleo.2013.07.167

Raheja, J. L., Das, K., & Chaudhary, A. (2011). Fingertip Detection: A Fast Method with Natural Hand. *International Journal of Embedded Systems and Computer Engineering, 3*(2), 85–89.

Rattarangsi, A., & Chin, R. T. (1992). Scale-Based Detection of Corners of Planar Curves. *Transactions on Pattern Analysis and Machine Intelligence, 14,* 430–449. doi:10.1109/34.126805

Ray, B. K., & Pandyan, R. (2003). ACORD – an adaptive corner detector for planar curves. *Pattern Recognition, 36,* 703–708. doi:10.1016/S0031-3203(02)00084-5

Razmi, S. M., & Saad, N. (2010). Vision-Based Flame Detection: Motion Detection & Fire Analysis. In *Proceedings of IEEE Student Conference on Research and Development.* IEEE.

Redner, R., & Walker, H. (1984). Mixture densities, maximum likelihood and the EM algorithm. *SIAM Review, 26,* 195–239. doi:10.1137/1026034

Roberts, M. J., Schimmelpfennig, D., Ashley, E., Livingston, M., Ash, M., & Vasavada, U. (2006). *The Value of Plant Disease Early-Warning Systems (No. 18).* Economic Research Service, United States Department of Agriculture.

Rocha, A., Hauagge, C., Wainer, J., & Siome, D. (2010). Automatic Fruit and Vegetable Classification from Images. *Computers and Electronics in Agriculture, 70*, 96–104. doi:10.1016/j.compag.2009.09.002

Rodrguez-Pulido, F., Gordillo, B., Gonzlez-Miret, M., & Heredia, F. (2013). Analysis of food appearance properties by computer vision applying ellipsoids to colour data. *Computers and Electronics in Agriculture, 99*, 108–115. doi:10.1016/j.compag.2013.08.027

Romberg, J., Choi, H., Baraniuk, R., & Kingsbury, N. (2000). Multi-scale classification using complex wavelets and hidden markov tree models. In *Proceedings of IEEE International Conference on Image Processing*, (pp.371-374). Vancouver, Canada: IEEE.

Ropelato, J. (2006). *Internet pornography statistics*. Retrieved from http://internet-filter-review.toptenreviews.com/internet-pornography-statistics.html

Rosenfeld, & Weszka. (n.d.). An Improved Method of Angle Detection on Digital Curves. *IEEE Transactions on Computers, 24*, 940-941.

Rosenfeld, A., & Johnston, E. (1973). Angle Detection on Digital Curves. *IEEE Transactions on Computers, 22*, 875–878. doi:10.1109/TC.1973.5009188

Ross, A. A., Nandakumar, K., & Jain, A. K. (2006). *Handbook of multibiometrics* (Vol. 6). Springer.

Rumelhart, D. E., Hinton, G. E., & Williams, R. J. (1986). Learning representations by back-propagating errors. *Nature, 323*(9), 533–536. doi:10.1038/323533a0

Rusu, C., & Tsaftaris, S. A. (September 2013). Estimation of Scribble Placement for Painting Colorization. *Image and Signal Processing and Analysis (ISPA)* (pp. 564-569). Trieste, Italy: IEEE.

Rutkowski, W. S., & Rosenfeld, A. (1978). *A comparison of corner-detection techniques for chain-coded curves (TR-623)*. Computer Science Center, University of Maryland.

Rutledge, R. (2009). *Just Enough SAS: A Quick-start Guide to SAS for Engineers*. SAS Institute Inc.

Ryu, T., Lee, B. G., & Lee, S. (2014). Image Compression System Using Colorization and Meanshift Clustering Methods. *Ubiquitous Information Technologies and Applications*, 165-172.

Saeed, K. (2014). Carathéodory–Toeplitz based mathematical methods and their algorithmic applications in biometric image processing. *Applied Numerical Mathematics, 75*, 2–21. doi:10.1016/j.apnum.2012.05.004

Saeed, K., & Mosdorf, R. (Eds.). (2006). *Biometrics, computer security systems and artificial intelligence applications*. Springer. doi:10.1007/978-0-387-36503-9

Saeed, K., & Nagashima, T. (Eds.). (2012). *Biometrics and Kansei Engineering*. Springer. doi:10.1007/978-1-4614-5608-7

Sankarana, S., Mishraa, A., Ehsania, R., & Davisb, C. (2010). A Review of Advanced Techniques for Detecting Plant Diseases. *Computers and Electronics in Agriculture, 72*, 1–13. doi:10.1016/j.compag.2010.02.007

Sarfraz, M., & Rasheed, A. (2007). A randomized knot insertion algorithm for outline capture of planar images using cubic spline. In *Proceedings of The 22th ACM Symposium on Applied Computing* (ACM SAC-07), (pp. 71 – 75). ACM.

Sarfraz, M., Asim, M. R., & Masood, A. (2004a). Capturing Outlines using Cubic Bézier Curves. In *Proc. of IEEE 1st International Conference on Information & Communication Technologies: from Theory to Applications*. IEEE.

Sarfraz, M., Asim, M. R., & Masood, A. (2004b). A Web Based System for Capturing Outlines of 2D Objects. In *Proceedings of The International Conference on Information and Computer Science*, (pp. 575 – 586). King Fahd University of Petroleum and Minerals.

Sarfraz, M., Hussain, M. Z., & Chaudary, F. S. (2005). Shape preserving cubic spline for data visualization. *Computer Graphics and CAD/CAM, 1*(6), 185-193.

Sarfraz, M. (2004). Some algorithms for curve design and automatic outline capturing of images. *International Journal of Image and Graphics, 4*(2), 301–324. doi:10.1142/S0219467804001427

Sarfraz, M. (2006). Computer-Aided reverse engineering using simulated evolution on NURBS. *International Journal of Virtual and Physical Prototyping, 1*(4), 243–257. doi:10.1080/17452750601130492

Sarfraz, M. (2010). Vectorizing outlines of generic shapes by cubic spline using simulated annealing. *International Journal of Computer Mathematics*, *87*(8), 1736–1751. doi:10.1080/00207160802452519

Sarfraz, M. (2013). *Intelligent Computer Vision and Image Processing: Innovation, Application, and Design*. Hershey, PA: IGI Global. doi:10.4018/978-1-4666-3906-5

Sarfraz, M. (2014). *Computer Vision and Image Processing in Intelligent Systems and Multimedia Technologies*. Hershey, PA: IGI Global.

Sarfraz, M., Asim, M. R., & Masood, A. (2006). A New Approach to Corner Detection. In *Computer Vision and Graphics*. Springer. doi:10.1007/1-4020-4179-9_75

Sarfraz, M., & Khan, M. A. (2004). An automatic algorithm for approximating boundary of bitmap characters. *Future Generation Computer Systems*, *20*(8), 1327–1336. doi:10.1016/j.future.2004.05.024

Sarfraz, M., & Raza, A. (2002). Visualization of Data using Genetic Algorithm. In *Soft Computing and Industry: Recent Applications*. Springer. doi:10.1007/978-1-4471-0123-9_45

Sarfraz, M., & Swati, Z. N. K. (2013). Mining Corner Points on the Generic Shapes. *Open Journal of Applied Sciences*, *3*(1B), 10–15. doi:10.4236/ojapps.2013.31B003

Sargano, A.B., Sarfraz, M., & Haq, N. (2014). An Intelligent System for Paper Currency Recognition with Robust Features. *Journal of Intelligent and Fuzzy Systems*.

Sawah, A. E., et al. (2007). A Framework for 3D Hand Tracking and Gesture Recognition Using Elements of Genetic Programming. In *Proceedings of 4th Canadian Conference on Computer and Robot Vision* (pp. 495-502). Montreal, Canada: Academic Press.

Schertz, C. E., & Brown, G. K. (1968). Basic considerations in mechanizing citrus harvest. *Transactions of the ASAE. American Society of Agricultural Engineers*, 66–131.

Schneier, B. (1996). *Applied cryptography: Protocols, Algorithms, and Source Code in C*. John Wiley & Sons.

Schroder, K., & Laurent, P. (1999). Efficient polygon approximations for shape signatures. In *Proceedings of International Conference on Image Processing*, (pp. 811-814). Kobe, Japan: Academic Press.

Scott, C., & Nowak, R. (2000). Pattern extraction and synthesis using a hierarchical wavelet-based framework. In *Proceedings of IEEE International Conference on Image Processing*, (pp. 383-386). Vancouver, Canada: IEEE.

Selesnick, I. W. (1999). The Slantlet Transform. *IEEE Transactions on Signal Processing*, *47*(5), 1304–1313. doi:10.1109/78.757218

Semary, N. A. (2012). *Image coloring Techniques and Applications*. Norderstedt, Germany: GRIN Verlag.

Semechko, A. (2013, December 8). *Fast segmentation of N-dimensional grayscale images*. Retrieved from http://www.mathworks.com/matlabcentral/fileexchange/41967-fastsegmentation-of-n-dimensional-grayscale-images

Serra, J. (1986). Introduction to mathematical morphology. *Computer Vision Graphics and Image Processing*, *35*(3), 283–305. doi:10.1016/0734-189X(86)90002-2

Shafri, H. Z. M., & Hamdan, N. (2009). Hyperspectral Imagery for Mapping Disease Infection in Oil Palm Plantation using Vegetation Indices and Red Edge Techniques. *American Journal of Applied Sciences*, *6*(6), 1031–1035. doi:10.3844/ajassp.2009.1031.1035

Shah Rizam, M. S., Farah Yasmin, A. R., Ahmad Ihsan, M. Y., & Shazana, K. (2009). Non-destructive Watermelon Ripeness Determination Using Image Processing and Artificial Neural Network (ANN). *International Journal of Intelligent Technology*, *4*(2), 130–134.

Shahbahrami, A., Borodin, D., & Juurlink, B. (2008). Comparison between color and texture features for image retrieval. *Proc. 19th Annual Workshop on Circuits, Systems and Signal Processing (ProRisc 2008)*. Veldhoven, The Netherlands: STW.

Shalhoub, G., Simon, R., Iyer, R., Tailor, J., & Westcott, S. (2010). Stylometry system–use cases and feasibility study. *Forensic Linguistics*, *1*, 8.

Shen, D., & Ip, H. H. S. (1999). Discriminative wavelet shape descriptors for recognition of 2-D patterns. *Pattern Recognition*, *32*, 151–165. doi:10.1016/S0031-3203(98)00137-X

Shin, M. C., Tsap, L. V., & Goldgof, D. B. (2004). Gesture Recognition using Bezier Curves for Visualization Navigation from Registered 3-D Data. *Pattern Recognition, 37*(5), 1011–1024. doi:10.1016/j.patcog.2003.11.007

Silva, R. S., Laboreiro, G., Sarmento, L., Grant, T., Oliveira, E., & Maia, B. (2011). 'twazn me!!!('automatic authorship analysis of micro-blogging messages. In *Natural Language Processing and Information Systems* (pp. 161–168). Springer. doi:10.1007/978-3-642-22327-3_16

Singh, C., Walia, E., & Mittal, N. (2011b). Magnitude and phase coefficients of Zernike and Pseudo Zernike moments for robust face recognition. In *Proceedings of the IASTED international conference on Computer Vision (CV- 2011)* (pp. 180-187). Vancouver, Canada: IASTED.

Singh, N., Dubey, S. R., Dixit, P., & Gupta, J. P. (2012, September). Semantic Image Retrieval by Combining Color, Texture and Shape Features. In *Proceedings of the International Conference on Computing Sciences (ICCS)*, (pp. 116-120). ICCS.

Singh, S., & Hemachandra, K. (2012). Content-Based Image Retrieval using Color Moment and Gabor Based Image Retrieval using Color Moment and Gabor Texture Feature. *IJCSI International Journal of Computer Science Issues, 9* (5).

Singhal, A. (2001). Modern information retrieval: A brief overview. *IEEE Data Eng. Bull., 24*(4), 35–43.

Singh, C. (2006). Improved quality of reconstructed images using floating point arithmetic for moment calculation. *Pattern Recognition, 39*, 2047–2064. doi:10.1016/j.patcog.2006.05.025

Singh, C., Walia, E., & Mittal, N. (2011a). Face Recognition using Zernike and Complex Zernike moment features. *Pattern Recognition and Image Analysis, 21*(1), 71–81. doi:10.1134/S1054661811010044

Singh, C., Walia, E., & Mittal, N. (2011c). Rotation Invariant Complex Zernike Moments Features and their Application to Human Face and Character Recognition. *IET Computer Vision, 5*(5), 255–265. doi:10.1049/iet-cvi.2010.0020

Slaughter, D. C., & Harrell, R. C. (1987). Color vision in robotic fruit harvesting. *American Society of Agricultural Engineers, 30*(4), 1144-1148.

Smith, P., Sinclair, D., Cipolla, R., & Wood, K. (1998). Effective Corner Matching. In *Proceedings of the 9th British Machine Vision Conference*, (vol. 2, pp. 545-556). BMVA Press.

Smith, S. M. (2002). Fast robust automated brain extraction. *Human Brain Mapping, 17*(3), 143–155. doi:10.1002/hbm.10062 PMID:12391568

Smith, S., & Brady, J. (1995). SUSAN—a new approach to low level image processing. *International Journal of Computer Vision, 23*, 45–78. doi:10.1023/A:1007963824710

Soman, S., Ghorpade, M., Sonone, V., & Chavan, S. (2012). Content Based Image Retrieval using Advanced Color and Texture Features. *Proc. International Conference in Computational Intelligence (ICCIA2012)*. New York, USA.

Sonka, M., Hlavac, V., & Boyle, R. (1999). *Image Processing, Analysis, and Machine Vision*. PWS Publishing.

Sourin, A. (2006). *Computer Graphics: From a Small Formula to Cyberworlds*. Singapore: Prentice-Hall, Inc.

Spafford, E. H., & Weeber, S. A. (1993). Software forensics: Can we track code to its authors? *Computers & Security, 12*(6), 585–595. doi:10.1016/0167-4048(93)90055-A

Spinelli, F., Noferini, M., & Costa, G. (2006). Near Infrared Spectroscopy (NIRs), Perspective of Fire Blight Detection in Asymptomatic Plant Material. In *Proceedings of the 10th International Workshop on Fire Blight*, (pp. 87-90). Academic Press.

Spinola, C. G., Canero, J., & Gonzalo, M.-A. (2011). Real-time image processing for edge inspection and defect detection in stainless steel production lines. In *Proceedings of the IEEE International Conference on Image and Graphics*. Hefei, China: IEEE.

Stanciu, S. G. (2012). *Digital Image Processing. InTech. Koprowski, R., & Wrobel, Z. (2011). Image Processing in Optical Coherence Tomography using Matlab*. University of Silesia.

Starck, J.-L., & Murtagh, F. (2006). *Astronomical Image and Data Analysis*. Berlin: Springer.

Starck, J., Murtagh, F. D., & Bijaoui, A. (1998). *Image Processing and Data Analysis: The Multiscale Approach*. Cambridge, UK: Cambridge University Press. doi:10.1017/CBO9780511564352

Stathaki, T. (2008). *Image Fusion: Algorithms and Applications*. London: Elsevier Ltd.

Statisticbrain. (n.d.). Retrieved from http://www.statisticbrain.com/twitter-statistics/

Stilla, U., & Michelses, E. (2002). Estimating vehicle activities using thermal image sequences and maps. In *Proceedings of the Symposium on Geospatial Theory, Processing and Applications*. Academic Press.

Strang, G., & Nguyen, T. (1996). *Wavelets and filter banks*. Wellesley-Cambridge Press.

Sturman, D., & Zeltzer, D. (1994). A Survey of Glove-Based Input. *IEEE Transactions on Computer Graphics and Applications*, *14*(1), 30–39. doi:10.1109/38.250916

Suckling, J., Parker, J., Dance, R., Astley, M., Hutt, I., & Boggis, M. ... Savage, J. (1994). The mammographic image analysis society digital mammogram database. In *Proceedings of the 2nd International Workshop on Digital Mammography*. Elsevier.

Suesut, T., Numsomran, A., & Tipsuwanporn, V. (2010). Vision-based Network System for Industrial Applications. *International Journal of Computer Systems Science and Engineering*, *3*(1), 22–26.

Suganthy, M., & Ramamoorthy, P. (2012). Principal Component Analysis Based Feature Extraction, Morphological Edge Detection and Localization for Fast Iris Recognition. *Journal of Computer Science*, *8*(9), 1428–1433. doi:10.3844/jcssp.2012.1428.1433

Sultana, M., Paul, P. P., & Gavrilova, M. (2014). Social Behavioral Biometrics: An Emerging Trend. *International Journal of Pattern Recognition and Artificial Intelligence*.

Sung, K., & Poggio, T. (1998). Example-based learning for view-based human face detection. *IEEE Transactions on Pattern Analysis and Machine Intelligence*, *20*, 39–51. doi:10.1109/34.655648

Superkids Educational Software Reviews. (n.d.). Retrieved january 2012, from http://www.superkids.com/aweb/pages/reviews/kidsafe/1/sw_sum1.shtml

Suralkar, S., Karode, A. H., & Pawad, P. W. (2012). Texture Image Classification Using Support Vector Machine. *International Journal of Computer Applications in Technology*, *3*, 71–75.

Surmacz, K., Saeed, K., & Rapta, P. (2013). An improved algorithm for feature extraction from a fingerprint fuzzy image. *Optica Applicata*, *43*(3), 515–527.

Syal, S., Mehta, T., & Darshni, P. (2013). Design & Development of Intelligent System for Grading of Jatropha Fruit by Its Feature Value Extraction Using Fuzzy Logics.[IJARCSSE]. *International Journal of Advanced Research in Computer Science and Software Engineering*, *3*(7), 1077–1081.

Sylvia, K. (2011). To block or not to block e European child porno law in question. *Computer Law & Security Report*, *27*, 573–584. doi:10.1016/j.clsr.2011.09.005

Takahashi, T., Zhang, S., & Fukuchi, H. (2002). Measurement of 3-D Locations of Fruit by Binocular Stereo Vision for Apple Harvesting in an Orchard. In *American Society of Agricultural Engineers. ASABE Paper No. 021102*. St. Joseph, MI: ASABE.

Tang, C. W., & Hang, H. M. (2003). A feature-based robust digital image watermarking scheme. *IEEE Transactions on Signal Processing*, *51*(4), 950–959. doi:10.1109/TSP.2003.809367

Tang, Y. L., Hwang, M. S., & Yang, C. R. (2002). An image authentication scheme based on digital signatures. *Pakistan Journal of Applied Sciences*, *2*(5), 553–557.

Tarrataca, L., Santos, A. C., & Cardoso, J. M. P. (2009). The current feasibility of gesture recognition for a smartphone using J2ME. In *Proceedings of the ACM Symposium on Applied Computing* (pp.1642-1649). ACM.

Taylor, P., Hajnal, S., Dilhuydy, H., & Barreau, B. (1994). Measuring image texture to separate difficult from easy mammograms. *The British Journal of Radiology*, *67*(797), 456–463. doi:10.1259/0007-1285-67-797-456 PMID:8193892

Teague, M. R. (1980). Image analysis via the general theory of moments. *Journal of the Optical Society of America*, *70*, 920–930. doi:10.1364/JOSA.70.000920

Teh, C. H., & Chin, R. (1990). On the detection of dominant points on digital curves. *IEEE Transactions on Pattern Analysis and Machine Intelligence, 11*(8), 859–873. doi:10.1109/34.31447

Teh, C. H., & Chin, R. T. (1988). On image analysis by the methods of moments. *IEEE Transactions on Pattern Analysis and Machine Intelligence, 10*, 496–511. doi:10.1109/34.3913

Tillett, J., Rao, T. M., Sahin, F., Rao, R., & Brockport, S. (2005). Darwinian Particle Swarm Optimization. In B. Prasad (Ed.), *Proceedings of the 2nd Indian International Conference on Artificial Intelligence* (pp. 1474-1487). Pune, India: IEEE.

Tom, I. (n.d.). *Review: CyberPatrol 4 & SurfWatch 3.* Retrieved january 2012, from http://www.atpm.com/4.11/page11.shtml

Trucco, E., & Verri, A. (1998). *Introductory Techniques for 3-D Computer Vision.* New York: Prentice Hall.

Turek, F. (2011). Machine Vision Fundamentals: How to Make Robots See. *NASA Tech Briefs Magazine, 35*(6), 60–62.

Turk, M. (2001). A random walk through Eigenspace. *IEICE Transactions on Information and Systems. E (Norwalk, Conn.), 84-D*(12), 1586–1595.

Twitter. (n.d.). Retrieved from https://twitter.com/BillGates

Twitter-glossary. (n.d.). Retrieved from https://support.twitter.com/articles/166337-the-twitter-glossary

Tzotsos, A. D. A. (2006). A support vector machine approach for object based image analysis. *in Proc. international conference on object based image analysis (OBIA06).* Salzburg, Austria.

Tzourio-Mazoyer, N., Landeau, B., Papathanassiou, D., Crivello, F., Etard, O., & Delcroix, N. et al. (2002). Automated anatomical labeling of activations in SPM using a macroscopic anatomical parcellation of the MNI MRI single-subject brain. *NeuroImage, 15*, 273–289. doi:10.1006/nimg.2001.0978 PMID:11771995

U.S.D.A . (1991). Retrieved March 2013, from United States Standards for Grades of Fresh Tomatoes, U.S. Dept. Agric./AMS, Washington, DC: http://www.ams.usda.gov/standards/vegfm.htm

Vailaya, A., Figueiredo, M. A. T., Jain, A. K., & Zhang, H. J. (2001). Image classification for content based indexing. *IEEE Transactions on Image Processing, 10*(1), 117–129. doi:10.1109/83.892448 PMID:18249602

Valle, Y. D., Venayagamoorthy, G. K., Mohagheghi, S., Hernandez, J. C., & Harley, R. (2008). Particle swarm optimization: Basic concepts, variants and applications in power systems. *IEEE Transactions on Evolutionary Computation, 2*(2), 171–195. doi:10.1109/TEVC.2007.896686

Van de Pol, L. A., Hensel, A., Van der Flier, W. M., Visser, P., Pijnenburg, Y. A., & Barkhof, F. et al. (2006). Hippocampal atrophy on MRI in frontotemporal lobar degeneration and Alzheimer's disease. *Journal of Neurology, Neurosurgery, and Psychiatry, 77*, 439–442. doi:10.1136/jnnp.2005.075341 PMID:16306153

van Schyndel, R. G., Tirkel, A. Z., & Osborne, C. F. (1994). A digital watermark. In *Proc. IEEE International Conference of Image Processing,* (vol. 2, pp. 86-90). IEEE.

Vanschoenwinkel, B., & Manderick, B. (2005). Appropriate kernel functions for support vector machine learning with sequences of symbolic data. *Deterministic and Statistical Methods in Machine Learning in Computer Science, 3635*, 256–280. doi:10.1007/11559887_16

Vapnik, V. N. (2000). *The Nature of Statistical Learning Theory* (2nd ed.). New York: Springer-Verlag New York, Inc. doi:10.1007/978-1-4757-3264-1

Venkatachalam, V. (2000). Image classification using pseudo power signatures. In *Proceedings of IEEE International Conference on Image Processing,* (pp.796-799). Vancouver, Canada: IEEE.

Venkatesan, R., Koon, S. M., Jakubowski, M. H., & Moulin, P. (2000). Robust image hashing. In *Proc. of the IEEE International Conference on Image Processing,* (vol. 3, pp. 664-666). IEEE.

Vetterli, M., & Kovacevic, J. (1995). *Wavelet and subband coding.* Englewood Cliffs, NJ: Prentice Hall.

Vezhnevets, V., Sazonov, V., & Andreeva, A. (2003). A survey on pixel-based skin color detection techniques. In *Proceedings of GraphiCon* (pp. 85–92). GraphiCon.

Vieira, L. F., Vilela, R. D., & Nascimento, E. R., Jr. F. A., Carceroni, R. L., & Araújo, A. d. (October, 2003). Automatically choosing source color images for coloring grayscale images. *Brazilian Symposium on Computer Graphics and Image Processing (SIBGRAPI)* (pp. 151-158). Sao Carlos, Brazil: IEEE.

Vincent, E., & Laganiere, R. (2005). Detecting and matching feature points. *Journal of Visual Communication and Image Representation*, 16(1), 38–54. doi:10.1016/j.jvcir.2004.05.001

Vincent, E., & Laganire, R. (2001). Matching feature points in stereo pairs: a comparative study of some matching strategies. *Machine Graphics and Vision*, 10, 237–259.

Viola, P., & Jones, M. J. (2001). Rapid Object Detection Using a Boosted Cascade of Simple Features. In *Proceedings of IEEE Conference Computer Vision and Pattern Recognition, CVPR (1)* (pp. 511-518). IEEE Computer Society.

Walton, S. (1995). Image authentication for a slippery new age. *Dr. Dobb's Journal of Software Tools for Professional Programmers, 20*.

Wang, H., & Brady, M. (1995). Real-time corner detection algorithm for motion estimation. *Image and Vision Computing*, 13(9), 695–703. doi:10.1016/0262-8856(95)98864-P

Wang, J. Y. A., & Adelson, E. H. (1994). Representing moving images with layers. *IEEE Transactions on Image Processing*, 3(5), 625–638. doi:10.1109/83.334981 PMID:18291956

Wang, Y., Berwick, R. C., Haykin, S., Pedrycz, W., Kinsner, W., Baciu, G., & Bhavsar, C. (2011). Cognitive Informatics and Cognitive Computing in Year 10 and Beyond. [IJCINI]. *International Journal of Cognitive Informatics and Natural Intelligence*, 5(4), 1–21. doi:10.4018/jcini.2011100101

Wang, Z., Bovik, A. C., Sheikh, H. R., & Simoncelli, E. P. (2004). Image quality assessment: from error visibility to structural similarity. *IEEE Transactions on Image Processing*, 13(4), 1–14. doi:10.1109/TIP.2003.819861 PMID:15376952

Wee, C.-Y., & Paramesran, R. (2007). On the computational aspects of Zernike moments. *Image and Vision Computing*, 25, 967–980. doi:10.1016/j.imavis.2006.07.010

Wei, Z., Wang, X., An, W., & Che, J. (2009, September 20-23). Target-tracking based early fire smoke detection in video. In *Proceedings of the IEEE International Conference on Image and Graphics*, (Vol. 3, pp. 172-176). IEEE.

Wellcome-Trust-Centre-for-Neuroimaging. (2009, April). *SPM8 - Statistical Parametric Mapping*. Retrieved from http://www.fil.ion.ucl.ac.uk/spm/software/spm8/

Wenyin, L., Wang, T., & Zhang, H. (2000). A hierarchical characterization scheme for image retrieval. In *Proceedings of IEEE International Conference on Image Processing*, (pp. 42-45). Vancouver, Canada: IEEE.

Weston, J., & Watkins, C. (1999). Support Vector Machines for Multi-Class Pattern Recognition. In *Proc European Symp Artif Neural Netw (ESANN)*, (Vol. 99, pp. 61-72). Bruges, Belgium: Univ. Cath. de Louvain - ICTEAM-ELEN - Machine Learning Group.

Winkler, S. (June 2001). Visual fidelity and perceived quality: Toward comprehensive metrics. *Photonics West 2001-Electronic Imaging* (pp. 114-125). San Jose, California, USA: International Society for Optics and Photonics.

Wolfe, N. (1976). Risk for breast cancer development determined by mammographic parenchymal pattern. *Cancer*, 37(5), 86–92. doi:10.1002/1097-0142(197605)37:5<2486::AID-CNCR2820370542>3.0.CO;2-8 PMID:1260729

Wolfgang, R. B., & Delp, E. J. (1996). A watermark for digital images. In *Proc. of IEEE International Conference of Image Processing*, (vol. 3, pp. 219-222). IEEE.

Wong, P. W., & Memon, N. (2001). Secret and public key image watermarking schemes for image authentication and ownership verification. *IEEE Transactions on Image Processing*, 10(10), 1593–1601. doi:10.1109/83.951543 PMID:18255501

Wu, Q., & Zhou, D.-X. (2006). Analysis of support vector machine classification. *Journal of Computational Analysis and Applications*, 8, 99119.

Wyawahare, M. V., Patil, D. P. M., & Abhyankar, H. K. (2009). Image Registration Techniques: An overview. *Internal Journal of Signal Processing. Image and Processing and Pattern Recognition*, 2(3), 11–28.

Xiang, C., Ding, S. Q., & Lee, T. H. (2005). Geometrical Interpretation and Architecture Selection of MLP. *IEEE Transactions on Neural Networks*, 16(1), 84–96. doi:10.1109/TNN.2004.836197 PMID:15732391

Xiang, Y., Zou, B., & Li, H. (2009). Selective color transfer with multi-source image. *Pattern Recognition Letters*, 30(7), 682–689. doi:10.1016/j.patrec.2009.01.004

Xiao, B. (2010). Principal component analysis for feature extraction of image sequence. *International Conference On Computer and Communication Technologies in Agriculture Engineering (CCTAE)*. 1, pp. 250-253. Chengdu, China: IEEE.

Xie, S., Shan, S., Chen, X., & Chen, J. (2010). Fusing Local Patterns of Gabor Magnitude and Phase for Face Recognition. *IEEE Transactions on Image Processing*, 19(5), 1349–1361. doi:10.1109/TIP.2010.2041397 PMID:20106741

Xu, Y., Zhang, D., Yang, J., & Yang, J.-Y. (2008). An approach for directly extracting features from matrix data and its application in face recognition. *Neurocomputing*, 71, 1857–1865. doi:10.1016/j.neucom.2007.09.021

Yampolskiy, R. V. (2011). Behavioral, cognitive, and virtual biometrics. In *Computer Analysis of Human Behavior* (pp. 347–385). London, UK: Springer. doi:10.1007/978-0-85729-994-9_13

Yampolskiy, R. V., & Govindaraju, V. (2008). Behavioral biometrics: a survey and classification. *International Journal of Biometrics*, 1(1), 81–113. doi:10.1504/IJBM.2008.018665

Yampolskiy, R. V., & Govindaraju, V. (2010). Game Playing Tactic as a Behavioral Biometric for Human Identification. In *Behavioral Biometrics for Human Identification: Intelligent Applications*. IGI Global.

Yang, M. H., & Ahuja, N. (1998). Detecting human faces in color images. In *Proceedings of International Conference on Image Processing (ICIP)*, (vol. 1, pp. 127–130). Chicago: ICIP.

Yang, C. M., Cheng, C. H., & Chen, R. K. (2007). Changes in Spectral Characteristics of Rice Canopy Infested with Brown Planthopper and Leaffolder. *Crop Science*, 47, 329–335. doi:10.2135/cropsci2006.05.0335

Yang, H., Wang, W., & Sun, J. (2004). Control point adjustment for B-spline curve approximation. *Computer Aided Design*, 36(7), 639–652. doi:10.1016/S0010-4485(03)00140-4

Yang, J., Chu, D., Zhang, L., Xu, Y., & Yang, J. (2013). Sparse Representation Classifier Steered Discriminative Projection with Applications to Face Recognition. *IEEE Transactions on Neural Networks and Learning Systems*, 24(7), 1023–1035. doi:10.1109/TNNLS.2013.2249088 PMID:24808518

Yang, X. (2004). Curve fitting and fairing using conic splines. *Computer Aided Design*, 36(5), 461–472. doi:10.1016/S0010-4485(03)00119-2

Yang, X. N., & Wang, G. Z. (2001). Planar point set fairing and fitting by arc splines. *Computer Aided Design*, 33(1), 35–43. doi:10.1016/S0010-4485(00)00059-2

Yang, Z., Deng, J., & Chen, F. (2005). Fitting unorganized point clouds with active implicit B-spline curves. *The Visual Computer*, 21(1), 831–839. doi:10.1007/s00371-005-0340-0

Yanushkevich, S., Gavrilova, M., Wang, P., & Srihari, S. (2007). *Image pattern recognition: Synthesis & analysis in biometrics*. Singapore: World Scientific Publishers.

Yatziv, L., & Sapiro, G. (2006). Fast image and video colorization using chrominance blending. *IEEE Transactions on Image Processing*, 15(5), 1120–1129. doi:10.1109/TIP.2005.864231 PMID:16671293

Ye, J., Chen, K., Wu, T., Li, J., Zhao, Z., Patel, R., et al. (2008). Heterogeneous data fusion for Alzheimer's disease study. In *Proceedings of International Conference on Knowledge Discovery and Data Mining* (pp. 1025-1033). New York: ACM.

Yeung, M. M., & Mintzer, F. (1997). An invisible watermarking technique for image verification. In *Proc. of the IEEE International Conference on Image Processing*. IEEE.

Yu, H., Li, M., Zhang, H.-J., & Feng, J. (2002). Color texture moments for content-based image retrieval, " in Proc. International Conference., *3*, pp. 929-932. Rochester, New York, USA.

Zawbaa, H. M., El-Bendary, N., Hassanien, A. E., & Abraham, A. (2011). SVM-based Soccer Video Summarization System. *in Proc. The Third IEEE World Congress on Nature and Biologically Inspired Computing (NaBIC2011)*, (pp. 7-11). Salamanca, Spain.

Zawbaa, H. M., El-Bendary, N., Hassanien, A. E., & Kim, T.-H. (2011). Machine Learning-Based Soccer Video Summarization System. In *Proc. Multimedia, Computer Graphics and Broadcasting FGIT-MulGraB (2). 263, pp* (pp. 19–28). Jeju Island, Korea: Springer. doi:10.1007/978-3-642-27186-1_3

Zeman, R., Fox, S., & Silverman, P. et al. (1993). Helical (spiral) CT of the abdomen. *AJR*, *160*, 719–725. doi:10.2214/ajr.160.4.8456652 PMID:8456652

Zeman, R., Zeiberg, A., & Davros, W. et al. (1993). Routine helical CT of the abdomen: image quality considerations. *Radiology*, *189*, 395–400. PMID:8210365

Zhang, Y., & He, M. (2009). 3D Wavelet Transform and Its Application in Multispectral and Hyperspectral Image Fusion. In *Proceedings of the 4th IEEE Conference on Industrial Electronics and Applications* (pp. 3643-3647). Xi'an, China: IEEE.

Zhang, Y., & Wang, R. (2004). Multi-resolution and multi-spectral image fusion for urban object extraction. In *Proceeding of 20th ISPRS Congress*, (Vol. 3, pp. 960-966). GeoICT.

Zhang, Y., Xie, X., & Cheng, T. (2010). Application of PSO and SVM in image classification. *in Proc. 3rd IEEE International Conference on Computer Science and Information Technology (ICCSIT), 6*, pp. 629-631. Chengdu, China.

Zhang, L., & McCarthy, M. (2011). Measurement and evaluation of tomato maturity using magnetic resonance imaging. *Postharvest Biology and Technology, 67*, 37–43. doi:10.1016/j.postharvbio.2011.12.004

Zhao, W., Chellappa, R., Phillips, P., & Rosenfeld, A. (2003). Face recognition: A literature survey. *ACM Computing Surveys, 35*, 399–458. doi:10.1145/954339.954342

Zheng, Y. (2011). *Image Fusion and Its Applications*. InTech. doi:10.5772/691

Zhi, R., & Ruan, Q. (2008). Two-dimensional direct and weighted linear discriminant analysis for face recognition. *Neurocomputing, 71*, 3607–3611. doi:10.1016/j.neucom.2008.04.047

Zhou, H., & Ruan, Q. (2006). A Real-time Gesture Recognition Algorithm on Video Surveillance. In *Proceedings of 8th international conference on Signal Processing*. Academic Press.

Zhou, X.-C. (2009). Image Segmentation Based on Modified Particle Swarm Optimization and Fuzzy C-Means Clustering Algorithm. In *Proceedings of Second International Conference on Intelligent Computation Technology and Automation* (pp. 611-616). IEEE Computer Society.

Zhou, C., Chan, P., Petrick, N., Helvie, A., Goodsitt, M., Sahiner, B., & Hadjiiski, M. (2001). Computerized image analysis: estimation of breast density on mammograms. *Medical Physics, 28*(6), 1056–1069. doi:10.1118/1.1376640 PMID:11439475

Zhou, H., Wu, J., & Zhang, J. (2010). *Digital Image Processing. BookBoon. Young, I., Gerbrands, J., & Vliet, L.V. (2009). Fundamentals of Image Processing*. Delft University of Technology.

Zhou, J., Civco, D. L., & Silander, J. A. (1998). A wavelet transform method to merge Landsat TM and SPOT panchromatic data. *International Journal of Remote Sensing, 19*(4), 743–757. doi:10.1080/014311698215973

Zoghlami, I., Faugeras, O., & Deriche, R. (1997). Using geometric corners to build a 2D mosaic from a set of images. In *Proceedings of the Conference on Computer Vision and Pattern Recognition*. IEEE Computer Society.

Zwiggelaar, R., Muhimmah, I., & Denton, E. (2005). Mammographic density classification based on statistical gray-level histogram modeling. In *Proc. Medical Image Understanding and Analysis*. Academic Press.

Zwiggelaar, R., Parr, C., Schumm, E., Hutt, W., Taylor, J., Astley, M., & Boggis, M. (1999). Model-based detection of spiculated lesions in mammograms. *Medical Image Analysis*, *3*(1), 39–62. doi:10.1016/S1361-8415(99)80016-4 PMID:10709696

About the Contributors

Muhammad Sarfraz is a Professor in Kuwait University, Kuwait. He received his Ph.D. from Brunel University, UK, in 1990. His research interests include Computer Graphics, CAD/CAM, Pattern Recognition, Computer Vision, Image Processing, and Soft Computing. He is currently working on various projects related to academia and industry. He has been keynote/invited speaker at various platforms around the globe. He has advised/supervised more than 50 students for their MSc and PhD theses. He is the Chair of the Information Science Department, Kuwait University. He has published more than 260 publications in the form of various books, book chapters, journal papers, and conference papers. He is member of various professional societies including IEEE, ACM, IVS, IACSIT, and ISOSS. He is a chair, member of the International Advisory Committees and Organizing Committees of various international conferences, symposiums, and workshops. He is a reviewer for many international journals, conferences, meetings, and workshops around the world. He is the Editor-in-Chief of the *International Journal of Computer Vision and Image Processing*. He is also Editor/Guest Editor of various international conference proceedings, books, and journals. He has achieved various awards in education, research, and administrative services.

* * *

Namita Aggarwal obtained B.Sc. (Hons.) Maths from University of Delhi, Delhi and Master of Computer applications from University of Delhi, Delhi. Currently, she is pursuing Ph.D. from School of Computer and Systems Sciences, Jawaharlal Nehru University, New Delhi. Her current area of research is pattern recognition and image processing. At the same time, she is working as Assistant Professor at University of Delhi, Delhi.

R. K. Agrawal obtained MTech. (Computer Application) from Indian Institute of Technology Delhi, New Delhi and PhD (Computational Physics) from University of Delhi, Delhi. Presently, he is working as an Professor at School of Computer and Systems Sciences, Jawaharlal Nehru University, New Delhi. His current research areas are: classification, feature extraction, and selection for pattern recognition problems in domains of image processing, security, and bioinformatics.

Abder-Rahman Ali received his BSc in Computer Science in 2006 from the University of Jordan (Jordan), MSc Software Engineering in 2009 from DePaul University (USA), and is currently pursuing his Ph.D. degree in France, in the area of fuzzy clustering and discrete geometry of MRI and ultrasound imaging sequences for Hepa-Tocellular Carcinoma (HCC). He is very passionate to the idea of applying computer science to medical imaging, and software engineering to medical device software systems, in an eventual goal to come up with algorithms and systems that aid in Computer Aided Diagnosis (CAD). He also likes to adopt fuzzy logic in his research.

Saif alZahir received his PhD and MS degrees in Electrical and Computer Engineering from the University of Pittsburgh and the University of Wisconsin - Milwaukee (UWM), respectively. Dr. alZahir is involved in research in the areas of image processing, digital forensic, mHealth, wireless networking, VLSI, ethics, and corporate governance. In 2003, The Innovation Council of British Columbia – Canada named him British Columbia Research Fellow. He has authored or co-authored nearly 100 journal and conference papers in several languages, 2 books, and 4 book chapters. He is the editor-in-chief of the *Signal Processing: International Journal*, editor-in-chief of *International Journal on Corporate Governance*, editor in several journal editorial boards, and member in many International Program Committees of international conferences. Prof. alZahir has chaired several International and National Conferences. Currently, he is with the Computer Science Department at UNBC, British Columbia – Canada.

Ahmed M. Anter Lecturer Assistant at the Computer Science Department, Faculty of Computer Science and Information System, Jazan University, KSA from 2011-now. Anter is interested in biomedical engineering, image processing, computer vision, neural network, programming and application development, Business Process Management Systems (BPMS), patient information and medical application systems, open source technologies; he is worked in communication and Information Technology Center "CITC" Mansoura University as a senior software development from 2007 – 2011 and junior software development in Mansoura E_Learing Center, Mansoura University from 2005 – 2007. Anter holds the Master Degree of Computer Science from Computer Science and Information System, Mansoura University, 2010. His Master in "Content-Based Mammogram Image Retrieval." He is now a Ph.D. student at the same faculty and working in "Automatic Computer Aided Diagnosis for CT Liver Tumors." Research Field include: Artificial Intelligence, Computer Vision, Image Processing, Neural Networks and Fuzzy, Optimization Techniques, Neutrosophic sets, Machine Learning, Algorithms, and Data Mining.

Amr Badr is a Professor at Cairo University, Dept. of Computer Science, Faculty of Computers and Information, Cairo University. He received his PhD degree in Computer Science from the Institute of Statistical Studies and Research (ISSR) - Cairo University in 1998. His main research interests are in the areas of Compilers Design, Expert Systems, Computational Intelligence, Soft Computing, Genetic Algorithms, Evolutionary Algorithms, Neural Networks, Fuzzy Logic, Expert Systems, Petri Nets, Cellular Automata, Bioinformatics, Immune Systems, Mathematics of Soft Computing, and Medical Imaging. Prof. Badr has authored/coauthored many research publications in peer-reviewed journals and conference proceedings. Furthermore, he is a member in the editorial board of a number of international journals. In addition, prof. Badr advises many M.Sc. and Ph.D. students as well as supervises various graduation projects.

Ankit Chaudhary received his Master of Engineering in Computer Science and Engineering from Birla Institute of Technology and Science, Pilani, India and Ph.D. in Computer Vision from Central Electronics Engineering Research Institute (CEERI), Pilani, India. His areas of research interest are

Computer Vision, Digital Image Processing, Artificial Intelligence and Robotics. Currently, he is with Dept. of Electrical and Computer Engg., The University of Iowa, USA. He is member of IEEE and also serves in the editorial board at many international journals.

Micael Santos Couceiro obtained the B.Sc. degree on Electrical Engineering - Automation in 2006, and the Teaching Licensure degree (BSc plus 2 years) on Electrical Engineering - Automation and Communications in 2008 and the M.Sc. degree on Automation and Communications in Energy Systems - Industrial Systems in April 2010, all at the Engineering Institute of Coimbra (ISEC). He obtained the Ph.D. degree on Electrical and Computer Engineering at University of Coimbra (FCTUC), having Rui Rocha (MRL-ISR) as his scientific supervisor and Nuno Ferreira as his co-supervisor. He worked at ISEC both as a researcher (RoboCorp) and as a Professor Assistant in the Department of Electrical Engineering (DEE). He is currently the CEO of Ingeniarius, Lda.

Karen Das received his M.Sc. in Electronics Science from Guwahati University, India and M.Tech in Electronics Engineering from Tezpur University, Assam, India. Currently, he is Assistant Professor at Dept. of Electronics Engg., Don Bosco University, Assam. His areas of research interest are Digital Image Processing, Artificial Intelligence, VLSI systems, and Digital Communication.

Manik Lal Das received his Ph.D. degree from Indian Institute of Technology, Bombay in 2006. He is an Associate Professor in Dhirubhai Ambani Institute of Information and Communication Technology, Gandhinagar, India. He has published more than 50 research articles in referred journals and conferences. He is a senior member of IEEE and life member of Cryptology Research Society of India. His research interests include Cryptography and Information Security.

Shiv Ram Dubey was a research fellow in Computer Vision lab, CSE, IIT Madras and currently pursuing PhD from Indian Institute of Information Technology Allahabad. His research was funded by DST, Govt. India. He received his B.Tech in Computer Science and Engineering in 2010 from the Gurukul Kangri Vishwavidyalaya Haridwar, India and his M.Tech in Computer Science and Engineering in 2012 from GLA University Mathura, India. His current research interests are Image Processing, Computer Vision, and Machine Learning.

Nashwa El-Bendary received her Ph.D. degree in 2008 in Information Technology from the Faculty of Computers and Information, Cairo University, Egypt. She is an assistant professor at the Arab Academy for Science, Technology, and Maritime Transport (AASTMT), Cairo - Egypt. During the year 2012, she received a post-doctoral fellowship in School of Computing and Information Systems, Athabasca University, Canada. She is a member in the Scientific Research Group in Egypt (SRGE). Dr. Nashwa El-Bendary has published several papers in major international journals and peer-reviewed international conference proceedings along with a number of book chapters. Her main research interests are in the areas of Ambient Intelligence, Ubiquitous Smart Systems, Smart Environmental Monitoring, Mobile Computing and Technologies, Wireless Sensor Networks, Image Processing, and Machine Learning. She currently co-advises master and Ph.D. students as well as leading and supervising various graduation projects. Dr. Nashwa is a member of the editorial boards of a number of international journals. She has also been a reviewer, technical program committee member, special session co-chair, and has been invited as a speaker to several workshops and international conferences.

Tarek Abd El-Hafeez received his Ph.D. degree in computer science from Minia University (Egypt) in 2009. In 2005, he has a Master in Computer Science in Software Engineering branch. Currently, he is Associate Professor there. His research interests include pattern recognition, Computer Vision, Web-Based Applications, and Data Mining.

Esraa Elhariri received her B.Sc. with honors in 2010 from Faculty of Computers and Information, Computer Science Department, Fayoum University. She received her Pre-Master in 2011 from Faculty of Computers and Information, Computer science department, Cairo University. She is a demonstrator at faculty of Computers and Information Fayoum University since 2010. She is a member in the scientific research group in Egypt (SRGE). Her M.Sc. topic is "Content-Based Image Retrieval for Agricultural Crops." Her main research interests are Machine Learning, Image Processing, and Cloud Computing Security.

Mohamed Abu ElSoud is an Assistant Professor of Computer Science at the Faculty of Computer and Information Sciences, Mansoura University. He is the Head of Computer Science Department, Director of the Unity of Quality Assurance and Accreditation, and a member of the Board of Counseling Center of Computing and Information Systems.

Marina Gavrilova is an Associate Professor in the Department of Computer Science, University of Calgary. Dr. Gavrilova's research interests lie in the area of biometric security, cognitive sciences, pattern recognition, social networking and cyberworlds. Prof. Gavrilova is founder and co-director of the Biometric Technologies Laboratory, with over 120 journal and conference papers, edited special issues, books and book chapters, including World Scientific Bestseller (2007) – *Image Pattern Recognition: Synthesis and Analysis in Biometric* and *Multimodal Biometrics and Intelligent Image Processing for Security Systems*. Together with Dr. Kenneth Tan, Prof. Gavrilova founded ICCSA series of international events in 2002. She was co-Chair of the International Workshop on Biometric Technologies BT 2004 and General Chair of International Conference on Cyberworlds CW2011, and currently serves as Founding Editor-in-Chief of *Transactions on Computational Science Journal*, Springer. Prof. Gavrilova has given Invited Keynotes and Invited Panel Lectures at such prestigious international events at INDIN 2003, 3AI'06, ICBAKE 2008, ICCSA 2010, ICCI*CC 2011, CyberWorlds 2012, GRAPHICON 2012, and appeared as panelist at 14th Security and Privacy Conference. She has given invited talks at DIMACS, Bell Labs, USA, Microsoft Research, Redmond, Samsung Research, South Korea and at numerous universities worldwide. Her research was profiled in newspaper and TV interviews, most recently being chosen to be featured in Exhibit at National Museum of Civilization, in National Film Canada production and on upcoming Discovery Channel biometric spoofing segment.

Aboul Ella Hassanien (Abo) received his B.Sc. with honours in 1986 and M.Sc. degree in 1993, both from Ain Shams University, Faculty of Science, Pure Mathematics and Computer Science Department, Cairo, Egypt. On September 1998, he received his doctoral degree from the Department of Computer Science, Graduate School of Science and Engineering, Tokyo Institute of Technology, Japan. He is a Full Professor at Cairo University, Faculty of Computer and Information, IT Department. Professor Abo is the founder and chair of the scientific research group in Egypt. He has authored/co-authored over 380 research publications in peer-reviewed reputed journals, book chapters, and conference proceedings.

He has served as the general chair, co-chair, program chair, program committee member of various international conferences and reviewer for various international journals. He has directed many funded research projects. Abo is the chair of the Computer Science and Information Technology Division at the Egyptian Syndicate of Scientific Professions (ESSP). His research interests include Computational intelligence, medical image analysis, security, animal identification and multimedia data mining.

Hung-Yao Hsu received Bachelor of Science in mechanical engineering from National Taiwan Institute of Technology at Taipei of Taiwan in 1985 and Master of Science in mechanical engineering from National Cheng Kung University at Tainan of Taiwan in 1987. He received his Ph.D. in manufacturing engineering from University of South Australia in 2002. He is currently a senior lecturer in the School of Engineering located in Mawson Lakes campus at University of South Australia. His research interests include kinematics, intelligent design for assembly, Micro-Electro-Mechanical-Systems (MEMS) design and applications and micro-joining and micro-manufacturing. His teaching interests include design for assembly evaluation, robotics and manufacturing automation, intelligent design and manufacturing.

Malik Zawwar Hussain is a Professor in University of the Punjab, Pakistan. He received his Ph.D. Degree in 2002 in the field of Computer Graphics from University of the Punjab. He did post-doctoral research fellowship from University of Birmingham, UK in 2007. His research interests include Computational Mathematics, Computer Graphics, CAGD, CAD/CAM, Image Processing, and Soft Computing. He has supervised more than 36 students for their M.Phil. and Ph.D. theses. He has published more than 65 publications in the form of journal and conference papers. He has been invited speaker in more than 20 international conferences/ Seminars/ Workshops and a member of organizing committee for several international conferences around the world. He also attended many international conferences/workshops and presented his research in most of them. He is also a life member of many renowned international societies. He is associated to many journals of international repute as editor and reviewer.

Misbah Irshad is a lecturer in Lahore College for women University, Lahore, Pakistan. She received her Ph.D. degree in 2013. Her research interests comprises of various fields like: Computational Mathematics, Computer Graphics, CAGD, CAD/CAM, Image and Signal Processing, and Soft Computing. She has published more than eight publications in different international journals and conference proceedings. She also presented couple of research papers in international conferences held in Singapore and UK.

Anand Singh Jalal received his MTech degree in Computer Science from Devi Ahilya Vishwavidyalaya, Indore, India. He received his PhD in the area of Computer Vision from Indian Institute of Information Technology (IIIT), Allahabad, India. He has 14 years of teaching and research experience and currently, he is working as Head and Professor in Department of Computer Engineering and Applications, GLA University, Mathura, India. His research interests include image processing, computer vision and pattern recognition.

Senthil Kumaran obtained PhD from Indian Institute of Science, Bangalore, India. Presently, he is working as an Associate Professor at Department of NMR, All India Institute of Medical Sciences, New Delhi, India. His current research areas are: Biomedical Applications of MR, Multinuclear Spectroscopy, Functional MRI.

Sang-Heon Lee received Bachelor of Engineering in aeronautical engineering from Inha University, Korea in 1988 and Master of Engineering and Science in Mechatronics from University of New South Wales in 1995. He received his Ph.D. in Systems Engineering from Australian National University in 1999. He has been a member of the Institute of Electrical and Electronics Engineers (IEEE) since 1995. He is currently a senior lecturer in the School of Engineering, the Mawson Lakes campus in the University of South Australia. His research interests include discrete-event systems, integrated on-line robot control systems, machine vision and fuzzy logic control and neural networks. He has published around 90 international journals or conference papers.

Peilin Li received Bachelor of Engineering in mechanical design manufacturing and automation from Shanghai Tong Ji University in China of P. R. in 2002 and Master of Engineering in advanced manufacturing technology from School of Advanced Manufacturing and Mechanical Engineering at University of South Australia in 2007. He has been pursuing Ph.D. degree with the School of Engineering under Division of Information Technology, Engineering and Environment at University of South Australia sponsored by the scholarship of University of South Australia President's Scholarship and Australian Postgraduate Award. His current research interests include the multisensor imaging data analysis by statistical learning methods in machine learning application and neural network architecture. The application includes pattern recognition by visual perception in agricultural application.

Tarek M. Mahmoud received his Ph.D. degree in engineering (computer science) from Bremen University (Germany) in 1997. Since 1997, he has been with the Department of computer science of Minia University. Currently, he is a Professor there and the Dean of the Faculty of Computers and Information, Minia University, Egypt. His research interests include wired and wireless networks, mobile applications, pattern recognition, data mining.

K. C. Manjunatha did his B.E in Instrumentation Technology in Malnad College of Engineering, Hassan, Karnataka state, under Visvesvaraya Technological University during 2008. Presently, he is pursuing part time MSc. Engineering by Research under Visvesvaraya Technological University. He served for about two years in the Department of IT in Malnad college of Engineering, Hassan, as Lecturer from Sept 2008 to June 2010. He is currently working as Process Manager in Prakash Steels and Power Private Limited, Challekere, Chitradurga, Karnataka. His research interests are in Industrial automation, Computer vision, Image processing and manufacturing process. He has around six research paper publications in reputed journals and conferences. He has procured five merit incentives for specified academic subjects and he nominated for better performance from the employer.

Neerja Mittal received her B.E. in Computer Science and Engineering from SLIET, Longowal, India in 2000. She received her M.Tech and Ph.D. in Computer Science from Punjabi University, Patiala, India in 2003 and 2012, respectively. Presently, she is working as a Scientist at CSIR-Central Scientific Instruments Organisation, Chandigarh, India. Earlier she has worked as an Assistant Professor in CSE department of Rayat & Bahra Institute of Engineering and Bio-Tech, Kharar, Distt. Mohali (Pb.), India. She has a number of International journal and conference publications to her credit. Her research interests include pattern recognition, image processing and particularly face recognition algorithms.

H. S. Mohana was born in the year 1965. He obtained B.E Degree in Electrical and Electronics Engineering from University of Mysore during 1986. Since then, he has served in the technical education field in various capacities. He obtained M.E from University of Roorkee, presently IIT ROORKEE, with the specialization in Measurement and Instrumentation. He worked as chairman and member of board of examiner and board of studies with several universities which include, University of Mysore, Kuvempu University, and VTU. He presented research findings in 12 national conferences and in 4 international conferences held across the world. He has published 10 journal papers in peer reviewed journals of international reputation and good impact factor. He is recognized as AICTE expert committee member in the inspection and reporting continuation of affiliation and Increase in intake of the engineering colleges. He is a life member of professional bodies: FIE, FIETE, MISTE, IACSIT-Singapore. He completed one AICTE/MHRD-TAPTECH project and one AICTE/MHRD-Research project successfully. He coordinated TWO ISTE Sponsored STTP for the technical college teachers. He was honored as session chair person in IEEE- Int. National conference (ICACC-09) at Singapore, 21 – 24 January 2009 and in IEEE- 2009 First International Conference on Computational Intelligence, Communication Systems and Networks, Indore, 22-24th July 2009.

Siva Charan Muraharirao obtained his Bachelor's degree from Dhirubhai Ambani Institute of Information and Communication Technology, Gandhinagar, India and an MBA from NITIE, Mumbai, India. Being an IT engineer, he worked in one of the largest IT companies in India and currently has been working as an Account Manager in another leading IT company. Besides IT, his interests lie in multimedia and advertising.

Ahmed Omar received his M.Sc. degree (Computer Science) from the Department of Computer Science of Minia University (Egypt) in 2013. Currently, he is Assistant Lecturer there. His research interests include pattern recognition and data mining.

Padma Polash Paul received the B.Sc. degree in Computer Science and Engineering from University of Rajshahi, Bangladesh, in 2006, the M.Phil. degree in Computer Science from City University of Hong Kong in 2010. He has over 25 international journal, conference papers, and book chapters. Padma Polash Paul joined as faculty member in the Department of Computer Science and Engineering, Ahsanullah University of Science and Technology, Bangladesh in 2007. He taught there for a year and started higher study. He is currently a PhD Student in the Department of Computer Science at University of Calgary, AB, Canada.

Jagdish Lal Raheja Received his M.Tech from Indian Institute of Technology, Kharagpur, India and Ph.D. from Technical University of Munich, Germany. Currently he is Senior Principal Scientist at Digital Systems Group, Central Electronics Engineering Research Institute (CEERI), Pilani, India and also Professor at CSIR. He has been a DAAD fellow. He has published more than 100 papers in International Journals and peer reviewed conferences. His areas of research interest are Digital Image Processing, Embedded Systems and Human Computer Interface. He is in the editorial board of several international journals and also reviewer for many reputed conferences. He has been Principal investigator in many important real life projects.

Shekhar Raheja received his B.Tech in electronics engineering from Rajasthan Technical University, India and M.S from Department of Computer Science, TU Kaiserslautern, Germany. His areas of research interest are digital image processing, real time and embedded systems, age-invariant person identification.

Bharti Rana is currently PhD scholar at School of Computer & System Sciences (SC&SS), Jawaharlal Nehru University (JNU), New Delhi, India. She has received her MTech. degree (Computer Science and Technology) from SC&SS, JNU, New Delhi, and MCA from GGSIPU, Delhi. Her current area of research is pattern recognition and image processing.

Noura A. Semary is an associated professor in Information Technology department, faculty of Computers and Information, Menofia University. She received her B.Sc in Computers and Information-Information Technology, faculty of Computers and Information, Cairo University, 2001. She received her M.Sc and Ph.D in Computers and Information- Information Technology, Faculty of Computers and Information, Menofia University, 2007 and 2011, respectively. She had participated in "Made in Arab world" (MIA) competition in 2009 by her project "Black and White Movie Colorization" and she won the 1st rank. She has about 15 publications in national/international conferences and journals. Her research interests are in Image and Video Processing, Computer Vision, Data Compression, Virtual Reality, Pattern Recognition fields, and Assistive Technologies.

Chandan Singh received undergraduate degree in science in 1975 and post graduate degree in Mathematics in 1977 both from Kumaon University, Nainital, India, and Ph.D. degree in Applied Mathematics from Indian Institute of Technology, Kanpur, India, in 1982. He joined M/S Jyoti Ltd., Baroda, India, in 1982, and later Thapar Corporate R&D Centre, Patiala, India, in 1987. In the year 1994, he joined the Department of Computer Science at Punjabi University, Patiala. He becomes Professor in the year 1995. He also served as Dean, Faculty of Engineering and Technology, from 1995 to 2000 and Dean, Faculty of Physical Sciences, during 2007-2008. Presently, he has been designated as Dean, Research at Punjabi University, Patiala, India. He has worked in many diverse areas such as Fluid Dynamics, Finite Element Analysis, Optimization, and Numerical Analysis. He has more than 33 years of teaching/research experience. For the last 16 years, he has been working in Pattern Recognition, Optical Character Recognition and Computer Graphics. He has published more than 50 papers in various international journals and more than 40 papers in various national and international conferences.

Madeena Sultana is pursuing Ph.D. in Computer Science at University of Calgary, Alberta, Canada. She received her Master of Science and Bachelor of Science in Computer Science and Engineering at Jahangirnagar University, Bangladesh. At present, she has over 20 publications in refereed journals and IEEE/ACM conferences. Madeena has a co-authored book titled *Efficient Trademark Retrieval using Weighted Image Features: A GPU Based Approach* which is published by VDM Verlag, Germany. Her research interests include biometric security, digital image processing, and GPU computing. She is a student member of IEEE and IACSIT.

P. A. Vijaya did her B.E in Electronics and Communication in Malnad College of Engineering, Hassan, Karnataka state, under University of Mysore during 1985. She did her M.E in 1991 and Ph.D in 2005 from Indian Institute of Science, Bangalore, India. She served for about 27 years in the Department of ECE in Malnad college of Engineering, Hassan, in various capacities (Lecturer, Asst Professor, Professor and HOD), from Jan 1986 to Jan 2013. She is currently working as a Professor in the Department of ECE, BNMIT, Bangalore. Her research interests are in pattern recognition, image processing, embedded and real time systems, operating systems and computer network protocols. She has around 82 research paper publications in reputed journals and conferences. She has produced 2 Ph.Ds and few more are doing Ph.D and M.Sc (Engg) under her guidance.

Ekta Walia received her Bachelor's degree in Computer Science from Kurukshetra University, India in 1995 and Masters in Computer Applications as well as Ph.D. in Computer Science from Punjabi University, Patiala, India in 1998 and 2006 respectively. She started her professional career as a software consultant with DCM DataSystems, New Delhi where she was actively involved in development of database applications like Medical Transcription system and Scheduling system. Later, she served as Lecturer and Senior Lecturer in the National Institute of Technical Teachers Training and Research (NITTTR), Chandigarh, India for approximately seven years. Later she worked as Reader in the Department of Computer Science, Punjabi University, Patiala, India. Thereafter, she worked as Professor and Head in the Department of Information Technology, M.M. University, Mullana, Ambala, India. At present, she is working as Associate Professor in the department of Computer Science of South Asian University, Delhi, India. Her academic achievements include University Gold medal in Graduation as well as in Post Graduation. She is the author of two textbooks. Her research interests include Computer Graphics, Data Bases and Image Processing. She has a number of International journal and conference publications to her credit. She was sponsored by DST, Govt. of India to attend an IEEE sponsored conference held at University of London in 2006. She has guided many M.Tech. thesis and students are also pursuing Ph.D. under her guidance. She is reviewer of a reputed annual international conference of Europe.

Index